DATA FILES FOR STUDENTS

To complete the activities in this book, students will need data files, which are available online.

To access the data files, follow these instructions:

1. Open your browser and access the companion website at NGL.Cengage.com/AdobePS

2. For data files to complete each activity within a chapter, select the chapter number from the drop-down box (below the book title), then click "Student Downloads" in the Book Overview section on the left panel.

3. For National Geographic Unit Projects and ACP Prep Guide data files, select "Student Downloads" in the Book Resources section on the left panel.

Adobe
Photoshop
REVEALED

CHRIS BOTELLO

NATIONAL
GEOGRAPHIC
LEARNING

CENGAGE

Acknowledgments

Grateful acknowledgment is given to the authors, artists, photographers, museums, publishers, and agents for permission to reprint copyrighted material. Every effort has been made to secure the appropriate permission. If any omissions have been made or if corrections are required, please contact the Publisher.

Cover Image Credit:

Christian Ziegler/National Geographic Image Collection

Adobe® Photoshop®, Adobe® InDesign®, Adobe® Illustrator®, Adobe® Flash®, Adobe® Dreamweaver®, Adobe® Edge Animate®, Adobe® Creative Suite®, and Adobe® Creative Cloud® are trademarks or registered trademarks of Adobe Systems, Inc. in the United States and/or other countries. Third party products, services, company names, logos, design, titles, words, or phrases within these materials may be trademarks of their respective owners.

Adobe product screenshot(s) reprinted with permission from Adobe Systems Incorporated.

For product information and technology assistance, contact us at Customer & Sales Support, 888-915-3276

For permission to use material from this text or product, submit all requests online at **www.cengage.com/permissions**

Further permissions questions can be emailed to **permissionrequest@cengage.com**

National Geographic Learning | Cengage
20 Channel Center Street
Boston, MA 02210

National Geographic Learning, a Cengage company, is a provider of quality core and supplemental educational materials for the PreK–12, adult education, and ELT markets. Cengage is a leading provider of customized learning solutions with employees residing in nearly 40 different countries and sales in more than 125 countries around the world. Find your local representative at **NGL.Cengage.com/RepFinder**

Visit National Geographic Learning online at **NGL.Cengage.com**

ISBN: 978-0-357-63587-2

Printed in the United States of America.

Print Number: 01
Print Year: 2021

CREATE A DIVERSION A bird zeroing in on
a flag-footed bug perched on a passionflower
might see the flutter of red "flags"—the
insect's attempt to divert the hunter's bite to
nonessential limbs, away from its vital core.
ANISOCELIS FLAVOLINEATA (INSECT); PASSIFLORA SP. (FLOWER)

A flag-footed bug perched on a passionflower distracts predators with appendices on hind legs.
Photo location: Bocas del Toro, Panama.

CONTENTS

UNIT 2 PROJECT

CONTENTS

UNIT 4 UNIFY ADVANCED SKILLS

UNIT 4 PROJECT

ABOUT THE AUTHOR

Chris Botello began his career as a print production manager for *Premiere* magazine. He designed and produced movie and TV campaigns for Miramax Films and NBC Television and was the art director for Microsoft's launch of sidewalk.com/boston. Chris is the author of the *Revealed* series of books on Photoshop, Illustrator, and InDesign, and the co-author of *YouTube for Dummies*. He lives in Los Angeles, where he teaches graphic design at a private high school and uses his own Revealed books as the text for his classes.

REVIEWERS

Dahlia Acosta
Socorro High School
El Paso, Texas

Andrea Bays
Charles Page High School
Sand Springs, Oklahoma

Rachele Hall
Yerington High School
Yerington, Nevada

Diana Johnston
Northside Health
Careers High School
San Antonio, Texas

Dr. Marilyn Proctor-Givens
Lincoln High School
Tallahassee, Florida

Linda Robinson
Winter Haven High School
Winter Haven, Florida

Natasha Smith
Union High School
Tulsa, Oklahoma

Alison Spangler
John Paul Stevens High School
and Northwest Vista College
San Antonio, Texas

CREATIVE STORYTELLING | *THE REVEALED SERIES VISION* |

The *Revealed* series extends step-by-step software instruction to creative problem solving for real-world impact with more projects than any other Adobe® curriculum. Through our exclusive partnership with National Geographic, students create unique and meaningful projects inspired by National Geographic Storytellers with a focus on how design principles create meaningful compositions, layouts, and infographics, all while meeting the most recent Adobe® Professional Certification requirements. This updated series includes professional examples of photographs, infographics, and visually impactful layouts from *National Geographic*® magazine. Students will connect concepts with real-world projects through featured interviews with National Geographic Explorers, Designers, and Creatives for an authentic, professional perspective. Flexible for a variety of digital devices, these programs include instruction for iPad users as well as desktop and Mac computers.

We recognize the unique learning environment of the digital media classroom, and we deliver a complete curriculum package that includes:

- Comprehensive step-by-step instructions
- In-depth explanations of the "why" behind each skill
- Creative projects for additional practice and critical thinking
- Full-color visuals for a clear illustration of concepts
- MindTap, the comprehensive online solution offering additional study tools, instruction, and skills practice

The *Revealed* series speaks directly to the digital media and design community and gives students the tools to pick up the conversation and make an impact with their work.

New to This Edition

Adobe Photoshop Creative Cloud—Revealed, 2nd edition, includes many exciting new features, some of which are as follows:

- Adobe Certified Professional Test Prep Guide with practice test
- Comprehensive exploration of working effectively with layers, layer masks, and vector masks
- In-depth exploration of the Grayscale, RGB, and HSB color modes
- Extensive coverage of core image adjustments and strategies for using them effectively
- Expert-level masking strategies and techniques
- Expert-level strategies for harnessing the power of blending modes
- Extensive coverage of retouching and healing tools
- Enhancements to Shapes
- Enhancements to the Image Size dialog box
- Coverage of artboards, libraries, and web graphics
- Core production strategies for managing resolution, actions, and image processing
- Advanced and sophisticated typographical designs
- A step-by-step guide for drawing complex paths, shapes, and clipping paths
- Cross-referenced projects between Photoshop and Illustrator, and between Photoshop and InDesign
- A step-by-step guide to produce a professionally designed movie poster

| AUTHOR'S VISION |

It has been a dream job to write this new edition of *Adobe Photoshop Creative Cloud—Revealed*. What a chance to revisit, explore, and share my favorite tips, tricks, strategies, and inspirations for working with Photoshop. The project put me back to work with Ann Fisher, my longtime friend and editor. Ann's work is invisible and everywhere in this book. It is the thread that holds the whole thing together.

A book like this is always a team effort. I have been honored (and humbled) by all the hard work, joy, and creativity the many people involved in this project have delivered. Thank you, Raj Desai, Product Manager, for your vision and willingness to have fun and brainstorm ideas. Thank you, Chris Jaeggi, Product Director, for your advice and confident leadership. Thank you, Karen Caldwell, Supervising Content Developer, for all that you do (which often seemed like everything) and for welcoming Ann and me into the group. Thank you to the design team of Michael Farmer, Alex von Dallwitz, and Brian Nehlsen, for the beautiful cover and the smart, readable, and sophisticated run of the book. As a designer myself, I was on pins and needles hoping I would like the new look (and terrified I wouldn't). I was blown away the day I first saw it. I hope you guys have enjoyed my design work as much as I've enjoyed yours. Thank you, Amy Ostenso for all the wise and thoughtful feedback. Thank you, Jessica Livingston, for developing the beautiful Nat Geo Storyteller projects. Thank you, Laura Bolesta, for being production manager extraordinaire. And a final thank you to Mary Ann Lidrbauch and the reviewers who kept us on track and clear-eyed as we worked our way through each chapter.

To the teachers, the students, and the readers: These are my favorite tricks and my best-kept secrets. Now they're yours. I've enjoyed an unimaginable career and lived the dreams of my childhood simply because Photoshop exists. I hope something of what I've shared with you here brings your dreams to reality and launches you on your own unimaginable journey.

—Chris Botello

INTRODUCTION TO
ADOBE® PHOTOSHOP CREATIVE CLOUD

Welcome to *Adobe Photoshop Creative Cloud—Revealed*. This book offers creative projects, concise instructions, and coverage of basic to advanced Photoshop skills, helping you to create polished, professional-looking artwork. Use this book both in the classroom and as your own reference guide. It also includes many of the new features of Adobe® Photoshop Creative Cloud. This edition is written for the 2021 Photoshop CC release.

Chapter Opener

To set the stage for learning, each chapter opens with an impactful, full-page image to engage students visually. The lesson topics and the Adobe Certified Professional Exam Objectives covered in the chapter are clearly laid out so students and instructors can easily track their progress in acquiring skills for preparing for the exam.

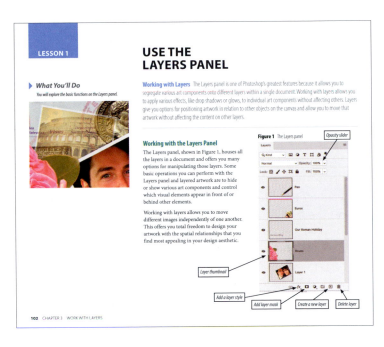

What You'll Do

A What You'll Do figure begins every lesson. This figure gives you an at-a-glance look at what you'll do in the lesson, by showing you either a file from the current project or a tool you'll be using.

Comprehensive Conceptual Lessons

Before jumping into the instruction, in-depth conceptual information tells you why skills are applied. This book provides the "how" and "why" through the use of professional examples. Also included in the text are tips and sidebars to help you work more efficiently and creatively or to teach you a bit about the history or design philosophy behind the skill you are learning.

Step-by-Step Instructions

This book combines in-depth conceptual information with concise hands-on steps to help you learn Photoshop Creative Cloud. Each set of steps guides you through a lesson where you will create, modify, or enhance a Photoshop file. Step instructions reference large colorful images, and quick step summaries round out the lessons.

Skills Review

A Skills Review at the end of the chapter contains hands-on practice exercises that mirror the progressive nature of the lesson material.

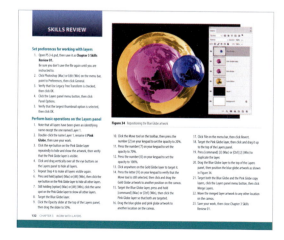

Chapter Projects

This book contains a variety of end-of-chapter projects for additional practice and reinforcement. Most chapters conclude with two Project Builders and one Design Project that require you to apply the skills you've learned in the chapter.

PROJECT BUILDER 2

Project Builder 2 is designed specifically to get you to remember the Stroke Emboss effect. So many designers aren't even aware of it, so that's even more reason to get it into your your skill set. Once you've completed the steps, take a moment to appreciate the sophisticated and stunning impact it has on the artwork.

1. Open PS 4-14.psd, then save it as **Sunset Stroke Emboss**.
2. Target the SUNSET layer on the Layers panel.
3. Click Layer on the menu bar, point to Layer Style, then click Stroke.
4. Click the Color box, type **128** in the R, G, and B text boxes, then click OK.
5. Set the Size to 10, then set the Position to Center.
6. In the Styles column at the left of the dialog box, click the words Bevel & Emboss.
7. Set the Style to Stroke Emboss, set the Technique to Chisel Hard, then set the Depth to 110%.
8. Set the Size to 2, then set the Soften value to 0.
9. Click the Gloss Contour list arrow, click the Ring - Double gloss contour, then verify that the Anti-aliased check box is checked.
10. Click OK, then compare your artwork to Figure 41.
11. Save your work, then close Sunset Stroke Emboss.

Figure 41 Bevel & Emboss layer style applied to the stroke

DESIGN PROJECT

Fine art school students are usually required to create still life artwork. The same can be done with digital art. You are given various fruits and asked to arrange them into a beautiful and balanced still life. This is a great challenge for working with layers, transforming images, and bringing images into a working file from other files.

1. Open PS 3-12.psd, then use it as **Still Life Composition**.
2. Target the Background layer.
3. Click File on the menu bar, click Open, then navigate to the Fruit folder in the Chapter 3 Data Files folder.
4. Open the file named Green Grapes. The file has been masked for you.
5. Drag the Green Grapes file by its name down from the Photoshop window so that it is a floating window. Your screen should resemble Figure 47.
6. Click the Move tool, then drag the Green Grapes layer into the Still Life Composition file. The artwork, along with the mask, is moved into the Still Life Composition file.
7. Close Green Grapes.
8. Open the file named Orange Navel.
9. Mask out the background.
10. Drag the Orange Navel artwork into the Still Life Composition file, then close Orange Navel.

Figure 47 Dragging the masked Green Grapes layer into the Still Life Composition file

11. Using the same method, open other fruit image files you want to work with, mask out their backgrounds, then add them to the Still Life Composition file until you have enough images to build a still life.

12. In the Still Life Composition file, transform artwork as needed and reposition artwork to build a still life collage. Figure 48 shows one outcome that you can use as a guide.
13. Save your work, close Still Life Composition.

DESIGN PROJECT

This project gives you the opportunity to incorporate the layer skills you have learned in Chapters 3 and 4. You are going to type the name of a city, then place images into the letters, as you did with the "JAPAN" artwork in Lesson 6 of this chapter.

The way to do this project is to work methodically, don't rush. Think about color and about finding the right typeface and images. Think about which layer styles would work best for you about how a gradient might add to the effect.

1. Open PS 4-16.psd, then save it as **City Images**. This file is blank, a clean slate to get you started.
2. Decide what city you want to work on. Keep in mind that the shorter the name, the larger the letters will be on the canvas, and the more of the images you'll be able to see inside those letters.
3. Type the name of the city on the canvas.
4. Choose the best typeface for the city. You have many considerations when choosing a typeface. Your most important consideration though, is finding a typeface that's very bold and thick so that when you put images into the type, they will show substantially.
5. Track and kern the type as necessary.

6. Go online and find a background image that you think will work and paste it in.
7. Research and choose the best image for the collage and clip them into the type.
8. Apply the layer styles you think will best make the type and images stand out from the background.
9. Incorporate a gradient over the background to perhaps darken it or lighten it. Figure 43 shows one result.

Figure 43 Final artwork

NATIONAL GEOGRAPHIC | STORYTELLERS

This edition of *Adobe Photoshop Creative Cloud—Revealed* provides eight opportunities for students to walk in the shoes of a National Geographic Storyteller and be inspired to pursue their own creative careers. Based on in-depth interviews and images chosen by each photographer, the features give students a window into the photographers' career development, creative process, and passion for their work. Students learn firsthand how accomplished creative professionals use their skill and talent to capture impactful, meaningful images that bring their stories to life.

Each feature also provides the opportunity to engage with the Storytellers and their work with hands-on projects. Four mid-unit features encourage students to analyze the image or create their own images based on the work they have just studied.

Four end-of-unit features incorporate longer creative projects that allow students to explore designing for impact, with an emphasis on visual storytelling, inspired by the work of the featured National Geographic Storytellers.

Writing Projects give graphic arts students a chance to become master storytellers by analyzing the intentional key elements of photographs, layouts, and compositions created by National Geographic professionals. Students

explore concepts such as placement, lighting, balance, depth, scale, and more, as they practice creative analysis. Students prepare for future careers as they develop an eye to pick up on the design elements in each example, learn and employ professional terminology, use critical thinking skills, and give feedback in these writing assignments before starting their own composition.

Design Projects give students hands-on practice telling their own stories, inspired by the theme or topic explored in the writing project. Using their own research and images downloaded from the companion site as a starting point, students build their own composition or layout. Design Projects include examples of pre-work including sketches, plans, and mockups that National Geographic Storytellers

and Designers have used in the Writing Project example to encourage student planning.

Portfolio Projects allow students to build a composition from scratch as they research their interests and incorporate more advanced skills from the current unit. Students have the freedom to be creative and choose from a list of recommended skills and tools to use in their project that are also assessed in the Adobe Certified Professional exam. These projects encourage students to tell stories that relate to their lives; to research local and community issues; and to incorporate photographs, data, or copy that directly impacts their school, community, and interests.

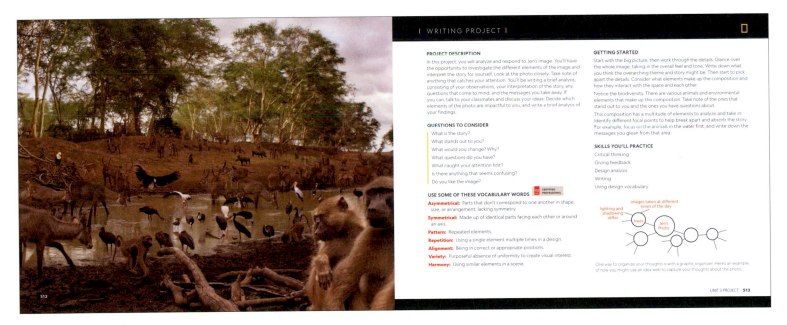

RESOURCES

A FULL SUITE OF SUPPORTING RESOURCES

Instructor Companion Site

Everything you need for your course in one place! This collection of product-specific lecture and class tools is available online via the instructor resource center. You'll be able to access and download materials such as PowerPoint® presentations, data and solution files, Instructor's Manual, Industry-Aligned Credential correlations, and more.

- Download your resources at companion-sites.cengage.com.

Instructor's Manual

The Instructor's Manual includes chapter overviews and detailed lecture topics for each chapter, with teaching tips.

Syllabus

A sample Syllabus includes a suggested outline for any course that uses this book.

PowerPoint Presentations

Each chapter has a corresponding PowerPoint presentation to use in lectures, distribute to your students, or customize to suit your course.

Solutions to Exercises

Solution Files are provided to show samples of final artwork. Use these files to evaluate your students' work, or distribute them electronically so students can verify their work.

Test Bank and Test Engine

Cognero®, Customizable Test Bank Generator is a flexible, online system that allows you to import, edit, and manipulate content from the text's test bank or elsewhere, including your own favorite test questions; create multiple test versions in an instant; and deliver tests from your LMS, your classroom, or wherever you want.

- K12 Teachers, log on at **nglsync.cengage.com**, or companion-sites.cengage.com.
- Higher Education Teachers, log on at **www.cengage.com**.

THE ONLINE SOLUTION FOR CAREER AND TECHNICAL EDUCATION COURSES

MindTap for *Adobe Creative Cloud—Revealed* is the online learning solution for career and technical education courses that helps teachers engage and transform today's students into critical thinkers. Through paths of dynamic assignments and applications that you can personalize, real-time course analytics, and an interactive eBook, MindTap helps teachers organize and engage students. Whether you teach this course in the classroom or in hybrid/e-learning models, MindTap enhances the course experience with data analytcs, engagement tracking, and student tools such as flashcards and practice quizzes. MindTap for Photoshop also includes the following:

- An Adobe Certified Professional Test Prep Guide with Practice Exam

- A bonus module for using Adobe Photoshop on the iPad

- A Career Readiness Module for the Arts, A/V Tech & Communications Career Cluster (available Spring 2022)

K-12 teachers and students who have adopted MindTap can access their courses at **nglsync.cengage.com**.

Don't have an account? Request access from your Sales Consultant at ngl.cengage.com/repfinder.

Higher education teachers and students can access their courses at **login.cengage.com**.

ACCESS RESOURCES ONLINE, ANYTIME

Accessing digital content from National Geographic Learning, a part of Cengage, has never been easier. Through our new login portal, NGLSync, you can now easily gain access to all Career & Technical Education digital courses and resources purchased by your district, including: MindTap, Cognero Test Bank Generator, and Instructor/Student Companion Sites.

Log on at **nglsync.cengage.com**, or **www.cengage.com**

SUBJECT MATTER EXPERT CONTRIBUTORS

Adobe Certified Professional Test Prep Guide
Debbie Keller
Director Career & Technical Education
Adobe Education Leader
Medina Valley Independent School District
Castroville, Texas

Adobe Photoshop on the iPad
Chana Messer
Artist, Designer, Educator
Adobe Education Leader
University of Southern California (USC), FIDM
Los Angeles, California

GETTING STARTED

INTENDED AUDIENCE

This text is designed for beginners who want to build basic skills and solid foundations in Photoshop. This text is also designed for experienced intermediate users who want to take their skills beyond the basics and explore advanced techniques and the "high end" of what Photoshop has to offer. The book is designed not only to educate you, but also to encourage you to explore the nuances of the program and of your own vision and design sense.

APPROACH

The text allows you to work at your own pace through step-by-step tutorials. A concept is presented, the process is explained, and then the actual steps are detailed. To learn the most from the use of the text, you should adopt the following habits:

- Proceed slowly: Accuracy and comprehension are more important than speed.

- Understand what is happening with each step before you continue to the next step.

- After finishing a skill, ask yourself if you could do it on your own, without referring to the steps. If the answer is no, review the steps.

Chapters 1–7 have been designed as an introduction to Photoshop and make up a perfect one-semester introductory course. If you're new to Photoshop, the first seven chapters in this book will provide you with a solid foundation in the program. Do not rush through these chapters. Photoshop is a big program with a lot of features and important concepts behind these features. Build your skills steadily and solidly.

If you're experienced with Photoshop but are self-taught, you should absolutely step through Chapters 1–7 as well. Being self-taught is admirable, but you need to understand what you're doing intellectually and in depth. These chapters provide that understanding, and that will launch you to the bigger, higher-end challenges Photoshop has to offer.

You could call Chapters 8–14 the "advanced" chapters, but really, they are more like in-depth explorations of more focused or challenging techniques or concepts. Again, don't rush to get there. Be sure you're solid with the core skills. You want a strong understanding of how Photoshop does what it does before you begin layering on advanced challenges.

GENERAL

Throughout the initial chapters, students are given precise instructions regarding saving their work. Students should feel they can save their work at any time, not just when instructed to do so.

Students are also given precise instructions regarding magnifying/reducing their work area. Once students feel more comfortable, they should feel free to use the Zoom tool to make their work area more comfortable.

FONTS

If a data file contains type, the type will often have been converted to outlines so that no font management will be necessary. If the data file does use actual fonts, they will be commonly used fonts, but there is no guarantee these fonts will be available on your computer. If any of the fonts in use are not available on your computer, you can make a substitution, but realize that the results may vary from those in the book.

WINDOWS AND MAC OS

Adobe Photoshop CC works virtually the same on Windows and macOS operating systems. In those cases where there is a significant difference, the abbreviations (Win) and (Mac) are used.

SYSTEM REQUIREMENTS

For a Windows operating system:

- Processor: Intel® or AMD processor with 64-bit support; 2 GHz or faster processor with SSE 4.2 or later

- Operating System: Windows® 10 (64-bit) version 1809 or later; LTSC versions are not supported

- RAM: 8 GB minimum; 16 GB or more recommended

- Graphics card: GPU with DirectX 12 support; 2 GB of GPU memory minimum or 4 GB of GPU memory for 4K displays and greater recommended

- Storage space: 4 GB of available hard-disk space; additional space is required for installation

- Monitor resolution: 1280 × 800 display at 100% UI scaling minimum; 1920 × 1080 display or greater at 100% UI scaling recommended

- Internet connection and registration are necessary for required activation, validation of subscriptions, and access to online services

For a macOS operating system:

- Processor: Intel® processor with 64-bit support; 2 GHz or faster processor with SSE 4.2 or later

- Operating System: macOS Mohave v10.4 or later minimum; macOS Big Sur v11, Mac OS Catalina v10.15 recommended

- RAM: 8 GB minimum; 16 GB or more recommended

- Graphics card: GPU with Metal support; 2 GB of GPU memory minimum or 4 GB GPU memory for 4K displays and greater recommended

- Storage space: 4 GB of available hard-disk space; additional space is required for installation

- Monitor resolution: 1280 × 800 display at 100% UI scaling minimum; 1920 × 1080 display or greater at 100% UI scaling recommended

- Internet connection and registration are necessary for required activation, validation of subscriptions, and access to online services

Rubén Salgado Escudero, Solar Portraits Project, Men
playing pool in the town center, Kalagala, Uganda

© Rubén Salgado Escudero

CHAPTER 1

GET STARTED WITH PHOTOSHOP

1. Learn About Photoshop and Digital Images
2. Set Important Photoshop Preferences for Using This Book
3. Create, Open, and Save Documents
4. Explore the Toolbar and the Options Panel
5. Create a Customized Workspace for Using This Book
6. Work with Grids, Guides, and Rulers

Adobe Certified Professional in Visual Design Using Photoshop CC Framework

2. Project Setup and Interface

This objective covers the interface setup and program settings that assist in an efficient and effective workflow, as well as knowledge about ingesting digital assets for a project.

2.1 Create a document with the appropriate settings for web, print, and video.
　A Set appropriate document settings for printed and onscreen images.
　B Create a new document preset to reuse for specific project needs.

2.2 Navigate, organize, and customize the application workspace.
　A Identify and manipulate elements of the Photoshop interface.
　B Organize and customize the workspace.
　C Configure application preferences.

2.3 Use non-printing design tools in the interface to aid in design or workflow.
　A Navigate a document.
　B Use rulers.
　C Use guides and grids.

2.4 Import assets into a project.
　A Open or import images from various devices.

5. Publishing Digital Media

This objective covers saving and exporting documents or assets within individual layers or selections

5.2 Export or save digital images to various file formats.
　A Save in the native file format for Photoshop (.psd).

LEARN ABOUT PHOTOSHOP AND DIGITAL IMAGES

▶ *What You'll Do*

In this lesson, you'll read about Photoshop, the history of its original launch, and learn about digital images.

About Adobe Photoshop

Adobe Photoshop is the famous and revolutionary image-editing program created by Thomas and John Knoll in 1988. The Knoll brothers sold the license for distribution to Adobe Systems, based in San Jose, California. Adobe released Photoshop 1.0 in February 1990 exclusively for the Macintosh platform.

Photoshop immediately captured the imaginations of not just graphic designers but the world. The idea that image editing—the ability to manipulate an image in any and all kinds of ways—was now available to the general public for $895 was revolutionary. The launch of Photoshop, along with the launch of Adobe Illustrator in 1988, reinvented graphic design as it is now known in the modern, computer-based world. Adobe Systems, along with other pioneering software companies, created a new platform that revolutionized the entire printing industry.

In 1993, Adobe chief architect Seetharaman Narayanan "ported" Photoshop to Microsoft® Windows®. The Windows port led to Photoshop reaching a wider mass market audience as Microsoft's global reach exploded over the next few years.

Over the next 10 extraordinary years starting with the launch of Photoshop in 1990, the entire offset printing process, which had evolved over centuries strictly as a table-based operation, changed to an entirely computer-based operation. Whole industries and new technologies were created, while other traditional systems were suddenly out of date. Jobs were lost, but thousands of new and unprecedented jobs were invented. Service bureaus were created to help people learn to print "camera-ready" type on "repro paper" from their desktop computers and to output the digital layouts they sent in on "floppy" disks. Then, suddenly, service bureaus were outputting not to paper but to film—film that could be used to burn plates to be used on a conventional offset printing press.

Film was the bridge. Once desktop computers could print to film, the connection between the desktop computer and the traditional offset printing press was established. And there was no turning back.

Today, even film has disappeared and people can print "direct to press," meaning they hit the Print button on their computers and are able to download directly—and wirelessly! — to multimillion-dollar "digital printers," often thousands of miles away, that produce professional-grade reproductions. That this has occurred over the course of just 30 years is astounding.

All of this happened because of the release of one program: Adobe Photoshop. Yes, Adobe Illustrator came first, but Illustrator wasn't unique. There was a competing software package called Aldus Freehand. But to date, Adobe Photoshop is a one and only. Think of it—there has never been another mass-market, image-editing software package. Never. No other software company has ever released "another Photoshop." There is no alternative to Photoshop. Photoshop is a monolith.

It's not overstating to say that Photoshop has freed the human spirit. With Photoshop, people could suddenly live the life of the artist. "Art" up to that point, be it "fine" art or "commercial" art, was accessible as a career only to a rarefied segment of society. Before Photoshop, the idea that you could make money as an artist or have a career as an artist was a daunting ambition. Going to art school was a must and something of a luxury, for betting all one's chips on a career in art was a genuine risk. "Help wanted" ads for artists were few and far between, and career jobs for artists existed almost exclusively in the big cities. There were, as always, the successful and celebrated artists, but for every David Hockney, Peter Max, and Roy Lichtenstein, there were thousands of innately gifted would-be artists working in obscurity, working as a hobby, or not working at all.

Photoshop changed all that too. It's not going too far to say that, like Prometheus giving fire to the mortals, Photoshop made a career in art possible for the everyman and everywoman. Suddenly, from their homes, on their computers, people were able to make art using Photoshop. They were able to *sell* art they made in Photoshop—and feed themselves, pay the rent, and get hired—because of Photoshop. Photoshop provided the tools and the venue for people who might never have even thought of themselves as artists to be able to express themselves as such.

So much has been written about the Photoshop software story. What has not been written about Photoshop is the human story.

About Adobe Creative Cloud

In the early days, you purchased Photoshop at a store, in a box. In the box, you found a couple of floppy disks that contained the software and a user's manual. As time went by, the floppy disk turned into a CD, and then into a DVD. Then the printed user's manual vanished and was relocated to the DVD as a digital document.

The question for Adobe, of course, was how to continue to make money on Photoshop. They didn't want Photoshop to be a one-time-only purchase, so versioning became the method for repeat sales. Every two years or so, Adobe would release an updated version of Photoshop with new features so people would pay to upgrade.

The advent of the Internet made purchasing software on physical disks obsolete, and Internet downloads became the delivery method of choice for Adobe. Around 2015, Adobe transitioned out of versioning Photoshop and its other products and switched to a monthly subscription-based model (and its stock skyrocketed).

That's where Adobe Creative Cloud comes in. Creative Cloud is the Adobe website that houses all Adobe programs. You subscribe to Creative Cloud for a monthly fee; then you can download and install the Creative Cloud software. Once you have the Creative Cloud software on your computer, you have access to all of Adobe's software packages to download, install, and use. Now, when there's an update to Photoshop or any of the other Adobe products, you simply click the Update button to access those new features.

Defining Image-Editing Software

Photoshop is an image-editing program. An **image-editing program** offers you a wide variety of tools and settings that allow you to manipulate electronic images. You can use those images for on-screen presentations, whether on the Internet or on a single laptop computer, and you can also print those images, either on your home printer or professionally with a high-quality printer. Because Photoshop is so versatile, you can open images from many different sources, including from your phone, your digital camera, and images you download from the Web.

The following are just some of the tasks you can use Photoshop to accomplish:

- **Acquire images from a variety of devices** Transfer images from CDs, DVDs, digital cameras, and scanners into Photoshop. Download images from the Web and open them in Photoshop. With some digital cameras, you can use Photoshop to preview images from your camera before you open them in Photoshop.

- **Apply basic processing procedures** Crop an image to get rid of unwanted elements or to focus more dramatically on your subject. Rotate an image if it is upside down, on its side, or crooked. Resize an image so it prints to fit the frame you just bought. All of these are essential and practical procedures that Photoshop can do quickly and efficiently.

- **Improve the color and quality of images** Photoshop has many sophisticated color tools that allow you to enhance the appearance of photographs. You can brighten images that are too dark or darken images that are overexposed. Turn an otherwise plain image into something striking with a quick increase in contrast. Make the color more vivid or remove it entirely to create a dramatic black-and-white image.

- **Fix image flaws** Photoshop's retouching tools and production filters offer you many options for fixing flaws in an image, such as dust and scratches, graininess, and red eye. You can also retouch photos of your family and friends. Best of all, retouch and restore old family photos, and give them as gifts to be treasured.

- **Add special effects**

  If you can think of it, you can probably do it in Photoshop. Turn a brand-new photo into an old-looking photo, or take a typical black-and-white photo and make it look hand-tinted. Add grain effects or blur effects to give an ordinary photo a custom look. Distort photos by giving your friends big heads on little bodies or making your sister appear to be a giant 40-foot woman crashing her way down Fifth Avenue. Photoshop makes your imagination a reality.

- **Batch-process image files**

  Photoshop is also a production workhorse. For example, Photoshop can automatically process a batch of files for one type of output, such as professional printing, and then reprocess the same batch of files by reducing their physical size and file size and changing their format for use on the Web. And that's literally with the click of one button.

- **Output to various devices**

  You can use Photoshop to create graphics for slide shows, video presentations, and electronic billboards. Photoshop is used every day to create elements for on-screen animation projects. Photoshop comes complete with software you can use to save images for your cell phone or your iPad. Photoshop can even process many different-sized images into one contact sheet.

Understanding an Electronic Image

A **digital image** is a picture in electronic form, and it may be referred to as a file, document, graphic, picture, or image. You can create original artwork in Photoshop, or you can manipulate images that you bring into Photoshop from your camera or online sources.

Every electronic or "digital" image is made up of very small squares, which are called **pixels**, and each pixel represents a single color or shade. The word "pixel" is a combination of the words *picture* and *element*. Pixels are always square, and they are the smallest component of an electronic image.

Digital cameras, like the one in your phone, create the digital image the moment you snap a photo. The light from the live image that you capture is recreated digitally; it is converted into pixels inside your camera. The number of pixels per inch that your camera can access to recreate the image is the **camera resolution**.

Modern-day phones, like your iPhone or Android, are amazing machines with amazing cameras able to store hundreds upon hundreds of high-resolution and large-file-size images. For example, an iPhone 10, by default, creates an image that is 3,024 × 4,032 pixels and 34 megabytes. That's more than 12 million pixels in each photo on your phone. You could print one photo as is, at high resolution, at 13 inches tall. That's the size of a coffee table book.

When Photoshop was introduced in 1989, these high resolution levels and storage capabilities were as fantastic as space travel would have been to the Wright brothers at Kitty Hawk. And think about it, that's just one of the hundreds and hundreds of photos you have on your phone!

LESSON 2

SET IMPORTANT PHOTOSHOP PREFERENCES FOR USING THIS BOOK

▶ *What You'll Do*

In this lesson, you'll set important preferences for working in this book.

Understanding Preferences

Think of the millions of people who use Photoshop every day and have used it for years and even decades. Just as with any traditional work area, Photoshop users like to set up their workspace to use the software in a particular way that they find logical and comfortable. For example, some users might prefer to work with tools that are arranged in two columns rather than one, and they might prefer dark panels with white type rather than light panels with black type. They might have created an arrangement of panels that are docked and positioned exactly as they want them to be, and they want that arrangement to be consistent every time they launch the software. For these reasons, Photoshop offers an array of options, which are referred to as **preferences**.

The Preferences dialog boxes are where users choose from a variety of preferences for using Photoshop, a list far too long to present here. Once chosen, these preferences become part of the software package itself. Whenever you launch Photoshop, even if you're opening a file that's not your own, the software will launch with *your* preferences intact.

Understanding Platform User Interfaces

Photoshop is available for both Windows and Mac OS platforms. Regardless of which platform you use, the features and menu commands are the same. Some Windows and Mac OS keyboard commands use different keys. For example, [command] and [option] keys are used on Macs and [ctrl] and [alt] keys, respectively, on the Windows platform. There are also cosmetic differences between the Windows and Mac OS versions of Photoshop due to the user interface differences found in each platform.

One glaring difference is the location of the Preferences command. On a Mac, to access the Preferences dialog box, click the Photoshop command on the menu bar, point to Preferences, and then choose the dialog box you want to open. On a Windows PC, the Preferences command is located at the bottom of the Edit menu.

Set important preferences for using this book

1. Launch Photoshop.

TIP You don't need to have any files open to set preferences.

2. If you are working on a Mac, click **Photoshop** on the menu bar, point to **Preferences**, then click **General**.

3. If you are working on a Windows PC, click **Edit** on the menu bar, point to **Preferences**, then click **General**.

4. Match your settings to Figure 1.

5. Click the word **Interface** in the left column to show the Interface preferences dialog box, then match those settings to Figure 2.

Continued on next page

Figure 1 General Preferences

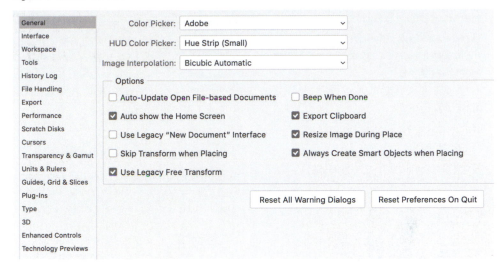

Figure 2 Interface Preferences

6. Click the word **Workspace** in the left column to show the Workspace preferences dialog box, then match those settings to Figure 3.

7. Click the word **Tools** in the left column to show the Tools preferences dialog box, then match those settings to Figure 4.

Figure 3 Workspace Preferences

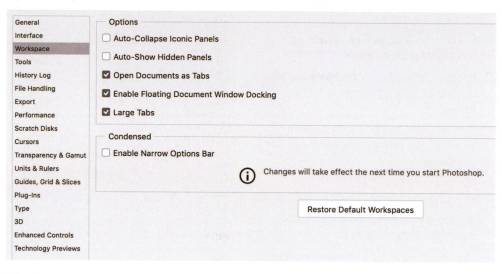

Figure 4 Tools Preferences

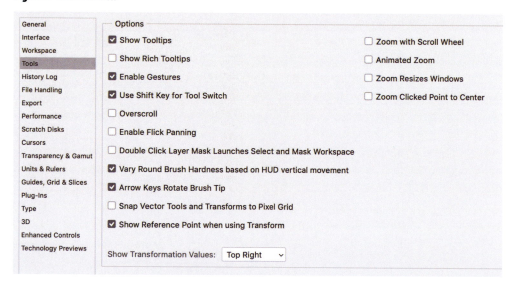

8. Click the word **Cursors** in the left column to show the Cursors preferences dialog box, then match those settings to Figure 5.

9. Click the words **Transparency & Gamut**, then match those settings to Figure 6.

Continued on next page

Figure 5 Cursors Preferences

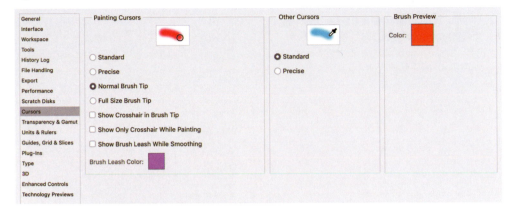

Figure 6 Transparency & Gamut Preferences

10. Click the words **Units & Rulers**, then match those settings to Figure 7.

11. Click the words **Guides, Grid & Slices**, then match those settings to Figure 8.

Figure 7 Units & Rulers Preferences

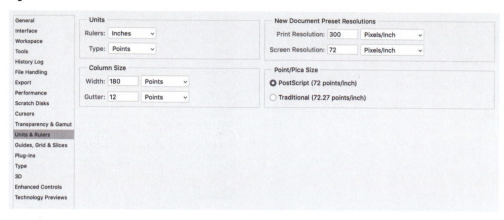

Figure 8 Guides, Grid & Slices Preferences

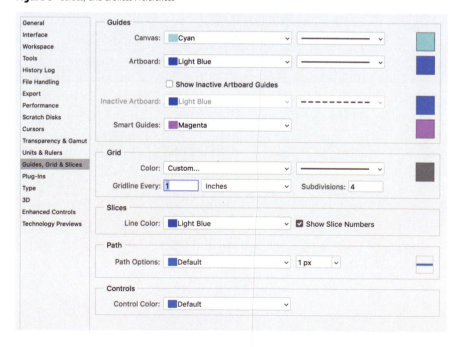

12. Click the word **Type**, match those settings to Figure 9, then click **OK**.

13. Exit Photoshop, then relaunch Photoshop.

You must exit and restart Photoshop for some of the changes you made to take effect.

You set preferences in nine different dialog boxes so your software behavior will mirror that which you see in the figures in this book.

Figure 9 Type Preferences

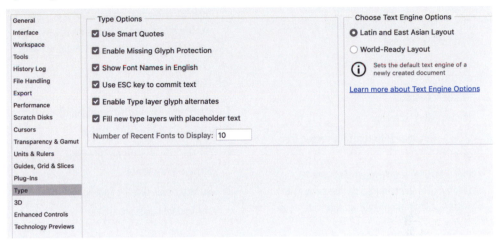

Remove the Siri keyboard shortcut on a Mac computer

1. On your Mac, click the **Apple menu**, then click **System Preferences**.

   If you are working on a Windows PC, skip this set of steps.

2. Click the **Siri icon**.

   The Siri dialog box opens.

3. Click the **Keyboard Shortcut list arrow**, then click **Off**.

   Your dialog box should resemble Figure 10. The keyboard shortcut for Siri is the same as an important Photoshop keyboard shortcut, so you need to disable this option or customize it to a sequence that doesn't involve the [shift] [control] [option] [command] or [spacebar] keys. A good key to use would be one of the [function] keys, which aren't used in any common Photoshop keyboard shortcuts.

4. Close the Siri dialog box.

Turn off the Spotlight keyboard shortcut on a Mac computer

1. On your Mac, click the **Apple menu**, then click **System Preferences**.

2. In the top row, click the **Spotlight button**.

   The Spotlight dialog box opens.

3. In the lower-left corner, click **Keyboard Shortcuts**.

   The Keyboard dialog box opens.

4. Uncheck both options so your Keyboard dialog box resembles Figure 11.

   The Mac keyboard commands for accessing the Spotlight search feature are the same keyboard commands Photoshop uses to access the Zoom tool, so they have been disabled.

5. Close the Keyboard dialog box.

You disabled a Mac system keyboard shortcut that conflicts with an important keyboard shortcut in Photoshop.

Figure 10 Turning the Siri keyboard shortcut off

Figure 11 Disabling the keyboard command for accessing the Spotlight search feature

CREATE, OPEN, AND SAVE DOCUMENTS

▶ *What You'll Do*

In this lesson, you'll create a new Photoshop document, open an existing document, and save both.

✓ Photoshop
Large Document Format
BMP
Dicom
Photoshop EPS
GIF
IFF Format
JPEG

Creating a New Document

After you start Photoshop, you can create a file from scratch using the New Document dialog box. In the New Document dialog box, you determine the dimensions of the file you want to create by typing values into the Width and Height text boxes. You also set the number of pixels you want, per inch, in the file. The number of pixels per inch in a Photoshop file is called the **image resolution**.

Opening an Existing Document

Much of the work you do in Photoshop will be working on image files you open from another source—in other words, image files you didn't create from scratch in Photoshop. Photoshop can open image files from a wide variety of sources, such as files from your phone camera, your digital camera, or files you download from the Internet. Once opened in Photoshop, those images are editable using all of Photoshop's features.

Saving Files

Photoshop provides several options for saving a file. Often the project you're working on determines the techniques you'll use for saving files. For example, you might want to preserve the original version of a file while you modify a copy. You can open a file and then immediately save it with a different filename as well as save files in many different file formats. When working with graphic images, you can open a Photoshop file that has been saved as a bitmap (.bmp) file and then save it as a JPEG (.jpg) file to use on a web page.

Understanding File Formats

When you save a Photoshop file, you must choose a file format in which to save it. You can think of file formats as different types of coding that an image can be saved with or, if you like, different languages. Photoshop can open images saved in many different file formats, and it can save those images in different file formats as well.

Perhaps the most important file format for you to understand is PSD. Saving a file as a PSD is saving it as a Photoshop file. The PSD format is called a **proprietary format**. That means it's the property of someone; in this case, it's Adobe's format for Photoshop files. Because the PSD format is itself the Photoshop format, it saves all Photoshop elements and features with the file with no compression and thus no loss of image quality. As a rule of thumb, you should always save your files as PSD files for your own work. If you need to deliver PSD files to others, ask them which file format they prefer. Make a note: Because the PSD format is proprietary, PSD files can only be opened and edited in Photoshop, and they can be placed only in other Adobe software packages, such as InDesign, Illustrator, or Dreamweaver.

Other file formats are **nonproprietary formats** and choosing them can have a big effect on how the image is saved. The following is a list of the most commonly used nonproprietary formats.

- **JPEG** (Joint Photographic Experts Group) Named for the group that created it, the JPEG file format is widely used, especially for web graphics. Because it is so common, many programs other than Photoshop are compatible with JPEGs. For example, Microsoft Word, PowerPoint, and Excel can all place and display JPEG files. On the contrary, these programs cannot place or display a PSD file, because that format is proprietary to Adobe.

Despite the fact that the JPEG format is so common, beware of choosing JPEG as a format for your work. The JPEG format cannot save layered artwork from Photoshop. If you save a file as a JPEG, the layered artwork will be "flattened" into one layer, and the layer structure lost.

Another reason to avoid the JPEG format is that it is "lossy," meaning that it degrades Photoshop image data to compress the image down to a smaller file size. Thus, you must think of JPEG as *only* an output file, as opposed to a file you'll use while you're working on a Photoshop document. You must always think of JPEG as a format you use for a *copy* of your artwork. The only real reason to use the JPEG format is to create a flattened copy of your artwork that you want to share for use online or in other programs where the quality of the image isn't a priority.

- **TIFF** Another common format is the TIFF (Tagged Image File Format). TIFF files are a good choice for saving a Photoshop file if you need it to be in a nonproprietary format. TIFF files save Photoshop files in their existing state; for example, TIFFs will save the Photoshop files with their layers intact. You must always be aware of compression when choosing a file format other than PSD. The TIFF format is "non-lossy compression," meaning that the compression algorithm will make the file size smaller without degrading the image data in any way.

- **GIF** (Graphics Interchange Format) The GIF format, pronounced with a hard or soft G, is a lossy compression format created in the late 1980s. You can think of GIF as only for output and sharing an image; it's not a format you'd ever use while working on a Photoshop document, because it doesn't save layers and it heavily compresses an image. GIFs have become very popular for creating low-resolution and small-file-size animations shared on the Internet because they are able to contain multiple images simultaneously.

- **PNG** (Portable Graphics Format) PNG is a relatively new format created to replace GIF files. One of the big benefits of the PNG file format is that it is "lossless"; it doesn't degrade the quality of the image like JPEG and GIF. PNG files, like GIFs, support transparent backgrounds, and they too can be animated. However, like GIF and JPEG, PNG files do not support layered artwork, so they are not an option for saving in-progress Photoshop documents.

To summarize, PSD is the format you want to always use when saving Photoshop documents because it saves everything with no loss in quality. Use the other formats only for copies of the artwork you want to use online or deliver to someone else who can't open or doesn't need layered Photoshop artwork.

TIP Photoshop files that are larger than 2 GB cannot be saved in the PSD format. Instead, they must be saved in the Large Document Format (PSB), which is also a proprietary Adobe format. PSB supports documents up to 300,000 pixels, keeping all Photoshop features such as layers, effects, and filters intact.

Using Save As Versus Save

Sometimes it's more efficient to create a new image by modifying an existing one, especially if it contains elements and special effects you want to use again. The Save As command on the File menu creates a copy of the file. It prompts you to give the duplicate file a new name, so it doesn't overwrite the original file.

Throughout this book, you will be instructed to open your data files and use the Save As command. Saving your data files with new names keeps the original data files intact in case you have to start the lesson over or you want to repeat an exercise.

TIP You can also create a copy of the active file by clicking Image on the menu bar and then clicking Duplicate. Click OK to confirm the name of the duplicate file.

Create a new Photoshop document

1. Start Photoshop.
2. Click **File** on the menu bar, then click **New** to open the New Document dialog box.
3. Click the **Print tab** at the top of the dialog box.
4. Click the preset template named **Letter** in the first row.
5. In the **Preset Details pane** on the right side of the dialog box, note the words **Untitled-1** at the top.

   Photoshop automatically names new documents with the word "Untitled" followed by a sequential number.

TIP Depending on how many Photoshop files you have open on your computer, your default name might be different.

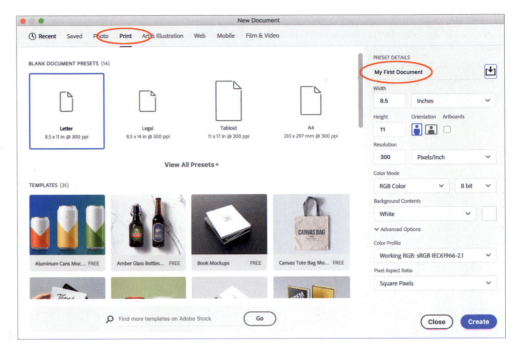

Figure 12 New Document dialog box

6. Change Untitled-1 to **My First Document**.

   Your New Document dialog box should resemble Figure 12.

   Entering a name for the document does just that—it gives the document a name. Understand that naming the document is *not* saving the document. This new document won't be saved on your computer until you actually save it.

7. Note the value in the **Resolution text box**.

   This file will have 300 pixels per inch, which is the default resolution when you choose Letter as your document type.

Continued on next page

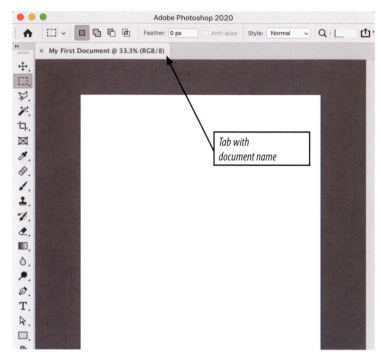

Figure 13 The new document opened in the Photoshop window

Figure 14 PS 1-1.psd file open in the Photoshop window

8. Click **Create**.

A document opens. As shown in Figure 13, the new document appears as a white rectangle, which is called the **canvas**, but it is actually a bed of millions of pixels, all of which can be colorized to render any image you can think of. Be sure to note that a tab appears at the top of the window with the name My First Document.

9. Press the **letter [D]** on your keypad to set the foreground color to black and the background color to white.

10. Click **Filter** on the menu bar, point to **Render**, then click **Clouds**.

The pixels on the canvas change to a pattern of clouds, which were rendered using the foreground and background colors on the toolbar.

11. Keep this document open as you move to the next set of steps.

You used the New command to open the New Document dialog box. You then loaded the Letter document type and noted its default dimensions and resolution. You created the document and then noted it appears as a white canvas. You then used the Render filter to see the pixels rendered as clouds.

Open an existing Photoshop document

1. Click **File** on the menu bar, then click **Open**.

2. Navigate to the folder where your data files are stored, then open **PS 1-1.psd**.

As shown in Figure 14, the file opens in a new tab with the name PS 1-1.psd.

3. Keep this document open as you move to the next set of steps.

You opened a second Photoshop document and noted that a second tab appeared in the window for this document.

Explore options for viewing multiple open documents

1. At the top of the Photoshop window, click the **My First Document tab**.

   Photoshop switches to the My First Document file, and it becomes the active file.

2. Click the **PS1-1.psd tab**.

   PS1-1.psd becomes the active file.

3. Click **Window** on the menu bar, point to **Arrange**, then click **Tile All Vertically**.

   As shown in Figure 15, the two documents now appear side by side.

AUTHOR'S **NOTE** As you work in Photoshop, you will often have many documents open simultaneously. Sometimes you'll even want to drag elements from one file into another. Use these commands on the Arrange menu when you need to see multiple documents at the same time.

4. Click **Window** on the menu bar, point to **Arrange**, then click **Consolidate All to Tabs**.

   The two documents revert to tabbed documents at the top of the Photoshop window.

5. Click **Window** on the menu bar, point to **Arrange**, then click **Float All in Windows**.

   Each document is no longer tabbed; each is now a "floating" window.

6. Click and drag **each document** by its name to move it to a different position in the window.

   Figure 16 shows one arrangement.

7. Click **Window** on the menu bar, point to **Arrange**, then click **Consolidate All to Tabs**.

8. Keep both documents open as you move to the next set of steps.

You used the Arrange commands to show the two open documents side by side and to return them to tabbed documents at the top of the Photoshop window.

Figure 15 Two documents arranged side by side in the Photoshop window

Figure 16 Two documents "floating" in the Photoshop window

Save and Save As

1. Click the **My First Document tab** to activate that document.

   This file has not been saved since you created it. It has been named in the New Document dialog box, but it hasn't been saved.

2. Click **File** on the menu bar, then click **Save**.

   TIP The first time you save a new file, you will be asked if you wish to save it on your computer or to cloud documents. If you do not wish to make this choice every time you save a Photoshop document, simply click the Don't show again check box in the lower-left corner.

3. Click **Save on your computer**, if necessary.

   The Save As dialog box opens. Note that the name you gave the file, My First Document, has automatically been loaded into the Save As dialog box.

4. Navigate to where you save your working files for this chapter.

5. Click the **Format list arrow**.

   As shown in Figure 17, the Format menu offers many file formats you can use to save your document.

6. Click **Photoshop** on the list.

7. Click **Save**.

8. Click the **PS 1-1.psd tab** to switch to that image.

9. Click **Image** on the menu bar, point to **Adjustments**, then click **Hue/Saturation**.

10. Drag the **Hue slider** left to **–77**, then click **OK**.

    All the colors in the image shift, and the bird's beak changes to red. If the file were saved now, it would over-write the original image with this altered image. This is undesirable because the original image may be needed at some other time.

11. Click **File** on the menu bar, then click **Save As**.

12. Type **Red Beak Eagle** in the Save As text box.

13. Verify that **Photoshop** is selected as the **Format**, then click **Save**.

    A new file is created; the original PS1-1.psd document has not been altered and is no longer open.

Figure 17 File formats available in the Save As dialog box

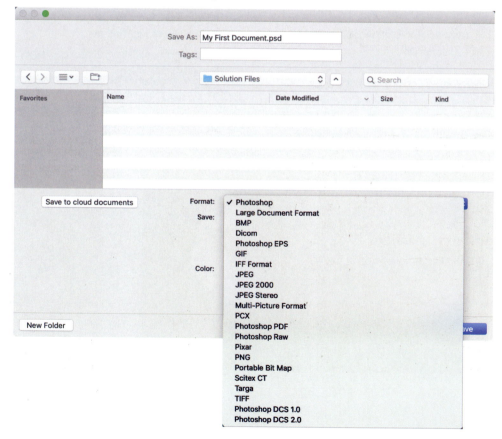

14. Close My First Document, and then close Red Beak Eagle.

Note that even though no documents are open, Photoshop is still open.

You saved the My First Document file. You used the Hue/Saturation dialog box to alter the PS 1-1.psd image, then you used Save As to save the altered image as a new file.

Save a custom document preset

1. Click **File** on the menu bar, then click **New**.

The New Document dialog box opens. Listed across the top of the dialog box are different types of output destinations for the new file.

2. Click **Photo**, then click **View All Presets**.

The window offers preset document sizes in both portrait and landscape orientations that you might use for a photo. For example, the preset Portrait, 5 × 7 would fit a standard-sized frame.

3. Click **Mobile**, then click **View All Presets**.

The window offers many presets for Apple devices, such as for the iPhone X or an Apple Watch. It also offers presets for an Android phone and a Microsoft Surface Pro 4, among others.

4. Click **Print**, then click **View All Presets**.

5. In the **Preset Details pane**, change the settings to those shown in Figure 18.

The standard size for a billboard, like what you'd see along a highway, is 14-feet by 48-feet. To design a billboard in Photoshop, you would build a high-resolution image file at a scale of 1-foot=1-inch. Therefore, the Photoshop file would be 14-inches by 48-inches.

6. Click the **Save Document Preset button** , identified in the figure.

7. Type **14 x 48 BILLBOARD** at the top of the window, then click **Save Preset**.

The new 14 x 48 BILLBOARD preset is now listed in the Saved window. You can use this preset as a template each time you want to create a file for a 14" × 48" billboard.

8. Click **Close** at the bottom of the New Document dialog box.

You explored different file output categories in the New Document dialog box to view different preset documents. You entered settings for a 14" × 48" billboard document and then saved those settings as a custom preset on the Saved tab.

Figure 18 Settings for a custom preset for a billboard document

EXPLORE THE TOOLBAR AND THE OPTIONS PANEL

▶ *What You'll Do*

In this lesson, you'll explore the toolbar and Options panel, set preferences for different tools, and learn important quick keys for accessing tools.

Explore the Toolbar

The **toolbar** presents a tool with an icon representing its function. For example, the Zoom tool shows a magnifying glass. You can place the pointer over each tool to display a tool tip, which tells you the name or function of that tool. Some tools have additional hidden tools, indicated by a small black triangle in the lower-right corner of the tool. Press and hold the tools with the small black triangle to reveal the hidden tools.

You can view the toolbar in a one-column or two-column format by clicking the expand arrow in its upper-left corner.

Each tool has a corresponding one-letter shortcut key. For example, the shortcut key to access the Type tool is T. If a tool has hidden tools, you can cycle through them by pressing and holding [shift] and then pressing the tool's shortcut key until the desired tool appears.

> **TIP** The Edit toolbar button on the toolbar (represented by a three-dot icon) opens the Customize Toolbar dialog box. Here you can customize the toolbar by placing tools into groupings based on your work style. Tools that are not used often can be dragged into the Extra Tools pane. You can choose whether to hide or show these tools.

Explore the Options Panel

The **Options panel**, located directly under the menu bar, displays the current settings for the selected tool. For example, when you select the Type tool, the default font and font size appear on the Options panel, which can be changed if desired. If you choose the Lasso tool (a selection tool), the Options panel switches to show options for the Lasso tool. As you work, whenever you select a tool, the first place your eye should go is to the Options panel to check the settings for the tool you're about to use.

Quick-Accessing the Move Tool and Zoom Tool

As you progress with Photoshop, you will often find yourself switching between the Move tool and the Zoom tool. This is because, no matter what other operation you're doing, the need to move artwork and zoom in or out to view artwork comes up regularly.

Moving your mouse pointer to click back and forth between the Move tool and the Zoom tool takes too much time and is too much of a distraction. Instead, you can use simple keyboard shortcuts that allow you to temporarily switch to those tools without clicking on them on the toolbar.

For example, let's say you are using the Brush tool to paint artwork. At any time, you can temporarily switch to the Move tool by pressing and holding the [command] (Mac) or [ctrl] (Win) key on your keypad. Your mouse pointer will switch to the Move tool for you to move artwork. Then, when you're done, simply release the key, and you're back to the Brush tool.

In the same scenario, let's say you need to access the Zoom tool. Press and hold [spacebar][command] (Mac) or [spacebar] [ctrl] (Win) and your Brush tool will change to the Zoom Plus tool, which you can use to enlarge the view of the canvas. Add [option] (Mac) or [alt] (Win) to switch to the Zoom Minus tool, which reduces the view of the canvas.

Explore the Toolbar and the Options panel

1. Open PS 1-1.psd.
2. Click **Window** on the menu bar, point to **Workspace**, then click **Reset Essentials**.

   Essentials is a default workspace, which refers to how the Photoshop window is arranged. Clicking Reset Essentials restores the window and its panels to the default arrangement.

3. Note the toolbar on the left side of the window, then note the Options panel at the top, under the menu bar.
4. At the very top of the toolbar, click the **two tiny arrows** pointing to the right.

   As shown in Figure 19, the toolbar switches from a single column to a double column. Clicking the arrows toggles between a single- and double-column toolbar.

   AUTHOR'S NOTE   It is suggested you work with a double column of tools when using this book to match the figures in the book.

5. At the top of the toolbar, note the series of **tiny vertical lines**.
6. Click and drag those **vertical lines** to move the toolbar away from the left edge and "float" it anywhere in the Photoshop window.

   Some Photoshop users like their toolbar locked against the window's edge, and others like to float it in different locations.

7. Position your mouse pointer over the **top-left tool** and keep it there.

   A tool tip appears, telling you the name of the tool. This is the Move tool. Note the letter V in parenthesis. That is the shortcut for the Move tool.

8. Press the **letter [V]** on your keypad (lowercase works too) and the **Move tool** ⊕ will be selected on the toolbar.

Continued on next page

Figure 19   Toolbar set to a double column of tools

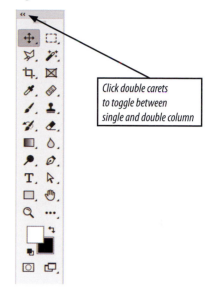

Click double carets to toggle between single and double column

Figure 20 Showing hidden Marquee tools

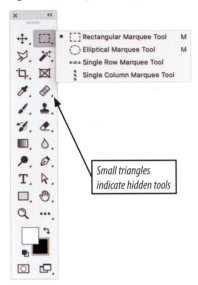

Small triangles indicate hidden tools

9. Press the **letter [M]** on your keypad.

The Rectangular Marquee tool is selected. Note the small black triangle at the lower-right corner of the tool. The triangle indicates that there are hidden tools behind the tool that is showing.

10. Press and hold the **Rectangular Marquee tool**.

As shown in Figure 20, all four marquee tools become visible.

11. Press and hold **[shift]**, then press the **letter [M]** on your keypad repeatedly.

Each time you press the letter [M], the toolbar toggles between the Rectangular and Elliptical Marquee tools. The combination of the [shift] key and a tool's keyboard shortcut will toggle through all hidden tools for that tool.

12. Press the **letter [V]** on your keypad to access the **Move tool**.

Note how the Options panel changes from the Marquee tool settings to show the Move tool settings.

13. On the Options panel, verify that **Auto Select:** and **Show Transform Controls check boxes** are not checked.

14. Press the **letter [Z]** on your keypad to access the **Zoom tool**.

15. On the Options panel, verify that none of the check boxes are checked.

Your Options panel should resemble Figure 21.

16. Note the two colors at the bottom of the toolbar.

The top color is the foreground color, and the color beneath the foreground color is the background color.

17. Click **Window** on the menu board, then click **Swatches**.

The Swatches panel opens. The Swatches panel contains numerous default colors for you to work with.

18. Click the **red swatch** at the top of the Swatches panel.

The foreground color changes to the red swatch you clicked. Clicking a swatch in the Swatches panel always changes the foreground color.

19. Press the **letter [X]** on your keypad repeatedly.

The foreground and background colors switch.

20. Press the **letter [D]** on your keypad.

Pressing [D] restores the foreground and background colors to their defaults, which are black over white.

You changed the toolbar to a double column, you viewed hidden tools, you selected tools using keypad shortcuts, and you selected tools and verified their settings on the Options panel.

Figure 21 Zoom tool settings on the Options panel

Use keyboard keys to quick-access the Zoom tool and Hand tool

1. Press the **letter [Z]** on your keypad to access the **Zoom tool** 🔍 .

2. On the Options panel, *remove* the **check marks** next to **Resize Windows to Fit**, **Zoom All Windows**, and **Scrubby Zoom**.

3. Press the **letter [L]** on your keypad to access the **Lasso tool** ⊘ .

    The Lasso tool is a selection tool that allows you to select a randomly shaped area of pixels. Let's practice working with the Lasso tool to quickly change the view of the canvas.

4. Use your index finger and your ring finger to press and hold **[spacebar] [command] (Mac)** or **[spacebar] [ctrl] (Win)** on your keypad.

    The Lasso tool ⊘ changes to the Zoom Plus tool 🔍 .

5. Click the **Zoom Plus tool** 🔍 three times between the eagle's eyes.

    The image of the eagle is so large now that it exceeds the window. You would have to use the scroll arrows or scroll bars at the side of the window to see other parts of the image, but there's a faster way.

6. Press and hold only **[spacebar]** with your index finger.

    The tool changes to the Hand tool ✋ , which is a panning tool.

7. Click and drag the **Hand tool** ✋ to pan to see different parts of the enlarged image.

8. With your index finger still on **[spacebar]**, bring down your middle and ring fingers so that you are pressing and holding three keys: **[spacebar] [command] [option] (Mac)** or **[spacebar] [ctrl] [alt] (Win)**.

    The tool changes to the Zoom Minus tool 🔍 .

9. Click the **Zoom Minus tool** 🔍 five times between the eagle's eyes.

> **AUTHOR'S NOTE** You *must* learn these keyboard shortcuts to access the Zoom tools quickly. You can easily remember these commands by the number of fingers needed to execute them: one finger = scroll, two fingers = zoom in, three fingers = zoom out. For the remainder of this book, you will never be asked to "click the Zoom tool." Instead, you will be asked to "access the Zoom tool" or "zoom in on the image."

10. Click **View** on the menu bar, then click **Fit on Screen**.

11. Use the keyboard shortcut to access the **Zoom Plus tool** 🔍 .

    Using Figure 22 as a guide, click and drag a box around both of the eagle's eyes, then release the mouse pointer.

    The area you drew the box around is enlarged in the window. This method is called a "marquee zoom," and it is a very effective way to zoom in on the area of the canvas that you want to see.

TIP If you are unable to create a marquee with the Zoom tool, it is because you have options activated for the Zoom tool that need to be turned off. Click the Zoom tool 🔍 , then uncheck Resize Windows to Fit, Zoom All Windows, and Scrubby Zoom.

12. Press and hold **[command] [0] (Mac)** or **[ctrl] [0] (Win)** to fit the artwork on the screen.

    These are the keyboard shortcuts for the Fit on Screen command on the View menu. You will do this thousands of times. Use the keyboard shortcut to do it quickly.

TIP The keyboard shortcuts are zeros, not the letter O.

13. Keep this file open for the next exercise.

You used keyboard shortcuts to access the Zoom Plus and Zoom Minus tools.

Figure 22 Executing a marquee-zoom

CREATE A CUSTOMIZED WORKSPACE FOR USING THIS BOOK

▶ *What You'll Do*

In this lesson, you'll explore the toolbar and the Options panel, set preferences for different tools, and learn important quick keys for accessing tools.

Working with Panels

Imagine you were a designer on the Photoshop interface. In the early days, you could use the menu commands on the menu bar to contain all the commands and launch all the dialog boxes necessary for users to use Photoshop. But that was a long time ago. Photoshop now has so many features that Adobe needed to create individual panels to house them.

Panels are small control windows that house settings you use to modify images. By default, panels appear in stacked groups at the right side of the window. A collection of panels is called a **panel group**.

The **panel dock** is a gray vertical bar that contains a collection of panels, panel groups, or panel icons. The arrows in the dock are used to expand and collapse the panels.

You can display a panel by simply clicking the panel tab, making it the active panel by clicking its name from the Window menu, or by clicking its icon in the icon dock (if it's displayed).

Panels can be separated and moved anywhere in the workspace by dragging their tabs to new locations. To manage screen space, you can package panels into groups, or you can dock them so that they move together as a unit.

Each panel has its own menu that you can access by clicking the Panel menu button in its upper-right corner.

Working with Rulers

Rulers in Photoshop are positioned along the top and down the left edge of the Photoshop window. Rulers can help you precisely measure and position an object in the workspace. Rulers do not appear the first time you use Photoshop, you display them by clicking Rulers on the View menu.

Photoshop offers a variety of units to choose from for your rulers. You can display rulers as pixels, inches, centimeters, millimeters, points, picas, or percentages.

Learning Shortcut Keys

Keyboard shortcuts can make your work with Photoshop faster and easier. For example, rather than clicking the Edit menu, then pointing to the word Transform, and then clicking the word Scale to scale an image, you can simply enter [command][T] (Mac) or [ctrl][T] (Win) to do the exact same thing. Commands on the menu bar list their keyboard shortcut to the right of the command.

As you become more familiar with Photoshop, you'll gradually pick up shortcuts for commands and tools you use most often, such as saving a file, opening a document, copying, pasting, duplicating a layer, or transforming artwork. You'll notice that as you learn to use shortcut keys, your speed while working with Photoshop will increase, and you'll complete tasks with fewer mouse clicks.

You can find existing keyboard shortcuts by clicking Edit on the menu bar and then clicking Keyboard Shortcuts. The Keyboard Shortcuts and Menus dialog box allows you to add shortcuts or edit those that already exist. You can also display the list of shortcuts by exporting it to an HTML file and then printing it or viewing it in a browser.

Customizing Your Workspace

The term **workspace** refers to how you set up your Photoshop window—specifically, which panels you keep open, how you group them, and where you position them. Once you establish the workspace the way you like it, you can name it and save it as a customized workspace, and it will be available to every document you create. Even if you modify your own customized workspace, you can always restore it to its default by hitting the Reset command under the Window/ Workspace command.

Many designers name and create different customized workspaces based on the work they might be doing. For example, if a project calls for a lot of work with type, you might want to create a workspace that has the type-formatting panels available, such as the Character, Paragraph, and Paragraph Styles panels. For a different project that involves a lot of color correction, you might create a workspace heavy with color adjustment panels, like Curves, Levels, Hue/Saturation, and Color Balance panels.

You can easily switch between different workspaces using the Workspace submenu command on the Window menu or the Workspace Switcher icon at the top right of the Photoshop window.

You can also change the color of your workspace by clicking Edit on the menu bar, pointing to Preferences, and then clicking Interface (Win) or by clicking Photoshop on the menu bar, pointing to Preferences, and then clicking Interface (Mac). Here you can choose one of four gray themes, from light gray to the darker charcoal gray.

Specify the keyboard shortcut for hiding extras

1. Verify that the file **PS 1-1.psd** is still open.

2. Click the **Rectangular Marquee tool** 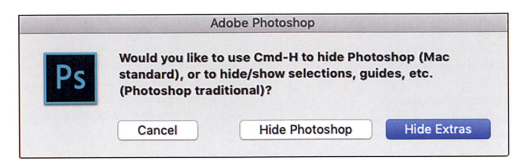 on the toolbar, then click and drag to make a rectangular marquee anywhere on the image.

   Occasionally, you may want to hide things Photoshop refers to as "extras" on the canvas. For example, you might want to work with this selection you just made, but you might want it to be invisible, or hidden, while you work. You can use a keyboard shortcut to do that, which you will do in the next step.

3. Press **[command] [H] (Mac)** or **[ctrl] [H] (Win)**.

   A dialog box may appear, as shown in Figure 23. (If the dialog box does not appear, skip to Step 5.) The shortcut you entered can be used to hide extras, which is what you want to do, or it can be used to hide Photoshop entirely, which you most definitely do not want to do.

Figure 23 Specifying the result of entering the Hide Extras keyboard shortcut

4. Click the **Hide Extras button**.

   The selection still exists, but the selection marquee is hidden.

5. Press **[command] [H] (Mac)** or **[ctrl] [H] (Win)** again.

   The selection marquee becomes visible. The keyboard shortcut toggles between hiding and showing extras.

6. Press **[command] [D] (Mac)** or **[ctrl] [D] (Win)** to deselect the pixels.

You made a simple selection and then tried to hide it using the keyboard shortcut for Hide Extras. If this was the first time you used that shortcut on a Mac, Photoshop wanted to know if you meant it to Hide Extras or to Hide Photoshop. You specified that you wanted to Hide Extras. You will not be asked to specify this again.

Customize the View menu and the Move tool

1. Click **View** on the menu bar, point to **Snap To**, then click **None**.

2. Click **View** on the menu bar, point to **Show**, then click **None**.

3. Click **View** on the menu bar, point to **Show**, then click **Selection Edges** to activate it.

    Always keep Selection Edges checked. Selection edges can be hidden or shown when you choose [command] [H] (Mac) or [ctrl] [H] (Win).

4. Click the **Move tool** ⊕ on the toolbar.

5. On the Options panel, verify the **Auto-Select** and **Show Transform Controls** options are not checked.

You customized options on the View menu and for the Move tool.

Customize the Photoshop workspace

1. Click **Window** on the menu bar, point to **Workspace**, then click **Reset Essentials**.

    The panel arrangement throughout the Photoshop window resets to a default workspace named Essentials.

2. At the very top of the toolbar, click the **two arrows** pointing to the right to make the toolbar a double column.

3. From the right side of the screen, click and drag the **Learn panel** by its name tab to the center of the window, so that your screen matches Figure 24.

Figure 24 "Floating" the Learn panel on its own at the center of the window

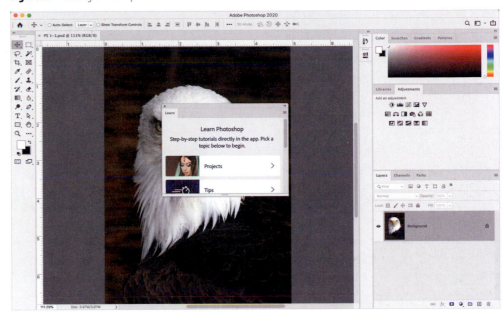

By clicking and dragging the Learn panel by its name tab, it is removed from the panel dock on the right edge of the window.

TIP The Learn panel is on the Window menu.

4. Click the **small x** at the upper-right corner of the Learn panel to close it.

5. Using the same method, close the following panels: **Adjustments**, **Libraries**, **Patterns**, and **Gradients**.

If you do not see the same panels mentioned in the steps, substitute them for panels that you do see to practice working with panels.

TIP Drag each panel to the center of the canvas and then click the x on the panel to close it.

Continued on next page

6. Drag the **Color panel** by its name toward the left side of the image, then drag the **Swatches panel** by its name toward the center.

Your figure should match Figure 25. Note that the Layers panel now takes up the full height of the window. You will be working with many layers (often dozens, sometimes hundreds!), so having this much vertical space for the Layers panel is a good thing.

TIP Note that the Color panel and the Swatches panel are now "floating" panels; you can move them to any area of the window that you like.

7. Note the tall, narrow panel dock outlined in red in Figure 25. Note also that two icons are stored at the top.

This tall, narrow panel dock is spring loaded. It contains full panels, but it displays them as small icons.

8. Click the **top icon** on the panel dock.

The top icon is a thumbnail for the History panel. When you click it, the History panel pops open to the left of the vertical bar.

9. Click the **top icon** again.

The History panel collapses.

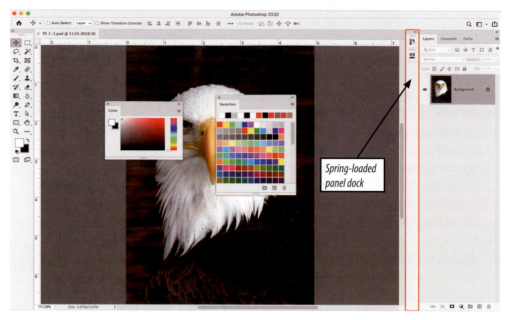

Figure 25 "Floating" the Color and Swatches panels

10. Click the **second icon** on the panel dock.

The second icon is a thumbnail for the Properties panel, one of the most important and most used panels in Photoshop.

11. Click the **second icon** again to collapse the Properties panel.

12. Note the **gray bar** across the top of the Color panel.

13. Click and drag the **Color panel** by the gray bar, position the **gray bar** over the bottom of the Swatches panel until you see a horizontal blue bar appear, then release the mouse pointer.

As shown in Figure 26, the two panels are now docked.

14. Click and drag the **Swatches panel** by its gray bar.

Both panels move together because they are docked.

15. Click and drag the **Color panel** by its name tab out of the dock.

The Color panel is released from the dock and is now a floating panel on its own.

16. Click and drag the **Color panel** by its name tab into the Swatches panel to the space at the right of the Swatches name tab.

As shown in Figure 27, the panels are grouped. You can click on each tab to view each panel.

17. Click and drag the **Color panel** by its name tab out of the group so that the two panels are separated again.

Continued on next page

Figure 26 The Color and Swatches panels docked

Figure 27 The Color and Swatches panels grouped

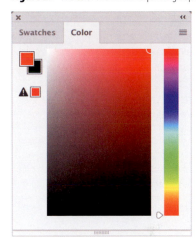

18. Click and drag the **Color panel** by its name tab beneath the second icon in the tall, narrow spring-loaded dock.

The Color panel is added to the dock and now appears as the third icon in the spring-loaded dock.

19. Click and drag the **Swatches panel** into the spring-loaded dock.

Your window should resemble Figure 28.

You closed panels that you didn't want open in your workspace. You docked two panels, you grouped two panels, and then you separated two panels. Finally, you dragged two panels into the spring-loaded dock.

Save a customized workspace

1. Click **Window** on the menu bar, point to **Workspace**, then click **New Workspace**.

The New Workspace dialog box opens.

2. Type **REVEALED WORKSPACE** in all caps.

Your dialog box should resemble Figure 29.

3. Click **Save**.

4. Click **Window** on the menu bar, then point to **Workspace**.

REVEALED WORKSPACE is now listed as a workspace and is checked because it is the active workspace.

5. Close PS 1-1.psd, and don't save it if prompted.

You named and saved the workspace you customized in the previous set of steps. You will use this workspace as the basis for the remainder of this book.

Figure 28 The Color and Swatches panels displayed as icons in the spring-loaded dock

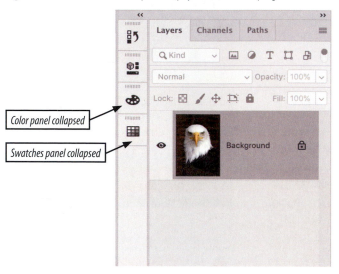

Color panel collapsed

Swatches panel collapsed

Figure 29 Naming the new workspace

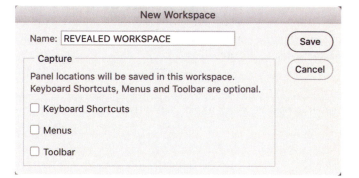

WORK WITH GRIDS, GUIDES, AND RULERS

▶ *What You'll Do*

In this lesson, you'll rotate and flip the canvas, and then you'll show rulers, create guides, modify guide colors, and view the document grid.

Using Guides

Guides are nonprinting horizontal and vertical lines that you can display on top of an image to help you position a selection. You can create an unlimited number of horizontal and vertical guides. You create a guide by displaying the rulers, positioning the pointer on either ruler, and then clicking and dragging the guide into position. You delete a guide by selecting the Move tool on the toolbar, positioning the pointer over the guide, and then clicking and dragging it back to its ruler. If the Snap feature is enabled, as you drag an object toward a guide, the object will be pulled toward the guide. To turn on the Snap feature, click View on the menu bar, and then click Snap. A check mark appears to the left of the command if the feature is enabled.

To delete a guide, first select the Move tool, and then click and drag the guide off of the canvas. You can also clear all guides from the document by clicking the Clear Guides command on the View menu.

You can lock guides on the canvas so they are not accidently moved. Click View on the menu bar, and then click Lock Guides. This menu also contains the Extras command, which you learned about in Lesson 5 of this chapter. The Extras command hides and shows guides along with other "extras" on the canvas, which are listed on the Show menu.

Using the Document Grid

In the pre-digital days, graphic designers and production artists designed and produced their layouts on grid paper—paper with intersecting lines that formed a grid. This was useful for aligning images and blocks of text. Photoshop documents have a document grid that you can hide or show using the Show/Grid commands on the View menu.

Changing the Color and Style of Guides and the Document Grid

The color and style of guides in a document are preferences that you set in the Preferences dialog box for Guides, Grid, and Slices. You use this same dialog box to change the space increments of the document grid. To access that dialog box quickly, double-click any guide. Change the color of guides or the document grid by clicking the appropriate Color list arrow, selecting a color, and then clicking OK.

Rotating and Flipping the Canvas

Another positioning element is the canvas itself. Sometimes an image will open on its side or even upside down and will need to be rotated. This happens most often when you download from a phone camera or other digital camera when the photographer has taken the photo with the camera in a side orientation.

In other circumstances, you might want to rotate the image just for artistic considerations. You might want to also flip the canvas so that you achieve a mirror image of the original.

To rotate or flip the canvas, click Image on the menu bar, point to Image Rotation, and then select the operation you want to execute.

Viewing the Canvas at 100%

Photoshop allows you to zoom in to enlarge an image or to zoom out to reduce an image on your screen. You can use the Fit on Screen command to view the entire canvas at the largest size it can fit on your screen.

When you click the 100% command on the View menu, you view the image at 100%. That sounds simple enough, but it actually requires some additional information to understand what that means. It's important to keep in mind that the monitor on your computer has its own screen resolution, which is by default 72 pixels per inch. At that setting, if you have a document that is 720 pixels × 720 pixels, that document at 100% would take up 10 inches × 10 inches on your screen.

Why does this matter? Because viewing a document at 100% is the minimum most accurate view of the document. As you progress with Photoshop, you will be adding very fine details to an image, such as noise or film grain or edge sharpening. In order to view those details with minimum accuracy, you must be viewing the document at a minimum of 100%. You may zoom in to enlarge the details but a view of less than 100% will not show a fully rendered view of the image.

Rotate and flip the canvas

1. Open **PS 1-2.psd**, then save it as **Bird Guides**.

2. Click **Image** on the menu bar, point to **Image Rotation**, then click **90° Clockwise**.

3. Click **Image** on the menu bar, point to **Image Rotation**, then click **Flip Canvas Horizontal**.

    The image is "flipped" to become its mirror image. Your canvas should resemble Figure 30.

4. Save the file.

You rotated the canvas 90° clockwise, and you flipped the canvas horizontally.

Figure 30 The image rotated and flipped

Morguefile

Work with guides and the document grid

1. Click **Image** on the menu bar, then click **Canvas Size**.

   The Canvas Size dialog box opens showing that the document is 7" × 10".

2. Click **Cancel**.

3. If you do not see rulers along the canvas, enter **[command] [R] (Mac)** or **[ctrl] [R] (Win)** so that the rulers are showing along the top edge and left edge of the canvas.

4. Double-click the **top-edge ruler**.

   The Preferences for Units & Rulers dialog box opens.

5. In the Units section, click the **Rulers list arrow** to see the list of measurements available.

   You can set your rulers to pixels, inches, centimeters, millimeters, picas, points, or percent.

   TIP Right-click the ruler to see a pop-up menu of the available measurements.

6. Verify that **Inches** is selected as the measurement, then click **OK**.

7. Click **View** on the menu bar, then click **100%**.

   The view of the canvas changes to 100%.

   TIP Memorize the keyboard shortcuts **[command][1]** or **[ctrl][1]** to view the canvas at 100%.

8. Click anywhere in the **top ruler**, then begin **dragging down** to create a horizontal guide across the image.

   As you drag, an info window appears, telling you, in inches, the position of the guide from the top edge of the canvas.

9. Position the guide so that it is **5"** from the top edge of the canvas.

10. Click anywhere in the **left ruler**, then begin **dragging right** to create a vertical guide.

11. Position the guide so that it is **3.5"** from the left edge of the canvas.

    As shown in Figure 31, the guides divide the image into four equal quadrants, and the intersection of the guides identifies the center of the document.

12. Press and hold **[command] (Mac)** or **[ctrl] (Win)**, then press the **semicolon key (;)** on your keypad to hide and show guides.

    TIP The semicolon key is one key to the right of the [L] key.

13. Press and hold **[command] (Mac)** or **[ctrl] (Win)**, then press the **apostrophe key (')** on your keypad to hide and show the document grid.

    TIP The apostrophe key is two keys to the right of the [L] key.

14. Click **View** on the menu bar, then click **Lock Guides**.

15. Save your work, then close Bird Guides.

You positioned a horizontal and a vertical guide at specific locations. You used keyboard commands to hide and show the guides and to hide and show the document grid. You used a View menu command to lock guides.

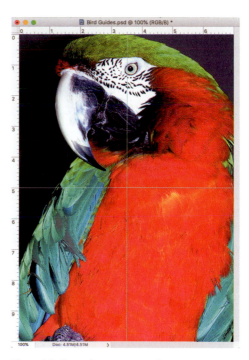

Figure 31 Two guides intersecting at the center point of the image

CHAPTER **2**

PAINT, SELECT, AND MOVE PIXELS

1. Fill the Canvas and Make Simple Selections
2. Paint with the Brush Tool
3. Make Selections with the Marquee and Lasso Tools
4. Explore a Grayscale Image with the Magic Wand Tool
5. Posterize an Image and Save Selections

Adobe Certified Professional in Visual Design Using Photoshop CC Framework

2. Project Setup and Interface

This objective covers the interface setup and program settings that assist in an efficient and effective workflow, as well as knowledge about ingesting digital assets for a project.

2.1 Create a document with the appropriate settings for web, print, and video.
   A Set appropriate document settings for printed and onscreen images.

2.5 Manage colors, swatches, and gradients.
   A Set the active foreground and background color.
   C Create, edit, and organize swatches.

3. Organizing Documents

This objective covers document structure such as layers and managing document structure for efficient workflows.

3.3 Differentiate between and perform destructive or nondestructive editing to meet design requirements.
   B Destructive editing: painting, adjustments, erasing, and rasterizing.

4. Creating and Modifying Visual Elements

This objective covers core tools and functionality of the application, as well as tools that affect the visual outcome of the document.

4.3 Make, manage, and manipulate selections.
   A Make selections using a variety of tools.
   B Modify and refine selections using various methods.
   C Save and load selections as channels.

FILL THE CANVAS AND MAKE SIMPLE SELECTIONS

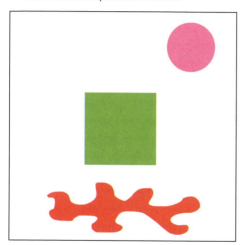

Photoshop is so popular and such a best seller that it's likely this is not your first time using it. You have probably done some exploring of the program and figured out how a lot of it works on your own. You might even be a self-taught user who has gone pretty far with the program. That's great! However, do not skip this chapter because you think it's too basic and you already know this content. Chapter 2 contains the ABC skills of Photoshop, and even the most accomplished self-taught user will find a valuable refresher course here. The chapter is designed to reinforce fundamental skills and behaviors. There are tips and tricks included and the selection tools are explored in depth. Don't pass this chapter over. You'll walk away a stronger user for the time you put in here.

Of course, if you are brand new to Photoshop, then this chapter is exactly what you are looking for. Welcome! And no matter what, don't rush! These are the skills that will strengthen your Photoshop muscles, and the time you put in here will build your entire foundation for working like a superhero with the program.

Filling with Color

"Filling" is one of the first commands most people learn in Photoshop. To fill in Photoshop means to choose a color and "fill" an area of the canvas—or the entire canvas—with that color. Even though filling is one of the most basic of Photoshop's operations, it's one you'll use over and over again, even in complex situations.

The Fill command on the Edit menu takes you to the Fill dialog box, which you use to fill a selection or the entire canvas with the foreground or background colors or other colors available in the dialog box. In most cases, however, you should use simple keyboard shortcuts to fill quickly. Press and hold [option] (Mac) or [Alt] (Win), then click the [delete] key to fill with your foreground color.

Understanding Pixels

All digital images are made up of small squares of color called **pixels**. The word pixel is a combination of two words—picture and element. The pixel is the smallest component, or element, of a digital image. There's no such thing as a half-pixel; the pixel is as small as it gets. Pixels are also only one color. A pixel is either black or white or red or pink or peach or brown. There are no "shades" in a pixel, and there are no "blends" of color. A pixel is one color and one color only.

Figure 1 shows an image, and it also shows an area of the image magnified so you can see the component pixels. When we see a digital image, we see the image and not the pixels because the pixels are so small. The number of pixels per inch is called the **resolution** of the image and is measured in pixels per inch (ppi). In an on-screen presentation such as a slideshow, on-screen images are saved with a resolution of 72 ppi. For high-quality printing, images are saved with a resolution of 300 ppi. Think of that—each pixel is so small that 300 of them can fit in one inch.

Filling Selections

To modify just some of the pixels on the canvas, you need to first select those pixels. Photoshop offers several selection tools that do just that—select pixels. These include the **Marquee tools**, which are the **Rectangular Marquee tool** and the **Elliptical Marquee tool**. As their names suggest, they create rectangular and square selections and elliptical and circular selections, respectively. The **Lasso tool** allows you to make freehand selections of any shape or size.

Once you make a selection, only those pixels on the canvas can be modified. For example, if you apply a fill color, only the selected pixels will be filled with the new color.

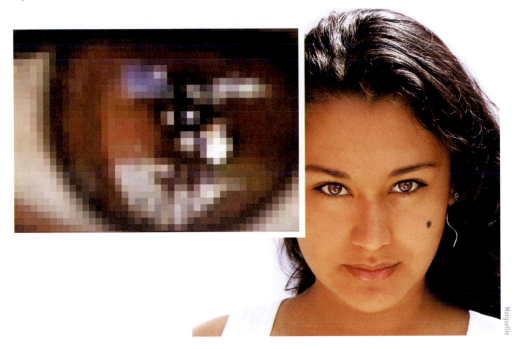

Figure 1 Image showing enlarged pixels

Morguefile

Fill the canvas

1. Open PS 2-1.psd, then save it as **Basic Fills**.

2. Click **Window** on the menu bar, point to **Workspace**, then click **Reset REVEALED WORKSPACE**.

   REVEALED WORKSPACE is the workspace you created in Chapter 1. Resetting a workspace restores it to the exact setup you saved and resets any modifications you might have made since.

3. Click **Window** on the menu bar, then click **Swatches**.

   The Swatches panel opens. This workspace has been saved with the Swatches panel as a thumbnail on the narrow spring-loaded panel dock. From this point on, rather than using the Window menu, you can access the Swatches panel by clicking the thumbnail.

   TIP All of Photoshop's panels are listed on the Window menu. This is a big help because whenever you are looking for a specific panel, you know it's located on the Window menu.

4. Click a **bright red swatch** on the Swatches panel.

   The foreground color on the toolbar changes to the red color you clicked.

5. Press the **letter [X]** on your keypad.

   The foreground and background colors switch. Red is now the background color.

6. Click a **blue swatch** on the Swatches panel.

   The foreground color changes to blue.

7. Click **Edit** on the menu bar, then click **Fill**.

   The Fill dialog box opens.

8. Match your settings to Figure 2, then click **OK**.

Figure 2 Fill dialog box

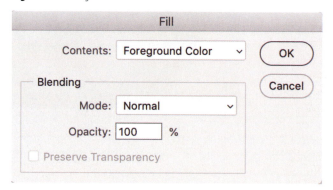

9. Compare your screen to Figure 3.

   The entire canvas fills with the foreground color.

10. Press the **letter [X]** on your keypad so that the foreground color changes to red.

TIP To switch the foreground and background colors, you can also click the Switch Foreground and Background Colors icon 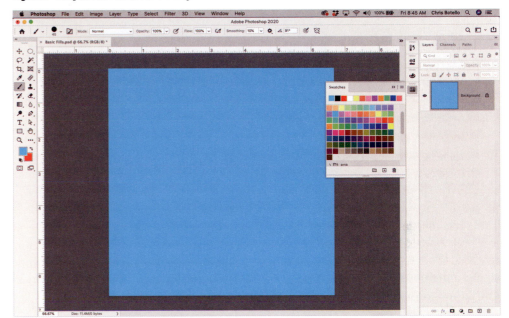 on the toolbar.

11. Press and hold **[option] (Mac)** or **[Alt] (Win)**, then press the **[delete] key** on your keypad.

   The canvas fills with the red foreground color. It is important that you memorize this keyboard shortcut for filling with the foreground color. This is an operation you will do countless times in your Photoshop work, so you need to know how to do it quickly, without having to use the Edit menu.

12. Save your work.

You reset the workspace. You selected a red foreground color and then switched the foreground and background colors. You then selected a blue foreground color. You used the Fill dialog box to fill the canvas with the blue foreground color. You switched the colors again and then used a keyboard command to fill the canvas with red.

Figure 3 Filling the entire canvas with the foreground color

Fill simple selections

1. Press the **letter [D]** on your keypad.

    The foreground and background colors change to their default colors, which are black over white.

2. Press and hold **[command] (Mac)** or **[Ctrl] (Win)**, then press the **[delete] key** on your keypad.

    The canvas fills with the white background color. Memorize this keyboard shortcut for filling with the background color.

3. Select the **Rectangular Marquee tool** [icon] on the toolbar, then make roughly a 2" square near the center of the canvas.

TIP Press the letter [M] on your keypad to access the Marquee tool. Hold [shift] and press the letter [M] repeatedly to toggle between the Rectangular and the Elliptical Marquee tools.

4. Click a **green swatch** on the Swatches panel.

5. Use the keyboard shortcut to **fill** the selection with the green foreground color.

    For the remainder of this chapter (and the whole book), use the keyboard shortcut to fill.

TIP The keyboard shortcut to fill a selection is **[command] (Mac)** or **[Ctrl] (Win)**, then **[delete]**.

6. Click **Select** on the menu bar, then click **Deselect**.

7. Select the **Elliptical Marquee tool** [icon] on the toolbar, then make roughly a 1.5" circle in the upper-right corner of the canvas.

8. Fill the circle with **pink**.

9. Press and hold **[command] (Mac)** or **[Ctrl] (Win)**, then press the **letter [D]** on your keypad.

    The circle is deselected. It's important that you memorize this keyboard shortcut to deselect; using the Select menu takes too long.

10. Select the **Lasso tool** [icon] on the toolbar.

    The Lasso tool [icon] makes freeform selections.

TIP Press the letter [L] on your keypad to access the Lasso tool [icon]. Hold [shift] and press the letter [L] repeatedly to toggle between all the Lasso tools.

11. Click and drag the **Lasso tool** [icon] to make any shape you like at the bottom of the canvas.

12. Fill the selection with **orange**.

13. **Deselect**, then compare your canvas to Figure 4.

14. Save your work.

You made three simple selections with the Rectangular Marquee tool, the Elliptical Marquee tool, and the Lasso tool and then filled them with green, pink, and orange.

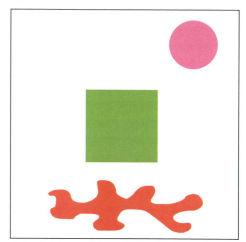

Figure 4 Three selected areas with three different fill colors

GROUPING, IMPORTING, AND EXPORTING NEW SWATCHES

The Swatches panel comes with default groups of swatches to make your design work easier. For example, you can choose colors from the Pastel group or the Dark group, depending on your needs. While these swatch groups are helpful, you may want to create your own group of colors to work with. To create a new swatch group, click the Swatches panel menu button, click New Swatch Group, name your group with a descriptive name, then click OK. Drag swatches from other groups into your new group or create new colors using the Color panel or the Color Picker. Clicking the Add to Swatches button in the Color Picker will place your new color in whichever swatch group is selected on the Swatches panel. To use your colors in another program or to send to someone else to use, you can export color swatches by first selecting all the swatches you want to export, click the Swatches panel menu button, then click Export Selected Swatches. Your swatches will be saved with the (*.ACO) filename extension. You can also import swatches by clicking the Swatches panel menu button, selecting Import Swatches, and then navigating to the (*.ACO) file on your computer.

PAINT WITH THE BRUSH TOOL

What You'll Do

In this lesson, you'll use the Brush tool with three different modes to paint on the canvas.

Painting with the Brush Tool

The Brush tool is Photoshop's version of a paintbrush. You click and drag it to paint, and it always paints with the foreground color. In addition to clicking and dragging to paint, you can single-click the brush and then [shift]-click the brush on a different area of the canvas. When you do that, a straight brush stroke will automatically connect the two points.

When you click the Brush tool on the toolbar, the Options panel at the top of the window changes to show settings for the Brush tool, and the **Brush Preset picker**, shown in Figure 5, becomes available. The Brush tool's size is measured in pixels. When the Brush tool is selected, the Options panel shows the current brush size and a rendering of the brush edge.

Clicking the Brush Preset picker list arrow reveals settings for the brush's **Size** and **Hardness**. The Hardness setting is measured in percentages. While 100% Hardness produces a brush that has a well-defined, smooth edge, 0% Hardness produces a brush with a very soft edge that fades or blends. These soft brushes

are often referred to as having a "feathered" edge. Even with a 0% Hardness setting, however, the center of the Brush tool will paint 100% of the foreground color.

While you can always use the Size slider on the Options panel to change the size of the Brush tool, you'll want to use the left and right bracket keys on the keypad to do so far more quickly. These keys are immediately to the right of the letter P on the keypad. The right bracket key ( ]) increases the brush size, and the left bracket key ([ ) decreases it.

The Options panel also displays the Opacity setting for the Brush tool. The word "opaque" means "not see-through," so the term **opacity** in Photoshop describes how opaque the Brush will paint. At 100% opacity, the brush paints 100% opaque; you can't see through the paint. At 50% opacity, the paint will be 50% see-through. Whenever the Brush tool is selected, you can quickly change the Opacity setting by pressing numbers on your keypad. Press [5] for 50% opacity, press [4] for 40% opacity, and so forth. For 100% opacity, press [0].

Figure 5 Brush settings on the Options panel

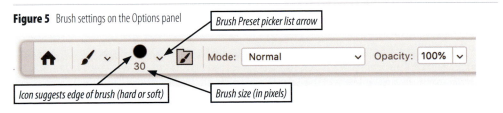

Brush Preset picker list arrow

Icon suggests edge of brush (hard or soft)

Brush size (in pixels)

Introducing Blending Modes

Blending modes are some of the most complex user algorithms in Photoshop, and they're available to you both for painting and for superimposing images and colors on the Layers panel. The basic definition of a blending mode is a computer **algorithm** (an ordered set of instructions to process data in a certain way) that controls how overlapping colors interact with one another. You will study and explore blending modes in great depth starting in Chapter 6. In this chapter, you will be introduced to blending modes as a concept when you use two of them to paint with the Brush tool.

When the Brush tool is selected, the Options panel displays a **Mode** setting with a list arrow, also identified in Figure 5. Click the list arrow to reveal all the blending modes available for you to paint with.

The default blending mode for the Brush tool is **Normal**, which you can think of as using no blending mode at all. In Normal mode, whatever color you paint changes the pixel to that color. For example, let's say your canvas is filled with bright yellow pixels, and you decide to paint with cyan. Wherever you paint, those yellow pixels will become cyan.

When the **Multiply** blending mode is activated, painting the same yellow canvas with the same cyan brush will yield green wherever you paint. This is because the Multiply blending mode causes the Brush tool to paint with transparent paint. One of the most useful features of the Multiply algorithm is that black pixels cannot

MULTIPLY BLENDING MODE

CYAN STOKE MULTIPLIED OVER A YELLOW STROKE PRODUCES GREEN

SAME COLORS MULTIPLIED OVER THEMSELVES PRODUCE DARKER COLOR

ANY COLOR MULTIPLIED WITH BLACK BECOMES BLACK

SAME PRIMARY COLORS MULTIPLIED DO NOT PRODUCED A RESULT

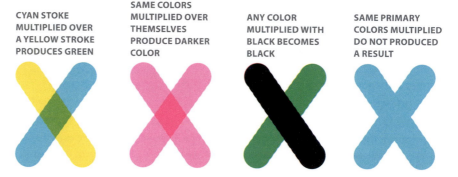

DARKER COLOR BLENDING MODE

CYAN STROKE DOMINATED BECAUSE IT IS THE DARKER COLOR

SAME COLORS PRODUCE NO CHANGE BECAUSE NEITHER IS DARKER

BLACK STROKE ALWAYS DOMINATES BECAUSE NO COLOR IS DARKER THAN BLACK

Figure 6 Multiply and Darker Color blending modes detailed

be altered by any other colors. Thus, Multiply mode is a great choice for painting white areas of an image without affecting any of the black areas, like in a coloring book.

You can think of using the Brush tool in Multiply mode like coloring with overlapping magic markers. If you overlap paint strokes of the same color, a darker color will appear where they intersect, as shown in the top section in Figure 6. This can be a cool effect. However, if it's an effect you don't want, you'll need to paint in a way that strokes don't overlap, or you can use a different blending mode.

In Multiply mode, the only colors that don't create a darker shade where they overlap themselves are the six primary colors—red, green, blue, cyan, magenta, and yellow. This is because the first three are the additive primary colors and the last three are the subtractive primary colors. You will learn *a lot* more about these six colors in later chapters.

The **Darker Color** blending mode, detailed in the lower section of Figure 6, is a straightforward algorithm. Wherever two colors overlap, the darker color will dominate and replace the lighter color. Painting with the Darker Color blending mode, as with the Multiply blending mode, leaves black pixels unaffected by any color. This is because no other color is darker than black.

The Fill dialog box on the Edit menu offers you the ability to fill a selection or the entire canvas with a color using a blending mode. Figure 7 shows a line art illustration composed of black lines after half the canvas is filled with a green color using the Multiply blending mode. The white areas become green, but the black areas are not affected.

Figure 7 Line art illustration half filled with the Multiply blending mode

Alka5051/Shutterstock.com

Paint with the Brush tool

1. Open PS 2-2.psd, then save it as **Paint Palette**.

2. Select the **Brush tool** ✐ on the toolbar.

   When you select the Brush tool, the Options panel at the top of the window changes to show options for the Brush tool.

3. Click the **Brush Preset picker list arrow** ⬤ to show Size and Hardness settings, as shown in Figure 8.

4. Drag the **Size slider** to **100 px**, then drag the **Hardness slider** to **100%**.

5. On the Options panel, verify that **Mode** is set to **Normal**, **Opacity** is set to **100%**, **Flow** is set to **100%**, and **Smoothing** is set to **10%**.

6. Open the Swatches panel, then click **any blue swatch**.

7. On your keypad, note the **left bracket ([ )** and **right bracket ( ])** keys, which are immediately to the right of the letter [P].

8. Press the **right bracket ( ])** key repeatedly until the **Size** on the Options panel reads **500 px**.

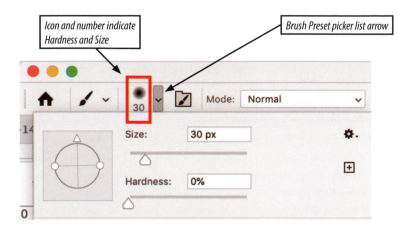

Figure 8 Brush Preset picker list arrow on the Options panel

Pressing the right bracket ( ]) key enlarges the brush size. Pressing the left bracket ([ ) key reduces the brush size.

9. Click the **brush** one time on the upper-left quadrant of the canvas.

   A circle with a hard, smooth edge is painted.

10. Change the **Hardness** setting to **0%**, then click the **brush** one time on the upper-right quadrant of the canvas.

    A circle with a soft, feathered edge is painted.

11. Reduce the brush size to **250 px**, then click one time on the bottom-left quadrant.

12. Press and hold **[shift]**, then click one time on the bottom-right quadrant.

    A straight stroke is painted connecting the two places you clicked. Your canvas should resemble Figure 9.

13. Change the **Hardness** setting to **100%**.

14. Change the **foreground color** to any of the **pink** swatches on the Swatches panel.

15. Press the **number [3]** on your keypad.

    On the Options panel, the Opacity for the brush now reads 30%.

16. Increase the brush size to **600 px**, then click and drag the **brush** over different areas of the canvas.

    Wherever you paint, a transparent pink color appears. It is only 30% opaque, so the blue lines you created are still visible.

17. Paint with the brush a second time, overlapping one of your pink brush strokes.

    Wherever you overlap the pink, the opacity doubles.

18. Press the **letter [D]** on your keypad, then press the **letter [X]** to change the foreground color to white.

19. Press and hold **[option] (Mac)** or **[Alt] (Win)**, then press the **[delete] key** on your keypad.

    The canvas is filled with white.

20. Save your work.

You examined a brush with a Hardness setting of 100% and a brush with a Hardness setting of 0%. You created an automatic brush stroke using the [shift] key, and you painted with opacity. Finally, you filled the canvas with white to erase your work.

Figure 9 Hard brush, soft brush, and an automatic brush stroke

Examine brush edges and opacity

1. Verify that the **Brush tool** is selected, then press **[0]** on your keypad to set the Opacity to 100%.

2. Set the brush size to **250 px**.

3. On the Swatches panel, click **any blue swatch**.

4. Click and drag to paint a curved arc approximately two inches long anywhere on the canvas.

5. Click a **red swatch** on the Swatches panel, then paint another **curved ark** anywhere on the canvas.

Continued on next page

Figure 10 Painting the wide, hard-edged strokes

Figure 11 Painting the narrow, soft-edged strokes

6. Using Figure 10 as an example of the look you are trying to achieve, paint the whole canvas with different colors.

    As you paint, observe that whenever you overlap colors, there's no "mixing" of colors. When the Mode is set to Normal for the Brush tool, the current color replaces whatever color was previously there.

7. Press and hold **[option] (Mac)** or **[Alt] (Win)**.

    The Brush tool changes to the Eyedropper tool.

8. Click the **Eyedropper tool** on any **yellow color** on the canvas.

    The foreground color changes to the yellow color you sampled with the Eyedropper tool.

9. Release **[option] (Mac)** or **[Alt] (Win)** to return to the **Brush tool**.

10. Click the **Brush Preset picker list arrow**, then set the **Hardness** to **0%**.

11. Click the **left bracket key ([ )** on your keypad until the brush size on the Options panel reads **60 px**.

12. Toggling between the **Brush tool** and the **Eyedropper tool**, paint thin, soft-edged strokes in different colors all over the canvas.

    Figure 11 represents an example of the look you are trying to achieve.

13. Save your work without making any other changes, and continue ***directly*** to the next set of steps.

You painted the canvas with wide, hard-edged, multicolored brush strokes. You toggled between the Brush tool and the Eyedropper tool to sample colors off the canvas, then you painted narrow, soft-edged strokes on top of the existing colors.

Use Keyboard Shortcuts to Undo and Redo

1. Press and hold **[command] (Mac)** or **[Ctrl] (Win)**, then press the **letter [Z]** on your keypad 12 times.

   This keyboard shortcut executes the Undo command, which is on the Edit menu. Every time you press [Z], you undo a previous move that you made. By default, Photoshop saves 50 "history states," so you can step backward 50 times.

2. Press and hold **[shift] [command] (Mac)** or **[Shift] [Ctrl] (Win)**, then press the **letter [Z]** on your keypad 12 times.

   This keyboard shortcut executes the Redo command, which is also on the Edit menu. Every time you press [Z], you step forward through the moves you made until you are back to the current state of the document.

3. Using the keyboard shortcut, undo 20 times.

4. Using the **Brush tool** , paint a stroke of color anywhere on the canvas.

   Because you made a new move after using the Undo command, you can no longer redo your way forward to the state of the artwork when you started this series of steps. The new stroke you painted is now the current state of the artwork. All you can do is undo from here.

5. Click **File** on the menu bar, then click **Revert**.

   The Revert command restores the file to the state it was in when you last saved, which, in this case, was Step 13 of the previous set of steps.

AUTHOR'S **NOTE** You can think of the Revert command as a "Super Undo" you can use to go way back if you really mess up, even if you've made hundreds of moves. This is an example of why you must make it a habit to save your work as you go.

You used keyboard shortcuts to undo and redo steps you made while working. After undoing a second time, you made a new move, which made it impossible to redo to the state of the artwork when you started this series of steps. You used the Revert command to restore the file to when it was last saved.

Use filters with painted artwork

1. Click **Filter** on the menu bar, point to **Blur**, then click **Gaussian Blur**.

2. Type **23** in the **Radius text box**, then click **OK**.

3. Click **Filter** on the menu bar, point to **Pixelate**, then click **Crystallize**.

4. Drag the **Cell Size slider** to **40**, then click **OK**.

5. Click **Filter** on the menu bar, point to **Stylize**, then click **Oil Paint**.

6. Set **Stylization** to **10.0**, **Cleanliness** to **2.0**, **Scale** to **6.0**, and **Bristle Detail** to **10.0**.

7. Verify that the **Lighting option** is checked, then click **OK**.

Continued on next page

8. Click **View** on menu bar, click **100%**, then compare your artwork to Figure 12.

   The result of the Oil Paint filter is a perfect example of why you must view the canvas at 100% to see fine details. You would not get an accurate rendering of the filters you applied if you viewed the canvas at anything less than 100%.

9. Press the **letter [F]** on your keypad two times to view the canvas in full screen mode against a black background.

AUTHOR'S **NOTE**   Considering the simple steps we took to paint the canvas, now that the filters have been applied, it's quite remarkable that this has become a reasonably interesting piece of artwork.

10. Press the **[esc] key** on your keypad to exit full screen mode.

11. Save your work, then close Paint Palette.

You applied three filters to the painted artwork to create the effect of an oil painting. You viewed the artwork at 100% in full screen mode against a black background.

Figure 12   Viewing the artwork with three filters applied

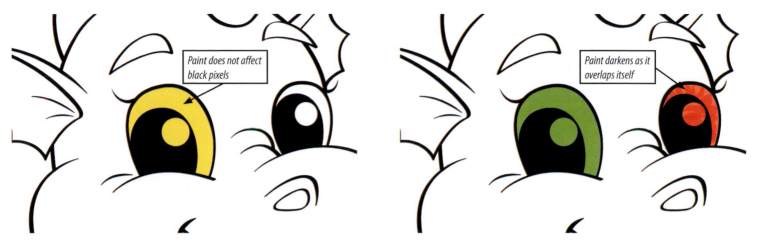

Figure 13 Painting the left eye yellow

Figure 14 Overlapping transparent paint strokes in the right eye

Paint with transparent paint in Multiply mode

1. Open PS 2-3.psd, then save it as **Coloring Book**.

2. Assess the image as a painting project, like a child's coloring book image.

   The challenge of trying to "color" the artwork with the same methods we've used so far in this lesson wouldn't be possible. That's because we'd have to paint right up to every black line without painting over the black lines. Fortunately, the Brush tool offers other options.

3. Select the **Brush tool** 🖌 on the toolbar; set the **Size** to **20 px** and the **Hardness** to **100%**.

4. On the Options panel, change the **Mode** to **Multiply**.

5. Click the **yellow swatch** at the top row of the Swatches panel.

6. Paint the **left eye yellow** so your artwork resembles Figure 13.

   When you paint over black areas in the eye, they aren't affected by the Brush tool and don't change color. In Multiply mode, black pixels don't change color; they will remain black, regardless of what color is being painted by the Brush tool.

7. Click the **cyan swatch** at the top row of the Swatches panel.

8. Paint over the **yellow area** of the same left eye.

   Even though you are painting with cyan, the color of the eye changes to green. This is because you are painting with transparent paint, and transparent cyan over yellow produces green.

9. Click a **peach-colored swatch** on the Swatches panel.

10. Using at least 10–12 short strokes, paint the **right eye** with overlapping strokes.

    As shown in Figure 14, because the paint is transparent, it darkens when it overlaps itself. The effect is just like overlapping magic markers. A challenge when painting with Multiply mode is that every area must be painted in one move. If not, the colors will darken when overlapped. We will use a different blending mode to avoid this problem.

    TIP The following colors will not darken when they overlap themselves in Multiply mode: red, green, blue, cyan, magenta, and yellow.

11. Click **File** on the menu bar, then click **Revert**.

    You set the Brush tool to Multiply mode, noting black pixels remain unaffected by any paint color. You painted cyan over yellow, noting these areas become green because they are transparent. You painted multiple strokes with a peach color, noting where they overlap themselves, they create a darker color. You reverted the file.

Paint in the Darker Color mode

1. On the Options panel, change the **Mode** to **Darker Color**.

2. Click an **orange swatch** on the Swatches panel. Then paint the **left eye** orange, except the circle; leave it white.

   When you paint over the black areas in the eye, they aren't affected by the Brush tool and don't change color. In Darker Color mode, when two colors overlap, the darker of the two dominates and remains. Because no color is darker than black, black cannot be replaced by any other color. Also, in Darker Color mode, colors do not darken when they overlap themselves, so you can feel free to paint with multiple strokes.

3. Using different colors and adjusting the brush size as necessary, paint the remaining areas of the head.

   Figure 15 shows one result. Take the time to finish the whole head to practice resizing the brush with the bracket keys.

4. Save your work.

You set the Brush tool to Darker Color mode, noting black pixels remain unaffected by any paint and the same color does not darken when it overlaps itself. Using different colors, you painted the remainder of the dragon's head.

Figure 15 An example of the painted dragon's head

Alka5051/Shutterstock.com

Fill selections with a blending mode

1. Use the **Eyedropper tool** to sample a **pink color** from the artwork, or select a **pink swatch** from the Swatches panel.

2. Select the **Magic Wand tool** on the toolbar.

   When you select the Magic Wand tool , the Options panel at the top of the window changes to show options for the Magic Wand tool .

3. On the Options panel, type **4** in the **Tolerance text box**, then verify that the **Anti-alias** and **Contiguous** options are both checked.

   For this lesson, you are going to use the Magic Wand tool to select large areas to fill.

4. Note the **circles** on the dragon's arms.

   There are 19 circles in the artwork.

5. Click the **Magic Wand tool** in the **center** of any of the circles.

   The entire white center of the circle is selected. The Magic Wand tool selects pixels based on their similarity in color, so it selected all the white pixels at the center of the circle. It didn't select the gray or black pixels that draw the circle because they are too dissimilar from the white center that you clicked.

6. Press and hold **[shift]**, then click the **Magic Wand tool** in the **centers** of the 18 other circles.

   Because you are pressing and holding [shift], you add to the selection.

7. Press and hold **[option] (Mac)** or **[Alt] (Win)**, press the **[delete] key** on your keypad, then deselect.

Figure 16 Fill dialog box with the Darker Color blending mode activated

The selection fills with the pink foreground color. Where the pink pixels meet the lines that draw the circles, there is potential for some white or light gray pixels to remain. We will use a different method in the next steps to address that.

8. Choose a **green foreground color** to paint the dragon's leg.

9. Click the **Magic Wand tool** on the dragon's tail.

   The white pixels in the tail and the dragon's front leg are all selected.

10. Click **Select** on the menu bar, point to **Modify**, then click **Expand**.

11. Type **1** in the Expand By text box, then click **OK**.

    The entire perimeter of the selection is expanded by one pixel. The selection now overlaps the black lines that draw the dragon.

12. Click **Edit** on the menu bar, then click **Fill**.

13. Enter the settings shown in Figure 16, click **OK**, then deselect.

    The leg and tail are filled with the foreground color, but the black lines you overlapped weren't affected because you used the Darker Color blending mode for the fill.

14. Using any of the methods you learned in this lesson, finish coloring the drawing.

    Figure 17, shown on the following page, is one result.

15. Save your work, then close Coloring Book.

You made selections with the Magic Wand tool, then you expanded the selections by one pixel to overlap the black line art. You then used the Fill dialog box to fill with the Darker Color blending mode activated, noting the black line art was not affected. This allowed you to be sure that no white or light gray pixels were left after applying the fill.

Figure 17 The colorized artwork

MAKE SELECTIONS WITH THE MARQUEE AND LASSO TOOLS

Understanding the Goals of this Lesson

While working your way through Lesson 3, imagine a collection of kids' toys that need to be stored neatly on three shelves. You will work with images of toys and put them all together into a final image. This type of work is called *compositing*. A **composite image** is one in which many different images are brought together—in a *composition*—to create one single image or effect.

The main goal of this lesson is for you to learn to make basic selections with the Marquee and the Lasso tools. The challenge of selecting and moving the objects onto the shelves will allow you to explore many options for working with these essential selection tools.

Along the way, you will be asked to notice aspects of the composite image that *don't work well* and to consider some of the challenges you would face if you were working at a more advanced or professional level. Therefore, while you're making basic selections and moving the artwork, you will also learn to think like a more advanced user about such topics as size, spatial relationships, perspective, and shadows, along with more advanced Photoshop features like layers. This will be a great opportunity for you to explore the considerations that professional designers must keep in mind when they work.

Selecting Pixels

Making selections is one of the most fundamental procedures you'll do in Photoshop. The toolbar houses three types of selection tools—the Marquee tools, the Lasso tools, and the Tolerance-based tools—the Magic Wand, the Quick Selection, and the Object Selection tools. Making selections is just one component of working with selections. In this lesson, you'll also learn how to define a selection edge—with a feather, for example—how to transform and save a selection, and how to refine a selection's edge. You'll also gain an understanding of issues involved with moving pixels to a new location on the canvas.

Using the Marquee Selection Tools

The Marquee tools are the most basic tools available for making selections in Photoshop. The Rectangular Marquee tool is used for making rectangular or square selections, and the Elliptical Marquee tool is used for making oval or circular selections. Press and hold [shift] while you drag to constrain the tools to make perfect squares and circles, respectively.

When you make any kind of a selection, what you see on your screen is called a **selection marquee**. Some users call the marquee "marching ants" because it appears as tiny creatures moving in a clockwise direction.

Actually, the term "marquee" refers to a real-world entity. Think of the great old movie palaces you find in the theater districts in big cities. The sign out front that announces the movie's title is called a marquee, and marquees are known for the blinking lights that attract attention, often blinking in patterns that create the illusion of movement. Thus, in Photoshop, the blinking result of making a selection is called a selection marquee.

You can add to an existing selection and remove pixels from an existing selection using simple quick keys. Press and hold the [shift] key to add pixels to an existing selection, and use the [option] (Mac) or [Alt] (Win) keys to remove pixels from a selection.

Doing Double Duty with the Shift Key

The [shift] key plays two important roles when making selections. It allows you to add to an existing selection, and it constrains the Marquee tools so that they create a perfect square or circle when dragging. But what if you want to do both? What if you select a square and you want to select an additional square? You'll need to use the [shift] key to select the second square, *and* you'll need the [shift] key to constrain the new selection to a perfect square. How can you use the same key to do both? First, press and hold [shift] to make a square marquee. Next, to make the second square, press [shift] to add to the first selection. Then, while dragging the second marquee, release the [shift] key and then press it again

to constrain the second marquee to a square shape. This method also works for making multiple perfect-circle selections.

Using the Lasso Selection Tools

The Lasso tool is a freeform selection tool. Unlike the Marquee tools, which limit you to rectangular and elliptical selections, you can use the Lasso tool to make selections of any shape. When selecting a complex shape with the Lasso tool, you will usually find it easier to make small selections and then add to them with the [shift] key.

The Polygonal Lasso tool functions like the Lasso tool, but it does so with straight lines. This makes the tool extremely effective for making quick selections or selecting areas of the canvas that are geometric in shape, as the tool's name implies.

The Magnetic Lasso tool will amaze you the first time you use it. Like the Lasso tool, it makes freeform selections. Its specialty, however, is that it "snaps" to the shape of the object you are trying to select, as if it knows what you are trying to do. For example, let's say you have an image of a black cat on a white background, and you want to select the cat. Drag the Magnetic Lasso tool near the cat, and it will align itself with the edge of the cat image automatically. The Magnetic Lasso tool achieves this ability because Photoshop recognizes contrasting pixels that abut. In this example, Photoshop is able to calculate that

the black pixels of the cat are abutting the white pixels of the background. The Magnetic Lasso tool "understands" that you are trying to make a selection around the black object (the cat) only. This makes the Magnetic Lasso tool valuable for selecting objects photographed against solid backgrounds of contrasting color.

Transforming a Selection Marquee

The word **transformation** means change. After you make a selection, you can enlarge, reduce, rotate, or distort the selection marquee using the Transform Selection command on the Select menu. A bounding box appears around the marquee you are transforming. A **bounding box** is a rectangle that contains eight handles you click and drag to change the dimensions of the marquee.

Press and hold [shift] while dragging a handle on the bounding box to maintain the proportion of the marquee when you are scaling it to be larger or smaller. Press and hold [option] (Mac) or [Alt] (Win) to scale it from its center; this can be very useful when scaling selection marquees. You can use transform commands individually or in a chain. In other words, you can first scale a marquee, and before committing the transformation, you can rotate it too. Once you are done, press [return] (Mac) or [Enter] (Win) to execute the transformation. Press [esc] to abandon the transformation.

Make selections with the Rectangular Marquee tool

1. Open PS 2-4.psd, then save it as **Marquee and Lasso Selections**.

2. Press the **letter [D]** on your keypad to change the foreground and background colors to the default black over white, then press the **letter [X]** to switch them.

3. Click the **Rectangular Marquee tool** , on the toolbar, then verify that **Feather** is set to **0 px** and **Style** is set to **Normal** on the Options panel.

4. Use the keyboard shortcut to access the **Zoom tool** .

   If you need a review of accessing the Zoom tool via the keyboard, see Chapter 1, Lesson 4, Exercise 2.

5. Use the **Zoom tool** to drag a box around **both comic books** at the top-right corner of the white section.

   The view of the two comic books is enlarged in the Photoshop window. If you don't see a selection marquee while dragging the Zoom tool, deselect the Scrubby Zoom option for the Zoom tool on the Options panel.

   TIP To make selections accurately, it is *essential* that you zoom in enough to see what you are doing. If you need to squint or move closer to your computer screen, you're not zoomed in enough.

6. With the **Rectangular Marquee tool** position the **center of the crosshair** on the upper-left corner of the blue comic book, drag downward until the center of the crosshair is on the lower-right corner, then release the mouse pointer.

7. Press and hold **[shift]**, position the **crosshair** over the upper-left corner of the red comic book, then drag a **second marquee** to add the red comic book to the selection.

   Both comic books are selected. Pressing and holding [shift] when making a selection adds to the existing selection.

8. Press the **letter [V]** on your keypad to access the **Move tool** .

   For the remainder of this chapter and the whole book, use this method to access the Move tool.

9. Drag the **two comic books** to the top shelf in the position shown in Figure 18, but don't deselect.

   When you move a selection, the current background color is used to fill the original location of the selection. In this example, the area is filled with black, which is the current background color on the toolbar.

Continued on next page

Figure 18 Positioning the two comic books

10. Deselect.

Once you deselect, the pixels are embedded into the canvas. If you wanted to move the comic books to another location, you'd have to select them again to do so. However, if you move the comic books a second time, you would leave behind the black background color. The blue back wall of the shelves "behind" the comic books is no longer there. This situation is a great example of why working with layered artwork is so important. If the comic books were on their own layer, you could move them without affecting any other pixels on the canvas. You will learn all about layers in Chapter 3.

11. Press the **letter [M]** on your keypad to access the **Rectangular Marquee tool** , use the keyboard shortcut to access the **Zoom tool** , then zoom in on the **pink frame** beneath the "WOW" poster.

You are going to select just the frame and then move it on top of the poster above it to frame the poster.

12. Select the **pink frame**.

We need just the frame, not the white interior, so we need to remove the white pixels from the selection.

13. Press and hold **[Alt] (Win)** or **[option] (Mac)**, then select the **white inner rectangle** inside the pink frame.

Pressing and holding [Alt] (Win) or [option] (Mac) when making a selection removes pixels from the existing selection. As shown in Figure 19, the white inner rectangle is removed from the selection, and just the frame is selected.

Figure 19 Deselecting the interior section of the pink frame

14. Access the **Move tool** , press and hold **[shift]**, drag the **frame** straight up, position it over the poster so that the poster completely fills the frame, then deselect.

Now we want to move the framed poster over to the shelves, so we need to *reselect* the frame.

15. Select the **pink frame**.

This time, the interior is not a problem; we *want* the image inside the frame.

16. Move the **framed artwork** to the second shelf in the position shown in Figure 20.

17. Save your work.

You used the [shift] key to select the two comic books. You used the [option] or [Alt] key to deselect the interior of the pink frame, positioned the frame over the poster artwork, and then positioned the framed artwork on the second shelf.

Figure 20 Positioning the framed artwork

Use the Elliptical Marquee tool and transform a selection marquee

1. Click the **Elliptical Marquee tool** ⬭ on the toolbar, then verify that **Feather** is set to **0 px** and **Style** is set to **Normal** on the Options panel.

2. Zoom in on the **dartboard** so that it fills the screen but remains fully visible.

3. Click and drag the **Elliptical Marquee tool** ⬭, and try to select the **dartboard**.

   Chances are you won't be able to select it accurately. For selecting circular objects, starting at the center is the best method.

4. Press and hold **[shift] [option] (Mac)** or **[Shift][Alt] (Win)**, position the **crosshair** over the **center** of the dartboard, then drag out a **circle** that is approximately 75% the size of the dartboard.

   The [option] and [Alt] keys draw the ellipse from its center, and the [shift] key constrains the result to a perfect circle. The circle is not as large as the dartboard, but it can be enlarged.

5. Click **Select** on the menu bar, then click **Transform Selection**.

   A bounding box appears around the selection marquee.

6. Press and hold **[shift] [option] (Mac)** or **[Shift] [Alt] (Win)**, then drag the **top-right corner handle** to enlarge the marquee until it selects the entire **dartboard**.

   Don't try to be perfect. Go just up to the edge of the dartboard, but leave a little room for error. The last thing you want is to have a white halo around the dartboard that will show against the blue background of the shelves.

Figure 21 Positioning the dartboard

7. When the selection is where you want it, press **[return] (Mac)** or **[Enter] (Win)** to execute the transformation.

8. Zoom out, move the **dartboard** to the position shown in Figure 21, then deselect.

9. Fit the whole canvas on the screen, then assess the "shelves" section of the artwork.

   AUTHOR'S NOTE The more you work with Photoshop, the more you will "learn to see." To the untrained eye, the three shelves are identical, but if you look closer, you will see that each is entirely different from the other two. We are looking straight on at the middle shelf; we see neither its top nor its bottom surface. We are looking up at the top shelf, so we see its bottom surface. We are looking down at the bottom shelf, so we see its top surface.

   Our perspective of the shelves affects how we view the objects on the shelves. The framed poster is believably standing at the front edge of the middle shelf because we are looking at it and the shelf straight on. It could also be believably back against the wall, except in that case, the shelf above would cast a shadow on it, so it must be at the front of the shelf.

The dartboard and the comic books on the top shelf don't pass the reality test. They appear to be standing at the very front edge of the shelf, but that makes no visual sense, because they couldn't stand on their own. Either they would have to lean back against the wall or they would be positioned deeper into the shelf and up against the wall. In that case, because we are looking at them from below, we would not see the bottoms of the dartboard or the comic books.

Figure 22 shows an example of an edit that looks more realistic. This was achieved by slicing off the bottom of the books and the dartboard. Because we see the bottom surface of the top shelf, it makes sense that we wouldn't see the bottom of the books or the dartboard. Now they appear as though they are up against the wall, deeper into the shelf. Note also a shadow was added to the top of the framed poster, which makes it appear to be positioned at the back of the shelf and under the top shelf. It's another touch that adds more reality points to the composite.

These are the kinds of complex perspective considerations you'll have to keep in mind when compositing multiple images on a more advanced level, which is exactly what you'll be doing in Chapter 3.

10. Save your work.

You used the Elliptical Marquee tool to select most of the round dartboard artwork. Rather than trying to get the selection dead on in just one move, you made just a 75% selection and then used the Transform Selection command to scale the marquee. This allowed you as many tries as you needed to get the best selection of the artwork. You then analyzed the top shelf of the artwork, noting the round dartboard could not be positioned on the shelf in a way that looks realistic.

Figure 22 A more realistic crop of top-shelf images

Use the Lasso tool and the Magnetic Lasso tool

1. Be sure your work is saved at this point.

2. Click the **Lasso tool** ⌀ on the toolbar, then verify that **Feather** is set to **0 px** and **Anti-alias** is checked.

3. Zoom in on the **teddy bear**.

4. Using Figure 23 as a guide, click and drag the **Lasso tool** ⌀ to make a rough selection of the interior of the artwork.

5. Using the **[shift] key**, click and drag to add to the selection to select the **whole teddy bear**. Use the **[option] (Mac)** or **[Alt] (Win)** key to remove from the selection if you accidentally select the white background.

   You will quickly realize that this is not the right tool for the job. The Lasso tool is good for making quick, inaccurate selections of areas of the canvas, but it's not a precision selection tool.

6. Deselect whatever selection you have made.

Figure 23 Rough selection of the interior of the artwork

7. Select the **Magnetic Lasso tool** 🔗 on the toolbar, then enter the settings shown in Figure 24 on the Options panel.

   The Width setting determines the number of pixels Photoshop samples to identify an edge. The Contrast setting is the minimum amount of contrast, measured in pixel brightness, for Photoshop to identify an edge. The Frequency is a measurement of how often the Magnetic Lasso tool will position an anchor point on the line. These are the default settings for the Magnetic Lasso tool. The Magnetic Lasso tool works by placing a selection line on the "edge" of artwork. Photoshop can't really "see" what the edge of any piece of artwork is in relation to other artwork. All Photoshop "sees" is pixels with different color and brightness values. In this case, Photoshop recognizes that a lot of brown-colored pixels are adjacent to white pixels and that the contrast between those pixels, in terms of their brightness values, is very different. Based on that information, Photoshop will position the Magnetic Lasso tool on the edge of the teddy bear artwork.

8. Zoom in so that you can see the **whole head** of the teddy bear.

9. Position the **Magnetic Lasso tool** 🔗 on the **left edge** of the head at the eye level, click just once, then drag along the edge until you have gone around both ears and are on the right edge of the head at the eye level.

TIP You don't need to hold down the mouse pointer while you drag; just drag. However, when you come to a corner or a sharp turn, you can click the mouse on that point. This will help you switch directions sharply.

10. When you reach the right side of the head, at the eye level, double-click.

   When you double-click, the Magnetic Lasso tool automatically closes the selection with a line. Your selection should be similar to Figure 25.

Continued on next page

Figure 24 Settings for the Magnetic Lasso tool

| Feather: | 0 px | ☑ Anti-alias | Width: | 10 px | Contrast: | 10% | Frequency: | 57 |

Figure 25 Selecting just the top half of the head

11. Starting in the *interior* of the current selection, press and hold **[shift]**, then add more to the current selection.

    It's tempting to try to go around the whole of the artwork in one move, but you'll do a better job if you stay zoomed in and make multiple selections, adding along the way. You should be able to finish selecting the entire teddy bear with five or six selections.

12. When you have finished selecting the perimeter of the teddy bear, press and hold **[option] (Mac)** or **[Alt] (Win)**, then *remove* the white triangle under the arm from the selection.

13. Zoom in on an **edge** of the teddy bear, press and hold **[spacebar]**, then pan around the artwork to assess the selection.

    You can use the "add to" or "remove from" technique to improve the selection if you need to.

14. Access the **Move tool** , then move the **teddy bear** to the position shown in Figure 26.

    While the Magnetic Lasso tool is not perfect, it does a remarkably good job.

15. Zoom in on the **dart** so that it fills the entire screen.

16. Use the **Magnetic Lasso tool** to select the **dart**, then move it to the position shown in Figure 27.

17. Save your work.

Figure 26 Positioning the teddy bear on the shelf

Figure 27 Positioning the dart

The teddy bear sits on the shelf in a way that looks very realistic; the angles all make sense. However, an issue you'd have to consider on the advanced level is that the bear would cast a shadow on the shelf. Figure 28 shows painted shadows for the bear. Note the shadow from the bear is complex, especially where its leg hangs off the shelf. Shadows, your ability to understand how they would be cast, and your ability to paint them, are all major challenges when making composite images.

You tried to use the Lasso tool to select the teddy bear but quickly realized that it's not accurate enough to do the job. You switched to the Magnetic Lasso tool, which was much more effective. Rather than trying to select the entire artwork in one move, you used [shift] to combine multiple selections as you worked.

Figure 28 Shadows on the bear artwork

Use the Polygonal Lasso tool

1. Zoom in on the **blue O block** so that it fills your screen.

2. Select the **Polygonal Lasso tool**  on the toolbar. Then, on the Options panel, verify that **Feather** is set to **0 px** and **Anti-alias** is checked.

3. Press the **[caps lock] key** on your keypad.

   With the [caps lock] key activated, the cursor switches to a crosshair, which is more precise.

4. Click the **crosshair** one time on the **top-left corner** of the O block.

5. Move the mouse pointer down, and click the crosshair on the **bottom-left corner** of the O block.

6. Click the **next two corners** of the O block.

7. Moving counterclockwise, work your way all the way around the blocks.

   As you move the mouse pointer, the screen will scroll automatically.

8. When you near the end, float over the **original point** you clicked so the Polygonal Lasso tool icon appears with a small "o" beside it, then click to close the selection.

TIP You can also double-click the mouse pointer to close the path. When you double-click the mouse pointer, the path will automatically close by drawing a straight line from your current location to the starting point.

9. Zoom out, then move the **blocks** to the second shelf, as shown in Figure 29.

   The blocks cannot realistically be positioned on the second shelf. We are looking straight on at the shelf, so the surface of the shelf is not at all visible. Therefore, as shown in the figure, the O block is floating in thin air. Even though the R block and the M block are touching the front edge of the shelf, they make no logical sense. They too are floating away.

10. Move the **blocks** down to the bottom shelf, then compare your work to Figure 30.

    The placement of the blocks on the bottom shelf makes visual sense. Both the blocks and the shelf are photographed from the same angle. Note how we see the tops of the O, R, and M blocks exactly as we see the top of the shelf itself. We see the surface of the bottom shelf, and we see the blocks resting on the shelf.

11. Save your work, then close Marquee and Lasso Selections.

You used the Polygonal Lasso tool to select the straight edges of the blocks. You positioned the blocks on the second shelf, noting the perspective was too far off to look real. You then positioned the blocks on the bottom shelf, which worked much better.

Figure 29 Positioning the blocks on the second shelf doesn't work

Shutterstock photo credits: Shelf: Lauritta; Comic books: benchart; Dartboard: Oleaon17; Picture frame: ABA Bitter; WOW: Irina Levitskaya; Teddy bear: Sararoom Design; Blocks: Gearstd

Figure 30 Assessing the final artwork

EXPLORE A GRAYSCALE IMAGE WITH THE MAGIC WAND TOOL

▶ What You'll Do

In this lesson, you'll gain an understanding of a grayscale image while learning to use the Magic Wand tool.

Moving a Selection Marquee vs. Moving Pixels

When you make a selection, as long as a selection tool is active on the toolbar, you can move the selection marquee to another location on the canvas without moving any pixels. When the Move tool is active, moving a selection marquee moves the selected pixels.

The arrow keys on your keypad are very useful when moving a selection marquee or moving pixels. Press an arrow key and the selection will move one pixel in that direction. Press and hold [shift] plus an arrow key, and the selection will move 10 pixels in that direction. Using arrows helps you to be very specific when moving pixels or a selection marquee.

Using the Magic Wand Tool

The Magic Wand tool is a powerful selection tool. Click any pixel on the canvas, and the Magic Wand tool selects other pixels based on the similarity of their color. The **Tolerance** setting on the Options panel will determine the number of pixels the Magic Wand tool either includes or doesn't include in the selection. The greater the Tolerance value, the greater the number of pixels the Magic Wand tool will select.

By clicking the **Contiguous check box** on the Options panel, you are specifying that the Magic Wand tool selects only pixels that are contiguous to (touching) the pixel where you click the image. Otherwise, it will select pixels throughout the image that are within the current Tolerance value.

Understanding the Grayscale Image and the Tolerance Setting on the Magic Wand Tool

The Magic Wand tool and other tools and dialog boxes in Photoshop do their work based on the function of tolerance. The key to understanding tolerance is to understand that every pixel in the image has a number between 0 and 255.

A **grayscale image** is a single-color image, one that you would normally refer to as black and white. The single color is black, and the image is produced as a range of grays, from black to white. You are already familiar with this concept if you've ever printed an image on a black-and-white printer. The printer has only black ink, but it can use that one color to reproduce an image by creating the *illusion* of a range of grays. The word "illusion" is appropriate because there are no actual gray inks coming out of your black and white printer; the printer just uses fewer dots of black ink in lighter areas to create the illusion that those areas are gray.

In a grayscale image, Photoshop produces an image using a range of 256 gray pixels, from black to white. Each pixel can be one—and only one—of 256 shades of gray. Keep the following important points clear in your understanding:

- Black pixels have a grayscale value of 0.
- White pixels have a grayscale value of 255.
- Values 1–254 are shades of gray.
- "Middle gray" has a grayscale value of 128.
- The range in a grayscale image is 0–255, for a total of 256 shades of gray available per pixel.

Tolerance settings for the Magic Wand tool are directly related to a pixel's **grayscale value**. When you click the Magic Wand tool on an "area" of an image, you are *only* clicking on one pixel, and that pixel has a grayscale value. Because pixels are so small, you won't know the specific pixel you are clicking or its grayscale value, but nevertheless, you are clicking on one pixel. The Magic Wand tool selects other pixels based on the grayscale value of the pixel you clicked and the Tolerance value that you set on the Options panel.

For example, let's say you set the Tolerance value for the Magic Wand tool to 10, and you click the Contiguous check box. Next, you click the Magic Wand tool on a pixel whose grayscale value is 75. The Magic Wand tool would select all contiguous pixels whose grayscale value falls within the range of 65–85, 10 grayscale values higher and 10 grayscale values lower than the pixel that you clicked. If the Contiguous option is *not* checked, the Magic Wand tool would select all the pixels whose grayscale values were 65–85 *throughout the image*.

When working with the Magic Wand tool, you don't need to know the number of the pixel you are clicking, that would be impractical. Your goal is simply to select pixels of similar color. Experiment with different tolerance settings until you get the selection you want.

This discussion of tolerance is a great example of how working effectively with Photoshop requires a broad understanding of the program itself. Sure, you can click around mindlessly with the Magic Wand tool and figure out, "Hey, it selects the same colors." That's great, but it's in no way an in-depth understanding of the program that will take you where you want to go. To understand how the Magic Wand tool *really* works requires that you understand what the grayscale image *really* is—a grid of tiny gray pixels, each of them having one grayscale value.

Understanding Selection Edges

The outline of a selection is called the **edge** of a selection; the type of edge that you choose will have a big impact on how your work appears. The edge of a selection is always either aliased or anti-aliased. An **aliased** edge is a hard edge—the hard "stair-stepped" pixels are very obvious. The edge is noticeably blunt and seldomly used. An **anti-aliased** edge is a crisp but smoother edge. With an anti-aliased edge, Photoshop creates a smooth transition between the edge and its background using many shades of the edge pixel color.

Think about it this way. The Photoshop canvas is made of square pixels. How could you possibly reproduce a round image, like an orange, if all you are using is square pixels? The answer is a combination of resolution and an anti-aliased edge. The resolution of the image, the number of pixels per inch, must be high enough that the pixels are too small to be seen individually. The anti-aliased edge uses edge pixels to create a visual color transition at the edge between the object and the background, so the viewer sees the *illusion* of a smooth, curved edge. That's what all curved objects are in Photoshop—an illusion created with an anti-aliased edge.

Most selection tools have an anti-alias option. Whenever you see it, 99.9% of the time you should activate it.

Working with a Feathered Edge

A **feathered edge** is a blended edge. Photoshop creates a blend at the edge of a selection between the selected pixels and the background image. Photoshop offers settings for controlling the length of the blend at the edge. The feather value is equal to the length of the feathered edge. When you apply a feathered edge to a selection, the edge is equally distributed inside and outside the selection edge. In Photoshop, vignettes are created with feathered edges. A **vignette** is a visual effect in which the edge of an image, usually an oval, gradually fades away.

Figure 31 shows three circles—one with an aliased edge, one with an anti-aliased edge, and one with a feathered edge.

Understanding the Relationship Between Computer Monitors and Viewing Selection Edges

Your computer monitor acts as the middleman between you and the Photoshop image. Everything you are seeing is through your monitor. Monitors have resolution as well; most have a resolution of 72 pixels per inch. This fact has a big impact on how you view your Photoshop image because your monitor's resolution is constantly trying to display the image's resolution. When you're viewing your image at less than 100%, your monitor is not giving you an accurate visual representation of the pixels in your image. When you're analyzing subtle components of your image—like selection edges!—be sure that you're viewing your image at least at 100%.

Sampling Pixels and Saving Swatches

The term **sampling** refers to either taking information from a pixel or accessing its color.

The Info panel offers readouts that tell you a pixel's color information. When you position your mouse pointer over a pixel, the Info panel gives you a readout on that pixel, and that readout can be in terms of RGB, CMYK, Grayscale, or HSB, among other settings you can choose. Most designers set the Info panel's readouts to RGB, which provides grayscale information on each pixel.

Click the Eyedropper tool on any pixel to sample its color. When you do, the color of the pixel you click becomes the foreground color on the toolbar. Press [option] (Mac) or [Alt] (Win) when you click a swatch or use the Eyedropper tool to change the background color.

When using the Brush tool, pressing [option] (Mac) or [Alt] (Win) changes the Brush tool to the Eyedropper tool.

If you click a swatch on the Swatches panel, the foreground changes to that color.

The Color panel is an interactive panel. You create a color on the Color panel by dragging the available color sliders, based on the current color mode. Any new color you make on the Color panel becomes the foreground color on the toolbar.

Figure 31 Examples of three selection edges

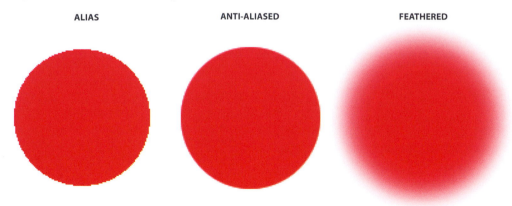

ALIAS   ANTI-ALIASED   FEATHERED

The Swatches panel houses lots of preset colors for you to work with. In addition to the default set of colors, the Swatches panel offers you different collections of swatches, such as Pastel, Dark, Light, and Pale.

When you create a new color by either using the Color panel or sampling a color with the Eyedropper tool, you can save it to the Swatches panel. The Swatches panel allows you to name and save your color using the Create new swatch button on the panel. The new color will appear at the bottom of the panel, under the default swatch categories.

You can also add a new color to the Swatches panel from the Color Picker dialog box. Click the Add to Swatches button in the dialog box. You will be prompted to name your new color and choose which library to add it to. To delete a swatch, click to select it, then click the Delete swatch button.

Move a selection marquee and move pixels

1. Open PS 2-5.psd, then save it as **Balloon Puzzle**.

2. Select the **Magic Wand tool** 🪄 on the toolbar.

3. On the Options panel, set the **Tolerance** to **8**, then verify that the **Contiguous** and **Anti-alias options** are both checked.

4. Use the **Fit on Screen** keyboard shortcut.

TIP The keyboard shortcut is [command] [0] (Mac) or [Ctrl] [0] (Win).

5. Click the **Magic Wand tool** 🪄 on the **center of the white circle** on the right side of the canvas that corresponds with the Number 4 puzzle piece on the left side of the canvas.

   The white circle, and only the white circle, is selected. The other white areas of the image are not selected because the Magic Wand tool is set to select *only* contiguous pixels.

6. Position your mouse pointer over the selection.

   Your mouse pointer changes to a move selection marquee cursor ▸□ .

7. Click and drag the **selection marquee**, and align it with the **Number 4 puzzle piece**.

8. Press and hold **[spacebar] [command] (Mac)** or **[spacebar] [Ctrl] (Win)** to access the **Zoom tool** 🔍 .

9. With the **Zoom tool** 🔍 , zoom in around the **Number 4 puzzle piece**, then release **[spacebar] [command] (Mac)** or **[spacebar] [Ctrl] (Win)**.

   The puzzle piece fills the window.

10. Use the arrow keys on your keypad to align the selection marquee exactly to the puzzle piece.

    The marquee moves one pixel every time you press an arrow key.

11. Click **View** on the menu bar, then click **Fit on Screen**.

12. Press and hold the **letter [V]** to switch to the **Move tool** ✛ .

13. Click and drag the **Number 4 puzzle piece** until it is close to aligning with the corresponding white circle on the right side of the canvas.

Continued on next page

14. Use the keyboard to access the **Zoom tool** , then zoom in on the selected circle.

15. Use the **arrow keys** to move the pixels to the best alignment, as shown in Figure 32.

Because the Move tool ✛ is the active tool on the toolbar, pressing the arrow keys moves the pixels along with the selection marquee.

16. Deselect.

17. Using the same methods, including zooming in and out of the image, finish the puzzle. Your result should resemble Figure 33.

There is no "perfect" in this exercise. The pieces will align, but there will be a white halo around all the pieces in the final image.

18. Save your work, then close Balloon Puzzle.

You used the Magic Wand tool to select white areas of the image. You moved the marquee selection to align it with pixels of the same shape. You used arrow keys to get the best alignment possible. You used the Move tool to move the image pieces into the puzzle. You used the arrow keys again, this time to move and align pixels. Throughout the exercise, you used keyboard commands to access the Zoom tool, to zoom in on the image, and to fit the image on the screen.

Figure 32 Positioning the Number 4 puzzle piece

Figure 33 Finishing the puzzle

Morguefile

Experiment with Tolerance settings

1. Open PS 2-6.psd.

   This file has a gradient that gradates horizontally from black to white. This is a grayscale image. In a grayscale image, each pixel can be one of 256 shades of gray. Black pixels have a grayscale value of 0, and white pixels have a value of 255. Thus, the range of black to white pixels is 0–255, for a total of 256 shades of gray per pixel. Each pixel is one of those shades.

2. Click **Window** on the menu bar, then click **Info**.

   The Info panel opens. You use the Info panel to sample the grayscale values of pixels. Since this might be the first time you are using the Info panel, we must first verify that your Info panel displays the same settings as this book.

3. On the left side of the Info panel, click the **Eyedropper icon** 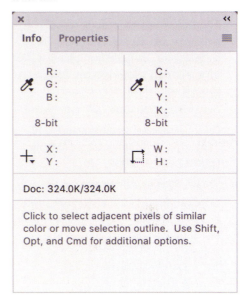, then click **RGB Color**.

Your Info panel should resemble Figure 34. It doesn't matter what the setting is on the right side of the Info panel. The RGB Color readout displays grayscale information for each pixel. If this were a color image, each pixel would have a different number for red, for green, and for blue. For example, a yellowish pixel would have high numbers for red and green and a low number for blue, because red and green produce yellow. In a grayscale image, no color dominates. Each is the same, and that produces a "gray" pixel. A black pixel is RGB 0/0/0. A white pixel is RGB 255/255/255. A middle gray pixel is RGB 128/128/128. And so forth.

4. Press the **letter [I]** on your keypad to access the **Eyedropper tool**, position it on the far-left edge of the image, then note the readout on the left side of Info panel.

   Because you are positioned over a black pixel, the RGB values on the Info panel are 0/0/0.

Continued on next page

Figure 34 The Info panel showing the left side set to RGB Color

5. Slowly move the **Eyedropper tool** 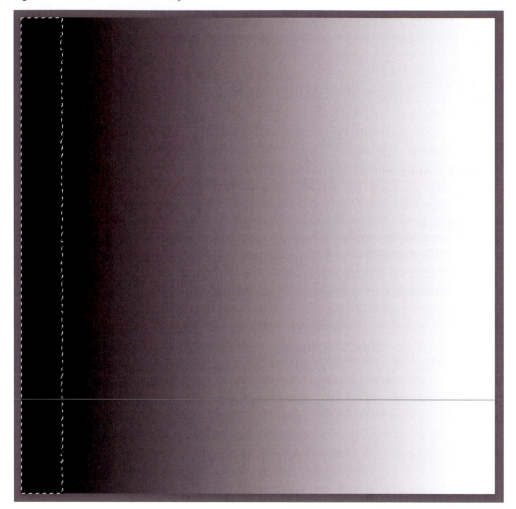 from left to right while noting the changes on the Info panel.

   As you move from left to right, the grayscale values on the Info panel move up incrementally. The gradient on the canvas goes from 0 (black) to (255) white, with every value in between. The lighter the pixel, the higher the grayscale value will be.

6. Click the **Magic Wand tool** on the toolbar.

7. On the Options panel, set the **Tolerance** to **10**, then verify that the **Contiguous** and **Anti-alias options** are not checked.

8. Click the **left edge** of the canvas.

   As shown in Figure 35, a small slice of the artwork is selected from top to bottom. You clicked a black pixel on the left edge, and black pixels have a grayscale value of 0. With the Tolerance set to 10, the Magic Wand tool selected pixels with a grayscale value of 0–10.

   AUTHOR'S **NOTE**   This explanation of how the Tolerance setting works on the Magic Wand tool is correct, but it's also simplified. Photoshop's computing algorithms are sophisticated and complex, and the Magic Wand tool will produce selections that won't always correspond exactly with the Tolerance setting that has been input. Don't worry about that; just keep in mind the essential understanding of how the tool works with the Tolerance setting.

Figure 35   Selection with a Tolerance setting of 10

9. Deselect, change the **Tolerance** to **64**, then click the **left edge**.

Roughly the left quarter of the canvas is selected because 64 is one-quarter of 256.

10. Deselect, change the **Tolerance** to **128**, then click the **left edge**.

Roughly half of the canvas is selected because 128 is half of 256.

11. Deselect, change the **Tolerance** to **20**, then click roughly the **center** of the canvas.

Roughly 40 pixels are selected. Let's agree that when you clicked, you clicked on a pixel whose grayscale value is 128. With tolerance set at 20, pixels in the range of 108–148 were selected. In the case of this specific graphic, that means 20 pixels to the right and 20 pixels to the left of where you clicked were selected.

12. Close the file.

You used a black-to-white gradient to better understand the concept of a tolerance-based tool like the Magic Wand tool and to better understand the concept of a grayscale image as a whole. You set the Info panel to display in RGB color, which shows pixel information as grayscale values. By increasing the tolerance, you saw that the selection was expanded. You also clicked the center of the gradient to better understand that a tolerance setting selects pixels that are higher and lower than the pixel that is clicked.

Experiment with the Contiguous setting

1. Open PS 2-7.psd, then save it as **Contiguous Concentration**.

2. Select the **Magic Wand tool** [✦]. Then, on the Options panel, set the **Tolerance** to **0**, verify the **Contiguous option** is checked, then verify that **Anti-alias** is *not* checked.

With a tolerance value of 0, the Magic Wand tool [✦] selects just the grayscale value of the pixel you click and *zero* others.

3. Click the **topmost pink square**.

Because the Contiguous option is activated, the other pink square is not selected. Only the pixels that are touching the pixel you clicked are selected (if they are within tolerance).

4. Click a **yellow swatch** on the Swatches panel, then click **[option] [delete] (Mac)** or **[Alt] [delete] (Win)** to fill with the foreground color.

5. Uncheck the **Contiguous option** on the Options panel.

6. Click **either** of the **blue squares**.

7. Fill the **blue squares** with **purple**.

8. Check the **Contiguous option** to activate it.

9. Click the **top-left black square**, press and hold **[shift]**, then add the three other **black corner squares** to the selection.

10. Fill the **corner squares** with **red**.

11. Uncheck the **Contiguous option**.

Continued on next page

12. Click any of the **green squares**.

   All four green squares are selected.

13. Check to activate the **Contiguous option**.

14. Press and hold **[option] (Mac)** or **[Alt] (Win)**, then click the **top-right green square**.

   The top-right green square is deselected. This was a *very tricky* move. Holding the [option] or [Alt] key removes from a selection. However, if the Contiguous option had remained off, all four of the green squares would have been deselected when you clicked the top-right green square. With the Contiguous option activated, only that square was deselected.

15. Fill the **three selected squares** with **orange**.

16. Select all the **black squares**.

17. Click **Select** on the menu bar, point to **Modify**, then click **Contract**.

18. Type **8** in the Contract By text box, then click **OK**.

   The Contract and Expand dialog boxes do exactly that. They contract or expand a selection marquee by a specific number of pixels. In this case, the selection was contracted by eight pixels.

19. Fill the selection with **blue**, then deselect.

   Your canvas should resemble Figure 36.

20. Save your work.

You alternated activating and deactivating the Contiguous option for the Magic Wand tool to fill different squares on the checkerboard.

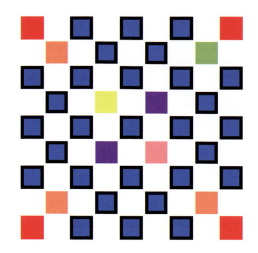

Figure 36   The multicolored checkerboard

Explore Select Inverse vs. Invert

1. Ask yourself how you could use the **Magic Wand tool** with one click to select all the different colored squares on the canvas.

2. Click the **Magic Wand tool** on any white area.

3. Click **Select** on the menu bar, then click **Inverse**.

   OK, so we cheated a little bit. You had to use the menu command as well. The Inverse command deselects the pixels that are selected and selects the pixels that aren't.

4. Fill the selection with **white**.

Figure 37   The black and white checkerboard

5. Click **Select** on the menu bar, click **Inverse**, fill the selection with **black**, then deselect.

   Your canvas should resemble Figure 37.

6. Verify that nothing is selected on the canvas, enter **[command] [I] (Mac)** or **[Ctrl] [I] (Win)** repeatedly to execute the Invert command.

   The Invert command inverts pixels' grayscale values. Black pixels (0) become white pixels (255) and vice versa.

7. Use the **Magic Wand tool** to fill the squares with **blue**.

8. Fill the background with **green**.

9. Deselect, then invert the canvas repeatedly.

   Colored pixels also invert their grayscale values and become their "opposite" colors.

10. Save your work, then close Contiguous Concentration.

You selected the background color of the checkerboard and then used the Inverse command to select the multicolored squares. You then used the Invert command to invert the canvas with nothing selected, noting that the black squares became white and vice versa.

Use the Magic Wand tool to select an image

1. Open PS 2-8.psd, then save it as **Orange Balloon**.

2. Click the **Magic Wand tool** , then on the Options panel, set the **Tolerance** to **64**, verify that **Contiguous** is not activated, then verify that **Anti-alias** is checked.

3. Click the **bright yellow area** of the balloon above the green diamond at the upper-left corner of the balloon.

4. Press and hold **[shift]**, then click **two other areas of darker yellow** so that your selection resembles Figure 38.

   Three clicks should be enough to get a clean selection of all yellow areas, as shown in the figure. Note the basket under the balloon was also selected. We will remove that from the selection.

   Continued on next page

Figure 38 Selecting the yellow areas of the balloon

The basket is also selected

5. Click the **Rectangular Marquee tool** [⬚] , press and hold **[option] (Mac)** or **[Alt] (Win)**, then drag a **box around the basket** below the balloon.

   The basket is deselected, so just the yellow areas of the balloon are selected.

6. Press **[command] [H] (Mac)** or **[Ctrl] [H] (Win)** to hide the selection marquee.

   If a dialog box appears asking what you want to hide, click Hide Extras.

7. Click **Image** on the menu bar, point to **Adjustments**, then click **Hue/Saturation**.

   The Hue/Saturation dialog box opens.

8. Drag the **Hue slider** left to **−99**, then click **OK**.

   The yellow pixels change to bright purple.

9. Click the **Magic Wand tool** [🪄] , increase the **Tolerance** to **100**, then activate **Contiguous**.

10. Click the **blue sky** at the top-left corner of the image.

    The entire sky, or background, is selected.

11. Click **Select** on the menu bar, then click **Inverse**.

    The sky is deselected, and the balloon is selected. Unfortunately, the basket is also selected, which you must now deselect.

12. Click the **Lasso tool** [◯] , press and hold **[option] (Mac)** or **[Alt] (Win)**, then deselect the basket.

13. Click **[command] [U] (Mac)** or **[Ctrl] [U] (Win)** to open the Hue/Saturation dialog box.

14. Drag the **Hue slider** to **+87**, click **OK**, then compare your artwork to Figure 39.

15. Save your work, then close Orange Balloon.

You used the Magic Wand tool to select only the yellow areas of the balloon, which you changed to purple. You then selected the sky and inversed the selection to select the balloon. You then removed the basket from the selection and changed the color of the whole balloon.

Figure 39 Changing the color of the whole balloon

Explore selection edges

1. Open PS 2-9.psd, then save it as **Selection Edges**.

2. Click the **Magic Wand tool** 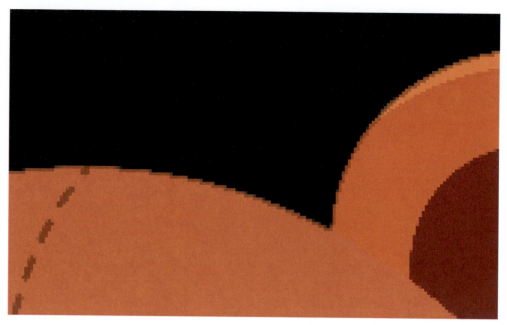, set the **Tolerance** to **8**, then verify that **Contiguous** is checked.

3. Uncheck **Anti-alias**.

4. Click the **white background**, press and hold **[shift]**, then click the **black background** to add it to the selection.

5. Click **Select** on the menu bar, then click **Inverse**.

6. Click the **Move tool** on the toolbar, press and hold **[option] (Mac)** or **[Alt] (Win)**, then drag the **bear** completely into the black area.

   Pressing and holding [option] (Mac) or [Alt] (Win) when dragging a selection makes a copy of the selection.

7. Zoom in to examine the aliased edge.

   The edge is hard and uneven. It is unacceptable.

8. Click **File** on the menu bar, then click **Revert**.

9. Click to activate **Anti-alias** on the Options panel.

10. Using the same method as before, select the **bear**, then move it into the black area.

Figure 40 Examining the anti-aliased edge

11. Zoom in to examine the anti-aliased edge.

    The edge is smooth. As shown in Figure 40, the Anti-alias option uses the edge pixels of the selection to create a color transition between the edge of the bear and the black background.

12. Revert the file, then using the same method, select the **bear**.

13. Click **Select** on the menu bar, point to **Modify**, then click **Feather**.

14. Type **24** in the Feather Radius text box, then click **OK**.

15. Move a **copy of the bear** into the black area.

    The artwork appears with a white glow. The bear gradates out to the illusion of a soft white "feathered" edge, which is really a range of white pixels blending with the black background.

16. Save your work, then close Selection Edges.

You used the Magic Wand tool to select the bear first with an aliased edge and then with an anti-aliased edge and examined both edges. Lastly, you applied a feather to the selection and then examined that effect against the black background.

Smooth selection edges

1. Open PS 2-10.psd, then save it as **Robot on White**.

    The robot was photographed against a black background for contrast. However, we want to position it over a white background. Removing a black background can often be challenging.

2. Click the **Magic Wand tool** , verify that the **Tolerance** is set to **8**, then verify that **Contiguous** and **Anti-alias** are both checked.

3. Click the **black background**, press and hold [**shift**], then click the **white background** to add it to the selection.

4. Click **Select** on the menu bar, then click **Inverse**.

5. Click the **Move tool** on the toolbar, press and hold [**option**] (**Mac**) or [**Alt**] (**Win**), drag a **copy** completely into the white area, then hide the selection marquee.

    A black edge surrounds the "silhouette" of the image, like a dark halo. Also, even though Anti-alias is activated, the pixels along the edge aren't smooth. Because the white robot abuts a black background in the original photograph, the Magic Wand tool cannot make a selection that visually appears smooth, not even with an anti-aliased edge. Adding a feathered edge will soften and fade the edge, which is not an option for a plastic and hard-edged toy.

TIP Press [**command**] [**H**] (**Mac**) or [**Ctrl**] [**H**] (**Win**) to hide the selection marquee.

6. Revert the file.

7. Using the same method, select the **robot**.

8. Zoom in so that you are viewing the artwork at **400%**.

9. Click **Select** on the menu bar, point to **Modify**, then click **Contract**.

10. Enter **2** in the Contract By text box, then click **OK**.

    Viewing the artwork at this magnification, we can see the selection edge shift. Contracting the selection will remove the black edge pixels from the selection. However, just contracting the selection won't make its edge any smoother.

11. Zoom out, click **Select** on the menu bar, then click **Select and Mask**.

    The Select and Mask workspace opens, with the Properties panel on the right and its own set of tools on the left. This workspace offers many options for altering selections. For our purposes in this lesson, we will use it for viewing the artwork and for simply smoothing a selection.

12. On the Properties panel, in the View Mode section, verify that **High Quality Preview** is the only one of the three check boxes that is checked.

13. Click the **View list arrow**, then click **Overlay**.

    The View menu offers options that will change the background of the artwork to help you better see the edges of the selection and the overall appearance of the silhouette.

14. Drag the **Opacity slider** to **100%**.

15. Click the **Color box** to open the **Color Picker**.

Continued on next page

16. Drag the **Hue sliders** (along the rainbow graphic) to a blue area. Then, in the large color square, click a **bright blue area** in the upper-right corner.

17. Click **OK**.

The selection of the robot appears against the blue background. With the Overlay view, you can preview your selection against any color. This can be very useful. For example, this preview would give you a good sense of how the robot would look against an image of a blue sky. In this case, however, we want to position the robot against a white background.

18. Click the **View list arrow**, then choose **On White**.

19. Press and hold **[command] [spacebar] (Mac)** or **[Ctrl] [spacebar] (Win)** to access the **Zoom tool** ⊕, then zoom in on the **inside of the robot's arm** on the left side of the image.

You should be viewing the inside of the arm at 500%. At this magnification, you can see clearly that the edge is not smooth.

20. On the Properties panel, drag the **Smooth slider** to **2**.

As shown in Figure 41, the edge pixels are made smoother without a feathering or fading effect taking place.

21. Click **OK**.

22. Zoom out, click the **Move tool** ⊕ on the toolbar, press and hold **[option] (Mac)** or **[Alt] (Win)**, then drag a **copy of the robot** completely into the white area.

Figure 41 Examining the smoother edge

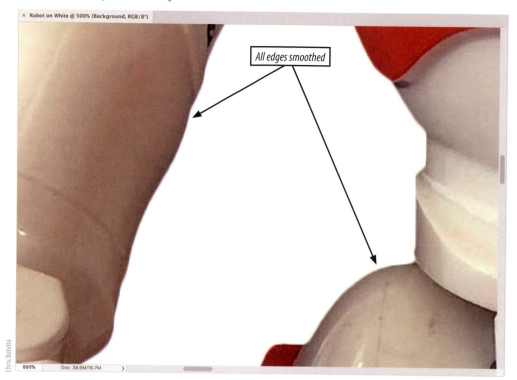

All edges smoothed

Chris Botello

23. Deselect, then examine the edge.

The edge is smooth, exactly as it was previewed in the Select and Mask workspace.

24. Save your work, then close Robot on White.

You used the Magic Wand tool to select the robot, then you contracted the selection trying to remove the black halo from the edge. You opened the selection in the Select and Mask workspace and viewed it against a custom blue background. You then used the Smooth option to smoothen the rough edge.

POSTERIZE AN IMAGE AND SAVE SELECTIONS

▶ What You'll Do

In this lesson, you'll gain a deeper understanding of a grayscale image while creating a posterized effect.

Saving Selections

After you've made a selection, especially a complex selection, you can save it for future use. The Select menu offers you the Save Selection command, which gives you the ability to name and save multiple selections with a file. Use the Load Selection command, also on the Select menu, to load any of the selections you've saved.

When you save a selection, Photoshop creates a new channel, called an alpha channel, on the Channel menu. An **alpha channel** is a grayscale image that Photoshop creates and uses to render the selection. Photoshop uses white pixels to represent pixels that are selected and black pixels to represent pixels that aren't selected. For example, let's say you selected an image of an airplane against a blue sky. When you save the selection, Photoshop will create a new channel with the shape of the airplane filled with white, meaning that those pixels are part of the selection. All the other parts of the image, the sky in this example, will be black, meaning they're not part of the selection. When you load a selection, Photoshop uses the channel information, the white pixels specifically, to know what will be selected.

Converting from RGB to Grayscale and Vice Versa

RGB is the color mode that Photoshop uses to render color images. In an RGB image, each pixel can be one of 256 shades of red, 256 shades of green, and 256 shades of blue. The pixel is just one color—"orange," for example—but that color is represented by its RGB components. One specific hue of orange can be rendered as 255R/128G/0B. In an RGB image, each pixel has three times the amount of color information than in a grayscale image, so the file size is three times larger. Given a combination of 255 potential reds, 255 potential greens, and 255 potential blues per pixel, the RGB mode can produce more than 16.5 million colors ($256 \times 256 \times 256$).

Sometimes, you will want to use an RGB image as a black and white image. To do so, use the Grayscale mode on the Image menu. The color data per pixel will be discarded, and the image will be rendered as a single-color black and white image.

You can also convert an image from Grayscale mode to RGB mode. For example, you might want to paint colors over a black and white image. You wouldn't be able to do that in

Grayscale mode because there are no colors available in Grayscale mode, only shades of gray. But if you convert to RGB mode, each pixel's *potential* to be one of 16.5 million colors is restored. However, the image will continue to appear as a black and white image.

Posterizing a Grayscale Image

Figure 42 shows a grayscale image and the same image posterized. Posterizing is an effect created by reducing the range of colors in an image. In the figure, the top image is rendered with 256 shades of gray available per pixel. It has a smooth range of color from black to white, also known as "continuous tone." The posterized image is rendered with just four shades of gray—black, dark gray, light gray, and white. The image is still recognizable, but the result is colors that "jump" drastically from black to white.

In the top image, each pixel can be one of 256 shades of gray. In the posterized version, each can be just one of four shades of gray. Photoshop runs this simple equation: 256/4 = 64. Photoshop then identifies all the pixels whose grayscale values are 0–64 and makes them all black. Pixels that were 65–128 become dark gray. Pixels that were 129–192 become light gray, and those that were 193–255 become white. So what appears to be a complex effect, from the computing perspective, is quite simple. Now that you know each pixel in a digital image has a number, you can understand that Photoshop is producing those effects by playing with the numbers.

Figure 42 A grayscale image posterized

Morguefile

Investigate an RGB image

1. Open PS 2-11.psd, then save it as **Posterized Eagle**.

2. Click the **Eyedropper tool** , then open the **Info panel**.

3. Zoom in on the image until you can see the individual pixels.

4. Move the **Eyedropper tool** over the pixels, and note the readout on the Info panel.

   This is an RGB image, and each pixel has a red, green, and blue component. Each pixel is one of 256 reds, one of 256 greens, and one of 256 blues. Thus, a yellow pixel in the bird's beak might read, in terms of RGB, 250/243/12.

5. Fit the image on the screen.

6. Click **Window** on the menu bar, then click **Channels**.

   The Channels panel opens.

7. Click the word **Red** on the Channels panel.

   Figure 43 shows the Red channel. In the Red channel, each pixel can be one of 256 shades of red. The color range in the channel is from black to red. Black pixels have a value of 0; red pixels have a value of 255. Everything in between is a range between black and red.

Figure 43 Viewing the Red channel in an RGB image

Marguefile

8. Click **Green** to see the Green channel.

9. Click **Blue** to see the Blue channel.

10. Click **RGB** to see the composite channel.

    As you learned in the beginning of this chapter, the word composite refers to one thing that is created by bringing other things together. The RGB channel is called the composite channel because it is rendered by combining the three color channels.

    AUTHOR'S NOTE You will learn a lot more nuances about the RGB color model as you progress through this book, but here you've already learned the most fundamental concept. The pixels in an RGB image are one color composed of a red, a green, and a blue component, each with 256 available shades per pixel per channel.

11. Click **Image** on the menu bar, point to **Mode**, then click **Grayscale**.

12. Click **Discard** to discard other channels, if a warning box appears.

    All of the color data per pixel is discarded, and the image changes to a black and white image.

13. Note the Channels panel.

    The Channels panel now contains only one channel named Gray. Grayscale mode is a single-channel mode.

    Continued on next page

14. Float the **Eyedropper tool**  over the pixels, and note the readout on the Info panel.

The RGB readout shows the same number in R, G, and B. The Info panel has a Grayscale readout, but that readout is in percentages; it doesn't give you information from 0 to 256. Therefore, when sampling a grayscale image, you use the RGB readout and infer that when you're looking at three identical numbers on the Info panel, they represent just one number in this single-channel image. Don't let this confuse you. This is a single-channel image, and the single channel is Gray. Each pixel has just **one** grayscale value, and that one grayscale value can be 0–255.

15. Save your work, then continue to the next set of steps.

You sampled pixels in RGB mode, noting each is one color with an RGB component. You looked at each of the three color channels that make up the image in the Channels panel. You then converted the image to Grayscale, noting it becomes a single-channel image named Black in the Channels panel.

Posterize an image and save selections

1. Click **Image** on the menu bar, point to **Adjustments**, then click **Posterize**.

2. Highlight the **number in the Levels text box**, then use the up and down arrows on your keypad to increase and decrease the number of levels.

3. Set the number of levels to **8**.

The Posterize dialog box is a valuable key for understanding the concept of rendering an image in Grayscale mode. For example, if you enter eight levels, that's what a black and white image would look like if only eight shades of gray were available per pixel—clearly not enough to create the illusion of an invisible transition, or "continuous tone," from black to white.

4. Set the number of levels to **16**.

At 16 shades of gray available per pixel, the image is still clearly posterized, and there's no illusion of continuous tone.

5. Set the number of levels to **32**.

At 32 shades of gray available per pixel, the illusion of continuous tone starts to take hold. Even in the eagle's beak, which is a smooth range of grays, the tone appears continuous. Consider that, if the image looks this good at just 32 shades of gray per pixel, imagine how invisible the transition from black to white is with 256 shades.

6. Set the number of levels to **4**, click **OK**, then sample the pixels with the **Eyedropper tool** .

Your canvas should resemble Figure 44. The pixels in this image are black, dark gray, light gray, or white. In grayscale values, they are 0, 107, 187, or 255.

7. Click the **Magic Wand tool** , set the **Tolerance** to **0**, then verify that **Contiguous** and **Anti-alias** are not checked.

8. Click **any white area** of the image to select all the white pixels in the image.

9. Click **Select** on the menu bar, then click **Save Selection**.

The Save Selection dialog box opens.

10. Type **White Pixels** in the Name text box, then click **OK**.

Note that on the Channels panel, a new alpha channel has appeared named **White Pixels**.

Figure 44 Viewing the image posterized at 4 levels

11. Deselect, then click the words **White Pixels** on the Channels panel.

As shown in Figure 45, the alpha channel uses white pixels to represent the area of the canvas that you selected, and it uses black pixels to represent the pixels that weren't selected.

TIP When you view channels, click the channel's name or the thumbnail image on the panel; don't click the eye icons on the left.

12. Click the **Gray channel** on the Channels panel to return to the posterized artwork.

Figure 45 Alpha channel representing the selection of the white areas of the posterized image

13. Click the **Magic Wand tool** on a **light gray area** of the image, then save the selection with the name **Light Gray Pixels**.

14. Select the **dark gray pixels**, then save the selection with the name **Dark Gray Pixels**.

15. Select the **black pixels**, then save the selection with the name **Black Pixels**.

Your Channels panel should resemble Figure 46.

16. Save your work, then continue to the next set of steps.

You used the Posterize dialog box to explore the concept of "number of shades of gray per pixel." You increased the number of shades available until the illusion of a smooth transition from black to white, or "continuous tone" was achieved. You then posterized the image to four levels. You used the Magic Wand tool to select each of the four colors and saved a selection for each as an alpha channel on the Channels panel.

Add color to a posterized image

1. Click **Image** on the menu bar, point to **Mode**, then click **RGB Color**.

Nothing appears to change. The image still looks like a black and white image. However, this is now an RGB image.

2. Click **Select** on the menu bar, then click **Load Selection**.

The Load Selection dialog box opens.

3. Click the **Channel list arrow**, click **Black Pixels**, then click **OK**.

The Black Pixels selection is loaded on the canvas.

4. On the Swatches panel, click a **dark blue swatch**, then fill the selection with that color.

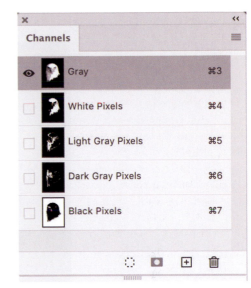

Figure 46 Channels panel showing four alpha channels for saved selections

5. Using the same methodology, load the **Dark Gray Pixels selection**, then fill it with a **medium green color**.

6. Load the **Light Gray Pixels selection**, then fill it with an **orange color**.

7. Load the **White Pixels selection**, then fill it with a **pale yellow color**.

8. Deselect, then compare your canvas to Figure 47, shown on the following page.

9. Save your work, then close Posterized Eagle.

You converted the grayscale image to an RGB image, noting that pixels in an RGB image are gray when none of the three colors dominates. You then loaded saved selections and filled them with a color, creating a dramatic color posterized effect.

Figure 47 The saved selections filled with color

Paint with the Brush tool

1. Open PS 2-12.psd, save it as **Connect the Dots**, then click the Brush tool.
2. Set the foreground color on the toolbar to black.
3. On the Options panel, set the Size to 32, set the Hardness to 100%, then set the Opacity to 100%.
4. Leave the Options panel, then press the right bracket ( ]) on your keypad until the brush size increases to 80 px.
5. Target the Hard brush layer on the Layers panel, then click point #1 on the canvas.
6. Press and hold [shift], then click point #2.
7. Using the same method, continue to point #6.
8. Target the Soft Brush layer on the Layers panel, then change the foreground color to white.
9. Click the left bracket ([ ) on your keypad until the brush size is 30 px.
10. Change the Hardness to 0%.
11. Click where point #1 would be if it were visible, press and hold [shift], then click point #2.
12. Using the same method, continue to point #6.
13. Save your work, then move directly into the next set of steps.

Use keyboard shortcuts to undo and redo

1. Press and hold [command] (Mac) or [Ctrl] (Win), then press the letter [Z] on your keypad 12 times.
2. Press and hold [shift] [command] (Mac) or [Shift] [Ctrl] (Win), then press the letter [Z] on your keypad 12 times.
3. Save your work, then close Connect the Dots.

Paint and fill with Darker Color mode

1. Open PS 2-13.psd, then save it as **Skills Coloring Book**.
2. Select the Brush tool on the toolbar; set the Size to 20 px and the Hardness to 100%.
3. On the Options panel, change the Mode to Darker Color.
4. Click a blue swatch on the Swatches panel to paint water.
5. Use the brush to paint the water drops coming from the elephant's trunk at the top of the illustration. Change the brush size as needed. Because you are painting in Darker Color mode, you can paint over the black lines of the image without affecting them.
6. Select the Magic Wand tool on the toolbar.
7. On the Options panel, type **4** in the Tolerance text box, then verify that the Anti-alias and Contiguous options are both checked.
8. Click the Magic Wand tool in the puddle of water at the bottom of the illustration.
9. Click Select on the menu bar, point to Modify, then click Expand.
10. Type **1** in the Expand By text box, then click OK.
11. Click the Edit menu, then click Fill.
12. Set the Contents to Foreground Color, set the Mode to Darker Color, set the Opacity to 100%, then click OK.
13. Using any of the methods you learned in this chapter, finish coloring the drawing.
Figure 48, shown on the following page, shows one result.
14. Save your work, then close Skills Coloring Book.

Use the Marquee and Lasso tools to make selections

1. Open PS 2-14.psd, then save it as **Skills Puzzle**. You used this same file in Lesson 4 to move marquees you made with the Magic Wand tool. In this exercise, you'll build the puzzle to review using the Marquee and Lasso selection tools.
2. Zoom in on the #1 piece, then click the Rectangular Marquee tool.
3. Position the center of the crosshair on the upper-left corner of the puzzle piece, drag downward until the center of the crosshair is on the lower-right corner, then release the mouse pointer.

4. Click View on the menu bar, click Fit on Screen, click the Move tool, drag the piece to the correct position on the hot air balloon image, then deselect.

5. Click the Rectangular Marquee tool, select the top square in the #2 piece, press and hold [shift], position the crosshair over the lower-right corner, drag a second marquee around the bottom square that overlaps the first square, then release the mouse pointer.

    Pressing and holding [shift] when making a selection adds pixels to the existing selection.

6. Move the selected pixels into place in the puzzle.

7. Select the outer square in the #3 piece, press and hold [option] (Mac) or [Alt] (Win), then select the white inner rectangle.

    The white inner rectangle is removed from the selection. Pressing and holding [option] (Mac) or [Alt] (Win) or when making a selection removes pixels from the existing selection.

8. Move the selected pixels into place in the puzzle.

9. Select the Elliptical Marquee tool, then position the crosshair icon over the green pixel at the center of the #4 piece.

Figure 48 Viewing the painted artwork

10. Press and hold [option] (Mac) or [Alt] (Win), begin dragging, add the [shift] key, then drag to the edge of the circle to complete the selection.
    Pressing and holding [option] (Mac) or [Alt] (Win) when no pixels are selected creates a marquee selection that starts in the center and grows outward. Pressing and holding [shift] while dragging a Marquee tool constrains the marquee selection to a perfect circle or square.
11. Move the selected pixels into position in the puzzle.
12. Zoom in on the #5 piece, then click the Lasso tool.
13. Click and drag to select just an interior section of the piece.
14. Press [shift], then use the Lasso tool to keep adding to the selection until the entire shape is selected.
    If necessary, press [option] (Mac) or [Alt] (Win) while using the Lasso tool to remove unwanted selected areas you might create outside of the shape. Your result will not be ideal. This selection calls for more precision than the Lasso tool can provide.
15. Move the selected pixels into place in the puzzle.
16. Zoom in on the #6 piece, click the Polygonal Lasso tool, then press [caps lock] so that the Lasso tool is a precise crosshair.
17. Position the crosshair at the tip of the upper-right point of the shape, click, and release the mouse button. Then move the mouse pointer to the next corner on the shape, and click.
18. Using the same method, move the mouse pointer around the shape, clicking on the next 12 corners of the shape.
19. Float over the original point you clicked so the Polygonal Lasso tool icon appears with a small "o" beside it, then click to close the selection.
20. Move the selected pixels into place in the puzzle.
21. Click the Magnetic Lasso tool.
22. Click and drag the Magnetic Lasso tool to select the #7 piece.
23. Move the selected pixels into place to complete the puzzle.
24. Save your work, then close Skills Puzzle.

Experiment with the Contiguous setting

1. Open PS 2-15.psd, then save it as **Contiguous Skills Test**.
2. Using Figure 49 as a reference, use the Magic Wand tool change the squares to match the figure using as few moves as possible. If you're working in a group, count the number of steps it takes you to finish, then compare with the group to see who used the fewest steps.
   If you have problems, refer to the third exercise in Lesson 4.
3. When you are finished, Invert the canvas.
4. Save your work, then close Contiguous Skills Test.

Figure 49 The multicolored checkerboard

Use the Magic Wand tool to select an image

1. Open PS 2-16.psd, then save it as **Blue Stop**.
2. On the Options panel, set the Tolerance to 32, then verify that Anti-alias and Contiguous are both checked.
3. Click the red area of the stop sign directly above the letter O.
   The Contiguous option is activated to avoid any of the pixels in the red bricks of the building being accidentally selected.
4. Press and hold [shift], then click the center of the red areas inside the letter O and inside the letter P.
5. Click Select on the menu bar, point to Modify, then click Expand.
6. Type **2** in the Expand By text box, then click OK.
7. Click Select on the menu bar, then click Select and Mask.
8. At the top of the Properties panel, in the View Mode section, verify that High Quality Preview is the only one of the three check boxes that is checked.
9. Click the View list arrow to see the viewing options available to you.
10. Click Black and White (K), then zoom in on the image to better see the edge pixels.
    Viewing the selection in black and white makes it easy to see that the selection edge is very uneven— not the straight and smooth edge one would expect when looking at color on a stop sign.
11. On the Properties panel, drag the Smooth slider to 3.
    The edge pixels are smoothed without a feathering or fading effect taking place.

Figure 50 The blue stop sign

12. Click OK.
13. Press [command] [H] (Mac) or [Ctrl] [H] (Win) to hide the selection marquee.
14. Click Image on the menu bar, point to Adjustments, then click Hue/Saturation.
    The Hue/Saturation dialog box opens.
15. Drag the Hue slider left to −128, then click OK.
    As shown in Figure 50, the stop sign is blue, but the white letters and border are not affected.
16. Save your work, then close Blue Stop.

Posterize an image and save selections

1. Open PS 2-17.psd, then save it as **Posterize Skills**.
2. Click Image on the menu bar, point to Mode, then click Grayscale.
3. Click Image on the menu bar, point to Adjustments, then click Posterize.
4. Set the number of shades to 4, then click OK.
5. Click the Magic Wand tool, set the Tolerance to 0, then verify that Contiguous and Anti-alias are not checked.
6. Select all the white pixels in the image.
7. Click Select on the menu bar, then click Save Selection.
8. Type **White Pixels** in the Name text box, then click OK.
   Note that in the Channels panel, a new alpha channel has appeared named White Pixels.
9. Deselect, then click the words White Pixels in the Channels panel.
   The alpha channel uses white pixels to represent the area of the canvas that you selected, and it uses black pixels to represent the pixels that weren't selected.
10. Click the Gray channel in the Channels panel to return to the posterized artwork.
11. Select all the light gray pixels in the image, then save the Selection with the name **Light Gray Pixels**.
12. Select the dark gray pixels, then save the Selection with the name **Dark Gray Pixels**.
13. Select the black pixels, then save the selection with the name **Black Pixels**.
14. Click the Gray channel to return to the posterized image.
15. Save your work.

Add color to a posterized image

1. Click Image on the menu bar, point to Mode, then click RGB color.
2. Click Select on the menu bar, then click Load Selection.
3. Click the Channel list arrow, click Black Pixels, then click OK.
4. On the Swatches panel, click a dark maroon or dark purple swatch, then fill the selection with that color.
5. Using the same methodology, load the Dark Gray Pixels selection, then fill it with a medium purple color.
6. Load the Light Gray Pixels selection, then fill it with a light purple color.
7. Load the White Pixels selection, then fill it with a pale purple color.
   You can use the Color panel to create a pale purple color.
8. Deselect, then compare your canvas to Figure 51.
9. Save your work, then close Posterize Skills.

Figure 51 The posterized, colorized image

1. Open PS 2-18 .psd, then save it as **Painting Skills**.
2. Click the Magic Wand tool, set the Tolerance to 8, then verify that Contiguous and Anti-alias are not checked.
3. Click one of the black eyes so all the black pixels in the image are selected.
4. Click Select on the menu bar, point to Modify, then click Expand.
5. Type **1** in the Expand By text box, then click OK.
6. Save the selection with the name **All Black Pixels**.
7. Deselect.
8. Zoom in on both eyes so they fill your screen.
9. Click the Magic Wand tool, set the Tolerance to 8, then verify that Contiguous is checked and Anti-alias is not checked.
10. Select both orange sections of the eyes, then hide the selection marquee.
11. Click the Eyedropper tool, then sample the orange color from the eyes so it becomes the foreground color.
12. Click the Brush tool, set the Size to 60 px, then set the Hardness to 0%.

13. Set the Opacity to 80%.
14. Set the Mode to Multiply.
    In Multiply mode, the orange foreground color will darken the orange eye color if painted.
15. Paint darker orange on the insides of both eyes so your artwork resembles Figure 52.
16. Change the foreground color to white.
17. Change the Opacity of the brush to 40%, then change the Size to 25 px.
18. Change the Mode of the brush to Screen.
    Screen blending mode functions as the opposite of Multiply. In Screen mode, lighter colors lighten a painted area. Note the selection is still active, so you cannot paint outside and affect the black lines that draw the eye.
19. Paint lighter orange on the outside of the eyes so your artwork resembles Figure 53.
20. Click Filter on the menu bar, point to Blur, then click Gaussian Blur.
21. Type **3** in the Radius text box, then click OK.
    The Gaussian Blur filter smooths the lines made by the brush. Instead of being one color, the eyes now have a range of tone from shadows to highlights in orange. Even though no black pixels are selected,

some of the black from the black lines blur into the orange.
22. Using the skills covered in steps 1–15, select different parts of the image, then paint shadows and highlights to create dimension.
    Use Figure 54 as a guide. You will need to alter the size and the opacity of the brush as well as the amount of the Gaussian Blur, depending on your preferences.
23. When you are done painting, load the All Black Pixels selection, then fill it with black.
    The fill replaces some of the blurring that occurs with the original black lines.
24. Save your work, then close Painting Skills.

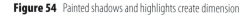

Figure 54 Painted shadows and highlights create dimension

Figure 52 Darkening the eye with Multiply mode

Figure 53 Lightening the eye with Screen mode

PROJECT BUILDER 2

1. Open PS 2-19.psd, then save it as **Pink Flip Flops**.
2. Click the Magnetic Lasso tool.
3. On the Options panel, verify that the Feather is set to 0, Anti-alias is checked, the Width is set to 10, the Contrast is set to 10, and the Frequency is set to 57.
4. Select both flip flops with the Magnetic Lasso tool. Use [shift] to add to the selection. Use [option] (Mac) or [Alt] (Win) to remove from the selection.
5. When you finish making the selection, use the Lasso tool to improve the selection by adding to or removing from it.
6. Click Select on the menu bar, then click Select and Mask.
7. Click the View list arrow, then click Black & White (K).
8. Type **3** in the Smooth text box, then click OK.
9. Press and hold [command] (Mac) or [Ctrl] (Win), then press the letter [U] on your keypad to open the Hue/Saturation dialog box.
10. Type **-100** in the Hue text box, click OK, then compare your results to Figure 55.
    These results were achieved using exactly these steps and no additional "extras" to help the process. The results are a testament to the ability and power of the Magnetic Lasso tool.
11. Save your work, then close Pink Flip Flops.

Figure 55 Viewing the altered flip flops

Morguefile

DESIGN PROJECT

1. Open PS 2-20.psd, then save it as **Contiguous Colors**.
2. Convert to the file to Grayscale.
3. Posterize the image to six levels.
4. Convert the file to RGB Color.
5. Set the Magic Wand tool to a Tolerance of 4, verify that Contiguous is checked, then verify that Anti-alias is not checked.
6. Make contiguous selections and fill them with color. Use Figure 56 as a guide. Filling contiguous selections with color will create a different effect than the other two posterize exercises from this chapter, both of which were done with the Contiguous option turned off. You should use all the selection techniques you learned in this chapter to create the final image.

Figure 56 Design Project completed

NATIONAL GEOGRAPHIC STORYTELLERS ❘ ALISON WRIGHT

Courtesy of Alison Wright

Alison Wright travels around the world to meet people and uses photography to tell their stories. Many of her photos focus on people who have suffered from disaster, war, or infringement of their basic human rights. Her goal is to create images that help people and their communities by increasing awareness of their situations and reminding viewers of the connection we all share as human beings.

Alison is passionate about the people of Tibet and has traveled there many times. In 2005, while working on a story about Tibet's nomads for *National Geographic*, she met a group of people returning from a horse festival. In this group, Alison saw a young girl dressed in traditional clothing and beautiful jewelry and asked for the opportunity to take her photo.

Because it was pouring rain, Alison took the girl indoors and used natural light from a side window to illuminate the photograph. Not knowing each other's languages, Alison said she and the girl connected through communication of the heart. The girl's expression was not coached. Instead, the moment unfolded naturally to produce an image that Alison feels captures not only the sadness of this girl's community and culture, but also its resilience and tenacity.

© Alison Wright

Alison Wright, Tibet girl, near Manigango, Kham, Tibet

PROJECT DESCRIPTION

In this project, you will analyze and respond to Alison's image. You'll have the opportunity to investigate the different elements of the image and interpret the story for yourself. After looking at the photo closely, you will write a brief analysis consisting of your observations, your interpretation of the story, any questions you may have, and the messages you take away.

QUESTIONS TO CONSIDER

❘ What stands out to you?

❘ What surprised you?

❘ What questions would you ask?

❘ What do you think the story is about?

GETTING STARTED

Research the Tibetan culture and people. Look into where they live and how they work. Understand how the culture has changed over time and what that means for Tibetan people today. Understanding the topic of the photo you're analyzing will help you better interpret and comprehend the story.

Analyze the photo. Take note of anything that catches your attention. Look closely at the girl and how she is posed. Pay attention to her facial expression and what she is wearing. Make observations about how the different visual elements are interacting with each other in the photo. If you can, talk to your classmates and discuss your ideas. Decide which elements of the photo are impactful to you and write a brief analysis of your findings.

Our Roman Holiday

Ps CHAPTER **3**

WORK WITH LAYERS

1. Use the Layers Panel
2. Transform Layered Artwork
3. Incorporate Layer Styles
4. Employ a Layer Mask
5. Mask Out the Background of an Image and Modify the Canvas Size

Adobe Certified Professional in Visual Design Using Photoshop CC Framework

3. Organizing Documents

This objective covers document structure such as layers and managing document structure for efficient workflows.

3.1 Use layers to manage design elements.
  A Use the Layers panel to manage visual content.
  C Recognize the different types of layers in the Layers panel.
3.2 Modify layer visibility using opacity, blending modes, and masks.
  B Create and edit masks.

4. Creating and Modifying Visual Elements

This objective covers core tools and functionality of the application, as well as tools that affect the visual outcome of the document.

4.4 Transform digital graphics and media.
  A Modify the canvas or artboards.
  B Rotate, flip, and modify individual layers, objects, selections, groups, or graphical elements.

USE THE LAYERS PANEL

▶ *What You'll Do*

You will explore the basic functions on the Layers panel.

Working with Layers The Layers panel is one of Photoshop's greatest features because it allows you to segregate various art components onto different layers within a single document. Working with layers allows you to apply various effects, like drop shadows or glows, to individual art components without affecting others. Layers give you options for positioning artwork in relation to other objects on the canvas and allow you to move that artwork without affecting the content on other layers.

Working with the Layers Panel

The Layers panel, shown in Figure 1, houses all the layers in a document and offers you many options for manipulating those layers. Some basic operations you can perform with the Layers panel and layered artwork are to hide or show various art components and control which visual elements appear in front of or behind other elements.

Working with layers allows you to move different images independently of one another. This offers you total freedom to design your artwork with the spatial relationships that you find most appealing in your design aesthetic.

Figure 1 The Layers panel

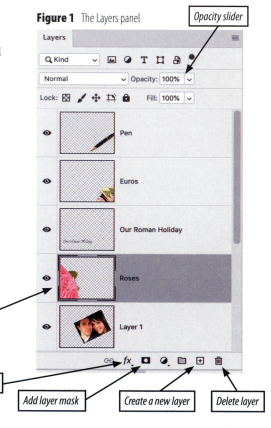

Opacity slider

Layer thumbnail

Add a layer style

Add layer mask

Create a new layer

Delete layer

Working with Layer Opacity

The Layers panel offers you controls to modify the opacity of artwork on the Layers panel. In Photoshop, the term **opacity** refers to how *opaque* artwork is. For example, if artwork has 100% opacity, it is completely opaque—no part of it is transparent. Conversely, artwork with 0% opacity is completely transparent and thus invisible. In between the two extremes is a whole range of transparency, from 99% down to 1%. For example, artwork with 50% opacity would be visible, but any artwork on a layer or layers beneath it would be visible *through* it.

Layer opacity can be a very effective design tool, especially when you want to merge multiple images by having them "blend" into one another.

Merging Layers

At any point during your design process, you can merge some or all of the layered artwork in a file onto one layer. The more layers in a file, the larger the file size, so merging layers reduces file size. Remember, though, that merging layers is a commitment: once artwork is merged onto a single layer, it can't be unmerged later on in the project (other than by using the Undo or Revert commands, which are very limited). For example, if you merge two layers and then exit Photoshop, there will be no way to unmerge that artwork.

Even though you'll learn how to merge layers in this lesson, it's almost always best to not merge. Generally speaking, it's best to keep artwork segregated on different layers simply to keep your options open for any modifications you might need to make as your project evolves.

Duplicating, Deleting, and Pasting New Layers

Layers are created in Photoshop in a variety of ways. For example, you can click Layer on the menu bar, point to New, then click Layer. The fastest and easiest way is to click the Create a new layer button on the Layers panel. This creates a new "empty" layer on the Layers panel.

Another common way that layers are created is when you duplicate an existing layer in the panel. Perhaps the most common way that new layers are created occurs when you copy and paste an image from another file into your current file. Whenever you copy artwork and then paste, the copied artwork is pasted onto a new layer, directly above the active layer on the Layers panel. This is a great feature in Photoshop because you can be confident that when you paste artwork, the new artwork will always be isolated on its own layer and will not directly affect any existing artwork in the file.

To delete a layer, simply drag it to the Delete layer button on the Layers panel.

Loading a Selection from a Layer

Any artwork on a layer is, by definition, selectable as a selection. Press and hold [command] (Mac) or [Ctrl] (Win), then click the layer's thumbnail to load a selection of the artwork on the canvas. You can then use that selection for different operations, such as adding a shadow behind the selected object.

Set preferences for working with layers

1. Open PS 3-1.psd, then save it as **Roman Holiday**. Be sure you don't save the file again until you are instructed to.

2. Click the **Photoshop menu** (Mac) or the **Edit menu** (Win) on the menu bar, point to **Preferences**, then click **General**.

3. Verify that **Use Legacy Free Transform** is checked, as shown in Figure 2, then click **OK**.

   "Legacy" is an option Photoshop Creative Cloud offers you for some tools, features, and dialog boxes. It allows you to work with older versions of features that have since been updated. Use Legacy Free Transform is the only legacy feature we use in this book. We do so because it allows you to transform layers in a way that is most consistent with making marquees and shapes in Photoshop and making shapes in Illustrator and in InDesign.

4. On the Layers panel, note the size of the "thumbnail" for each layer.

   The thumbnail icons present a visual of the artwork that is on each layer. These icons are currently very small and would be more helpful if they were larger.

5. Click the **Layers panel menu button** 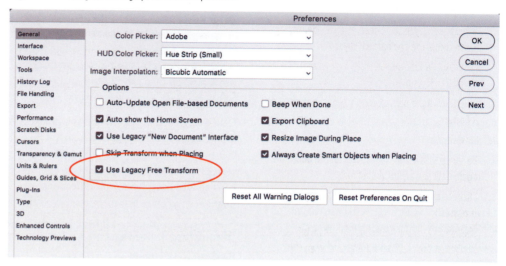, then click **Panel Options**.

6. Click the **largest thumbnail option**, then click **OK**.

You set a preference to use the legacy version when transforming, and you changed the size of the thumbnails on the Layers panel.

Figure 2 Activating the Use Legacy Free Transform preference

Perform basic operations on the Layers panel

1. Note that all layers have been given an identifying name except the one named "Layer 1."

   By default, whenever you create a new layer, it is assigned a layer number.

2. Double-click the name **Layer 1**, then rename it **Couple**.

3. Save the file.

   Be sure you save the file in this step, and don't save again until you are instructed to.

4. Click the **eye button** 👁 on the **Pen layer** repeatedly.

   The layer toggles between visible and invisible. Verify that the pen artwork is visible when you're done with this step.

5. Click and drag vertically over **multiple eye buttons** 👁 on the Layers panel.

   Clicking and dragging over multiple eye buttons hides those layers.

6. Repeat Step 5 to make **all layers** visible again.

7. Press and hold **[option] (Mac)** or **[Alt] (Win)**, then click the **eye button** 👁 on the **Couple layer**.

   Only the artwork on the Couple layer is visible. Pressing and holding [option] (Mac) or [Alt] (Win) while clicking an eye button shows only that layer and hides all other layers.

8. Still holding **[option] (Mac)** or **[Alt] (Win)**, click the **eye button** 👁 on the **Couple layer**.

   All the layers become visible again.

9. Target the **Colosseum layer**.

10. Click the **Opacity slider** at the top of the Layers panel, then drag the **slider** to **50%**.

    As shown in Figure 3, the Colosseum artwork is now 50% transparent. You might have noticed that dragging a slider to an exact number can be difficult. There's a better way to change opacity.

11. Click the **Move tool** ⊕ on the toolbar, then press the **number [2]** on your keypad.

    The Colosseum artwork opacity changes to 20%. With the Move tool activated, pressing numbers on the keypad changes the opacity and the Opacity setting is updated on the Layers panel. 5 = 50%, 2 = 20%, 1 = 10%, and 0 = 100%.

12. Click anywhere on the **Coin layer** to target it.

    In Photoshop, you don't "select" a layer; you *target* it. Designers use this distinction to avoid confusion with making "selections" with the selection tools.

    Continued on next page

Figure 3   The Colosseum artwork at 50%

13. Press the **letter [V]** on your keypad to verify that the Move tool ⊕ is still selected, float over the **coin artwork**, then click and drag it to another position on the canvas.

The Move tool moves artwork only on the targeted layer. You will use the Move tool all the time when working with layers. Get used to using the [V] shortcut key to access the Move tool.

14. Target the **Couple layer**, press and hold **[command] (Mac)** or **[Ctrl] (Win),** then click the **Pen layer** so that both layers are targeted.

Pressing and holding [command] (Mac) or [Ctrl] (Win) allows you to target multiple and nonadjacent layers on the Layers panel.

15. Drag the **Couple** and **Pen artwork** to another location on the canvas.

Because both layers are targeted on the Layers panel, the artwork on both layers moves as you drag.

16. Click **File** on the menu bar, then click **Revert.**

The artwork returns to the state when you last saved it. Note, however, that the thumbnails on the Layers panel are still large. Preferences are saved separately from individual files, so when you reverted this file, it did not revert the preference you changed.

17. Target the **Coin layer**, then click and drag it up to the top of the Layers panel.

As you drag, a blue horizontal line appears, indicating where the layer will be repositioned when you release the mouse pointer. Changing the *stacking order* of layers changes which artwork is in front of or behind other artwork.

TIP Photoshop has hundreds (if not thousands) of features for you to keep track of. Knowing the names of different features helps you keep track of all your options. So, when

Figure 4 Moving the coin with the arrow key

you learn a term like *stacking order*, it's worth your time to incorporate it into your understanding of the program.

18. Verify that the **Coin layer** is still targeted, then press **[command] [J] (Mac)** or **[Ctrl] [J] (Win).**

The coin layer is duplicated. A new layer named Coin copy automatically appears on the Layers panel above the original Coin layer.

19. Enter **[command] [J] (Mac)** or **[Ctrl] [J] (Win)** again.

A third Coin layer is created.

20. Click and drag the **Coin copy 2 layer** to the **Delete layer button** 🗑 on the Layers panel.

The layer is deleted.

21. Target the **Coin copy layer**, press and hold **[shift]**, then press the **right arrow** on your keypad six times.

Your coins should resemble Figure 4.

TIP Pressing an arrow key on the keypad moves artwork on the targeted layer **one** increment in that direction. Holding [shift] and pressing an arrow key moves artwork on the targeted layer **10** increments in that direction.

22. Target both the **Coin** and the **Coin copy layers**, click the **Layers panel menu button** ≣ , then click **Merge Layers**.

The artwork is merged onto one layer. Even though you are being taught that you *can* do this, you seldom should merge layers. Think of Photoshop as a "Hansel & Gretel" application—you always want to have a trail of breadcrumbs so that you can backtrack if you need to. Once you merge artwork, you're stuck with it, other than using the Undo command.

23. Click **File** on the menu bar, then click **Revert.**

You named a layer, made layers hidden and visible, changed the opacity of layers, then moved artwork on layers and duplicated layers.

Load a selection from artwork on a layer

1. Target the **Couple layer**.

2. Press and hold **[command] (Mac)** or **[Ctrl] (Win)**, then click the **Create a new layer button**  on the Layers panel.

   A new blank layer is created below the Couple layer. Pressing and holding [command] (Mac) or [Ctrl] (Win) when you click the Create a new layer button adds a new layer below the currently targeted layer.

3. Rename the new layer **Couple Shadow**, then verify that the Couple Shadow layer remains targeted.

4. Press and hold **[command] (Mac)** or **[Ctrl] (Win)**, then click the **thumbnail image on the Couple layer**.

   A selection of the couple artwork is loaded.

5. Click **Select** on the menu bar, point to **Modify**, then click **Feather**.

6. Enter **4** in the Feather Radius text box, then click **OK**.

7. Press the **letter [D]** on your keypad to set the default colors on the toolbar to black (foreground) and white (background).

8. Press and hold **[option] (Mac)** or **[Alt] (Win)**, then press **[delete]** on your keypad.

   The selection is filled with the foreground color on the Couple Shadow layer and remains selected.

9. **Deselect**, then click the **Move tool** on the toolbar.

10. Press and hold **[shift]** on your keypad, then press the **down arrow** on your keypad three times.

11. Set the **Opacity** on the Couple Shadow layer to **50%**, then compare your canvas to Figure 5.

12. Save your work, then close Roman Holiday.

You created a new layer beneath a targeted layer, you loaded a selection from artwork on a layer and feathered it, then you filled it with black to create a drop shadow effect.

Figure 5 Viewing the drop shadow

LIFE WITHOUT LAYERS

It seems quite hard to believe now, but in the early versions of Photoshop, there were no layers! It was possible to overlap various components of artwork, but once you deselected, those components would become embedded in the canvas, totally integrated with all the other pixels. So, if the montage we worked on in this lesson was created in an early version of Photoshop, all the elements would have existed on one canvas, one bed of pixels. If you think about that for a moment, you get a real sense of the true benefit of working with layers: the options to edit, rethink, and redesign.

TRANSFORM LAYERED ARTWORK

▶ *What You'll Do*

In this lesson, you'll scale and rotate artwork on layers.

Using the Transform Commands

Any kind of transformation is a change. In Photoshop, transforming artwork means doing any of the following:

■ moving

■ scaling

■ rotating

■ skewing

■ distorting

You can **transform** (change the shape, size, perspective, or rotation of) an object or objects on a layer using one or more of the Transform commands on the Edit menu. You can transform a single layer or transform multiple layers simultaneously.

When you use some of the transform commands, a bounding box appears around the object you are transforming. A **bounding box** is a rectangle that surrounds an image and contains eight handles that you click and drag to change the dimensions of the artwork.

After you transform an object, you can apply or execute the changes by pressing [return] (Mac) or [Enter] (Win). Alternatively, clicking the Move tool on the toolbar will also execute the transformation.

You can use transform commands individually or in a chain. After you choose your initial transform command, you can try out as many others as you like before you apply the changes by pressing [return] (Mac) or [Enter] (Win). In other words, you can first scale artwork, and before committing the transformation, you can rotate it too.

You don't have to keep going back to the Edit menu every time you want to transform. A faster method is to simply enter [command] [T] (Mac) or [Ctrl] [T] (Win). This causes the bounding box to appear around the artwork on the targeted layer so you can begin transforming. Drag any handle with your mouse pointer to scale the artwork. Float your pointer outside of the bounding box, and it turns into the rotate icon. Click and drag the rotate icon to rotate the artwork.

Transforming artwork is one of the preeminent features of Photoshop. Transforming is a key skill in Photoshop, especially when creating a montage, because montages involve specific positioning and size relationships between elements.

Flipping and Rotating Artwork

Flipping and rotating are two transformations that can be especially useful when creating a montage of various images. **Flipping** artwork creates a mirror image of the artwork. You can flip images horizontally or vertically. **Rotating** an object moves it clockwise or counterclockwise around its center point, just like a windmill spins. You can rotate an image by hand or by entering a specific rotation value on the Options panel.

Rotating and flipping are very different transformations that produce different results. You can compare rotating artwork with your tire rotating as you drive. By default, artwork in Photoshop is rotated around its center point unless you move the crosshair icon from the center point to a new location.

Figure 6 shows an image flipped horizontally and vertically.

Flipping an image can produce odd results, especially when the image shows peoples' faces. Flipping the image of a person's face may yield unexpected results because nobody's face is perfectly symmetrical. Also remember, if there's text anywhere in an image when flipped, that text is going to read backwards or upside down, which is a dead giveaway that the image has been flipped!

Figure 6 The same image, flipped horizontally and vertically

ORIGINAL

FLIP HORIZONTAL

FLIP VERTICAL

Chris Botello

Understanding the Point of Origin in a Transformation

The **point of origin** defines the point from which a transformation occurs. In Photoshop, the point of origin is represented by the crosshair icon, as shown in Figure 7.

When you click and drag *outside* the bounding box to rotate, by default, the artwork will be rotated at the location of the crosshair icon. By default, the crosshair is at the center of the artwork when you first apply a transform command. However, you can move the crosshair icon. Figure 8 shows the crosshair

icon moved to the upper-left corner of the image. Clicking and dragging outside the bounding box will rotate the image around that point.

Scaling artwork functions differently than rotating. To scale artwork, you drag a handle on the bounding box. The transformation occurs at the location of the handle you drag. Press and hold [option] (Mac) or [Alt] (Win) while dragging a handle and the crosshair will become the point of origin for the scale. For example, if you create a 2" × 2" square and then reduce it by 50% using its center point as the point of origin, all four sides of the square

will move equally toward the center until the new size of the square is 1" × 1". This is a very powerful technique for managing your artwork when doing scale transformations.

Remember, before you make any kind of transformation, you can move the crosshair icon to any point that you want to remain fixed, then transform the artwork using that point as the point of origin.

Rather than click and drag to scale or rotate, you can enter values on the Options panel. When you do, the crosshair icon determines the point of origin automatically.

Figure 7 The crosshair icon, representing the point of origin for the transformation

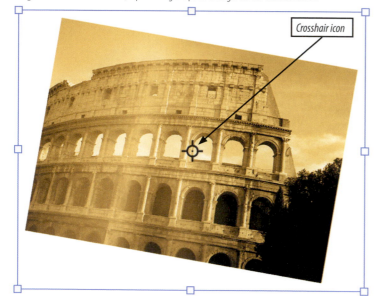

Crosshair icon

Figure 8 The crosshair icon, relocated

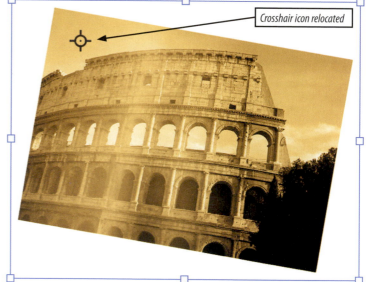

Crosshair icon relocated

Scale artwork

1. Open PS 3-2.psd, then save it as **Roman Holiday 2.**

2. Target the **Colosseum layer**, click **Edit** on the menu bar, point to **Transform**, then click **Scale.**

   As shown in Figure 9, the bounding box appears around the artwork. The bounding box has a square handle at each corner that you click and drag to transform the artwork. The handles are sometimes referred to as resizing handles.

TIP If you do not see the crosshair pointer in the center of the bounding box, click **Edit (Win)** or **Photoshop (Mac)** on the menu bar, point to **Preferences**, click **Tools**, and then click the **Show Reference Point when using Transform check box**.

3. Position the mouse pointer on the **lower-right corner handle** until a double-headed arrow appears, click and drag in different directions to modify the image, then release the mouse pointer.

   Clicking and dragging the corner handle allows you to enlarge, reduce, and/or distort the image.

4. **Undo** your last step.

5. Position the mouse pointer on the **lower-right corner handle**, press and hold **[shift]**, click and drag in different directions, then release the mouse pointer.

   The [shift] key constrains the scale proportionately. Using the [shift] key, you can enlarge or reduce the artwork, but you can't modify the proportional relationship between the width and height.

6. **Undo** your last step.

Continued on next page

Figure 9 The bounding box and crosshair icon

7. Note the crosshair icon in the middle of the bounding box.

   The crosshair icon is automatically positioned at the center of the bounding box and therefore at the center of the artwork.

8. On the Options panel, double-click the **W text box**, type **80**, press **[tab]**, type **80** in the **H text box**, press **[tab]**, then compare your screen to Figure 10.

   The artwork is scaled 80% at the crosshair, which is at the artwork's center point. By default, when you enter a scale value in the W and/or H text boxes on the Options panel, the artwork is scaled using the crosshair icon as the point of origin for the scale.

9. Press the **[Esc]** key on your keypad to cancel the last transformation.

   Note that throughout these steps, we have been experimenting with different transformations. All of them were previewed, but none of them were executed. The bounding box allows you to experiment endlessly without necessarily committing.

10. Click and drag the **Coin layer** to the top of the Layers panel so that the coin artwork is the topmost artwork.

11. Click the **Coin layer**, then enter **[command] [J] (Mac)** or **[Ctrl] [J] (Win) two times** to create two duplicate coin layers.

12. Rename the layers **Bottom Coin**, **Middle Coin**, and **Top Coin**.

Figure 10 Scaling the artwork 80% at its center

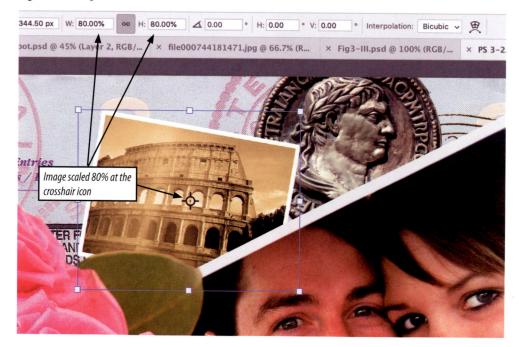

13. Drag the **Bottom Coin layer** down below the Couple layer, then position the artwork as shown in Figure 11.

14. Target the **Bottom Coin layer**, press **[command] [T] (Mac)** or **[Ctrl] [T] (Win)**, then drag the **crosshair icon** to the position shown in Figure 12.

Entering [command] [T] (Mac) or [Ctrl] [T] (Win) is a fast way to access the bounding box.

15. Press and hold **[shift][option] (Mac)** or **[Shift][Alt] (Win)**, position the mouse pointer over the **lower-left handle**, drag to experiment with resizing the coin artwork, then release the mouse pointer.

Pressing and holding the [option] (Mac) or [Alt] (Win) key ensures that any transformation will be executed using the location of the crosshair as the point of origin. The [shift] key is used in this step to constrain the width and height ratio of the artwork while scaling.

16. Undo the last step.

Rather than resizing by dragging, we are going to enter a specific value for the scale.

17. Double-click the **W text box** on the Options panel, type **67**, press **[tab]**, type **67** in the **H text box**, then press **[tab]**.

By default, when you transform by entering values on the Options panel, the transformation uses the crosshair icon as its point of origin.

TIP If you activate the link icon 🔗 between the W and H text boxes on the Options panel, the value you enter in one box automatically appears in the other. This forces a scale transformation to be in proportion. The link icon's official name is Maintain aspect ratio.

18. Click **[return] (Mac)** or **[Enter] (Win)** to execute the transformation.

19. Save your work.

You scaled artwork using the bounding box and by entering width and height percentage values on the Options panel.

Figure 11   Repositioning the bottom coin artwork

Figure 12   Repositioning the crosshair icon

Crosshair icon

Rotate and Flip artwork

1. Target the **Couple layer**, click **Edit** on the menu bar, point to **Transform**, then click **Flip Horizontal.**

   The artwork is flipped horizontally.

2. Position the **couple artwork** as shown in Figure 13.

3. Click the **Bottom Coin layer,** then press **[command] [T] (Mac)** or **[Ctrl] [T] (Win).**

   The bounding box appears.

4. Press and hold **[shift]**, then position your mouse pointer *outside* of the bounding box so that it changes to the rotate icon ↱ .

5. Click and drag counterclockwise outside the bounding box to rotate the bottom coin **−45°**, then click the **Move tool** ✛ on the toolbar.

   Clicking the Move tool executes the transformation. The bottom coin is rotated and no longer appears as an obvious duplicate of the larger coin. Holding [shift] while you rotate constrains the rotation to 15° increments as you drag. Rotating counterclockwise produces a negative rotation. In terms of spatial relationships, the coin is now a bit too far from the couple, so we're going to move the coin.

   TIP Note that the rotation uses the crosshair as the point of origin for the rotation—even though you weren't pressing [option] (Mac) or [Alt] (Win); those keys are only required when you are scaling artwork from the point of origin.

6. Position the coin as shown in Figure 14.

7. Using the same techniques, scale and rotate the top coin to resemble Figure 15.

   Save your work, then close Roman Holiday 2.

You flipped artwork horizontally and rotated artwork.

Figure 13 Flipping and repositioning the couple artwork

Figure 14 Repositioning the rotated coin

Figure 15 Scaling and rotating the top coin

INCORPORATE LAYER STYLES

▶ **What You'll Do**

In this lesson, you'll add Drop Shadow and Outer Glow layer styles to artwork. You'll also copy layer styles between layers.

Adding Layer Styles to Artwork

Layer styles are built-in effects that you can apply to layers; they include glows, shadows, bevels, embosses, and chiseled edges, among many others. When you apply layer styles to artwork on a layer, they will be listed on the Layers panel beneath the layer they've been applied to. Click the small black caret icon to the right of the layer to expand or collapse the list of layer effects for that layer. Click the eye button to hide or show the effect. Once a layer style has been applied, all the artwork on that layer takes on the effect.

Using the Layer Style Dialog Box

The Layer Style dialog box houses all the styles available to add effects to your work. You have several options to add a layer style to a targeted layer. You can click Layer on the menu bar, then click Layer Style, or you can click the Add a layer style button on the Layers panel. Either of these actions will open the Layer Style dialog box. The fastest and easiest way to open the Layer Style dialog box is to simply double-click a layer on the Layers panel.

The Layer Style dialog box is "sticky," meaning any styles you apply will remain in the dialog box even if you close and open the dialog box repeatedly.

All styles you've applied will be checked in the dialog box. Note that you must target the *name* of a style on the left column to display the settings associated with it.

Working with Layer Styles Settings

The Layer Style dialog box contains 10 styles, and each of these styles offers many options for modifying and customizing the style you are applying. When working with layer styles, you will run into many different terms for these options. In this chapter, you will encounter terms such as *distance*, *size*, and *spread* for applying a drop shadow and an outer glow. While those terms might seem self-explanatory, they can get confusing because they overlap. For example, the "spread" option for a drop shadow appears to alter the size of a drop shadow more than the "size" option does. These three options are covered in context in the steps in this lesson.

Generally speaking, most designers don't overthink the options available for a given layer style. Instead, they experiment with the options while watching the visual changes to the artwork. In this sense, applying styles is more about the visual result rather than a calculation of every option.

Copying Layer Styles Between Layers

The ⨍x icon on the Layers panel indicates that one or more layer styles have been applied to that layer. If you drag the ⨍x icon to a different layer, the layer styles will move to that layer and the styles will be applied to the artwork on that layer. Press [option] (Mac) or [Alt] (Win) and drag the ⨍x icon to copy styles between layers.

Copying styles between layers is a good solution for applying styles quickly; however, don't fall into the trap of just assuming that the settings for one style work for all the artwork you copy them to. Take the time to adjust the settings to customize the effect for all the artwork to which you apply styles. The differences might be subtle, but you'll find with experience that subtle customization is what makes all the difference.

Apply a Drop Shadow layer style

1. Open PS 3-3.psd, then save it as **Roman Holiday 3**.

   This file picks up where the previous lesson left off.

2. Target the **Couple layer**.

3. Click **Layer** on the menu bar, point to **Layer Style**, then click **Drop Shadow**.

   The Layer Style dialog box, shown in Figure 16, opens. Because you clicked Drop Shadow when you opened the dialog box, Drop Shadow is checked and activated in the left column, and the settings shown are those of the Drop Shadow layer style (your specific settings will be different).

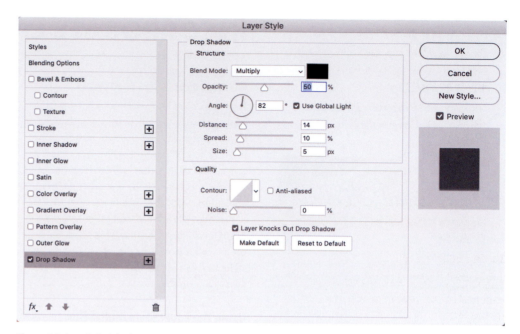

Figure 16 Layer Style dialog box

4. Position the Layer Style dialog box so that you can see as much of the artwork on the canvas as possible.

   As you work with the Layer Style dialog box, the selections you make are updated dynamically on the artwork on the canvas. Even though the Layer Style dialog box is quite large, you want to be able to see as much of the artwork as possible.

5. Experiment with the **Opacity slider**, then set it to **50%**.

   The Opacity setting determines how opaque the shadow is. A 100% opacity shadow is totally opaque—you can't see through it no matter what color it is. A 0% opacity shadow is not

visible. Since you want to see a shadow and see through it, a midrange Opacity setting is usually the best choice.

6. Experiment with the **Distance slider**, then set it to **35**.

   The Distance slider determines how far away from the object the shadow will appear. The greater the distance, the more the object will appear to "float" above the background.

7. Experiment with the **Spread slider**, then set it to **10**.

   The Spread slider expands the size of the shadow itself before it is blurred by the Size slider.

8. Experiment with the **Size slider**, then set it to **20**.

   The Size slider determines the size of the feathered edge of the shadow. A value of 0 would create a hard-edged shadow.

9. Experiment with dragging the **Angle wheel** and notice the effect it has on the shadow in the collage.

   The Angle setting determines the position of the shadow in terms of the artwork casting the shadow. The angle of a shadow and the distance of a shadow in relationship to the object casting the shadow is often referred to as the "offset" of the shadow.

10. Set the **Angle** to **19°**.

AUTHOR'S NOTE In a collage like the one you're creating here, generally speaking, you'll want all shadows to move in the same direction. Your choice of angle for a drop shadow will be based on the shadows in the photos in the collage. For example, when choosing an angle for the shadow on the picture of the couple, you should match the angle of the shadow that's in the photo of the euros. That shadow is not a layer style; it's in the photograph itself.

11. Click **OK**, then compare your artwork to Figure 17.

12. Save your work, then continue to the next set of steps.

You added a Drop Shadow layer style to artwork and specified settings for the style.

Figure 17 Viewing the Drop Shadow layer style on the couple artwork

Copy layer styles between layers

1. Note the layer styles listed on the Layers panel.

   As shown in Figure 18, the Drop Shadow layer is now listed on the Layers panel as a subset of the Couple layer. The *fx* icon indicates that layer styles have been applied to this layer.

2. Press and hold **[option] (Mac)** or **[Alt] (Win)**, then drag the *fx* icon to the Colosseum layer.

   The shadow is copied to the Colosseum layer. You must hold [option] (Mac) or [Alt] (Win) to copy the layer style. Simply dragging the *fx* icon only moves the style from one layer to another.

   TIP Even if you can't see the Colosseum layer on the Layers panel when you begin dragging, you can still do this step. The layers on the Layers panel will scroll as you drag, so you can get to the layer you want.

3. Using the same method, copy the **layer style** from the **Colosseum layer** to the **Top Coin layer**.

Figure 18 Layer style listed on the Layers panel

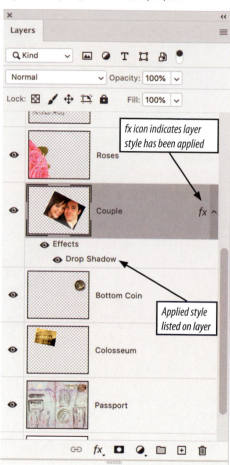

fx icon indicates layer style has been applied

Applied style listed on layer

4. On the Layers panel, double-click **Drop Shadow** under the Colosseum layer to open the Layer Style dialog box.

5. Change the **Distance value** to **18**, then click **OK**.

6. Double-click **Drop Shadow** under the Top Coin layer, change the **Distance value** to **14**, change the **Size value** to **5**, then click **OK**.

7. Drag and drop the **Drop Shadow layer style** from the **Top Coin layer** to the **Middle Coin** and the **Bottom Coin layers**.

8. Compare your artwork to Figure 19.

9. Save your work, then continue to the next set of steps.

You copied a Drop Shadow layer style from one layer to another, then modified the settings for the drop shadow to better fit the new artwork.

Figure 19 Shadows copied and customized to multiple layers

Apply an Outer Glow layer style

1. Hide and show the **Our Roman Holiday layer**.

   In a collage design like this one, type plays an important role. In this collage, it explains the collage. When you read the type, you understand immediately that this is a couple who took a trip to Rome together. They saw the Colosseum. The coins indicate that they experienced the old-world charm of this ancient city, and the euros remind us that it's also a modern city. The passport in the background conveys travel, and the flowers tell us it was romantic. All of this information comes to us through the type. Perhaps they wrote home with the pen, or perhaps they wrote the headline itself with the pen. When you hide the type, you can still understand the image, but not quite so specifically.

2. Verify that the **Our Roman Holiday layer** is visible.

   As a design element, the type is well positioned in its own space in the lower-left quadrant. It has plenty of "air" around it—it's not crammed in there. However, the type overlaps both the image of the roses and the image of the couple, and it is slightly difficult to read. The typeface itself is elegant and charming, but it's also thin, and this too makes it difficult to read.

3. Double-click the **Our Roman Holiday layer**.

   The Layer Style dialog box opens. This is the fastest and easiest way to access the Layer Style dialog box. Note that no specific layer style is targeted in the left column when you open the dialog box using this method.

4. Click the words **Outer Glow** in the left column.

   The settings for the Outer Glow layer style appear. It is tempting to just click the check box and be done. Clicking the check box activates the style, but if you want to see the settings for the style, you must click on the words themselves.

Continued on next page

5. In the **Structure** section, set the **Blending Mode** to **Screen**, then set the **Opacity** to **75**.

The Screen blending mode makes bright colors visible and darker colors invisible. We cover this extensively in later chapters. For the time being, just know that you want the Screen blending mode for any bright glows like hot whites, pinks, yellows, blues, etc.

6. Position your pointer over the unlabeled **black square** in the lower-left corner of the Structure section until **Set color of glow** appears.

This is the official name of the black square.

7. Click the **square**.

The Color Picker dialog box opens, offering you 16.5 million choices for the color of the outer glow. For the remainder of this chapter and this book, we will refer to the square you clicked as the "Color Picker square."

8. Choose **white** for the color, then click **OK**.

9. In the **Elements** section, set the **Spread** to **20** and the **Size** to **60**.

10. Click **OK**, then compare your artwork to Figure 20.

Not only does the Outer Glow layer style add an interesting (and charming) visual element to the collage, look what it does for legibility. The glow makes the type stand out—it's effortless to read the type. Because the glow hides so much of the background elements (the image of the roses and the image of the couple), those elements no longer compete with the type for your attention.

11. Save your work for the next set of steps in Lesson 4.

You added an Outer Glow layer style to type outlines so they would be more legible. You specified settings for the glow in the Layer Style dialog box.

Figure 20 The Outer Glow layer style applied to the type

EMPLOY A LAYER MASK

▶ *What You'll Do*

In this lesson, you'll use a layer mask to hide aspects of layered artwork.

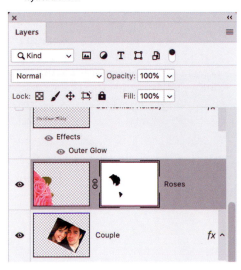

About Layer Masks

You use layer masks to hide or reveal specific artwork on a layer. A layer mask can affect an entire layer or specific areas within a layer. When a layer has a mask, the layer mask thumbnail appears on the Layers panel between the layer thumbnail and the layer name.

The basic concept of a layer mask is that you use black to hide specific areas of the artwork on that layer, or you use white to show specific areas. You add black or white by painting in the layer mask or making selections and filling them with black or white. **Note**: You may also use shades of gray in a layer mask, which is covered in Chapter 4. For this chapter, we are sticking with black or white to get the basic concept down.

As you hide or reveal portions of a layer, the layer mask thumbnail mirrors the changes you are making, and the artwork hides or shows dynamically. One of the many great features about layer masks is that they are endlessly editable. Simply repaint or refill areas you altered previously, and those areas will be updated. Furthermore, nothing you do in a layer mask is permanently altering the actual

artwork. You can disable the layer mask or delete it if you want. Because you alter the mask and not the image, no actual pixels are modified in the artwork.

TIP You can think of a layer mask as a type of temporary eraser. When you add black to the mask, you erase pixels from the image—they disappear. If you go back and add white to the mask, those pixels from the image reappear.

Creating a Layer Mask

To add a layer mask to a layer, first target the layer, then click the Add layer mask button on the Layers panel.

By default, Photoshop adds an all-white mask, meaning no artwork is hidden and essentially nothing changes. Note the frame around the layer mask thumbnail. The frame indicates that the mask is activated, so when you paint on the canvas, for example, you are painting in the mask, not on the actual artwork. Because you can switch between activating the artwork or the mask on a given layer, it's important to be aware of which is activated. If you lose track, it is easy to accidentally paint the artwork when you think you're painting in the layer mask.

Figure 21 conveys the entire concept of a mask. The designer made a rectangular marquee selection in the mask and filled it with black. Therefore, the corresponding artwork (the image of the man on the Couple layer) is no longer visible. The frame around the mask indicates that the mask is active. If the designer were to paint black anywhere *on the artwork*, more of the Couple layer artwork would disappear because the mask is activated.

Viewing, Editing, Disabling, and Deleting a Mask

Once you've painted a mask, you can actually view the mask rather than the artwork. Press and hold [option] (Mac) or [Alt] (Win), then click the mask to view it. When you do, you'll see the black and white sections of the mask. Note that you can paint directly in the mask! You might see a spot you missed—for example, a small white area in a field that is supposed to be all black. You can paint that small white area you missed black directly in the mask. This is a great method for ensuring that all the areas of the mask that you intend to be black are indeed black.

At any time, you can disable or "turn off" a mask simply by shift-clicking the mask. A red X will appear over the layer mask thumbnail. To delete a layer mask, simply drag the layer mask thumbnail to the Delete layer button on the Layers panel.

TIP The term "mask" has its origin in printing. Traditionally, a mask was opaque material or tape used to block off an area of the artwork that you did not want to print.

Figure 21 The activated layer mask with a black rectangle and its effect on the corresponding artwork

Masked area in the layer mask and on the artwork

Add and employ a layer mask

1. Open Roman Holiday 3.psd from Lesson 3, then hide the **Our Roman Holiday layer**.

2. Target the **Roses layer**.

   You are going to "mask out" the two green leaves to see if the roses look better without them.

3. Click the **Add layer mask button** 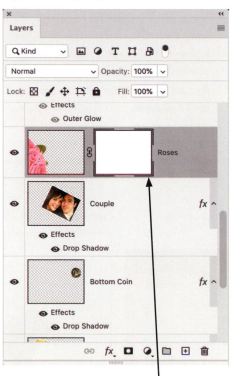 on the Layers panel.

   As shown in Figure 22, an all-white mask is added to the layer, and by default, a frame appears around the mask thumbnail, indicating that the mask is activated. Because the mask is all white, nothing is hidden on the layer, so adding a mask has no immediate effect on the artwork.

4. Note the foreground and background colors on the toolbar.

   No matter what colors you currently have displayed on the toolbar, when you activate a layer mask, the foreground and background colors change to black, white, or a shade of gray because you can only paint black, white, or a shade of gray in a layer mask.

5. Press the **letter [D]** on your keypad to access the default colors, which are foreground (white) and background (black) when a mask is activated.

6. Press the **letter [X]** on your keypad to reverse the foreground and background colors.

   When you paint, you will now be painting with the foreground color, which is black. In other words, anything you paint will disappear.

TIP Get in the habit of using the [D] and [X] keys when you're working in a layer mask to be sure you're painting with pure black and pure white.

Figure 22 Adding the layer mask

Frame around the layer mask thumbnail indicates it is activated

---

7. Type the **letter [B]** on your keypad to access the Brush tool, click the **brush settings** on the Options panel, then set the **Brush Size** to **30** and the **Hardness** to **75**.

   If you need a refresher on brush settings, refer back to Chapter 2, Lesson 2. To mask effectively, it is critical that you use the best brush size and brush hardness (which is essentially the brush "edge") to get the job done. This cannot be overstated. Your willingness to take the time to experiment with the best brush size and especially the best hardness setting will have a huge impact on the success of any mask you ever create.

8. **Zoom in** on the **top green leaf** to enlarge it.

   Taking the time to enlarge the view of the area that you intend to mask is another critical choice for success in masking. Condition yourself to make zooming in a default step when you work with masks.

9. **Paint on the green leaf** so the entire leaf disappears.

   Use the left and right bracket keys (to the right of the letter [P] on your keypad) to adjust the size of the brush, as necessary. Taking the time to adjust your brush size as you work is key to success in masking.

10. Using the same method, mask out the **small lower leaf**.

Continued on next page

11. Compare your artwork and your Layers panel to Figure 23.

12. Press **[command] [0] (Mac)** or **[Ctrl] [0] (Win)** (Fit on Screen), press and hold **[option] (Mac)** or **[Alt] (Win)**, then click the **layer mask thumbnail**.

As shown in Figure 24, the entire mask becomes visible. You can see where you painted black in the mask. Evaluate the mask. Note, if you missed a spot—if there's a bit of white in a field of black that you intended to be all black—you could paint that spot black directly in the mask.

13. Click the **Roses layer thumbnail** (the artwork thumbnail) on the Layers panel.

The view switches back to the artwork. Note that the double border around the artwork thumbnail indicates that the artwork is activated, not the layer mask.

14. Press and hold **[shift]**, then click the **layer mask thumbnail**.

The layer mask is disabled, and a red X appears over the layer mask thumbnail. Because the mask is disabled, the two green leaves are visible again.

15. Evaluate the image.

Let's agree that you decide you like the artwork better with the green leaves visible. You decide the leaves add some unique color, and you like the way the big green leaf overlaps the couple image. Should you delete the layer mask? No. You've already put in the work, and you never know if you might change your mind later in the process, so don't discard the mask. Simply keep it disabled.

16. Save your work, then close Roman Holiday 3.

You used a layer mask along with the Brush tool to mask out parts of artwork and make them invisible.

Figure 23 Viewing the roses without the green leaves and the corresponding layer mask thumbnail on the Layers panel

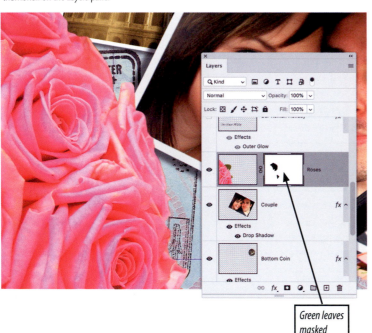

Green leaves masked

Figure 24 Viewing (and evaluating) the mask itself

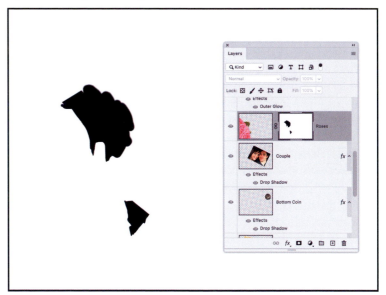

MASK OUT THE BACKGROUND OF AN IMAGE AND MODIFY THE CANVAS SIZE

▶ *What You'll Do*

In this lesson, you'll use a layer mask to remove the background from an image. You'll also enlarge the canvas size to make room for a frame.

Masking Out the Background of an Image

In Lesson 4, you used a layer mask to make two leaves on the roses artwork disappear. That type of work—removing unwanted details from artwork—is a common task layer masks are used to achieve.

Layer masks are most often used to remove the background of an image so that the main subject of the image can be used in a collage or positioned in a different environment. For example, when you see a movie poster that shows the movie's star floating in space or hanging from the edge of a cliff or standing in the middle of Manhattan with no cars or people to be seen, that movie star was not photographed in those locations. He or she was photographed in a studio, most likely against a white screen. Designers then use layer masks to remove the white background. Once the subject is "isolated" or "silhouetted" and the background is removed, the subject can be positioned against any other background—like in space, or hanging from a cliff, or standing in an empty New York street.

Masking out a background is a fundamental skill in Photoshop, a skill that must be practiced and honed. Professional designers are expected to be able to quickly "drop out" a background so that they can begin building their designs, and when a design is chosen, advertising agencies and other types of art departments hire highly skilled (and highly paid) "finishers" to do exactly that—finish the artwork. Finishing the artwork includes painting a flawless mask. You might ask, is that really so hard to do? What if the actor has curly hair? How do you mask out the background but keep the curls? What if the actress's hair is blowing in the wind? How do you mask around that? What if the actress is wearing a cape that is somewhat transparent and the white background is partially showing through? How do you keep the see-through cape and lose the white background? As you can see, masking out a background can be very challenging, so much so that it requires professional-level skills.

When you mask out a background, you can do so in the original image file, then drag the masked layer from the original file into the collage file you are building. Alternatively, you can copy and paste the original file into the collage file and mask it in the collage file.

Pasting an Image

When you paste an image into a Photoshop file, Photoshop automatically creates a new layer for the pasted artwork and assigns it a number. It's always a good idea to rename the layer with a descriptive term.

Here's a great tip: use the Fit on Screen command on the View menu so the entire canvas is visible before you paste. Now when you paste, the pasted artwork will be centered on the canvas. This simple move can be very useful in the right time and place for alignment considerations.

About the Canvas Size

The canvas size is the size of the artwork on your screen. If you fit the artwork in the window so that you can see all of it, you are seeing all the canvas. If you create a new document in Photoshop that is 8" × 8", the canvas size for that document is 8" × 8". If you open an image from the camera on your phone, the canvas size for that image is whatever size your phone is set to. Imagine for a moment that you have an image from a recent vacation, and you want space below the image to type the location and the date you were there. Let's be clear: you don't want to type over the image— you want *more* space to type the info. You can add that space by increasing the canvas size in the Canvas Size dialog box.

The Canvas Size dialog box allows you to add more pixels to the canvas at the bottom, top, left, right, or all around the image. Figure 25 shows an image with added space at the bottom to accommodate type.

Figure 25 An image with pixels added to the bottom to create space for type

Bleeding an Image off the Canvas

Once you've pasted an image, you can use the Move tool to position the pasted artwork anywhere you want on the canvas, including partially off the canvas. When you position artwork off the canvas, it does not show—only that which is on the canvas is visible.

Figure 26 shows the same image with a robot pasted in the foreground. The robot has been positioned so that it *bleeds* off the canvas. "Bleed" is a term from the days of conventional printing that has survived into modern lingo.

Any artwork that extends all the way to the edge of the canvas is said to bleed. In this image, the parts of the robot image that are not on the canvas are not visible, but at any time, you could move the robot artwork back on to the canvas to show more of the artwork that's not currently visible. It's still there; it's just not visible.

When you position artwork off the canvas, Photoshop creates space to accommodate that artwork. It does NOT change the canvas size— the new space is virtual. However, you should consider that the file size of the image—how

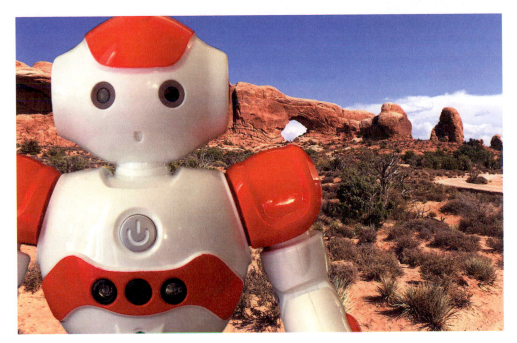

Figure 26 The same image with a robot bleeding left and bottom

The risk of cropping a file is that all the off-canvas data will be lost with the crop. In the preceding example, if you cropped the image, you would lose all options for showing more of the robot artwork in the future. On the other hand, if you manage your files properly, you will have saved another copy of the entire robot artwork for future access, so cropping here would be a good choice to manage the file size.

Instead of using the Crop tool, you can quickly crop the entire image by choosing All on the Select menu, then clicking the Crop command on the Image menu.

Figure 27 The Reveal All command exposes all the artwork

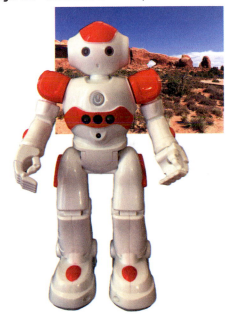

Using the Reveal All Command

The Reveal All command on the Image menu expands the canvas size to show you the totality of all artwork that bleeds off the canvas. This is not a much-used command, but it can be useful to remind yourself of the artwork that's not visible and how much content is placed off of the canvas.

much memory it takes up—increases based on how much virtual space needs to be added to accommodate the bleed image.

Figure 27 shows the canvas after the Reveal All command has been applied. Like an iceberg, there was a lot more to this file than could be seen. The file size, in terms of memory, was also a lot bigger than one might have guessed looking at the original file.

Cropping an Image with the Crop Command

Sometimes designers choose to crop an image to delete content that's off the canvas and reduce the file size. When you crop an image, anything that's outside of the crop is deleted.

Paste an image

1. Open PS 3-4.psd, then save it as **Roman Holiday Final**.

   This collage is in the same state as it was at the end of Lesson 4.

2. Target the **Top Coin layer** at the top of the Layers panel.

3. Open PS 3-5.psd, click **Select** on the menu bar, then click **All**.

4. Copy the artwork, then close the file.

5. In the Roman Holiday Final document, click **View** on the menu bar, then click **Fit on Screen**.

6. Paste the artwork.

   The ring artwork is pasted into the document and a new layer is created above the Top Coin layer. Pasted artwork is always placed in a new layer above the targeted layer on the Layers panel.

TIP When you choose Fit on Screen, any artwork you paste will be pasted at the center of the canvas. This can be a strategic choice in the right situation.

7. Rename the new layer **Ring**.

8. Save your work.

You pasted artwork into a working document.

Use a layer mask to remove a background

1. Target the **Top Coin layer**, then click the **Create a new layer button** ⊞ on the Layers panel.

   A new layer is created above the Top Coin layer and below the Ring layer. Since the new layer has no content, it doesn't change the image in any way.

2. Click the **Foreground color** on the toolbar to open the Color Picker.

3. Choose a **bright lime green color**, then click **OK**.

4. Press and hold **[option] (Mac)** or **[Alt] (Win)**, then press **[delete]** on your keypad to fill the layer.

   Your canvas should resemble Figure 28.

5. Name the layer **Temp Green Bkg**.

   You will use this green background as a visual aid when masking the ring artwork. Rather than mask the ring against the busy collage artwork, you will mask it against this simple green background, which will make it easier for you to see the outline you are creating.

6. Click the **Ring layer**, then click the **Add layer mask button** ▭ on the Layers panel.

Figure 28 Filling the entire layer with green

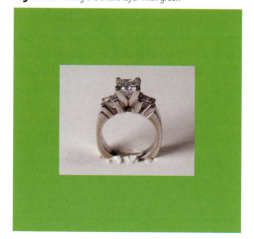

7. Press the **letter [B]** on your keypad to access the Brush tool ✎, then **zoom in** on the ring so you can analyze its edge.

   The edge is fairly hard.

8. Click the **Brush Preset picker arrow** ● ⌄ on the Options panel, choose an appropriate brush size, then set the **Hardness** to **75**.

9. Press the **letter [D]** on your keypad, then press the **letter [X]** to verify that your foreground color is black.

10. **Mask** the **ring** so your artwork resembles Figure 29.

    Don't go past the point shown in Figure 29.

    The best method for masking this ring would be to use the click + [shift]-click. If you need a refresher on this, go back to Chapter 2, Lesson 3.

Figure 29 Masking around the ring

Morguefile

TIP Remember, there are no "mistakes" in masking. If you want to undo a move you made at any time, you can always paint white to show the image.

11. Press and hold **[option] (Mac)** or **[Alt] (Win)**, then click the **layer mask** to see the mask.

    We want to find a fast way to get rid of all the white in the mask that's outside the mask you've painted so far.

12. Click the **Magic Wand tool** 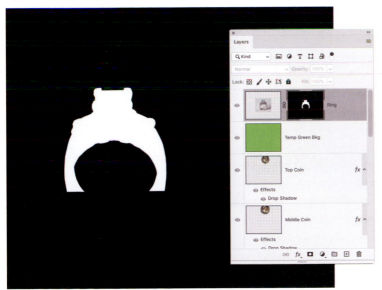, set the **Tolerance** to **16**, then verify that the **Contiguous option** is checked.

13. Click the **Magic Wand tool** anywhere in the white background.

    The entire white background is selected, up to the edge of the mask you painted.

14. Click **Select** on the menu bar, point to **Modify**, then click **Expand**.

15. Enter **3**, then click **OK**.

    The selection is expanded by three pixels to overlap the mask you painted. This is like painting a wall in your house with a roller—you overlap the previous roll a little bit to be sure you don't miss a spot. In this case, we want to be sure we don't leave a white line around the painted mask.

16. Fill the selection with the **black foreground color**, then **deselect**.

    Your mask should resemble Figure 30.

17. Click the **Ring artwork thumbnail** to show the artwork.

18. Hide the **Temp Green Bkg layer**.

19. Enter **[command] [T] (Mac)** or **[Ctrl] [T] (Win)**, scale the artwork **75%**, rotate the artwork **28°**, then click the **Move tool** on the toolbar to apply the transformation.

20. Position the ring as shown in Figure 31.

21. Save your work.

You created a new layer with a bright green background so you could mask artwork against a simple background. You masked around the ring artwork, viewed the mask, then masked the entire background of the ring image.

Figure 30 Filling the layer mask background with black

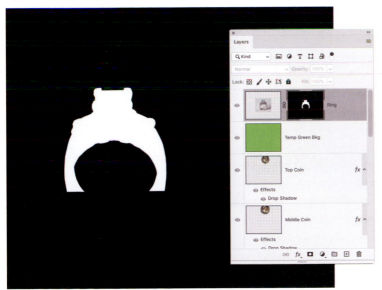

Figure 31 Positioning the scaled and rotated ring artwork

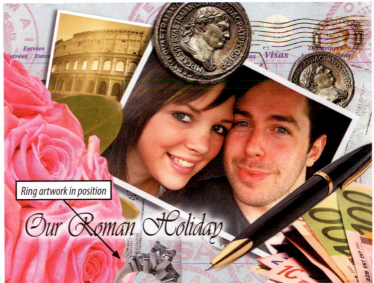

Ring artwork in position

Our Roman Holiday

Change the canvas size to create a frame

1. Click **Image** on the menu bar, then click **Reveal All**.

   All the artwork that bleeds off the canvas is now revealed, including the ring artwork you positioned.

2. **Undo** the last step.

3. Click **Select** on the menu bar, then click **All**.

4. Click **Image** on the menu bar, then click **Crop**.

   The image is cropped at the edge of the canvas. All the images end at the canvas edge. You wouldn't be able to use the Reveal All command now because there's nothing to reveal.

5. Click **Image** on the menu bar, then click **Canvas Size**.

   The Canvas Size dialog box opens, revealing that the canvas is 6.573" wide and 4.987" tall. You are going to add a thin black frame around the canvas.

6. Click once in the **Width dialog box** to the immediate right of 6.573, then type **+.25**.

7. Press **[tab]** on your keypad.

   Note that Photoshop automatically does the calculation for you. The new width will be 6.823".

8. Click once in the **Height dialog box** to the immediate right of 4.987, then type **+.25**.

   Your dialog box should resemble Figure 32.

9. Press **[tab]** to execute the calculation.

   The new height will be 5.237".

10. Click the **Color Picker square** at the bottom of the dialog box.

11. Set the color to **black**, click **OK**, then click **OK** to close the dialog box.

12. Compare your canvas to Figure 33.

    A black frame appears around the image. The frame is .125" on all four sides, because you expanded the canvas by .25" on the width and .25" on the height.

13. Save your work, then close Roman Holiday Final.

You enlarged the canvas size to create a black frame around the image.

Figure 32 Adding .25" to the height

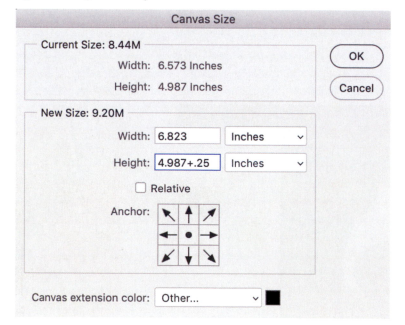

Figure 33 Viewing the final artwork with the frame

SKILLS REVIEW

Set preferences for working with layers

1. Open PS 3-6.psd, then save it as **Chapter 3 Skills Review 01.**
   Be sure you don't save the file again until you are instructed to.
2. Click Photoshop (Mac) or Edit (Win) on the menu bar, point to Preferences, then click General.
3. Verify that Use Legacy Free Transform is checked, then click OK.
4. Click the Layers panel menu button, then click Panel Options.
5. Verify that the largest thumbnail option is selected, then click OK.

Perform basic operations on the Layers panel

1. Note that all layers have been given an identifying name except the one named Layer 1.
2. Double-click the name Layer 1, rename it **Pink Globe**, then save your work.
3. Click the eye button on the Pink Globe layer repeatedly to hide and show the artwork, then verify that the Pink Globe layer is visible.
4. Click and drag vertically over all the eye buttons on the Layers panel to hide all layers.
5. Repeat Step 4 to make all layers visible again.
6. Press and hold [option] (Mac) or [Alt] (Win), then click the eye button on the Pink Globe layer to hide all other layers.
7. Still holding [option] (Mac) or [Alt] (Win), click the same spot on the Pink Globe layer to show all other layers.
8. Target the Blue Globe layer.
9. Click the Opacity slider at the top of the Layers panel, then drag the slider to 50%.

Figure 34 Repositioning the Blue Globe artwork

10. Click the Move tool on the toolbar, then press the number [2] on your keypad to set the opacity to 20%.
11. Press the number [7] on your keypad to set the opacity to 70%.
12. Press the number [0] on your keypad to set the opacity to 100%.
13. Click anywhere on the Gold Globe layer to target it.
14. Press the letter [V] on your keypad to verify that the Move tool is still selected, then click and drag the Gold Globe artwork to another position on the canvas.
15. Target the Blue Globe layer, press and hold [command] (Mac) or [Ctrl] (Win), then click the Pink Globe layer so that both are targeted.
16. Drag the blue globe and pink globe artwork to another location on the canvas.
17. Click File on the menu bar, then click Revert.
18. Target the Pink Globe layer, then click and drag it up to the top of the Layers panel.
19. Press [command] [J] (Mac) or [Ctrl] [J] (Win) to duplicate the layer.
20. Drag the Blue Globe layer to the top of the Layers panel, then position the blue globe artwork as shown in Figure 34.
21. Target both the Blue Globe and the Pink Globe copy layers, click the Layers panel menu button, then click Merge Layers.
22. Move the merged layer artwork to any other location on the canvas.
23. Save your work, then close Chapter 3 Skills Review 01.

Figure 35 Reordering and repositioning the globes

Figure 36 Repositioning the scaled globes

Scale artwork

1. Open PS 3-7.psd, then save it as **Chapter 3 Skills Review 02.**

2. Reorder and reposition the globes as shown in Figure 35.

3. Target the Pink Globe layer, click Edit on the menu bar, point to Transform, then click Scale.

4. Position the mouse pointer on the lower-right corner handle until a double-headed arrow appears, click and drag in different directions to modify the image, then release the mouse pointer.

5. Undo your last step.

6. Position the mouse pointer on the lower-right corner handle, press and hold [shift], click and drag in different directions, then release the mouse pointer.

7. Undo the move.

8. Note the crosshair icon in the middle of the bounding box.

9. On the Options panel, double-click the W text box, type **80**, press [tab], type **80** in the H text box, press [tab], then click the Move tool on the toolbar to execute the transformation.

10. Target the Blue Globe layer, then press [command] [T] (Mac) or [Ctrl] [T] (Win).

11. Press and hold [shift] [option] (Mac) or [Shift] [Alt] (Win), position the mouse pointer over the lower-left handle, drag to experiment with resizing the globe artwork, then release the mouse pointer.

12. Undo the last step so you can enter specific values.

13. Double-click the W text box on the Options panel, type **60**, press [tab], type **60** in the H text box, press [tab], then click [return] (Mac) or [Enter] (Win) to execute the transformation.

14. Position the globes as shown in Figure 36.

15. Save your work.

Rotate and flip artwork

1. Target the Gold Globe layer, click Edit on the menu bar, point to Transform, then click Flip Vertical.
2. Click the Blue Globe layer so it is the only targeted layer, then press [command] [T] (Mac) or [Ctrl] [T] (Win).
3. Press and hold [shift], then position your mouse pointer *outside* of the bounding box so it changes to the rotate icon.
4. Click and drag outside the bounding box to rotate the blue globe –60 degrees, then click the Move tool to execute the transformation.
5. Save your work, then close Chapter 3 Skills Review 02.

Apply an Outer Glow layer style

1. Open PS 3-8.psd, then save it as **Chapter 3 Skills Review 03**.
2. Double-click the thumbnail on the Gold Globe layer.
3. Click the words Outer Glow in the left column of the Layer Style dialog box.
4. In the Structure section, set the Blend Mode to Screen, then set the Opacity to 75.
5. Position your mouse pointer over the Color Picker square in the lower-left corner of the Structure section, then click it. Choose a similar shade of yellow/gold to the golden globe artwork, then click OK.
6. In the Elements section, set the Spread to 14 and the Size to 200, then click OK.
7. Save your work.

Figure 37 Viewing the scaled green globe

Copy layer styles between layers

1. Note that the Outer Glow layer style is now listed on the Layers panel as a subset of the Gold Globe layer. The *fx* icon indicates that layer styles have been applied to this layer.
2. Press and hold [option] (Mac) or [Alt] (Win), and drag the *fx* icon to the Blue Globe layer.
3. Using the same method, copy the layer style from the Gold Globe layer to the Pink Globe layer.
4. On the Layers panel, double-click Outer Glow under the Pink Globe layer to open the Layer Style dialog box.
5. Change the color of the glow to the same hot pink as the globe.
6. Drag the Size slider to 120, then click OK.
7. On the Layers panel, double-click Outer Glow under the Blue Globe layer to open the Layer Style dialog box.

8. Change the color of the glow to the same blue as the globe.
9. Drag the Size slider to 100, then click OK.
10. Save your work.

Add and employ a layer mask

1. Duplicate the Blue globe layer, then rename it **Green Globe**.
2. Move the green globe artwork to the lower-right quadrant of the canvas.
3. Enter [command] [U] (Mac) or [Ctrl] [U] (Win) to open the Hue/Saturation dialog box.
4. Drag the Hue slider to -57, then click OK
5. Scale the Green Globe layer 75% proportionally.
6. On the Layers panel, click the eye button to hide the Outer Glow layer style on the Green Globe layer. Your artwork should resemble Figure 37.

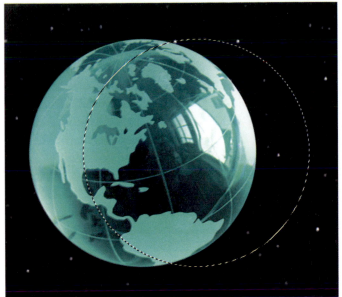

Figure 38 Moving the selection marquee with the arrow key

Figure 39 Four glows

7. Verify that the Green Globe layer is still targeted, then click the Add layer mask button on the Layers panel.
8. Press and hold [command] (Mac) or [Ctrl] (Win), then click the thumbnail image on the *artwork* thumbnail on the Green Globe layer.
9. Press the letter [M] on your keypad to access a marquee tool on the toolbar.
10. Press and hold [shift], then press the right arrow on your keypad eight times.
    Your Green Globe artwork should resemble Figure 38.
11. Set the foreground color on the toolbar to black.
12. Press and hold [option] (Mac) or [Alt] (Win), then press [delete] on your keypad.

13. Deselect.
14. Show the Outer Glow layer style on the Green Globe layer on the Layers panel.
15. Change the outer glow color to the same green as the green globe artwork.
16. Compare your canvas to Figure 39.
17. Save your work.

Paste an image

1. Target the Green Globe layer at the top of the Layers panel.
2. Open PS 3-9.psd, click Select on the menu bar, then click All.

3. Copy the artwork, then close the file.
4. In the globes document, click View on the menu bar, then click Fit on Screen.
5. Paste the artwork.
6. Rename the new layer **Rocket**.
7. Save your work.

Use a layer mask to remove the background

1. Verify that the Rocket layer is targeted.
2. Press and hold [command] (Mac) or [Ctrl] (Win), then click the Create a new layer button on the Layers panel.

(continued)

3. Click the foreground color on the toolbar to open the Color Picker.
4. Choose a bright lime green color, then click OK.
5. Press and hold [option] (Mac) or [Alt] (Win), then press [delete] on your keypad to fill the layer.
6. Name the layer **Temp Green Bkg**.
7. Click the Rocket layer, then click the Add layer mask button on the Layers panel.
8. Press the letter [B] on your keypad to access the Brush tool, then zoom in on the rocket artwork so you can analyze its edge.
   The edge is fairly hard.
9. Click the Brush Settings panel button on the Options panel, choose an appropriate brush size, then set the Hardness for the brush to 75.
10. Press the letter [D] on your keypad, then press the letter [X] to verify that your foreground color is black.
11. Mask the rocket so your artwork resembles Figure 40. Don't go past the point shown in Figure 40.
    The best method for masking the rocket would be to use the click + [shift]-click method. If you need a refresher on this, go back to Chapter 2, Lesson 3.

12. Press and hold [option] (Mac) or [Alt] (Win), then click the layer mask to see the mask.
13. Click the Magic Wand tool, set the Tolerance to 16, then verify that the Contiguous option is checked.
14. Click the wand anywhere in the white background.
15. Click Select on the menu bar, point to Modify, then click Expand.
16. Enter **3**, then click OK.
17. Fill the selection with the black foreground color, then deselect.
18. Click the Rocket artwork thumbnail to show the artwork.
19. Hide the Temp Green Bkg layer.
20. Enter [command] [T] (Mac) or [Ctrl] [T] (Win), scale the artwork 63%, rotate the artwork 45°, then click the Move tool on the toolbar to execute the transformation.
21. Copy the Outer Glow layer style from the Blue Globe layer to the Rocket layer.
22. Position the rocket as shown in Figure 41.
23. Save your work, then close Chapter 3 Skills Review 01.

Figure 40 Masking the rocket

Morguefile

Figure 41 Positioning the rocket

Using a layer mask to remove an object from a background is one of the most important skills in Photoshop, and one you'll have to master if you want to achieve larger goals with the program. This project builder uses an image of flip flops, an item you are likely very familiar with. The goal is to use a mask to remove the background, but it's also for you to use the right brush size and the right hardness setting to get the best edge for the mask. These sandals would have a relatively hard edge, even though the rubber material is flexible. Think about that when you choose the hardness for your brush and when you're painting the mask.

1. Open PS 3-10.psd, then save it as **Flip Flop Mask.**
2. Duplicate the Background layer, then rename the new layer **Flip Flops**.
3. Target the Background layer, then fill it with red.
4. Target the Flip Flops layer, then add a layer mask.
5. Zoom in on the image until you are viewing the image at minimum 500%.
6. Select the Brush tool, set the Size to 10 pixels, then set the Hardness to 80%.
7. Mask both flip flops so your mask resembles Figure 42.
   The best method for masking the flip flops would be to use the click + [shift]-click. If you need a refresher on this, go back to Chapter 2, Lesson 3.

TIP Remember, there are no "mistakes" in masking. If you want to undo any move you made at any time, you can always paint white to show the image.

Figure 42 Masking the flip flops

8. Press and hold [option] (Mac) or [Alt] (Win), then click the layer mask to see the mask.
9. Click the Magic Wand tool, set the Tolerance to 16, then verify that the Contiguous option is checked.
10. Use the Magic Wand tool to select all the white areas that need to be filled with black.
11. Click Select on the menu bar, point to Modify, then click Expand.
12. Enter 3, then click OK.
13. Fill the selection with the black foreground color.
14. Click the flip flop artwork thumbnail to show the artwork.
15. Compare your artwork to Figure 43.

Figure 43 The flip flops fully masked

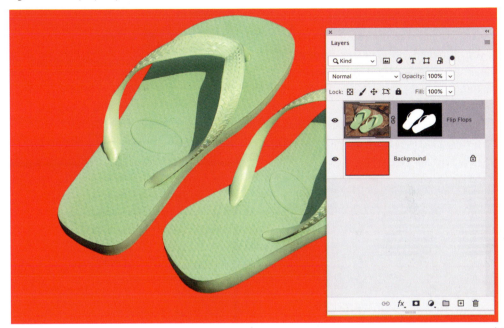

(continued)

Working with layers in Photoshop is a game of strategy. This project builder is designed to teach you a fundamental strategy for layering one image "inside" another. Starting with an image of an empty basket, you'll be asked to arrange fruit "inside" the basket. You'll use the front of the basket strategically with a layer mask to create the illusion. This technique is fundamental and can be applied to other projects with similar objectives.

1. Open PS 3-11.psd, then save it as **Still Life**.
2. Click Select on the menu bar, click Load Selection, verify that your Load Selection dialog box matches Figure 44, then click OK.
3. Click the Rectangular Marquee tool on the toolbar, press and hold [shift] to add to the selection, then select the top-half of the canvas.
   Your selection should resemble Figure 45.
4. Click Select on the menu bar, then click Inverse.
5. Target the Background layer, copy the selection, then paste.
   A new layer is created.
6. Name the new layer **Basket Front**, then drag it to the top of the Layers panel.

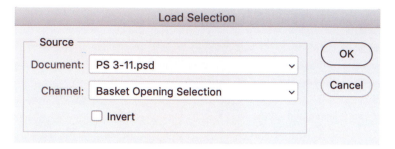

Figure 44 The Load Selection dialog box

Figure 45 Adding to the elliptical marquee

Figure 46 The final effect

7. Make the Purple Grapes layer visible, then move the artwork around the canvas to see the effect you've created.

   The grapes appear to be "inside" the basket because they are behind the Basket Front artwork.

8. Undo your last move so the grapes are in the same location as when you made the layer visible.

9. Duplicate the Purple Grapes layer, rename it **Purple Grapes in Front**, then drag it to the top of the Layers panel.

10. Add a layer mask, then fill the layer mask with black so that the Purple Grapes in Front artwork is not visible.

11. Painting with white, "unmasks" some of the purple grapes so that the artwork appears to be "hanging over" the front of the basket. Use Figure 46 as a guide. The illusion is very effective because some of the grapes appear to be "inside" the basket while others are hanging "outside" the basket.

12. Save your work, then close Still Life.

DESIGN PROJECT

Fine art school students are usually required to create still life artwork. The same can be done with digital art. You are given images of various fruits and asked to arrange them into a beautiful and balanced still life. This is a great challenge for working with layers, transforming images, and bringing images into a working file from other files.

1. Open PS 3-12.psd, then save it as **Still Life Composition**.
2. Target the Background layer.
3. Click File on the menu bar, click Open, then navigate to the Fruit folder in the Chapter 3 Data Files folder.
4. Open the file named Green Grapes.
   The file has been masked for you.
5. Drag the Green Grapes file by its name down from the Photoshop window so that it is a floating window. Your screen should resemble Figure 47.
6. Click the Move tool, then drag the Green Grapes layer into the Still Life Composition file.
   The artwork, along with the mask, is moved into the Still Life Composition file.
7. Close Green Grapes.
8. Open the file named Orange Navel.
9. Mask out the background.
10. Drag the Orange Navel artwork into the Still Life Composition file, then close Orange Navel.

Figure 47 Dragging the masked Green Grapes layer into the Still Life Composition file

11. Using the same method, open other fruit image files you want to work with, mask out their backgrounds, then add them to the Still Life Composition file until you have enough fruit images to build a still life.

12. In the Still Life Composition file, transform artwork as needed and reposition artwork to build a still life collage.
    Figure 48 shows one outcome that you can use as a guide.
13. Save your work, then close Still Life Composition.

Figure 48 One example of the completed still life

Morguefile

CHAPTER 4

WORK WITH TYPE AND
GRADIENTS

1. Set and Format Type
2. Create Bevel & Emboss Effects on Type
3. Create and Apply Gradients
4. Clip a Gradient and an Image into Type
5. Fade Type with a Gradient and a Layer Mask
6. Clip Multiple Images into Type

Adobe Certified Professional in Visual Design Using Photoshop CC Framework

2. Project Setup and Interface

This objective covers the interface setup and program settings that assist in an efficient and effective workflow, as well as knowledge about ingesting digital assets for a project.

2.5   Manage colors, swatches, and gradients.
   B   Create, customize, and organize gradients.

4. Creating and Modifying Visual Elements

This objective covers core tools and functionality of the application, as well as tools that affect the visual outcome of the document.

4.1   Use core tools and features to create visual elements.
   A   Create and edit raster images.

4.2   Add and manipulate text using appropriate typographic settings.
   A   Use type tools to add typography to a design.
   B   Organize and customize the workspace.
   C   Convert text to graphics.

SET AND FORMAT TYPE

▶ **What You'll Do**

In this lesson, you'll use the Type and the Character panels to set and format type. You'll rasterize type and learn to lock transparent pixels so that you can paint type outlines.

Working with Type and Gradients

When people think of Photoshop, their first thought usually is of images, photographs, and special effects. But another great Photoshop feature is the ability to create sophisticated typographical effects. Photoshop makes it easy to create classic effects like beveled and embossed text, chiseled text, and text that shines as though it were made of chrome. Even better, you can combine type with photographic images to produce truly unique typographical designs.

When you start working extensively with type, you often find yourself working with gradients as well. **Gradients** are blends between two or more colors, and they are visually striking when applied to type and typography. A white-to-black gradient can add weight to a title, or a green-to-yellow gradient can make for a vibrant headline that appears to glow. Gradients offer many more options than a simple solid color for filling type.

Setting Type

Adobe has outfitted Photoshop with all the text-editing capabilities you'd expect from any top-notch word processing or page layout package. When you create type in Photoshop, it is "live type" just like in any other application; you can select it, copy it, paste it, and so on. The toolbar offers you a tool to set type horizontally and a tool to set type vertically.

When you set type, a new type layer is shown on the Layers panel. A type layer is a "live type" layer: the type can be edited at any time. Simply by targeting the layer on the Layers panel, you can change the type size, typeface, and color of the type. You can do this without clicking and dragging to highlight and select the type as you would in a word processing program.

Type layers can be transformed like any other artwork. In fact, rather than change the font size on type, most designers simply scale the type to the size they think looks good. In addition to scaling, type can be rotated, skewed, warped, and flipped horizontally and vertically.

Working with the Character Panel

The Character panel is command central for formatting type in Photoshop. You can do all formatting you need to do—setting the typeface, the size, the tracking, the kerning, and so forth—on the Character panel.

Figure 1 shows the Character panel and identifies the many options available to you when working with type. The Tracking and Kerning options are used to perfect the appearance of typography in terms of spacing. Tracking controls the overall spacing between letters in a given word or paragraph. Kerning controls the spacing between any two specific letters. The Horizontal and Vertical scale options resize selected text, making it wider or taller, respectively. Be sure to experiment with the style buttons at the bottom of the panel, which are useful for making all caps, small caps, superscripts, and other classic examples of typographical formatting.

Figure 1 The Character panel

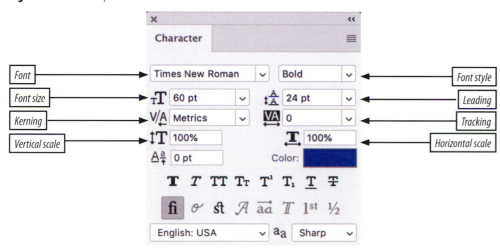

Working with the Paragraph Panel

Most designs in Photoshop that call for type usually call for what is referred to as display type. Headlines and other large, free-standing typographical elements in a design are examples of display type. Some designs, however, call for type to be laid out in paragraph format. In those cases, you will rely on the Paragraph panel. The Paragraph panel offers standard paragraph formatting tools, including margin indents, first line indents, space after and space before paragraph measures, and text alignment.

Tracking and Kerning Type

When setting type in Photoshop, don't just assume that the way the type lays out when you type it is visually satisfying. Many fonts, when they are typed, leave you with awkward or inconsistent spacing between letters. Neglecting to address these issues is neglecting the typographical considerations that are critical for producing elegant and sophisticated type. Unfortunately, many inexperienced designers either overlook or don't bother correcting this. You'd be amazed at how many posters, flyers, and advertisements—even billboards!—are printed and released to the public with obviously neglected typographical considerations.

Tracking and **kerning** are options on the Character panel that control the space between letters. Tracking is the more global of the two. When tracking type, you select the whole word (or words) then reduce the space or increase the space between letters evenly. Kerning is more specific. With kerning, you click the cursor between two letters and affect the spacing only of that pair of letters. With both tracking and kerning, a negative value brings letters closer together, and a positive value moves letters further apart.

Rasterizing Type

Sometimes a designer will want to create an effect or a look that can't be done with live type. For example, live type cannot be painted, you can't apply filters to live type, and you can't apply the Distort command with the transform bounding box. If you want to do these or other operations to type, the only option is to first rasterize the type using the Rasterize command on the Type menu.

To **rasterize** type means to convert type to pixels. Adobe users refer to this as changing the live type to "outlines." Once rasterized, the type outlines don't appear to change, but they can be manipulated like all other Photoshop artwork.

That's because, once rasterized, type outlines are just that, outlines. They're not type. They're simply pixels.

Rasterizing type is a commitment. Once you do so, other than using the Undo command or reverting the file, you can never go back and convert the rasterized text back into live type.

Another reason designers rasterize type is to avoid font issues. When you share a Photoshop file that includes font information, the person who opens your file will need the same font installed on their computer to render the type. When type is rasterized, you no longer need the font installed because the type has been converted to pixels.

Understanding Transparency on a Layer

When you create a new layer in Photoshop, you'll see no changes to the artwork on your canvas. This is because each new layer is automatically a transparent layer. It's empty because it has no artwork on it. Until you fill the layer or paint in the layer, you can think of the pixels on the layer as being transparent, or "empty."

Transparency on a layer is rendered visually as a gray and white checkerboard.

The idea that a layer or part of a layer is transparent is an important concept to understand, especially when working with type. On a type layer, the pixels on the layer that *aren't* used to render the type are transparent by default. Similarly, if you have masked artwork on a layer, like a coin or a pen, the pixels on the layer that aren't used to render the artwork are transparent by default.

Filling and Painting Live Type and Rasterized Type

Live type can be filled with any solid color, but it can't be filled with a gradient. Live type also cannot be painted with multiple colors.

Once rasterized, type outlines can be painted like any other artwork. When painting or filling rasterized type with colors, you'll want to preserve the shapes of the type outlines. To do so, click the **Lock Transparent Pixels button** on the Layers panel, or activate the Preserve Transparency option when it appears in dialog boxes, like the Fill dialog box.

When you lock transparent pixels or preserve transparency, the transparent pixels on the layer won't be affected by any fills or painting that you do on the layer.

Set type

1. Open PS 4-1.psd, then save it as **Typography**.

2. Press the **letter [D]** on your keypad to set the foreground and background colors on the toolbar to the default black over white.

3. Click the **Horizontal Type tool** **T.** on the toolbar, set your type size to 24 points on the Options panel, then set your foreground color to black.

4. Float over the canvas, then click the cursor on the left side of the canvas.

   A blinking type cursor appears, prompting you to begin typing.

   TIP When you click the Type tool, default "Greek" text appears that reads "Lorem ipsum." This is intended to give you a preview of the typeface and the type size you have preset before you started typing. The Greek text disappears the moment you type a character.

5. Type the word **Typography**.

   A type layer appears on the Layers panel. The word or words you type will be set in whatever typeface, type size, and foreground color you have active when you click the Type tool. Make a note of this, because you want to be set up to succeed before you start typing. For example, if your foreground color were set to white, you wouldn't see the type against the white background. Or, if your type size were set to 150 points, it would be too large to fit on the canvas.

6. Click the **Move tool** **+.** on the toolbar.

   Once you click the Move tool, the name of the new layer becomes the same as the word or words you typed.

   TIP Clicking the Move tool is a good way to escape from type mode when you're done typing.

7. On the Character panel, click the **Font family list arrow**, then choose **Times New Roman** (or a similar typeface).

   Even though the Move tool is selected, the typeface changes. In Photoshop, when a type layer is targeted on the Layers panel, changing the typeface on the Character panel changes the typeface of the type on the canvas. Also note that when the Move tool is selected, type formatting options are no longer available on the Options panel.

   TIP If you don't see the Character panel, click Window on the menu bar, and then click Character.

8. Move the type so that it's centered on the canvas.

9. Click the **Font style list arrow**, click **Bold**, click the **Set the font size list arrow**, then click **60 pt**.

10. Show the Swatches panel, then click **any blue swatch**.

    Your Character panel should resemble Figure 2.

You used the Type tool and the Character panel to set and format type.

Figure 2 Formatting the type

Typography

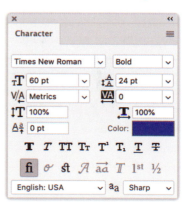

Track and kern type

1. Click the **Horizontal Type tool** on the toolbar, then double-click the word **Typography** on the canvas to select the whole word. On the Character panel, enter **–75** in the **Tracking text box**, then compare your results to Figure 3.

2. Change the **Tracking value** to **–25**.

3. Click the **cursor** between the letters **p** and **h**.

4. On the Character panel, enter **–25** in the **Kerning text box**.

5. Click the **cursor** between the letters **h** and **y**, then enter **–25** in the **Kerning text box**.

   The two letters move closer together.

6. Save your work.

You used the Character panel to track and kern type.

Rasterize and paint type

1. Verify that the **Typography layer** is targeted, click **Layer** on the menu bar, point to **Rasterize**, then click **Type**.

   When you rasterize a type layer, all layer content is converted from type to pixels. The type icon disappears from the layer on the Layers panel, and the layer is no longer editable as type.

2. Hide the Background layer.

   The many transparent pixels on the Typography layer are rendered as a gray and white checkerboard.

3. Press the **letter [D]** on your keypad to access the default foreground and background colors.

4. Press **[option] [delete] (Mac)** or **[Alt] [Delete] (Win)** to fill the layer with the black foreground color.

   All the pixels on the layer—transparent and nontransparent—are filled with black.

   AUTHOR'S NOTE For the remainder of this chapter, use [option] [delete] (Mac) or [Alt] [Delete] (Win) when you are instructed to "fill."

Figure 3 Tracking type

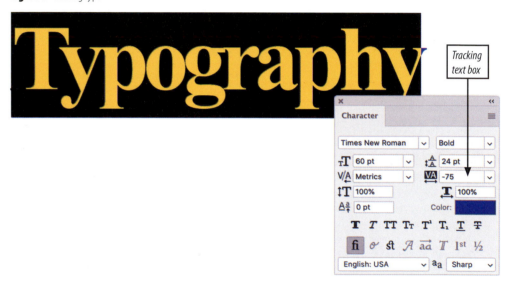

5. Undo the fill, then click the **Lock transparent pixels button** 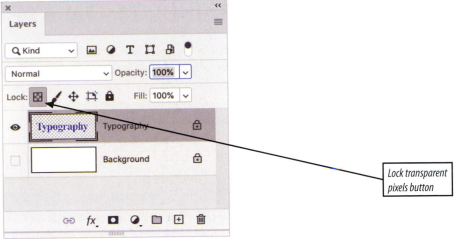 on the Layers panel, as shown in Figure 4.

A padlock icon appears at the right of the layer on the Layers panel. Locking the transparent pixels on the layer ensures that they will remain transparent when other pixels are being modified.

6. Fill the layer with the black foreground color.

The type outlines are filled with black, but the transparent pixels on the layer are not filled.

7. Click a **bright red swatch** on the Swatches panel, press **the letter [B]** on your keypad to access the Brush tool, set the **brush size** to **50 px**, set the **Hardness** to **100%**, then set the **Opacity** to **100%** on the Options panel.

8. Paint different areas of the type red, then compare your result to Figure 5.

Because transparent pixels are locked, only the black pixels are affected by the Brush tool.

9. Show the Background layer, save your work, then close Typography.

You rasterized type, converting it to pixels on a transparent layer. In order to fill only the rasterized type with the foreground color (and not the whole layer), you first had to click the Lock transparent pixels button for that layer on the Layers panel. You were then able to paint only in the type outlines with the Brush tool.

Figure 4 Locking transparent pixels on the Typography layer

Lock transparent pixels button

Figure 5 Painting parts of rasterized type with transparent pixels locked

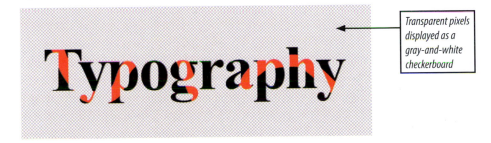

Transparent pixels displayed as a gray-and-white checkerboard

CREATE BEVEL & EMBOSS EFFECTS ON TYPE

▶ *What You'll Do*

In this lesson, you'll apply the Bevel & Emboss layer style to type.

Creating Bevel & Emboss Effects on Type

Prepare to fall in love with Bevel & Emboss, especially when you use it to design type. Bevel & Emboss is a layer style—a built-in effect that you can apply to layers—just like the Drop Shadow and Outer Glow layer styles you learned in Chapter 3. Bevel & Emboss is especially effective for type because you can use it to create classic effects like raised text and chiseled text. Rather than offering only a single option, the Bevel & Emboss dialog box features a number of different styles and techniques that you can use to create a variety of bevel and emboss effects. It's a great opportunity to experiment to see the different looks you can achieve.

Figure 6 shows an illustration of type that has been carved with a chisel into stone, type you'd expect to see carved into ancient Greek buildings or, in modern times, carved into everything from banks to gravestones. Note that, because of the carving, each letter has an angle with a highlight and a shadow. The effect that results is a letterform with a bright edge and a contrasting dark edge.

The Bevel & Emboss layer style in Photoshop mimics this real-world look. The Bevel & Emboss layer style dialog box offers you myriad options to create different bevel and emboss effects, including inner bevels, outer bevels, chisel effects, and emboss effects. These are

Figure 6 Type chiseled in stone

some of the most popular effects designers use when working with type. The results can be both sophisticated and eye-popping.

Using a Stroke Layer Style

A **stroke** is a basic artistic element that places an outline on an object or on type. For example, you can apply a black fill to type and then apply a colored stroke as an outline. In Photoshop, the best method for applying a stroke is to apply it as a layer style. This method allows you to apply the stroke and choose its color and its size. As with all layer styles, you can modify it or remove it at any time. Figure 7 shows a Stroke layer style applied to type with a Bevel & Emboss layer style.

Once you've applied the Stroke layer style, you can then apply a Bevel & Emboss layer style to the stroke. To do this, click the Style list arrow in the Layer Style dialog box and then choose Stroke Emboss. As a result, only the stroke will be beveled and embossed.

Applying Gloss Contours to Layer Styles

Gloss contours are a set of 12 preset adjustments that affect the brightness and contrast of a layer style to create dramatic lighting effects. They are available for many different kinds of layer styles, not just Bevel & Emboss. Gloss contours fall into the "click and choose" category of Photoshop features—you simply click through them to see what they do and how they affect the current artwork you're working with, then choose the one you like best. After a while, you'll get a sense of what to expect from each of them. However, the gloss contours will produce different results for different types of artwork.

Understanding the Use Global Light Option with Layer Styles

Many layer styles produce their effects by adjusting the brightness and contrast of the artwork they're applied to. The effect is often created with a "light source," meaning that the artwork appears to be brightened from a certain direction. For example, if you apply a Bevel & Emboss layer style to text and set the light source to light the artwork from the right, you will create interesting shadows on the left side of the artwork.

You will apply multiple layer styles to multiple pieces of artwork when working in Photoshop, especially when creating collages. The **Use Global Light** option exists as a simple solution to help you maintain a consistent light source for multiple layer styles. With the Use Global Light option checked, all your layer styles will create their individual effects using "light" from the same direction.

Sometimes consistency is desired, and if you want a consistent light source, the Use Global Light feature is a great option. But don't think that you *must* have a consistent light source. Sometimes different layer styles applied to the same artwork look even more interesting when they strike the artwork from different angles or light sources. You can turn off the Use Global Light option and manually set the angle and the altitude of the light source by dragging the Direction of light source icon in the Shading section of the Layer Style dialog box.

Be open to experiment when working with any feature associated with layer styles. Experimenting will lead to surprising yourself with a new look or a new effect, and that's always a great moment.

Figure 7 Stroke layer style

Creating a Double Emboss Effect

Layer styles are a lot of fun, and they produce interesting and useful effects. But at some point, you're bound to feel that you're not really *creating* artwork with a layer style, because the result is something anyone could achieve by dragging the sliders to the same settings you did. That is the truth about layer styles—they are canned effects, manufactured by Adobe Systems and packaged with the program. As a designer, it's your job to see past this built-in limitation of layer styles and figure out how to create *unique* artwork with these effects. The key to doing so is to work with *many* layer styles, combining them in inspired and insightful ways to produce artwork that is unexpected and brand-new.

One way you can achieve this is by duplicating artwork and applying different layer styles that work together to create one visual effect. A double emboss effect is achieved by creating two copies of the text. One copy has an outer bevel, and the other has an inner bevel. The result appears to be one block of type with a complex bevel and emboss effect.

Figure 8 Bevel & Emboss effect

Figure 9 Different settings produce a different bevel and emboss effect

Apply a Bevel & Emboss layer style to type

1. Open PS 4-2.psd, then save it as **Bevel & Emboss**.

2. Click the **HEADLINE layer** on the Layers panel, click **Layer** on the menu bar, point to **Layer Style**, then click **Bevel & Emboss**.

   The Layer Style dialog box opens with the default Bevel & Emboss settings selected.

3. Set the **Style** to **Emboss**, set the **Technique** to **Smooth**, then set the **Depth** to **100%**.

4. Set the **Size** to **24 px**, set the **Soften value** to **0 px**, then click **OK**.

   Your canvas should resemble Figure 8.

5. Double-click the **Bevel & Emboss layer style** on the Layers panel to open the Layer Style dialog box.

6. Set the **Style** to **Inner Bevel**, set the **Technique** to **Chisel Hard**, then set the **Depth** to **120%**.

7. Set the **Size** to **44**, set the **Soften value** to **0**, then click **OK**.

   As shown in Figure 9, the modified settings produce an entirely different bevel and emboss effect.

8. Save your work.

You applied a Bevel & Emboss layer style to type outlines.

Apply a gloss contour to a layer style

1. Double-click the **Bevel & Emboss layer style** on the Layers panel to open the Layer Style dialog box.

2. Move the **Layer Style dialog box** out of the way so you can see at least one of the letters on your canvas.

3. Click the **Gloss Contour list arrow**, then position the mouse pointer over the **third square in the second row**.

   The gloss contour is identified in Figure 10. If you position the mouse pointer over this gloss contour, a tool tip appears, revealing the name of the gloss contour, which is Ring - Double.

4. Click **Ring - Double**, then move the dialog box out of the way to see the effect on the artwork.

5. Click **each of the remaining 11 gloss contours** to see its effect on the type artwork.

6. Click the **second gloss contour**, named **Cone**, on the top row.

7. Click the **Anti-aliased check box** beside the Gloss Contour list arrow, then click **OK**.

   Your artwork should resemble Figure 11. You can use the Undo/Redo commands to see a before and after view of the change.

8. Save your work.

You applied a Gloss Contour preset in the Layer Style dialog box.

Figure 10 The Ring - Double gloss contour

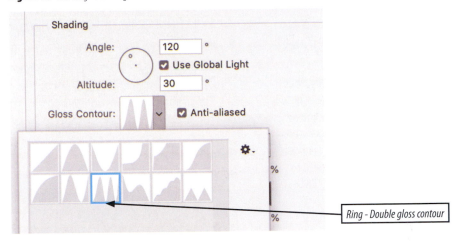

Ring - Double gloss contour

Figure 11 The Cone gloss contour applied to the type outlines

Apply an Outer Bevel layer style to create a double emboss effect

1. Verify that the **Headline layer** is targeted, then press **[command] [J] (Mac)** or **[Ctrl] [J] (Win)** to duplicate the layer.

2. Rename the new layer **Inner Bevel**, then **hide** it.

   In this exercise, we are hiding the Inner Bevel layer style so you can see the Outer Bevel layer style being built. However, if you were designing this type in a real-world project, you would probably want to show the Inner Bevel layer style to see the final effect of both layer styles together as you are designing.

3. Target the **Headline layer**, then rename it **Outer Bevel**.

4. Drag the **Layer effects button** fx on the Outer Bevel layer to the **Delete layer button** on the Layers panel.

   Your Layers panel should resemble Figure 12.

5. Double-click the **Outer Bevel layer** to open the Layer Style dialog box, then click the words **Bevel & Emboss** in the left column.

6. Set the **Style** to **Outer Bevel**, set the **Technique** to **Chisel Hard**, then set the **Depth** to **100%**.

7. Set the **Size** to **13**, then set the **Soften value** to **0**.

8. Uncheck the **Use Global Light option**.

   We want to change the lighting on this layer style. However, we do not want to change the lighting on the Inner Bevel layer style, so we must uncheck Use Global Light.

Figure 12 Two layers, one hidden

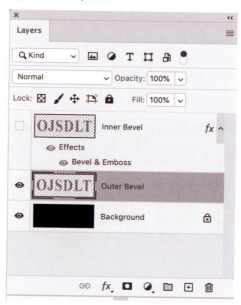

9. Set the **Angle** to **139**, then set the **Altitude** to **32**.

10. Click the **Cove - Deep gloss contour**.

    Your Layer Style dialog box should resemble Figure 13.

Figure 13 Layer Style settings

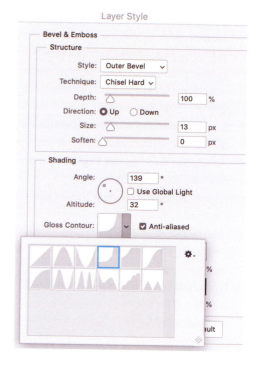

11. Click **OK**, then compare your artwork to Figure 14.

12. Show the **Inner Bevel layer**, then compare your artwork to Figure 15.

The two layer styles work together to create one single visual effect. If you hide and show the Outer Bevel layer, you can see the top layer with and without the effect.

13. Save your work, then close Bevel & Emboss.

You duplicated the type layer, then applied an Outer Bevel layer style to the copy. The result was two layer styles working together to produce a more complex and dimensional effect.

Figure 14   The Outer Bevel effect on its own

Figure 15   The Outer Bevel and Inner Bevel effects combined

CREATE AND APPLY GRADIENTS

▶ What You'll Do

In this lesson, you'll use the Gradient tool and the Gradient Editor dialog box to create and apply gradients to the canvas and to type.

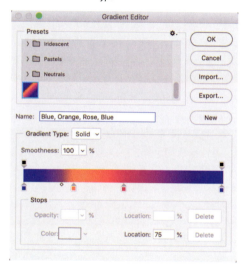

Applying a Gradient

A **gradient** is a blend of two or more colors. Often, a gradient between two colors creates a third distinct color. For example, any gradient between red and yellow will produce orange somewhere in between.

The Gradient tool is the tool that you use to apply gradients. It determines the placement and the length of the gradient. The tool works by clicking, dragging, and releasing. Where you click determines where the gradient begins, where you drag determines the length of the gradient, and where you release determines where the gradient ends.

When you click the Gradient tool on the toolbar, the Options panel changes to show the Gradient Picker box and list arrow, identified in Figure 16. Click the list arrow beside the box, which shows you a menu that contains dozens upon dozens of preset gradients that come with the program. These presets are housed in different folders. Click the caret beside the folder to see the preset gradients. This menu is also the location that automatically stores gradients you create on your own in the Gradient Editor dialog box.

In addition, when you click the Gradient tool, the Options panel shows options that allow

you to determine the *type* of gradient you are applying. A **linear** gradient blends from one color to another in a straight, linear fashion. A **radial** gradient blend radiates outward from one color to another, like a series of concentric circles.

Creating a New Gradient

In addition to the preset gradients that come with Photoshop, you can create your own customized gradients in the Gradient Editor dialog box, shown in Figure 17. The colors that make up a gradient are called **color stops**. In the Gradient Editor dialog box, you create a customized gradient on the **gradient ramp**. You can create gradients between two color stops or between multiple color stops. You add color stops simply by clicking the gradient ramp, and you remove them by dragging them down and off the gradient ramp. You determine the length of the gradient between color stops by moving color stops closer to or farther away from each other. The diamond-shaped **color midpoint slider** between color stops determines where the gradient is a 50–50 mix between color stops. The **Location** text box below the gradient ramp identifies a selected color stop's location, from left to right, on the gradient ramp.

Figure 16 Gradient picker box and list arrow

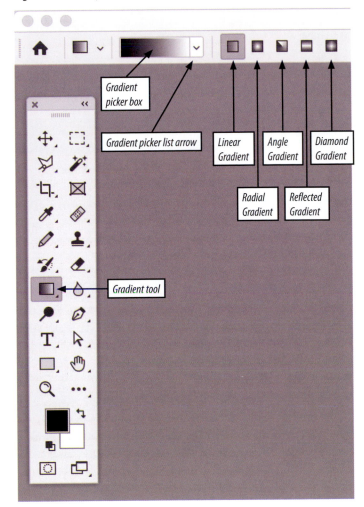

Gradient
picker box

Gradient picker list arrow

Linear
Gradient

Angle
Gradient

Diamond
Gradient

Radial
Gradient

Reflected
Gradient

Gradient tool

Figure 17 Gradient Editor dialog box

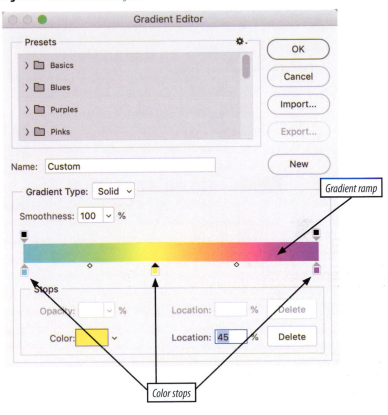

Gradient ramp

Color stops

Apply a gradient

1. Open PS 4-3.psd, then save it as **Making the Gradient**.

2. Click the **Gradient tool** ◼️, on the toolbar.

3. Click the **Gradient picker list arrow**, identified in Figure 18.

As shown in the figure, clicking the list arrow shows a list of folders, all of which contain preset gradients that come with Photoshop.

4. Expand the **Reds folder**, then click the **first gradient** in that folder.

The Options panel updates to show the gradient you clicked.

5. Click the **Linear Gradient button** ◼️ on the Options panel.

TIP See Table 4-1, which describes the five types of gradients available on the Options panel.

Figure 18 Gradient picker on the Options panel

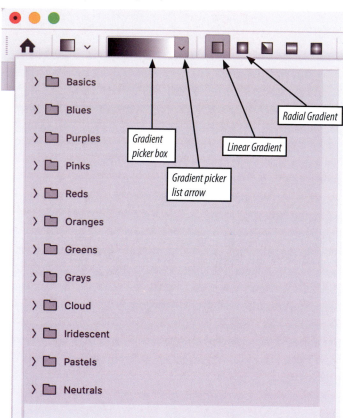

Radial Gradient

Gradient picker box

Linear Gradient

Gradient picker list arrow

> Basics
> Blues
> Purples
> Pinks
> Reds
> Oranges
> Greens
> Grays
> Cloud
> Iridescent
> Pastels
> Neutrals

TABLE 4-1: FIVE TYPES OF GRADIENTS		
Type of Gradient	**Button Icon**	**Description**
Linear	◼️	Blends from the start color to the end color in a straight line.
Radial	◼️	Blends from the start color to the end color in a circular pattern, with the start color in the center.
Angle	◥◣	Blends in clockwise sweep from the start color to the end color. Think of an angle gradient as the big hand and the little hand being in the same place on a clock, like at midnight. The gradient is created from the foreground color to the background color from the big hand to the little hand in a clockwise direction.
Reflected	▬	Blends using symmetric linear gradients on either side of the starting point. Think of a reflected gradient as a mirror. Click and drag from your foreground to background color, and it creates a linear gradient *plus* a mirror image of that gradient at the point where you first clicked. Practically speaking, this type of gradient would be useful for making something that looks like a lead pipe or some other kind of metal tube.
Diamond	◼️	Blends from the start color outward in a diamond pattern. The end color defines one corner of the diamond. The result appears three-dimensional and could be especially useful for creating flares or web graphics.

6. Position the mouse pointer at the **left edge** of the canvas, click and drag to the **right edge** of the canvas, then release the mouse button.

   A linear gradient is created from the left edge of the canvas to the right edge of the canvas. The gradient blends from gray to rose to dark purple.

7. Click and drag from the **top** of the canvas to the **bottom** of the canvas.

   The gradient is re-created from top to bottom.

8. Click and drag from the **upper-left** to the **lower-right corner** of the canvas.

   The gradient is re-created diagonally from the upper-left to the lower-right corner of the canvas.

9. Click near the **center** of the canvas and drag from **left to right** for approximately one inch, then compare your result to Figure 19.

   The length of the entire gradient is approximately one inch long. Any pixels outside of the one inch range are filled with solid start and end colors, which in this case are gray and dark purple.

10. Click the **Radial Gradient button** 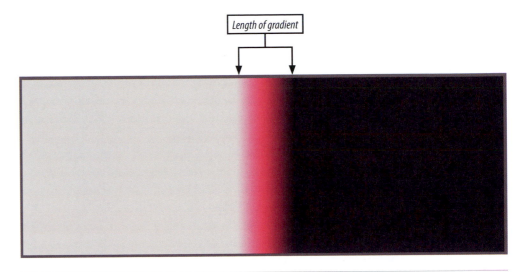 on the Options panel.

11. Position your pointer at the **center** of the canvas, click and drag approximately one inch to the right, then compare your result to Figure 20.

   The gradient starts where you click and ends where you release. With a radial gradient, however, the gradient "radiates" out from a center point, like concentric circles, with the start color as the center color.

12. Save your work.

You used the Gradient tool and a preset gradient to create a gradient on the canvas.

Figure 19 Short linear gradient

Length of gradient

Figure 20 Radial gradient with the start color at the center by default

Create a new gradient

1. Click the **Gradient picker box** 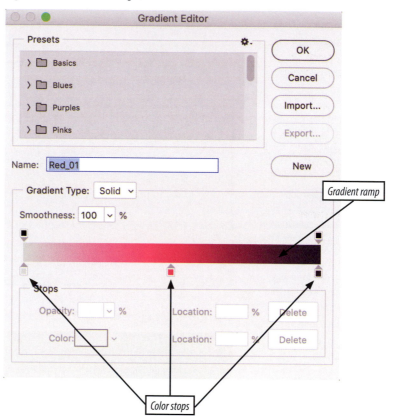 on the Options panel.

   The Gradient Editor dialog box opens, shown in Figure 21. The Gray/Rose/Dark Purple gradient appears in the gradient ramp in the dialog box. The color stops on the gradient ramp from left to right represent gray, rose, and dark blue. Note that the name given to the preset gradient is Red_01.

2. Click the **first (leftmost) color stop**.

   The name of the gradient in the Name text box changes to "Custom" once you click the color stop.

3. Click the **Color box** below the gradient ramp to open the Color Picker.

4. Type **29** in the **R text box**, type **5** in the **G text box**, type **170** in the **B text box**, then click **OK**.

   The color stop on the gradient ramp changes to a royal blue.

5. Click the **last color stop**, then change its color to the same royal blue, 29R/5G/170B.

6. Click **right below the gradient ramp** between the first and second color stops.

   A new color stop is added to the gradient ramp where you clicked.

Figure 21 Gradient Editor dialog box

Gradient ramp

Color stops

7. Drag the **new color stop** until the Location text box reads **25%**.

   The Location text box indicates where a color stop is positioned on the gradient ramp, from left to right. For example, at 25%, the new color stop is exactly between the first stop at 0% and the middle stop at 50%.

8. Change the color of the new color stop to **246R/142G/86B**.

9. Drag the **Color Midpoint diamond slider** between the first and second color stop to 75%, as shown in Figure 22.

   The blue and orange color stops are blended equally three-quarters of the way between the two stops.

10. Type **Blue, Orange, Rose, Blue** in the Name text box, then click the **New button.**

    The new gradient is added to the group of presets in the Gradient Editor.

11. Click **OK**.

   TIP The new gradient is also added to the bottom of the list of gradient preset folders on the Options panel.

12. Save your work, then close Making the Gradient.

You used the Gradient Editor dialog box to modify and save a new gradient.

Figure 22 Changing the midpoint between two color stops

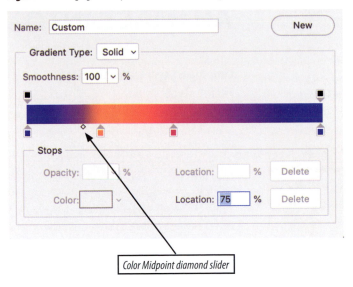

Color Midpoint diamond slider

CLIP A GRADIENT AND AN IMAGE INTO TYPE

▶ **What You'll Do**

In this lesson, you'll use the Layers panel to clip a layer filled with a gradient into type.

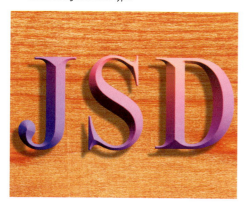

Clipping a Layer with a Gradient Fill into Type

Clipping refers to using artwork on one layer to mask the artwork on a layer (or multiple layers) above it. The simplest example of clipping and a clipping mask would be of a type layer with a layer above it filled with a gradient. If you target the gradient layer and then create a clipping mask, the gradient will be clipped into the type layer beneath it and will be visible only within the type. The transparent areas of

the type layer will mask the gradient artwork. Figure 23 shows a radial gradient clipped into type and visible only in the type.

The layer functioning as the clipping mask—the type layer in the preceding example—is referred to as the **base layer**. For artwork to be clipped, it must be immediately above the base layer. Base layers can have multiple layers clipped into them, but all those layers must be immediately above the base layer on the Layers panel.

Figure 23 Radial gradient clipped into type

Clipping Layers on the Layers Panel

Let's say you have two layers on the Layers panel—Layer A and Layer B—and you want to clip Layer B into Layer A. Select Layer B, then click the Create Clipping Mask command on the Layers panel menu.

A faster way to clip a layer is to use a quick and easy keyboard technique. Using the previous example, press and hold [option] (Mac) or [Alt] (Win), then float your cursor over the line between the two layers on the Layers panel. A square icon with a small black arrow will appear. Click the small black arrow on the line that separates the two layers, and the top layer will be clipped into the layer beneath it.

Clipping Imagery into Type

Clipping imagery into type works the same way as clipping a gradient into type, except that you are clipping a picture instead of a gradient fill. Figure 24 shows a landscape image clipped into type.

Another good example of clipping a picture into type would be an old-fashioned postcard with the word *FLORIDA* and different scenes of Floridian attractions inside the letters. Clipping an image into type is a classic type of design that is visually interesting and communicates an idea with strength and clarity. Remember, when you clip an image into text that has layer styles applied to it, the image takes on the effects of the layer style.

Applying a Gradient Directly to Live Type

You're already familiar with "filling" type with color. You can also apply a gradient to live type using the Gradients panel. The Gradients panel houses all the gradients that come preset with Photoshop and all the custom gradients you create in the Gradient Editor dialog box. When you target a live type layer and click a gradient on the Gradients panel, the gradient is applied directly to the live type as a Gradient Overlay layer style. When you apply a gradient with this method, you can't use the Gradient tool to control how the gradient fills the live type. Instead, use the Gradient Overlay layer style dialog box to control how the gradient is applied.

Clip a layer with a gradient fill into type

1. Open PS 4-4.psd, then save it as **Clipped Gradient**.

2. On the **TYPE layer**, click the **eye button** 👁 beside the word Effects to hide the layer styles that have been applied.

3. Create a new layer above the TYPE layer, then name the new layer **Gradient**.

4. Click the **Gradient tool** ▭, then click the **Gradient picker box** ▬ on the Options panel.

Continued on next page

Figure 24 Landscape image clipped into type

5. Click the **Blue, Orange, Rose, Blue gradient** at the bottom of the list of presets in the Gradient Editor dialog box, then click **OK**.

   This is the gradient you created in the previous set of steps.

6. Click the **Radial Gradient button** on the Options panel.

7. Verify that the **Gradient layer** is targeted on the Layers panel, position the mouse pointer at the top edge of the canvas, then click and drag the **Gradient tool** from the top edge to the bottom edge of the canvas.

   Your canvas should resemble Figure 25.

8. Click the **Layers panel menu button**, then click **Create Clipping Mask**.

   As shown in Figure 26, the Gradient layer is clipped into the TYPE layer, indicated by the bent arrow on the Gradient layer. The gradient artwork is visible only where there is artwork on the TYPE layer. The gradient artwork is not visible—it is masked—where there are transparent pixels on the TYPE layer.

9. Click the **Move tool**, then drag the **gradient artwork** around the canvas to show different areas of the clipped artwork.

   The gradient artwork moves but continues to be masked by the TYPE layer.

Figure 25 Radial gradient

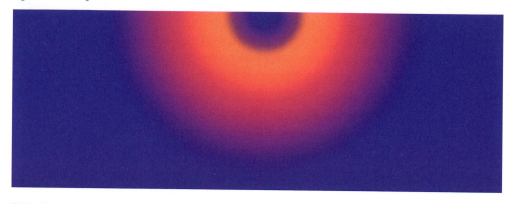

Figure 26 Clipping the gradient

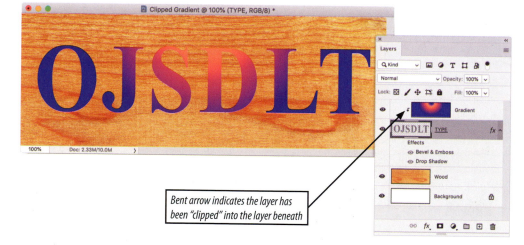

Bent arrow indicates the layer has been "clipped" into the layer beneath

10. Undo your last step.

11. Make the **Effects layer** visible on the Inner Bevel layer, then compare your canvas to Figure 27.

The gradient artwork is beveled and embossed. When a layer style is applied to a layer, any artwork that is clipped into the layer will take on the appearance of the layer style. The colors of the gradient have lightened because they are taking on the highlight and shadow colors specified in the Bevel & Emboss layer style.

12. Save your work.

You used a radial gradient on a layer then used the Create Clipping Mask command to clip the gradient layer into the type layer beneath it, noting that the gradient took on the layer effects from the type layer when clipped.

Clip an image into type

1. Hide the effects on the **TYPE layer**.

2. Drag the **Wood layer** to the top of the Layers panel.

3. On the Layers panel, press and hold **[option] (Mac)** or **[Alt] (Win)**, then float your mouse pointer over the line between the **Gradient layer** and the **Wood layer**.

The clip icon  will appear. The clip icon is a small white square with a bent black arrow .

Figure 27 Making the styles on the base layer visible

Figure 28 Layer styles on the base layer affect the clipped image

4. Click the **line between the layers** with the clip icon .

The wood artwork is clipped into the TYPE artwork. It's important to understand that the Wood layer is being clipped into the TYPE layer, not into the Gradient layer. The gradient artwork has no visual impact on the final artwork because the gradient artwork is beneath the wood artwork.

5. Show the effects on the **TYPE layer**, then compare your canvas to Figure 28.

6. Save your work, then close Clipped Gradient.

You used a keyboard command to clip an image layer into the type layer beneath it, noting that the image took on the layer effects from the type layer when clipped.

Apply a gradient directly to live type

1. Open PS 4-5.psd, then save it as **Overlay Gradient**.

2. On the Layers panel, click the **Typography layer** to target it.

3. Open the **Gradients panel**.

    The Gradients panel houses all the gradients that come preset with Photoshop and all the customized gradients you create in the Gradient Editor dialog box. A thumbnail for the Blue, Orange, Rose, Blue gradient you created is at the bottom of the Gradients panel.

4. Click the **Blue, Orange, Rose, Blue gradient thumbnail** on the Gradients panel.

    The gradient is applied to the type and a layer style named Gradient Overlay appears beneath the layer. When you target a live type layer and click a gradient swatch on the Gradient panel, the gradient is applied with this method. The gradient cannot be manipulated with the Gradient tool. Instead, you manipulate the gradient as you would any other layer style.

5. Double-click the **Gradient Overlay layer style** to open it.

    The Layer Style dialog box opens with the Gradient Overlay settings, as shown in Figure 29.

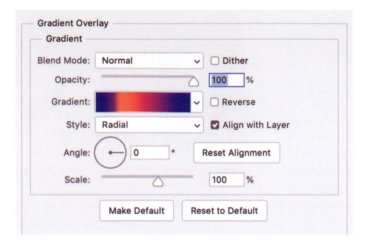

Figure 29 Gradient Overlay layer style settings

6. In the Layer Style dialog box, set the **Angle** to **0**.

    The gradient now fills the type from left to right.

7. Change the **Style** to **Radial**, then click **OK**.

8. Click the **Gradient tool** , position your pointer over the **type** on the canvas, then note that the tool won't work.

    You cannot use the Gradient tool on a gradient applied as a Gradient Overlay layer style. Because using the Gradient tool is a faster and more direct method for manipulating a gradient, many designers prefer to clip a layer with a gradient fill into type, as you did in the first exercise in this lesson. With that method, you can use the Gradient tool to modify the gradient rather than using slider controls.

9. Save your work, then close Overlay Gradient.

You applied a gradient directly to type and used the Gradient Overlay layer style to modify the gradient settings.

FADE TYPE WITH A GRADIENT AND A LAYER MASK

▶ *What You'll Do*

In this lesson, you'll use a gradient in a layer mask to fade type.

Using a Gradient in a Layer Mask to Fade Artwork

Gradients play an important visual and artistic role when they function as a color element in artwork. Gradients play an important *practical* role when used in layer masks. The fundamental rule of a layer mask is that white areas of the mask reveal 100% of the artwork on the layer, and black areas of the mask hide or mask 100% of the related artwork on the layer. Therefore, it follows logically that gradients in a layer mask that blend from white to black affect the artwork as a blend from "revealed" to "masked." Thus, a gradient in a layer mask becomes a powerful tool for gradually fading artwork on the layer.

Use a layer mask to fade type

1. Open PS 4-6.psd, then save it as **Fade Type**.

2. Target the **FADE OUT layer**, then click the **Add layer mask button** on the Layers panel.

   An all-white layer mask is added to the layer.

3. Press the **letter [D]** on your keypad to set default colors to a white foreground color and a black background color.

4. Click the **Gradient tool**, on the toolbar, then click the **Linear Gradient button** on the Options panel.

5. Click the **Gradient picker list arrow** on the Options panel, expand the Basics folder, then click the **Foreground to Background thumbnail**.

   We want to make a white-to-black gradient in the mask, so a white-to-black gradient must be active.

Continued on next page

6. Click and drag from the **top edge** of the type down to the **bottom edge** of the type, then compare your result to Figure 30.

   Because the layer mask was targeted, you applied the gradient to the layer mask. The layer mask graduates from white to black from the top to the bottom of the type. Thus, the type is fully visible at its top edge, completely invisible at its bottom edge, and gradually fades from top to bottom.

7. Click and drag from the **top edge** of the type down to the **bottom edge** of the canvas, then compare your result to Figure 31.

   The bottom edge of the text is no longer invisible.

8. Press and hold **[option] (Mac)** or **[Alt] (Win)**, then click the **layer mask** to view the layer mask.

   The area of the mask that corresponds to the bottom of the type is dark gray, not black. Thus, the type does not fully disappear at its bottom edge because the gradient in the mask becomes fully black only at the bottom of the canvas.

9. Press and hold **[option] (Mac)** or **[Alt] (Win)**, then click the **layer thumbnail** to view the layer artwork.

10. Save your work, then close Fade Type.

You used a linear gradient in a layer mask to fade type artwork from visible to transparent.

Figure 30 Fading the type with a gradient in a layer mask

Figure 31 Changing the way the type fades

CLIP MULTIPLE IMAGES INTO TYPE

▶ *What You'll Do*

In this lesson, you'll clip multiple images into one type layer, using transformations and layer masks to achieve the final look.

Clipping Multiple Images into Type

Clipping images into typography has a long and much-beloved history in graphic arts. Figure 32 shows an old postcard with images of Paris clipped into the word. The appeal of the effect never gets old, never gets dated, and never gets tired. Clipping multiple images into type inevitably involves transforming the images to achieve the best fit between the images and the type itself. It also involves using layer masks to isolate the images in the targeted letter outlines. Clipping multiple images into type will challenge you on many levels and offers the potential for producing charming and eye-popping results.

Figure 32   Old postcard with images clipped into type

Delpixel / Shutterstock.com

Clip images into type

1. Open PS 4-7.psd, then save it as **Japan Postcard**.

2. Show the **Mt. Fuji layer**, then show the **Blue push-back layer**.

3. Target the **Blue push-back layer**, then reduce its **Opacity** to **40%**.

4. Click **File** on the menu bar, click **Open**, navigate to where you store your data files, open the folder named **Japan Images**, then open the file named **Waterfall.psd**.

5. Select all, copy, then close Waterfall.psd.

6. In the **Japan Postcard file**, target the **JAPAN layer**, then paste the **waterfall artwork**.

7. Name the new layer **Waterfall**, then hide it.

8. Using the same method, open, copy, and paste the following four files: **Pagoda.psd**, **Arch.psd**, **Blossom.psd**, and **Bamboo.psd**.

9. When you're done pasting and naming the new layers, hide them all.

   Your Layers panel should resemble Figure 33, with the layers named the same and in the same order.

Figure 33 All five images pasted into the document

Figure 34 Positioning the clipped waterfall image

10. Show the **Waterfall layer**, then clip it into the **JAPAN layer**.

TIP Float your mouse pointer over the line between the Waterfall layer and the JAPAN layer, then click when you see the clip icon ⬇▢. Use the **Move tool** ✛, to position the waterfall into the J of Japan.

11. **Scale** the **waterfall artwork** so that it's positioned in the J in a way you find appealing.

    Figure 34 shows one possibility.

TIP If you need a refresher on scaling and transforming, see Chapter 3.

Figure 35 Positioning the clipped pagoda image

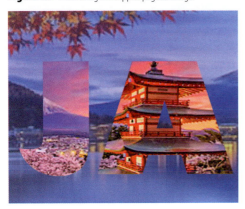

Figure 36 Masking unwanted parts of the pagoda image

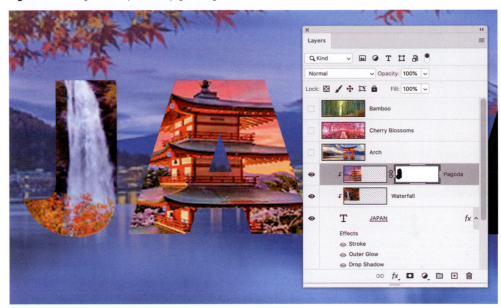

12. Show the **Pagoda layer**, clip it, then scale it and position it as shown in Figure 35.

    The pagoda artwork is extending into the letter J and covering the waterfall artwork.

13. Add a **layer mask** to the **Pagoda layer**.

14. Click the **Brush tool** , then use a hard-edged brush to mask out the pagoda artwork where it overlaps the waterfall artwork.

    Your canvas and your Layers panel should resemble Figure 36.

Continued on next page

Figure 37 Clipping and positioning all five images

You have a faster alternative than using the brush. You can use the Rectangular Marquee tool ⬚ to drag a rectangular selection around the J and then fill the selection with black. The black fill will fill the selection in the mask because the mask is targeted. The objective is to get black into the layer mask, you can use whatever means you like to achieve that objective.

15. Using the same methods and skills, clip, transform, and mask the remaining images so that your canvas and Layers panel resemble Figure 37.

16. Show all the layer styles on the JAPAN layer, then compare your artwork to Figure 38.

17. Hide and show the Blue push-back layer to see the role it plays in the finished artwork.

When you hide the layer, the colors in the background image are so deep and vivid that they *compete* with the images inside the letters. As a designer, you must resolve this competition so there is one clear focal point. In this image, the first thing the viewer should see is the word JAPAN in vivid color. Therefore, we use the Blue push-back layer to dull the background and make it more uniform in color.

18. Save your work, then close Japan Postcard.

You pasted five images into the working file, clipped them, transformed them, and positioned them in a type layer.

Shutterstock photo credits: Mt. Fuji: Guitar photographer; Waterfall: PixHound; Pagoda & Bamboo: Sean Pavone; Cherry blossoms: picture cells

Figure 38 The final artwork

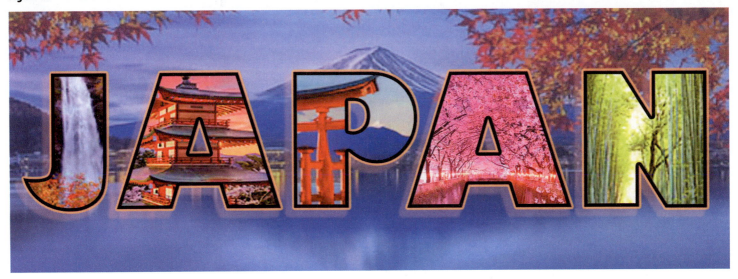

Don't overlook the critical role the layer styles play in this artwork. Without them, the word JAPAN is hardly legible against the background image. The layer styles, especially the black stroke and the bright orange outer glow, define the letter outlines from the background and make the word readable. The drop shadow behind the layers plays a subtle role, but also contributes to making the letters stand out from the background.

AUTHOR'S NOTE I am pleased to share this stunning piece of artwork created by my student, Kishan Shah, in our Digital Design class at Sierra Canyon High School in Chatsworth, CA. At the time, Kishan was a freshman who signed up for the course and likely never thought he'd be published. We were working on clipping images into type as I was writing this chapter, and when he showed me this artwork, I knew it had to be part of this book. This story says a lot about how rapidly young people can learn and how far they can go when empowered by learning a great program like Photoshop. Thank you, Kishan.

Set type

1. Open PS 4-8.psd, then save it as **Skills Type**.
2. Click the Horizontal Type tool, then click on the left side of the canvas.
3. Type the words **Type It**.
4. Click the Move tool.
5. On the Character panel, click the Fonts list arrow, then choose Impact (or a similar typeface).
6. Set the font size to 96 pt by typing **96** in the Set the font size text box.
7. Center the type on the page, then click a red swatch on the Swatches panel.
8. Save your work.

Lock transparent pixels

1. Verify that the Type It layer is targeted, click Layer on the menu bar, point to Rasterize, then click Type.
2. Hide the Background layer.
3. Press the letter [D] on your keypad to access the default foreground and background colors.
4. Press [option] [delete] (Mac) or [Alt] [Delete] (Win) to fill with the black foreground color.
   The entire layer fills with black.
5. Undo the fill, then click the Lock transparent pixels button on the Layers panel.
6. Fill the layer with the black foreground color.
   Only the type outlines are filled with black.
7. Click a bright red swatch on the Swatches panel, click the Brush tool, set the Size to 50 px, then set the Hardness to 100%.

8. Paint different areas of the type.
9. Show the Background layer, save your work, then close Skills Type.

Create bevel and emboss effects on type

1. Open PS 4-9.psd, save it as **Bevel Skills Type**, then target the HEADLINE layer on the Layers panel.
2. Double-click the HEADLINE layer to open the Layer Style dialog box, then click the words Bevel & Emboss in the left column.
3. Set the Style to Emboss, set the Technique to Smooth, then set the Depth to 100%.
4. Set the Size to 24, set the Soften value to 0, then click OK.
5. Double-click the Bevel & Emboss layer style on the Layers panel to reopen the dialog box.
6. Set the Style to Inner Bevel, set the Technique to Chisel Hard, then set the Depth to 100%.
7. Set the Size to 48, set the Soften value to 0, then click OK.
8. Save your work.

Apply gloss contours to layer styles

1. Double-click the Bevel & Emboss layer style on the Layers panel to open the dialog box.
2. Click the gloss contour named Cone.
3. Click the Anti-aliased check box, then click OK.
4. Save your work.

Create a double emboss effect

1. Duplicate the HEADLINE layer, rename the new layer **Inner Bevel**, then hide it.
2. Target the HEADLINE layer, then rename it **Outer Bevel**.
3. Drag the Layer effects icon *fx.* on the Outer Bevel layer to the Delete layer button on the Layers panel.

4. Click Layer on the menu bar, point to Layer Style, then click Bevel & Emboss.
5. Set the Style to Outer Bevel, set the Technique to Chisel Hard, then set the Depth to 100%.
6. Set the Size to 12, then set the Soften value to 0.
7. Apply the Ring - Double gloss contour, then activate the Anti-aliased check box.
8. Click OK, then show the Inner Bevel layer.
9. Save your work, then close Bevel Skills Type.

Apply a gradient

1. Open PS 4-10.psd, then save it as **Gradient Skills**.
2. Click the Gradient tool on the toolbar.
3. Click the Gradient picker list arrow.
4. Expand the Oranges folder, then click the 12th gradient in that folder, named Orange_12.
5. Click the Linear Gradient button on the Options panel.
6. Position the mouse pointer at the left edge of the canvas, click and drag to the right edge of the canvas, then release the mouse button.
7. Click and drag from the top of the canvas to the bottom of the canvas.
   The gradient is recreated from top to bottom.
8. Click and drag from the upper-left to the lower-right corner of the canvas.
   The gradient is recreated diagonally from the upper-left to the lower-right corner of the canvas.
9. Click near the center of the canvas and drag from left to right for approximately one inch.
   The length of the entire gradient is approximately one inch long. Any pixels outside of the one inch range are filled with solid start and end colors, which in this case are yellow and purple.
10. Click the Radial Gradient button on the Options panel.

11. Position your pointer at the center of the canvas, then click and drag approximately two inches to the right. The gradient starts where you click and ends where you release. With a radial gradient, however, the gradient "radiates" out from a center point with the start color as the center color.
12. Save your work.

Create a new gradient

1. Click the Gradient picker box on the Options panel to open the Gradient Editor dialog box.
2. Click the first (leftmost) color stop, then click the Color box below the gradient ramp to open the Color Picker.
3. Type **255** in the R text box, type **208** in the G text box, type **0** in the B text box, then click OK.
4. Click the last color stop, then change its color to 29R/5G/170B.
5. Click just below the gradient ramp roughly in the middle of the two color stops.
   A new color stop is added to the gradient ramp where you clicked.
6. Drag the new color stop until the Location text box reads 65%.
7. Change the color of the new color stop to 0R/211G/194B.
8. Drag the Color Midpoint diamond slider between the second and third color stop to 20%.
9. Type **Yellow, Cyan, Blue** in the Name text box, then click the New button.
10. Click OK.
    The new gradient is added to the bottom of the Gradient Editor dialog box.
11. Save your work, then close Gradient Skills.

Figure 39 Clipping the granite image into type

Clip a layer with a gradient fill into type

1. Open PS 4-11.psd, then save it as **Clipping Skills**.
2. Hide the effects on the TYPE OUTLINES layer.
3. Create a new layer above the TYPE OUTLINES layer, then name the new layer **Gradient**.
4. Click the Gradient tool.
5. Click Gradient picker list arrow, then click the Yellow, Cyan, Blue gradient thumbnail at the bottom of the menu.
6. Click the Linear Gradient button on the Options panel.
7. Verify that the Gradient layer is targeted on the Layers panel.
8. Position the mouse pointer at the top edge of the letters, then create a gradient from the top to the bottom of the letters.
9. Click the Layers panel menu button, then click Create Clipping Mask.
10. Make the effects visible on the TYPE OUTLINES layer, then save your work.

Clip imagery into type

1. Hide the effects on the TYPE OUTLINES layer.
2. Move the Granite layer to the top of the Layers panel.
3. Press and hold [option] (Mac) or [Alt] (Win), then click the line between the Granite layer and the TYPE OUTLINES layer to clip the Granite layer. Show the effects on the TYPE OUTLINES layer, then compare your result to Figure 39.
4. Save your work, then close Clipping Skills.

Fade type

1. Open PS 4-12.psd, then save it as **Fade Skills**.
2. Target the FADE AWAY layer, then click the Add layer mask button on the Layers panel.
3. Set the foreground color to white and the background color to black.
4. Click the Gradient tool on the toolbar, then click the Linear Gradient button on the Options panel.
5. Click the Gradient picker list arrow on the Options panel, expand the Basics folder, then click the Foreground to Background thumbnail.
   We want to make a white-to-black gradient in the mask, so a white-to-black gradient must be active.
6. Click and drag the Gradient tool from the left edge of the letter F to the right edge of the letter Y.
7. Click and drag the Gradient tool from the middle of the letter D to the right edge of the canvas.
8. Press and hold [option] (Mac) or [Alt] (Win), then click the layer mask to view the layer mask.
9. Press and hold [option] (Mac) or [Alt] (Win), then click the layer thumbnail to view the layer artwork.
10. Save your work, then close Fade Skills.

This exercise focuses on creating a simple type-based post card for an event. It's a terrific example of how a gradient can so effectively make a basic layout visually interesting.

1. Open PS 4-13.psd, then save it as **Sunset Gradient**.
2. Fill the Background layer with black, then lock transparent pixels on both type layers.
3. Fill the type on the two type layers with white.
4. Click the Gradient picker box on the Options panel to open the Gradient Editor dialog box.
5. In the Presets section, expand the Basics folder, then click the first Gradient thumbnail, which is named "Foreground to Background."

TIP Position the mouse pointer over a gradient and wait for a moment for its name to appear.

6. Change the color of the left color stop to 255R/228G/0B.
7. Verify that the color of the right color stop is 0R/0G/0B.
8. Add a third color stop between the first and second color stops.
9. Change the color of the new color stop to 255R/0G/0B, then change its location to 75%.
10. Add a new color stop between the first color stop and the new color stop.
11. Change the color of the new color stop to 255R/132G/0B, and change its location to 50%.

Figure 40 Gradient clipped into type

12. Name the new gradient **Sunset Gradient**, click New, then click OK.
13. Create a new layer above the SUNSET layer, then name the new layer **Sunset Gradient**.
14. Click the Gradient tool on the toolbar, then verify that the Linear Gradient button is selected on the Options panel.
15. Position your cursor at the top edge of the SUNSET type, then create a linear gradient from the top of the SUNSET type to the bottom of the SUNSET type.
16. Click the Layers panel menu button, then click Create Clipping Mask.
17. Compare your canvas to Figure 40.
18. Save your work, then close Sunset Gradient.

Project Builder 2 is designed specifically to get you to remember the Stroke Emboss effect. So many designers aren't even aware of it, so that's even more reason to get it into your skill set. Once you've completed the steps, take a moment to appreciate the sophisticated and stunning impact it has on the artwork.

1. Open PS 4-14.psd, then save it as **Sunset Stroke Emboss**.
2. Target the SUNSET layer on the Layers panel.
3. Click Layer on the menu bar, point to Layer Style, then click Stroke.
4. Click the Color box, type **128** in the R, G, and B text boxes, then click OK.
5. Set the Size to 10, then set the Position to Center.
6. In the Styles column at the left of the dialog box, click the words Bevel & Emboss.
7. Set the Style to Stroke Emboss, set the Technique to Chisel Hard, then set the Depth to 110%.
8. Set the Size to 2, then set the Soften value to 0.
9. Click the Gloss Contour list arrow, click the Ring - Double gloss contour, then verify that the Anti-aliased check box is checked.
10. Click OK, then compare your artwork to Figure 41.
11. Save your work, then close Sunset Stroke Emboss.

Figure 41 Bevel & Emboss layer style applied to the stroke

The entire focus of this Project Builder is on clipping. Clipping is where many of the "magic tricks" in Photoshop happen. In this case, your result will have what appears to be the same image used twice, but look closer and you'll see a neat visual trick being played.

1. Open PS 4-15.psd, then save it as **Sunset Image Clipping**.
2. Verify that only the Background and Original Image layers are showing on the Layers panel.
3. Show, then hide the Sunset layer, comparing the artwork to the Original Image artwork. The Sunset artwork is a duplicate of the Original Image artwork. It has been colorized orange, and sunset artwork has been added at the center.
4. Show all layers, then drag the Sunset layer above the HEADLINE layer.
5. Clip the Sunset layer into the HEADLINE layer.
6. Add a layer mask to the Sunset layer.
7. Set the foreground and background colors to white and black, respectively.
8. Click the Gradient tool, then position it at the horizon line in the image.
9. Make a white-to-black gradient in the layer mask from the horizon line to bottom edge of the artwork.

Figure 42 Viewing the final effect

10. Press [command] [J] (Mac) or [Ctrl] [J] (Win) to duplicate the Sunset layer, then move the Sunset copy layer to the top of the Layers panel.
11. Drag the layer mask on the Sunset copy to the Delete layer button on the Layers panel, then click Delete when prompted.
12. Clip the Sunset copy layer into the type layer beneath it.
13. With the Sunset copy layer still targeted, drag the Opacity slider on the Layers panel to 70%.
14. Compare your Layers panel and your artwork to Figure 42.

The eye recognizes immediately that it's the same image inside the letters as outside the letters but, on second glance, realizes that the sunset is only inside the letters. The stroke emboss delineates the word "SUNSET" from the background but is thin enough that it doesn't interrupt the continuity between the two images. You can create a lot of tricky effects like this by duplicating and modifying an image and clipping it strategically into type.

15. Save your work, then close Sunset Image Clipping.

DESIGN PROJECT

This project gives you the opportunity to incorporate the layer skills you have learned in Chapters 3 and 4. You are going to type the name of a city, then place images into the letters, as you did with the "JAPAN" artwork in Lesson 6 of this chapter.

The way to do this project is to work methodically, don't rush. Think about color and about finding the right typeface and images. Think about which layer styles would work best for you about how a gradient might add to the effect.

1. Open PS 4-16.psd, then save it as **City Images**. This file is blank, a clean slate to get you started.
2. Decide what city you want to work on. Keep in mind that the shorter the name, the larger the letters will be on the canvas, and the more of the images you'll be able to see inside those letters.
3. Type the name of the city on the canvas.
4. Choose the best typeface for the city. You have many considerations when choosing a typeface. Your most important consideration though, is finding a typeface that's very bold and thick so that when you put images into the type, they will show substantially.
5. Track and kern the type as necessary.

Figure 43 Final artwork

6. Go online and find a background image that you think will work and paste it in.
7. Research and choose the best images for the collage and clip them into the type.
8. Apply the layer styles you think will best make the type and images stand out from the background.
9. Incorporate a gradient over the background to perhaps darken it or lighten it. Figure 43 shows one result.

Shutterstock photo credits: Christ the Redeemer: Dmitri Kalvan; Night view of Rio de Janeiro & Mosaic sidewalk: Catarina Belova; Brazilian woman: Gold Stock Images

DEVELOPING A MEANINGFUL PROJECT

Rubén Salgado Escudero, Solar Portraits
Project, Fishermen in Odisha, India

© Rubén Salgado Escudero

Rubén Salgado Escudero has a passion for finding sustainable solutions to environmental issues and climate change. He knows that using solar energy can have a substantial positive impact on Earth's carbon footprint. Rubén travels around the world to photograph the ways small, inexpensive photovoltaic solar lights have improved people's lives. He hopes to inspire people with his Solar Portraits and demonstrate how solar energy has the potential to change the lives of millions.

THE BEGINNING OF THE SOLAR PORTRAITS PROJECT

Rubén went to Myanmar in Southeast Asia in 2013. As he traveled around the country, he was struck by the fact that most rural communities do not have access to electricity. In order to work in the evening hours between sunset and dark, people must use non-electric lamps to light their living spaces.

Rubén noticed a difference between communities with solar lamps and those without. Villages with solar lights were much more active in the evenings. Non-solar lamps have serious drawbacks—they are often dangerous, expensive, or both. For instance, candles can start fires, and batteries cost a lot of money, while kerosene and other fuels are expensive and give off noxious fumes. In contrast, solar lamps are safe and use free and plentiful sunlight as their power source. For these reasons, villagers are likely to use lights more frequently for evening tasks when they are solar-powered.

Rubén saw firsthand how solar-powered lights changed people's lives in dramatic ways and knew he needed to document this. He talked to people about their lives before and after solar lights and began to take photos—lit only by solar-powered light bulbs—to tell peoples' stories and reveal the impact solar lights have had on their lives. The first photos taken in Myanmar became the foundation of Rubén's ongoing Solar Portraits Project.

LIGHT FOR FINDING FISH

The men in this photo live in a rural village in eastern India. Rubén met them while on assignment for *National Geographic*. It was close to sunset when he saw the group gathering beside a mud pond with their solar lanterns. The men were getting ready to fish. As they walked through the field, they used the light from the solar lanterns to look for bubbles in the mud, which let them know there were fish below the surface. Once a fish was spotted, a man would slam a basket down into the mud to trap it. Then he would reach down through a hole in the top of the basket to catch the fish with his hands.

THE SOLAR SOLUTION

The people in this image are farmers. When the sun is out, they must work in their fields. At night, without lights, they cannot see the fish well enough to catch them. The solar lanterns allow these men to use the evening hours to provide their families with additional protein-rich food that would not otherwise be available to them.

RUBÉN'S POINTS OF INTEREST

1. A solar-powered light bulb was placed on a lily pad to maintain a balance of light throughout the image.

2. A light bulb hanging off a stick hovered over the man to illuminate and bring attention to his face. Rubén kept the bulb in the photo when he saw it looked like the moon.

3. A man was placed farther back to show the size and depth of the mud pond they were fishing in.

PROJECT DESCRIPTION

In this project, you will analyze and respond to Rubén's image. You'll have the opportunity to investigate the different elements of the image and interpret the story for yourself. Look at the photo closely. Take note of anything that catches your attention. You'll be writing a brief analysis consisting of your observations, your interpretation of the story, any questions that come to mind, and the messages you take away. If you can, talk to your classmates and discuss your ideas. Decide which elements of the photo are impactful to you, and write a brief analysis of your findings.

QUESTIONS TO CONSIDER

What is the story?

What stands out to you?

What would you change? Why?

What questions do you have?

What caught your attention first?

Is there anything that seems confusing?

Do you like the image?

USE SOME OF THESE VOCABULARY WORDS

Form: The assembly of 2D shapes to represent a third dimension. Form shows measurable dimensions of length, width, and depth of an object.

Shape: A defined area in 2D space. There are two different types of shapes: geometric and organic.

Line: The path between two points. A line is most often used to define a boundary.

Value: The use of light and dark to add highlight, shadows, or shading.

Space: The area of volume in a scene.

Movement: An applied action.

Balance: The arrangement of objects so that no one section overpowers any other part.

Foreground: The part of a view that is nearest to the viewer.

Background: The part of a view that is farthest from the viewer. The background is the area behind the main focus of an image.

GETTING STARTED

Analyze the photo. Look closely at each individual person and how he is posed. Pay attention to what is around them. Use the vocabulary words to help you think about the relationships between the different parts of the scene. Make observations about the environment as a whole and about the natural elements that are present.

Mark details that catch your eye. Look for elements in the scene that you can't identify. Note the parts of the image that you find most interesting.

Organize your thoughts. Think about how you want to present your observations and questions. Make a list of your ideas, and create bullet points with the observations you want to write about and discuss.

SKILLS YOU'LL PRACTICE

Critical thinking

Giving feedback

Design analysis

Writing

Using design vocabulary

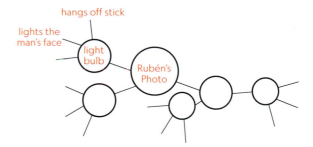

One way to organize your thoughts is with a graphic organizer. Here's an example of how you might use an idea web to capture your thoughts about the photo.

PROJECT DESCRIPTION

In this project, you'll investigate sustainable solutions and the environment to tell a relevant story from your own perspective. You'll need to research and figure out what sustainability means to you. This can be done by searching the Internet for relevant articles and news, having conversations with classmates, watching topical videos, etc.

After gathering a base understanding of your topic, establish the stance and angle you want to take. Think about which parts of the story are worth telling. Decide what the important points are and how you can communicate those in a digital composition.

Using at least three of the images provided, in addition to any of your own taken or found images, create a composition that tells a story.

SKILLS TO EXPLORE

- Access an image from the Internet
- Work with the layers panel
- Make basic selections
- Paint inside selections
- Create and edit symbols and graphic styles
- Create and edit brushes and patterns
- Convert text to graphics
- Create vector shapes

FILES YOU'LL USE

- Ps_u1_globe.JPEG
- Ps_u1_lightbulb.JPEG
- Ps_u1_solar.JPEG
- Ps_u1_wave.JPEG
- Ps_u1_sun.JPEG

You will use Photoshop for this project to create an image that is inspired by Rubén's photographic work.

SKILLS CHALLENGE
USE QUICK MASK MODE FOR PRECISE LOCALIZED ADJUSTMENTS

Step 1: Double-click the Quick Mask Mode button in the toolbox.

Step 2: Choose from the following display options: Selected Areas. It is okay to leave the color as red and the opacity at 50%. Recommendation: If you are having trouble viewing your painted area, choose a contrasting color, and increase the opacity to 80%.

Step 3: Choose the object or area you want to select, and paint the area using the brush tool. Recommendation: Increase brush hardness to 100%.

Step 4: Press Q on the keyboard to enter Quick Mask mode. The object or area you selected will become a selection.

Step 5: Adjust the selected object or area as you desire. For example, you can cut and move the selected area, remove the selected area, paint the selected area, etc.

FOLLOW RUBÉN'S EXAMPLE

1. Understand the space and environment. Think about all the elements that live in the environment you are working with. Consider how all the different elements interact with one another and identify which of those elements are needed to tell the story.

2. Think about balance. Keep the image balanced and focused. Consider where you want the focus to be and how the other elements support that idea.

3. Consider the smaller details. Stories, especially human-centered stories, are often complex. The small details help give viewers a closer look at a unique perspective.

4. Find the focus of the story. Consider what specific message you want your viewers to take away from your image. Think about what part of the bigger picture you want to tell viewers.

GETTING STARTED

The planning and brainstorming step of your creative process can often be the most difficult and unstructured part, but it is also where you get to do the most exploring. In this section, you are encouraged to research and explore your ideas without too many constraints. You might be surprised how one idea connects to another.

1. Find some inspiration. Look online and at books and your favorite magazines. Find imagery and photos that you find visually appealing. Look for editing styles and visual effects you think effectively communicate a message.

2. Do your research. Gather background information on sustainability and the environment. Think about varying viewpoints, and determine whether you agree or disagree. This will help you identify a story and create a composition that is authentic and well informed.

While doing research, the student noted and sketched information about sustainability and the environment.

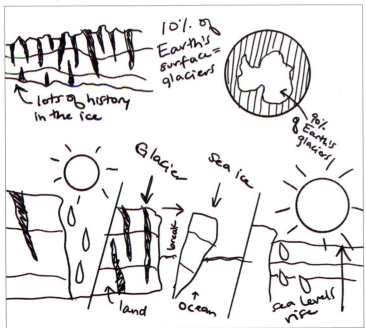

3. Sketch out your ideas. Think about what elements you want to focus on and where they will sit on the page. Decide what role each piece will play in your story and how it will interact with other elements. Sketch out what you want each element to look like. Write down words and phrases that relate to your drawings.

After deciding to focus on glaciers, the student experimented with texture, balance, and perspective by brainstorming different ways to view the landscape.

PROJECT DESCRIPTION

In this project, you'll continue your investigation of sustainable solutions for the environment by exploring your own community. You'll need to examine a location familiar to you. This could be your school, neighborhood, local forest preserve, or another location that resonates with you.

Use whatever is available to you: camera, phone, pen and paper, Internet, etc., to gather pieces of evidence that help you tell a story. Think about what elements you'll need to create a full composition. Use journaling to record questions you want to answer and conversations you have with the people around you; then reflect on how you want to convey this information.

The goal of this project is to create an image or series of images that tells a story about how sustainability and the environment relate to your community.

THINK LIKE RUBÉN

1. Find a topic you're passionate about. Think about one subject that has always stuck in your mind. Consider lessons and conversations that have sparked your interest and made you want to explore and know more.

2. Explore the people related to that topic. Be curious and leave no stone unturned. Research and explore the people, environments, challenges, solutions, and other relevant information that could help you find a lead or unique perspective worth communicating.

3. Think about the message you want to convey. Think about what you like about the subjects you are working with. Evaluate which ideas you want to share with people through your work.

SKILLS TO EXPLORE

- Research
- Design mapping and sketching
- Explore burn and dodge tools
- Explore smudge and blur tools
- Make basic selections
- Paint inside selections
- Move selected pixels
- Examine selection edges
- Use magic wand selection
- Flatten and merge layers

SKILLS CHALLENGE
TRANSFORMATIONS WITH THE CONTENT-AWARE MOVE

Step 1: In the toolbar, hold down the Spot Healing Brush and select the Content-Aware Move tool.

Step 2: In the options bar, do the following:
Mode: Use the Move mode to place selected objects in a different location. Use the Extend mode to expand or contract objects.
Structure: Enter a value between 1 and 7 to specify how closely the patch should reflect the existing image patterns. Value 1 adheres very loosely, while value 7 adheres very strongly to the existing image pattern.
Color: Enter a value between 0 and 10 to specify the extent to which you want Photoshop to apply color blending to the patch. Value 0 disables color blending, while value 10 applies maximum color blending.
Sample All Layer: Enable this option to use information from all layers to create the result of the move in the selected layer. Select the target layer in the Layers panel.

Step 3: Select an area to move or extend. You can use any of the selection tools to draw your selection.

Step 4: Drag the selection over the area you want to generate a fill form.

GETTING STARTED

Telling an original story about a new topic can be challenging. Use your ideas, and work from the previous project as a stepping stone for this project. Consider the story you told in your previous composition. Think about if and how that story relates to your community. You can adjust your previous composition or copy parts of it into your new one. You might even build upon your previous composition and turn it into a series of images.

1. Brainstorm and list places in your community that might be of interest to you. These could be places you think have a direct connection to sustainability and the environment or places you feel lack a connection to sustainability and environment. Investigate these places and decide what story you want to tell about a particular location as it relates to your topic and community.

2. Start a conversation. Take the social temperature of the people around you. Conversations are often stepping stones to new ideas. Use the people around you as a creative resource to ensure your story will resonate with your audience.

3. Map out your story. Picture a grid in your mind, and imagine placing the elements of your composition on it. This will ensure your image is balanced and that you have thought out all elements of the composition. Consider the hierarchy of the page. Decide how you want each individual element of your composition to attract attention. Create a layout that catches the viewer's eye in an effective manner.

While taking a walk around the community, the student stopped to observe and sketch different parts of a garden.

After talking with a member of the garden, the student explored ways to illustrate all the work that goes into making a garden flourish year-round.

ADJUST AND MANIPULATE IMAGES AND FILES

Anand Varma, Hummingbird using its forked
tongue to drink

CHAPTER 5

EMPLOY ADJUSTMENT LAYERS

1. Explore Fundamental Adjustments
2. Adjust Levels
3. Investigate the RGB Color Model
4. Investigate the HSB Color Model

Adobe Certified Professional in Visual Design Using Photoshop CC Framework

3. Organizing Documents

This objective covers document structure such as layers and managing document structure for efficient workflows.

3.1 Use layers to manage design elements.
- **C** Recognize the different types of layers in the Layers panel.

3.2 Modify layer visibility using opacity, blending modes, and masks.
- **A** Adjust a layer's opacity, blending mode, and fill opacity.
- **B** Create and edit masks.

3.3 Differentiate between and perform destructive or nondestructive editing to meet design requirements.
- **A** Nondestructive editing: adjustment layers.
- **B** Destructive editing: painting, adjustments, and erasing.

4. Creating and Modifying Visual Elements

This objective covers core tools and functionality of the application, as well as tools that affect the visual outcome of document elements.

4.5 Use basic reconstructing and retouching techniques to manipulate digital graphics and media.
- **A** Apply basic auto-correction methods and tools.
- **C** Evaluate or adjust the appearance of objects, selections, or layers using various tools.
- **D** Apply photographic changes to images using tools and adjustments.

EXPLORE FUNDAMENTAL ADJUSTMENTS

Improving Images with Adjustments

Our digital world offers unprecedented access to professional-level, high-quality photography, images that are flawless and require no improvements or corrections. On the contrary, our digital world has put phone cameras in the hands of almost everyone, and while these cameras are also high quality, the photos an amateur photographer captures are often just average.

Photoshop offers many practical adjustment operations to improve the quality of images—their color, contrast, and overall effect. Brightness/Contrast, Levels, and Color Balance are three common, powerful, and highly useful adjustments for improving the overall appearance of an image.

Once you understand the concepts of the Grayscale, RGB, and HSB color modes, you'll be ready and able to dramatically alter or improve your images with a variety of adjustments.

Understanding Nondestructive Editing

In the course of a project, you will execute hundreds and even thousands of moves that affect the original image or images you are working with. Regardless of all changes you make, you never want to permanently change your original artwork, which is also referred to as the **base artwork** or the **base image**. You want all your changes to be editable or removable, if necessary. You can achieve this by working effectively with the Layers panel, which gives you the ability to execute all operations on *layers* rather than on the base image itself.

Nondestructive editing is the term used to describe this working behavior. With nondestructive editing, your original artwork is protected from permanent changes.

One of the big misconceptions new designers have regarding more experienced designers is that they know where they're going and what their goal is at all times, and the finished product is exactly what they planned from the start. That is very seldom (if ever) the case. Design is a process, one that often involves experimentation, trial and error, and redirection. Nondestructive editing allows you endless flexibility to experiment, to try something out. If it works, great, and if it doesn't, edit and move in a new direction. Once you are close to finishing the piece, the fact that all your steps are editable allows you to tweak everything to perfect the final look.

Working with Adjustments

Photoshop offers 22 types of operations, called **adjustments**, that affect the appearance of an image. These include fundamental adjustments such as Levels, Curves, Hue/Saturation, and Brightness/Contrast. Adjustments can be applied using commands on the Image menu, but you should always make adjustments using the Layers panel. If you make adjustments using the commands on the Image menu, those fall under the category of **destructive editing** because they are applied directly to the image.

Adjustments made using the Layers panel are referred to as **adjustment layers**. When an adjustment is applied as a layer, it is always editable. You can hide or show the adjustment, you can delete it if you no longer want it, and you can change its settings whenever you like. For example, if you create a new adjustment layer to brighten an image with the Brightness/Contrast adjustment, the base image will be affected only as long as the Brightness/Contrast adjustment layer is showing. In addition, you can return to this Brightness/Contrast adjustment at any time to change its settings.

Adjustment layers are created on the Layers panel by clicking the Create new fill or adjustment layer button on the panel and then choosing the type of adjustment you want. Once created, the Properties panel opens showing the adjustment's default settings. Settings on the Properties panel allow you to change the appearance of the adjustment. For example, Figure 1 shows a Brightness/Contrast adjustment layer and the settings for it on the Properties panel.

You can use the Opacity setting on the Layers panel to decrease or increase the effect an adjustment has on the base artwork. By default, all new adjustment layers are created at 100% opacity. All adjustment layers are also created with a layer mask, which you can use to hide or show the adjustment in different areas. The ability to "brush in" adjustments this way, in specific areas and with specific strengths, is a powerful option for working with adjustments.

Figure 1 Brightness/Contrast adjustment layer and settings on the Properties panel

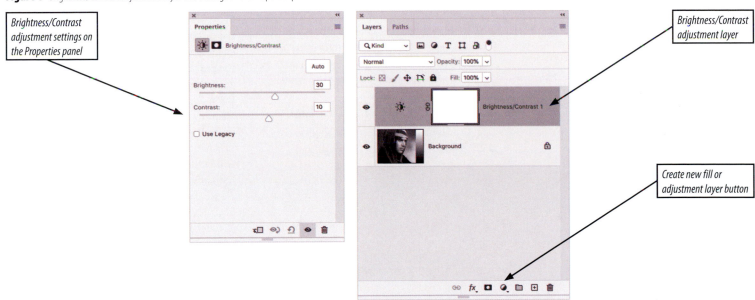

Understanding Grayscale

A grayscale image is a digital image in which each pixel can be one—and only one—of 256 shades of gray. With 256 shades of gray available per pixel, the illusion of a continuous tone image can be created. The grayscale range is 0–255. Pixels with a grayscale value of 0 are black. Pixels with a grayscale value of 255 are white. Any number in between 0 and 255 is gray—light gray or dark gray—with 128 being the middle point in the grayscale range.

The first step in analyzing the appearance of any image is to identify the highlights, midtones, and shadows. **Highlights** are the lightest areas of the image and are represented by pixels whose value falls in the upper third of the grayscale range. **Shadows** are the darkest areas represented by pixels in the lower third of the grayscale range. **Midtones**, as the name suggests, fall into the middle of the grayscale range.

When you look at a digital image, you don't see individual pixels; you see the illusion of continuous tone, a smooth transition from shadows to midtones to highlights. To create this illusion, there must be enough grays available per pixel so that the eye perceives smooth transitions between tones.

Applying an Invert Adjustment

The **Invert adjustment** achieves its effect by flipping the grayscale range. Black pixels change to 255 and become white, and white pixels change to 0 and become black. In a black and white image, applying the Invert adjustment creates an x-ray effect.

Applying a Threshold Adjustment

Like the Posterize effect you explored in Chapter 2, the **Threshold adjustment** creates its effect by manipulating the number of colors available per pixel. The Threshold adjustment forces each pixel to be either black or white, thus creating the ultimate high-contrast effect. By default, the adjustment splits the image right down the middle: pixels with a grayscale value of 128 or higher all become white; pixels with a grayscale value of 127 or lower all become black. You can adjust where that split occurs by dragging the Threshold Level slider left or right. The number you stop on specifies the grayscale value at which pixels become white.

Applying a Gradient Map Adjustment

The **Gradient Map adjustment** applies a gradient to the transition from shadows to highlights. For example, if you created a gradient from dark blue to yellow and used it as a Gradient Map adjustment, the image would transition from dark blue shadows to yellow highlights. You can use any gradient you create in a gradient map, including multicolor gradients. Thus, with the Gradient Map adjustment, you can create dynamic images that transition through multiple hues from shadow to highlight.

Applying a Brightness/Contrast Adjustment

The Brightness/Contrast adjustment, as the name suggests, affects the brightness and contrast in an image. **Brightness** is defined by a pixel's grayscale value. The higher the number, the brighter the pixel, because the closer it is to white.

Contrast is represented by the relationship between the shadows and highlights of the image. Good contrast is created when shadows and highlights are distinctly different in tonal range—that is, when shadow areas are richly dark and highlights are gleaming white and there's a "dynamic range" between shadows and highlights. On the other hand, when the highlights aren't bright enough and the shadows aren't dark enough, the image will lack contrast and appear drab and "flat" in its tonal range.

Bad contrast can also occur "in camera" when the available lighting is poor or the camera settings are not correct for the given lighting conditions. In these cases, the highlights can "blow out and "bleach" the image, or the shadows can "plug up" to the point that there's no range of gray in the dark areas. When this occurs in the camera, there is very little that can be done to fix it. On the other hand, be sure you don't overdo the Brightness/Contrast adjustment in Photoshop and create these problems yourself!

Figure 2 shows an example of good contrast and three examples of bad contrast.

Understanding Legacy Settings

Photoshop is more than 30 years old, and some users have been using it for that long. Many users find their groove with Photoshop and are resistant to changes or evolutions Adobe might make to long-standing features. For some of these features, Adobe offers the *Use Legacy* option, which restores the functionality of a given feature to its *classic* state. The Brightness/Contrast adjustment is one of many Photoshop features that offers the "Use Legacy" option.

Figure 2 Four examples of contrast

Poor contrast: "weak" shadows and "closed" highlights

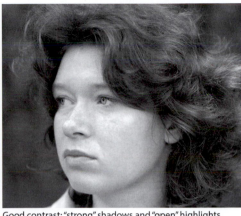

Good contrast: "strong" shadows and "open" highlights

Poor contrast: shadows are "plugged" and have no range

Poor contrast: highlights are "blown out" and have no detail

Morguefile

Sample shadows, midtones, and highlights in an image

1. Open PS 5-1.psd, then save it as **Basic Adjustments**.

2. Click **Image** on the menu bar, point to **Mode**, then note that **Grayscale** is checked.

   This image has been saved in Grayscale mode, meaning that one of 256 shades of gray is available per pixel.

3. Open the **Info panel**, then verify that the left-side readout is set to **RGB**.

4. Click the **Eyedropper tool** 🖋 on the toolbar, then position it over different areas of the image, noting the readouts on the Info panel.

5. Position the **Eyedropper tool** 🖋 at the very bottom of the gradient on the right, then move it slowly to the top of the gradient.

   The pixels in the gradient range from 0 at the bottom to 255 at the top. Try to see the image of the young man as a similar gradient from black to white.

6. Make the **Chart layer** visible on the Layers panel.

   The chart shows the general ranges for shadows, midtones, and highlights on the gradient. Try to see these ranges in the image of the young man.

7. Assess the image for its **shadows**. Which areas do you identify as the shadow areas of the image?

   The dark area under the young man's chin and the dark jacket on his shoulder are the shadow areas. Note that a *range* of dark gray pixels exists at his shoulder. They are not all black, and there is detail in the jacket; therefore, you can see the folds in the cloth and the scrunching of the material along the

collar. Note too that even though the area under the chin is very dark, you can still see the detail of the *inside* of the hood. These are great examples and reminders that shadow areas *must* have a range of dark grays to show detail. Otherwise, all you'd be looking at is a field of black.

8. Assess the image for its **highlights**. Which areas would you guess contain the brightest pixels in the image?

   The pixels with the highest grayscale value can be found in the highlight along the man's nose. His face and the lighter stripes of the knit cap are the highlights in the image.

9. Assess the image for its **midtones**. Which areas would you guess contain pixels closest to 128?

   If you're thinking it's the man's hood, you'd be wrong. Those pixels are darker than you might first guess, somewhere in the range of 64. The midtones in the image are the blurry background to the right of the man's nose.

   | AUTHOR'S **NOTE**   In terms of contrast, the hood is an interesting component of the image. The fabric is not shiny, so there's no bright highlight, and the fabric is not overly dark in color, so there's no deep shadow. Nevertheless, try to see that there is a *range of tone* that renders the hood. The vertical, diagonal shadow has grayscale values from 20 to 40, and the soft highlight at the back of the hood is rendered with grayscale values from 90 to 105. Consider, therefore, that even though the hood is not rendered with deep shadows or bright highlights, there is a limited range of contrast in the hood.

10. Hide the **Chart layer** on the Layers panel.

11. Assess the whole image in terms of **shadows**, **midtones**, and **highlights**.

    | AUTHOR'S **NOTE**   As shown in Figure 3, this image has great contrast. The shadows are deep and dark, yet they never go black or lose detail. The face is bright, the highlight along the nose delivers, and there's detail in all areas of the face. Note how this good contrast serves the whole image. The pupils in the young man's eyes are dark and intense. There's a highlight on his bottom lip and a very sharp and bright highlight on the edge of his hood where it meets the knit cap. The image is a study in textures. The outer jacket reads as a smooth nylon, like a windbreaker; the softness of the hood is visible, and the texture of the knit cap is rendered with bright pixels abutting very dark pixels at the holes in the knitting. When you view the image in terms of shadow, midtones, and highlights, there's much to appreciate.

Figure 3 Identifying shadows, midtones, and highlights

12. Continue to the next set of steps.

You used the Eyedropper tool in conjunction with the Info panel to explore the shadows, midtones, and highlights in the image.

Create an Invert adjustment layer

1. Drag the **Chart layer** to the **Delete layer button**  on the Layers panel.

The Chart layer is deleted.

2. Click **Image** on the menu bar, point to **Adjustments**, then click **Invert**.

This image is inverted. By using the menu command, the change is applied directly to the image on the Background layer. This is an example of destructive editing.

TIP For every adjustment layer on the Layers panel, there is a corresponding adjustment menu item on the Image/Adjustments menu. Remember that adjustment layers are nondestructive, making them a far superior method for applying adjustments than using the commands on the Image/Adjustments menu, which permanently alter the base image.

3. Undo the last step.

Next, you will apply the same adjustment using an adjustment layer.

4. Click the **Create new fill or adjustment layer button** on the Layers panel, then click **Invert**.

As shown in Figure 4, an Invert adjustment layer appears on the Layers panel with a default layer mask. As indicated on the gradient to the right, the entire range from black to white has been inverted: black pixels have changed from 0 to 255, and white pixels have changed from 255 to 0.

5. Hide and show the **Invert adjustment layer**.

Because the adjustment has been applied as an adjustment layer, it can be made visible or invisible like any other layer. The original artwork is affected only when the adjustment layer is visible. This is an example of nondestructive editing.

Continued on next page

Figure 4 Invert adjustment layer and the inverted artwork

6. Save your work and continue to the next set of steps.

You applied the Invert menu command, noting that it affected the image directly. After undoing that move, you applied the Invert adjustment as an adjustment layer, noting that you could hide and show the adjustment and the original image was not permanently affected.

Create a Threshold adjustment layer

1. Verify that the **Invert adjustment layer** is hidden and the **Background layer** is targeted.

2. Click the **Create new fill or adjustment layer button** 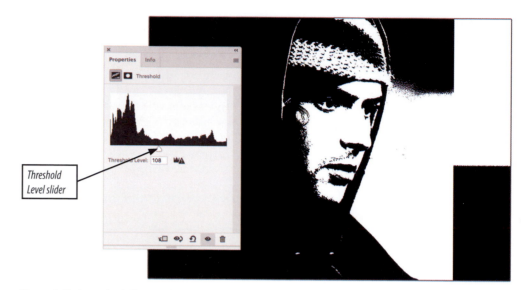 on the Layers panel, then click **Threshold**.

   All the pixels in the image become either black or white.

3. Verify that the **Properties panel** is visible.

   The Properties panel shows the settings for the current selected adjustment layer. For a Threshold adjustment, the default setting is 128, the midpoint of the grayscale range. Thus, in the image, the pixels whose grayscale values were 128 or above have all changed to white, and the pixels that were 127 or below have all changed to black. Note that the gradient on the right is now split vertically at the halfway point, its top half is white, and its bottom half is black.

4. Assess the effect on the image.

   It's a pretty cool effect. The man is recognizable, but his eyes and eyebrows are almost completely black and lack detail.

5. On the Properties panel, drag the **Threshold Level slider** to **108**.

Threshold Level slider

Figure 5 The image threshold set to 108

As shown in Figure 5, all pixels with a grayscale value of 108 or above are white. Note that the gradient on the right is no longer split 50-50 white over black; there's now more white than black. More pixels in the image of the man are now white, and his eyes are now rendered with more detail.

6. Show the **Invert adjustment layer**.

   The Threshold effect is inverted. Multiple adjustment layers affect other adjustments.

7. Hide the **Invert adjustment layer**, save the file, then continue to the next set of steps.

You created a Threshold adjustment layer then adjusted it to render the effect with more white pixels.

Create a Gradient Map adjustment layer

1. Hide both **adjustment layers**, then target the **Background layer**.

2. Click **Image** on the menu bar, point to **Mode**, then click **RGB Color**.

   If a warning box opens asking whether or not you want to flatten the image, click **Don't Flatten**.

3. Press the **letter [D]** on your keypad to set the foreground color to black and the background color to white.

4. Click the **Create new fill or adjustment layer button** 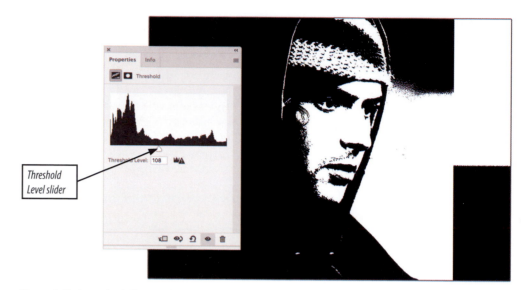 on the Layers panel, then click **Gradient Map**.

5. On the Properties panel, click the **black-to-white gradient** directly above the **Dither option**.

The Gradient Editor dialog box opens.

6. In the **Gradient Editor dialog box**, click the **left color stop**, click the **Color box**, choose a **dark blue**, then click **OK**.

The image changes from a black-to-white color range to dark blue to white.

7. Change the **right color stop** to a pale yellow color.

8. Add a **color stop** in the middle of the gradient, change its color to **orange**, then set its location to **45%**.

Your gradient settings should resemble Figure 6.

TIP Click the base of the gradient bar to add a new color stop.

9. Click **OK**, then compare your artwork to Figure 7.

10. Save your work, then close Basic Adjustments.

You added a Gradient Map adjustment layer, and then you specified the colors of the gradient applied to the image.

Adjust Brightness/Contrast

1. Open PS 5-2.psd, then save it as **Adjust Brightness and Contrast**.

2. Click **Select** on the menu bar, click **Load Selection**, click the **Channel list arrow**, click **Gradient at Bottom**, then click **OK**.

The gradient is darker on the left side than it is on the right, but the tonal range is short, from 108 to 212.

Continued on next page

Figure 6 Customizing the colors of the gradient

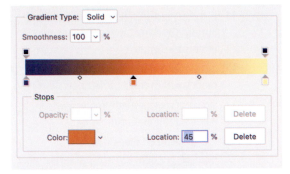

Figure 7 Viewing the Gradient Map adjustment

3. Click **Image** on the menu bar, point to **Adjustments**, then click **Brightness/Contrast**.

The Brightness/Contrast dialog box opens.

4. Click the **Use Legacy check box**, then drag the **Contrast slider** to **60**.

The darker pixels in the gradient are darkened to black, and the lighter pixels are lightened to white. Adding contrast moves pixels toward the extremes of the grayscale range

5. Drag the **Contrast slider** to **–60**.

The ends of the gradient move toward the middle of the grayscale range. These two steps are illustrated in Figure 8.

6. Click **Cancel**, click **Select** on the menu bar, then click **Inverse**.

7. Click **Image** on the menu bar, then click **Crop** to remove the gradient from the image.

8. Take a moment to assess the image and its tonal range.

As was the case with the gradient at the bottom, the shadows in the image are weak, and there are no highlights.

9. Using the Info panel, sample the highlight areas of the face, including the whites of the eyes, to get a general range of the values of the highlights in the image.

The values are generally 140–170, far too low for highlights, which should be greater than 200. This image is not bright enough.

10. Sample the hair and the image background area to the left of the face to get an idea of the general range of the shadows in the image.

The values are generally 40–70, which puts them at the high end of the shadow range.

11. Click the **Create new fill or adjustment layer button** 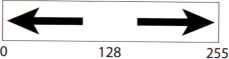 on the Layers panel, then click **Brightness/Contrast**.

12. On the Properties panel, click the **Use Legacy check box**, then drag the **Brightness slider** to **50**.

Increasing brightness increases the grayscale values of all the pixels in the image.

13. Drag the **Contrast slider** to **78**.

The shadows darken, and the highlights brighten. The shadows are improved dramatically, especially in the hair and the dark details of the face, like the pupils and the eyelashes.

14. Hide and show the **Brightness/Contrast adjustment layer** to see its effect.

Figure 9 shows the before and after views of the image. The improvement in the image is stunning.

Figure 8 Illustration of the relationship between contrast and grayscale

Increasing contrast moves values toward the black or white ends of the grayscale range

0   128   255

Decreasing contrast moves values toward the gray center of the grayscale range

0   128   255

Compared to the improved image, the original image looks like you're seeing it through a dusty and dirty window.

15. Save your work, then close Adjust Brightness and Contrast.

You added a Brightness/Contrast adjustment layer, then adjusted both the brightness and the contrast to dramatically improve the image.

Figure 9 Before and after views of the Brightness/Contrast adjustment

ADJUST LEVELS

Understanding the Levels Adjustment

Levels is an adjustment in Photoshop that allows you to manipulate the range of tone in an image, from shadow to highlight. The word "levels" refers to the concept that a grayscale image has 256 "levels" of gray and that an RGB image has 256 "levels" of in each channel. You can use the Levels adjustment to define the darkest and brightest point in an image, and you can define the middle tone between the two extremes. Making these adjustments with levels redistributes the image data along the grayscale range. Generally speaking, you use the Levels adjustment to improve the contrast in an image.

Adjusting Black and White Points with Levels

In addition to the shadow, midtone, and highlight ranges, every image has a **black point**, the very darkest pixel in the image, and a **white point**, the very lightest pixel in the image. The black and white points are critical to the appearance of the image because they represent the start and the end of the tonal range.

Today's digital cameras, including the camera in your phone, are so sophisticated that most images need little or no correction for contrast or color balance. However, when an image is captured in poor lighting conditions, the image quality will also be poor, regardless of how sophisticated the camera is. That's where Photoshop adjustments can help.

In some cases, professional photographers will define their camera settings so the darkest pixel will be no darker than 15, and the brightest pixel will be no lighter than 240. This forces the camera not to make shadows too dark or highlights too white. It results in an image that has a smooth tonal range from shadow to highlight, and it allows for the black and white points to be improved in Photoshop.

When adjusting images with levels, the first standard move is to verify that the black and white points are at their optimal grayscale value—that is, that the black point is at or close to zero and that the white point is at or close to 255.

Figure 10 shows the Levels adjustment settings on the Properties panel. Notice the three eyedropper tools on the left. These are sampling tools for setting the black (shadow) point, gray (midpoint) point, and white (highlight) point. You use these tools by clicking in the image. For example, where you click the white point eyedropper determines the whitest point in the image, and where you click the black point eyedropper determines the darkest point. Use these tools to get a sense of what the image might look like with different white and black points. The moves are not permanent, and you can always readjust. Not everyone uses the eyedroppers to set black and white points, but it's a great way to identify the 255 and 0 pixels before you make any adjustments.

These tools offer another great feature. If you click the white point eyedropper, then press [option] (Mac) or [Alt] (Win), the entire image turns black, except for the pixels with a grayscale value of 255, which remain white. This is a great way to know where you can find white pixels in the image. (If the entire canvas displays black, that's because the image contains no white pixels.)

Conversely, when you click the black point eyedropper, then press [option] (Mac) or [Alt] (Win), the entire image turns white, except for the pixels with a grayscale value of 0, which remain black.

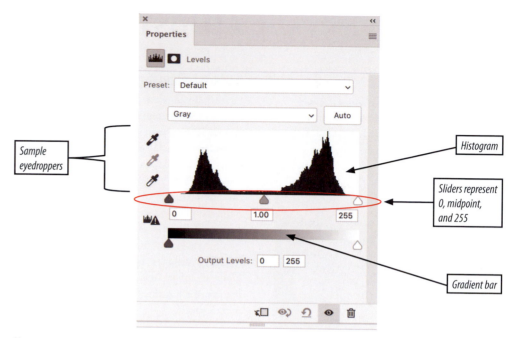

Figure 10 Levels adjustment on the Properties panel

Understanding the Histogram

The most striking component of the Levels adjustment is the histogram. The **histogram** is a graph of the image data and where that data is positioned on the grayscale range.

Using Figure 10 as a reference, imagine that the Levels adjustment has 256 slots between the black triangle on the left and the white triangle on the right, one slot for each of the 256 available colors in the grayscale image. The slot for the 0-value pixels is on the left, and the slot for the 255-value pixels is on the right. Imagine that the image is composed of 100,000 pixels and 1,000 of them have a grayscale value of 64. Using a black marble to represent each pixel, imagine that you drop 1,000 marbles into the 64-value slot on the slider. Next, imagine that the image contains 2,000 pixels with a grayscale value of 72, and you drop 2,000 black marbles into the 72-value slot. The marbles in that slot will go twice as high as in the 64-value slot.

Imagine that you do this for each of the 256 slots on the slider. Your result would be the histogram—exactly what you see on the Properties panel. From left to right, the histogram shows the distribution of the pixels in the image, from 0 to 255. The varying heights of the histogram show the concentration of pixels at any given point on the grayscale range.

Understanding How the Levels Adjustment Works

With the Levels adjustment, you modify the tonal range of the image by manipulating the sliders directly below the histogram. The black triangle represents 0 on the grayscale range. The white triangle represents 255. The gray triangle represents the midpoint between the two.

When you move any of the triangles, you readjust how the histogram relates to the full *potential* grayscale range, from shadow to highlight. For example, wherever you place the white triangle, the grayscale values of the pixels at that spot on the histogram change to 255. Wherever you place the black triangle, those pixels change to 0. All the data between those two points will now be redistributed.

The gray triangle, or midpoint slider, separates the light half of the image from the dark half. Wherever you place the gray triangle sets those pixels at 128; therefore, any part of the histogram to the right of the gray triangle must have grayscale values higher than 128, and any pixels to the left must have grayscale values 127 or lower. To put it another way, the more you move the gray triangle to the left, the brighter the image will become, because more of the histogram will be to the right of the gray midpoint triangle.

Adjusting the tonal range of an image is a lot like knowing which fork to use in fine dining—you start at the outside and work your way in. First, set your black and white points—the extremes. If that one move delivers satisfactory contrast throughout the image, you are ready to (if you want) adjust the midpoint. Essentially, the midpoint darkens or lightens the image. Interestingly, a midpoint adjustment is often only subjective, depending on your preference for a lighter or a darker image overall.

TIP Because of the complexity of Photoshop's algorithms, where you place the gray channel will define those pixels as the middle value of the histogram, but not necessarily as 128. We used the number 128 in the preceding explanation because 128 is the middle number between 0 and 255. Photoshop's calculation of the midpoint won't be quite so simple. Nevertheless, you should think of the gray midpoint slider as the "middle gray" of the image.

Understanding the Relationship Between Contrast and Color

When improving a black and white image, a dynamic range of shadow to highlight produces a dynamic black and white image. When it comes to color images, the relationship between contrast and color isn't quite as intuitive. This is because, when considering the improvement of color in a color image, most people think that means shifting the color balance of the image, for example, making the photo less red or less yellow or more neutral.

In fact, good contrast and good color are inextricably linked. For an image to have vibrant color, it's necessary to have a dynamic tonal range with deep shadows and bright highlights. Just like a black and white image with poor contrast, you can't get bright yellows and deep blues in a color image with poor contrast.

Today's digital cameras are of such high quality and so finely calibrated—even those in most smart phones—that color balance problems and contrast problems have become somewhat rare. Even in poor lighting conditions, most cameras will produce an image with neutral, balanced color. For those images, you will find that correcting the highlight and shadow points and improving the overall contrast will be enough to bring out vibrant and balanced color in the image.

Using Layer Masks with Adjustments

When you create an adjustment layer, it is created with a layer mask by default. The layer mask is often an essential component of working with adjustment layers. Sometimes, you will make an adjustment that you can apply completely to the artwork, but more often, you will want to use the layer mask to apply the adjustment selectively in different strengths to different areas.

Some designers make it an automatic part of their process to mask the adjustment completely and then use a low-opacity brush to paint white in the mask, thus "brushing in" the adjustment gradually in specific areas. Working with this method allows you to apply an adjustment in a way that is more customized and unique to the given artwork.

Because masking is so essential, you need to choose the right brush for the job. This means using the best brush size and edge hardness for a given goal. The decisions you make—especially for the edge hardness—will have a direct effect on the success of the mask.

Brush settings allow you to specify the edge of a brush in terms of hardness: 100% is the hardest-edged brush, and 0% is the softest-edged brush. You can think of a hard brush as having a smooth, crisp, anti-aliased edge, and you can think of a brush with 0% hardness as having a feathered edge. The size of the feathered edge increases and decreases proportionately with the size of the brush.

In other words, if you're using a soft brush with a brush size of 100 pixels, the feathered edge on that brush will be much wider than the feathered edge on a brush with a brush size of 10 pixels.

Investigate the histogram

1. Open PS 5-3.psd, then save it as **Adjusting Levels**.

2. Enter **[command] [L] (Mac)** or **[Ctrl] [L] (Win)**.

   The Levels dialog box opens. The histogram shows the distribution of the pixels in the image, from the darkest pixels to the lightest pixels. For this exercise, you are going to make selections and note where those pixels appear on the histogram.

To keep things simple, you're going to use the Levels dialog box on the Image menu, not a Levels adjustment on the Layers panel.

3. Click **Cancel**.

4. Click the **Rectangular Marquee tool** [⬚], then make a small selection of the **interior of one of the petals**.

5. Enter **[command] [L] (Mac)** or **[Ctrl] [L] (Win)**.

   As shown in Figure 11, the histogram now shows only the selected pixels. The petal is a lighter area of the image, and those pixels are located at the upper half of the histogram.

6. Click **Cancel**, then make a selection of the **top-left corner of the background**.

Figure 11 A selection of lighter pixels represented on the histogram

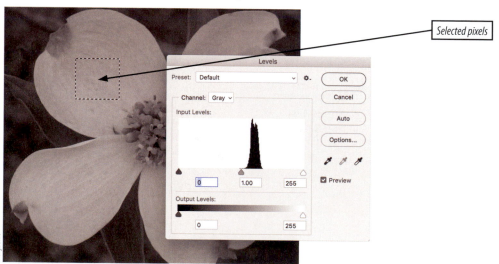

Selected pixels

Morguefile

7. Enter **[command] [L] (Mac)** or **[Ctrl] [L] (Win)**.

As shown in Figure 12, the selected pixels appear on the lower half of the histogram, closer to the black triangle.

8. Click **Cancel**.

9. Deselect, click **Image** on the menu bar, point to **Adjustments**, click **Posterize**, enter **3** in the Levels text box, then click **OK**.

The pixels in the image are now black, gray, or white. There are far fewer white pixels compared to gray and black.

10. Enter **[command] [L] (Mac)** or **[Ctrl] [L] (Win)**.

As shown in Figure 13, the histogram is just three vertical lines: one at the 0 representing the black pixels; a taller line at the center, representing the majority gray pixels; and a short line at 255, representing the few white pixels.

11. Click **OK**, click **File** on the menu bar, then click **Revert**.

The file is returned to its original state to be used in the next set of steps.

You explored how the histogram represents the image by selecting light and dark areas of the image and noting where they appear on the histogram. You posterized the image to three levels and then noted that the histogram showed just three lines.

Figure 12 A selection of darker pixels represented on the histogram

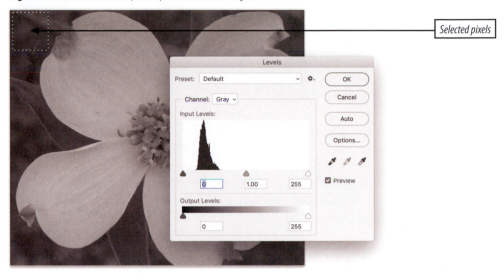

Selected pixels

Figure 13 The posterized image represented by three lines on the histogram

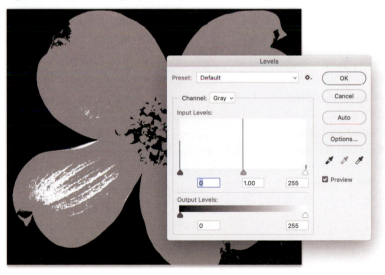

Employ the Levels adjustment

1. Click the **Create new fill or adjustment layer button** 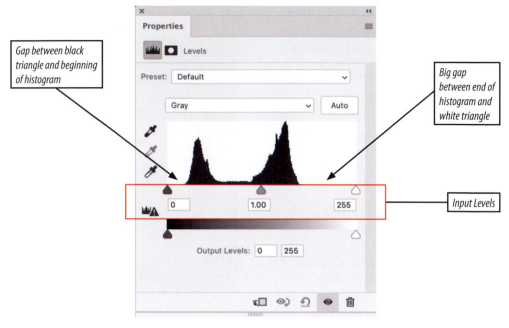 on the Layers panel, then click **Levels**.

   Note that merely creating a new adjustment layer does nothing to affect the image. Only when you manipulate the settings in an adjustment layer do you affect the image.

2. Assess the image for contrast and assess the histogram on the Properties panel.

   The image has poor contrast. The shadows are weak, and the highlights are gray and dull. As shown in Figure 14, the histogram reflects this assessment of the image. Left to right, the histogram has a short range. On the left side, it does not extend into the darker areas of the grayscale range, and on the right side, there's a big gap between the end of the histogram and the white triangle. That gap represents a range of high-numbered bright pixels on the grayscale range not being used to render the highlights in the image. The same is true for the darker pixels on the left side of the histogram.

3. Drag the **black triangle**, directly below the histogram, to the right to line it up with the beginning of the histogram.

   The shadow input level should be 22. Before you moved the black triangle, the darkest pixels in the image had a grayscale value of 22. Now those pixels have a grayscale value of 0 (black).

   TIP In this lesson, you will only drag the triangles in the Input Levels section—those immediately below the histogram, not those in the Output Levels section.

Gap between black triangle and beginning of histogram

Big gap between end of histogram and white triangle

Input Levels

Figure 14 Assessing the histogram

4. Click the **set black point eyedropper tool** on the Properties panel float over the image, then press **[option] (Mac)** or **[Alt] (Win)**.

   The entire canvas turns white except for any pixels that have a grayscale value of 0, which remain black. In the case of this image, those pixels are very few and at the center of the canvas.

5. Drag the **white triangle** to the left to line up with the end of the histogram.

   The highlight input level should be 183. Before you moved the white triangle, the brightest pixels in the image data had a grayscale value of 183. Now, those pixels have a value of 255 (white).

6. Click the **set white point eyedropper tool** , float over the image, then press **[option] (Mac)** or **[Alt] (Win)**.

   The entire canvas turns black except for any remaining white pixels. There are very few of those pixels on the bottom-left petal, where it folds over itself. The fact that so few pixels are 0 and 255 tells you that the image is using the full range of the grayscale, but not overly so.

7. Drag the **gray triangle**, directly below the histogram, to the left so that the **midtone input level** is **1.04**.

   The image is slightly brighter.

8. Assess the improvements to the image.

The petals in the image are now white, not light gray. They are dramatically brighter, but the fine detail in the petals has all been retained. The shadows are darker, but there is still detail throughout.

9. Select the **Eyedropper tool** 🖋, on the toolbar, then float it over the shadow and highlight areas of the image.

The Info panel shows before and after readouts that reflect darker shadows and brighter highlight areas. These changes are particularly dramatic on the petals, where you can find before and after readouts with a difference of more than 50 grayscale levels.

10. Add a **second Levels adjustment layer**, then compare its histogram to Figure 15.

The image data in the histogram is now distributed across the length of the grayscale, from 0 to 255. Thus, the shadows are deep and dark, and the highlights are bright. Compare this histogram in Figure 15 to the histogram in Figure 14, and you can see that the work you did in Steps 3–5 affected the *entire* image. All the data has been *redistributed*; the tonal range has been *extended* to take full advantage of the available range of tones.

11. Drag the **white triangle** left to change the **highlight input level** to **218**, drag the **black triangle** to the right to change the **shadow**

input level to **17**, then compare your results to Figure 16.

These changes are not acceptable for the flower because the highlights on the petal are blown out. Note that the petals are now just "flat" white; there's no longer any detail. This is represented on the histogram. All the data to the right of the white triangle—all those pixels—are now all 255. At the left side of the histogram, all the pixels to the left of the black triangle, which used to be a range of shadow values, are now black.

TIP Read the *Explore Extreme Adjustments* sidebar.

Continued on next page

Figure 15 Assessing the adjusted histogram

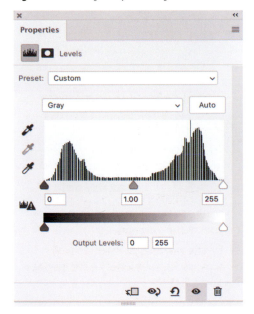

Figure 16 Blown-out highlights on the image reflected in the histogram

12. Focus on the **buds** at the center of the flower, then hide and show the **second Levels adjustment layer**.

    The second Levels adjustment layer is an improvement to the buds, despite being bad for the petals. The buds' highlights are brighter without blowing out, and the shadows are deeper.

13. Enter **[command] [I] (Mac)** or **[Ctrl] [I] (Win)** to invert the second Levels adjustment layer.

    The entire Levels adjustment is masked.

14. Click the **Brush tool** 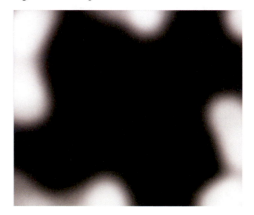 on the toolbar, set the **Size** to **100 px**, set the **Hardness** to **0%**, set the **Mode** to **Normal**, then set the **Opacity** to **30%**.

15. Set the **foreground color** to **white**, then paint over the buds to "brush in" the Levels adjustment in that location only.

16. Look past the flower petals and focus only the background of the image.

    The leaves in the background have brighter edges, but those brighter edges are a dull gray. We will use a third adjustment layer to improve the dullness of the leaf edges.

17. Add a **third Levels adjustment**, then assess the histogram.

    By now, you've noted that the histogram for this image has the appearance of two mountains. If you look at the image itself, it only makes sense

that the larger mountain on the right represents all the brighter pixels that render the petals, and the smaller mountain on the left represents the darker pixels that make up the background.

18. Drag the **white triangle** left past the right "mountain" until the **highlight input level** is **158**, then drag the **black triangle** to the right until the **shadow input level** is **8**.

    The entire flower is blown out to white, and the background lightens dramatically. The shadows in the background are darker. The tonal range of the background is now using the full range of the grayscale, as you can see on the highlights of the edges of the leaves, which are now brighter.

19. Invert the mask.

    The entire adjustment is masked.

20. Change the brush **Size** to **200 px**, then change the **Opacity** to **40%**.

21. Working from the outside in, gradually "brush in" the adjustment on the background only without affecting the petals.

If you're a new user, you might have the instinct to brush this adjustment in at 100% opacity with a hard line along the flower so as to not affect the petals. That's not the way you want to go. Think of this adjustment as a subtle adjustment. You want to gradually "bump up" the areas you can get

to with the big soft brush. Consider avoiding small, "surgical" moves in narrow areas such as those between the petals. If you do go into those areas with a small brush, it will be challenging to show the adjustment while keeping your presence invisible. Smaller brushes have a smaller feather at their edges and leave behind harder lines.

22. Press and hold **[option] (Mac)** or **[Alt] (Win)**, then click the **mask** to view the mask.

    Figure 17 shows the **mask** the author painted.

23. Click the **histogram thumbnail** on the Levels 3 layer on the Layers panel to view the image instead of the mask.

Figure 17 Viewing the mask

24. Shift-click to select all **three adjustment layers** on the Layers panel, then enter **[command] [G] (Mac)** or **[Ctrl] [G] (Win)** to place them into a group.

    The three Levels adjustment layers are grouped into a new group layer (named Group 1 by default).

25. Hide and show the **Group 1 layer**.

    Figure 18 shows the image before and after the adjustments.

26. Save your work, then continue to the next set of steps.

AUTHOR'S NOTE This exercise is a great example of how gratifying adjusting images can be. One enjoyable element of this work is the designer's invisible role. If you executed this assignment well, there should be no trace of you anywhere in the image. You shouldn't see any kind of a white halo at the center where you brushed in the brighter buds, and you shouldn't see any "hot spots" on the edges of the petals where you brushed in the background. None of your Levels adjustments should have been so extreme that they catch the eye. It should not appear manipulated or doctored in any way. Instead, the image should be simply beautiful on its own. The greatest compliment you, as the designer, can get is the viewer's total lack of awareness that you were ever there at all.

You made a Levels adjustment to correct the shadow and highlight points for the flower image, thereby improving the contrast throughout the entire image. You then used two more Levels adjustments in conjunction with layer masks to adjust specific areas of the image. Finally, you grouped the three adjustment layers so you could hide and show all three simultaneously to see a before and after view of the image.

EXPLORE EXTREME ADJUSTMENTS

Sometimes, the best method for making effective adjustments is to walk the fine line between going far enough to make the adjustment the best it can be and then going too far. As a designer, you can do exactly that—push the adjustment to the extreme to see what it looks like when it's too much. When you find that line, pull back a bit, and you'll know you've gone far enough but not too far. When you work this way, seeing what you don't want can make it easier to find what you do want. You're training your eye to recognize when an image looks its best, and recognizing when an image looks *bad* is a big part of that training.

Figure 18 Before and after views of the Levels adjustments

Adjust levels on a color image

1. Verify that the **Group 1 layer** is showing.

2. Click **Image** on the menu bar, point to **Mode**, click **RGB Color**, then click **Don't Flatten** if a dialog box appears.

   When the flower image and the three Levels adjustments are converted from Grayscale to RGB Color, the adjustments affect the flower image differently. The lower petals are now blown out. The Levels 1 adjustment needs to be readjusted.

3. Expand the **Group 1 layer**, then target the **Levels 1 adjustment**.

4. On the Properties panel, drag the **white triangle** to **203**, drag the **black triangle** to **29**, then collapse the **Group 1 layer**.

   With minor tweaks, the image once again has excellent contrast and is visually dynamic.

5. Save your work and keep this file open.

6. Open PS 5-4.psd.

   This is the same image in color that you've been working on in black and white.

7. Select all, copy, close the file, then return to the Adjusting Levels file.

8. Verify that the **Group 1 layer** is collapsed and targeted, then paste.

   Because the Group 1 layer was collapsed and targeted, the pasted image was placed in a new layer above the Group 1 layer and not inside it.

9. Target the **Group 1 layer**, click **Layer** on the menu bar, then click **Duplicate Group**.

   The Duplicate Group dialog box opens.

10. Type **Color Adjustments** in the As text box, then click **OK**.

11. Drag the new **Color Adjustments group layer** above Layer 1 on the Layers panel.

    As shown in Figure 19, the impact that the three Levels adjustments have on the color flower is dramatic. The highlights are bright without being blown out, the shadows have substance, the colors are rich, and the whole image is vibrant. The same adjustments that were applied to improve the black and white image did the exact same thing for the color image. The color is much more vibrant in the corrected image because the highlight and shadow points are on target and the contrast is excellent. You could not achieve this level of vibrant color without excellent contrast.

    AUTHOR'S NOTE Converting modes with adjustments, as we did in Step 2, is something you'll likely never do in your own work. As you saw, it adversely affected the adjustments. We did this only as part of a teaching exercise.

12. Save your work, then close Adjusting Levels.

You converted the grayscale file to RGB Color. You noted that the shift to a different color mode negatively affected how one of the Levels adjustments was affecting the image, so you tweaked that adjustment. You duplicated the adjustments and applied them to a color version of the same image, noting

that the same adjustments improved the color in the image and making the connection that excellent contrast is the key to excellent color.

Figure 19 Before and after views of the same Levels adjustments on a color image

INVESTIGATE THE RGB COLOR MODEL

What You'll Do

In this lesson, you'll learn about the RGB Color model in depth.

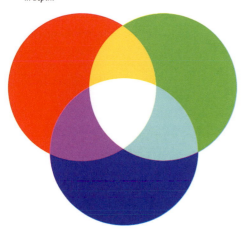

Investigating RGB in Photoshop

A **color model** is a mathematical model that describes how colors can be represented as numbers, usually as a way for computers to process color. Photoshop incorporates many different color models, including RGB, HSL, CMYK, Lab color, and Hexadecimal color.

RGB (Red, Green, Blue) is the primary color model that Photoshop uses to render color images. In an RGB image, each pixel can be one of 256 shades of red, 256 shades of green, and 256 shades of blue.

On the Channels panel, you will find a Red, a Green, and a Blue channel. Each is a grayscale image displaying pixels from 0 to 255 for that channel. In the Red channel, for example, the range is from black, at 0, to red, at 255.

Whenever red, green, and blue values are equal, the pixel's color will be black, white, or a range of gray in between. Black pixels have an RGB value of 0R/0G/0B. White pixels are 255R/255G/255B. Middle gray pixels have an RGB value of 128R/128G/128B.

Whenever red, green, and blue values are not equal, they produce colors. For example, orange colors are created with a high percentage of red and a lower percentage of green and little or no blue. One specific hue of orange can be rendered as 255R/128G/0B.

Investigating RGB on Your Computer Screen

Think of a white screen on your computer. Imagine, for example, that you're looking at a blank document in Microsoft Word or a white canvas in Photoshop. That white screen is actually composed of three colors—red, blue, and green, mixed together in equal measure. Now imagine a rainbow across your screen, perhaps a gradient in Photoshop with a spectrum of pink, purple, orange, yellow, cyan, and magenta. Those colors, too, are all produced on your monitor with the same three colors: red, green, and blue. In fact, in the actual hardware of your computer screen, the light emitting components are red lights, green lights, and blue lights. Figure 20 shows an illustration of this concept. With those three colored lights, your computer can render all the color you see every day on your screen.

If you flick a few drops of water onto a computer monitor, the water droplets will magnify and refract the light on the computer screen, enabling you to see the tiny red, green, and blue lights that are the light source for the computer screen. The white that you see on the screen is actually red, green, and blue monitor pixels combining equally to produce white light.

Investigating RGB in the Natural World

Red, green, and blue lights making all the colors on your computer screen, including white, mimics color in the natural world. Use Figure 21 as an illustration for this discussion. The great light source in our world is, of course, the sun. The sum total of light radiation from the sun is called the **electromagnetic spectrum**. The spectrum is measured in waves and includes such familiar components as radio waves, microwaves, x-rays, and ultraviolet rays.

Figure 20 Illustration of red, green, and blue light on a computer monitor

Oleg Gawriloff/Shutterstock.com

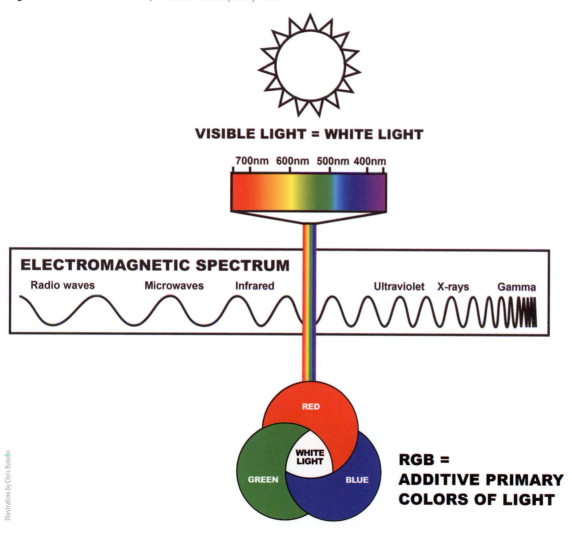

VISIBLE LIGHT = WHITE LIGHT

700nm 600nm 500nm 400nm

ELECTROMAGNETIC SPECTRUM

Radio waves   Microwaves   Infrared   Ultraviolet X-rays Gamma

RED

WHITE LIGHT

GREEN   BLUE

RGB =
ADDITIVE PRIMARY
COLORS OF LIGHT

Illustration by Chris Botello

Only a small subset of the electromagnetic spectrum is visible to the human eye. The typical human eye can see wavelengths between 380 and 750 nanometers. This subset is called **visible light**. As humans, we perceive all visible light as colorless; therefore, the visible spectrum is also called **white light**.

Through the process of **refraction**, white light can be broken down to make its component wavelengths visible. Figure 22 shows a prism refracting white light, making the visible spectrum visible. The **visible spectrum** is red, orange, yellow, green, blue, indigo, and violet, which has the nickname *roygbiv*.

Red light, green light, and blue light (RGB) are the **additive primary colors** of white light. The term "additive" refers to the fact that RGB light can combine in infinite measures to produce all the colors of the visible spectrum; the term "primary" refers to the fact the red light, green light, and blue light cannot themselves be refracted or broken down. For example, yellow light is a component of the visible spectrum, but it is not primary, because yellow light is created when red light and green light combine. Therefore, yellow light can be broken down to red light and green light. Those two primary colors, however, cannot be broken down.

This phenomenon occurs in nature, as you know, when you see a rainbow. For a rainbow to occur, there must be rain and bright sunlight. The droplets of water function as tiny prisms that refract the sunlight and make the visible spectrum visible in the sky. It's quite profound to consider that something so beautiful and magical to our human eyes exists as a scientific fact of nature.

When RGB combine in equal measure, they produce white light. Therefore, what we perceive as white is the combination of all colors. Black, on the other hand, is the absence of light, and therefore the absence of all colors.

Investigating How Our Eyes Interpret RGB

It is fascinating to think of our tiny human eyeball as the receptor for the immense ball of light that we call the sun, but the identification is correct. Light makes human vision possible, and the only true light in the world is sunlight. Consider the millions of years of evolution that have fashioned the human eye not only to perceive our world but also to perceive the infinite range of beautiful color in our world. It is a consideration both astounding and humbling.

Figure 22 Illustration of a prism refracting white light into the visible spectrum

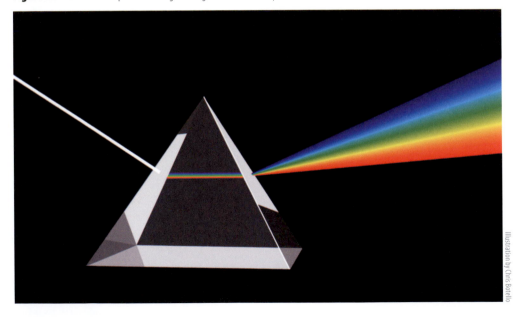

Illustration by Chris Botello

Figure 23 shows an illustration of the human eye. Our eyes contain receptor cells called **rods** and **cones**.

Rod cells process and perceive light as a range from highlight to shadow. Therefore, our perception of shape and size and distance and perspective relies on the rod receptors in the physiology of our eyes. It has likely never occurred to you how bizarre it is that we watch old black and white movies and fully accept them as reality, when in fact not one of us has ever lived in a black and white world. The rod receptors in our eyes make sense of those images, and that suggests we don't rely on color as much as we think we do to understand our world.

Cone cells perceive color. Some cone cells are sensitive to red light, some to green light, and some to blue light. Therefore, our eyes essentially break down white light into reds, greens, and blues.

One can only imagine the delicate balance and calibration our eyes rely upon to process and perceive color. People who are color blind have a deficiency in the cone cells in their eyes for a specific color. Red-green colorblindness is the most common, and those people have difficulty distinguishing between some red and green hues.

Humans have discovered all kinds of ways to manipulate (and have fun with) these physiological realities of color perception. You are probably familiar with old-fashioned 3-D glasses with a red plastic lens on one side

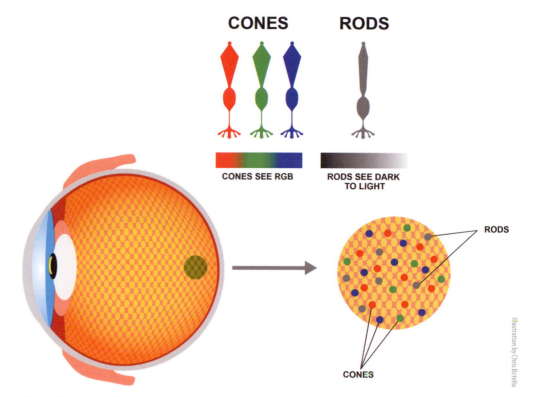

Figure 23 Illustration of rods and cones in the human eye

Illustration by Chris Botello

and a blue plastic lens on the other. Those glasses created a three-dimensional effect by separating the perception of red and blue light in each eye and using that separation to create an artificial perception of different depths. In the late 1960s, people would create outdoor "red rooms," which were small rooms lit with only red light. Standing in that room for a short amount of time would overstimulate the red cone receptors in their

eyes and simultaneously starve the green and blue receptors. Then, when they stepped out into the bright white light of day, their minds would "see" the intense greens of nature's flora and the profound blues of an immense sky. What was really happening was that those starved green and blue receptor cells were drinking in all the sudden green and blue light while the overstimulated red receptors had had their fill.

Another interesting optical color phenomenon is called a green flash. You can see a green flash shortly after sunset or just before sunrise. When the sun is almost entirely behind the horizon, with only the barest edge still visible, the eye might perceive a sky full of green for just a few seconds.

All of this is a great reminder that color is perception and entirely dependent on the lighting conditions in our world.

Investigating Subtractive Primary Colors

Cyan, magenta, and yellow (CMY) are the **subtractive primary colors**. Each is created by *subtracting* one of the additive primary colors. To put it a different way, each is created by combining two additive primaries. Figure 24 shows the subtractive primary colors.

Cyan is created by removing red light and combining green and blue light equally. Thus, cyan is also referred to as "minus red."

Magenta is created by removing green light and combining red and blue light equally. Thus, magenta is also referred to as "minus green."

Yellow is created by removing blue light and combining red and green light equally. Thus, yellow is also referred to as "minus blue."

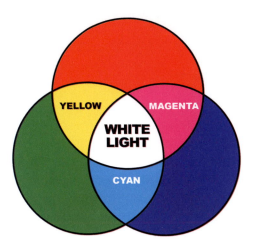

Figure 24 Subtractive primary colors

This relationship between CMY and RGB is reflected in the Color Balance adjustment, shown in Figure 25. The Color Balance settings show that Cyan is opposite Red, Magenta is opposite Green, and Yellow is opposite Blue. Therefore, any adjustment you make is either a move toward or away from an additive primary.

The world of subtractive primary colors is a world unto itself. For the purposes of this discussion, think of cyan, magenta, and yellow as "primary" *not for light* but only for human-made colors, such as pigments, inks, paints, and the like. For example, you might know that cyan, magenta, and yellow are the three

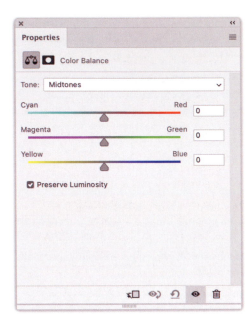

Figure 25 Color Balance adjustment settings

ink colors used to produce all other colors in conventional offset printing. When it comes to working with Photoshop (and using this book), all you should focus on is that CMY are each created by subtracting red, green, and blue light, respectively. Only RGB are the primary colors of light because they can't be refracted and broken down to other colors. Based on that definition, cyan, magenta, and yellow are *not* primary colors of light because each is composed of two additive primary colors.

View RGB on your computer monitor

1. Open PS 5-5.psd, then verify that only the **Background layer** is showing.

2. Make the **Freak Flag layer** visible.

3. Move the **Layers panel** out of the way so you can see the entire flag.

4. Position the mouse pointer over the **eye button** 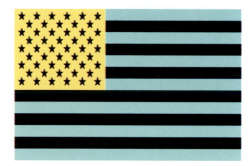 on the **Freak Flag layer** so you will be ready to hide the layer in the next step without looking away from the flag.

5. Stare at the **lower-right black star** for a full 30 seconds then, without looking away, click the **eye button** 👁 to hide the flag and stare at the white canvas for 45 seconds longer.

   Instantly you see the red, white, and blue American flag on the white canvas. If you continue to stare, it will fade in and out. As you stare at the flag, shown in Figure 26, your eyes are starved for red light in the stripes, blue light in the square, and all light in the black areas. When the white screen is restored, all colors are present in equal measure. However, the color receptors in your eyes that were deprived of certain colors are now overly sensitive to them. They are "drinking them in," so to speak. Therefore,

Figure 26 Minus red, minus white, and minus blue flag

your eyes are literally pulling red light out of the white light for the stripes and pulling blue light out of the white light in the rectangle. Even the white stripes on the flag are brighter white.

6. Show the **RGB layer**.

7. Stare for 30 seconds at the center blue and red stripes, then hide the layer.

   You instantly see cyan, magenta, and yellow stripes. When you stare at the red stripes, your eyes are starved for green light and blue light. When the red stripes are removed, your eyes pull green light and blue light from the white light in those

areas. Those areas appear as cyan, because cyan is created from combining green and blue light. The same principle explains why you see magenta and yellow stripes in place of the other two additive primary colors.

8. Close the file without saving changes.

You used two illustrations to perceive the color receptors in your own eyes.

Mix colors with RGB

1. Open PS 5-6.psd, then verify that your computer screen is turned up to full brightness.

2. Move the **Green circle** left so it overlaps the **Red circle**.

   The overlap is yellow because red light and green light combine to make yellow light.

3. Move the **Green circle** down so it overlaps the **Blue circle**.

   The overlap is cyan because green light and blue light combine to make cyan light.

4. Overlap the **Blue circle** with the **Red circle**.

   The overlap is magenta because red light and blue light combine to make magenta light.

Continued on next page

5. Overlap all three circles, as shown in Figure 27.

Where the three circles overlap, the area is white, with an RGB value of 255R/255G/255B. Overlapping RGB in equal measure produces white when the RGB components are each 255. White is the combination of all three additive primaries.

6. Reduce the **Opacity** on all three layers to **50%**.

The overlap area is gray, with an RGB value of 128R/128G/128B. At lower values, the overlap produces gray.

7. Increase the **Opacity** on the **Red layer** to **100%**.

As shown in Figure 28, the red/green overlap creates orange, the green/blue overlap creates a dark cyan, and the blue/red overlap creates a dark magenta. The area where all three colors overlap is a muted pink color. The RGB value of that pink is 255R/128G/128B.

8. Set the **Opacity** on the **Red layer** to **50%**, the **Green layer** to **20%**, and the **Blue layer** to **100%**.

As shown in Figure 29, purple hues are created when blue dominates and green is highly reduced. Note that where the red and green overlap produces a dark orange, bordering on a brown.

9. Close the file without saving changes.

You experimented with RGB in different combinations to produce white, gray, and different colors.

Figure 27 Mixing RGB to produce white

Figure 28 Mixing RGB with red dominating

Figure 29 Mixing RGB with blue dominating

Manipulate RGB in a Photoshop image

1. Open PS 5-7.psd, then save it as **RGB Color Balance**.

   This image has a yellow tone overall, which makes for a beautiful image. However, the color balance can be manipulated to create other tones that are equally interesting.

2. Verify that the **Sunset layer** is targeted, click the **Create new fill or adjustment layer button** on the Layers panel, then click **Color Balance**.

   Color Balance adjustment settings appear on the Properties panel. Each of the subtractive primaries is opposite its additive primary—Cyan is opposite Red, Magenta is opposite Green, and Yellow is opposite Blue.

3. On the Properties panel, note that **Tone** is set to **Midtones**. Drag the **top slider** to **+43**, then drag the **middle slider** to **−36**.

4. Click the **Tone list arrow**, then choose **Highlights**.

5. Drag the **top slider** to **+26**, then drag the **middle slider** to **−21**.

   Your screen should resemble Figure 30. Moving the midtones and highlights toward red and away from green has produced an overall red color balance to the image.

6. Click the **Reset to adjustment defaults button** on the Properties panel.

   The adjustments you made are removed.

7. Drag the **top slider** to **−28**, then drag the **bottom slider** to **+44** to adjust the midtones.

Continued on next page

Figure 30 Shifting the overall color balance to red

Morguefile

USE THE ERASER TOOL

The Eraser tool is a quick way to erase pixels from an image. When a layer is targeted, the Eraser tool will erase pixels leaving transparent areas. In a flattened image (all layers are flattened to one background layer), the Eraser tool paints with the current background color.

8. Click the **Tone list arrow**, choose **Shadows**, drag the **top slider** to **–27**, then drag the **bottom slider** to **+37**.

9. Click the **Tone list arrow**, choose **Highlights**, drag the **top slider** to **–20**, then drag the **bottom slider** to **+15**.

   Your screen should resemble Figure 31. Moving the midtones and highlights away from red and toward blue has produced an overall blue color balance to the image. If you compare the two figures from this exercise, you can see the dramatic difference in color that can be achieved by adjusting the color balance.

10. Save your work, then close RGB Color Balance.

You used the Color Balance adjustment to shift the color dramatically from its original overall yellow effect to an overall red then an overall blue effect.

Explore shape vs. color

1. Open PS 5-8.psd, then save it as **Rods and Cones**.

2. Click **Select** on the menu bar, click **Load Selection**, load the selection named **Circle**, then click **OK**.

3. Click **Edit** on the menu bar, click **Fill**, click the **Contents list arrow**, click **50% Gray**, then click **OK** to fill the circle with **50% Gray**.

4. Hide the **selection marquee**, click the **Brush tool** , then set the **foreground color** on the toolbar to **white**.

TIP To hide the selection marquee, press [command] [H] (Mac) or [Ctrl] [H] (Win).

5. Set the Brush tool **Size** to **400 px**, then set the **Hardness** to **0%**.

Figure 31 Shifting the overall color balance to blue

6. Set the **Opacity** to **20%**, then position the brush at the **center of the gray circle**.

7. Click the **brush** one time.

8. Move the brush **slightly to the right**, then click again to paint a highlight.

9. Repeat the preceding step 14 times (moving the brush slightly to the right each time) to complete the highlight.

   Your artwork should resemble Figure 32.

10. Change the **foreground color** to **black**.

11. Approaching the circle from the outside and overlapping slightly, paint a shadow counterclockwise from 9 o'clock to 5 o'clock.

12. Repeat Step 11 two or three times to create a deeper shadow without going all the way to black.

Your artwork should resemble Figure 33. With shadows and highlights, the flat gray circle has transformed into a sphere. As a circle, its shape was defined by its perimeter. As a sphere, its shape is defined by its dimensionality.

13. Click the **Create new fill or adjustment layer button** ⊘ on the Layers panel, then click **Hue/Saturation**.

14. On the Properties panel, click the **Colorize check box**.

   The Colorize option applies a single hue, or color, to each pixel; however, it does not change the brightness of the pixel. The sphere now appears red.

15. Drag the **Saturation slider** to **50**.

   Increasing the saturation increases the intensity of the color.

16. Drag the **Hue slider** to **205**.

   Your artwork should resemble Figure 34. The sphere changes from red to blue.

17. Drag the **Hue slider** to different locations to see the sphere with different colors.

   Regardless of how you change the color, the sphere remains a sphere. This exercise is a great example of how we perceive shape through highlight to shadow, not through color.

18. Save your work, then close Rods and Cones.

You filled a circle with gray and then created the illusion of a sphere by first painting highlights using white and then painting shadows using black. You applied the Hue/Saturation adjustment to colorize the sphere, then changed it to different hues, noting that changing the hues did not change your perspective of the object as a sphere.

Figure 32 Painting a highlight

Figure 33 Painting a shadow

Figure 34 Shifting the hue to blue does not change the dimension of the sphere

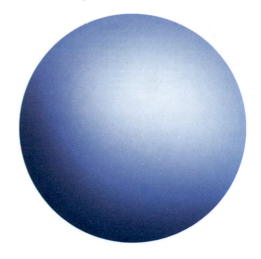

As a teacher, one of the concepts I love to share with my students is the idea that they must "learn how to see." Each of them looks at me with a "does not compute" expression. One is born, and if one is fortunate, one sees. What is there to learn?

When we are children, we are amazed by what we see. Shapes and colors are endlessly fascinating. The color receptors in our eyes are brand new, so the colors we see are the most vivid of our lifetimes. Perspective, on the other hand, is mysterious (and seemingly impossible for us to render). Thus, with our crayons, we draw the stick-figure family and the red square house with the triangle roof and the round yellow sun and the blue rectangle sky, and it's all on one plane.

As we get older, our vision becomes for us, first and foremost, a *function*—our most essential *tool* for navigating the adult world of responsibility and goals. What we call "seeing" is how we parse and process the world around us—how we put a plate on a table, how we avoid an oncoming car, how we recognize the face of our loved ones in a crowd, how we find our own face in a group photo. Even our language recognizes this functionality. Consider that we use the same word, "sense," to describe our five mechanisms for perceiving the world *and* our concept of logic. We say, "It makes sense."

Somewhere in all this visual *function*, we "lose sight" of the miracle and the beauty in everything we are seeing. We say, "This coat is red," as though it were a fact, and we don't even consider that, in a room with no light, the coat is, in fact, *not red*. We say, "This coat is red," as though it is one thing, and even as we look at it, we fail to see that it is a *range of reds*, with darker reds in the folds and more vibrant reds where the light strikes.

With all that is visible, so much becomes invisible. We fail to notice the blue hue on the shadowy side of the white building. We barely perceive the dart of white light glinting off the ripple in the brook as it babbles by. We aren't fascinated by the polygons of negative space created by the telephone wires crossing diagonal tree branches in the gray light of winter.

We look at ourselves in the mirror and tell ourselves, "This is what I look like," oblivious to the reality that we look completely different the moment we leave that spot, the moment we leave that light. We look different in every room we enter. On a rainy day, we look different than we do in the sunshine. We look different in the morning than we do in the afternoon and in the evening. When we bump into a long-lost friend, we are shocked at how much they've changed, yet we are blind to the fact that the face we see in the mirror would be a total stranger to our younger selves.

As the shadows move across our world from morning to night, week to week, year to year, all the shapes and all the colors in our visual space change constantly before our eyes, yet we seldom mark the difference.

Photoshop demands that we see again. Photoshop insists that we notice the difference in contrast between two images that we put together in a composite. It insists that we adjust them so that they share the same highlight and the same depth of shadow; otherwise, what's the point? Photoshop expects us to see that the shadows on this layer are inconsistent with the shadows on that layer. Photoshop challenges the logic centers in our brain to "make sense" of the perspective of one image merged with another.

Photoshop asks that we debate between this red, or maybe that red, but not this yellow, because it's too green, and not this blue, because it's too red. In Photoshop, we find ourselves torn between one percentage point either way when resizing an image to fit in a collage. We negotiate the size and the space relationship between this shape and that, and we attempt to make peace with the negative space that is created between the two. Photoshop even, at times, asks us to harmonize that which is not visible with that which is.

Over time, Photoshop teaches us. Then, at some point, we transcend Photoshop. We find ourselves seeing the actuality of the world again, as Photoshop demands that we do. Ultimately, we can work truthfully in Photoshop only when we learn, once again, to bother, to

pause,

to stop,

to look,

and to see,

once again,

to see.

INVESTIGATE THE HSB COLOR MODEL

Investigating HSB in Photoshop

HSB (Hue, saturation, and brightness) is a color model that is based on 360 colors or hues. In the HSB color model, 360 hues exist on an imaginary circle or color wheel, one hue for each of the 360 degrees on a circle. Figure 35 shows an illustration of a color wheel.

One could legitimately ask, "Does that mean there are only 360 hues in the HSB color model?" The answer would be yes … sort of. For each of the 360 hues, there is a Saturation component and a Brightness component, each of them measured in percentages from 0% to 100%.

Saturation is the intensity of the hue. At 0% saturation, there is no color; the hue is a neutral gray. The full intensity or vibrance of the hue is 100% saturation.

Hues in the HSB color model also have a brightness component: 0% brightness represents the absence of light and is black, and 100% brightness is the full illumination of the hue.

With a range of 0–100% saturation and 0–100% brightness available for each hue, each hue can be one of 10,000 colors ($100 \times 100 = 10,000$). With 360 hues available, that creates a total of 3,600,000 color combinations available in the HSB color model.

Figure 35 Illustration of a color wheel

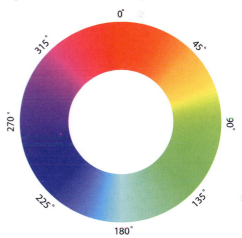

Figure 36 shows the Color Picker dialog box, which is one of the most essential dialog boxes in Photoshop. It allows you to choose any color as the foreground or background color. The Color Picker dialog box uses the HSB color model for its interface. In the figure, the color wheel is represented by the vertical rainbow rectangle. Move the sliders on the rectangle to choose a hue from 0° to 360°. In the figure, hue 225° has been chosen. Each hue number is followed by the degree symbol (°) to show its placement in the 360° color wheel.

The large rectangle that dominates the dialog box represents all the combinations of saturation and brightness available for hue 225°. Saturation increases horizontally from left to right. Brightness increases vertically from bottom to top. Therefore, the most vivid combinations are in the top-right corner, which all have higher saturation and brightness values. All the colors on the left edge are grays because they have 0% saturation. Those grays range from black on the bottom (0% brightness) to white at the top (100% brightness). All the pixels along the bottom edge are black, regardless of their saturation, because they have 0% brightness. The top-right corner of the rectangle represents the "pure hue" with 100% saturation and 100%

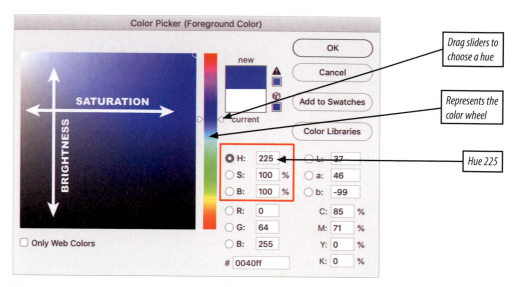

Figure 36 Color Picker dialog box

brightness. What's interesting is that the colors you see in the rectangle are all the same hue: 225°.

RGB and HSB Working in Tandem

In the Color Picker dialog box, you can specify color as RGB or HSB. They are independent of one another, but they don't conflict. It's like reading the same novel in English and in Italian—same story, just a different language.

The best way to approach the two color models is to keep them separate in your mind. When you are evaluating an image in terms of color balance, you're looking at the image in terms of RGB. Is it too red? Is the green too heavy in the highlights? At other times, you'll be evaluating images in terms of brightness/contrast, or you'll want to make the color of an image more intense. In that case, you're looking at the image in terms of HSB. Become comfortable with both because each offers a powerful and effective way to assess a color image.

Using the Hue/Saturation Adjustment

As much as you've gotten used to thinking of each pixel in a color image as having a red/green/blue component, you must also think of each as simultaneously having a hue/saturation/brightness component. That comes into play with the Hue/Saturation adjustment, which offers three controls (Hue, Saturation, and Lightness, along with a Colorize option) to manipulate HSB values in each pixel. The Hue/Saturation adjustment is one you will use often for both practical reasons and for special effects.

Hue is the name of a color. Red, blue, green, and yellow are all hues. The Hue slider shifts selected pixels' hues around the color wheel. In the Hue/Saturation adjustment, the Hue slider isn't listed as degrees. Instead, hues are listed as moving in two directions, toward +180 or –180. You can think of this as moving clockwise and counterclockwise around a 360° color wheel.

When you alter the hue of a given image, the brightness component is not affected by moving the Hue slider, so the tonal range from shadow to highlight is not affected. Therefore, the object simply appears to only change color. With this in mind, imagine that you have an online store selling sweaters, and you sell those sweaters in different colors. You could photograph a single red sweater; bring the image into Photoshop; and then use the Hue slider to quickly create new versions of the image for the orange, yellow, green, blue, and purple sweaters you also sell.

The Saturation slider either intensifies the color or removes color. When you desaturate an image, you set the saturation percentage for each pixel to 0%, thus creating what appears to be a "black and white" image. In that case, remember that the file is still a "color" file, because it's in RGB mode; it just appears black and white because the saturation is at 0%. In terms of your online sweater business, you could desaturate the image of the red sweater to create a gray sweater.

The third slider is the Lightness slider. (In the Color Picker dialog box, the third component is called "Brightness"; in the Hue/Saturation dialog box, it's called "Lightness." One must get used to this minor inconsistency.) The Lightness slider alters pixels' brightness values from black to white.

As a general rule, think of the Lightness slider as an option when using the Hue/Saturation adjustment for special effects; however, don't think of the Lightness slider as an alternative to brightening an image as you would with the Brightness/Contrast or the Levels adjustments. Those adjustments also offer controls for maintaining contrast; the Lightness slider does not. Therefore, looking back at your online sweater business, if you create a gray sweater image that is darker than the actual gray sweater you're selling, use the Brightness/Contrast or the Levels adjustment to brighten it, not the Lightness slider.

Colorizing an Image

When you click the Colorize option on the Hue/Saturation adjustment, it changes the hue of all selected pixels to 0°, which is a red hue.

You can change that hue by moving the hue slider; when you do, all the selected pixels will have that new hue. The result is that an image appears to be one color, like a black and white image that's been tinted with a single color. You can also modify the saturation and lightness when colorizing.

Loading Selections from Layer Masks

A layer mask is itself a selection. The act of painting in a layer mask is the act of making a selection. For example, let's say that you want to change a person's hair color from blond to blue. You would use a Hue/Saturation adjustment to colorize the image blue. You would then fill the layer mask with black and then paint white only in the areas that correspond with the person's hair. When you're done, the white area you painted in the mask represents a selection of the person's hair. At any time, you can load a layer mask as a selection by pressing [command] (Mac) or [Ctrl] (Win) and then clicking the layer mask.

Using the Replace Color Dialog Box

When you want to modify the color in areas of an image that are difficult to select with the selection tools, the Replace Color dialog box can be very useful. The Replace Color dialog box offers tools that allow you to target various areas of an image based strictly on similarity in color. When you target an area, the dialog box shows you a black and white mask, with the white areas representing the pixels that will be affected by any changes you make. Drag the Fuzziness slider to increase white in the mask and the pixels that will be affected. Use the Add to sample tool to click a specific area to add that area to the selection. Once you have targeted the areas of the image you want to affect, changing the Hue and Saturation values in the dialog box will modify the color only in those areas.

The Replace Color feature is another example of destructive editing—it directly affects the targeted artwork. Unless you use the Undo command (or the History panel), the change is permanent. Therefore, whenever you use the Replace Color feature, you should duplicate the layer you want to modify and apply the Replace Color feature to the duplicate artwork. That way, you preserve the original artwork, and you can use a layer mask on the duplicate artwork layer to control how the Replace Color alteration affects the original.

USING TOOLS TO MAKE LOCAL ADJUSTMENTS TO BRIGHTNESS AND SATURATION

Most of the work you do to brighten and darken an image and adjust color saturation will be done with adjustment settings. However, the toolbar offers tools to make these moves by hand to specific (or *local*) areas of an image.

The Dodge tool 🔍 brightens areas that you paint. When the Dodge tool is selected, the Options panel offers an Exposure setting, which controls the strength of the tool and its effect. The Options panel also offers a Range menu, which allows you to choose to brighten shadows, midtones, or highlights with the tool.

The Burn tool ✋ is the Dodge tool's partner and opposite. Use the Burn tool to darken local areas in an image. The Options panel offers the same settings for Burn tool as it does the Dodge tool.

Use the Sponge tool 🧽 to saturate or desaturate color in specific locations of an image. The Mode menu on the Options panel allows you to toggle between Saturate and Desaturate mode for the tool.

COLOR MODELS IN PHOTOSHOP	
Grayscale	Single-channel mode. Pixels can be one of 256 shades of gray, numbered 0–255. Grayscale mode is used to render black and white images.
RGB	Red, Green, Blue. This three-channel color mode offers 256 shades in the red channel, the green channel, and the blue channel, thus making more than 16 million colors available. RGB mode is the most-used color mode in Photoshop.
HSB	Hue, Saturation, Brightness. Each pixel can be one of 360 available hues. That hue is modified by saturation and brightness, each of which is measured in percentages. Saturation describes the vividness of the color and is measured from a neutral gray at 0% saturation to full intensity at 100%. Brightness is measured from 0% brightness, which is black, to 100% brightness, which is white. A pixel with a "pure hue" has 100% saturation and 100% brightness.
CMYK	Cyan, Magenta, Yellow, Black. This color mode is used for images that are to be printed using the conventional four-color printing process. Some modern-day digital printing presses work with RGB images, so talk to your printer about whether or not your color images should be saved in RGB or CMYK mode.
Indexed Color	The Indexed Color mode renders color images using a palette of 256 colors. When a color image is rendered with just 256 colors, it can appear as continuous tone, or it can appear to be posterized, depending on the image. Indexed color was used often in the early days of the Internet to render color images with small file sizes that could be downloaded quickly.
Lab Color	Lab Color is a color space in which color is described with a value for universal lightness (L) and four chromatic colors, the red/green axis (a) and the blue/yellow axis (b). The Lab color space is considered "device independent" meaning that it can be used to achieve the exact same color in different mediums. Lab Color is widely used in the plastics, automotive, and textile industries.

Explore hue, saturation, and brightness in the Color Picker

1. Open PS 5-9.psd, then save it as **Hue Sat Stripes**.

2. Press the **letter [D]** on your keypad to set the foreground and background colors to their defaults.

3. Click the **foreground color** on the toolbar.

   The Color Picker dialog box opens.

4. Verify that the **option button** 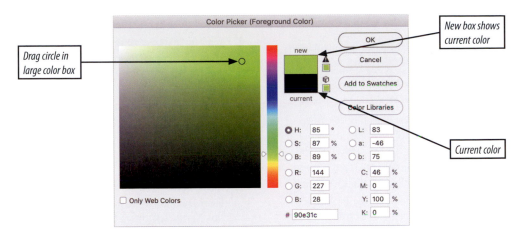 next to **H (Hue)** is activated, then drag the **Hue slider** up and down, noting the changes in the H text box.

   The H value refers to the hue number on a 360° color wheel.

5. Drag the **Hue slider** until the H value reads **85°**.

6. Click and drag **in the large color box** to the left of the Hue slider.

   As you click and drag in the large color box, the values in the S (Saturation) and B (Brightness) text boxes change depending on the direction you drag. Figure 37 illustrates this. The new box at the top of the dialog box shows the current color you are sampling, and the current foreground color is below it. Note, however, that wherever you sample, the H value remains at 85°. Any new colors you are sampling are all hue 85° with varying percentages of saturation and brightness.

7. Drag the **circle in the color box** all the way to the upper-right corner.

   In the upper-right corner, the S and B values are 100%. This color is the "pure" hue 85°—the brightest and most saturated.

Figure 37 Sampling a color with high saturation and brightness percentages

8. Drag the **circle in the color box** down along the right edge of the color box.

   As you drag down, the brightness is reduced, and the color is darkened. A color with 0% brightness is black, regardless of the hue and saturation values.

9. Click the **upper-left corner**, then drag the **circle** down along the left edge of the color box.

   Wherever you click along the left edge, you will see a shade of gray. At the left edge, there is 0% saturation, which means that only a shade of gray is possible. The left edge changes from white to black as the brightness decreases.

10. Click **near the center** of the color box, then drag the **circle** right and left, noting the changes in the S (Saturation) text box.

    As you drag to the right, the saturation increases. As the saturation increases, the intensity of the color increases.

11. Click **near the center**, then drag slowly toward the upper-right corner.

    As shown in Figure 37, as you drag up and right, both the saturation and the brightness increase, and the color is brightened and intensified dramatically.

12. Click **OK** to close the Color Picker dialog box.

You sampled Hue 85° in the Color Picker dialog box and dragged the circle in the color box to better understand how to change the saturation and brightness of the hue.

Apply Hue/Saturation adjustment layers

1. Click the **Create new fill or adjustment layer button** on the Layers panel, then click **Hue/Saturation**.

2. Drag the **Hue slider** to **−125**.

    The stripes on the shirt change to blue. White pixels are not affected by changes in hue because white pixels have HSB values of 0%/0%/100%. Since a white pixel has 0% saturation, it has no color, and a hue shift cannot affect it. Note in the image, however, wherever there are shadows in the white stripes, those are visibly affected by the adjustment.

3. Rename the adjustment layer **Blue**.

4. Verify that the **layer mask** is selected, then invert it by pressing **[command] [I] (Mac)** or **[Ctrl] [I] (Win)**.

    The layer mask on the adjustment layer is inverted to black.

    TIP Whenever you rename the layer, the layer mask becomes deselected, and the adjustment thumbnail becomes selected. You must select the mask to use it.

5. Choose a **brush size**, **hardness**, and **opacity**, then paint with a **white foreground color** to "brush in" the adjustment so your artwork matches Figure 38.

6. Add a second **Hue/Saturation adjustment layer**, drag the **Hue slider** to **+123**, then drag the **Saturation slider** to **−40**.

7. Rename the adjustment layer **Green**.

8. Invert the mask, then brush in the adjustment only on the **stripe immediately below the blue stripe** you just painted (including the sleeves).

9. Using the same steps for the blue and green stripes, add four more Hue/Saturation adjustment layers and paint each stripe a different color. Name each new adjustment layer by color.

    Your artwork should resemble Figure 39.

Figure 38 Changing the hue of a stripe to blue

Figure 39 Different Hue/Saturation adjustments applied to different stripes

10. Zoom in on the **sleeve** at the right side of the canvas.

White is the most reflective color, and the white stripes above and below the green stripe are red in the shadows. They are reddish because they reflected the original red stripe, which is now green. Also, there are red reflections near the blue stripe.

11. Target the **Green layer**, then brush in the adjustment to change the pink reflections on the white stripes to green.

12. Target the **Blue layer**, then brush in the adjustment to change the pink reflections on the white stripes to blue.

Your result should resemble Figure 40. When doing a project like this, reflections are always a challenge. For example, note the pink reflection on the skin on the inside of the man's arm. In this case, the reflection is not a problem because the stripe beside it is pink.

13. Zoom in and pan over the image, looking for other reflection color issues and correct them.

TIP Look for another issue under the other sleeve.

14. Target **all the adjustment layers**, then click the **Create a new group button**  on the Layers panel.

15. Set the **Opacity** on the **Group 1 layer** to **50%**.

As shown in Figure 41, reducing the opacity of all the adjustment layers reduces the opacity of the colored stripes.

16. Save your work, then continue to the next set of steps.

You used multiple Hue/Saturation adjustments and their layer masks to change colors throughout the image.

Figure 40 Adjusting red/pink reflections on the white stripes

Figure 41 Reducing the opacity on all the adjustments

Desaturate an image and load selections from layer masks

1. Target the **Group 1 layer**, then add a new **Hue/Saturation adjustment layer**.

   The new adjustment layer appears above the Group 1 layer on the Layers panel.

2. Drag the **Saturation slider** all the way to the left to **–100%.**

   The entire image appears as a black and white image. White stripes on the shirt are not affected because they have 0% saturation to begin with.

3. Invert the layer mask.

   The adjustment no longer shows.

4. Expand the **Group 1 layer** to show the adjustments inside.

5. Press and hold **[command] (Mac)** or **[Ctrl] (Win)**, then click the **layer mask** on the **Blue layer**.

   The mask is loaded as a selection.

6. Add the **[shift] key** so that you're holding **[shift] [command] (Mac)** or **[Shift] [Ctrl] (Win)**, then click the **five other masks**.

   All six masks are loaded as selections.

7. Target the **layer mask** on the new Hue/Saturation layer at the top of the Layers panel.

8. Fill the selection with **white**.

9. Deselect, hide the **Group 1 layer**, then compare your results to Figure 42.

10. Save your work, then close Hue Sat Stripes.

You used a Hue/Saturation adjustment layer to desaturate the whole image. You then loaded selections from all the masks you painted on other adjustment layers to mask the desaturation adjustment to affect only the stripes on the shirt.

Figure 42 Desaturated stripes

Clip adjustment layers

1. Open PS 5-10.psd, then save it as **Clipped Adjustments**.

   This is the layers project you worked on in Chapter 3. The goal of this exercise is to desaturate the two coins.

2. Target the **Middle Coin layer**, then **add a Hue/Saturation adjustment layer**.

3. On the Properties panel, drag the **Saturation slider** all the way to the left.

   All the artwork on layers below the Middle Coin layer are affected.

4. Press and hold **[option] (Mac)** or **[Alt] (Win)**, then float over the horizontal line between the adjustment layer and the Middle Coin layer on the Layers panel.

   When you float over the line, your mouse pointer changes to a bent arrow icon.

5. Click the **horizontal line**.

The adjustment is clipped into the Middle Coin layer and now affects only that artwork. As shown in Figure 43, the adjustment layer now shows the bent arrow icon, indicating that it is

Figure 43 Bent arrow icon indicates clipped layer

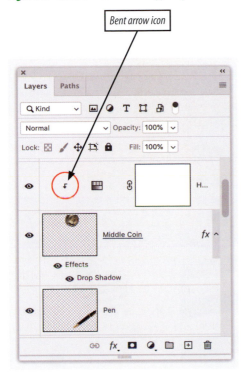

Bent arrow icon

a clipped layer. The method you used to clip the layer is the manual method. Next, you will learn an alternative method.

6. Target the **Bottom Coin layer**.

7. Press and hold **[option] (Mac)**, then click the **Create new fill or adjustment layer button** ⬢ or press and hold **(Alt) (Win)** and **right-click** the **Create new fill or adjustment layer button** ⬢ on the Layers panel, then click **Hue/Saturation**.

The New Layer dialog box opens.

8. Click the **Use Previous Layer to Create Clipping Mask check box**, then click **OK**.

The new adjustment layer appears on the Layers panel as a clipped adjustment.

9. Desaturate the **Bottom Coin artwork** by dragging the **Saturation slider** all the way to the left.

10. Add a **Levels adjustment layer**, then clip it.

AUTHOR'S **NOTE** When working with multiple clipped adjustments, think of the adjustments as all being clipped into the base artwork. For example, in this case, don't think of the Levels adjustment being clipped into the Hue/Saturation adjustment. Instead, think of both adjustments as being clipped into the Bottom Coin artwork.

11. On the Properties panel, drag the **white triangle** to **215**.

12. Press and hold **[option] (Mac)** or **[Alt] (Win)**, then drag the **Levels adjustment** above the Hue/Saturation adjustment clipped into the Middle Coin layer.

A copy of the Levels adjustment is created. Pressing and holding [option] (Mac) or [Alt] (Win) when dragging a layer copies the layer. The new adjustment layer is unclipped and is affecting all artwork on layers beneath it.

13. Clip the Levels adjustment into the Hue/Saturation adjustment and thus the Middle Coin artwork.

14. Save your work, then close Clipped Adjustments.

You clipped two Hue/Saturation adjustment layers and two Levels adjustment layers into two different components of the collage.

Use the Replace Color dialog box

1. Open PS 5-11.psd, then save it as **Replace Color**.

2. Duplicate the **Background layer**, then rename the new layer **Replace Color**.

3. Click **Image** on the menu bar, point to **Adjustments**, then click **Replace Color**.

The Replace Color dialog box opens with the Eyedropper tool selected 🖉 in the upper-left corner.

4. Click the **Eyedropper tool** 🖉 on the **red stripe** at the center of the man's chest.

The mask turns white in areas representing what is selected.

Continued on next page

5. Drag the **Hue slider** to **−125**, then compare your screen to Figure 44.

   As shown in the figure, most but not all the red stripes have been affected by the hue shift. Some red patches remain.

6. Drag the **Fuzziness slider** to **94**.

   Fuzziness expands or contracts the selection based on where you sampled. The greater the Fuzziness value, the more white data will show in the mask and the more pixels will be affected by any changes you make.

7. Click the **Add to Sample tool**  at the top of the dialog box.

8. Click the **Add to Sample tool** on a remaining red patch on the shirt, which is likely in shadow areas.

   Clicking the Add to Sample tool adds that area and similar areas of the image to the selection.

9. Click the **Add to Sample tool** until the stripes on the shirt are completely blue, as shown in Figure 45.

10. Click **OK**.

11. Add a **layer mask** to the Replace Color layer, then invert the mask.

12. Paint with white to brush in the blue stripes from the Replace Color layer.

Figure 44 Results of the first sample

Figure 45 Using the Add to Sample tool adds reddish areas to the selection

13. Save your work, then close Replace Color.

You used the Replace Color dialog box to sample areas to change their hues.

Colorize an image

1. Open PS 5-12.psd, then save it as **Colorize**.

The sweater in this image is an excellent example of range of tone in shadows. Despite being overall a dark charcoal gray throughout, there is an abundance of detail in the sweater. You can see shadows in the fold under the sleeves and where the folded-over turtleneck meets the sweater. Furthermore, you can see the pattern of the knitting throughout.

2. Open the **Info panel**, click the **Eyedropper tool** on the *right half* of the panel, then click **HSB Color**.

3. Click the **Eyedropper tool** on the toolbar, then float over the **sweater**, noting the HSB information on the Info panel.

The pixels that make up the sweater have a range of hues from approximately 60° to 90° degrees, but their Brightness values are all less than 20 percent, so there's very little color in the sweater.

4. Add a **Hue/Saturation adjustment layer**, then drag the **Hue slider** slowly left and right.

No matter where you drag the Hue slider, the color of the sweater doesn't change.

5. Click **Colorize** on the Properties panel, then float the **Eyedropper tool** over the image to sample pixels' HSB values on the Info panel.

The Info panel shows before and after values. As shown in Figure 46 and on your Info panel, all the pixels in the image now have 0° as their hue, which is red.

6. Drag the **Hue slider** slowly to the right.

As you drag, the hue for all the pixels in the image changes. At all times, all the pixels in the image have the same hue.

Continued on next page

Figure 46 Viewing all pixels at Hue: 0°

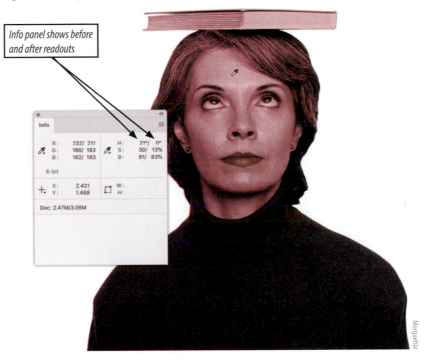

Info panel shows before and after readouts

7. Target the **layer mask** on the adjustment layer, click **Select** on the menu bar, click **Load Selection**, load the selection named **Sweater Mask**, then click **OK**.

8. Fill the selection with **black**, then **deselect**.

9. Invert the **mask**.

10. Select the **adjustment layer thumbnail**.

11. On the Properties panel, drag the **Hue slider** to **124**, then drag the **Saturation** slider to **50**.

   The sweater appears as a dark forest green.

12. Drag the **Lightness slider** to **13**.

   The color of the sweater lightens, and the sweater is now clearly green. However, the shadows were weakened with the Hue/Saturation adjustment, which you will now fix with a Levels adjustment.

13. Add a **Levels adjustment** above the Hue/Saturation adjustment.

14. On the Properties panel, drag the **black triangle** to **19** to darken the shadow point, drag the **white triangle** to **203**, then drag the **gray triangle** to **0.87**.

15. Select the **Hue/Saturation adjustment layer**, then reduce the **Saturation** to **45**.

   As shown in Figure 47, considering that was originally a dark charcoal gray sweater, the adjusted sweater is now very believably green.

16. Save your work, then close the Colorize file.

You colorized the image, masked the adjustment so that it affected the sweater only, then you brightened the sweater so the hue and saturation shifts became visible. You then used the Levels adjustment to restore contrast to the sweater without losing the new green hue.

Figure 47 Viewing the green sweater

Apply an Invert adjustment layer

1. Open PS 5-13.psd, then save it as **Skills Trio**.
2. Click the Create new fill or adjustment layer button on the Layers panel, then click Invert.
   The grayscale values of the pixels in the image are inverted: black pixels have changed from 0 to 255, and white pixels have changed from 255 to 0. As indicated on the gradient on the left, the entire range from black to white has been inverted.
3. Hide and show the Invert adjustment layer. Because the adjustment has been applied as an adjustment layer, it can be made visible or invisible like any other layer. The original artwork is affected only when the adjustment layer is visible.
4. Save your work, then continue to the next set of steps.

Apply a Threshold adjustment layer

1. Hide the Invert adjustment layer, then target the Background layer.
2. Click the Create new fill or adjustment layer button on the Layers panel, then click Threshold.
   All the pixels in the image become either black or white.
3. On the Properties panel, drag the Threshold Level slider to 74.
   All pixels with a grayscale value of 74 or greater are now white.
4. Save your work then continue to the next set of steps.

Apply a Gradient Map adjustment layer

1. Hide all the adjustment layers, then target the Background layer.
2. Click Image on the menu bar, point to Mode, then click RGB Color.
   If a warning box opens asking whether or not you want to flatten the image, click Don't Flatten.
3. Click the Create new fill or adjustment layer button on the Layers panel, then click Gradient Map.
4. On the Properties panel, click the gradient above the Dither option.
   The Gradient Editor dialog box opens.
5. Click the left color stop, click the Color box, choose a dark purple or maroon, then click OK.
6. Change the right color stop to a pale yellow color.
7. Add a color stop in the middle of the gradient, change its color to green, then set its location to 50%.
8. Click OK, then compare your artwork to Figure 48.
9. Save your work, then close Skills Trio.

Figure 48 Viewing the Gradient Map adjustment

imtmphoto/Shutterstock.com

Adjust Brightness/Contrast

1. Open PS 5-14.psd, then save it as **Skills Brightness and Contrast**.
2. Sample the image, looking for the brightest pixels and darkest pixels.
   The brightest pixels are over the man's shoulder, but they are in the 120–124 range, which is below even a middle gray. The shadows overall are weak, with the darkest being around 30.
3. Click the Create new fill or adjustment layer button on the Layers panel, then click Brightness/Contrast.
4. On the Properties panel, click the Use Legacy check box, then drag the Brightness slider to 65.
5. Drag the Contrast slider to 65.
6. Sample the highlights over the man's shoulder, on his forehead, and in the white of his eye.
   The highlights are bright and white.
7. Sample the shadows in the man's hair.
   The shadows in the image are still too bright in the 28–32 range.
8. Reduce the Brightness to 55, then increase the Contrast to 69.
9. Hide and show the Brightness/Contrast adjustment layer to see its effect.
   Figure 49 shows the before and after views of the image.
10. Save your work, then close Skills Brightness and Contrast.

Employ the Levels adjustment

1. Open PS 5-15.psd, then save it as **Skills Adjusting Levels**.
2. Click the Create new fill or adjustment layer button on the Layers panel, then click Levels.

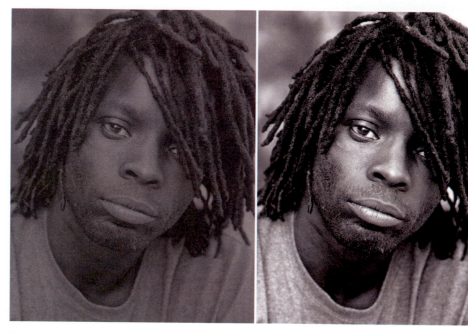

Figure 49 Before and after views of the Brightness/Contrast adjustment

3. Assess the histogram.
   On the right side of the histogram, it appears that some data goes all the way to the white triangle, but there's very little of that data. The bulk of the histogram ends halfway between the gray triangle and the white triangle. On the left side of the histogram, there's a gap between the black triangle and the data on the histogram, meaning there are no black pixels in the image.
4. Click the Set white point eyedropper tool on the Properties panel, float over the image, then press [option] (Mac) or [Alt] (Win).
   The entire canvas turns black except for any pixels that have a grayscale value of 255, which remain white. In the case of this image, those pixels are very few and in a line on the right side of the image.
5. Drag the black triangle right to 15 at the start of the histogram.
6. Click the Set black point eyedropper tool on the Properties panel, float over the image, then press [option] (Mac) or [Alt] (Win).
   The entire canvas turns white except pixels with a grayscale value of 0, which remain black.

7. Add a second Levels adjustment layer.
8. Drag the white triangle to 175—the end of the bulk of data on the histogram.
   The image is brightened, but many of the very bright areas have blown out to white and will need to be masked from this adjustment.
9. Click the Set white point eyedropper tool  on the Properties panel, float over the image, then press [option] (Mac) or [Alt] (Win).
   With this technique, you can see which highlights blew out to white.
10. Click the Brush tool, set the Opacity to 30%, then use a soft-edged brush to gradually mask out the second Levels adjustment where it blew out the highlights. When you are done, no highlight areas on the image should be overly blown out or glaring white.
11. Drag the gray triangle to the right to change the midtone input level to 0.92.
12. Shift-click to target both adjustment layers on the Layers panel, then enter **[command] [G] (Mac)** or **[Ctrl] [G] (Win)**.
13. Hide and show the Group 1 layer.
    Figure 50 shows the image before and after the adjustments.
14. Save your work, then continue to the next set of steps.

Figure 50 Before and after views of the adjustments

Morguefile

Adjust levels on a color image

1. Verify that the Group 1 layer is showing.
2. Click Image on the menu bar, point to Mode, click RGB Color, then click Don't Flatten if a dialog box appears.
3. Open PS 5-16.psd.
4. Select all, copy, close the file, then return to the Skills Adjusting Levels file.
5. Verify that the Group 1 layer is collapsed and targeted, then paste.

    Because the layer is collapsed, the image was pasted above the layer, not inside the group.
6. Target the Group 1 layer, click Layer on the menu bar, then click Duplicate Group.

    The Duplicate Group dialog box opens.
7. Change the name of Group 1 to **Color Adjustments**, then click OK.
8. Drag the new Color Adjustments group layer above the Group 1 layer on the Layers panel.

    Figure 51 shows the image before and after the adjustments.
9. Save your work, then close Skills Adjusting Levels.

Figure 51 Before and after views of the same Levels adjustments on a color image

Apply Hue/Saturation adjustments

1. Open PS 5-17.psd, then save it as **Skills Stripes**.
2. Click the Create new fill or adjustment layer button on the Layers panel, then click Hue/Saturation.
3. Drag the Hue slider to +118.
4. Rename the adjustment layer **Green**.
5. Verify that the layer mask is selected, then invert it by pressing **[command] [I] (Mac)** or **[Ctrl] [I] (Win)**. The layer mask on the adjustment layer is inverted to black.

TIP Whenever you rename the layer, the layer mask becomes deselected, and the adjustment thumbnail becomes selected. You must select the mask to invert it.

6. Paint with a white foreground color to "brush in" the adjustment so that the longest stripe is green.
7. Add a second Hue/Saturation adjustment layer, drag the Hue slider to −63, then drag the Saturation to −26.
8. Rename the new adjustment layer **Purple**.
9. Select the mask, invert the mask, then brush in the adjustment on only the bottom-most stripe.
10. Using the same steps for the green and purple stripes, add three more Hue/Saturation adjustment layers to create three more colors, and paint the remainder of the shoe. Name each adjustment layer with its color.
    Figure 52 shows one example.
11. Target all the adjustment layers, then click the Create a new group button on the Layers panel.
12. Set the Opacity on the Group 1 layer to 50%.
13. Save your work, then continue to the next set of steps.

Desaturate an image and load selections from layer masks

1. Target the Group 1 layer, then add a new Hue/Saturation adjustment layer.
   The new adjustment layer appears above the Group 1 layer on the Layers panel.
2. Name the new adjustment layer **Desaturate**, then drag the Saturation slider all the way to the left.
   The entire image is affected and appears as a black and white image. White stripes on the shoe are not affected because they have 0% saturation to begin with.
3. Invert the layer mask.
   The adjustment no longer shows.

4. Expand the Group 1 layer to show all the adjustments inside.
5. Press and hold [command] (Mac) or [Ctrl] (Win), then click the layer mask on the Green layer.
   The mask is loaded as a selection.
6. Add the [shift] key so that you're holding [shift] [command] (Mac) or [shift] [Ctrl] (Win), then click all the other layer masks.
   All masks are loaded as selections.
7. Target the layer mask on the Desaturate group layer, then fill the selection with white.
8. Deselect, then hide the Group 1 layer.
9. Paint white in the Desaturate layer's layer mask to desaturate any areas of the image that are still in color, then compare your results to Figure 53.
10. Save your work, then continue to the next set of steps.

Figure 52 Different Hue/Saturation adjustments applied to different stripes

Morguefile

Figure 53 Desaturated stripes

Use the Replace Color dialog box

1. Open PS 5-18.psd, then save it as **Replace Color Skills**.
2. Duplicate the Background layer, then rename the new layer **Replace Color**.
3. Click Image on the menu bar, point to Adjustments, then click Replace Color.
   The Replace Color dialog box opens with the Eyedropper tool selected in the upper-left corner.
4. Click the Eyedropper tool on the light purple sleeve on the woman's left arm.
   The goal is to change the purple elements of her costume to green.
5. Drag the Hue slider to −180 and the Saturation slider to +15.
6. Drag the Fuzziness slider to 40.
7. Click the Add to Sample tool 🖊 at the top of the dialog box.
8. Click the Add to Sample tool 🖊 on a darker purple area of the costume.
   Clicking the Add to Sample tool 🖊 adds that area and similar areas of the image to the selection.
9. Click the Add to Sample tool 🖊 until the purple areas are completely green, as shown in Figure 54.
10. Click OK.
11. Add a layer mask to the Replace Color layer, then mask the face and hands to fix any areas that may have changed color.

AUTHOR'S NOTE You will repeat this exercise in this chapter using a layer mask instead of the Replace Color dialog box. As you will see, doing this with a mask will be a lot of work. This image is one for which Replace Color is a faster and more effective choice than using a mask.

12. Save your work, then close Replace Color Skills.

Colorize an image

1. Open PS 5-19.psd, then save it as **Colorize Skills**.
2. Add a Hue/Saturation adjustment layer, then drag the Hue slider slowly left and right.
   The color of the car changes very subtly—not a dramatic change or a vivid color.
3. Click the Colorize check box on the Properties panel.
4. Drag the Hue slider all the way to the left to 0.
5. Drag the Lightness slider to +10, then drag the Saturation slider to 60.
6. Mask the adjustment where it needs to be masked; you'll need to figure out what needs to be color and what should remain as is.

TIP Consider avoiding looking at the finished image on this page as you decide what stays and what gets masked. "Processing reality" is itself a challenge when masking.

7. When you're finished masking, change the Hue to 216, then compare your choices and your results to Figure 55.
8. Save your work, then close Colorize Skills.

Figure 54 Purple areas replaced with green

MorgueFile

Figure 55 Viewing the results of colorizing

Dimitris Leonidas/Shutterstock.com

PROJECT BUILDER 1

This project is designed to give you more experience adjusting with levels. Creating the best contrast possible with levels is something you'll need to do often, and the only true way to get good at it is to practice on lots of images and develop an eye for tonal range, both in black and white and in color images.

For this project, you've been given seven images in black and white and the same images in color. All of them require adjustments for contrast. Feel free to use multiple Levels adjustments when necessary, and definitely feel free to use layer masks to brush in adjustments to specific areas. Don't use any other adjustments, such as Hue/Saturation or Color Balance.

Work on the black and white images first. When you move to the color images, don't go back and check the adjustments you made on the black and white versions. Instead, remember what you learned on the black and white versions to inform you how to approach the color versions.

The goal for both the black and white and color images is to produce the best contrast and tonal range while maintaining reality and leaving no evidence of your involvement in modifying the images.

1. Open the folder named Project Builder Images, then open the folder named Grayscale.
2. Open all seven images.

3. Working methodically, use the skills you learned in Lesson 2 of this chapter to use Levels adjustments to improve the contrast in each image.

TIP You might want to read through Lesson 2 again for a refresher on how we approached the work in those exercises.

4. When you are done with each image, save a separate PSD file for each.
5. Close each of the black and white images before moving on to the color images.

6. Open the seven color images in the Color Images folder.
7. Using what you learned when improving the black and white versions, adjust the color images for better contrast and, as a result, better color.
8. Save a separate PSD file for each.
   Figure 56 shows a before and after example of one set.

Figure 56 Before and after results of Levels adjustments

Morguefile

This project is designed to reinforce your skills using brush work for creating layer masks. You will first mask out the background of an image; then you will brush a Hue/Saturation adjustment into a complex costume. The image has only medium resolution, so fine details are missing, and you'll have to decide for yourself what to affect and what to leave alone as you work toward the goal. This exercise will also reinforce the need to clip adjustments when working with multiple images, as you learned to do in Chapter 3.

1. Open PS 5-20.psd, then save it as **Multiple Hues**.
2. Add a layer mask to the Purple layer.
3. Select the Brush tool, then set its Hardness to 75%.
4. Mask the image to remove the white background.
5. When you finish the mask, fill the Background layer with white.
6. Click Image on the menu bar, then click Canvas Size.
7. Click the Canvas extension color list arrow, then click White.
8. Click the arrow in the middle-left anchor box ⬅, change the Width to 8.25, then click OK.
9. Duplicate the Purple layer, then rename it **Green**.
10. Move the Green layer artwork directly to the right, as shown in Figure 57.
11. Press and hold [option] (Mac), then click the Create new fill or adjustment layer button or press and hold (Alt) (Win) and right-click the Create new fill or adjustment layer button on the Layers panel, then click Hue/Saturation.

Figure 57 Duplicating and moving the artwork

Figure 58 Changing the purple hues to green

12. Click the Use Previous Layer to Create Clipping Mask check box, then click OK.
    The new Hue/Saturation adjustment layer is clipped into the Green layer and therefore will affect only the Green layer.
13. Drag the Hue slider to −180, then drag the Saturation slider to +27.
    The entire layer is affected.
14. Invert the layer mask on the Green layer.
15. Paint with white to brush in the adjustment in all the purple areas.
    Use Figure 58 as your guide. Expect to spend at least 30 minutes brushing in the adjustment.

16. Target both the Green layer and its clipped adjustment layer on the Layers panel.
17. Press and hold [option] (Mac) or [Alt] (Win), then drag the artwork directly to the right as you did in Step 10. A copy of the artwork and the adjustment layer is created.
18. Shift the Hue and Saturation so the third costume is orange, not green.
19. Using the same steps as you did to create the green and orange costumes, create a yellow and blue version so your canvas resembles Figure 59 on the following page.
20. Save your work, then close Multiple Hues.

Figure 59 The finished project

DESIGN PROJECT

This project will show you how to create a "tinted black and white" effect in which parts of the image appear in color and other parts appear as a faintly colored black and white image. After you have progressed through the exercise, find your own images and experiment with different techniques for creating this effect.

1. Open PS 5-21.psd, then save it as **Tinted Black and White**.
2. Add a Hue/Saturation layer mask, then drag the Saturation slider all the way to the left.
3. Mask the adjustment so the apples are in full color and the remainder of the image is black and white.
4. Reduce the Opacity on the adjustment layer to 80% so your work resembles Figure 60.
5. Save your work, then close Tinted Black and White.

Figure 60 Vibrant apples and a tinted background

mythja/Shutterstock.com

CHAPTER 6

DESIGN WITH ESSENTIAL BLENDING MODES AND FILTERS

1. Use the Multiply Blending Mode
2. Explore the Screen Blending Mode
3. Apply the Overlay Blending Mode
4. Design with Blending Modes

Adobe Certified Professional in Visual Design Using Photoshop CC Framework

3. Organizing Documents

This objective covers document structure such as layers and managing document structure for efficient workflows.

3.2 Modify layer visibility using opacity, blending modes, and masks.

   A Adjust a layer's opacity, blending mode, and fill opacity.

4. Creating and Modifying Visual Elements

This objective covers core tools and functionality of the application, as well as tools that affect the visual outcome of the document.

4.6 Modify the appearance of design elements by using filters and styles.

   A Use filters to modify images destructively or non-destructively.

USE THE MULTIPLY BLENDING MODE

▶ What You'll Do

In this lesson, you'll use the Multiply blending mode for different effects.

Working with Blending Modes

Because Photoshop offers the ability to work with layered artwork, it follows logically that pixels on one layer will directly overlap pixels in the same location on layers below it. **Blending modes** are mathematical algorithms that define how pixels affect pixels on layers beneath them. The Layers panel houses 27 blending modes (including Normal), many of which you'll use often and some you might never use. You'll use blending modes to create special effects, but the most essential blending modes have highly practical functions as well.

You specify the blending mode for a given layer on the blending mode menu, shown in Figure 1. Note that the list of blending modes is grouped into sections based on how they function. Four commonly used groups are as follows:

Darken blending modes (Darken, Multiply, Color Burn, Linear Burn, Darker Color): With these modes, white pixels become invisible, and black pixels are unaffected and remain opaque. These modes darken the areas of overlap.

Lighten blending modes (Lighten, Screen, Color Dodge, Linear Dodge, Lighter Color): With these modes, black pixels become invisible, and white pixels are unaffected and remain opaque. These modes lighten the areas of overlap.

Figure 1 Blending modes on the Layers panel

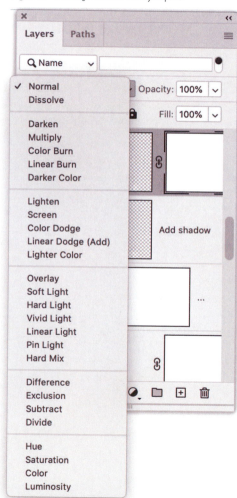

Overlay blending modes (Overlay, Soft Light, Hard Light, Vivid Light, Linear Light, Pin Light, Hard Mix): With these modes, gray pixels become invisible, and all pixels become transparent. These modes increase the contrast and saturation where pixels overlap.

Hue blending modes (Hue, Saturation, Color, Luminosity): These modes affect the color of pixels, specifically in terms of their hue, saturation, or brightness (luminosity).

The default blending mode for a layer is Normal, which is no blend at all. In Normal blending mode, the pixels on one layer completely hide pixels on layers below it. With other blending modes, pixels blend to create all kinds of color and special effects.

A good strategy for understanding blending modes is to think of three colors: the **base color** is the color of the pixel on the lower layer, the **blend color** is the color above it on the layer with the blending mode applied, and the **result color** is the color produced by blending the base and blend colors.

Figure 2 shows an example of the Multiply blending mode. The blue diamond is the base color, and the pink diamond is the blend color. In Normal mode, the pink color obscures the blue diamond below it where they overlap. When the Multiply blending mode is applied to the pink diamond, a third color is created where they overlap. This third color is the result color. If you were to apply a different blending mode to the pink diamond, the result color would be different; with some modes, there would be no change at all.

Figure 2 Example of the Multiply blending mode

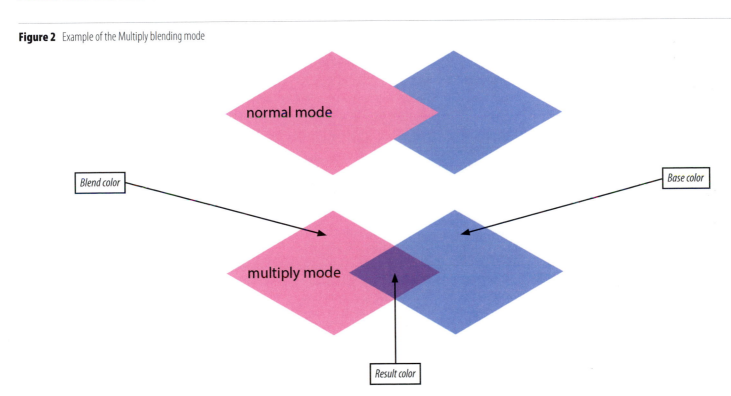

Examining the Multiply Blending Mode

The Multiply blending mode is one of the first blending modes most new Photoshop users encounter, primarily because it makes white pixels "invisible," and all colors appear "see-through" (except black). Figure 3 demonstrates this. In the top photo, an image of a blue car with a white background is positioned above an image of an orange and gray checkerboard. In the bottom photo, the Multiply blending mode has been applied to the layer with the car on it. The white background has disappeared completely. The car is now transparent: you can see the checkerboard through the car—except in the black areas like the tires, which are not affected by the blending mode.

What's fun about the Multiply blending mode is that its mathematical algorithm is basic enough for anybody to understand, so let's examine how it does what it does.

The calculation for the Multiply blending mode is the following:

(pixel 1 × pixel 2) / 255 = pixel 3

where pixel 1 is the base color, pixel 2 is the blend color, and pixel 3 is the result color. Figure 4 shows four examples of how pixels will blend with this calculation. In the top equation, a pixel with a grayscale value of 100 is multiplied with a pixel with a grayscale value

Figure 3 Multiplying the car image over the checkerboard

of 210, and then the result is divided by 255. The result is a pixel whose grayscale value is 82. It only makes sense that the resulting pixel (pixel 3) is darker than the base pixel (pixel 1) because you divided by a number (255) that is higher than the number you multiplied by (210). Thus, the Multiply blending mode always darkens an image, as you can see in Figure 3. The blue of the car in Multiply mode is noticeably darker.

The second equation in Figure 4 shows what happens when you multiply with white. In the figure, a 100 pixel is multiplied by a 255 pixel and then divided by 255; thus, the resulting pixel (pixel 3) is 100. This explains why, in Figure 3, the white background behind the car disappears. The resulting pixel (pixel 3) is identical to the base pixel (pixel 1), so the blend color (the white pixel) has no role in the resulting image. Essentially, it "disappears."

The third equation in Figure 4 shows how colors blend in the Multiply mode. In this case, yellow and cyan are being multiplied to make green. You can see how each of the RGB components are run through the equation to produce the green result. (Note: this discussion of blending modes and their calculations has no relation to the additive primary and subtractive primary color model discussions from Chapter 5. They are two different and unrelated topics.)

The fourth equation in Figure 4 shows what happens when you multiply with black. A black pixel has a grayscale value of 0. Anything multiplied by zero is zero. Thus, anything multiplied with black results in black. This explains why the black tires and other black parts of the car do not change in Figure 3.

With all of this in mind, you can understand better what a *practical* tool the Multiply blending mode can be, offering you the ability to make images and colors transparent and make white disappear.

Figure 4 Examples of different calculations with the Multiply blending mode

MULTIPLY MODE
(Pixel 1 x Pixel 2) / 255 = Pixel 3

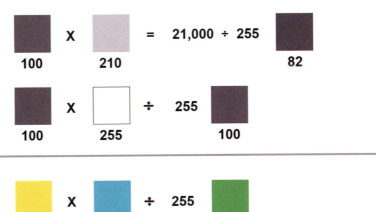

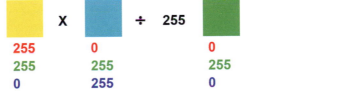

Applying a Blending Mode to a Group

The Layers panel offers you the ability to use **groups**, which are like folders, to organize your layers. When you're working with multiple layers, especially when you're building collages that involve numerous pieces of artwork, a group becomes very useful for collecting related layers in one place, segregating different components of a project, and making the Layers panel more manageable.

By default, when you create a layer group, its blending mode will be Pass Through. **Pass Through mode** indicates that the group functions only as an organizational tool to house layers, nothing more complicated than that. Therefore, the act of grouping layers will cause no change to how layers with blending modes applied to them will affect one another or how they affect images outside the group.

Blending modes can be applied to groups themselves. When you apply a blending mode to a group, all the layers in the group take on that blending mode. For example, if you apply the Multiply blending mode to a group, all the layers inside the group will be multiplied. This offers you a powerful method for quickly applying blending modes to multiple layers.

Applying the Normal Blending Mode to a Group

Applying the Normal mode to a group prohibits blending modes on layers in the group from affecting images outside the group. For example, if you have two overlapping images set to Multiply inside a group that is set to Normal, they will only multiply over one another and over images *inside* the group. They will *not* multiply over any images on layers that are not inside the group.

You can think of a group set to Normal mode as being a collection of isolated layers—a world unto itself.

Using Adjustment Layers in Groups

An adjustment layer inside a group, such as Hue/Saturation or Levels, affects artwork outside the group only when the group is set to Pass Through. When a group is set to any other blending mode, an adjustment layer inside the group affects only the layers in that group.

Consider for a moment the time-saving opportunity this provides. Imagine that you have 10 layers of artwork, and you want to colorize all of them with a Hue/Saturation layer. Without creating a group, you'd need to create 10 Hue/Saturation layers, all with the same settings, and clip each into the 10 images. Instead, if you put all 10 images into a group and set it to Normal, you could create one Hue/Saturation adjustment layer to affect them all, and only them, with no clipping required.

Experiment with Multiply mode

1. Open PS 6-1.psd, then save it as **No Surrender**.

2. Show and target the **Magenta layer**, click the **blending mode list arrow** on the Layers panel, then click **Multiply**.

   The magenta fill becomes transparent. The effect is similar to looking at the brick wall through glass that is tinted magenta. All black areas, such as the shadow underneath the sofa, remain black.

3. Show the **Cyan layer**.

   Because the layer is set to Normal mode, the cyan rectangle obscures everything beneath it.

4. Set the **Cyan layer's** blending mode to **Multiply**.

   The cyan rectangle becomes transparent, and the overlapping area becomes blue. Figure 5 shows the Multiply blending mode calculation that creates this blue color.

5. Delete the **Magenta layer**.

6. Delete the **Cyan layer**.

7. Show and target the **Yellow-White Gradient layer**, then multiply it.

   The yellow-white gradient becomes transparent. The yellow-white gradient now transitions from transparent yellow to clear. The white area of the gradient at the bottom is no longer visible.

8. Delete the **Yellow-White Gradient layer**.

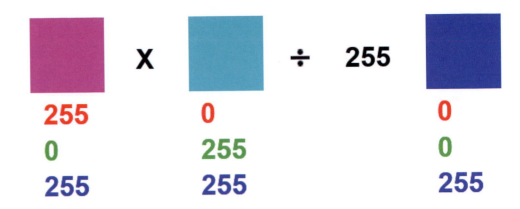

Figure 5 Calculation of magenta multiplied with cyan and producing blue

9. Show and target the **Black-White Gradient layer**, then multiply it.

   The black-white gradient transitions from black to clear. The black area at the top remains black. Black pixels have an RGB value of 0/0/0, and anything multiplied by zero becomes zero. Thus, the resulting pixel at the top of the image will be 0/0/0, regardless of what image is blended with it.

10. Delete the **Black-White Gradient layer**.

11. Save your work, then continue to the next set of steps.

You multiplied two solid fill colors to see their effect on the base image and on each other. You multiplied two gradients to demonstrate that multiplying white makes white disappear and multiplying anything with black results in black.

Applying blending modes to groups

1. Show and target the **Cyan Circle layer**, then multiply it.

2. Show and target the **Yellow Circle layer**, then multiply it.

   Where the yellow circle is multiplied over the cyan circle, a green area appears at the overlap. Both circles are multiplied over the background image.

3. Target **both layers**, then click the **Create a new group button**  on the Layers panel to create a new group.

   The two circles are moved into a group named Group 1. The blending mode applied to the Group 1 is Pass Through, by default. Pass Through indicates that the group functions only as an organizational tool to house the two layers. As shown in Figure 6, the effect of the two multiplied circles "passes through," continuing to multiply over the brick wall.

TIP You can also press and hold [command] (Mac) [G] or [Ctrl] (Win) [G] to create a group.

Figure 6 Yellow circle multiplied over cyan circle; both circles multiplied over the background

Poprugin Aleksey/Shutterstock.com

4. Change the blending mode on the **Group 1 layer** to **Normal**.

   As shown in Figure 7, the yellow circle continues to multiply over the cyan circle, but the two circles no longer multiply over the brick wall. When a group layer is set to Normal, you can think of it as a closed container. The elements inside the group only affect each other. Layers outside the group are not affected.

5. Target **Group 1**, then click the **Delete layer button** 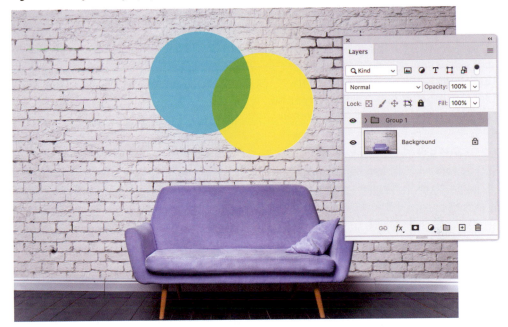 on the Layers panel.

   When you delete a group, a dialog box opens, asking if you want to delete Group and Contents, Group Only, or Cancel. If you delete Group Only, the contents remain as individual layers.

6. Click **Group and Contents**.

7. Save your work, then continue to the next set of steps.

You moved two multiplied circles into a group, noting that, by default, the group was set to Pass Through, and the effect of the multiplied circles was not changed. You then changed the blending mode on the group to Normal, noting that the multiplied circles no longer affected the background image.

Figure 7 Blending mode on group layer set to Normal

Remove a white background with the Multiply blending mode

1. Open PS 6-2.psd, then see Figure 8.

    AUTHOR'S NOTE In Figure 8, the spray paint letters spell out NO RETREAT NO SURRENDER, which is a lyric from an old Bruce Springsteen song. In this exercise, you will layout the same phrase, because it has many repeating letters and will spur you to work more quickly by duplicating layers.

2. Select the **Rectangular Marquee tool** [⬚], drag a **box** around the **letter N**, copy it, then paste it into the No Surrender document.

3. Name the new layer "**N**" and then apply the **Multiply blending mode**.

    The white background disappears.

    TIP Be sure to name every layer in this exercise.

4. Copy, paste, and multiply the following letters: **O**, **R**, **E**, and **T**.

5. Press and hold **[option] (Mac)** or **[Alt] (Win)**, then drag the **R layer** to the top of the Layers panel.

    A duplicate of the R layer is created.

    It is directly on top of the original R.

6. Move the **second R artwork** in place.

7. Duplicate the **E layer**, then move the **second E artwork** in place.

8. Using this method, finish the phrase so your artwork resembles Figure 8.

    This 20-letter phrase uses only eight different letters, so there are many opportunities for you to duplicate layers rather than copy and paste.

9. Target the **NO RETREAT letters**, then press and hold **[command] (Mac) [G]** or **[Ctrl] (Win) [G]**.

    The targeted layers are collected into a group called Group 1 with the Pass Through blending mode applied by default. Nothing changes in the artwork; the letters continue to multiply over the background image.

10. Rename the **Group 1 layer NO RETREAT**.

11. Create a new group for the **NO SURRENDER letters**, then rename the group **NO SURRENDER**.

12. Move the **NO RETREAT group** to the top of the Layers panel.

    It's always a good idea to organize your Layers panel logically.

13. Save your work, then continue to the next set of steps.

You copied and pasted letters into a document, and set their blending modes to Multiply to make their white backgrounds invisible. You created two groups to store each line of the phrase, noting that the Pass Through blending mode was applied to each group by default.

Figure 8 "Spray painted" phrase on the background image

Tomas Jasinskis/Shutterstock.com

Apply adjustment layers inside groups

1. Assess the No Retreat, No Surrender image.

   The type looks good, but because the letters are black, nothing of the brick shows through the "paint." It would be more effective if the details of the brick showed through the paint.

2. Expand the **NO RETREAT group**, target the **top layer** in the group, add a **Hue/Saturation adjustment layer**, then click the **Colorize check box** on the Properties panel.

   Because the blending mode of the NO RETREAT group is set to Pass Through, the adjustment affects the background image of the sofa.

3. Change the blending mode on the **NO RETREAT group** to **Normal**.

   Two things happen when the NO RETREAT group's blending mode changes to Normal. The Hue/Saturation adjustment continues to affect the letters because they are in the group, but it does not affect the background image because it is not in the group. In addition, the letters are no longer multiplied over the brick wall because the Normal blending mode prohibits blending modes on layers in the group from affecting images outside the group.

4. Change the blending mode on the **NO RETREAT group** to **Multiply**.

   The letters multiply over the brick wall. The Hue/Saturation adjustment layer affects all the letters, but it does not affect the background image.

TIP An adjustment layer in a group will only affect artwork on layers outside of the group when the blending mode is set to Pass Through.

5. Select the **Hue/Saturation layer**, set the **Hue** to **15**, set the **Saturation** to **40**, then set the Lightness to **+45**.

   The paint becomes rust colored, and the texture of the bricks is visible through the paint.

6. Change the blending mode on the **NO SURRENDER group** to **Multiply**, then expand it.

7. Duplicate the **Hue/Saturation adjustment layer**, then drag it into the **NO SURRENDER group** so that it's the top layer in the group.

8. Compare your artwork to Figure 9.

Continued on next page

Figure 9 Viewing the brick texture through the spray paint

It's important to understand that the letters in each group are multiplying over the background image but the Hue/Saturation adjustments are not affecting the image even though they are in the same groups as the letters. The decision to make the spray paint lighter and give it a color is an example of the opportunities you look for as a designer. The black letters certainly had presence, but the ability to see the texture of the brick through the paint brings in additional detail and integrates the effect through the interaction between the paint and the wall. Also consider that if you didn't bother to use groups, you would have had to create 20 Hue/Saturation adjustment layers, one for each letter, and you would have had to clip each of those adjustment layers into its corresponding letter. This demonstrates how useful a group can be.

9. Save your work, close No Surrender, then close PS 6-2.psd.

You added an adjustment layer to a group, noting that it affected the background image outside of the group because the group's blending mode was set to Pass Through. You changed the group's blending mode to Normal, noting that the adjustment layer no longer affected the background image. You then set the group's blending mode to Multiply to multiply the letters, noting that the Hue/Saturation adjustment continued to only affect the letters and not the background image.

Multiply images

1. Open PS 6-3.psd, select all, copy, then close the file.

2. Open PS 6-4.psd, then save it as **The Man with the Dragon Tattoo**.

3. Paste the copied image into The Man with the Dragon Tattoo file, then name the new layer **Dragon**.

4. Add a **Hue/Saturation adjustment layer**, then clip it into the **Dragon layer**.

5. Click **Colorize**, drag the **Hue slider** to **100**, then drag the **Saturation slider** to **20**.

6. Target the **Dragon layer**, then multiply it.

7. Scale the **dragon artwork 50%**.

8. With the **Dragon layer** still targeted, add a **Levels adjustment layer**.

9. On the Properties panel, drag the **white triangle** to **219**, then drag the **middle gray triangle** to **1.05**.

10. Position the **dragon** so it is centered on the man's upper arm near his shoulder.

TIP If you have trouble moving the dragon, remove the check mark next to Auto-Select on the Options panel if it is checked.

11. Zoom in on the tattoo to **300%**.

The image of the dragon is a bit too sharp-edged and highly detailed to resemble an actual tattoo. You will use a filter to blur it slightly.

12. Click **Filter** on the menu bar, point to **Blur**, then click **Gaussian Blur**.

13. Drag the **Radius slider** to **0.5 Pixels**, then click **OK**.

The slight blur makes the illustration look more like an actual tattoo. Considering that the tattoo is supposed to be on the man's shoulder muscle, the artwork is too flat; it should be more rounded. You will use a different filter for that.

14. Press and hold **[command] (Mac)** or **[Ctrl] (Win)**, then click the **Dragon layer thumbnail**.

A selection of the artwork on the layer is loaded. The selection is rectangular because, even though the artwork's white background is not visible in Multiply mode, it is still there and thus part of the selection.

TIP It is necessary to load this selection so the Distort filter you are going to use will use the center of this artwork as the center point for the effect.

15. Click **Filter** on the menu bar, point to **Distort**, then click **Pinch**.

The Pinch filter makes images either convex or concave.

16. Drag the **Amount slider** to **−15**, then click **OK**.

The filters' effects are subtle but necessary.

17. On the Layers panel, change the **Opacity** to **80%**, then compare your results to Figure 10.

18. Save your work, then close The Man with the Dragon Tattoo.

You colorized artwork green, then multiplied it over an image to create what appears as a tattoo. You used filters to blur and distort the artwork slightly.

Figure 10 Viewing the "tattoo"

PanicAttack/Shutterstock.com

EXPLORE THE SCREEN BLENDING MODE

What You'll Do

In this lesson, you'll use the Screen blending mode for different effects.

Working with the Screen Blending Mode

The Screen blending mode functions as the exact opposite of the Multiply blending mode. With Screen, black pixels become invisible, and white pixels are unaffected and remain opaque. Regardless of what colors you use, Screen mode always lightens the overlapped area, and all colors except white become transparent.

Screen blending mode has many practical uses. In Photoshop, you can take a PDF file with black type on a white background, invert the page, and then screen it to position white type over an image. Screen mode is also commonly used and very effective for lighting effects such as flares, smoke, fog, steam, and lightning. All of these can be photographed against a black background, which can then be screened out, leaving only the light component. For example, professional photographers are known to photograph smoke against a black background because they know the background can be "dropped out" using the Screen blending mode.

Experiment with Screen blending mode

1. Open PS 6-5.psd, then save it as **Flares**.

2. Show and target the **Yellow-Purple Gradient layer**, then set its blending mode to **Screen**.

    The gradient becomes transparent, and the entire image is brightened. The brightening is most apparent in the deep shadow of the water ripple at the bottom, which is now bright yellow.

3. Delete the **Yellow-Purple Gradient layer**.

4. Show and target the **White-Black Gradient layer**, then screen it.

    The white-black gradient now transitions from white to clear. The white area at the bottom remains white.

5. Delete the **White-Black Gradient layer** and the **Water Droplet layer**.

6. Show the **Outer Bevel** and **Inner Bevel layers**, then target the **Inner Bevel layer**.

7. Create a new layer, name it **Lens Flare**, then fill it with black.

8. Click **Filter** on the menu bar, point to **Render**, then click **Lens Flare**.

   Lens flare artwork is created by the Lens Flare filter. Note that the filter must have a pre-existing fill on the layer to render the artwork. Knowing that black will be dropped out with the Screen blending mode, it is the best color choice for the fill.

9. Set the **Brightness** to **100%**, then click **OK**.

10. Change the blending mode on the **Lens Flare layer** to **Screen**.

    The black background becomes clear, and the underlying type artwork becomes visible.

11. Move the **center of the lens flare artwork** over the **letter S**, as shown in Figure 11.

    When you move the lens flare artwork over the letter S, a hard line is revealed where the bottom of the lens flare artwork meets the black background. With the Screen blending mode, only black pixels with a grayscale value of 0 become 100% transparent. The Lens Flare filter lightened

Figure 11 Positioning the flare

most of the black fill; therefore, there's a faint line at the bottom because those pixels are a dark gray—not black—being screened. They must be made black.

12. Add a **Levels adjustment layer**, then clip it into the **Lens Flare layer**.

13. On the Properties panel, drag the **black triangle** right to **25**, then drag the **gray middle triangle** left to **1.32**.

    The hard line at the bottom is darkened and is no longer visible. The midtones are brighter, so they remained vibrant with the adjustment.

    Continued on next page

14. Add a **Hue/Saturation adjustment layer** above the Levels adjustment layer, then clip it.

15. On the Properties panel, click **Colorize**, drag the **Hue slider** to **223**, then drag the **Saturation slider** to **40**.

16. Target the **Lens Flare layer** and the **two adjustment layers**, then group them.

17. Verify that the **Group 1 layer** is targeted, click the **Layers panel menu button** ≡, then click **Duplicate Group**.

18. Click **OK** in the Duplicate Group dialog box to keep the name **Group 1 copy**.

TIP You can also right-click a group, then click Duplicate Group or drag the group to the Create a new layer button ⊞ on the Layers panel. If you drag the group to the Create a new group button ▢, the new group will be placed inside the original group.

19. Drag the **Group 1 copy layer** down below the Outer Bevel layer.

Figure 12 Duplicating, resizing, and repositioning lens flares

20. Expand the **Group 1 copy layer**, target the **Lens Flare layer**, scale the **lens flare artwork** to be larger, then position it **behind the letter O**.

21. Using Figure 12 as a guide, create two more duplicates of the original group, scale the lens flares to different sizes, then position them in different areas of the artwork.

22. Save your work, then close the Flares file.

You used the Lens Flare filter to create lens flare artwork on a black background. You screened the artwork to make the black background invisible and create the effect of a light shining on the type. You used a Levels adjustment to darken the background back to black after applying the filter. You then used a Hue/Saturation adjustment for a color effect.

APPLY THE OVERLAY BLENDING MODE

▶ *What You'll Do*

In this lesson, you'll use the Overlay blending mode for different effects.

Understanding the Basics of the Overlay Blending Mode

Overlay is a blending mode that adds contrast where images or color fills overlap. Given that it adds contrast, it follows logically that Overlay lightens some parts of an image and darkens others.

The key component to remember about the Overlay blending mode is that gray pixels, exactly those at 128 at the middle of the grayscale, become invisible when overlayed. Pixels lighter than 128 lighten the image as they increase to 255. Pixels darker than 128 darken the image as they decrease to 0.

See Figure 13. The original image is at the top. The bottom image has been overlayed with black, gray, and white. The area overlayed with gray is not changed. The area overlayed with white is brightened significantly, and the area overlayed with black is darkened.

Figure 13 An image overlayed with black, gray, and white

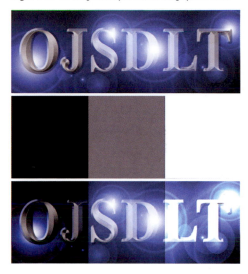

Sharpening with Overlay Mode

Sharpening is a technique for making an image appear less blurred and more in focus. Sharpening digital images is necessary because digital cameras have an anti-alias function in the lens that blurs the image slightly when it's captured to avoid creating artificial patterns (known as moire patterns).

Understanding sharpening with Overlay mode requires that you understand two concepts: edges and the results of overlaying an image on top of itself.

- The term **edges** in Photoshop refers to areas of the image where highly contrasting pixels meet. A black and white checkerboard would be an example of an image with extreme edges, because so many white pixels line up against so many black pixels.
- When you position a copy of an image on a layer on top of itself and then apply the Overlay blending mode, the result is a dramatic increase in contrast.

Sharpening with the Overlay blending mode utilizes these two concepts via the High Pass filter. As its most basic function, the High Pass filter fills a layer with gray. The High Pass filter allows you to manipulate the radius. The **radius** is a value that determines how many pixels to change on each side of the edge. When you increase the radius, the gray fill is gradually removed from the edge areas of the image; you could say those edge areas are exposed. Figure 14 shows the High Pass filter applied with a four-pixel radius. Notice the edge areas that have been exposed.

Figure 14 High Pass filter applied and exposing edge areas

The sharpening effect is achieved when this filtered image is overlayed upon itself. With Overlay blending mode, all the gray areas of the image are rendered invisible. Thus, once the High Pass filter is applied and the image is overlayed, only the edge areas are overlayed, and the dramatic increase in contrast occurs only at the edge areas of the image. The result is the appearance of an increase of focus and detail in the image.

As you can see in Figure 14, a typical image contains many edge areas. Sharpening is very effective for bringing detail to hair, beards, clothing, and eyes. Sharpening with the Overlay blending mode is something you do at the end of a project because the high pass image must match the image underneath exactly. Otherwise, halo effects will appear as a result of overlayed edges that are not aligned.

Adding Noise with Overlay Mode

One of the last steps you'll take in any project is to add noise. **Noise**, created by the Add Noise filter, refers to tiny, random, pixel-sized squares of color or gray. When overlayed, they create a texture over the image, similar to grain you might see in conventional photography.

It might seem counterintuitive that you would want to make an image grainy, but noise is used pretty much in every commercial image you see, especially artistic and photographic images such as movie posters, album covers, and magazine covers. Look closely and you'll see the noise.

As previously stated, all digital cameras blur an image slightly when it is captured due to an anti-alias function in the lens. When you create noise, however, there's no anti-aliasing; those pixels are all hard squares. When they are overlayed over the image, those tiny, hard-edged, right-angle squares convey a subtle sense of sharpness, focus, and detail.

Adding noise is particularly useful for composite image projects where you're working with multiple images from different sources. Applying noise across the entire composite adds a consistent texture throughout. It may be subtle, but that consistency creates a familiar relationship between all images, making them appear that they all exist in the same universe.

One last major reason for adding noise is it does an incredible job of hiding subtle flaws left behind, such as softness from brush edges, aliasing from masks, and subtle color halos from Hue/Saturation adjustments. Professional designers will often comment, "Don't worry, you can hide that under the noise."

Sharpen with the Overlay blending mode

1. Open PS 6-6.psd, then save it as **Sharpen and Noise**.

2. Target the **Ring layer** on the Layers panel, click **Select** on the menu bar, then click **All**.

3. Click **Edit** on the menu bar, then click **Copy Merged**.

   The Copy Merged command copies the composite of all visible layers, regardless of which layer in a layered document is targeted.

4. Click **Edit** on the menu bar, then click **Paste**.

   A flattened composite of the artwork is pasted.

5. Name the new layer **Merge Overlayed**, then set its blending mode to **Overlay**.

As shown in Figure 15, the effect of overlaying the image over itself results in a high-contrast version.

6. Duplicate the **Merge Overlayed layer**, then hide the **Merge Overlayed layer**.

7. Rename the **Merge Overlayed copy** layer **High Pass**, then set its blending mode to **Normal**.

8. Click **View** on the menu bar, then click **100%**.

   Whenever you are doing fine detail work like sharpening, you must view the image at 100% for the most accurate representation of the effect on the image.

9. Click **Filter** on the menu bar, point to **Other**, then click **High Pass**.

10. Drag the **Radius slider** all the way to the left until it reads **0.1**.

The image is filled with gray. Gray pixels set to the Overlay blending mode become invisible, so with this setting in the High Pass filter, all the artwork on the layer would be invisible.

11. Drag the **Radius slider** slowly to the right until it reads **3.0**.

As shown in Figure 16, the High Pass filter fills the artwork with gray, then, as you increase the Radius value, it finds edge areas of the image where highly contrasting pixels meet and makes them visible. Compare the roses with the coins. The coins are so much brighter because they contain so many more highly contrasting pixels that touch and are therefore exposed. The roses are more even in color, so the filter has less effect on them.

Continued on next page

Figure 15 Overlaying an image on top of itself creates a high-contrast version

Figure 16 The High Pass filter results

12. Click **OK**, set the layer's blending mode to **Overlay**, then hide and show the layer to see its effect.

The overall effect is that the image appears sharper and more in focus. The effect is stronger in high-contrast areas, such as the eyes, the coins, the diamond ring, and the details on the passport in the background. In some areas, it is not flattering. The man's skin tone is too detailed and ruddy. The rose petals and the coins are too sharp, and the line where the passport meets the black border is also too sharp.

AUTHOR'S NOTE Consider this: the High Pass layer and the Merge Overlay layer produce the same result, with the one big difference being that the High Pass layer is filled with lots of gray. The High Pass layer produces its "sharpening" effect because the high-contrast overlay is happening only where high-contrast edge pixels meet. Therefore, those "edges" are more distinct and appear "sharper."

13. Add a **layer mask** to the **High Pass layer**, click **Edit** on the menu bar, then click **Fill**.

14. Set the **Contents** to **50% Gray**, set the Mode to **Normal**, set the **Opacity** to **100%**, then click **OK**.

The mask is filled with 50% Gray; therefore, the effect is reduced by half.

15. Paint **white** in the mask where you want to see more sharpening, and paint **black** in the layer mask where you want to see less sharpening. Consider increasing it in the eyes and the diamond and reducing it in the man's face, the passport, and the border.

16. Save your work.

You used the Copy Merged command to create a composite copy of all the visible artwork. You then overlayed that artwork to see the effect of overlaying an image on itself. You created a High Pass layer and overlayed it to sharpen the edges in the image. You used a layer mask to determine where in the image you wanted to increase and decrease the sharpening effect.

Add Noise with the Overlay blending mode

1. Target the **High Pass layer**, then add a new layer.

2. Name the new layer **Noise**, then fill it with **50% Gray**.

TIP To fill the layer with 50% Gray, use the same method as you did in steps 13 and 14 in the previous exercise.

3. Click **Filter** on the menu bar, point to **Noise**, then click **Add Noise**.

4. Enter the settings shown in Figure 17, then click **OK**.

5. Set the **blending mode** of the **Noise layer** to **Overlay**.

6. Zoom in to **200%**, then hide and show the **Noise layer**.

The effect on the artwork is that of a texture of slightly darker or lighter pixels, similar to grain in a photograph.

AUTHOR'S NOTE The appeal of adding a noise layer is that it creates a consistent texture across the composite image. That consistency helps to unite the images into a whole, making them appear more

related to one another, as though they come from the same source. Typical noise values range from 8 to 12. In this exercise, 16 was used to make the effect very noticeable.

7. Save your work, then close Sharpen and Noise.

You filled a layer with 50% Gray, knowing that gray becomes invisible when multiplied. You then used the Add Noise filter to add noise to the gray layer. When you set the layer to Overlay mode, it became entirely transparent, and the noise added a grainy texture across the composite image.

Figure 17 Settings for the Add Noise filter

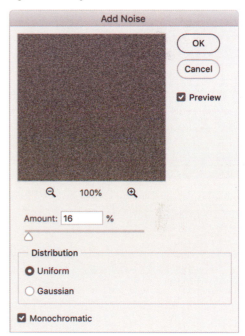

DESIGN WITH BLENDING MODES

▶ What You'll Do

In this lesson, you'll apply blending modes to adjustment layers and use them to design various effects with images.

Applying a Blending Mode to an Adjustment Layer

Let's say you have a single-layer image and you add an adjustment layer. If you don't modify the adjustment, it makes no change to the image. If you add a blending mode to the adjustment layer, the result is the same as if you copied the image, pasted the copy above it, and then applied the same blending mode to the copied image.

Even though the results are identical, applying the blending mode with the adjustment layer is the far better method, because you have all the controls available with the adjustment to modify the effect of the blending mode.

Blending modes can be applied to every type of adjustment layer. For example, you could create a Hue/Saturation adjustment layer, apply a blending mode, and then adjust the Hue, Saturation, and Lightness settings to modify the effect.

Using the Overlay and Soft Light Blending Modes to Enhance Images

The Overlay blending mode is known for making everyone and everything look better because of the dramatic increase in contrast it provides. Employing the Overlay blending mode brings with it more rich, vibrant, and intense color that results in images that take on a heightened reality and shine as though lit from within.

The Soft Light blending mode produces a similar effect to the Overlay blending mode, except that Soft Light is less intense. You can think of Soft Light as "baby Overlay."

Using Solid Color Adjustment Layers

In different situations, you'll want to fill a layer with a solid color. Often, you'll want to use the solid color with a blending mode, a technique that produces many dramatic and unexpected results. To fill a layer with a solid color, you can use the Fill command, but if you want to change the color of the fill again, you have to pick a new color and fill again. If you want to experiment with lots of different colors, it would become cumbersome.

A better method for working with fills is to add a Solid Color adjustment. When you do, the Color Picker opens for you to choose a color. You can then reopen the Color Picker, and as you sample different colors, the Solid Color adjustment updates dynamically. This can be particularly useful when you've applied a blending mode to the Solid Color adjustment because you can see the change of the effect dynamically as you sample different colors.

Using the Hue, Saturation, Color, and Luminosity Blending Modes

The Hue, Saturation, Color, and Luminosity blending modes are first cousins to the Hue/Saturation adjustment; they produce some of the same effects, and they produce different affects as well. These blending modes work well with solid color adjustments.

Let's say you choose a solid color with the HSB value of 10/80/70. Applying these four blending modes would result in the following:

Hue blending mode: All the pixels below the solid color will take on the hue of 10.

Saturation blending mode: All the pixels will take on the saturation of 80.

Color blending mode: All the pixels will take on both the hue of 10 and the saturation of 80.

Luminosity blending mode: All the pixels will take on the brightness of 70.

Knowing Which Blending Mode to Use

When introduced to blending modes, most new Photoshop users ask, "How do you know which one to use and when?" The best answer is probably, "Most of the time, you don't."

Once you understand the basic functions of the essential blending modes, situations arise in which you know for certain which mode to use. If you need to drop out a white background, you know to use Multiply. If you have an image of white smoke on a black background, you know to use Screen to just show the smoke. If you want to make artwork more vibrant and luminescent, you know to use Overlay, and if that effect is too dramatic, you know you can switch to Soft Light for a similar but diminished effect.

In addition to knowing the basic functions of the essential blending modes, you also know that they are grouped by similarity of effect. All the modes in the Darken section darken, all in the Lighten section lighten, and all in the Overlay section increase contrast. It also helps that Photoshop gives you a preview of a blending mode's effect just by floating your cursor over it.

Once you've worked a few hundred hours in Photoshop, you start to get a feel for specific blending modes, and you also start to create your own patterns and habits for working with them. Success, too, is a great instructor. For example, if you're going for a specific effect and you achieve it with a combination of blending modes, that naturally becomes a technique in your repertoire—one that you remember and one that you almost certainly will use again, perhaps with modifications. After a few thousand hours in Photoshop, you'll find that you have discovered and built more techniques for your repertoire.

Ultimately, though, blending modes are about experimentation, and when it comes to design, you're seldom, if ever, certain which blending mode to use and at which setting. Instead, you try one out, combine it with another, bring in opacity as a factor, maybe add another adjustment, and before you know it, you've achieved a look you like.

Experiment with blending modes applied to adjustment layers

1. Open PS 6-7.psd, then save it as **Adjustments and Blending Modes**.

2. Target and show the **Merge Overlayed layer**.

    This is the same merged layer you created in the previous lesson. It is overlayed over the image, resulting in a dramatic increase in contrast across the image.

3. Hide the **Merge Overlayed layer**.

4. Create a new **Hue/Saturation adjustment layer**, then set its blending mode to **Overlay**.

    The result of overlaying the Hue/Saturation blending mode is identical to overlaying the merged copy of the artwork. Adding a blending mode to any adjustment layer has the same effect as duplicating the artwork and applying the same blending mode. The great difference is that, with the adjustment layer, you have all the controls available to you to adjust the effect of the blending mode.

5. Save your work.

You viewed the effect of the composite copy of the artwork overlayed upon itself. You then created a Hue/Saturation adjustment layer and set its blending mode to Overlay, noting that the effect is identical.

Enhance an image with the Overlay and Soft Light blending modes

1. Hide and show the **Hue/Saturation adjustment layer**.

   The bump in contrast makes the image more vibrant and saturated.

2. On the Properties panel, drag the **Saturation slider** all the way left to **–100**.

   As shown in Figure 18, this creates an entirely new effect. Even though the Saturation is set to –100, the image retains color because the Overlay blending mode is applied to the Hue/Saturation adjustment. The effect is a somewhat harsh, high-contrast image drained of color. The grittiness of the Noise layer adds to that effect.

TIP The term "desaturated" doesn't necessarily mean "black and white"; it refers to a reduction of color or vibrancy in an image.

TIP A good way to reference these two effects is as "pretty" and "gritty." The overlay with the saturation is pretty, and the desaturated overlay is "gritty." Associating your own words and phrases with effects you create is a great way to relate to them and remember them for future use.

Continued on next page

Figure 18 A gritty desaturated effect with the Overlay blending mode

3. Evaluate the "gritty overlay" effect for this image.

   Visually, it's a stunning image, but it's not at all right for this collage. This collage is about romance and a happy couple getting engaged on a trip to Rome. If perhaps they were spies working undercover or planning an art heist, then maybe this effect would work, but for a romantic story, it's all wrong.

4. Drag the **Saturation slider** back to **0**.

   The overlayed Hue/Saturation adjustment is "too hot," especially in the man's face, which appears bright red.

5. Change the blending mode on the Hue/Saturation layer to **Soft Light**.

   The effect is reduced in Soft Light mode and better for this image. The color isn't so harsh or glaring.

6. Hide and show the layer.

   Compared to the original, the blending mode effect creates a heightened reality in its vibrancy. However, the effect is making the man's face still too red.

7. Verify that the **Hue/Saturation adjustment** is showing, then paint **50% black** in the layer mask to reduce the adjustment by one-half.

8. Save your work, then close Adjustments and Blending Modes.

You modified the Hue/Saturation adjustment by dragging the Saturation slider all the way to the left. You noted that the image did not become desaturated because of the Overlay blending mode. Instead, the move created a dramatic desaturated effect that was not right for the tone and content of the artwork. You applied the Soft Light blending mode, which worked best for the artwork overall but required that you reduce the effect over the man's face.

Experiment with Darken blending modes

1. Open PS 6-8.psd, then save it as **Designing Modes**.

2. Target the **Background layer** on the Layers panel.

3. Add a **Hue/Saturation adjustment**, then name the layer **Sweater**.

4. On the Properties panel, click **Colorize**, then drag the **Hue slider** to **109**.

5. **Invert** the **layer mask**, then use a soft brush to brush the adjustment into the sweater only.

6. Press and hold **[option] (Mac)** or **[Alt] (Win)**, then click the **layer mask** to view it.

7. Verify that you did not miss any spots brushing in the adjustment on the sweater, paint white if you did, then click the **layer thumbnail** to return to the image.

8. Show the other **five adjustment layers**.

   These adjustments were created with the same method you used for the sweater layer. All are set to Colorize, and all are masked in with a soft brush. All six adjustment layers have the Normal blending mode applied.

9. Target the **Backdrop layer**, change the blending mode to **Linear Burn**, set the **Saturation** to **90**, then set the **Lightness** to **–27**.

   The background becomes a deep, rich gold. The goal in this exercise is to modify the other layers to mimic this look.

10. Set the **Sweater layer** to **Multiply**, set the **Saturation** to **77**, then set the **Lightness** to **–11**.

    The goal is not to use the same blending modes; the goal is to find the best blending modes to achieve the desired effect.

11. Set the **Face layer** to **Multiply**, then set the **Saturation** to **82**.

12. Set the **Mouth layer** to **Linear Burn**, then set the **Saturation** to **55**.

13. Set the **Eyes layer** to **Linear Burn**, set the **Saturation** to **47**, then set the **Lightness** to **+15**.

14. Set the **Hair layer** to **Multiply**, set the **Saturation** to **82**, then set the **Lightness** to **+37**.

    Your artwork should resemble Figure 19.

15. Save your work, then continue to the next set of steps.

You applied the Multiply and Linear Burn blending modes with different Hue, Saturation, and Lightness values to darken the image with bold colors.

Figure 19 A darkened image with bold colors

Experiment with Lighten blending modes

1. Target all **six adjustment layers**, then create a new group.

2. Name the new group **Darkening modes**.

3. Drag the **Darkening modes group** on top of the **Create a new layer button**  to duplicate it.

   The duplicated adjustments create a dramatically different effect on the image.

4. Rename the new group **Lightening modes**, then hide the **Darkening modes group**.

5. Expand the **Lightening modes group**, then set the **Sweater layer** to **Color Dodge**.

6. Set the **Backdrop layer** to **Color Dodge**, set the **Saturation** to **70**, then set the **Lightness** to **−58**.

7. Set the **Face layer** to **Color Dodge**, set the **Saturation** to **50**, then set the **Lightness** to **−29**.

8. Set the **Mouth layer** to **Color Dodge**, set the **Saturation** to **73**, then set the **Lightness** to **−26**.

9. Set the **Eyes layer** to **Color Dodge**, set the **Saturation** to **55**, then set the **Lightness** to **−32**.

10. Set the **Hair layer** to **Color Dodge**, set the **Hue** to **44**, set the **Saturation** to **60**, then set the **Lightness** to **+5**.

11. On the **Backdrop layer**, change the **Hue** to **249**, then change the **Lightness** to **−39**.

    Your artwork should resemble Figure 20.

12. Save your work, then continue to the next set of steps.

You applied the Color Dodge blending mode with different Hue, Saturation, and Lightness values to create a bright, light, and glowing version of the artwork.

Experiment with Overlay blending modes

1. Collapse, then duplicate the **Lightening modes group**.

2. Rename the new group **Overlay modes**.

3. Hide the **Lightening modes group**.

4. Expand the **Overlay modes group**, set the **Sweater layer** to **Linear Light**, set the **Hue** to **190**, then set the **Lightness** to **−32**.

5. Set the **Backdrop layer** to **Vivid Light**.

Figure 20 A light and glowing version of the artwork

6. Set the **Face layer** to **Vivid Light**, then set the **Lightness** to **−32**.

7. Set the **Mouth layer** to **Vivid Light**.

8. Set the **Eyes layer** to **Vivid Light**, then set the **Lightness** to **−42**.

9. Set the **Hair layer** to **Linear Light**, set the **Saturation** to **49**, then set the **Lightness** to **+24**.

   Your artwork should resemble Figure 21.

10. Save your work, then continue to the next set of steps.

You applied the Vivid Light and Linear Light blending modes to create a version of the artwork with deep, rich colors and good contrast from shadow to highlight.

Figure 21 A version of the artwork with deep, rich colors

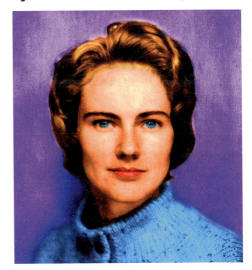

Use a Solid Color adjustment with blending modes that affect color

1. Hide the **Overlay modes group**, then show the **Darkening modes group**.

2. Create a new **Solid Color adjustment layer** at the top of the Layers panel above the **Overlay modes group**.

3. In the **Color Picker dialog box**, type **5** in the **H text box**, type **80** in the **S text box**, type **70** in the **B text box**, then click **OK**.

   The layer is filled with the color you specified.

4. Change the blending mode to **Hue**.

   All the pixels adopt the same hue (5) as the solid color.

5. Change the blending mode to **Color**, then compare your artwork to Figure 22.

   All the pixels adopt the same hue and saturation (5 and 80, respectively) as the solid color. The effect is similar, but if you click back and forth between the two, you will see there's a real difference.

6. Change the blending mode to **Saturation**.

   All the pixels adopt the 80% saturation of the solid color.

Figure 22 A version of the artwork with deep, rich colors

7. Change the blending mode to **Luminosity**.

   All the pixels adopt the 70% brightness of the solid color.

8. Change the blending mode to **Linear Dodge (Add)**.

9. Double-click the **solid color layer thumbnail** to open the Color Picker.

10. Drag the **Hue slider** to **150**.

11. Click and drag in the **color square** to sample different colors.

    As you sample different areas, the color updates dynamically on the canvas.

12. Choose a color that creates an effect you like.

13. Save your work, then close Designing Modes.

You created a Solid Color adjustment, then applied the Hue, Saturation, Color, and Luminosity modes. You then applied the Linear Dodge mode and sampled different colors in the Color Picker, noting that the artwork updated as you sampled.

Use the Multiply blending mode

1. Open PS 6-9.psd, then save it as **Multiply Skills**.
2. Hide the Original layer.
   The Masked layer is a duplicate of the Original layer with the sheet music behind the violin and carpet masked out.

TIP For an extra challenge and to practice critical masking skills, you should mask the violin yourself after completing this exercise.

3. Hide the Masked layer, then show the Sky and Clouds and Original layers.
4. Set the blending mode on the Original layer to Multiply.
   The entire image is multiplied, including the violin.
5. Add a Levels adjustment layer, clip it, drag the black triangle to 14, then drag the white triangle to 174.
   The adjustment makes the musical notes darker.
6. Show and target the Masked layer, add a Levels adjustment layer, then clip it.
7. Drag the black triangle to 13, drag the white triangle to 245, then drag the middle gray triangle left to 1.32.

8. Add a Hue/Saturation layer above the Levels adjustment layer, and don't clip it.
9. Set the blending mode to Hard Light, then drag the Lightness slider to +17.
10. Create a new layer above the Hue/Saturation layer, name it **Noise**, then fill it with 50% Gray.
11. Click Filter on the menu bar, point to Noise, then click Add Noise.
12. Set the Amount to 12, click Uniform, click to activate Monochromatic, then click OK.
13. Set the Noise layer blending mode to Overlay.
    Your artwork should resemble Figure 23.
14. Save your work, then close Multiply Skills.

Use the Screen blending mode

1. Open PS 6-10.psd, then save it as **Screen Skills**.
2. Open PS 6-11.psd, select all, copy, then close the file.
3. In the Screen Skills document, paste, then name the new layer **Coleridge**.
4. Press and hold [command] [I] (Mac) or [Ctrl] [I] (Win) to invert the layer.
5. Set the blending mode on the Coleridge layer to Screen.
6. Position the type where you like it.
7. Save your work, then close Screen Skills.

Figure 23 Sheet music multiplied over clouds image

Ingeborg Knol/imagebroker/Shutterstock.com

(continued)

Enhance an image with the Overlay blending mode

1. Open PS 6-12.psd, then save it as **Gritty Overlay**.
2. Target the Hue/Saturation layer, then add a second Hue/Saturation adjustment layer.
3. Name the new layer **Gritty Overlay**, then set its blending mode to Overlay.
   The image becomes more vibrant and saturated with higher contrast.
4. Drag the Hue slider to −100.
   The image is desaturated. The shadow on the front apple has become too black.
5. Add a Levels adjustment layer, then drag the middle gray slider left to 1.55.
6. Invert the layer mask, then brush in the adjustment to lighten the shadow on the front apple.
7. Add a new layer, name it **Noise**, then fill it with 50% Gray.
8. Open the Add Noise dialog box, specify 24 for the Amount, then click OK.
9. Set the blending mode on the Noise layer to Overlay.
10. Save your work, then close Gritty Overlay.

Add a lens flare

1. Open PS 6-13.psd, then save it as **Skills Flare**.
2. Target the Color Balance 1 adjustment layer, add a new layer, fill it with black, then name it **Flare**.

3. Click Filter on the menu bar, point to Render, then click Lens Flare.
4. Set the Brightness to 100%, verify that the 50–300mm Zoom option is chosen in the Lens Type list, then click OK.
5. Remove the check mark next to Auto-Select on the Options panel if it is checked.
6. Set the Flare layer's blending mode to Screen, then drag it below the Color Balance adjustment layer.

7. Position the flare in the sky at the horizon as though it's a sunrise or a sunset between the two rightmost trees.
   As shown in Figure 24, the green and blue parts of the flare are especially visible against the darkness of the large tree at right. The overall effect is that the photographer's camera created a lens flare while photographing a sunrise.
8. Save your work, then close Skills Flare.

Figure 24 Positioning the lens flare

Design with blending modes

1. Open PS 6-14.psd, then save it as **Skills Blending Modes**.
2. Show each of the hidden Hue/Saturation adjustment layers one at a time.

   The Face, Shirt, and Backdrop layers have been colorized. The Eyes and Hair layers are not colorized, so those adjustment layers are not affecting the image in any way.
3. Set the blending mode on the Face layer to Overlay, set the Saturation to 58, then set the Lightness to +21.
4. Set the blending mode on the Shirt layer to Hard Light.
5. Set the Hue to 11, set the Saturation to 63, then set the Lightness to −2.
6. Set the blending mode on the Backdrop layer to Linear Light.
7. Set the Hue to 49, set the Saturation to 20, then set the Lightness to −13.

   The image is dramatically higher in contrast and more vivid in color. However, the hair and the eyes have not been altered from the original image. Even though the goal is not to add color to those areas, they still require the contrast bump from the blending modes to match the surrounding areas.
8. Set the Eyes layer to Overlay.
9. Set the Hair layer to Hard Light, then drag the Lightness slider to +23.
10. Press [command] [A] (Mac) or [Ctrl] [A] (Win) to select all, click Edit on the menu bar, then click Copy Merged.
11. Target the top layer, paste, then name the new layer **High Pass**.
12. Click Filter on the menu bar, point to Other, then click High Pass.
13. Enter **5** in the Radius text box, then click OK.

    Because the blending mode effects are so sharp and vivid, adding the High Pass filter at a high level makes sense.
14. Set the High Pass layer to Overlay.

    Your artwork should resemble Figure 25.
15. Save your work, then close Skills Blending Modes.

Figure 25 Blending modes making the artwork more vivid

To create this fun and highly effective zombie image, you'll have to rely on many different skills you've learned so far in this book; those include making accurate selections and masks, crafting smart layer strategies, clipping layers, and using blending modes to achieve a desired visual effect. You will be given two flattened images: the cityscape and the zombie. Study the final image, then ask yourself if you can figure out on your own how to achieve it. Try it on your own to see how far you can get. If you can't complete it, follow the steps to the end. Have fun!

AUTHOR'S NOTE In the steps, you'll be instructed to select the zombie with the Magic Wand tool. If this were a professional project, you'd be expected to mask it with the Brush tool and a layer mask. When you're done with the project, you should take 30–40 minutes to mask the zombie anyway, which will give you more valuable experience masking images—one of the most important skills for any advanced Photoshop user to master.

1. Open PS 6-15.psd, then save it as **Hancock Tower**.
2. Click the Magic Wand tool, set the Tolerance to 32, then verify that the Contiguous option is activated.
3. Select the entire sky, and only the sky, in as few clicks as possible.
4. Click Select on the menu bar, click Inverse, copy, then paste.
5. Name the new layer **Skyline Only**.

6. Open PS 6-16.psd, use the Magic Wand tool to select the background, click Select on the menu bar, then select Inverse to select the zombie.
7. Click Select on the menu bar, click Select and Mask, type **4** in the Smooth text box, then click OK.

8. Copy the zombie.
9. Return to the Hancock Tower document, target the Background layer, paste, then name the new layer **Zombie**.
10. Using the Options panel, scale the layer 55%, then position it as shown in the Figure 26.

Figure 26 Positioning the zombie

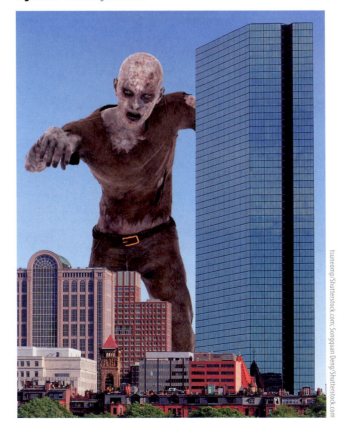

tsuneomp/Shutterstock.com; Songquan Deng/Shutterstock.com

11. Duplicate the Zombie layer, then rename it **Zombie Reflection**.

12. Drag the Zombie Reflection layer to the top of the layer stack, click Edit on the menu bar, point to Transform, then click Flip Horizontal.

13. Clip the Zombie Reflection layer into the Skyline Only layer.

14. Change the Opacity to 50%, click Edit on the menu bar, point to Transform, then click Scale.

15. Using the Options panel, scale *only the width* 86%, position the artwork as shown in Figure 27, then execute the transformation.

    Skewing the artwork creates the effect that the reflection is on the same angle as the building.

16. Add a layer mask.

17. Click the Rectangular Marquee tool, select **only** the front face of the Hancock Tower, then fill it with black. The zombie couldn't possibly be reflected on this plane.

18. Set the Opacity back to 100%, deselect, then mask the Zombie Reflection where the legs are in front of the buildings.

19. Sample through the list of blending modes to see the different effects available.

20. Set the blending mode to Overlay, then set the Opacity to 50%.

21. Add a Noise layer with an Amount of 8.

22. Compare your artwork to Figure 28 on the following page.

23. Save your work, close Hancock Tower, then close PS 6-16.psd.

Figure 27 Skewing and positioning the reflection

Figure 28 The final image

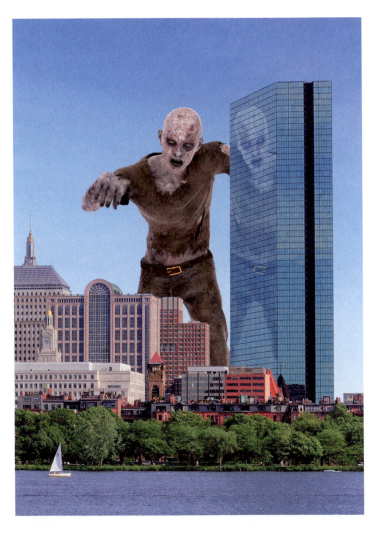

PROJECT BUILDER 2

Get your Brush tool ready for this exercise, which will ask you to do the most precise masking yet. The stunning aspect of the image is not only the smashed glass; it's also how we can see the tail inside the house as well as on either side of the windows. In many ways, it's seeing the tail *inside* the house that really makes the illusion work. This exercise provides great examples of blending modes (specifically the Screen mode), layer masks, transformations, and opacity choices all working together to produce an eye-popping effect. What you learn here can be applied to countless other situations.

1. Open PS 6-17.psd, then save it as **Komodo Attack**.
2. Show the Komodo layer, then show the House layer so you can see how the file has been built.
3. Open PS 6-18.psd, target the Tail layer, select all, copy, then close the file.
4. In the Komodo Attack document, target the House layer, paste the tail artwork, then name the layer **Tail**.
5. Remove the check mark next to Auto-Select on the Options panel if it is checked.

Figure 29 Positioning the tail

6. Position the tail exactly as shown in Figure 29, then hide the layer.
7. Save your work.
8. Open PS 6-19.psd, select all, copy, then close the file.

9. Target the House layer, paste, then name the new layer **Front Window**.
10. Set the blending mode to Screen.
11. Click Edit on the menu bar, point to Transform, then click Distort.

12. Align the four corners of the bounding box to the position shown in Figure 30, then execute the transformation.

13. Add a layer mask, choose a soft brush, set the Opacity to 40%, then fade out the breaks in the glass where they near the edge of the window.
The center of the glass should remain bright white and not be masked.

14. Save your work.

15. Show the Side Window layer, then change its blending mode to Screen.

16. Press [shift], then click the layer mask to activate it.

17. Show the Tail layer, duplicate it, then name the new layer **Tail Left**.

18. Duplicate the Tail Left layer, name the new layer **Tail Inside**, then hide the two new layers so only the original Tail layer is showing.

19. On the Tail layer, add a layer mask, then invert the mask so that the tail is completely masked.

20. Brush in the tail so that it conforms to the line where it meets the broken glass in the front window. Use Figure 31 as a guide. You can use a big brush to bring back the tail, but when you get to the glass, use a small brush (around 9 pixels or smaller if necessary) at 70% Hardness and 100% Opacity. Be sure to zoom in.

Figure 30 Distorting the front window glass

Figure 31 Mask where the tail meets the glass

21. Show the Tail Left layer, add a layer mask, invert the mask, then brush in the tail as shown in Figure 32.
22. Fit in window, then set the Opacity on the Front Window layer to 70%.
    Because that window is in shadow, the smashed glass would not be so white.
23. Hide the Tail and Tail Left layers, then show the Tail Inside layer.
24. Show the Tail Inside layer, then drag it down below the Front Window layer.
25. Set the Tail Inside layer to Hard Light, then reduce its Opacity to 70%.
26. Show the Tail and Tail Left layers, then compare your results to Figure 33 on the following page.
27. Save your work, then close Komodo Attack.

Figure 32 Mask where the Tail Left meets the glass

Figure 33 The final image

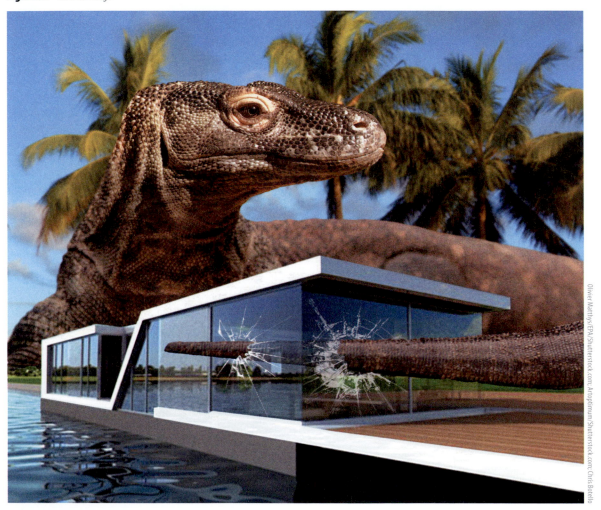

Olivier Matthys/EPA/Shutterstock.com; Artoptimum/Shutterstock.com; Chris Botello

Producing this image of the rainbow-colored giraffe will put you squarely into advanced Photoshop territory. You're going to see the Threshold adjustment used for a different purpose here. It will be a great lesson for you of how Photoshop interrelates and interconnects strategically in ways you might not first notice. Starting at step 14, this exercise will also challenge you to work effectively with multiple adjustment layers and their masks. Finally, you'll see the power that one blending mode can have to turn a colorized image instantly into art.

1. Open PS 6-20.psd, then save it as **Chromatic Giraffe**.
2. Hide and show the Red adjustment layer.
   The goal is to colorize only the giraffe's spots, which would be a very painstaking challenge to attempt with the Brush tool. Instead, we will take a smart shortcut to create a usable mask.
3. Hide the Red layer, create a Threshold adjustment layer, then drag the Threshold Level slider on the Properties panel to 138.
4. Select all, click Edit on the menu bar, click Copy Merged, then paste.
5. Click Image on the menu bar, point to Adjustments, then click Invert.
   Based on what's white and what's black, this image can be used as a mask to affect just the spots on the giraffe.
6. Select all, copy the inverted image, then hide the layer.
   Do not deselect.
7. Delete the Threshold adjustment layer, then show the Red layer.
8. Press and hold [option] (Mac) or [Alt] (Win), then click the layer mask on the Red layer.
9. Click Edit on the menu bar, point to Paste Special, then click Paste Into.
   The canvas must be selected for the Paste Into command to be available.
10. Click the thumbnail on the Red layer to view the effect.
11. Deselect, duplicate the Red layer, name the new layer **Orange**.
12. Set the Hue to 25, Saturation to 66, and Lightness to +3.
13. Mask out the orange color in the head so the giraffe shifts from red to orange.
14. Using the same method, duplicate the Red layer four more times to create layers for the following colors: yellow, green, blue, and purple.
15. Use masks to make the giraffe's colors to shift through the six colors, from left to right.
16. Create a new Hue/Saturation adjustment layer at the top of the layer stack, then set its blending mode to Vivid Light.
    Your artwork should resemble Figure 34 on the following page.
17. Save your work, then close Chromatic Giraffe.

Figure 34 Vivid Light blending mode applied to the artwork

Omer Messinger/EPA-EFE/Shutterstock.com

NATIONAL GEOGRAPHIC **STORYTELLERS**

GABRIELE GALIMBERTI

© Gabriele Galimberti

When the Italian government issued lockdown orders on March 9, 2020, as a response to COVID-19, Gabriele Galimberti was staying in the city of Milano. Rather than return to his home in Tuscany, Gabriele decided to remain in the city and document the COVID-19 quarantine for *National Geographic*.

Gabriele's photography projects explore people's daily lives around the world. They include "In Her Kitchen," a cookbook featuring grandmothers and their best recipes, and "Toy Stories," portraits of children and their toys.

Gabriele wanted to use this approach to tell the story of COVID-19 in a meaningful way. Because public places were closed and people were not allowed to meet or socialize indoors, he spent a few days figuring out how to approach the project.

When Gabriele visited his friend Veronica Strazzari, he stood out on the sidewalk and talked through her window while she stayed inside. After taking a photo of her framed in the window, he realized photos like this could show the shared common experience of isolation during quarantine. He called the project "Inside Out."

Gabriele says that because his subjects helped him by placing sanitized lights inside their homes, they became his assistants. The result is that each portrait is also a conversation.

PROJECT DESCRIPTION

In this project, you will explore distance and connection by creating a composition that tells a personal story about COVID-19. Reflect on your own experiences during the pandemic, and communicate how the distance between you and the people around you affected your sense of connection.

Use what you have available to you — your own photos, found photos, pieces of writing, art, etc.,— and create an image that tells your personal story as it relates to being quarantined, socially distanced, and separated from the people you once interacted with regularly.

QUESTIONS TO CONSIDER

What stands out to you?

Can you relate to the subject?

What do you think the story is?

GETTING STARTED

Reflect on what your life was like before COVID-19. Make a list of the activities that made up your everyday routine. Think about tasks that were so regular they became a habit.

© Gabriele Galimberti

Gabriele Galimberti, Inside Out Project, Veronica Strazzari, Milano, Italy

Working from the list you made, note which of those activities and tasks changed the most. Describe how they changed and what was most challenging about the adjustment.

Reflect on the descriptive list you've made, and using what's available to you, create a group of illustrations that visually express your feelings and experiences. These illustrations will help guide the imagery, perspective, and overall tone of your story.

CHAPTER **7**

INVESTIGATE PRODUCTION
TRICKS AND TECHNIQUES

1. Resize Images
2. Crop Images
3. Create Actions and Use the Image Processor
4. Use the History Panel and History Brush
5. Open an Image in Camera Raw

Adobe Certified Professional in Visual Design Using Photoshop CC Framework

1. Working in the Design Industry

This objective covers critical concepts related to working with colleagues and clients as well as crucial legal, technical, and design-related knowledge.

1.4 Demonstrate knowledge of key terminology related to digital images.

   A Demonstrate knowledge of digital image terminology.

1.5 Demonstrate knowledge of basic design principles and best practices employed in the design industry.

   C Demonstrate knowledge of common photographic/cinematic composition terms and principles.

2. Project Setup and Interface

This objective covers the interface setup and program settings that assist in an efficient and effective workflow, as well as knowledge about ingesting digital assets for a project.

2.4 Import assets into a project.

   C Use the Adobe Camera Raw interface to import images.

4. Creating and Modifying Visual Elements

This objective covers core tools and functionality of the application, as well as tools that affect the visual outcome of the document.

4.1 Use core tools and features to create visual elements.

   A Create and edit raster images.

4.4 Transform digital graphics and media.

   A Modify the canvas or artboards.

RESIZE IMAGES

Understanding Image Resolution

All digital images are bitmap graphics. All bitmap graphics are composed of pixels. The word **pixel** is derived from the words picture and element—pixel. You can think of a **bitmap image** as being a grid of pixels—thousands of them.

Resolution is a term that refers to the number of pixels per inch (ppi) in a digital image. For example, if you had a 1"×1" Photoshop file with a resolution of 100 pixels per inch, that file would contain a total of 10,000 pixels (100 pixels width × 100 pixels height = 10,000 pixels).

Often you will hear people refer to "high-resolution files" or "high-res files." High-resolution files are simply images that have more pixels. For any files that will be professionally printed, 300 ppi is considered a high resolution. For your home desktop printer, 150 ppi is generally enough resolution for a good-looking print. For web and other "on-screen" graphics, the standard resolution is low—just 72 ppi.

Image size refers to the dimensions of the Photoshop file. Image size is not dependent on

resolution; in other words, you could create two 3"×5" files, one at 72 ppi and the other at 300 ppi. They would have the same image size, but different resolutions.

Image size however, is related to resolution, because anytime you modify a file's image size, that will have a direct effect on its resolution. And because resolution is so closely associated with image quality, resizing an image can affect quality.

Changing an Image's Size and/or Resolution

Many situations come up in which you will want to change an image's size or resolution. Here are some examples:

■ You have a high-resolution image being used for a print project, but you also want to use the image on your website, so you must reduce its resolution from 300 ppi to 72 ppi.
■ You have a 5" × 7" image that you want to use as an 8" × 10" image for a magazine cover.
■ You've downloaded an image from a stock photography website. It is 11" × 17" at 300 ppi. The file size is 50 MB, and that's just too big for your needs.

All three of these cases require resizing, but only the second case is problematic, because it requires enlarging the image.

To best understand the ramifications of changing image size, the first thing you need to understand is the definition of captured data. **Captured data** is the digital image on your camera. The pixels in that image are the data your camera captured.

To keep the numbers easy, let's say your digital camera captures an image at 2,400 pixels wide and 1,800 pixels deep for a total of 4,320,000 pixels per image. Those numbers would be the resolution of the camera.

The image resolution is the number of pixels per inch, but that number is arbitrary and dependent on the output size of the document. For example, if you wanted to print your camera's image professionally, you would need 300 pixels per inch for the output file. Therefore, you could print an 8" × 6" image (300 pixels per inch times 8 inches equals 2,400 pixels).

Reducing the image resolution is not problematic, because all that you are doing is giving up captured data. Using your camera as an example, let's say you wanted to present the image at 8" × 6" on your website. The resolution for a web image is only 72 ppi, so you would reduce the resolution of your original image from 300 ppi to 72 ppi. If you run the numbers, that means your web image will be 248,832 pixels. So reducing the resolution from 300 ppi to 72 ppi means reducing the original image of 4,320,000 pixels to an image with just 248,832 pixels. Is this a problem? It is not, because the reduced image is still composed of original captured data.

Increasing image resolution is where the problems occur. Continuing with this example of your camera, let's say you wanted to use that original 8" × 6" image at twice the size, 16" × 12," for a poster. You are asking Photoshop to start with an image with 4,320,000 pixels and "res up" to an image of 17,280,000 pixels. You need all those extra pixels so that your 16" × 12" has the required 300 pixels per inch for professional printing. Photoshop can do that for you, but what is the reality of what's happening? Where are those "extra" 12,960,000 new pixels coming from?

When you increase resolution as in the preceding example, Photoshop creates the new pixels based on a process called **interpolation**. Photoshop uses the captured data as its source and then creates new pixels based on that data. In the preceding example, the resulting image would be 75% interpolated data. The quality of the image would be degraded substantially, and the image would become blurry and lose fine detail. If you had no other choice but to use it, you could sharpen the image and add noise to add artificial sharpness and detail.

There's one saving grace regarding this example: at least when the image size was doubled, it had a high-resolution of 4,320,000 pixels! Trouble occurs when someone expects you to print a 5" × 7" image at 72 ppi as an 8" × 10" image at 300 ppi. This is called a "garbage-in/garbage-out" scenario. Starting with such a low-resolution image, there's nothing Photoshop can do to make it print at high quality. There's simply not enough captured data to work with.

Understanding "Effective Resolution" in an InDesign Document

Often, you will create images that will be used in a layout in Adobe InDesign. When the image is placed in InDesign, it's easy to enlarge it to your heart's content. However, once again, you must ask yourself exactly what it is you're doing.

Let's say you are building a layout in InDesign for a print document. That means all photos must be printed at 300 pixels per inch. Now let's say you have a Photoshop image that is 1" × 1" at 300 ppi that you place in the document, and you size it up to 2" × 2". InDesign does not do interpolation when you scale the image. It simply takes the data you give it and spreads it out over a larger area. Thus, at 2" × 2," the **effective resolution** of the image is 150 ppi, which is half of what's needed for professional printing. Figure 1 illustrates this concept.

Effective resolution in InDesign is the resolution of the image at its current size in the layout. The takeaway from this is example is that you should save your image in Photoshop at a high resolution and at the size you want to use it in your InDesign layout. In other words, if you need a 2" × 2" image in InDesign, start with a high-resolution image in Photoshop at that size.

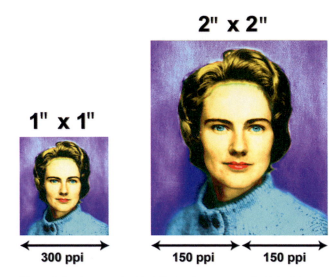

Figure 1 Resolution is reduced by half when the image size is doubled in InDesign

Reduce image size and resolution

1. Open PS 7-1.psd, then save it as **Resizing Images.**

2. Click **Image** on the menu bar, then click **Image Size**.

   The Image Size dialog box shows that this is a 2" × 2" file with a resolution of 300 ppi—thus making this a high-resolution file. The Dimensions section specifies that the full width of the file is 600 pixels (300 ppi × 2 inches), and the height is 600 pixels. Thus, this image is composed of exactly 360,000 pixels.

3. Click the **Resample check box** to remove the check mark.

   The Resample check box is the most important option in this dialog box. When Resample is **not** checked, the total number of pixels in the image must remain the same. In other words, no matter how you resize the image or change the resolution, no pixels can be added or discarded.

4. Type **100** in the **Resolution text box**, press **[tab]**, then note the changes in the Width and Height values.

The width and height of the file changes to 6". Because the total number of pixels cannot change, when the number of pixels per inch is reduced to 100, the file must enlarge to 6" wide and high to accommodate all the pixels. In other words, no pixels were added or discarded with the change in resolution—they were simply redistributed.

5. Press and hold **[option] (Mac)** or **[Alt] (Win)** so that the Cancel button changes to the Reset button, then click the **Reset button**.

The Image Size dialog box returns to its original values, and the Resample check box is once again checked.

6. Click the **Resample menu**, then choose **Bicubic Sharper (reduction)** from the menu, as shown in Figure 2.

The Resample menu contains algorithms Photoshop uses to enlarge and reduce images with resampling. Bicubic Sharper is the best choice for the highest-quality result when reducing the image size or resolution.

7. Change the resolution to **150**, press **[tab]**, then note the changes to the Width and Height values and to the pixel dimensions.

As shown in the Image Size dialog box, the image size remains at 2" × 2". Note, however, that the pixel dimensions are now 300 pixels × 300 pixels. This means that when you click OK, the total number of pixels will be 90,000. In other words, 75% of the original 360,000 pixels will be discarded because of the reduction in resolution from 300 to 150 ppi. This reduction is reflected in the Image Size reading at the top, which has gone down to 263 KB from 1.03 MB.

8. Click **OK**.

Though the image doesn't look much different on your screen, 75% of its original data has been discarded.

9. Click **File** on the menu bar, then click **Revert**.

You removed the Resample check mark then changed the resolution of the image, noting that the pixels were merely redistributed. You then reset the Image Size dialog box, which activated the Resample check box, allowing pixels to be added or discarded. When you reduced the resolution by 50%, you noted that 75% of the pixels in the original image were discarded, and the file size also went down by 75%.

Figure 2 Decreasing resolution with resampling

Increase Image Size and Resolution

1. Open the **Image Size dialog box**.

   Note that the Resample check box is checked by default. When the Resample check box is checked, pixels can be added or discarded when you resize an image. This file is 2" × 2", but it needs to be 4" × 4".

2. Type **4** in the Width text box.

   The Height value changes automatically because the Constrain Proportions feature is activated; this is represented by the link beside the width and height text boxes.

3. Note the **Resolution value**.

   The resolution remains at 300 ppi even though the image is being doubled in size. To maintain 300 ppi at the new, enlarged size, Photoshop must use interpolation to create the thousands more pixels necessary for this enlarged size. In fact, Photoshop will create three times the number of the original pixels.

4. Click the **Resample menu**, then click **Bicubic Smoother (enlargement)**, as shown in Figure 3.

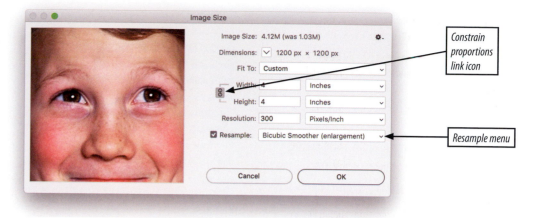

Figure 3 Increasing image size and resampling pixels

This is Photoshop's best algorithm for enlarging images with resampling.

5. Click **OK**, then view the image at **100%** to evaluate the enlargement in terms of image quality.

   Photoshop has done a good job enlarging the image, and it still looks good overall. However, as a high-resolution image for quality print reproduction, this image would be considered problematic because it is composed of 75% interpolated data. In other words, only 25% percent of the pixels are actual pixels captured in a digital camera.

6. Revert the file.

7. Open the Image Size dialog box, and ensure that the **Resample check box** is checked.

   Next you will resize the file so it could be used on a website. Resolution for images to be used on-screen is 72 ppi.

8. Change the Width and Height values to **4**, change the Resolution to **72**.

9. Click the **Resample menu**, click **Bicubic Sharper (reduction)**, then compare your dialog box to Figure 4.

   All you need to do is look at the before and after Image Size values at the top of the dialog box to see that the new size requires fewer pixels than the original size. At the new specifications, the file size will be reduced from 1.03M (megabytes) to 243.0K (kilobytes). Even though the image doubled in size from 2" × 2" to 4" × 4", the reduction in resolution from 300 ppi to 72 ppi resulted in the need for fewer than 25% of the number of original pixels.

10. Click **OK**, then evaluate the enlargement in terms of image quality.

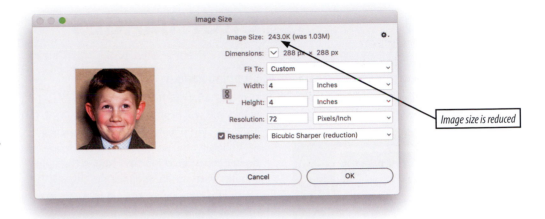

Figure 4 Decreasing image size and resampling pixels

Viewed at 100%, the image looks great on-screen, which is the goal, given that it will be used on a website. Even though Photoshop has discarded more than 75% of the original number of pixels, the reduced image contains only original data and no interpolated data.

11. Save your work, then close Resizing Images.

You increased the size and resolution of an image in the Image Size dialog box using the Bicubic Sharper (enlargement), noting that 75% of the data was interpolated. Because the quality of the image would not be acceptable, you reverted the file and then resized it using the Bicubic Sharper (reduction) option, noting that this method resulted in a better-quality image because it did not include interpolated data.

CROP IMAGES

▶ What You'll Do

In this lesson, you will use the Crop tool and the Straighten tool to crop images.

Cropping Images

Cropping might be the most underappreciated option and skill in all of Photoshop. Think of it this way: the iPhone 11 captures images at a width:height ratio of 4:3. Is 4:3 the best image size for every photo you take? Almost certainly not. But when was the last time you cropped any photo on your phone, or any of the images you post on Instagram or Snapchat?

Cropping can do wonders for an image. Figure 5 shows an uncropped image taken with an iPhone 10. It's a great photo of a great location in Utah, but the crop is not servicing the photo. There's too much unnecessary content in the foreground, and the left side also has redundant detail. In addition, the focal point of the image, where the two mountains meet, is off to the right side of the image.

Figure 5 Uncropped image from an iPhone 10

Chris Botello

Figure 6 shows the image cropped. Note the center of the image, and note also how the wideness of the crop conveys the expanse of the view.

The two images illustrate a central truth about graphic design: a designer's' fundamental role is to put the viewer immediately at ease with the sense of "I know what I'm supposed to look at first." When a layout or a single image has too much information competing for attention, it creates unconscious stress for the viewer. When the message is focused and finessed, as with this crop, the viewer can fall into the image with no resistance.

Using the Crop Tool

The Crop tool crops images to any size or rectangular shape that you desire. In addition to cropping to change the shape of an image, the Crop tool has a rotate option, allowing you to crop and rotate the image so that the resulting image is rotated by the crop. This is a good method for resolving images that need straightening.

The Crop tool also offers the option to crop to a specific aspect ratio and to a specific

Figure 6 Cropped image

size. For example, you might have an 8" × 10" image at 300 ppi, but you can set the Crop tool to crop at 4" × 4" at 150 ppi. Regardless of what size you set the crop with the Crop tool, once executed, the image will be reduced to that size and resolution.

When the Crop tool is selected, the Options panel displays options for working with the tool and techniques for cropping. The default option is Rule of Thirds, in which the Crop tool preview is divided into three rows and three columns; the points where the vertical and horizontal lines meet are where the focal points of your image should be.

Using the Straighten Tool

Another option for the Crop tool is the ability to crop an image by straightening it. The Straighten tool is a built-in tool option for the Crop tool on the Options panel. The Straighten tool draws a temporary line as you drag it across the photo. To straighten an image, drag the tool along an element in the image that should be horizontal or vertical.

Crop an image

1. Open PS 7-2.psd, then save it as **Mother's Love**.

2. Assess the image.

   This is a charming image of a mother and child. What's particularly lovely about it is how much the mother and her daughter look alike, and how similar their haircuts are as well. The key to the image is the closeness between the two, with their faces pressed together, and the way their eyes and mouths meet. Uncropped, this closeness is not being expressed to its full potential, and their faces are off-center.

3. Press the **letter [C]** on your keypad to access the **Crop tool** 🔲.

   The eight-handled crop frame appears around the image.

4. On the Options panel, click the **Clear button** to clear any prior ratio values.

   The Clear button only clears the existing values in the aspect ratio text boxes on the Options panel. It does not clear the crop grid from the image.

5. On the Options panel, click the **preset aspect ratio list arrow**, then click **Ratio**.

TIP The aspect ratio is also known as the crop size.

6. Click the **Overlay menu list arrow** ⊞ , then verify that **Rule of Thirds** and **Always Show Overlay** are both checked.

7. Drag the **center-left handle** of the crop frame to the right until the mother's and daughter's faces are centered.

8. Click and drag the **image** with the **Crop tool pointer** ▸ to position the crop as shown in Figure 7.

   In the crop, the faces are centered, and the little girl's head is centered top to bottom.

9. Press **[return] (Mac)** or **[Enter] (Win)** to execute the crop.

   The crop now emphasizes the closeness of the mother and daughter. All parts of the image that weren't part of the crop are discarded.

10. Save your work, then close Mother's Love.

You set the Overlay option for the Crop tool to Rule of Thirds. You then cropped the image.

Figure 7 Positioning for the crop

Morguefile

Rotate an image with the Crop tool

1. Open PS 7-3.psd, then save it as **Bird of Prey**.

2. Select the **Crop tool** ⬚, then position the crop frame as shown in Figure 8.

3. Position your mouse pointer at the **bottom-right corner** of the crop frame, about ¼ inch outside of the frame.

   The Crop tool pointer ▸ changes to a rotate icon ↲.

4. Click and drag counterclockwise until your screen resembles Figure 9.

   As you drag, the image is rotated behind the crop frame. Note that the eagle's eye is now at the intersection of the top-left squares.

5. Execute the crop, then compare your result to Figure 10.

   What was a very stagnant snapshot of a bird looking left is transformed into a dynamic and forceful square image. The eagle's beak pointing down diagonally toward the corner of the crop creates remarkable tension, and the diagonal white feathers in the top-right corner backed by the diagonal brown lines from the background now bring movement to the whole image. The original image was a photo of a bird. The cropped image is a bird of prey, swooping down for the kill. This is a stunning example of how much change a crop can bring to an image.

6. Save your work, then close Bird of Prey.

You rotated an image behind the crop frame, producing an entirely different effect with the resulting image.

Figure 8 Positioning for the crop

Figure 9 Rotating the image behind the crop frame

Figure 10 The dynamic cropped image

MorgueFile

Crop to a specific size and resolution

1. Open PS 7-4.psd, then save it as **Bird Bookmark**.

   The goal of this exercise is to create a tall, thin bookmark from this image. The resulting image must be high resolution at 300 ppi.

2. Click **Image** on the menu bar, then click **Image Size**.

   This image has a resolution of 72 ppi.

3. Click **Cancel**.

4. Click the **Crop tool** , click the **preset aspect ratio list arrow** on the Options panel, then click **W × H × Resolution**.

5. On the Options panel, type **2** in the **set the width text box**, then press **[tab]** to set the height.

6. Type **6** in the **set the height text box**, then press **[tab]** to set the resolution.

7. Type **300** in the **px/in text box**.

   Your Options panel should resemble Figure 11.

TIP Be sure your ruler units are set to inches.

8. Position the crop as shown in Figure 12.

   As you drag the Crop tool, the image's width and height are constrained to the 2:6 proportion.

9. Execute the crop.

10. Open the **Image Size dialog box**.

    The image is 2" wide and 6" tall at a resolution of 300 ppi. In this case, there were enough pixels in the image that interpolation was not necessary to achieve this resolution at this size. However, had there not been enough original data, the crop would have interpolated the data to "res up" the image.

11. Save your work, then close Bird Bookmark.

You specified a width, height, and resolution for the crop. The resulting crop was produced at exactly those settings.

Figure 11 Options panel for the crop

Figure 12 Positioning for the crop

Straighten an image with the Crop tool

1. Open PS 7-5.psd, then save it as **Straighten and Crop**.

2. Assess the image.

   The image is the front entrance of a hotel named Cathedral. It is on a steep hill, so the doorway is on an angle from the horizontal bottom of the image.

3. Click the **Crop tool** ⌸, then click **Clear** on the Options panel.

4. Click the **Straighten button** on the Options panel, then float your mouse pointer over the image.

   The cursor changes to the Straighten tool ⊹.

5. Click and drag the **Straighten tool** ⊹ down the **far-left edge of the door frame**, as indicated by the red line in Figure 13, then release the mouse pointer.

The image is rotated so the door frame is parallel to the left edge of the image.

6. Crop the image using Figure 14 as a guide.

7. Save your work, then close Straighten and Crop.

You used the Straighten tool to straighten the doorway of a building and then cropped the image. By doing so, the doorway and building were in alignment with the edge of the entire image.

Figure 13 Using the Straighten tool to straighten an image

Drag Straighten tool along door frame

Figure 14 The straightened and cropped image

CREATE ACTIONS AND USE THE IMAGE PROCESSOR

In this lesson, you will use the Actions panel, the Image Processor, and the Batch feature to automate working with files.

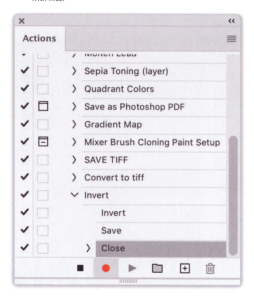

As designers, we like to focus on the big projects: the magazine covers, the posters, the billboards, the CD covers. But in the real world, it's not only the big projects that come across our desks; it's often the small stuff that you've got to handle as well. And the small stuff usually requires repetition. For example, you might receive 25 RGB files and be asked to convert them to CMYK and resize them so they are all seven inches wide. Or you might be given a folder full of PSD files and asked to convert them all to Grayscale mode and save them as 72 dpi JPEG files that can be used on a website. Sound like fun?

Fortunately, Adobe has made an enormous commitment to automation, especially since the advent of the Internet and the huge amount of image processing that creating and maintaining a website demands.

You might have played with the Actions panel before, but in this lesson, you're going to take a more rigorous and in-depth tour, and you're going to use more advanced features like batch processing and modal controls. You will also use Photoshop's Image Processor, which is a file conversion dream come true.

Using the Image Processor Dialog Box

In a professional ad agency or design firm, it's often the case that a client will send a folder full of images that need to be converted from one file format to another. This is where the Image Processor dialog box comes into play. The Image Processor can take a folder full of .psd files and quickly convert them into .tiff copies or .jpeg copies (or both) and put them into new folders. A situation in which literally hundreds or thousands of files need to be converted can be commonplace in some digital environments, and the Image Processor makes easy work of it.

Creating Actions on the Actions Panel

Once you've put 10,000 hours into Photoshop, you'll be amazed at how many repetitive sequences you do on a regular basis. For example, think of the sequence needed for creating a new noise layer: create a new layer, fill the layer with 50% Gray, open the Add Noise dialog box, enter the amount of Noise, click or don't click Monochromatic check box, click OK, set the layer's blending mode to Overlay. That's a lot of steps.

The Actions panel is designed to record a sequence just like this. Once recorded, you'll never have to step through it again. Instead, simply run the action on the Actions panel.

You might be thinking at this point, "But what about the amount of noise? What if I don't want the same amount of noise every time? What if I want to choose every time?" That's where modal controls come into play. A **modal control** stops the action at a specified step; a dialog box opens, allowing you to enter specific settings for that step. Continuing with the noise example, once you put a modal control on the Add Noise step, the action will stop when the Add Noise dialog box opens, allowing you to specify the amount of noise you want to use for the given project. Modal controls allow you to save an action sequence once and use it in different ways for different projects in perpetuity.

Using the Batch Dialog Box

The Batch dialog box gives you the power to apply an action sequence to a folder of files. Where the Image Processor is focused on changing file formats of a group of files, the Batch dialog box can apply more complex actions. For example, let's say you had a folder with 100 images downloaded from your camera. All of them are high resolution, and each of them is exactly the same size: 50 MB. You will give low-resolution images to your design team to produce ideas, because you don't want everybody working with 50 MB files. So you create an action that opens the Image Size dialog box and resizes the images to 6" × 8" at 150 ppi. That's when the Batch dialog box comes into play. Rather than you having to open each of the 100 files and apply the action, the Batch dialog box applies the action to all

the images in an instant. The Batch dialog box can save new, modified copies of the originals in the same folder and overwrite the originals, or you can create a new destination folder for the copies, leaving you with two sets.

Use the Image Processor

1. Open the seven files in the Automation folder located in the Chapter 7 Data Files folder.

    The files are all Photoshop (PSD) files. The goal of this lesson is to create one TIFF and one JPEG copy of each of the seven files.

2. Click **File** on the menu bar, point to **Scripts**, then click **Image Processor**.

3. In **Section 1 (Select the images to process)**, click the **Use Open Images button**.

    The Image Processor will only process the currently opened Photoshop files.

4. In **Section 2 (Select location to save processed images)**, click the **Save in Same Location button**.

5. In **Section 3 (File Types)**, click the **Save as JPEG check box**, then type **12** in the **Quality text box**.

6. In **Section 3**, click the **Save as TIFF check box**.

7. Verify that nothing is checked in **Section 4 (Preferences)**, then compare your Image Processor dialog box to Figure 15.

Continued on next page

Figure 15 Image Processor dialog box

8. Click **Run**.

The seven original PSD files remain open after the Image Processor is done.

9. Navigate to the **Automation folder**, then open it.

The Automation folder contains the seven original PSD files. It also contains a folder named JPEG and a folder named TIFF. These two folders contain the JPEG and TIFF copies generated by the Image Processor.

10. Return to Photoshop and keep all files open for the next set of steps.

You used the Image Processor dialog box to convert seven PSD files into seven new TIFF copies and seven new JPEG copies. You were able to specify where the files were saved to, and you were able specify the quality for the JPEG files.

Create and run an action on the Actions panel

1. Click **Window** on the menu bar, then click **Flowers.psd** at the bottom of the menu.

2. Click **Window** on the menu bar, then click **Actions**.

3. Click the **Actions panel menu button** ☰ , then verify that **Button Mode** is not checked.

4. Click the **Actions panel menu button** ☰ again, then click **New Action**.

5. Type **Invert** in the **Name text box**, then click **Record**.

A new action named Invert appears in the list on the Actions panel and is highlighted. The Begin recording button is activated. Any step you make at this point will be recorded as part of the action, so you need to be ready to go when you click the Begin recording button.

6. Click **Image** on the menu bar, point to **Adjustments**, then click **Invert**.

The Flowers.psd image is inverted.

7. Click **File** on the menu bar, then click **Save**.

8. Click **File** on the menu bar, then click **Close**.

9. Compare your Actions panel to Figure 16.

The three commands that you executed—Invert, Save, and Close—are listed as commands under the Invert action.

10. Click the **Stop playing/recording button** ◼ on the Actions panel.

11. Click **Window** on the menu bar, then click **Marble.psd**.

12. Click **Invert** on the Actions panel so that it is highlighted.

This is an easy step to miss—you must go back and target the action by its name before you can run it.

13. Click the **Play selection button** ▶ on the Actions panel.

You will only see the image closing. This is because "Close" is the final command of the action.

14. Repeat the **Invert action** for the remaining open images.

15. Open all **seven PSD files** in the **Automation folder**.

All seven images have been inverted.

16. Close all seven PSD files.

You used the Actions panel to create and specify a simple action of inverting an image, saving it, and then closing it. You applied that action to six other images.

Figure 16 Invert action with three commands

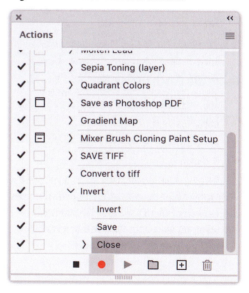

Batch process an action

1. Click **File** on the menu bar, point to **Automate**, then click **Batch**.

   No files need to be open.

2. In the Play section, click the **Action list arrow** to see all the actions available, then click **Invert**.

3. In the **Source section**, verify that **Folder** is chosen, then click **Choose**.

4. Navigate to and select the **Automation folder**, click **Select Folder**, then click **Choose (Mac)** or **OK (Win)**.

5. Verify that **none** of the **four check boxes** in the **Source section** are checked.

   Remember that the Automation folder now contains two subfolders—JPEG and TIFF—created from the first lesson of this chapter. This action should not be applied to the contents of those folders, so the *Include All Subfolders* option should not be checked.

6. In the **Destination section**, verify that **None** is chosen.

   No destination means that we want to affect the targeted images in the folder and for those images to be saved with the change. If you wanted to affect a *copy* of the images and save it in a new location, you would need to specify a destination for the copies.

7. In the **Errors section**, verify that **Stop for Errors** is chosen, then compare your Batch dialog box to Figure 17.

8. Click **OK**.

   The seven images are all affected by the action and then closed.

9. Open all seven PSD files from the Automation folder.

   All seven files have been inverted again and therefore appear as they did originally.

10. Keep all seven files open and continue to the next set of steps.

You used the Batch dialog box to apply the Invert action to a folder of images.

Figure 17 Batch dialog box

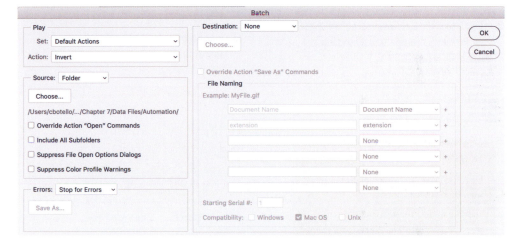

Create a complex action

1. Click **Window** on the menu bar, then click **Bricks.psd**.

2. Click the **Actions panel menu button** ☰, then click **New Action**.

3. Type **Processed Textures** in the **New Action dialog box**, then click **Record**.

4. Click **Image** on the menu bar, point to **Mode**, then click **CMYK Color**.

5. Click **Image** on the menu bar, then click **Image Size**.

6. Type **120** in the **Resolution text box**, then verify that your **Image Size dialog box** resembles Figure 18.

7. Click **OK**.

8. Click **Filter** on the menu bar, point to **Sharpen**, then click **Unsharp Mask**.

   Unsharp Mask is a sharpening filter. It produces similar results to the High Pass/Overlay technique you learned in Chapter 6.

9. Enter the settings shown in Figure 19, then click **OK**.

10. Click **File** on the menu bar, then click **Save As**.

11. Navigate to the **Automation folder**, open it, then create a new folder inside named **Processed Textures**.

12. Save **Bricks** as a PSD file in the **Processed Textures folder**.

13. Click the **Stop playing/recording button** ■ on the Actions panel.

14. Click ❯ to expand the **Unsharp Mask item** on the Actions panel.

    The settings for the Unsharp Mask are listed.

15. Click ❯ to expand the **Save action** on the Actions panel.

    The file format and the destination folder are recorded with the Save command.

16. Collapse the **Unsharp Mask** and **Save** items by clicking ⌄ .

17. Click **Window** on the menu bar, click **Wood.psd**, then click the **Processed Textures action** on the Actions panel.

Figure 18 Image Size dialog box

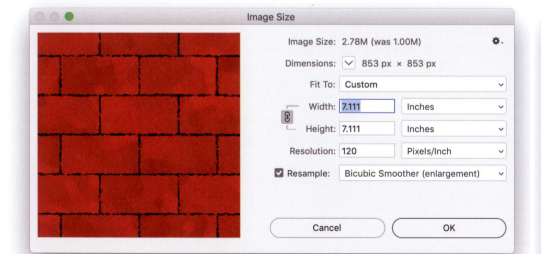

Figure 19 Unsharp Mask dialog box

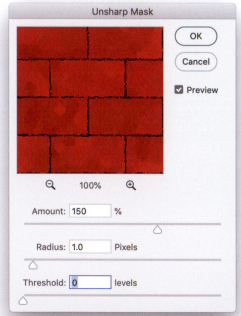

18. Click the **Play selection button** ▶ on the Actions panel.

The original file is left unchanged. The action is applied to a copy of the original whenever you choose a destination folder. The copy was saved as a PSD file with the same name in the Processed Textures folder. Both the original Wood.psd file and the new CMYK version remain open.

19. Continue to the next set of steps.

You used the Actions panel to create a complex action that involved converting an image's mode, resizing it, applying a filter, and saving a copy as a PSD file in a new folder.

Apply modal controls to an action

1. Click **Window** on the menu bar, then click **Water.psd**.

2. Click the **Toggle dialog on/off button** ☐ to the left of the **Unsharp Mask command** to activate it.

This button is known as a **modal control** ☐. With the modal control turned on, the action sequence will stop when it gets to the Unsharp Mask step and open the Unsharp Mask dialog box so you can adjust the settings if you so choose. Your Actions panel should resemble Figure 20.

3. Click the **Processed Textures action** on the Actions panel.

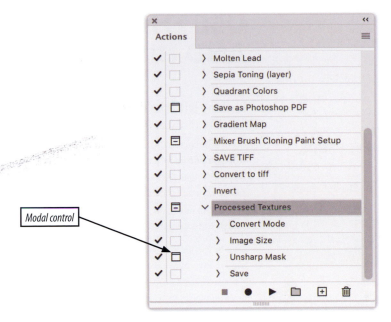

Figure 20 Modal control on the Actions panel

4. Click the **Play selection button** ▶.

The Processed Textures action pauses at the Unsharp Mask command, opens the dialog box, and awaits your input.

5. Change the **Amount value** to **75%**, then click **OK**.

The command is executed.

6. Apply the **Processed Textures action** to the remaining four PSD files, entering whatever settings you like for the Unsharp Mask filter.

7. Close all open files.

You added a modal control to the Unsharp Mask step, which pauses the action and gives you the option to enter new settings for that step.

USE THE HISTORY PANEL AND HISTORY BRUSH

▶ What You'll Do

In this lesson, you will learn how to return to a saved version of your work using the History panel, snapshots, and the History Brush tool.

Working with the History Panel

The History panel is like a visual version of the Undo command on the Edit menu. As you work, the History panel records all moves you make and lists them as steps in a sequence. At any time, you can click on a previous step that you made, and your work on the canvas will return to that step in the process.

One of the keys to understanding the value of the History panel is to consider that you will work on Photoshop projects that can take days or even weeks to finish. When you see a project from this perspective, it becomes clearer how important it is that you save iterations of the project at different stages.

The History panel allows you to take a snapshot of your project at any given time. A **snapshot** is a record of the project as it is at that given moment. The snapshot is listed at the top of the History panel. Once you've created a snapshot, you can be assured that you can always return to that state of the artwork simply by clicking

the snapshot. Even if you've worked for days before realizing you've gone in the wrong direction and want to return to a previous state, you can simply click the snapshot on the History panel and instantly get back to the state. It's like a super Undo command.

Before the advent of the History panel, designers would save copies of the file at different stages to achieve this same ability to return to a state of the work. That method came at the cost of saving numerous large files and having to organize and manage them. With the History panel, saving a project at a certain iteration is as simple as clicking a button on the History panel.

Using the History Brush Tool

The History Brush tool is used for restoring part of the artwork back to what it was at an earlier stage of the project. You should think of the History Brush tool as a production tool *rather* than a creative tool.

The History Brush tool allows you to paint from any step that's been recorded in the History panel. Let's say you are working on an image that requires a lot of painting and masking. Now let's say you've made 100 moves with the Brush tool, and you realize that in one area, you liked it better the way it was when you saved a snapshot at step 40. You don't want to return the whole canvas to step 40 for just one object. In that case, you can use the History Brush tool to paint in just that object as it was recorded at step 40.

Using the Fill with History Option

The Fill command on the Edit menu offers the opportunity to fill a selection from a previous state. In the Fill dialog box, choose History from the Use menu. When you execute the fill, the selected pixels will be reverted to what they were when the image was last saved.

Use the Fill dialog box to fill using history

1. Open PS 7-6.psd, then save it as **Fill from History**.
2. Open the History panel.
3. Click **Image** on the menu bar, point to **Mode**, click **Grayscale**, then click **Discard**.

   On the History panel, the step is listed as Grayscale.
4. Click **Image** on the menu bar, point to **Mode**, then click **RGB Color**.

   RGB Color is listed as the next step on the History panel.
5. Click the **Rectangular Marquee tool** , then make a selection that encompasses the **eyes**, **nose**, and **mouth**.
6. Click **Edit** on the menu bar, then click **Fill**.
7. Enter the settings from Figure 21 in the Fill dialog box.
8. Click **OK**.

   The selection is filled with color because the pixels in this selection were in color when the file was opened.
9. Save your work, then close Fill from History.

You converted the file to Grayscale then back to RGB Color, producing a black and white image in RGB Color mode. You made a selection, then chose History from the Contents menu on the Fill dialog box. The fill restored the pixels in the selection to their status when the file was first opened.

Figure 21 Fill dialog box set to fill Contents using History

Revert to a snapshot on the History panel

1. Open PS 7-7.psd, then save it as **History Snapshot**.

2. Open the **History panel**.

3. Click the **Brush tool**, set the **Opacity** to **100%**, then set the **Hardness** to **100%**.

4. Set the **Size** to **500 px**, then set the **Mode** to **Soft Light**.

5. Choose a **red foreground color**, then click the brush **seven times** using different brush sizes so that your artwork resembles Figure 22.

6. Click the **Create new snapshot button** 📷 on the History panel.

   A new snapshot appears at the top of the History panel named Snapshot 1.

7. Double-click the name **Snapshot 1** to select it, then rename it **Red Circles**.

   Your History panel should resemble Figure 23.

8. Choose a **yellow foreground color**, then click the **Brush tool** to make **seven yellow circles** of different sizes that overlap the red circles.

   Note that the yellow circles *should* overlap the red circles.

Figure 22 Red circles painted on the canvas

Chris Botello

Figure 23 Red Circles snapshot on the History panel

9. Choose a **green foreground color** and a **smaller brush size**, then make **seven green circles** on the canvas that **overlap only red circles**.

   Figure 24 shows one example of what your canvas might look like. The green circles should *not* overlap yellow circles.

10. Decide that you might have preferred the artwork with just red circles, then click the **Red Circles snapshot** at the top of the History panel.

    The artwork is restored to its state when you created the snapshot.

11. Decide that you prefer the artwork with all the colors, scroll to the bottom of the History panel, then click the **bottommost Brush tool snapshot**.

    The artwork returns to your last brush move.

12. Decide that there are too many yellow and green circles on the canvas, and you need to remove two of each.

13. Note the **Sets the source for the history brush icon** beside the **top snapshot (PS 7-7.psd)** on the History panel.

14. Click the **empty box** beside the **Red Circles snapshot** so appears on the **Red Circles snapshot**.

15. Click the **History Brush tool** on the toolbar.

16. Paint over **any two yellow circles** and **any two green circles**.

    The green and yellow circles are "removed." Wherever you paint, the canvas is restored

Figure 24 Yellow and green circles added to the artwork

to the state it was when you created the Red Circles snapshot.

AUTHOR'S **NOTE** Building the file this way would be silly because it's so destructive. You could just as easily have put the red circles on one layer, the yellow circles on another, and the green circles on another and set the blending modes for all three to Soft Light. That would have allowed you to mask out any circle you wanted to. However, this exercise was meant to demonstrate how the History Brush tool can save you from a tricky situation. Those situations often occur when you make a destructive move that you cannot undo or revert. In those cases, sometimes it's

the History Brush tool that can bail you out. One of the key takeaways from this lesson is to save often and to save snapshots often in the History panel, especially when you're working on long and involved projects. All it takes is losing three hours' work to learn the lesson the hard way.

17. Save your work, then close History Snapshot.

You painted red circles over an image and then saved a snapshot of that state in the History panel. You then painted yellow and green circles. You explored the option of restoring the artwork to the Red Circles state in the History panel. You then used the History Brush tool to restore just parts of the image to the Red Circles' state.

OPEN AN IMAGE IN CAMERA RAW

▶ What You'll Do

In this lesson, you'll open and edit an image in the Camera Raw utility window.

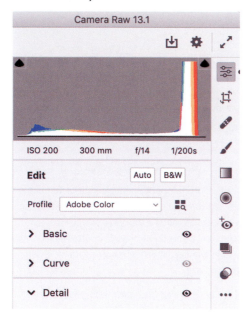

Investigating Camera Raw

A **Camera Raw** image is a digital image that hasn't been compressed or otherwise processed. When you set your digital camera to capture data in Camera Raw, the digital file that you download from your camera is as close to the actual image that was captured as possible. A Camera Raw file is not reduced by any compression algorithms, nor is the image manipulated by other algorithms that "ride" with the compression algorithms; therefore, the file size of a Camera Raw image is larger than compressed images.

The main alternative to shooting in Camera Raw is shooting in JPEG (or JPG) mode. JPEG is a compression algorithm that reduces the file size of images as they are captured. JPEG has become a standard format for digital cameras because it allows you to store more images on a photo card, and it allows the camera to capture frames more rapidly. Camera Raw images have file sizes that are much larger, so fewer of them fit on a card, and it's possible that your camera will take a fraction of a second longer to process before shooting the next image.

Despite the larger file size, many photographers prefer to shoot in Camera Raw because they want an image to be pure and unadulterated.

Once downloaded, rather than work in Photoshop, many workers open the Camera Raw file in the Camera Raw utility. This utility offers many image-adjustment controls that will look familiar to you from Photoshop: Shadows, Highlights, Hue, Saturation, and so forth. It also offers controls you've not seen in Photoshop, such as Temperature, Tint, Clarity, and Dehaze.

As a Photoshop designer, you might initially feel that you want to do all your work, including image adjusting, in Photoshop. That's fine. However, the more and more involved you get working with Photoshop, the more involved you are likely to get with digital photography. In the process of searching out more photography to work with, you will meet photographers, and you will likely purchase your own equipment and start shooting your own images to get exactly what you want for your projects. Once you start working with photographers or with your own camera, you too will be put in the position of choosing to shoot in Camera Raw or in JPEG. You'll also be put into the position of having to sift through dozens, if not hundreds, of images downloaded from your camera, and you might find yourself exploring possibilities with those images quickly in Camera Raw rather than going immediately into Photoshop.

Editing an image in Camera Raw

1. In Photoshop, navigate to where you store your Chapter 7 Data Files, then open PS 7-8.rw2.

   The RW2 file extension indicates that this is a Camera Raw file. The image opens in the Camera Raw utility with an Edit panel on the right side of the image.

   TIP If the Set Up Camera Raw window opens asking you to choose from two user interface (UI) styles, choose a style, then click OK.

2. On the **Edit panel**, drag the **Exposure slider**, under the **Basic section**, to **+1.40**.

   The Exposure setting represents the amount of light that was captured for the photograph. Increased exposure brightens the image overall.

3. Click the **White balance list arrow**, above Temperature, then click **Cloudy**.

   White balance is a process by which unrealistic color casts are removed from areas of an image that are meant to appear as neutral white.

4. Click the **Set zoom level list arrow** in the bottom-left corner, choose **100%**, then use the **Hand tool** 🖐 to center the eagle's head in the view window.

5. Drag the **Vibrance slider** to **+28**.

6. Expand the **Detail section** on the Edit panel.

7. Drag the **Sharpening slider** to **60**, then drag the **Noise Reduction slider** to **20**.

   Your Camera Raw utility window should resemble Figure 25.

8. At the bottom-right corner of the window, note the two buttons **Done** and **Open**.

9. Click **Done**.

   Clicking Done applies the changes you made in the Camera Raw window and closes the file.

10. Open the file PS 7-8.rw2 again.

    The image reopens in Camera Raw with all the adjustments you made still active. However, these edits were *not* saved with the image file. Instead, another file, followed by an .xmp suffix, was created in the same folder as PS 7-8.rw2. This file contains the code of the edits you made. When you reopen the image file, it references the code to restore your edits in the Camera Raw dialog box.

11. Click **Open**.

The image opens in Photoshop in RGB Color mode.

12. Open the Image Size dialog box.

    The image is roughly 17" × 13" at 300 ppi. Since the file is so large, you won't save a Photoshop version; you always have the Camera Raw data file should you want to do further work.

13. Click **Cancel**, then close the file without saving changes.

You opened an image in Camera Raw and improved it dramatically with the control functions in the utility. You clicked Done, which applied and saved the changes with the file. You reopened the file, noticed the changes were saved, then opened the image in Photoshop.

Figure 25   The Camera Raw utility window

SKILLS REVIEW

Reduce image size and resolution

1. Open PS 7-9.psd, then save it as **Eagle Comp**.
2. Click Image on the menu bar, then click Image Size. This is a huge digital file. It's roughly 17" × 11" at 300 ppi.
3. Verify that the Resample check box is checked, click the Resample menu, then click Bicubic Sharper (reduction).
4. Change the Width to 8, then change the Resolution to 150.
   Your Image Size dialog box should resemble Figure 26. Note at the top that the new file size will be 2.57M, reduced from 48.1M.
5. Click OK.
   While this is no longer a high-resolution file at this size, there is no interpolated data in the resulting image because Photoshop does not manufacture pixels in a reduction; on the contrary, it discards them.
6. Save your work, then close Eagle Comp.

Figure 26 Image Size dialog box set for reduction

Enlarge image size and increase resolution

1. Open PS 7-10.psd, then save it as **Reflecting Pool**. Imagine your client sent you this image from his website and asks you to use it as an 8" × 10" image to be printed as the cover image on his company's annual report. Right away, you realize that he does not understand anything about image resolution.

2. Click Image on the menu bar, then click Image Size. This image is low resolution. It has just 423 pixels as its width. This image is 6" × 4" at 72 ppi. This makes sense, because it was being used on the client's website, and 72 ppi is the resolution for on-screen images. When you explain to your client that the image can't be used at the large size he wants, he asks you to "res it up" with hopes that it won't look so bad.

3. Verify that the Resample check box is checked, click the Resample menu, then click Bicubic Smoother (enlargement).

4. Change the Width to 10.
   The Height changes to 6.667, which is less than the client needs for an 8" × 10" final image. Not only is this image's resolution too low to work with, it's also not proportional to the client's needs and will need to be cropped.

5. Change the Height to 8.
   The Width increases to 12.

6. Change the Resolution to 300.

Your Image Size dialog box should resemble Figure 27. The Image Size information at the top of the dialog box indicates that the file size will increase from 364.5K to 24.7M. The 423-pixel width that you started with will be interpolated to 3,600 pixels, nearly a 900% increase. This is becoming a mission that cannot succeed.

7. Click OK, click View on the menu bar, then click 100%.

The resulting image is obviously low quality and unacceptable for any professional publication like an annual report. The entire image is blurry and pixelated and lacks any semblance of detail. When your client sees the results of trying to "res up" a file, he finally understands why his original photo will never work for print. He hires a photographer to capture the same image at the correct resolution needed for a high-quality print job, like an annual report.

8. Save your work, then close Reflecting Pool.

Figure 27 Image Size dialog box set for enlargement

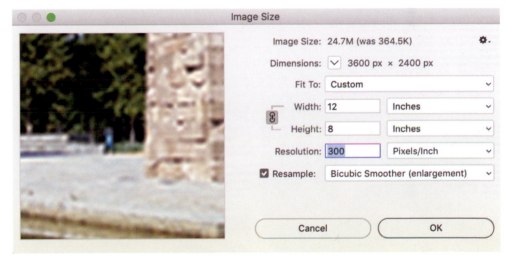

Straighten an image with the Crop tool

1. Open PS 7-11.psd, then save it as **Skyline Straighten**.
2. Press the letter [C] on your keypad to access the Crop tool, then click the Straighten button on the Options panel.
3. Note the line where the buildings meet the water line.
4. Drag the Straighten tool approximately 1 inch along the water line.
   The image is rotated so that the waterline is parallel to the bottom edge of the image.

5. Click [return] (Mac) or [Enter] (Win) to execute the crop.
6. Save the file, then close Skyline Straighten.

Crop images to a specific size and resolution

1. Open the three Construction photos in the Construction folder.
   You will resize each image to 2" × 2" at 300 ppi so they can be positioned side by side as a trio.
2. Click the Crop tool, click the preset aspect ratio list arrow, then click W × H × Resolution on the Options panel.
3. Type **2** in the set the width text box, then press [tab] to set the height.
4. Type **2** in the set the height text box, then press [tab] to set the resolution.

5. Type **300** in the px/in text box.
6. View the Construction 1 image, then crop it in a way that you think looks good.
7. Switch to the Construction 2 image, then crop it in a way that makes it a partner to the first image.
8. Switch to the Construction 3 image, then crop it as the third in the series.
   Figure 28 shows one example of the three crops.
9. Save Construction 1 as **Construction 1 cropped**, then close the file.
10. Save Construction 2 as **Construction 2 cropped**, then close the file.
11. Save Construction 3 as **Construction 3 cropped**, then close the file.

Figure 28 Three crops at 2" × 2" and 300 ppi

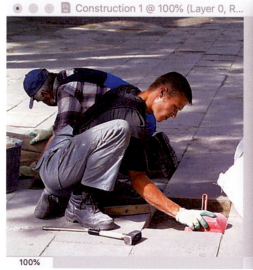
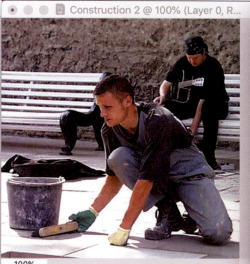
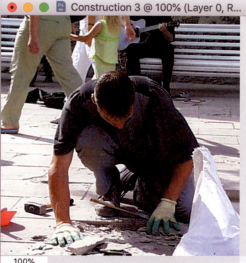

Create and apply an action

1. Open the Patterns folder, then open all seven images in the folder.
2. Click Window on the menu bar, then click Blue at the bottom of the menu to switch to the Blue file.
3. Open the Actions panel, click the Actions panel menu button, then click New Action.
4. Type **Resolution 300 to 72** in the Name text box.
5. Click Record.
6. Click Image on the menu bar, then click Image Size.
7. Verify that the Resample check box is checked, click the Resample menu, then click Bicubic Sharper (reduction).
8. Change the Resolution to 72, then click OK.
9. Click File on the menu bar, then click Save As.
10. Create a new folder, then name it **72 ppi**.
11. Set the file type as Photoshop, then click Save.
12. Click File on the menu bar, then click Close.
13. Click the Stop playing/recording button on the Actions panel.
14. Switch to the Yellow file, then target the Resolution 300 to 72 action on the Actions panel.
15. Click the Play selection button.
    The Yellow file vanishes because the last step in the action is Close.
16. Apply the Resolution 300 to 72 action to the remaining four files.
17. Open the 72 ppi folder.
    The folder contains six files that all have 72 ppi as their resolution.

Batch process an action

1. Click File on the menu bar, point to Automate, then click Batch.
2. In the Play section, click the Action list arrow, then click Resolution 300 to 72.
3. In the Source section, click the Choose button, navigate to the Halftones folder, click to select it, then click Choose.
4. Verify that none of the four check boxes are checked.
5. Click OK.
6. Navigate to the 72 ppi folder in the Patterns folder, then open it.
   As shown in Figure 29, seven files with the name Halftone have been added to the 72 ppi folder with the pattern files.

Figure 29 Seven Halftone images added to the 72 ppi folder

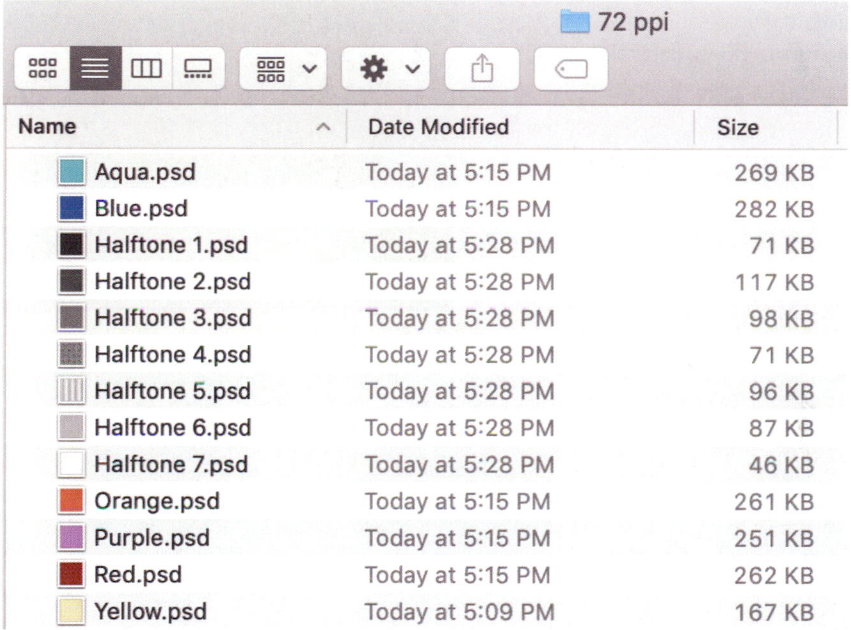

Edit an image in Camera Raw

1. In Photoshop, navigate to where you store your Chapter 7 Data Files, then open PS 7-12.rw2. The image opens in the Camera Raw utility.
2. In the Basic section, drag the Temperature slider to 5300.
3. Drag the Exposure slider to +0.15.
4. Drag the Clarity slider to +24.
5. Drag the Vibrance slider to +33, then drag the Saturation slider to +10.
   Your Camera Raw window should resemble Figure 30.
6. Click Done.

Figure 30 The Camera Raw utility window

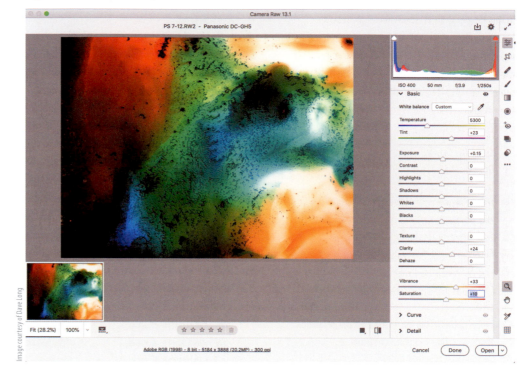

Image courtesy of Dave Long

PROJECT BUILDER 1

In this Project Builder, you will create an action for a High Pass sharpening layer, one that you can use over and over in your work. Because you will use the filter at different strengths for different projects, you will use a modal control for the filter step in the action.

1. Open PS 7-13.psd, then save it as **Sharpen Stripes**.
2. Target the Cyan layer on the Layers panel.
3. Open the Actions panel, click the Actions panel menu button, then click New Action.
4. Name the new action **High Pass Sharpen**, then click Record.
5. Click Select on the menu bar, then click All.
6. Click Edit on the menu bar, then click Copy Merged.
7. Click Edit on the menu bar, then click Paste.
8. Click Filter on the menu bar, point to Other, then click High Pass.
9. Type **3** in the Radius text box, then click OK.
10. Set the layer's blending mode to Overlay.
11. Click the Stop playing/recording button on the Actions panel.
12. Click the empty square beside the High Pass step on the Actions panel to add a modal control to that step.
    Your Actions panel should resemble Figure 31.
13. Save your work, then close Sharpen Stripes.
14. Open PS 7-14.psd, then save it as **Violin Sharpened**.
15. Hide the Noise layer, then target the Hue/Saturation 1 adjustment layer.
    When you sharpen, never include a noise layer in the sharpening.
16. Target the High Pass Sharpen action on the Actions panel, then click the Play selection button.
    Because of the modal control, the action stops when the High Pass dialog box opens.
17. Type **2** in the Radius text box, then click OK.
18. Rename the new layer **HP2.0**, then show the Noise layer.
19. Save your work, then close Violin Sharpened.

Figure 31 High Pass Sharpen action on the Actions panel

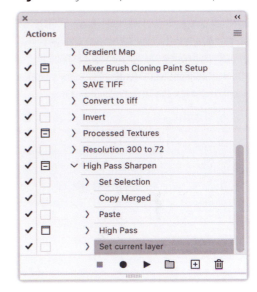

In this Project Builder, you will create an action for a Noise layer, one that you can use over and over in your work. Because you will want to add noise in different amounts for different images, you will use a modal control for the filter step in the action.

1. Open PS 7-15.psd.
2. Target the Cyan layer on the Layers panel.
3. Open the Actions panel, click the Actions panel menu button, then click New Action.
4. Name the new action **Add Noise Layer**, then click Record.
5. Click the Create new layer button.
6. Click Edit on the menu bar, then click Fill.
7. Fill the layer with 50% Gray.
8. Click Filter on the menu bar, point to Noise, then click Add Noise.
9. Type **8** in the Amount text box, then click OK.
10. Set the layer's blending mode to Overlay.
11. Click the Stop playing/recording button on the Actions panel.
12. Click the empty square beside the Noise step to add a modal control to that step.
    Your Actions panel should resemble Figure 32.
13. Close the file without saving changes.

Figure 32 Add Noise Layer action on the Actions panel

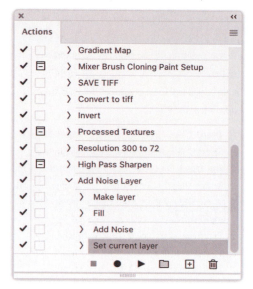

DESIGN PROJECT

This Design Project uses an abstract image to give you the opportunity to explore more artistic aspects of cropping. You will crop one image multiple times at different sizes. There will be no "right" answers. Crop in a way that feels right and looks interesting to you.

1. Open PS 7-16.psd.
   This is the image that you edited in the Camera Raw lesson.
   You will crop the image to be framed at four different sizes, all at 300 ppi.
2. Click Image on the menu bar, then click Duplicate.
3. Repeat Step 2 to make three more duplicate files.
4. Click the Crop tool, then use the W × H × Resolution Ratio setting to crop the first image at 2" wide × 2" high at 300 ppi.
5. Repeat Step 4 to create four more cropped images at the following sizes:
   2" × 8", 3" × 6", 5" × 7", and 6" × 6".
6. When you are done, save all five images, and name them by their size dimensions.
   Figure 33 shows an example of the five cropped images.

Figure 33 One image cropped five different ways

CHAPTER **8**

DISTORT AND
LIQUIFY IMAGES

1. Use the Distort Command
2. Create a Cast Shadow
3. Investigate the Liquify Filter
4. Create a Puppet Warp
5. Distort Text

Adobe Certified Professional in Visual Design Using Photoshop CC Framework

4. Creating and Modifying Visual Elements

This objective covers core tools and functionality of the application, as well as tools that affect the visual outcome of the document.

4.1 Use core tools and features to create visual elements.

  A Create and edit raster images.

4.4 Transform digital graphics and media.

  B Rotate, flip, and modify individual layers, objects, selections, groups, or graphical elements.

4.5 Use basic reconstructing and retouching techniques to manipulate digital graphics and media.

  B Use various tools to repair and reconstruct images.

USE THE DISTORT COMMAND

What You'll Do

In this lesson, you'll distort artwork to match the perspective of the images they're being placed into.

Using the Distort Command

Distort is a one of the commands on the Transform submenu—along with Scale, Rotate, and Perspective. When you apply the command, an eight-handle bounding box appears around the artwork. You distort an image by moving any or all of the four corner handles independently of one another.

Using the Distort Command to Create an "In Situ" Presentation

Imagine you are a designer working on artwork for a billboard. Your client will want to see an example of the artwork as it would appear in a real-life situation (referred to as "in situ"). This requires you to paste your artwork into a photograph of an existing billboard to show how the artwork would look as a billboard. The Distort command is useful whenever you paste rectangular artwork into a scene and need to match the perspective of the image you are pasting into. In Lesson 1, you will be the designer replacing an old billboard with a new one.

Use the Distort command

1. Open PS 8-1.psd, then save it as **Charlie & Me In Situ**.

   This image is of a hotel on the Sunset Strip in Los Angeles—one mile of billboard after billboard advertising everything from movies to TV shows, to high-end fashion.

2. Open the file named Charlie Key Art.psd, select all, click **Edit** on the menu bar, then click **Copy**.

3. Close the Charlie Key Art file.

4. In the Charlie & Me In Situ file, target the **Bottom Billboard layer**, then paste.

5. Name the new layer **Charlie Key Art**, then clip it into the **Bottom Billboard layer**.

6. Click **Edit** on the menu bar, point to **Transform**, then click **Distort**.

7. Align **all four corners** of the **Charlie Key Art artwork** with the four corners of the bottom billboard, as shown in Figure 1.

Figure 1 Aligning the four corners of the bounding box

Chris Botello

8. Execute the transformation by pressing **[return] (Mac)** or **[Enter] (Win)**.

9. Open Charlie Billboard.psd, select all, click **Edit** on the menu bar, click **Copy**, then close the file.

10. In the Charlie & Me In Situ file, target the **Top Billboard layer**, then paste.

11. Name the new layer **Charlie Billboard**, then clip it into the **Top Billboard layer**.

12. Click **Edit** on the menu bar, point to **Transform**, then click **Distort**.

13. Align **all four corners** of the Charlie Billboard artwork with the four corners of the top billboard.

14. Execute the transformation, then compare your results to Figure 2.

   This exercise is remarkably effective at providing a realistic example of what the artwork would look like in a real-world environment. Most projects that involve outdoor advertising use in situ examples like this.

15. Save your work, then close Charlie & Me In Situ.

You distorted two pieces of artwork to fit into an outdoor advertising setting.

Figure 2 Aligning the four corners of the bounding box

CREATE A CAST SHADOW

▶ **What You'll Do**

In this lesson, you'll access a selection of masked artwork, fill it with black, then distort it to create a cast shadow.

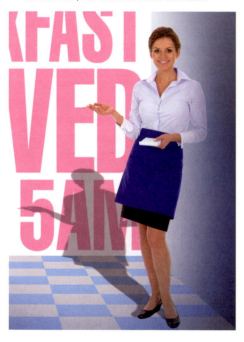

Exploring and Identifying Shadows

Understanding shadows, dealing with shadows, and creating shadows are all milestones in the arc of a Photoshop user's journey. Shadows are inevitable. As soon as you copy and paste one image into another, you can't avoid asking if it would create a shadow and what that shadow would look like. That question gets magnified when building a collage with multiple images, because then you must decide how all those images would create shadows, not only on the background but on each other.

The ultimate instruction for understanding shadows is to look at the real world itself. The first question with shadows is always, "What's the light source?" In a natural environment, the sun is the greatest of all light sources. At any given time on any given day, our world has abundant shadows whenever the sun is in the sky. But that doesn't mean shadows are consistent. Shadows on a bright day will be darker and have a sharper edge. Shadows on a gray day will be lighter and more diffuse. If you are familiar with sun dials, you know shadows change constantly based on the angle of the sun.

Observing and studying shadows in the natural environment is an exercise in learning to see. You'll be amazed at how many preconceived notions you have about shadows that turn out to be incorrect once you look more closely. For example, we often think that one object casts one shadow. That may be the case in most outdoor settings, where the sun is the only light source, but in many settings, one object will cast two or more shadows.

Another visually fascinating aspect of shadows is how they adapt themselves to the setting. For example, you could be standing in direct sunlight and cast a long shadow behind you. That shadow will extend in that direction until it encounters a different surface. For example, you might cast a shadow on the cement behind you, but if there's also a wall, when your shadow encounters that wall, it will change direction and climb the wall. Shadows are almost liquid in the way they instantly conform to any given environment.

Shadows are how we interpret our world. Shadows give dimensionality to our world. A sphere can only appear as a sphere if there's a highlight rounding its way gradually to a shadow. A cube can only be a cube with one bright plane and two other darker planes. A cone is only a cone when it shifts from highlight to shadow as only a cone does. Keep this in mind as you look at Figure 3 and consider the light source, where light strikes the object directly, and where light strikes the object indirectly.

You can think of shadows as falling into three categories.

- **Cast shadows:** When you shine a light directly onto something, it throws or casts a shadow in the direction completely opposite of the light source. Figure 4 shows an example of a cast shadow. Note that, just by looking at the direction of the shadow, you know the direction from which the light source is coming.
- **Touch shadows:** These shadows occur at the point where an object makes contact

with another object. At that point, even if there's a cast shadow formed, the point of contact creates a darker shadow within the cast shadow.
- **Secondary shadows:** These shadows occur when there are two or more light sources; you will see them most often indoors when you have natural light coming in from a window and other light coming from an artificial source, like a lamp or a TV screen. In that case, you will see two shadows moving in two different directions. Usually, one is darker than the other.

Figure 3 Observing shadows and highlights on three-dimensional graphics

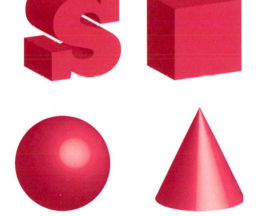

Figure 4 Illustration of a cast shadow

In addition to these three types of shadows, there's another type of shadow to consider, and it's not really a shadow at all. Let's say you photograph a person with a bright light aimed at just one side of his or her face. The lighted side of the face will be clearly visible, bright, and saturated with color. The unlit side of the face will be in relative darkness. We would say that there's a shadow on that side of the face, but think about it: yes, it's darker, but not because anything is casting a shadow on it. That side of the face is darker only because there's no light shining on it. It's "in shadow" because of the absence of light shining on it.

Keep these concepts in mind when you study shadows, and certainly when you attempt to paint them in Photoshop. If you're using the Brush tool, stay very conscious of your brush edge as well. Shadow edges are hardest when they are closest to the object casting the shadow, and they diffuse as they gain distance from the object.

Lastly, remember that all shadows are transparent. If you're standing on a blue and white checkerboard floor and you're casting a shadow, you will see the checkerboard through the shadow. With this in mind, it becomes

clear why Multiply mode, (in conjunction with Opacity settings) is the go-to blending mode when working with shadows in Photoshop.

Creating Shadows in Photoshop

Sometimes creating a shadow is as simple as applying a little bit of transparent black where two objects meet. This is especially the case for touch shadows.

Cast shadows can be just as easy, or seemingly impossible. Some shadows are so challenging to create that doing so crosses the line into illustration and demands the "hand talent" that you'd get from a gifted art school student or professional illustrator.

The essential question to ask yourself when creating a cast shadow is this: "Can I use the selection of the object casting the shadow to create the shadow itself?" Figure 5 shows a man casting a shadow on a wall behind him. This would be an easy shadow to create, because the man and his shadow are essentially the same shape. All you'd need to do is select the shape of the man; copy it; fill it with black; then use opacity, a feathered edge, and perhaps some distortion to create the shadow behind him.

Figure 5 The shadow and the subject casting the shadow are the same shape

Figure 6, on the other hand, presents a far more difficult situation. If you only had the image of the woman walking, how would you recreate the shadow in Photoshop? The key problem is that the shape of the woman is in no way the shape of the shadow she is casting. Unless you had a photo of the same image shot simultaneously from the angle representing the shadow, you'd have no alternative but to paint the shadow from scratch.

Figure 7 shows a most difficult scenario. Not only is the shadow of the glass not the shape of the glass itself, the detail in the shadow of the glass is abstract, complex, and recognizably realistic. Rendering this from scratch in Photoshop would require the talents of a gifted illustrator. It would be easier to photograph the glass and its shadow yourself rather than trying to render so complex and demanding a shadow by hand.

The Internet is filled with websites devoted to "bad Photoshop art." They're a lot of fun and highly instructive. You'd be amazed how much you can learn about getting things right by studying work other people got wrong. One big category on these sites is "impossible shadows." In almost every case, the impossible shadow results from the Photoshop artist using a selection of an object to cast a shadow that couldn't possibly be cast from that shape.

Figure 6 The shadow and the subject casting the shadow are two different shapes

Michael Dietrich/Shutterstock.com

Figure 7 The glass casts a shadow that would be very difficult to recreate with the Brush tool

Syda Productions/Shutterstock.com

Create a complex cast shadow

1. Open PS 8-2.psd, then save it as **Cast a Shadow**.

   This image is designed as an online advertisement for a restaurant's website.

2. Target the **Waitress layer**, press and hold **[command] (Mac)** or **[Ctrl] (Win)**, then click the **Create a new layer button** ⊞ on the Layers panel.

   A new layer is created *below* the targeted layer.

3. Name the new layer **Shadow 1**.

4. Press and hold **[command] (Mac)** or **[Ctrl] (Win)**, then click the **thumbnail** on the **Waitress layer**.

   The waitress artwork is loaded as a selection. The selection will be used to create a shadow.

5. With the **Shadow 1 layer** still targeted, fill the selection with **black**.

6. Deselect.

7. Show the **Shadow 1 Template layer**.

   The Shadow 1 Template layer is there as a guide for you to align the shadow you're about to make.

8. Verify that the **Shadow 1 layer** is targeted, click **Edit** on the menu bar, point to **Transform**, then click **Distort**.

9. Drag the **top-middle handle** and then the **bottom-middle handle** to distort the shadow and align it to the Shadow 1 Template, as shown in Figure 8.

10. Press **[return] (Mac)** or **[Enter] (Win)** to execute the Distort transformation.

11. Hide the **Shadow 1 Template layer**.

12. Click the **Rectangular Marquee tool** ⬚, then select the **top of the shadow** with the bottom line of the selection aligned to where the white wall meets the checkerboard floor.

    Use Figure 9 as a guide for making the selection.

13. Click **Edit** on the menu bar, click **Cut**, then press **[command] [V] (Mac)** or **[Ctrl] [V] (Win)** to paste.

    A new layer appears above the Shadow 1 layer. You cut the top half of the shadow and pasted it on a new layer so that you can distort it separately from the bottom half.

14. Name the new layer **Shadow 2**, then use the **Move tool** ✛ to realign it with the bottom half of the shadow.

15. Set the **Opacity** of the **Shadow 1** and **Shadow 2 layers** to **50%**.

Figure 8 Distorting the shadow

pixelstock/Shutterstock.com

Figure 9 Selecting the top half of the shadow

16. Show the **Shadow 2 Template layer**.

17. Verify that the **Shadow 2 layer** is targeted, click **Edit** on the menu bar, point to **Transform**, then click **Skew**.

18. Move the **cross hair** from the **center** of the **bounding box** down and position it over the **bottom-center handle** of the bounding box.

19. Press and hold **[option] (Mac)** or **[Alt] (Win)**, then drag the **top-center handle** to the right until the Shadow 2 artwork aligns with the Shadow 2 Template.

20. Hide the **Shadow 2 Template layer**.

21. Set the **blending mode** of the **Shadow 1** and **Shadow 2 layers** to **Multiply**.

22. Set the **Opacity** on the **Shadow 1 layer** to **40%**, then set the **Shadow 2 layer** to **30%**.

23. Zoom in on the **waitress's shoes**.

    The point where the shadow makes contact with its source is always a critical spot.

24. Target the **Shadow 1 layer**, then access the **Distort command**.

25. Drag the **bottom-middle handle** to reposition the shadow in relation to the shoes as shown in Figure 10.

    While it may seem risky to distort the artwork and disrupt the alignment of the two shadows, moving just the bottom handle will have no effect on the artwork at the top. This kind of exercise often requires these little tweaks at the end.

26. Compare your results to Figure 11 on the following page.

Figure 10 Positioning the shadow behind the shoes

AUTHOR'S **NOTE** One sure way to know the shadow is successful is that it's not the first thing you notice when you look at the artwork. The eye has a brilliant ability to instantly spot anything that goes against reality, so when creating shadows, there's no greater compliment. Note the powerful role the shadow plays in this artwork. The setting is clearly an illustration and not real. The woman, however, is real. Look at how the shadow builds a bridge connecting the real woman with the unreal setting. The shadow creates an interrelationship between the woman and the setting. If she's real, and she's casting a shadow, and that shadow is interfacing with the setting, then it's so much easier to believe in the entire illustration. In fact, most viewers won't notice that the setting is an illustration on first and even second glance. That's because of the power of the shadow. The shadow sells the illusion.

27. Save your work, then close Cast a Shadow.

You made a selection of the waitress, then filled it with black to create artwork for a shadow. You distorted the shadow artwork two different ways to create the illusion that the waitress is casting a shadow on the floor that goes up the back wall.

Figure 11 Final image with a realistic cast shadow

INVESTIGATE THE LIQUIFY FILTER

▶ What You'll Do

In this lesson, you'll use different features of the Liquify filter to distort images.

Using the Liquify Tools

Liquify is a powerhouse filter used to distort images in a variety of ways. The filter has its own set of tools, shown in Figure 12, each of which offers a specific type of distortion. Some of the most useful include the following:

- **Forward Warp tool** 🖐 : Like the Smudge tool, when you drag the Forward Warp tool over an area, it moves those pixels in the direction you drag. The Forward Warp tool is perhaps the most important tool in the Liquify window because it can be used for many practical purposes and fine corrections.

- **Reconstruct tool** 🖌 : This is a revert brush. Wherever you paint with the Reconstruct tool, the image is reverted to its state when you opened the Liquify window. Because you can use this with a soft brush at different sizes, it's very powerful for restoring unwanted changes that occur when Liquifying.

Figure 12 Liquify tools

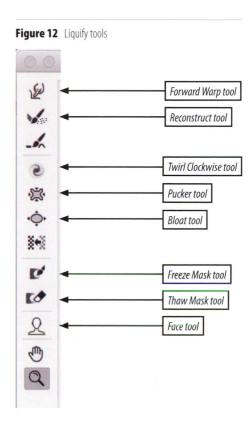

- **Twirl Clockwise tool** ⊛ : This tool functions like the Twirl filter; it rotates pixels clockwise from the center of the brush to create a whirlpool effect. Hold down [option] (Mac) or [Alt] (Win) and the tool will twirl counterclockwise. This isn't the most practical tool, but it is fun.
- **Pucker tool** ⊛ : Think of your lips puckering; they pull in your whole mouth toward the center. The Pucker tool does the same with pixels, pulling them toward the center of the brush in a concave movement. The general result is that the Pucker tool will reduce the size of imagery it paints.
- **Bloat tool** ◈ : The Bloat tool is the opposite of the Pucker tool. The Bloat tool moves pixels outward from the center in a convex movement. The result is a fisheye distortion.
- **Freeze Mask tool** 📝 : The Freeze Mask tool protects any area that you paint from being modified by any of the Liquify tools.
- **Thaw Mask tool** 📝 : Removes the protection from areas painted by the Freeze Mask tool.

- **Face tool** 👤 : The Face tool has been programmed to recognize universal facial features such as eyes, noses, mouths, jaws, chins, and head shapes. The Face tool places shapes and handles around different facial features, allowing you to drag those handles and make precise distortions.

The Liquify filter is Photoshop's funhouse mirror, but its value is not only about making bizarre distortions. The Liquify filter offers many practical solutions for common problems. If your subject is squinting a bit in an image, use Liquify to open the eyes. If you work with lots of faces, Liquify is great for small cosmetic changes such as giving a double chin a quick tuck. And it is a godsend for making motion and stretching images to make them appear to be speeding by.

Experiment with the Liquify tools

1. Open PS 8-3.psd, then save it as **Investigate Liquify Tools**.

   In this exercise, you will focus mostly on learning the Liquify tools. You will explore other Liquify features such as the much discussed and controversial face recognition tools in Chapter 10.

2. Duplicate the **Background layer**, then name the new layer **Liquify**.

3. Click **Filter** on the menu bar, then click **Liquify**.

   The artwork opens in the Liquify window.

4. Click the **Freeze Mask tool** 📝 , then paint the **dog's nose** so it resembles Figure 13.

   Freezing the nose protects it from any changes made in the window.

Figure 13 Freezing the dog's nose

5. Click the **Pucker tool** ⚏, then set the **Size** to **400** on the Properties panel.

TIP Resizing a brush in the Liquify window is done with the same keyboard keys as with the Brush tool. Use the right bracket ( ]) on your keypad to enlarge the brush size and the left bracket ([ ) to reduce it. The Size text box, on the Properties panel, shows the exact size of the brush.

6. Press and hold down the **Pucker tool** ⚏ over the **left eye** to make it increasingly smaller.

7. Reduce the size of the **right eye** to the same size you did for the left.

8. Click the **Thaw Mask tool** 🖌, then paint to remove the freeze mask from the dog's nose.

   Figure 14 shows one example of potential results so far.

9. Click the **Reconstruct tool** 🖌, then paint over the **eyes** to restore them to their original size.

The Reconstruct tool reverts the image's appearance to before it was opened in the Liquify window.

10. Click the **Bloat tool** ⬩, then set its **Size** to **400**.

11. Press and hold down the **Bloat tool** ⬩ over the **left eye** to make it larger.

12. Enlarge the size of the **right eye** to the same size you did for the left.

13. Click the **Forward Warp tool** 🖑, then set its **Size** to **90**.

14. Click and drag the **dark fur under the dog's nose** to put a smile on his face, as shown in Figure 15.

15. Enlarge the **Size** to **600**.

16. Click and drag strategically to enlarge the **dog's ears** substantially.

Figure 16 shows one example. Compare this to using the Forward Warp tool to put the smile on the dog's face. With a much larger brush, moves you make with the Forward Warp tool are far less concentrated and less obvious. You can pull at the dog's ears in different directions and move lots of pixels at one time. The effect is stronger at the center, but the large brush spreads out the effect.

17. Click **OK**.

18. Hide and show the **Liquify layer** to see the changes you made.

19. Save your work, then close Investigate Liquify Tools.

You opened an image of a dog in the Liquify window and used various Liquify tools to enlarge and then reduce the dog's eyes and ears. You also made the dog smile.

Figure 14 Using the Pucker tool to make the dog's eyes smaller

Figure 15 Using the Bloat tool to make the dog's eyes larger and the Forward Warp tool to make him smile

Figure 16 Enlarging the dog's ears

Use the Forward Warp tool with precision

1. Open PS 8-4.psd, then save it as **Face-Aware Liquify**.

2. Duplicate the **Background layer**, then name it **Straighten Nose**.

   You can see by the highlight on the man's nose that his nose is not straight. As we look at him, it bends to the right. This can be straightened quickly with the Liquify filter.

3. Open the **Liquify window**, click the **Forward Warp tool** , then set its **Size** to **300**.

4. Center the **Forward Warp tool** over the **man's nose** so the bottom of the brush aligns exactly with the very bottom of the man's nose.

5. Click and drag slowly to the left until the highlight on his nose straightens out.

6. Reduce the **brush size** to **175**, make any fine tweaks to the nose you think are necessary, then click **OK**.

   Figure 17 shows before and after results.

7. Save your work, then continue to the next set of steps.

You applied the Liquify filter to an image of a man and used the Forward Warp tool to straighten his nose.

Mirror a face

1. Select all, click **Edit** on the menu bar, then click **Copy**.

2. Verify that the **Straighten Nose layer** is targeted, then paste.

3. Hide the **Background layer** and the **Straighten Nose layer**.

4. Name the new layer **Mirror Distort**.

5. Click **Edit** on the menu bar, point to **Transform**, then click **Flip Horizontal**.

6. Click the **Add layer mask button** on the Layers panel.

7. Click the **Gradient tool** on the toolbar.

Figure 17 Nose straightened with the Forward Warp tool

8. Set the **foreground color** to **white**, then set the **background color** to **black**.

9. On the Options panel, choose the **Foreground to Background gradient** in the **Basics folder**.

TIP Verify that the Linear Gradient button is selected on the Options panel.

10. Position the **Gradient tool** on the **left side of the highlight on the man's nose**, then drag and release approximately **one-quarter inch to the right side of the highlight**, as shown in Figure 18.

    The right half of the face disappears and becomes transparent. The gradient creates a very short transition.

Figure 18 Dragging the Gradient tool to create a white-to-black linear gradient

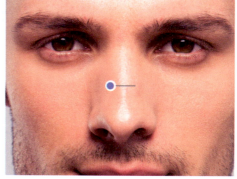

11. Show the **Straighten Nose layer**.

Your results should resemble Figure 19. What you're seeing is the same half of the face flipped and mirrored to create the whole face. The line where they meet does not show because the gradient in the mask creates a seamless transition between the two mirrored halves.

12. Invert the layer mask.

Inverting the mask shows the ***other*** half of the face flipped and mirrored to create the whole face. As shown in Figure 20, the second face is remarkably different, considering this is the same person. This is because the man is not looking at us exactly straight on in the original image. His head is slightly turned to the right of the screen. This slight difference between left and right is enough to make the two versions vastly different from one another.

13. Save your work, then continue to the next set of steps.

You created a mirror image of the man's face on a new layer. Then you added a layer mask and used the Gradient tool to hide half of the man's face on the mirrored image, which resulted in a view of the man's entire face made up of two identical halves.

Figure 19 Right side of the original face mirrored with a gradient transition

Figure 20 Left side of the original face mirrored

Use the Face tool in the Liquify window

1. Hide the **Mirror Distort layer**, but keep it targeted.

2. Select all, copy merged, paste a new layer, then name it **Face Tool**.

3. Click **Filter** on the menu bar, click **Liquify**, then click the **Face tool** 👤.

4. Float your cursor over the **eyes, nose, mouth, and chin**.

   White handles appear around the eyes, at the bottom of the nose, on the mouth, and around the face shape.

5. Position the **Face tool** 👤 at the **bottom of the nose**.

   A three-handled V shape appears.

6. Click and drag the **center handle** straight up as far as it will go.

   The nose is shortened.

7. Click and drag the **right handle** under the nose to the right as far as it will go.

   Both sides of the nose are widened.

8. Position the tool over the **mouth**.

   Along with two handles, curved white lines appear at the top and bottom of the lips.

9. Drag the **right handle** all the way to the right.

10. Drag the **top curved white line** straight up to widen the top lip.

11. Position the tool at the **bottom-center of the right eye**, then drag the **handle** down to widen the eye vertically.

12. Repeat Step 11 for the **left eye**.

13. Position the tool at the **bottom of the right ear** where it meets the face, then drag the **handle** all the way to the right.

14. Drag the **handle** at the **center of the chin** all the way down.

15. Drag the **top center handle** at the **forehead** all the way up, then click **OK**.

    Figure 21 shows before and after results.

16. Save your work, then continue to the next set of steps.

You used the Face tool in the Liquify window to manipulate the man's forehead, eyes, nose, mouth, ears, and chin.

Use the Face-Aware sliders in the Liquify window

1. Hide the **Face Tool layer**, but keep it targeted.

2. Paste a new layer, then name it **Face-Aware**.

   The pasted image is the same image pasted from the previous set of steps.

3. Click **Filter** on the menu bar, then click **Liquify**.

4. Enter **60** in both **Eye Size text boxes**, then enter **−40** in both **Eye Tilt text boxes**.

5. In the **Face-Aware Liquify pane** to the right of the image, drag the **Nose Height slider** to **−60**, then drag the **Nose Width slider** to **60**.

6. Drag the **Smile slider** to **65**, then drag the **Mouth Width slider** to **66**.

7. Drag the **Jawline slider** to **50**, then drag the **Face Width slider** to **−42**.

8. Drag the **Forehead slider** to **65**, then drag the **Chin Height slider** to **33**.

9. Click **OK**.

   Figure 22 shows before and after results.

10. Save your work, then close Face-Aware Liquify.

You used the Face-Aware sliders in the Liquify window to manipulate the height and width of the nose, smile, mouth width, eye size and eye tilt, jawline, face width, forehead, and chin height.

Figure 21 Distortions created with the Face tool

Figure 22 Distortions created with the Face-Aware Liquify sliders

CREATE A PUPPET WARP

► *What You'll Do*

In this lesson, you'll use the Puppet Warp command to distort an image, leaving no trace of evidence that the image was manipulated.

Using the Puppet Warp

Like the Scale, Rotate, and Perspective commands, Puppet Warp is a transform command that allows you to modify targeted artwork. Puppet Warp gives you a high degree of control when distorting artwork. The Puppet Warp command creates a mesh over targeted artwork. You interact with the mesh tool by placing "pins" on the mesh grid. The pins function like handles and give you control of which parts of the mesh move and which parts remain static. It's that control that makes the Puppet Warp feature so powerful: you can leave some areas as is while radically transforming others.

You can use Puppet Warp for subtle transformations, like reshaping clothing or hair, and you can use it for dramatic transformations, like moving a subject's arms and legs. You can make a cat's tail curl in the opposite direction, or reshape a pencil into a question mark. The range of possibilities and practical applications the Puppet Warp provides is quite amazing.

Working with Options for a Puppet Warp

The following list will familiarize you with some additional settings and techniques you can experiment with when using the Puppet Warp:

- The **Mode** setting determines the elasticity of the mesh. The default is normal. The **Rigid** setting causes the mesh to move with less ease, while the **Distort** setting moves the mesh fluidly and dramatically distorts the artwork.
- The **Density** setting determines the spacing of mesh points—how closely you can position them. The more points you add increases precision but also demands more processing from your computer.
- The **Expansion** setting expands or contracts the outer edge of the mesh. Use this setting when the choice for whether or not to warp the edge is a factor in the transformation. Use a negative value to contract the mesh and leave the edge unaffected.
- Deselect the **Show Mesh check box** to show only the pins, not the mesh itself.
- Click a pin to select it. Press [delete] to remove a selected pin. Click the **Remove All Pins** button on the Options panel to clear all pins from the mesh.

Use the Puppet Warp

1. Open PS 8-5.psd, then save it as **Puppet Warp**.

   Note that the swan artwork is on its own layer.

2. Target the **Swan layer**, click **Edit** on the menu bar, then click **Puppet Warp**.

   A mesh appears, covering the entire contents of the layer, and the cursor changes to the Add Pin pointer  .

   TIP Verify that the Show Mesh check box is checked on the Options panel to view the mesh.

3. Using Figure 23 as a guide, click the **areas of the mesh circled in red** with the **Add Pin pointer** to add **10 pins**.

   Areas where you add a pin remain unaffected if you transform other areas of the mesh.

Figure 23 Positioning ten pins

Figure 24 Adding a pin at the base of the head

Figure 25 Moving the base-of-the-head pin

Figure 26 Adding a pin at the center of the neck

4. Add a **pin** at the **base of the head**, as shown in Figure 24.

5. Place the **pointer** on top of the pin so that your cursor changes to an arrow, then click and drag right to move the head and neck to resemble Figure 25.

6. Add a **pin** near the **center of the neck**, as shown in Figure 26.

7. Move the **center-neck pin** to the left, as shown in Figure 27.

8. Click and drag the **pin** you created at the **base of the head** to reshape the image, as shown in Figure 28.

9. Add a **pin** on the **swan's eye**, then drag the **head** straight down to create an elegant arc at the top of the neck.

10. Press **[command] [H] (Mac)** or **[Ctrl] [H] (Win)** repeatedly to hide and show the mesh.

    When you hide the mesh, the pins remain visible.

11. Click and drag the **single pin on the neck** in the reflection in the water to mirror the change to the swan's neck.

12. Click the **Move tool** , click **Apply**, then compare your result to Figure 29.

    The final image gives absolutely no hint that it's been manipulated in any way. Compared to the original image, the final image is so much more visually pleasing and beautiful.

13. Save your work, then close Puppet Warp.

You applied the Puppet Warp feature to an image of a swan and added pins to the mesh so that you could manipulate only the head and neck of the swan, leaving the rest of the swan's body in the exact same position.

Figure 27 Moving the center-neck pin

Figure 28 Moving the base-of-the-head pin

Figure 29 The final image does not appear to have been distorted

DISTORT TEXT

▶ *What You'll Do*

In this lesson, you will explore various methods for distorting text.

Distorting Text

When people think of Photoshop, they think of images—often WOW images. When you work in Photoshop regularly, you become aware of how much of your work is so often about text. It's great when you get a project that is mainly image based, but most of the work that comes across designers' desks are banners, signage, and informational graphics, all of which are text heavy.

As a designer, you'll find yourself looking for other options than just placing straight text on a colored background. Fortunately, you can leverage all that Photoshop has to offer at designing eye-catching text graphics, and one category of eye-catching text graphics is distorted text. Text that enlarges as it comes at you, text that fades into the distance, text that bends and twists like a pretzel, and text that ebbs and flows like a wave on the ocean—all of this is possible in Photoshop.

Using Warps

The Warp Text dialog box houses a collection of 15 preset warps that create specific distortions on text. These include Flag, Wave, Fisheye, Squeeze, and Twist. Each preset comes with horizontal and vertical distortion controls, allowing you to customize the effect. They can only be applied to live text. Once you rasterize text, you can no longer apply these warps.

Using the Perspective Warp

The Perspective Warp command offers you the power to warp text and images in various perspectives. When you choose the Perspective Warp command, you can draw multiple grids on your artwork. Those grids represent potential planes for the artwork. You can customize the grids to best fit the given artwork. Once in place, you can then manipulate the grids as planes and bend the artwork onto different perspective planes. The Perspective Warp provides endless opportunities for you to bend and stretch text away from the standard one-liner into text that demands to be noticed.

Add a cast shadow to text with the Skew command

1. Open PS 8-6.psd, then save it as **Skew Text**.

2. Duplicate the **Text layer**, then name it **Shadow**.

3. Click the **Lock transparent pixels button**  on the Layers panel, then fill the letters with **black**.

4. Unlock the transparency on the **Shadow layer**, then drag the **Shadow layer** below the **Text layer**.

5. Click **Edit** on the menu bar, point to **Transform**, then click **Skew**.

6. Click and drag the **top-middle handle** to the right so that your artwork resembles Figure 30.

7. Click **Edit** on the menu bar, point to **Transform**, then click **Scale**.

8. Drag the **top-middle handle** straight up until your artwork resembles Figure 31.

   The scale occurs on the same skew angle.

9. Press **[return] (Mac)** or **[Enter] (Win)** to execute the transformation, zoom in on the **first letter T**, then use the **left arrow key** to align the **letter T** on the shadow with the **red T**.

10. Set the **Opacity** on the **Shadow layer** to **20%**.

11. Select **both layers**, click **Edit** on the menu bar, point to **Transform**, then click **Distort**.

12. Drag the **left-middle handle** straight up, then drag the **right-middle handle** straight down until your artwork resembles Figure 32.

13. Press **[return] (Mac)** or **[Enter] (Win)** to execute the transformation, save your work, then continue to the next set of steps.

You duplicated a text layer to create a drop shadow effect. You applied the Skew, Scale, and Distort commands to the text layers to create a dramatic text effect.

Figure 30 Skewing the text

Figure 31 The Scale command scales the text on the same skew angle

Figure 32 Distorting both layers simultaneously

Force perspective on text with the Perspective command

1. Select **both layers**, click **Edit** on the menu bar, point to **Transform**, then click **Perspective**.

2. Drag the **bottom-right handle** straight down, then drag the **top-left handle** straight down until your bounding box resembles Figure 33.

3. Press **[return] (Mac)** or **[Enter] (Win)** to execute the transformation.

4. Save your work, then close Skew Text.

You further manipulated the look of the final text by applying the Perspective command and dragging the bottom-right and top-left handles of the bounding box.

Use the Warp Text command

1. Open PS 8-7.psd, then save it as **Warped Text**.

2. Target the **Text layer**.

   This is a live text layer. The Text Warp command is available only for live text.

TIP The typeface in the data file is Chunk Five. If you don't have that font, use any other bold font.

3. Click **Type** on the menu bar, then click **Warp Text**.

4. Click the **Style list arrow**, then sample all **15 warps** listed to see what they do.

5. Click the **Fish warp**.

6. Set the **Bend** to +59, then set the **Horizontal Distortion** to +13.

7. Set the **Vertical Distortion** to +21, then click **OK**.

   Your artwork should resemble Figure 34.

AUTHOR'S NOTE Even though these warps might feel a little bit "canned," they look great and

Figure 33 Applying the Perspective command

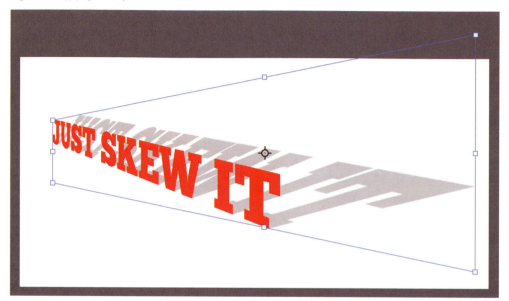

Figure 34 Applying the Fish text warp

offer hundreds of different looks when you include the distortion sliders. Keep them in mind when working with type.

8. Save your work, then close Warped Text.

You used the Warp Text command to sample all 15 types of warps that can be applied to live text, then settled on the Fish warp and adjusted the Fish warp settings in the Warp Text dialog box.

Apply a Perspective Warp to Text

1. Open PS 8-8.psd, then save it as **Perspective Warp Text**.

2. Target the **Text layer**.

3. Click **Edit** on the menu bar, then click **Perspective Warp**.

4. Using Figure 35 as a guide, create a **grid**, as shown.

5. Position the **cursor** at the **top-right of the letter G**, drag left to make a second grid, and release the mouse pointer when the edges of the two grids turn blue.

   Your canvas should resemble Figure 36. With two grids in place, the type can be warped into two different perspectives.

6. On the **Options panel**, click the **Warp button**.

   The grid lines disappear, and the handles turn to hollow circles.

   Drag the **two left handles** and the **two right handles** to the positions shown in Figure 37.

7. Execute the Perspective Warp, save your work, then close Perspective Warp Text.

You applied the Perspective Warp to text by first creating two grids covering the text. Then you were able to drag the two halves of the text onto two different perspective planes.

Figure 35 Positioning the grid on the left side of the text

Figure 36 Joining two grids together

Figure 37 Dragging the two halves of the text onto two different perspective planes

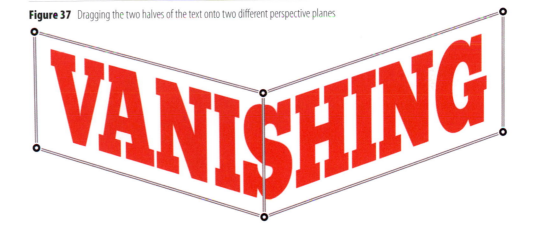

Use the Distort command

1. Open PS 8-9.psd, then save it as **Charlie DVD Display**.

   This image is a template for a DVD counter display.

2. Open the file named Charlie Backer, select all, click Edit on the menu bar, then click Copy.

3. Close the Charlie Backer file.

4. In the Charlie DVD Display file, target the Blue Back layer, then paste.

5. Name the new layer **Charlie Backer**, then clip it into the Blue Back layer.

6. Click Edit on the menu bar, point to Transform, then click Distort.

7. Align all four sides of the Charlie artwork with the four sides of the Blue Back artwork.

   It's a minor curve ball that the Blue Back art has rounded corners. Aligning the four sides will make the rounded corners not an issue.

8. Execute the transformation.

9. Open the Charlie Key Art.psd file, select all, click Edit on the menu bar, click Copy, then close the file.

10. In the Charlie DVD Display file, target the Cases layer, then paste.

11. Name the new layer **Charlie Key art**, then clip it into the Cases layer.

12. Click Edit on the menu bar, point to Transform, then click Distort.

13. Align all four corners of the artwork with the four corners of the leftmost green case.

14. Paste the same Charlie Key Art artwork two more times, then clip and distort each into the other two green cases.

    Note that you do not duplicate the artwork you pasted the first time for the other two cases. That would mean resizing the same artwork three times, which degrades the quality. Instead, you are resizing the copied art once for each case.

15. Compare your results to Figure 38.

16. Save your work, then close Charlie DVD Display.

Figure 38   Distorting four pieces of artwork into a dimensional display

Create a complex cast shadow

1. Open PS 8-10.psd, then save it as **Horse Shadow**.
2. Press and hold [command] (Mac) or [Ctrl] (Win), then click the thumbnail on the Horse layer to load the artwork as a selection.
3. Target the Shadow layer, fill the selection with black, then deselect.
4. Open the file named Race Track.psd, select all, copy, then close the file.
5. In the Horse Shadow file, target the Background layer, paste, then name the new layer **Race Track**.
6. Target the Shadow layer, click Edit on the menu bar, point to Transform, click Distort, then distort the shadow as shown in Figure 39.

   Because the time of day in the image appears to be mid-afternoon, and it's not a sunny day, the cast shadow will not be too far from the horse, and the shadow will be soft and not very dark.
7. Execute the transformation.
8. Set the Opacity on the Shadow layer to 30%.
9. Click Filter on the menu bar, point to Blur, then click Gaussian Blur.
10. Enter **5** in the Radius text box, then click OK.

    Your results should resemble Figure 40.
11. Save your work, then close Horse Shadow.

Figure 39 Distorting the shadow

Figure 40 Blurring the shadow

dikkenss/Shutterstock.com; Nadezda Murmakova/Shutterstock.com

SKILLS REVIEW

(continued)

Use the Puppet Warp

1. Open PS 8-11.psd, then save it as **Pencil Warp**.
2. Target the Pencil layer, click Edit on the menu bar, then click Puppet Warp.
3. Using Figure 41 as a guide, add eight pins.
4. Using Figure 42 as a guide, drag the middle pin to the right.
5. Add as many pins as necessary to reshape the pencil into a question mark, as shown in Figure 43.
6. Save your work, then close Pencil Warp.

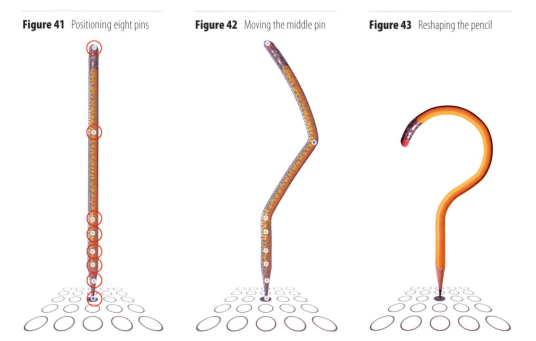

Figure 41 Positioning eight pins

Figure 42 Moving the middle pin

Figure 43 Reshaping the pencil

Perspective Warp Text

1. Open PS 8-12.psd, then save it as **Welcome Warp**.
2. Target the Welcome layer.
3. Click Edit on the menu bar, then click Perspective Warp.
4. Using Figure 44 as a guide, create the three grids where the first grid ends on the letter C, the second grid ends on the letter M, and the third grid covers the letter E and any remaining part of the letter M.
5. Click Warp on the Options panel.
6. Drag the handles to the positions shown in Figure 45.
7. Execute the Perspective Warp, then compare your results to Figure 46.
   Use the Puppet Warp to make any tweaks to the final art you deem necessary.
8. Save your work, then close Welcome Warp.

Figure 44 Positioning three grids side by side

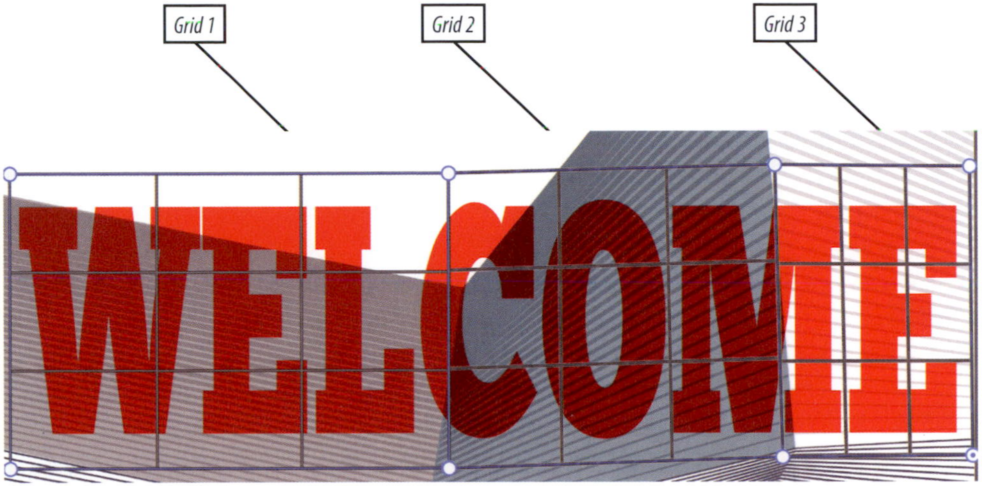

Grid 1   Grid 2   Grid 3

Figure 45 Distorting the text onto perspective planes

Figure 46 The Puppet Warp tool can be used for tweaks on the Perspective Warp

SilverCircle/Shutterstock.com

Project Builder 1 offers you another opportunity to place artwork in a real-life situation. In this case, you have a great photo of a real billboard to work with and a billboard version of the artwork you will create as a movie poster in Chapter 11.

1. Open PS 8-13.psd, then save it as **King's Wager Billboard**.

2. Hide and show the layers to see how the file has been built.

   The white billboard has been copied to its own layer to provide the opportunity to clip in the artwork.

3. Open 14 x 48 Billboard.psd, select all, copy, then close the file.

   The artwork is proportioned to be scaled to be a 14-foot-by-48-foot billboard.

4. In the King's Wager Billboard file, target the Billboard layer, paste, then name the new layer **King's Wager**.

5. Clip the King's Wager artwork into the Billboard layer.

6. Distort the artwork to align with the four corners of the billboard.

   Your result should resemble Figure 47.

7. Save your work, then close King's Wager Billboard.

Figure 47 The billboard image

This Project Builder offers you an alternative to the method you used on this artwork in Lesson 2. In Lesson 2, you cut the shadow and put the top half on its own layer to distort it separately from the bottom half. In this exercise, you will work toward the same goal, this time using the Perspective Warp that you learned in Lesson 4.

1. Open PS 8-14.psd, then save it as **Perspective Warp Shadow**.
2. Target the Shadow layer, click Edit on the menu bar, then click Perspective Warp.

3. As shown in Figure 48, create two perspective grids over the shadow that meet at the line where the wall meets the floor.
4. Click the Warp button on the Options panel.
5. As shown in Figure 49, drag the top two handles to the right to distort the shadow so it's reflected straight up on the wall.
6. Execute the warp.
7. Set the Opacity on the Shadow layer to 40%.
8. Click the Rectangular Marquee tool, then drag a marquee around the top half of the shadow that you distorted.
   Brightening the shadow where it overlaps the wall creates some nuance between it and the shadow on the floor.

9. Add a Brightness/Contrast adjustment layer, then clip it into the Shadow layer.
10. Click the Use Legacy option, then drag the Brightness slider to 40.
    Your results should resemble Figure 50.
11. Save your work, then close Perspective Warp Shadow.

Figure 48 Creating two perspective grids

Figure 49 Moving the top half of the shadow to a different plane

Figure 50 The distorted cast shadow

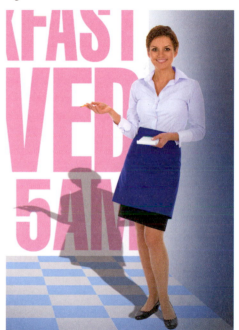

Shadows are like water in the sense that they conform to their surroundings. You might cast a shadow behind you that runs along the floor, up the wall, and across the ceiling. To create shadows realistically in Photoshop, you must first study them to understand them. This Design Project is set up for just that. You will apply perspective warps to cast a shadow across a complex background of three different "walls" or "panels," one of them on an angle. The shadows will have different edges and different levels of brightness against the different walls. As you work, and when you finish, use this exercise as an opportunity to deepen your awareness of how one cast shadow can take on different appearances based on where it's being cast.

1. Open PS 8-15.psd, then save it as **Shadow Challenge.**
2. Hide the Man layer so you can see the background.
3. Show and target the Shadow layer, then set its Opacity to 40%.
4. Make three perspective warp grids over each of the "wall" panels behind the shadow, all of them the same height as the left panel.
5. Click the Warp button on the Options panel.
6. Distort the grids so they align with the tops and bottoms of each panel, as shown in Figure 51.
7. Execute the Perspective Warp.

Figure 51 Warping the shadows to conform with the panels

8. With the Shadow layer still targeted, load the selection from the Left Panel layer, then apply a Gaussian Blur to the shadow with a Radius of 4.

9. Load the selection from the Middle Panel layer, then apply a Gaussian Blur to the shadow with a Radius of 12.

10. Load the selection from the Right Panel layer, then apply a Gaussian Blur to the shadow with a Radius of 8.

11. Load the selection from the Middle Panel layer.

12. Add a Brightness/Contrast adjustment layer, then clip it into the Shadow layer.

13. On the Properties panel, click the Use Legacy option, then drag the Brightness slider to 86.

14. Load the selection from the Right Panel layer.

15. Using the same method, add and clip a Brightness/Contrast layer, then drag the Brightness slider to 48 to brighten the shadow over the right panel.

16. Show the Man layer.

   Your results should resemble Figure 52. The middle part of the shadow would need to be brighter because the middle panel is brighter. It would need to have a softer edge because the middle panel is at an angle. The right part of the shadow would need to be smaller and have a soft edge because it is the farthest away from the man. For that reason, it can't be as large or as dark as the shadow on the left. The shadow on the left has the hardest and most defined edge because it's the closest to the man. It's the darkest because there's less ambient light between the man and the left panel to diffuse the shadow. These (and many more) are considerations you must consider to better understand working with shadows.

17. Save your work, then close Shadow Challenge.

Figure 52 Three different shadows behind the man

MAKING THE HIDDEN WORLD VISIBLE

Anand Varma, Hummingbird shaking off water droplets

© Scott Randall / National Geographic Image Collection

Science photographer Anand Varma has always found inspiration, stimulation, and wonder in the natural world. During college, he began working as an assistant to *National Geographic* photographer David Liittschwager. He also had his first opportunity to work with a scientist to solve a research question using the medium of photography. These experiences led him to realize he could use a camera as a means of both communication and discovery, to explore scientific observations made by others, and to uncover new information about the natural world.

DEVELOPING THE PROCESS

Anand's first project was a collaboration with Dr. Christopher Clark on his work with hummingbirds. His task was to figure out how to use still photography to capture images of the birds flying inside a wind tunnel. Solving this puzzle was exciting and helped Anand decide he wanted to pursue this type of work for his career.

When Anand starts a project, he works with the researcher to define the question he wants to answer using photography. Then through a trial-and-error process, he uses his camera to gather data about the subject. He evaluates the way light interacts with it and looks for structures, textures, and details that normally go unnoticed or that are not visible without the aid of a camera. He then designs the apparatus and the experiment to recreate conditions that allow him to capture these variables. The process can take months.

CAPTURING THE IMAGE

For this image, Anand worked with researchers who were studying the motions that hummingbirds use to dry themselves off. The movement is so quick, it happens within a fraction of a second, much faster than the eye can see.

From talking with the researchers, Anand knew he could use a tiny misting nozzle from a grocery store produce section to get the bird just wet enough to encourage the natural behavior of shaking its feathers. Then he had to decide how to compose the image. Because he wanted to focus on the behavior, he chose to use a dark background and zoom the shot in tight around the bird.

Next, he had to figure out how to use lighting to shape the viewer's attention and highlight specific details. He wanted to show both the bird and the motion of the water droplets as the bird shook them off. He used a very bright, very fast flash to light the bird from the front and kept the shutter open for 1/15 of a second while lighting the scene from behind to capture the trajectories of the water drops. It took many attempts, but he ultimately was able to capture the bird at exactly the right moment.

THE RESULT

The image perfectly reveals the complexity of motion as the bird shakes itself off. It surprises the viewer by capturing the richness of one tiny moment in time and space. The image inspires a sense of wonder and a joy of discovery and encourages viewers to observe hummingbirds more closely when they see them. According to Anand, a successful image is one that rewards the viewer for paying attention, where the longer you look, the more you see.

ANAND'S POINTS OF INTEREST

1. Circular lines form and surround the beak. These lines communicate the motion in which the beak is moving when the hummingbird shakes.

2. Squiggly and seemingly fast-moving lines spray from the hummingbird's head. These lines demonstrate the speed at which the hummingbird is shaking in an effort to dry itself.

3. The wings of the hummingbird look to be layered and at various opacities. This effect communicates the rapid movement of the bird when it spreads its wings wide and opens up to shake off water.

PROJECT DESCRIPTION

In this project, you will analyze and respond to Anand's image. You'll have the opportunity to investigate the different elements of the image and interpret the story for yourself. Look at the photo closely. Take note of anything that catches your attention. You'll be writing a brief analysis consisting of your observations, your interpretation of the story, any questions that come to mind, and the messages you take away. If you can, talk to your classmates and discuss your ideas. Decide which elements of the photo are impactful to you, and write a brief analysis of your findings.

QUESTIONS TO CONSIDER

What is the story?

What stands out to you?

What would you change? Why?

What questions do you have?

What caught your attention first?

Is there anything that seems confusing?

Do you like the image?

USE SOME OF THESE VOCABULARY WORDS

Hierarchy: Used to communicate the importance of each element on the page by manipulating things like color, size, etc.

Opacity: The transparency of an image or element.

Hue: A color or shade.

Tint: A lighter hue created by adding white. This lightens the hue and makes it less intense.

Texture: The surface characteristic of an element.

Contrast: Occurs when two elements on a page are different.

Color: Combination of hues applied to a line or shape.

GETTING STARTED

Analyze the photo. Look at the bird's wings, and make observations about the overlap and motion. Use a pen to mark the areas that catch your attention.

Follow the lines of motion. Consider the shape of the lines and the direction in which they travel. Think about what this communicates about the movement and motion of the bird.

Organize your thoughts by creating a list of your ideas and findings. Figure out what parts of the image are important for you to point out and how those points influenced your interpretation of the story.

SKILLS YOU'LL PRACTICE

Critical thinking

Giving feedback

Design analysis

Writing

Using design vocabulary

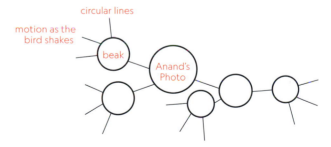

One way to organize your thoughts is with a graphic organizer. Here's an example of how you might use an idea web to capture your thoughts about the photo.

PROJECT DESCRIPTION

In this project, you will be exploring storytelling as a way to learn about science. Using one of the photos provided as a starting point, you will be investigating motion and movement as it relates to an animal.

You'll need to research your chosen animal, examine what kinds of movements it makes, and determine why it makes that particular movement. Once you have found your unique story, you will communicate your findings by creating a composition made up of various design elements, effects, and layers that depict the animal, its motion, and the environment in which the motion occurs.

The goal of this project is to communicate a scientific explanation of an animal's motion in a particular environment using a single composition.

SKILLS TO EXPLORE

- Paint inside selections
- Move selected pixels
- Examine selection edges
- Explore vector selection tools
- Explore shape tools
- Use magic wand selection
- Work with channels panel
- Create and customize gradients

FILES YOU'LL USE

- Ps_u2_hummingbird.JPEG
- Ps_u2_bee.JPEG
- Ps_u2_beaver.JPEG
- Ps_u2_mantisshrimp.JPEG
- Ps_u2_snake.JPEG

You will use Photoshop for this project to create an image that is inspired by Anand's photographic work.

SKILLS CHALLENGE
CREATE AN ACTION ZOOM BLUR EFFECT

Step 1: Create a duplicate background layer.

Step 2: Make sure the layer copy is selected in the Layers panel. On the Filter menu, point to Blur, then choose Radial Blur. A Radial Blur dialog box should appear. Enter the following settings:

Amount: The higher the amount, the more blur is applied. Start at 50, and increase until you reach your desired blur level.

Blur Method: Select Best.

Quality: Select Zoom.

Blur Center: Use this box to set the point from where the blur will appear to be "zooming" out. Click inside the box to set the point. Click OK.

Step 3: Make sure the layer copy is selected. Click on the Layer Mask icon at the bottom of the Layers panel.

Step 4: Make sure the layer mask is selected by looking for a thin white border around the mask.

Step 5: Select the Gradient Tool from the Tools panel. Look at the Options Bar and select Radial Gradient, then apply the gradient by clicking and dragging your mouse.

Step 6: Click on the center of your focal point, and drag the mouse out until you think you have created enough space around the focal point. The area between the start and end points of the gradient will become a smooth transition between the two layers.

FOLLOW ANAND'S EXAMPLE

1. Think about what new information you can provide. Your composition should give viewers information they probably didn't know before. This is an opportunity for you to teach your viewers something about science in a creative way.

2. Consider this project as a puzzle that needs to be solved. Capturing movement that is often invisible to the naked eye is not an easy task. When conducting your research, look for videos and images that capture motion in a unique way, and see if any of those techniques can be applied to your own work.

3. Decide what needs to be included in the environment to tell the story. Establishing the environment in which your chosen animal conducts its unique motion is a critical element in telling the full story. Think about what causes the animal to make its motion and how those circumstances might be communicated in your composition.

1. Do your research. Use what's available to you to learn about the animal you chose. Find videos, images, drawings, blog posts, personal accounts, and other resources that give you information about a critical movement your animal makes in a particular situation.

2. Find some inspiration. Make guesses and predictions about what you might find. Chances are, this is not the first time you have heard of the animal you are working with. Use what you already know about the animal to guide your hunt for information.

3. Sketch out what you're thinking. Use pen, pencils, paper, or notepad, to jot down a few ideas for design elements. Doing this will help guide the development of your composition, and help you build upon your different ideas.

Most interested in the wings, the student experimented with proximity, variety, and foreground to communicate the different position and forms a bat's wings can take.

The student spent time exploring the different parts of a bat's anatomy, as well as the bat's common resting position.

PROJECT DESCRIPTION

In this project, you will continue your exploration of motion and movement by examining the movement of an animal in your own vicinity. You'll need to make your own observations and research your chosen specimen to learn about how it moves. You will create a composition that communicates an important action and movement in a particular environment.

Take time to figure out what animals are around you. This could be a squirrel in a tree, an ant on the sidewalk, or even a spider on the wall. Using whatever tools are available to you, document your observations.

Create a composition using your taken and/or found images, and visualize your subject in motion. The goal of this project is for you to communicate a scientific description of motion that takes place in a location familiar to you and to encourage people to take a closer look at what's around them.

SKILLS TO EXPLORE

- Create and edit swatches
- Explore tools to repair and reconstruct images
- Create custom layer styles
- Use guides and grids
- Create a stamp visible layer
- Adjust layer opacity and fill opacity
- Use level adjustments
- Explore hue and saturation

THINK LIKE ANAND

1. Embrace trial and error. One of the most effective ways to learn your tools is by experimenting with them and trying new techniques. In this project, you are encouraged to be experimental and to see what you can create without being rigid in your approach.

2. Look for new ideas. Think outside the box with this composition. If your original idea doesn't seem to be working, don't be afraid to go back to the drawing board. Identifying what doesn't work can often be a productive part of the creative process.

3. Reward viewers for paying attention. Make small details a big part of your composition. You want your viewers to learn more about your scientific concept the longer they look at it, so ensure there are plenty of intricate, crucial, and communicative details for them to see.

SKILLS CHALLENGE
CORRECT COLOR CONTRAST

Step 1: On the Layers panel, click the Create new fill or adjustment layer icon, and choose Levels.

Step 2: To make sure the Levels adjustment layer in the Layers panel is selected, go to the Properties panel to access the controls for the adjustment.

Step 3: On the Properties panel, click on the Gray Eyedropper.

Step 4: Click on something in the image that should be a neutral color, such as gray, black, or white. When you click, the other colors in the image will shift.

GETTING STARTED

In this project, you'll get to interact with something in your environment. This can be both exciting and daunting. Being patient and diligent will be key to capturing the different parts of your story. In this section you are encouraged to spend ample time exploring and having conversations before starting your composition.

1. Explore your immediate vicinity and community. Take a walk around town. You may be surprised how many small living creatures exist in your daily life.

The student brainstormed and sketched the key elements needed for a story about honeybees.

2. Take notes of observations and conversations. While exploring your area, use what you have available to you to document your findings. Who might be a good person to talk to about this project? It could be your biology teacher, the janitor who knows the school grounds, or a science enthusiast in your class or family.

3. Consider a collaboration. Maybe your story and your classmate's story are one in the same, and maybe they explore similar ideas. Consider working together and bringing your ideas together in one collaborative project.

4. Always keep safety in mind when working on a project that requires interaction with an object you are unfamiliar with. It is not recommended that you pick up or handle any animals while working on this project. It is best to safely observe from a distance. Use your resources to get a closer look at your subject's different behaviors.

Fascinated by the different types of bees, the student experimented with repetition, shape, and scale to display key distinctions and establish focus.

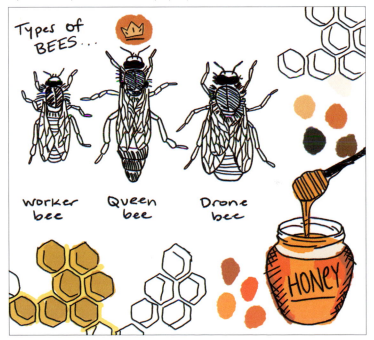

MASTER COMPLEX CONSTRUCTIONS AND TECHNIQUES

Jen Guyton, Dung Beetles

CHAPTER **9**

CREATE SPECIAL EFFECTS
WITH TYPE

1. Convert Layer Styles to Editable Artwork
2. Design Plastic Text Effects
3. Design Recessed Type
4. Use Images as Textures for Type

Adobe Certified Professional in Visual Design Using Photoshop CC Framework

4. Creating and Modifying Visual Elements

This objective covers core tools and functionality of the application, as well as tools that affect the visual outcome of the document.

4.6 Modify the appearance of design elements by using filters and styles.

    B   Apply, modify, copy, and remove layer styles.

    C   Create, manage, and save custom layer styles.

CONVERT LAYER STYLES TO EDITABLE ARTWORK

▶ *What You'll Do*

In this lesson, you'll convert layer styles to editable artwork in order to create a sliced text effect.

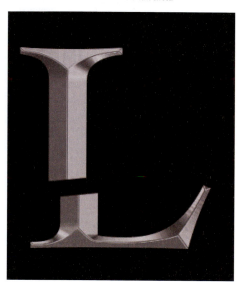

Converting Layer Styles to Editable Artwork

As you learned in Chapter 3, layer styles are built-in effects that you can apply to layers; they include glows, shadows, bevels, embosses, and chiseled edges, among many others. Layer styles are applied at the edges of artwork. If you have a layer with type, for example, and you apply the Outer Glow layer style, the style is applied to the edges of the type. This makes sense; having the glow at the edge of the type is exactly the effect you seek.

This can become a challenge, however, when you want to mask artwork with layer styles applied. Using the same example of working with type, if you mask one of the letters, the layer style updates to the new edge created by the mask.

Figure 1 shows type with a Bevel & Emboss layer style applied, and it shows how that style updates when parts of the letters are masked. The result is not necessarily a problem, but what if you didn't want the Bevel & Emboss effect to appear where you masked the type?

You will find yourself in situations when you want to mask artwork with a layer style applied, and you want the layer style to be masked as well. This can't be done with a layer mask alone because a layer style always updates to the new edge when the underlying artwork is masked.

There is no way to selectively mask a part or section of a layer style. The only way to achieve the goal is to convert the layer style to editable artwork. To do so, click Layer on the menu bar, point to Layer Style, then click Create Layers. This converts the layer style to artwork, which is clipped into the base layer. Once converted, the artwork is editable like any other artwork. It can be selectively masked.

The Create Layers command is one of Photoshop's lesser-known options for working with layer styles. Now that you've learned about it, make a mental note that it's available to you. It can come in very handy in the right situation. It's also fascinating to see Photoshop's layer style effects rendered as artwork.

Figure 1 The layer style is applied at the edge everywhere the artwork is masked

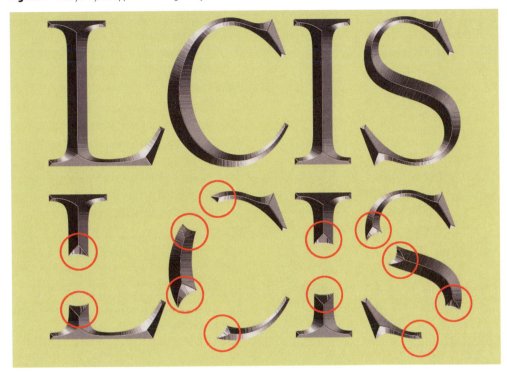

Figure 2 Simple "slice" of rasterized text

Convert a layer style to editable artwork

1. Open PS 9-1.psd, then save it as **Sliced Text**.

2. Target the **TEXT layer**.

    This text layer has been rasterized. When designing text, it's usually a good idea to start with gray text using 128R/128G/128B because this gives you the full upper half of the grayscale range to create highlights and the full lower half of the grayscale range to create shadows.

3. Click **Select** on the menu bar, click **Load Selection**, click the **Channel list arrow**, choose the selection named **Diagonal Cut**, then click **OK**.

4. Click the **Move tool** ⊕. , then drag the **selected pixels** down and slightly right so that your artwork resembles Figure 2.

    As you can see, it's a simple effect to achieve with rasterized text. However, it's much more of a challenge when layer styles have been applied to the text, which we will explore in this lesson.

5. Revert the file.

6. Click **Layer** on the menu bar, point to **Layer Style**, then click **Bevel & Emboss**.

Continued on next page

7. Apply all the settings shown in Figure 3, then click **OK**.

8. Target the **TEXT layer**, then, on the **Select menu**, load the selection named **Diagonal Cut**, as you did in Step 3.

9. Move the **selected text** straight down approximately ½ inch.

   The text is not split in a clean line. With the layer style active, the Bevel & Emboss style applies itself at all edges, including the slice line. It's not necessarily a bad effect, but the goal is to slice the text on a clean line. A layer style cannot be selectively edited or masked, so we will convert the layer style to artwork.

10. Undo the last step and deselect.

11. Click **Layer** on the menu bar, point to **Layer Style**, then click **Create Layers**.

   The artwork doesn't appear to change. However, on the Layers panel, the Bevel & Emboss layer style is no longer listed below the TEXT layer; it has been removed as a layer style and replaced by two new layers and clipped into the TEXT layer. These layers are artwork, editable like any other artwork in Photoshop.

12. **Save** your work so you can revert to this step.

   Be sure not to skip this step because you will be coming back to this point in the project later on.

13. Right-click the **TEXT's Inner Bevel Highlights layer**, then click **Release Clipping Mask.**

   Now you can see the artwork and how it recreates the Bevel & Emboss layer style.

   Note that the artwork that represents the highlights of the Bevel & Emboss layer style are

Figure 3 Settings for the Chisel Hard layer style

Bevel & Emboss

Structure

Style:	Inner Bevel
Technique:	Chisel Hard
Depth:	120 %
Direction:	● Up ○ Down
Size:	42 px
Soften:	0 px

Shading

Angle:	45 °
	☑ Use Global Light
Altitude:	30 °
Gloss Contour:	☑ Anti-aliased
Highlight Mode:	Screen
Opacity:	72 %
Shadow Mode:	Multiply
Opacity:	50 %

applied with the Screen blending mode, and the artwork that represents the shadows of the Bevel & Emboss layer style are applied with the Multiply blending mode. When each is clipped into the TEXT layer, you see only the chiseled effect within the letterforms.

14. Revert the file.

   The two Bevel & Emboss artwork layers are once again clipped into the TEXT layer.

15. Load the **Diagonal Cut selection**, as you did in Step 3, then use the **Move tool** ✛ to split the two groups apart so your artwork resembles Figure 4.

16. Save your work, then close Sliced Text.

You applied a Bevel & Emboss layer style to create a chisel effect on text. You then used a saved selection and pulled it apart to create a "slice" effect. You noted that the layer style was applied to the sliced edges when the text was pulled apart. You then converted the layer style to editable artwork so the text could be sliced on a clean line without the Bevel & Emboss effect being applied to that the slice lines.

Figure 4 Chiseled text "sliced" on a clean line

DESIGN PLASTIC TEXT EFFECTS

▶ **What You'll Do**

In this lesson, you'll use Adobe Illustrator to reshape text for a plastic effect done with a filter.

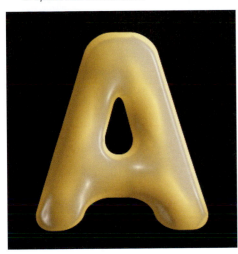

Applying Real-World Textures to Type

Type is a world unto itself in Photoshop. The number of typefaces and your ability to manipulate type seem endless. Some designers and agencies commit their entire practice to specializing in and working with type and typography. These are the people and businesses that create title treatments for TV shows, movies, magazine covers, and credits at the end of a program. There's no shortage of demand for type in our streaming and social media age.

Often, you will find yourself wanting to reproduce real-world textures when working with type. One often-used choice is generating type with a metallic appearance, which is easy to do with the Bevel & Emboss layer style. Other type textures you might want to create could include wooden, glass, or stone.

One of the great things about working with type is that it allows you to use some of the more extreme filters—ones that would have little or no application for a realistic image. The Plastic Wrap filter is one of those filters—a very cool effect, but one that is rarely used. Plastic type, unlike chiseled type, is unusual and not regularly seen, which makes it a great technique for you to have in your skill set.

When you learn how to render a plastic effect for text, it opens the door for many practical applications: it's fun, it's playful, and it's an especially great look if you're doing a project to appeal to young children.

Generating Text in Adobe Illustrator for Use in Photoshop

Photoshop is a robust application for creating and editing type; however, it has some limitations. Adobe Illustrator, because it's a drawing program, offers many options for manipulating type that are not available in Photoshop.

One such option is rounded corners. When you set type in Illustrator, you can apply an effect that rounds the corners of the letters. This simple effect can have major visual impact, making text fun, playful, and childlike. As you will see in this lesson, having type with rounded corners is essential for producing a plastic type effect.

Adobe Illustrator and Adobe Photoshop work very effectively together. Once you get to know Illustrator well, it becomes a powerful extension of your ability to achieve your goals in Photoshop.

Create text with rounded corners in Adobe Illustrator

1. Open PS 9-2.ai in Adobe Illustrator, then save it as **Round Corners**.

2. Select all, click **View** on the menu bar, then click **Hide Edges.**

3. Click **Effect** on the menu bar, point to the first **Stylize** command, then click **Round Corners**.

4. Type **.1"** in the Radius text box, then click **OK**.

5. Click **Object** on the menu bar, then click **Expand Appearance**.

6. Click **Edit** on the menu bar, click **Copy**, then save your work.

7. Switch to Photoshop, open PS 9-3.psd, then save it as **Plastic**.

8. Click **Edit** on the menu bar, click **Paste**, then, in the Paste dialog box, click the **Pixels button**, then click **OK**.

   The artwork is pasted on its own layer with a bounding box around it.

9. Press **[return] (Mac)** or **[Enter] (Win)**.

   The bounding box disappears, and the text is rendered as pixels.

10. Set the **foreground color** to **128R/128G/128B**.

11. Click the **Lock transparent pixels button** 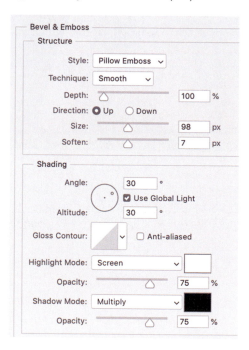 on the Layers panel to activate it, then fill the **text** with the foreground color.

    Your canvas should resemble Figure 5.

12. Name the new layer **Pillow Emboss**, then save your work.

You applied the Round Corners effect to text in Illustrator, knowing that Photoshop doesn't have a utility that rounds the corners of text. You then pasted the text from Illustrator into Photoshop to be further edited.

Use the Pillow Emboss layer style

1. Click **Layer** on the menu bar, point to **Layer Style**, then click **Bevel & Emboss**.

2. Enter the settings shown in Figure 6, then click **OK**.

The Pillow Emboss layer style creates a great effect for the letters. However, it also creates a soft gray shadow behind the letters, and this is not something that will work for the final effect. Therefore, the text needs to be isolated and the shadow discarded.

3. Press and hold **[command] (Mac)** or **[Ctrl] (Win)**, then click the **thumbnail** on the **Pillow Emboss layer**.

   The pixels on the layer are loaded as a selection.

Figure 6 Settings for the Pillow Emboss layer style

Figure 5 Text forms with rounded edges pasted from Illustrator

4. Click **Edit** on the menu bar, then click **Copy Merged**.

As you learned in Chapter 6, when you apply the Copy Merged command to layered artwork, it copies the selected artwork as though all the layers were merged and the image was flattened. To put it in other terms, the Copy Merged command copies selected artwork as it *appears*, regardless of how many different layers are involved in creating the appearance. In the case of this layer, if you had just used the Copy command, all you would have copied would be the flat gray text on the layer. With the Copy Merged command, you copied the letters along with the emboss effect.

7. Click **Edit** on the menu bar, click **Paste**, then name the new layer **Plastic Text**.

8. Hide the **Pillow Emboss layer**.

9. Save your work, then continue to the next set of steps.

You applied a Pillow Emboss layer style to the type. You noted that you wanted to work with the type without the shadow that comes with the Pillow Emboss layer style, so you pasted a Copy Merged layer. This put the artwork all on one editable layer. You selected just the type and then isolated it onto its own layer.

Apply a Solid Color adjustment

1. Click **Layer** on the menu bar, point to **New Fill Layer**, then click **Solid Color**.

Figure 7   Saturated yellow text mimics the appearance of plastic

2. Type **Gold** in the Name text box, click the **Use Previous Layer to Create Clipping Mask check box**, then click **OK**.

3. Type **255R/234G/94B** in the Color Picker, then click **OK**.

4. Set the blending mode on the **Gold layer** to **Soft Light**.

5. Press and hold **[option] (Mac)** or **[Alt] [right-click] (Win)**, click the **Create new fill or adjustment layer button** on the Layers panel, then click **Hue/Saturation**.

TIP   When you use this method to create an adjustment layer, the New Layer dialog box opens. The dialog box offers a quick method for giving the layer a name and clipping it.

6. Click the **Use Previous Layer to Create Clipping Mask check box**, then click **OK**.

7. Drag the **Saturation slider** to **+50**, then compare your result to Figure 7.

The combination of the Soft Light blending mode and the increased saturation mimics the vibrant color and muted sheen of plastic. Note that the overall texture is smooth and round because the shadows are not too deep. Though the highlights are distinct, they are not harsh or glaring.

8. Save your work, then continue to the next set of steps.

You created a Solid Color layer style, applied the Soft Light blending mode, and clipped it into the type artwork.

Apply the Plastic Wrap filter

1. Verify that the **Hue/Saturation adjustment layer** is targeted, select all, click **Edit** on the menu bar, then click **Copy Merged**.

2. Click **Edit** on the menu bar, click **Paste**, then name the new layer **Plastic Wrap**.

3. Hide **all other layers** except the **Background layer**.

4. Click the **Rectangular Marquee tool** , then select the **entire left side** of the **Plastic Wrap layer** from top to bottom including the **black background** and the **letters PLAS**.

   The letters PLAS should be included in the selection.

5. Click **Filter** on the menu bar, then click **Filter Gallery**.

6. Open the **Artistic folder** in the Filter Gallery dialog box, then click **Plastic Wrap**.

7. Drag the **Highlight Strength slider** to **15**, drag the **Detail slider** to **8,** then drag the **Smoothness slider** to **7**.

8. Click **OK**.

   The Plastic Wrap filter has different effects on different selections. For example, if we had selected the entire image, the letters at the sides would have not been sufficiently affected. Therefore, we are applying the filter twice.

9. Click **Select** on the menu bar, then click **Inverse**.

10. Click **Filter** on the menu bar, click **Filter Gallery** at the top of the Filter menu, then compare your result to Figure 8.

    TIP The Filter menu lists the last filter used (with the settings last used) at the top of the menu.

11. Deselect.

12. Press and hold **[command] (Mac)** or **[Ctrl] (Win)**, then click the **thumbnail** on the **Pillow Emboss layer**.

    The pixels on the layer are loaded as a selection.

13. Press and hold **[option] (Mac)** or **[Alt] (Win)**, then click the **Add layer mask button** on the Layers panel.

14. **Invert the mask**, then compare your results to Figure 9.

15. Save your work, then close the Plastic file.

In order to apply the Plastic Wrap filter to all the visible artwork, you had to first make a Copy Merged layer with all the artwork on one layer. You selected the left half of the image and applied the Plastic Wrap filter, then you selected the right half and applied it again. You selected just the text and masked out the other areas of the layer, leaving the text on its own with the Plastic Wrap filter effect.

Figure 8 Plastic Wrap filter applied to two different areas

Figure 9 Final plastic text

DESIGN RECESSED TYPE

▶ What You'll Do

In this lesson, you'll explore different techniques for designing text to appear inset or recessed.

Creating Recessed Type Effects

One of the interesting behaviors that develops when working in Photoshop is the desire to *build up*: to make artwork three-dimensional, to make it jump off of the canvas. This is only natural when working with layered artwork. One piece of artwork goes on top of another, and slowly but surely, you "build" toward a final piece of artwork.

Keep in mind, however, that Photoshop also provides the ability to *build down*. This lesson is designed to remind you that dimensionality can also be created by pushing things back, pushing them in, and pushing them away. One example is recessed type.

Recessed type is one of those effects that always looks good. Figure 10 shows an example of recessed type. At first glance, it appears to be a rendering of gold type. On closer inspection it becomes apparent that the type forms are created by the negative space in a foreground element. The foreground element casts a shadow, making the type appear even further behind or recessed.

Figure 10   A copper foreground element casts a shadow creating recessed type

Removing the Fill from an Object with a Layer Style

In some situations, you will apply a layer style to an object and want to show just the layer style and not the object itself. For example, let's say you have text with an outer glow layer style applied, and you only want to show the outer glow, not the actual text. This is achieved with the Fill option on the Layers panel, shown in Figure 11. When an object has a layer style applied, you use the Fill option to control the opacity of just the object; the opacity of the layer style is not affected. Therefore, if you set the Fill to 0%, the object will disappear, leaving just the layer style visible.

Create recessed text using the Inner Shadow layer style

1. Open PS 9-4.psd, then save it as **Recessed Text Effects**.

2. Press and hold **[command] (Mac)** or **[Ctrl] (Win)**, then click the **thumbnail** on the **Recessed Red layer** to load the selection.

3. Click **Select** on the menu bar, point to **Modify**, click **Expand**, then expand the selection by **20 pixels**.

4. Target the **Recessed White layer**, fill the selection with white, and don't deselect.

5. Expand the selection by **14 pixels**, then target the **Gray Metal layer**.

6. Copy.

7. Paste a new layer, then name the new layer **Gray Metal Inner Shadow**.

8. Add an **Inner Shadow layer style** with the settings shown in Figure 12.

   The Inner Shadow layer style makes the area appear indented or set back from the gray metal artwork that surrounds it.

Figure 11 Fill option on the Layers panel

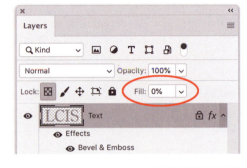

Figure 12 Inner Shadow settings

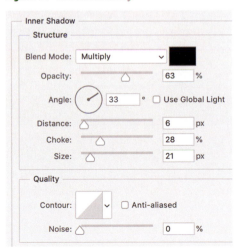

TIP Use the [tab] key to move from field to field in the dialog box.

9. Target the **Recessed White layer**, then add a **Bevel & Emboss layer style** with the settings shown in Figure 13.

   Note how this layer style on the Recessed White layer unites the entire illustration. The thick beveled and embossed edges create a bridge between the gray metal indentation and the white outline surrounding the red text.

Continued on next page

Figure 13 Bevel & Emboss settings for the Recessed White layer

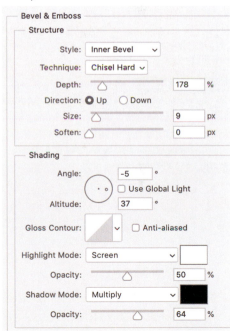

10. Target the **Recessed Red layer**, then add an **Inner Shadow layer style** with the settings shown in Figure 14.

Your artwork should resemble Figure 15. Note that the round edges of the white embossed text are not very smooth, especially compared with the red text. This is a limitation of the Expand command, which you used to create the white outline from the selection of the red text. For this reason, many designers would have used the Offset Path command in Adobe Illustrator, which would have rendered a smoother outline. You will learn more about Offset Path in the next lesson and in the end-of-unit material at the end of this chapter.

11. Save your work, then close Recessed Text Effects.

You combined two Inner Shadow layer styles with a Bevel & Emboss layer style to produce one visual effect of red text inset into a white beveled outline itself inset into an indentation in a metal background.

AUTHOR'S NOTE This is a very cool effect, and one that you see often, especially with rubber goods, such as logos on the sides of sneakers or kids' toys. It's very bold and sporty, and the contrast between the built-up beveled edges and the recessed type areas is visually quite pleasing.

Figure 14 Inner Shadow settings for the Recessed Red layer

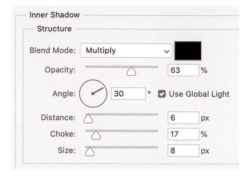

Figure 15 Three layer styles producing one effect

Combine Inner Shadow and Bevel & Emboss layer styles for complex recessed type effects

1. Open PS 9-5.psd, then save it as **Jazz 2096**.

2. Show each layer, one by one, to see how the file has been built.

   This artwork was created in Adobe Illustrator and then placed in Photoshop. The red type was set in the Universe bold typeface. The Offset Path command was used to create the orange, green, and blue offset outlines. Note that this illustration could not have been created in Photoshop because

Photoshop doesn't offer an Offset Path command. You will have the opportunity to create Offset Path artwork from scratch in Adobe Illustrator at the end of this chapter.

3. Set the **foreground color** to **128R/128G/128B**.

   From this point on in this lesson, we'll refer to this color as "neutral gray."

4. Hide the **Red** and **Orange layers**.

5. Target the **Blue layer**, then fill it with **neutral gray**.

   Note that the Lock transparent pixels option is activated on all four layers, so you can quickly fill them with gray.

6. Add a **Bevel & Emboss layer style** with the settings shown in Figure 16.

7. Click **OK**, then compare your results to Figure 17.

   With the 100-pixel Size setting, the chiseled edge butts up against the edge of the green artwork.

8. Target the **Green layer**, then fill it with **neutral gray**.

9. Add an **Inner Shadow layer style**.

Continued on next page

Figure 16 Bevel & Emboss settings

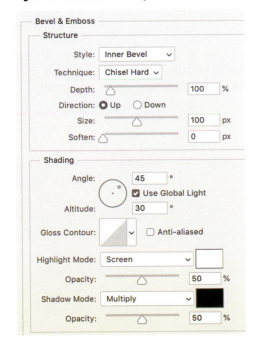

Figure 17 The beveled edge is sized to meet the edge of the green artwork

10. Verify that the **Blend Mode** is set to **Multiply**, the **Opacity** is set to **75%**, the **Angle** is set to **45°**, and the **Use Global Light check box** is checked.

The Use Global Light option allows you to set one "master" lighting angle that you can apply to layer styles that use shading. This is a great option for quickly applying a consistent light source to all your layer styles.

11. Drag the **Distance slider** to **11**, drag the **Choke slider** to **14**, drag the **Size slider** to **16**, then click **OK**.

Compare your results to Figure 18. The illustration at this point is composed of two pieces of artwork on two different layers. The two layer styles are working in conjunction so that the artwork appears as one object. The bevel and emboss effects create the outer edge of the object. The inner shadow creates indentations to the interior of the object. Take a moment to analyze the overall effect because it's a fine example of an important concept: don't get caught up in trying to make one layer style do the whole job. More often than not, it's *many* layer styles working together that create a *single* effect.

Figure 18 Two layer styles producing one effect

12. Show and target the **Orange layer**, then fill it with **neutral gray**.

13. Add a **Bevel & Emboss layer style**.

14. Verify that the **Style** is set to **Inner Bevel**, click the **Technique list arrow**, then click **Chisel Hard**.

15. Drag the **Size slider** to **9**.

16. Click the **Gloss Contour list arrow**, click **Ring**, then click the **Anti-aliased check box** to activate it.

Figure 19 Bevel & Emboss settings

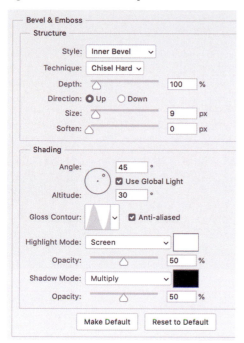

17. Set the **Highlight Mode** to **50%**, then set the **Shadow Mode** to **50%**.

Your dialog box should resemble Figure 19.

18. Click **OK**, then compare your results to Figure 20.

Continued on next page

Figure 20 The Orange layer beveled and embossed

19. Show and target the **Red layer**, then fill it with **neutral gray**.

20. Add an **Inner Shadow layer style** with the settings shown in Figure 21, then click **OK**.

21. Compare your artwork to Figure 22.

Figure 21 Inner Shadow settings

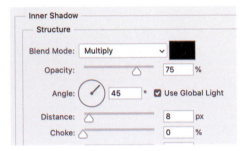

Figure 22 Four layer styles creating one piece of art

22. Click the **Create new fill or adjustment layer button** 🌓 on the Layers panel, then click **Solid Color**.

23. Create a color that is **199R/75G/195B**, then click **OK**.

24. **Clip** the **new fill layer** into the **Red layer**.

 Now that the illustration is almost finished, you will make final adjustments to brighten highlights and add contrast.

25. Double-click the **Bevel & Emboss layer style** on the **Orange layer** to open the Layer Style dialog box.

26. Increase the **Opacity** of the **Highlight Mode** to **80%**, then click **OK**.

This small change makes a big difference. Sometimes it's the little adjustments at the end that make the biggest difference in the final image.

27. Set the **foreground color** to **210R/210G/210B**.

28. Fill the **Blue layer** with the **foreground color**, then compare your artwork to Figure 23 on the following page.

29. Save your work, then close Jazz 2096.

This exercise was an exploration of using multiple layers and layer styles all working together to produce one visually complex piece of artwork. The combination of the Bevel & Emboss effect on the Blue layer with the Inner Shadow effect on the Green layer is a great way for you to see how two layer styles on two different pieces of artwork work together to produce one cohesive effect.

AUTHOR'S NOTE If you look back at the original artwork, it's pretty amazing that Photoshop can make an illustration this visually complex with just four layers and four layer styles. That said, the design itself works very well for this effect. The letter J is extra large, so it integrates the two lines of text into one piece of artwork: the J is the bridge, so to speak. But even more importantly, the hook of the letter J delivers an interesting shape on the left side of the artwork that shows off the embossing and the inner shadow effects quite dramatically. This is mirrored on the right side of the artwork by the number 6. Note how the point at the top extends farther to the right than the Z above it. That sharp point, along with the zigzag of the letter Z above it, creates a unique and interesting sharp edge on the right that resolves itself with the friendly circle of the number 6 below it. These shapes all work so well with the layer styles and their effects.

Figure 23   The final artwork

USE IMAGES AS TEXTURES FOR TYPE

▶ *What You'll Do*

In this lesson, you'll use photographic imagery as textures clipped into type.

Using Images as Textures for Type

In this lesson, you're going to create lots of different effects using type to mask images. The lesson is not designed to show you how to do it—clipping images into type is straightforward and something you already know how to do. Instead, this lesson is designed to show you how to *think* about clipping images into type. With time and practice, you'll develop an eye for images that work well with a given style of typography, and you'll get the knack for combining different blending modes to achieve an effect that you have in mind. You'll also learn the value of deliberate random behavior.

That might sound like a contradiction, but it's actually a smart working method. Make the deliberate choice to try out random moves just to surprise yourself with what the result might be. Duplicate layers, invert them, transform them, and apply blending modes to branch off into unexpected directions.

In Chapter 4, you placed images inside of type; those images were meant to be seen. In this lesson, you'll be using images more as textures for type, and you'll find that they can be remarkably effective.

Clip images into chiseled type

1. Open PS 9-6.psd, then save it as **Chisel Type Images**.

2. Show the **Wave layer**, clip it into the **Text layer**, then compare your artwork to Figure 24.

   The image adds an interesting color dynamic that works very well with the silver layer style and texture overlay. Because the image is so abstract, there's no sense that this type has a "photo" pasted into it.

3. Invert the **Wave layer**.

   This is a simple move that yields a dramatic effect. Inverted, the whites of the wave image overlaying the chiseled text creates a sheen that fades into steel blues—perfect for this illustration.

4. Change the blending mode to **Linear Light**.

   Employing blending modes brings in many options. In this case, the colors become more saturated and the text glows brightly.

Figure 24 The Wave image clipped

5. Hide the **Wave layer**, then show the **Wood layer.**

6. Clip the **Wood layer** into the **Wave layer**.

   The Wood layer is shiny because it's taking on the gloss contour of the Bevel & Emboss layer style on the Text layer. Though the effect is visually interesting, it's too shiny for a wooden texture.

7. Double-click the **Bevel & Emboss layer style** on the **Text layer** to open the dialog box, change the **Gloss Contour** to **Linear**, then click **OK**.

   The Linear Gloss Contour creates a realistic wood texture for the letter forms.

8. Hide the **Wood layer**, then show the **Granite layer**.

9. Clip the **Granite layer** into the **Wood layer**, then compare your result to Figure 25.

The result is quite stunning. The granite texture is perfect for this chiseled text; it looks like something from Ancient Rome.

10. Change the blending mode to **Color Burn**.

Color Burn darkens the effect and creates a shadowy high-contrast version of the granite text.

11. Show the **Wood layer**, change its blending mode to **Overlay**, then invert it.

The inverted Wood layer combined with the Granite layer creates a rich blue stone effect.

12. Save your work, then close Chisel Type Images.

You used a watery image, a wood image, and a stone image as textures for chiseled type. You experimented with different moves, such as inverting images or applying blending modes, just to see what might result. You also noted that some settings in a layer style work with some images and not with others. In this exercise, the gloss contour that made the watery chiseled text shine beautifully did not work with a clipped-in wood image.

Figure 25 The Granite image clipped

Clip images into plastic type

1. Open PS 9-7.psd, then save it as **Plastic Type Images**.

2. Show the **Abstract Blue layer**, clip it, then change its blending mode to **Overlay**.

3. Hide the **Abstract Blue layer**.

4. Show the **Mountains layer**, clip it, then change its blending mode to **Overlay.**

   As shown in Figure 26, the bright blue colors work very well with the plastic effect.

5. Hide the **Mountains layer**, show the **Geometry layer**, clip it, then change its blending mode to **Color**.

   With this artwork, the Color blending mode produces a great effect, like paint dripping down across the type.

6. Hide the **Geometry layer**, show the **Flowers layer**, clip it, then change its blending mode to **Overlay**.

   As shown in Figure 27, the bright colors and the textures of the flowers combined with the smoothness of the letterforms work beautifully together.

7. Save your work, then close Plastic Type Images.

This set of steps was the same as the previous set in the sense that you clipped images into letterforms. In this set of steps, however, because the letters are rounded and have a plastic appearance, you noted that the color of the clipped images played an even more important role. The clipped images appeared to wrap around the smooth rounded text, and they took on the appearance of plastic.

Figure 26 Mountains artwork clipped

Figure 27 Flowers artwork clipped

Clip images into recessed type

1. Open PS 9-8.psd, then save it as **Recessed Type Images**.

   TIP Before moving forward, check to see that your Photoshop software is updated on the Creative Cloud app. If it's not, consider quitting Photoshop and updating. This exercise uses multiple blending modes, and previewing multiple blending modes on the Layers panel might cause layer styles to vanish if the Photoshop software is not updated.

2. Open PS 9-9.psd, select all, copy, then close the file.

3. Hide the **Red**, **Orange**, and **Green layers**, then target the **Blue layer**.

4. Paste the copied image, then clip the image into the **Blue layer**.

   Your artwork should resemble Figure 28.

5. Show and target the **Green layer**, paste the image again, then clip it into the **Green layer**.

6. Change the blending mode on this clipped image only to **Hard Light**.

   TIP If the Bevel & Emboss layer style on the Blue layer disappears after this step, or if any other layer style vanishes during this set of steps, it's because your Photoshop software needs to be updated. As a work-around, hiding and showing vanished layer styles on the Layers panel will make them reappear.

7. Show and target the **Orange layer**, paste the image again, then clip it into the **Orange layer**.

Figure 28 Clipping the image into the Blue layer

Andrey Burmakin/Shutterstock.com

8. Change the blending mode on this clipped image only to **Multiply**.

9. Show and target the **Red layer**, paste the image, then clip the image into the **Red layer**.

10. Add a **Hue/Saturation adjustment layer** at the top of the Layers panel, then set its blending mode to **Overlay**.

11. Drag the **Lightness slider** to +16.

    Your artwork should resemble Figure 29, shown on the following page.

12. Save your work, then close Recessed Type Images.

You placed the same image four times, clipping each into a different layer of the layered artwork. In each case, the image took on the effects of the layer style applied, and you used different blending modes to create contrasting effects as the image progressed through the layers. Lastly, you applied a Hue/Saturation layer with an Overlay blending mode to produce a high-contrast, glowing, and genuinely stunning piece of artwork.

Figure 29 The final image

When we think of working with type, our imaginations often go to words like "bold" and "powerful" and "eye-catching." That's because we often use type to get an important message across to the viewer, so it's only natural to have the instinct to design the type as forceful. An alternative is to go elegant and stylized. You see this often with invitations: a curved and elegant typeface with thin lines and flourishes catches the eye and attracts the attention. This Project Builder is designed to get you to think of a third approach: subtlety. The result of this exercise is type that is barely visible, beautifully so. It's a great reminder that it's not always the squeaky wheel that gets the attention.

1. Open PS 9-10.psd, then save it as **White on white**. What you see is a well-known effect. White type is positioned on a white background. A black drop shadow makes the white letters visible. This exercise will show you a neat variation.
2. Change the foreground color to 235R/235G/235B.

3. Fill the Background layer with the foreground color, then fill the white on white layer with the foreground color.
4. Double-click the Drop Shadow effect on the white on white layer to open the Layer Style dialog box, then remove the check mark next to Drop Shadow.
5. Click Bevel & Emboss, then enter the settings shown in Figure 30.
6. Click OK, then compare your artwork to Figure 31. The effect is that of white paper that has been embossed, with the elegant white highlight defining the right edge of the letterforms. We darkened the image in Figure 31 so the type would be visible in the printed book. The artwork on your screen will be lighter (and more subtle) than what is shown here. This effect is too risky to try to reproduce in most print jobs, but it works beautifully for screen presentations like a slideshow or on a web page. Keep it in mind for those types of projects.
7. Save your work, then close White on white.

Figure 30 Bevel & Emboss settings

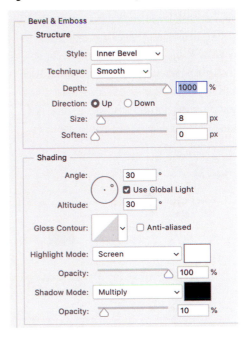

Figure 31 Final embossed variation

The indented, carved, and recessed effects that come with the Inner Shadow layer style can be quite lovely and a great alternative to relying on the Bevel & Emboss layer style over and over again. This Project Builder uses an image of wood to give you the experience of creating the illusion of text carved into wood. You've already seen the Inner

Shadow layer style do its job; in this exercise, focus especially on Step 11. In this step, you will apply a Bevel & Emboss layer style with a white color used for both the highlight and the shadow. This is not something you've done before. Note that both the highlight and shadow must use the Screen blending mode. The result is the sharp edge you'd expect if you successfully cut letters into wood. It's subtle, and it makes the whole effect work. Keep an eye on it.

1. Open PS 9-11.psd, then save it as **Carved Wood**.
2. Target the Logo layer, then add an Inner Shadow layer style.
3. Apply the settings shown in Figure 32, then keep the Layer Style dialog box open.
4. Click the words Inner Glow on the left side of the Layer Style dialog box.
5. Enter the settings shown in Figure 33.
6. Click OK, then set the Logo layer to Multiply.

Figure 32 Inner Shadow settings

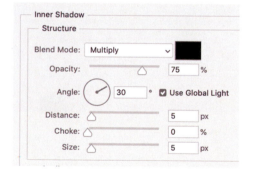

Figure 33 Inner Glow settings

7. Press and hold [command] (Mac) or [Ctrl] (Win), then click the Logo layer thumbnail to load it as a selection.
8. Click Select on the menu bar, then click Inverse.
9. Target the Wood layer, copy, then paste a new layer.
10. Name the new layer **Wood Emboss**.
11. Add a Bevel & Emboss layer style to the Wood Emboss layer, then enter the settings shown in Figure 34.

Note that, for this Bevel & Emboss, both the highlight and shadow at the bottom are set to screen a yellow highlight. The yellow color's RGB values are 255/255/150 for both.
12. Click OK.
    The thin bright edges convey the effect of a sharp highlight where the wood has been carved.
13. Target the Logo layer, then duplicate it.

This move really makes the whole effect work. The one issue is that the indented letters are too gray and too dark, so you will make a subtle but important color shift.
14. On the Logo copy layer, double-click the Inner Glow layer style to open the dialog box.
15. In the Structure section at the top, set the color of the glow to 196R/25G/25B.
16. Click OK, then compare your artwork to Figure 35.
17. Save your work, then close Carved Wood.

Figure 34 Bevel & Emboss settings

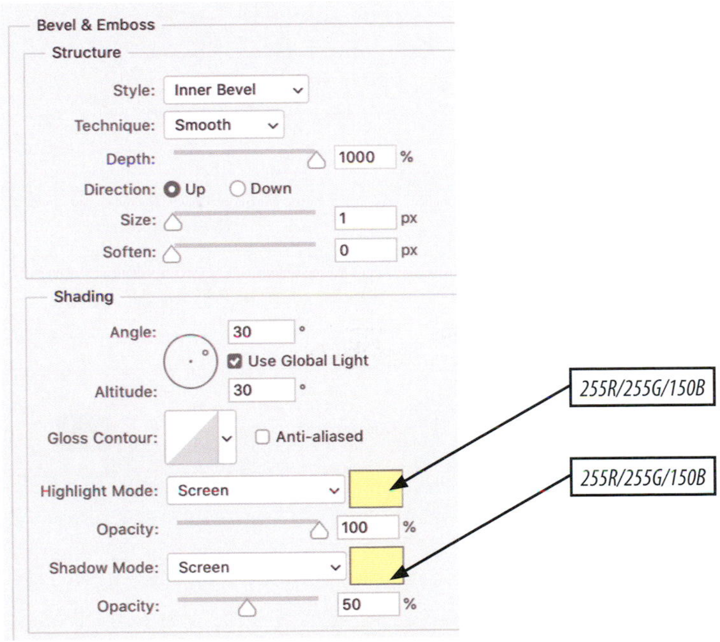

Figure 35 Final effect

This Project Builder shows you a really beautiful effect and an important set of skills for you to add to your roster. You've seen how the Inner Shadow layer style works; this exercise teaches you how to go one giant step further. In this lesson, what appears as type is literally on a layer behind the foreground element, and the foreground element is literally casting a shadow onto the "type" behind it. Keep your eyes peeled for two smart and strategic moves. In Steps 3 and 4, note that the type layer is first used only to load a selection that gets cut out of the Copper layer. There's actually no "type" in this artwork; what we perceive as type is the hole in the copper foreground element. Keep a close eye on Step 16, where that type layer gets used again, this time as the base artwork to create the beautiful smooth outer bevel for the edge of the copper foreground element. Step 17 is the most important step in the exercise; it's when you make the type element invisible, leaving only the Bevel & Emboss layer style showing. This exercise contains important and really smart strategies; make a note of them.

1. Open PS 9-12.psd, then save it as **Copper Cutout Text**.
2. Show each layer so you can see how the file was built.
3. Press and hold [command] (Mac) or [Ctrl] (Win), then click the thumbnail on the Text layer to load it as a selection.
4. Hide the Text layer, target the Copper layer, then add a layer mask.
5. Invert the layer mask.
6. Create a new layer above the Background layer, then name it **Shadow**.
7. Load the hidden Text layer as a selection again (as you did in Step 3), click Select on the menu bar, point to Modify, then click Feather.
8. Enter 4 in the Feather Radius text box, then click OK.
9. Click Select on the menu bar, then click Inverse.
10. Set the foreground color to black.
11. Target the Shadow layer is targeted, then fill the selection with black.
12. Deselect.
13. Click the Move tool, press the left arrow on your keypad 17 times, then press the down arrow 14 times.
14. Set the Opacity on the Shadow layer to 80%.
15. Show and target the Text layer, then add a Bevel & Emboss layer style.

16. Enter the settings shown in Figure 36. Because this is an outer bevel set to a size of 10 pixels, the bevel is 10 pixels outside of the text. In other words, there are 10 pixels that overlap the copper texture.

Figure 36 Bevel & Emboss settings

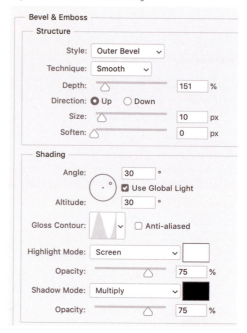

17. On the Layers panel, drag the Fill slider to 0%. The gray text disappears, leaving only the Bevel & Emboss layer style visible. Your artwork should resemble Figure 37.

18. Save your work, then close Copper Cutout Text.

Figure 37 Final recessed text

DESIGN PROJECT

The Jazz 2096 artwork in Lesson 4 is a stunning and complex piece of artwork. It relies on the Offset Path feature in Adobe Illustrator to produce the base artwork. Once you have the artwork in Photoshop, it becomes a case of applying layer styles and blending modes; the true secret in the sauce is the Offset Path technique that produces the artwork in the first place. This Design Project takes you into Illustrator and through the steps for producing the Offset Path technique necessary for achieving the final illustration. Learning this is truly empowering, especially because so many designers are so focused on Photoshop, they neglect to explore Illustrator on this level. Their loss; your gain.

Part 1: Illustrator

1. Open PS 9-13.ai, then save it as **Offset Path.**
   This first part is designed to show you how the Offset Path technique is created in Adobe Illustrator. If you prefer, you can bypass this and move to Part 2, which is entirely in Photoshop.
2. Select all, click Object on the menu bar, point to Path, then click Offset Path.
3. Type **.25"** in the Offset text box, then click OK.
4. Open the Pathfinder panel, then click the first pathfinder on the top row named Unite [icon].
5. On the Swatches panel, click a light orange swatch.

6. Click Object on the menu bar, point to Arrange, then click Send to Back.
7. Select all, click Object on the menu bar, point to Path, then click Offset Path.
8. Type **.25"** in the Offset text box, then click OK.
9. Click the Unite pathfinder [icon] on the Pathfinder panel.
10. On the Swatches panel, click a green swatch.
11. Click Object on the menu bar, point to Arrange, then click Send to Back.
12. Select all, click Object on the menu bar, point to Path, then click Offset Path.
13. Enter **.25"** in the Offset text box, then click OK.
14. Click the Unite pathfinder [icon] on the Pathfinder panel.

15. On the Swatches panel, click a blue swatch.
16. Click Object on the menu bar, point to Arrange, then click Send to Back.
    Your artwork should resemble Figure 38.
17. Save your work, then close the file.

Part 2: Photoshop

1. Open PS 9-14.psd, then save it as **Just Chillin**.
2. Using the skills you learned doing the "Jazz 2096" exercise in Lesson 3, apply Bevel & Emboss and Inner Shadow layer styles to the "Just Chillin" artwork to give it dimension.
   Figure 39 shows one example that also incorporates noise and a drop shadow.

Figure 38 Four paths in Illustrator

Figure 39 "Just Chillin" artwork with layer styles and noise

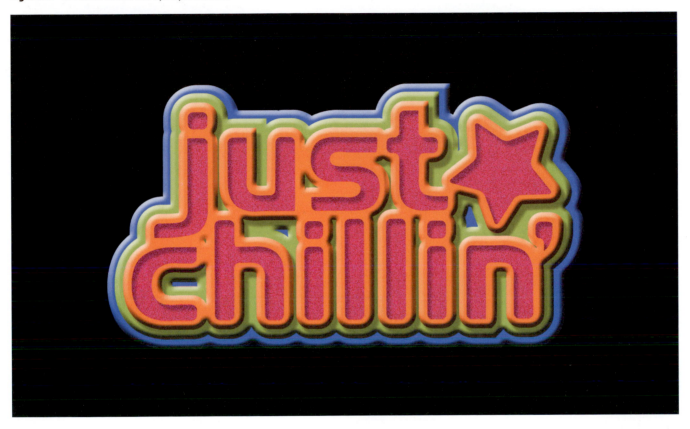

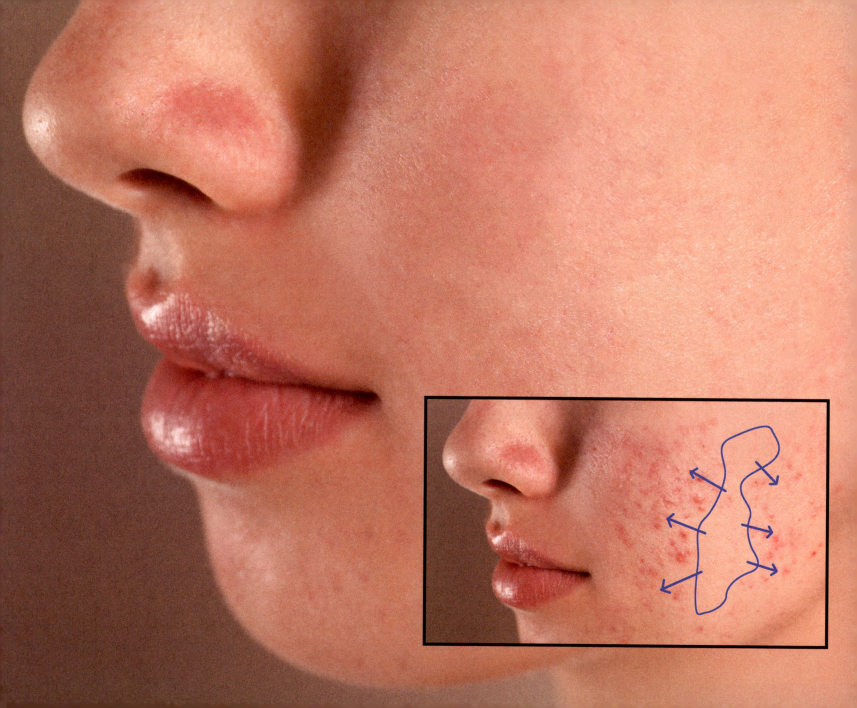

CHAPTER

10

ENHANCE AND
RETOUCH IMAGES

1. Apply Curves Adjustments

2. Use a Channel as a Mask

3. Use the Clone Stamp Tool

4. Explore Content-Aware Features

5. Retouch an Image with the Healing Brush Tools

Adobe Certified Professional in Visual Design Using Photoshop CC Framework

4. Creating and Modifying Visual Elements

This objective covers core tools and functionality of the application, as well as tools that affect the visual outcome of the document.

4.1 Use core tools and features to create visual elements.

   A Create and edit raster images.

4.3 Make, manage, and manipulate selections.

   C Save and load selections as channels.

4.5 Use basic reconstructing and retouching techniques to manipulate digital graphics and media.

   B Use various tools to repair and reconstruct images.

APPLY CURVES ADJUSTMENTS

▶ What You'll Do

In this lesson, you'll use curves to adjust the brightness, contrast, and color of an image.

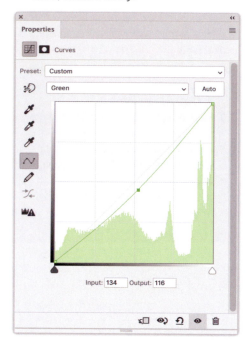

Working with the Curves Adjustment

The **Curves adjustment** is a color and tonal range manipulation utility in Photoshop, like the Levels and Brightness/Contrast adjustments. The Curves adjustment is the most nuanced and most powerful option for manipulating the dynamic range of an image because of the precision it offers. With curves, you have up to 14 different points throughout an image's tonal range to adjust, and you can target specific ranges on the grayscale. You can also make very precise adjustments to specific color channels.

Figure 1 shows a Curves adjustment for a grayscale image. The point in the bottom-left corner represents 0—which is black, or the shadow point. The point in the top-right corner represents 255—which is white, or the highlight point. The line in between the two points represents all values between 0 and 255.

Figure 1 Curves adjustment

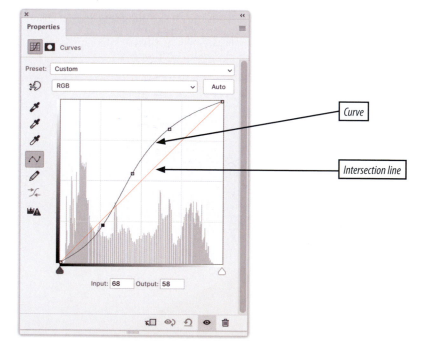

In the figure, the red line is the intersection line (note, this line is red in the figure only to make it easier to see; it's actually light gray in the adjustment). The **intersection line** represents the image before any adjustment was made to the curve. The differential between the curve and the intersection line represents the modifications that have been made. Where the curve is above the intersection line, that range of tone of the image has been brightened. Where the curve is below the intersection line, that range has been darkened. As you can see in the figure, a substantially larger range of the image has been brightened compared to the range that has been darkened.

Curves are often referred to as a "color" adjustment, and curves are highly effective for altering the color balance of an image. However, it's important to remember that curves are most often used to adjust contrast, shadow points, and highlight points to improve the dynamic range of the image. Curves are not only about changing the color balance of an image.

With time and practice, you will develop a reliable sense of how to work with curves to achieve a desired effect, such as brightening an image or increasing contrast. At other times, you'll want to make adjustments that can't be achieved with a standard curve. That's when the Curves adjustment will really test you. In these situations, you'll need to bring all your experience and knowledge to the task and experiment while working your way toward your goal.

Adjusting Tonal Range and Color Balance with Curves

In the Curves adjustment, RGB is the **composite curve**. When you modify the RGB curve, the change affects all three channels equally. For example, if you drag the RGB curve up to brighten the image, all three color channels are brightened by the same measure.

Similarly, if you create an S-shaped curve, that will brighten the highlight areas in all three channels and darken the shadows in all three equally. The effect will be an increase in contrast, but it will not change the color relationships between the three color channels.

The Curves adjustment has a separate curve for the red, the green, and the blue component channels of the image, allowing you to alter those colors individually. To adjust one of these curves, choose the channel color from the Channel menu on the Properties panel. Figure 2 shows the green curve reducing the green component in the image.

Figure 2 Reducing green in an image

Choose color channel from Channel menu

Green curve

Adjusting the component color channels individually is done most often to remove a color cast. A **color cast** occurs when a camera produces an image in which one of the RGB channels dominates the color balance. For example, a poorly calibrated camera or one specified to the wrong lighting settings might produce an image that is too red and weak in the blue component. It would be necessary to adjust the individual color curves to correct that color cast.

Color casts occur even when a camera isn't malfunctioning. For example, if you photograph a sunset with all its intense color, you might want to adjust individual channels simply to tweak the overall color story toward the hues you think look best. Or if you shoot in low light, you might find when you brighten the image that you want to shift the color balance toward hues that are warmer.

Before you even consider making changes to the color balance between the individual RGB channels, you first need to analyze the overall tonal range of the image. A correct range from shadow to highlight has more impact on achieving good color than any other consideration. Therefore, the first adjustments you make when trying to improve an image is to determine the best highlight point, the best shadow point, and the best contrast for the image. Only then should you move on to consider the color balance.

Think of it this way: if there's poor contrast, if the shadows are weak, if the white point is too dark, or if the midrange of the image is too dark or too light, trying to make color adjustments is futile. When you correct those problems, you'll be amazed at how dramatically color throughout the image is improved. Dull, muddy color suddenly becomes vivid and vibrant. For this reason, you will find that using the Curves adjustment to improve the tonal range is often enough to produce optimal color and that manipulating the color balance between the RGB channels is not necessary.

Adjust shadow and highlight points with a Curves adjustment

1. Open PS 10-1.psd, then save it as **Curves Black and White Points**.

   This is a grayscale image. Pixels in a grayscale image can be one, and only one, of 256 shades of gray. Using a single-channel image as opposed to a three-channel RGB image is the best way to learn about curves because, in the single-channel image, you can easily understand what's happening to the numbers when you make adjustments.

2. Show the **Info panel**, then verify that at least one of the **color readouts** is set to **RGB**.

   If you do not see at least one RGB read out on the panel, click ✎ , then click **RGB Color**.

3. On the Layers panel, click the **Create new fill or adjustment layer button** ◑ , then click **Curves**.

4. Click the **Properties panel menu button** 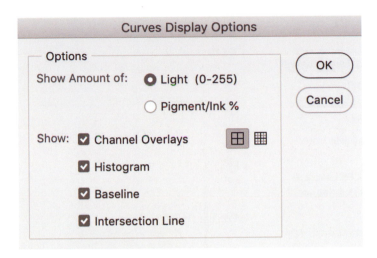,
   click **Curves Display Options**, choose the settings
   shown in Figure 3, then click **OK**.

<table>
<tr><td>AUTHOR'S **NOTE**</td></tr>
</table>

AUTHOR'S **NOTE** The Light (0–255) vs
Pigment/Ink % option determines how the Properties
panel displays the curve information. If you choose
the Light (0–255) option, the curve is displayed in
terms of grayscale, from 0 to 255. This is true for
color or black and white images. With the Pigment/
Ink % option, the Properties panel provides tonal
information for printing, as though it were evaluating
what percentages of ink on paper are represented
by the tonal areas in the image. This book focuses on
designing, not preparing files for print; therefore, for all
the exercises in this chapter, you will choose the Light
(0–255) option in the Curves Display Options dialog box.

5. Note the **black to white gradients** along the
   bottom and left side of the curves grid.

   These gradients have no practical function and
   don't change as a result of any changes you make to
   the curve. Their function is simply to represent the
   movement of shadow to highlight. In other words,
   the bottom gradient shows that the tonal range
   moves from shadow to highlight as you move from
   left to right in the grid. The vertical gradient on the
   left side shows that the tonal range moves from
   black to white as you move from bottom to top.

6. Note the **histogram** behind the curve.

   The histogram is the same histogram you
   would see in the Levels dialog box for this

Figure 3 Curves Display Options dialog box

image. The histogram and the black and white
triangle sliders are the components of the
Curves adjustment that function most like the
Levels adjustment. The concept is the same:
dragging the black triangle sets the shadow
point, and dragging the white triangle sets the
highlight point.

TIP The histogram is explained in detail in Chapter 5.

7. On the Properties panel, drag the **black triangle**
   right until the **Input text box** reads **15**, then drag
   the **white triangle left** until the **Input text box**
   reads **225**.

You darkened the shadow point and brightened
the highlight point. These steps are identical in
concept to those you made in the Levels dialog box
in Chapter 5. The darkest pixels on the histogram
are now 0, and the lightest pixels on the histogram
are now 255.

8. Save your work, then close Curves Black and
   White Points.

*You explored the Curves adjustment. You chose the Light
(0–255) option so the Curves adjustment displayed settings
in terms of grayscale (0–255). You then made an adjustment
using the histogram as a reference, similar to your experience
working with the Levels adjustment.*

Adjust brightness and contrast with curves

1. Open PS 10-2.psd, then save it as **Curves Contrast**.

2. Add a **Curves adjustment layer**.

3. On the Properties panel, click the **approximate center** of the grid to add a point.

   The cursor becomes a crosshair pointer when positioned over the grid.

4. Drag the **point** up so the **Input text box** reads **128** and the **Output text box** reads **160**, as shown in Figure 4.

   TIP You can enter values directly into the Input and Output text boxes.

   The image is brightened. Creating this point and dragging it upward is a simple example of what the Curves adjustment is all about. Pixels that had a grayscale value of 128 now have a value of 160. Therefore, those pixels are lighter by 32 shades of gray. But it's not only those specific pixels that have changed; the entire tonal range of the image has changed. Note how the curve deviates from the light gray intersection line (the intersection line is red in the figure to make it easier to see). Pixels in the middle range of the grayscale are most affected by the move, with the adjustment

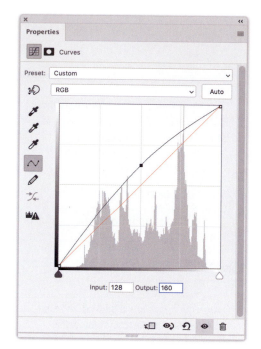

Figure 4 Brightening an image

tapering off in equal measure at the brightest highlights and darkest shadows.

5. Drag the **point** straight down, so the **Input text box** reads **128** and the **Output text box** reads **100**.

When you drag the curve below the intersection line, the image is darkened.

6. Drag the **point** straight up and off the grid.

   The point is deleted, and the curve returns to its original state.

7. Click the **Eyedropper tool** on the toolbar.

8. Press and hold **[command] (Mac)** or **[Ctrl] (Win),** then click and drag the **Eyedropper tool** over different areas of the image while noting the effect on the Curves adjustment.

   A small circle appears on the curve showing where the sampled pixels in the image appear on the curve. This is a useful method for identifying different areas on the image in terms of where they are on the curve.

9. Release the **mouse pointer**.

   A point is added to the curve, and it is targeted. The point represents the sampled pixel you were hovering over when you released the mouse pointer.

10. Type **191** in the **Input text box**, then type **218** in the **Output text box**.

11. Click the **curve** anywhere near the **center** to add a second point.

12. Type **64** in the **Input text box**, then type **40** in the **Output text box**.

As shown in Figure 5, the image's contrast is increased. The pixels above the midpoint have been brightened, and the pixels below the midpoint have been darkened. S-shaped curves always represent an increase in contrast.

13. Save your work, then continue to the next set of steps.

You used the Curves adjustment to brighten, darken, and add contrast to an image. In terms of contrast, you explored the idea that creating an S-shaped curve increases contrast. You also sampled pixels on the image with the Eyedropper tool to see where those pixels appeared on the curve.

Invert an image with curves

1. On the Layers panel, click the **Create new fill or adjustment button** , then click **Invert**.

The image is inverted. Based on your understanding of curves, ask yourself how this adjustment works. Before moving forward, take a few moments to imagine creating this effect with curves. What would the curve look like?

2. Delete the **Invert adjustment layer**, then verify that the **Curves adjustment layer** is targeted.

3. Create a second **Curves adjustment layer**.

4. On the Properties panel, drag the **black point** from the **lower-left corner** up to the **upper-left corner**.

The Input value of the black point, which was 0, changes to an Output value of 255. Because the entire curve now sits at the very top of the grid, every pixel now has an Output value of 255. Thus, the entire image is white.

5. Drag the **white point** down to the **lower-right corner** so your image and the Properties panel resemble Figure 6.

The curve is now inverted. The black point has changed from 0 to 255 and is now white. The white point has changed from 255 to 0 and is now black. All the points in between are also inverted. Pixels that were in the bottom half are now in the top half and vice versa.

Continued on next page

Figure 5 An S-shaped curve always represents an increase in contrast

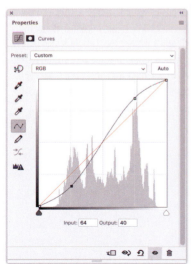 

Figure 6 Inverting an image

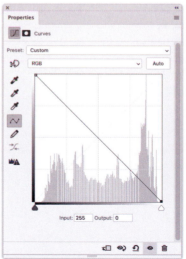 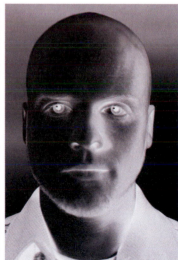

6. Add a **point** at the very **center** of the curve.

The Input and Output values are both 128. Pixel 128 is the middle gray pixel—128 is the median point between 0 and 255. The curve has not changed location at the 128 point on the grid. All the other pixels have swapped values with their counterparts on the other side of the midpoint: 129 is 127, 130 is 126, 245 is 10, and so on.

7. Save your work, then close the file.

To better understand the Curves adjustment, you inverted the curve to invert the image.

Remove a color cast

1. Open PS 10-3.psd, then save it as **Curves Color Cast**.

2. Assess the overall appearance of the image in terms of color.

With landscapes, it's seldom the case that the color is "wrong," as it might be with objects that are more specific in color, like fruit. This image clearly has a yellow color cast overall. The foliage that would naturally be green is closer to yellow and orange. This would be expected if the image had been shot at sunrise or sunset.

3. Sample different areas of the image with the **Eyedropper tool** 🖋, noting the **RGB values** on the Info panel.

Pretty much anywhere you sample in the image, other than the sky, the red component dominates the green and the blue significantly. The Blue channel appears to be the weakest of the three.

4. Create a new **Curves adjustment layer**.

5. On the Properties panel, click the **Channel menu list arrow**, click **Blue**, then add a **point** to the **blue curve** at **Input 128** and **Output 150**.

Yellow is composed of red and green; yellow is minus-blue. Since the image has a yellow color cast overall, a smart first move is to increase blue. With the increased blue, it is now clear that there's an overall red cast to the image. This makes sense: the yellow cast appears to have been the result of too little blue and too much red.

6. Using the **Channel menu**, switch to the **Red channel**.

7. Add a **point** to the **red curve**, then experiment by moving the point to various locations below the intersection line.

Experimenting this way is a smart solution for adjusting color. One can never be certain up front what the best adjustment is. It's best to scout around for clues. Different reductions of red in this image result in different qualities of green showing through in the foliage.

8. Drag the **new point** on the red curve to **Input 147/Output 100**.

9. Hide and show the **Curves adjustment layer** to see the change.

The change is dramatic and proves that the original image did indeed have a heavy red/yellow cast throughout. Another improvement is the increase in detail overall. Look at the tree trunk. Note how the sunny side of the tree trunk is now a genuine brown. Note how the mountains in the background are more differentiated from the middle ground, and how the fencepost is more prominent. One clue the balance is correct is that the red dirt below the foliage is still a vibrant red. This indicates that the red component of the image is strong where it needs to be. Finally, note how the plants in the foreground show so much more color variation and detail.

10. Assess the overall appearance of the image in terms of color.

When you make a color adjustment that improves an image dramatically, it's easy to jump to the conclusion that your work is done, because the image looks so much better. Instead, after every step, stop and assess the image. In this case, the improvement is dramatic, but the overall color tone of the image is cold. The greens are cold—like the color of evergreen trees. This suggests the blue adjustment might have been overdone.

11. Switch back to the **Blue channel**, then experiment with reducing the Blue channel by various degrees, noting the impact on the image.

12. Decrease the **Blue channel** to **Input 128/ Output 139**, then compare your results to Figure 7.

Though it was a small change, it improved the greens and warmed up the image overall.

13. Save your work, then close Curves Color Cast.

You manipulated the red and blue curves independently to remove a color cast from the image.

Figure 7 Before and after

USE A CHANNEL AS A MASK

▶ *What You'll Do*

In this lesson, you will use a channel as a mask to access difficult-to-select areas of an image.

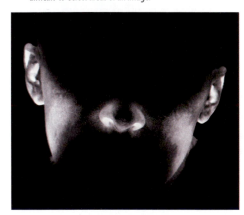

Some selections are difficult to make. Often it will be the case that you will want to adjust specific areas of an image, but isolating that area—either with a selection or a mask—is highly difficult or impossible.

Color channels can be used as layer masks to affect specific areas of the image in subtle ways. Because the channel is the image itself, it has all the ranges and nuances of the image, and you can use that to your favor to access subtle, nonspecific areas to adjust.

Figure 8 shows an image that has great color overall, but there's very little detail in the model's hair, especially over her shoulder. If you used a Curves adjustment to brighten the hair, the adjustment would brighten everything in the hair equally; the range of contrast in the hair would be diminished.

In Figure 9, two Curves adjustments and a Hue/Saturation adjustment were applied to brighten and add saturation to the hair, and they're all using the Red channel from the image inverted as a mask. Because it's inverted, the black areas of the hair are white. The mask has been painted so the face and other areas are black, allowing the adjustment to affect only the model's hair. However, because the channel is from the image itself, the hair area isn't one flat white area; it has a range of grays, so the brightening is being applied more in shadows and less in the highlights, thus maintaining good contrast. The hair has dramatically more detail and more range of color. As a bonus, the model's diamond earring is also brighter and more eye-catching.

Figure 8 Poor detail in the shadows of the hair

Figure 9 Adjustments with channels as masks to brighten hair

Reduce red areas in a flesh tone

1. Open PS 10-4.psd, then save it as **Channel Mask**.

2. Assess the image.

   The goal of this lesson is to reduce the distinct red flesh tones in the man's cheeks, the ears, and nostrils. The challenge is how to isolate those areas in order to affect them only. Trying to use the selection tools or a layer mask won't work. Instead, using one of the RGB channels as a readymade layer mask will be very effective.

3. Show the **Hue/Saturation adjustment layer**.

   The Hue/Saturation adjustment layer has been set to Overlay, which adds dramatic contrast and saturation overall and intensifies the red on the cheeks. Intensifying the red areas will make them easier to access in the channels.

4. If you're working on a Mac, click **Photoshop** on the menu bar, point to **Preferences**, then click **Interface**.

5. If you're working on a PC, click **Edit** on the menu bar, point to **Preferences**, then click **Interface**.

6. In the **Options section**, remove the **check mark** next to **Show Channels in Color**, then click **OK**.

7. Show the **Channels panel**, then view the **Red**, **Green**, and **Blue channels** one at a time by hiding the others.

   The goal is to identify the channel in which the red cheeks are most distinct from the adjacent flesh tones. The Green channel best meets this criterion.

8. Show all channels, target the **Green channel**, click the **Channels panel menu button** ≡ , then click **Duplicate Channel**.

9. Keep the name **Green copy**, then click **OK**.

   A new channel named **Green copy** is created. Channels reflect the image in its current state; therefore, the cheeks and the sides of the nose in the Green copy channel are dramatically darker than the adjacent flesh tones.

10. Verify that the **Green copy channel** is targeted, click **Image** on the menu bar, point to **Adjustments**, then click **Invert**.

    The Green copy channel is inverted. The red areas were dark areas in the original channel. Inverted, they are light areas. When this channel is used as a mask, the cheeks will be more selected than other areas of the image, because light areas in a mask are more selected than dark areas.

11. Click **Image** on the menu bar, point to **Adjustments**, then click **Levels**.

12. Type **24** in the **first Input text box**, type **.90** in the **second Input text box**, type **199** in the **third Input text box**, then click **OK**.

    The Levels adjustment pushed the image further toward the goal of making the cheek areas as light as possible and the adjacent flesh tones as dark as possible.

13. Click the **Brush tool** ✎, set the **Opacity** to **100%**, choose a big soft brush, then paint **black** so that your channel resembles Figure 10.

    Don't paint too close to the cheeks. As a mask, this channel has effectively isolated the ears, nose, and cheek areas as white.

14. Switch the **foreground color** to **white**, then change the Brush tool **Opacity** to **20%**.

15. Click the **Mode list arrow** on the Options panel, then click **Overlay**.

16. Paint the **cheeks**, the **sides of the nose**, and the **ears** to lighten them so your mask resembles Figure 11.

    When painting with the Overlay blending mode, the brush does not paint white—it lightens. What's really powerful in this case is that the brush can't affect the black areas, so you can effectively brighten the areas you want to affect.

17. Click the **RGB channel** to return to the composite channel.

18. Return to the **Layers panel**, then **delete** the **Hue/Saturation adjustment layer**.

19. Click **Select** on the menu bar, click **Load Selection**, click the **Channel list arrow**, click **Green copy**, then click **OK**.

    The Green copy channel is loaded as a selection. The red areas of the image are selected.

20. Click **Select** on the menu bar, point to **Modify**, click **Feather**, type **4** in the **Feather Radius text box**, then click **OK**.

    Modifying the feather value to 4 softens any hard lines.

21. Click the **Create new fill or adjustment layer button** ◕ on the Layers panel, then click **Hue/Saturation**.

    A Hue/Saturation adjustment layer is added. Because the selection was active when the Hue/Saturation adjustment was created, the selection is automatically added as a layer mask.

22. Drag the **Hue slider** to **+14**, drag the **Lightness slider** to **+12**, then compare your result to Figure 12.

Seen side by side, it's amazing how glaring the red areas in the original image are. There's no hint that the image has been manipulated or doctored in any way. The work is invisible. Remember this exercise as a great example of how powerful and useful channels can be for targeting and manipulating hard-to-select areas of an image.

23. Save your work, then close Channel Mask.

You used and manipulated a channel to perform a delicate color move on a nonspecific area of an image. You overlayed a Hue/Saturation adjustment layer to increase contrast in the image and in the channel. You painted black in the channel to remove areas from the eventual selection, and you painted white in Overlay mode to brighten areas while leaving black areas unaffected.

Figure 10 Painting black in areas to be unaffected

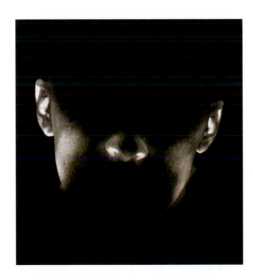

Figure 11 Using the Brush tool in Overlay mode to brighten bright areas of the channel

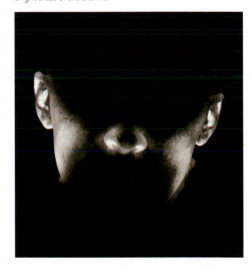

Figure 12 Before and after results

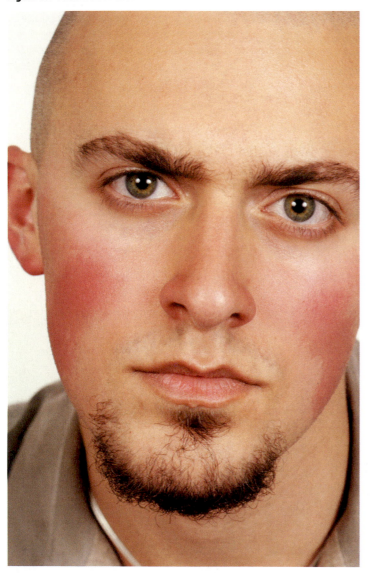

Ken Weingart/Getty Images

USE THE CLONE STAMP TOOL

What You'll Do

In this lesson, you'll use the Clone Stamp tool to extend parts of a rotated image to fill the canvas.

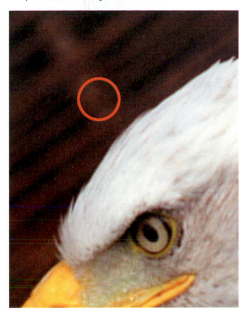

Imagine selecting a small area of an image, copying it, and pasting it somewhere else. That's essentially what the Clone Stamp tool does, but the big difference is that the Clone Stamp tool does it with a brush. Using the Clone Stamp tool, you first establish the point in the image that's being copied or cloned. Press and hold [option] (Mac) or [Alt] (Win), and then click the canvas to set the clone source. With that established, wherever you "paint" with the Clone Stamp tool, it will copy the clone source and its surrounding areas to that new location.

The Clone Stamp tool fills many different needs. For example, if you had an image of a field of flowers in one area, you could clone them to put flowers in a different area. For a different task, you might need to extend an image's height or width, and the Clone Stamp tool can help you do that.

The Clone Stamp tool is also used for retouching. If you had an image of a person with a tattoo and wanted to remove the tattoo, you could clone skin

from an untattooed area to replace the tattoo. And of course, if you need to put a third eye at the center of someone's forehead, the Clone Stamp tool is the first tool you'll go to.

The Clone Stamp tool has two modes, **Aligned** and **Non-aligned**, which you specify on the Options panel. With the Aligned option checked, if you stop cloning then start again, the next clone will pick up where you left off and continue the clone. In other words, the second clone is aligned with the previous clone.

If the Aligned option is not checked, whenever you stop and restart cloning, the new clone goes back to the clone source to create the next clone. In other words, every new clone you make will be from the clone source. Thus, the Non-aligned option is useful if you want to repeat the clone source area multiple times. For example, if you had an image of stars in the night sky and you quickly wanted to create more stars, you could clone them over and over with a Non-aligned clone.

Generally speaking, you almost always want the Aligned option checked when you use the Clone Stamp tool.

Cloning Strategically with Adjustment Layers

Often you will find that you need to do some retouching after you've applied adjustment layers like Curves or Hue/Saturation. In these cases, where you position your retouching layer in the Layers panel relative to the adjustment layers becomes a critical decision. Also critical is what layer you sample from to establish the clone source.

The key is to clone in a way that the adjustment layers can still be modified after the fact. The method for achieving this goal is to position the clone layer below any adjustment layers. Thus, if the adjustment is modified, both the original image and the clone are subject to the same adjustment.

This introduces a second critical consideration when cloning with adjustment layers. You cannot include the adjustment layer as part of the clone source for the clone you create because if you later modify the adjustment, the previous clone becomes unusable.

Use the Clone Stamp tool to fill empty areas of the canvas

1. Open PS 10-5.psd, then save it as **Cloned Eagle**.

   The image of the eagle was pasted into this file and rotated to a specific angle. The resulting problem is there's not enough image to fill the two corners. The only solution is to clone existing areas to fill the negative spaces.

2. Click the **Clone Stamp tool** 👤. on the toolbar, verify that its **Opacity** is set to **100%**, then verify that the **Aligned check box** is checked on the Options panel.

3. Create a **new layer** above the Eagle layer, then name it **Clones**.

Cloning should not be done directly on any image you are manipulating. In this case, you would not clone directly on the image of the eagle. That would be destructive editing. Instead, you will do all the cloning on the new, empty Clones layer you just created.

4. On the Options panel, click the **Sample list arrow**, then choose **Current & Below**.

   With this setting, the Clone Stamp tool will sample pixels from the current Clones layer and all layers beneath it. The Clones layer is empty, but the Clone Stamp tool will sample pixels from the Eagle layer beneath it as well.

5. Assess the upper-left corner of the image.

   The background image behind the eagle is a brown basket with straw that is woven horizontally and vertically (everything is now diagonal because the image has been rotated). It will be necessary to extend the lighter vertical line that is perpendicular to the bird's head in the upper-left corner.

6. On the Options panel, set the **Size** to **80**, then set the **Hardness** to **0%**.

Since the background image is slightly blurry and out of focus, a soft-edge brush will work in this case.

7. Press and hold **[option] (Mac)** or **[Alt] (Win)**.

The cursor changes to a sample icon, indicating the Clone Stamp is ready to set the sample location.

8. Click to sample the **area circled in Figure 13**, then release [option] (Mac) or [Alt] (Win).

9. Position the **Clone Stamp tool** in the location shown in Figure 14, then click and drag to paint over the **white triangle**.

Your result should resemble Figure 15. The goal was to extend and continue the light vertical line with no apparent break between the original and cloned areas.

Continued on next page

Figure 13 Choosing an area to sample

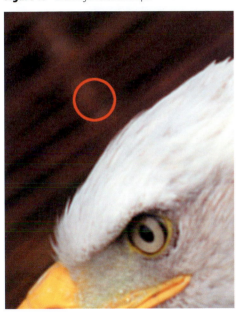

Figure 14 Choosing an area to start the cloning

Figure 15 Cloned areas of the image

10. Using the same method, clone out the **three distracting light gray spots** on the basket, two in front of the bird and one behind.

    You'll have to strategically choose sources for the clones to replace the light gray spots.

11. Assess the needs of the **lower-right corner** of the image.

    This is a more challenging area to clone. There are two patterns of feathers to consider. The feathers on the bird's chest point downward. The feathers behind them on the wing are layered in a scalloped pattern. The goal is to continue each of these patterns.

12. Clone the **front short feathers** to extend them horizontally into the white triangle, as shown in Figure 16.

13. Strategically clone **single large feathers** from the wing to extend them as shown in Figure 17 on the following page.

    This is a good opportunity to hone your cloning skills. The feathers must end in a scalloped edge when they meet the short feathers. This will require strategic sampling and cloning of individual feathers, as shown in the figure. With a little time and practice, you will be able to produce a similar result.

14. Save your work, then close Cloned Eagle.

You cloned areas of the image to fill two empty areas of the canvas. You also cloned to remove three distracting light spots in the original image. You did all cloning on a new layer above the artwork so your work was nondestructive to the original image.

Figure 16 Cloning the short front feathers

Figure 17 Cloning the larger wing feathers

Sample strategically with the Clone Stamp tool

1. Open PS 10-6.psd, then save it as **Sample Strategically**.

2. Hide and show the **Hue/Saturation adjustment layer** to see its effect on the base image.

3. Verify that the **Hue/Saturation adjustment layer** is showing.

4. Add a **new layer** above the Hue/Saturation adjustment layer.

    In this step, you are creating the clone layer in the *wrong* location above the Hue/Saturation adjustment layer. You are doing this incorrectly so you will see what goes wrong when cloning is done incorrectly in this manner.

5. Click the **Clone Stamp tool** , sample an **area of the woman's face** to set the clone source, then clone out the **beauty mark** on the woman's cheek.

6. Double click the **Hue/Saturation adjustment layer** to see its settings on the Properties panel, then change the **Hue** to **0**.

    As shown in Figure 18, adjusting the Hue/Saturation adjustment affects the base image beneath the adjustment layer, but the cloned pixels above the adjustment layer remain the blue color that was sampled before the adjustment change.

7. Revert the file.

8. Target the **Background layer**, add a new layer, then name it **Clones**.

    The new layer is below the adjustment layer.

9. Verify that the **Sample menu** on the Options panel reads **Current & Below**.

    The Current & Below setting specifies that the Clone Stamp tool will sample pixels only from the layer currently targeted and the layers below it.

10. Clone out the **beauty mark** on the woman's cheek.

11. Change the **Hue value** on the Properties panel to **0**.

    Both the base image and the cloned pixels are affected by the change and turn to red.

12. Hide the **Hue/Saturation adjustment layer**.

    The base image and the cloned pixels are shades of gray. The Clone Stamp tool never cloned the original blue color of the adjustment layer because it was not current or below.

13. Show the **Hue/Saturation adjustment layer**, save your work, then close the file.

You removed a beauty mark from a woman's face using the Clone Stamp tool twice. The first time you did it incorrectly by placing a new layer above a Hue/Saturation adjustment layer and cloning from that layer. When you modified the Hue value, you noticed that the cloned area did not update with the change on the adjustment layer. You reverted the file, then created a new layer above the Background layer from which to clone. Because this layer was set to Current & Below, the cloning only occurred on the current and Background layer. Additional changes to the Hue/Saturation adjustment layer did not affect the cloned area.

Figure 18 Error in cloning

EXPLORE CONTENT-AWARE FEATURES

▶ **What You'll Do**

In this lesson, you'll use the Content-Aware Fill, Content-Aware Move tool, and Content-Aware Scale features.

Making Content-Aware Fills, Scales, and Moves

In many science fiction movies, the question of whether a computer is alive or aware is a great existential question. This concept is explored in great sci-fi movies like *Blade Runner*, *The Terminator*, and *2001: A Space Odyssey*, just to name a few. The term artificial intelligence inspires humans to imagine what a computer knows or understands—or even feels.

It's interesting to consider what Photoshop really "knows." When the software was created, all Photoshop "knew" was pixels: the number of pixels, the HSB values of pixels, the RGB values of pixels, and the location of pixels on the pixel grid.

That has changed. For example, Photoshop is now able to recognize faces. People generally have two eyes, one nose, and one mouth in generally the same location on the face with similar spatial relationships to one another. Using thousands of images of faces, programmers have been able to "teach" Photoshop to recognize pixel combinations that are eyes and noses and mouths and cheeks and jaws and jawlines. Thus, the Liquify utility, which you explored in Chapter 8, now features a Face tool and face-aware controls that allow you to manipulate specific areas of faces without ever having to select them.

Photoshop also features many sophisticated content-aware utilities and tools. The content-aware tools involve cloning, moving, or scaling pixels. With content-aware utilities and tools, these operations can be done in a way that Photoshop is "aware" of the image and runs algorithms to match your work with the image. The following are some examples of content-aware operations.

A **Content-Aware Fill** will fill a selection in a way that mimics or matches the areas surrounding the selection. If you had an overhead shot of a rowboat on a wavy pond, you could select the boat and fill the selection with "wavy pond" pixels. The fill would match the surrounding wavy pond areas, but what's really amazing is that the content-aware fill wouldn't be cloned or copied wavy pond pixels. Instead, the algorithm creates new and original wavy pond pixels based on the available data.

The **Content-Aware Move tool** moves pixels from one location to another. The pixels that are moved are blended into the surrounding areas of the new location in terms of color, texture, and shading. The tool also performs a content-aware fill on the area left behind. Thus, the object is moved, and the original location is filled with pixels that match the surrounding area.

The **Content-Aware Scale tool** allows you to distort an image without distorting critical components of the image. Imagine you had an image of a sports car parked on an expanse of gold sand in the desert. Behind the car is a blue sky with puffy white clouds. Let's say you needed to stretch that image from a 5" × 5" square to a 5" × 9" rectangle. A content-aware scale would stretch the image by adding new sand, new sky, and new clouds, but it would recognize the car as a car and not distort it at all.

The content-aware operations in Photoshop will amaze you. However, it's good to see them as a means to an end. Using the rowboat on the wavy pond example, you might use the Content-Aware Fill tool to get you 90% of the way toward your goal, and then do a little bit of tweaking on your own with the Clone Stamp tool, the Brush tool, or both to perfect the result.

Cloning with the Patch Tool

The Patch tool is a content-aware cloning tool you can use to relocate one part of an image to another part of the image seamlessly. To work with the Patch tool, you first make a selection of the area you want to replace, then you drag the selection to the area you want to use as the replacement content. As you drag the selection, the Patch tool shows dynamic previews of what the replacement content will look like. When you release the mouse pointer, the area where you stop fills the original selection seamlessly with a content-aware fill.

Designers who use the Patch tool do so because of the dynamic previews of how the replacement area will fill the original selection. For example, let's say you had an image of a perfectly blue sky except for one cloud. You could make a lasso selection around the cloud, then drag the cloud to different areas of blue sky to preview which would area best replace the cloud.

Remove unwanted content with a content-aware fill

1. Open PS 10-7.psd, then save it as **Duck Alone**.

    There are three birds in this photo, but imagine that you would prefer it with just the one duck swimming alone. To try to clone out the two flying birds and their reflections would be a bit

of a challenge because there is a range of color that would need to be matched exactly. This is the type of challenge a content-aware fill can address efficiently.

2. Click the **Rectangular Marquee tool** , then drag a selection around the **flying bird and its reflection**.

3. Click **Edit** on the menu bar, click **Fill**, enter the settings shown in Figure 19, then click **OK**.

    The selection is filled with pixels that extend and match the background, removing the bird and its reflection from the scene.

4. Save your work, then close Duck Alone.

You removed an image of a duck from the document by using the Content-Aware option on the Fill dialog box. The selection was filled with pixels that matched the blue sky background.

Figure 19 Content-Aware option on the Fill dialog box

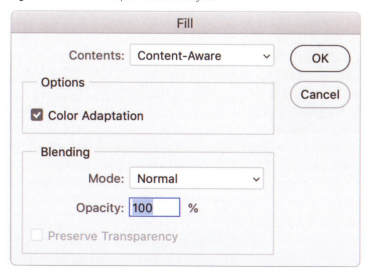

Create a content-aware fill on a layer

1. Open PS 10-8.psd, then save it as **Three Birds**.

   Imagine that you prefer this image with three birds, not four. You decide you're going to remove either the third or fourth bird from the left, but you're not sure which one. Rather than use the Fill command on the Edit menu, you decide to use the Content Aware dialog box so the content-aware fill will be saved to a layer rather than directly to the image.

2. Click the **Lasso tool** ![lasso icon], then draw a selection around the **third bird from the left**, leaving approximately 1/8" of space around the bird, as shown in Figure 20.

3. Click **Edit** on the menu bar, then click **Content-Aware Fill**.

The Content-Aware dialog box opens, showing a preview of the image with the selected bird removed and replaced with a content-aware fill. On the canvas, a green area appears, indicating the areas of the image Photoshop will use to calculate the fill. You could modify the area Photoshop has chosen to use, but why would you match wits with Photoshop?

TIP If you do not see a green area on the canvas, click Auto under Sampling Area Options in the Content-Aware pane on the right.

4. In the **Output Settings section**, click the **Output To list arrow**, click **New Layer**, then click **OK**.

   The content-aware fill is executed, and the fill is saved to a new layer called Background copy on the Layers panel.

5. Target the **Background layer**.

6. Select the **bird** in the **lower-right corner**, then use another content-aware fill to remove it.

   Your results should resemble Figure 21. The content-aware algorithm does an amazing job of replacing the birds with clouds that look real and not duplicated.

7. Decide which bird you want to keep in your final image, save your work, then close the file.

   Hiding the Background copy layer will show the bird that was removed. Showing the Background layer will hide the bird.

   You created two content-aware fills. You used the Content-Aware Fill dialog box to save the two fills to separate layers, allowing you the option to show the one you preferred.

Figure 20 Selecting the bird

Figure 21 Two birds removed from the image

Execute a content-aware fill on a complex image

1. Open PS 10-9.psd, then save it as **Just Mountains**.

2. Use the **Lasso tool**  to create the selection shown in Figure 22.

3. Execute a content-aware fill.

   Incredibly, Photoshop can create a believable fill. As shown in Figure 23, the fill is composed of original artwork. Nothing is cloned or duplicated. The only problem is that the algorithm created a little mountain in the middle of the road. That could be fixed easily with the Clone Stamp tool and the Brush tool.

4. Save your work, then close Just Mountains.

You executed a content-aware fill on an image with visually complex content, noting that Photoshop was able to duplicate the content realistically and without cloning.

Figure 22 Selecting the balloon

Xinhua/Shutterstock.com

Figure 23 New and original mountains replace the balloon

Use the Content-Aware Scale command and the Content-Aware Move tool

1. Open PS 10-10.psd, then save it as **Reach the Beach**.

   This image presents a real-world challenge that occurs often. The image is a rectangle; however, it needs to be substantially wider for the layout it's going into—let's imagine for a newspaper or for a website. Often the layout dictates the proportions of the image, and that can create really challenging situations like this one. In this case, you can't scale the image to this new width because there's important content at the bottom and at the top. If you tried to scale it, losing the man at the bottom wouldn't be an option, so you'd have no choice but to lose the wave at the top, and that's the best part of the image. This is where a content-aware scale can save the day.

2. Target the **Distort Scale layer**, click **Edit** on the menu bar, point to **Transform**, then click **Scale**.

   The bounding box appears. For this artwork, you are going to stretch the artwork just to see how distorted it would need to be to fill the width of the canvas.

3. Drag the **right-middle handle** all the way to the right edge of the canvas.

   This is an example of scaling the image not in proportion and with no content-aware algorithms involved. The image is stretched to a point that makes it unusable.

4. Press **[command] [Z] (Mac)** or **[Ctrl] [Z] (Win)** to undo the scale.

5. Hide the **Distort Scale layer**, then target the **Content-Aware Scale layer**.

6. Click **Edit** on the menu bar, then click **Content-Aware Scale**.

   The bounding box appears.

7. Drag the **right-middle handle** all the way to the right edge of the canvas.

The content-aware scale strategically increased the width of the image by adding new data in areas where that new data won't show, such as the beach, sky, rocks and, water. Figure 24 shows a before-and-after image. Note how much further from the left edge of the canvas the man now sits. Note also that his sandal is much farther away from him than in the original; that's because the content-aware scale added width in that area. Fortunately, we can easily move the sandal closer to the man.

8. Click the **Content-Aware Move tool** ✖, , then drag a **lasso selection** around the **sandal**.

The Content-Aware Move tool makes its own selections.

9. Drag the **sandal** to the right so it is close to the box the man is sitting on, as in the original image.

When you move a selection, the Cancel transform button ⊘ and the Commit transform button ✓ appear on the Options panel.

10. Click the **Commit transform button** ✓ to execute the move.

The sandal is moved with a content-aware setting, meaning it blends in to its new location. In addition, a content-aware fill is applied in its previous location.

11. Save your work, then close Reach the Beach.

You first stretched a copy of the image to see the degree to which it would be unusable with a traditional, noncontent-aware scale. You then did essentially the same stretch with the Content-Aware Scale tool, which resulted in a flawless scale that did not affect the man or the umbrella. You noted that the man's sandal was far from him with the new scale, so you used the Content-Aware Move tool to quickly move it closer.

Figure 24 Before-and-after image of the scene with a content-aware scale

Genaro Molina/Los Angeles Times/Shutterstock.com

Use the Patch Tool

1. Open PS 10-11.psd, then save it as **Patch the Bicycle**.

   This image presents another real-world challenge that you likely will encounter at some point. The design calls for the headline and type to be positioned in the lower half of the right page. The problem is there's content in that area—a man on a bicycle—that needs to be removed to create space for the type. Moving the type to the space at the upper-left corner could be a simple solution, but this design requires that the headline and type remain on the right-hand side of the image—a more prominent focal point. Therefore, the image of the man on the bicycle must go.

2. Hide the **TYPE layer**.

3. Click the **Rectangular Marquee tool** ⬚, then make a selection that completely surrounds the **manhole cover** and the **square of cement** that's around it.

4. Click **Edit** on the menu bar, then click **Fill**.

5. Fill the selection with a **Content-Aware fill** to make the manhole cover disappear.

   You removed the manhole cover to create a "clean" area of cement-only texture, which you will use to replace the man on the bicycle with the Patch tool.

6. Click the **Patch tool** ⬚ on the toolbar, then drag a **selection around the man on the bicycle** that resembles Figure 25.

Figure 25 Selecting the area to be replaced

Figure 26 Dragging the selection to the location for the replacement

7. Drag the **selection** to the location shown in Figure 26, then release the mouse pointer.

   A content-aware fill is applied to the selection of the man on the bicycle, using the content of the area you dragged to. The Patch tool allowed you to specify the source for the content-aware fill.

8. Deselect, show the **TYPE layer**, then compare your canvas to Figure 27 on the following page.

You used a content-aware fill to remove the manhole cover and create a "clean" area of cement. You used the Patch tool to select the man on the bicycle, then you dragged the selected area to the "blank" cement area, thus specifying the source for the content-aware fill to remove the man on the bicycle.

Figure 27 The final image shows no trace of the work done

ZOOMING AHEAD
Duis autem vel eum iriure dolor in hendrerit in vulputate velit esse consequat, illum dolore eu feugiat nulla facilisis at vero eros.

RETOUCH AN IMAGE WITH THE HEALING BRUSH TOOLS

▶ *What You'll Do*

In this lesson, you'll use the content-aware Healing Brush and Spot Healing Brush tools to remove blemishes on an image.

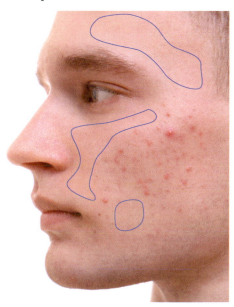

Employing Content-Aware Cloning Tools

Photoshop's content-aware abilities have had a big impact on cloning and retouching. For a long time, the Clone Stamp tool was the only cloning tool available. It's a capable and useful tool, but its big limitation is its reliance on the clone source. If you don't have many (or any) usable areas of the image to clone from, that can limit the work you can get done with cloning. For example, let's say you were retouching an image of a man's face, and one side of his face is bright from a light, and the other is in shadow. The shadow makes the left side of the face unusable as the clone source to retouch any areas on the bright side of the face, because the clone would be too dark to blend with the surrounding areas.

The **Healing Brush tool** is the content-aware version of the Clone Stamp tool. When you use it for retouching, it blends the clone source into the surrounding areas using content-aware

algorithms. Using the same example, you could use the Healing Brush tool to sample skin on the dark side of the face and clone it on the bright side of the face. Even though the clone source is darker, the Healing Brush tool will match the clone to the surrounding areas in the new location in terms of hue, saturation, brightness, and texture. Thus, the Healing Brush tool greatly expands upon the function of the Clone Stamp tool by increasing potential clone sources.

The **Spot Healing Brush tool** is the first cousin to the Healing Brush tool and the only cloning tool that does not require that you first sample before cloning. Instead, simply drag the Spot Healing Brush tool over the area you want to remove or correct, and it will replace that area with pixels that match the surrounding area in terms of hue, saturation, brightness, and texture. It's an amazing content-aware tool that can make otherwise impossible retouching possible.

Retouch with the Healing Brush tool

1. Open PS 10-12.psd, then save it as **Healing Brush Skin Retouch**.

2. Create a **new layer**, then name it **Healing Brush**.

3. Click the **Healing Brush tool** on the toolbar.

4. On the Options panel, verify that **Aligned** is not checked and the **Sample menu** reads **Current & Below**.

5. On the Options panel, set the **Size** of the brush to **150 px**, then set the **Hardness** to **60%**.

   Because the Healing Brush tool is content-aware, it automatically blends the clones you create with the surrounding areas. Therefore, it's not necessary to use a very soft brush. This is a major benefit because the relatively hard brush won't blur the image the way a soft brush would.

6. Press and hold **[option] (Mac)** or **[Alt] (Win)**, sample from any of the **areas circled in Figure 28**, then click to replace any one of the **red blemishes**.

   The Healing Brush tool works most effectively with a sample-click, sample-click working method. It's generally not a good idea to drag the brush around trying to clone large areas. Instead, think of the Healing Brush tool as making small clone patches. Because each clone is blended into its surroundings, the results don't look like patchwork.

7. Repeat the previous step 10 times on different blemishes.

   As you "heal" the image, you create more areas from which to sample.

8. Using the same steps, retouch all the blemishes on the image.

   Figure 29 shows one result. It was retouched entirely with the Healing Brush tool at 150 pixels and 60% Hardness with approximately 100 samples and clicks.

9. Work for as long as it takes for you to create a similar result. Practice is key. Revert the file if you need to start from scratch.

10. Save your work, then close Healing Brush Skin Retouch.

You used the Healing Brush tool to remove numerous blemishes from an image.

Figure 28   Identifying good areas to sample from

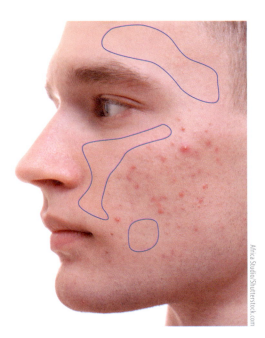

Africa Studio/Shutterstock.com

Figure 29   The image retouched using only the Healing Brush tool

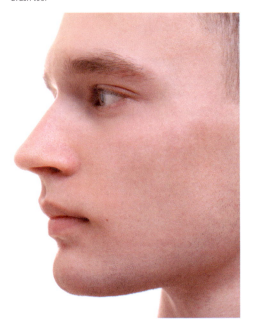

Retouch with the Spot Healing Brush tool

1. Open PS 10-13.psd, then save it as **Spot Healing Brush Skin Retouch**.

2. Duplicate the **Background layer**, then name it **Spot Healing Brush**.

3. Click the **Spot Healing Brush tool** on the toolbar, set the **Size** to **40 px**, then set the **Hardness** to **60%**.

4. On the Options panel, click the **Sample All Layers check box**.

5. Click and drag the **Spot Healing Brush tool** over one of the **blemishes**.

   The Spot Healing Brush tool is not a cloning tool; you don't sample. Clicking and dragging the Spot Healing Brush tool over an area blends it with the surrounding area in terms of color, texture, and shade. The blemish changes color slightly to adapt to the surrounding pixels.

6. Using Figure 30 as a guide, work your way from the center of the image outward to remove the blemishes.

   The skin at the center is the model's natural skin tone and unblemished. Working outward from that

area, the unblemished skin tone and texture will be expanded. Figure 31 shows one result, produced with only the Spot Healing Brush tool at these settings. The image has been greatly improved but still needs work to even out the flesh tone. That can be accomplished with the Healing Brush, Clone Stamp, and Brush tools.

7. Save your work, then close Spot Healing Brush Skin Retouch.

You used the Spot Healing Brush tool to retouch blemishes in an image.

Figure 30 Identifying the direction for retouching the image

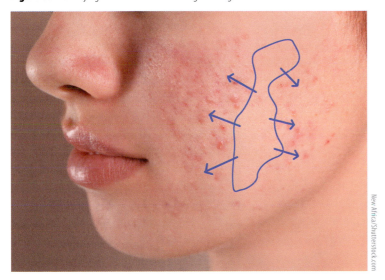

New Africa/Shutterstock.com

Figure 31 The image retouched using only the Spot Healing Brush tool

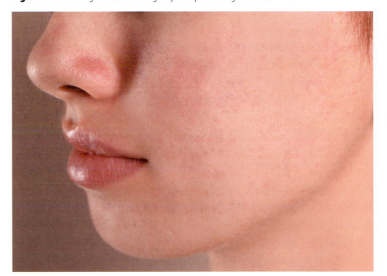

Adjust a grayscale image with curves

1. Open PS 10-14.psd, then save it as **Curves Skills Grayscale**.
2. Add a Curves adjustment.
3. Drag the white triangle left until the Input value reads 156.

   Pixels whose grayscale values were 156 are now 255.
4. Drag the black triangle right until the Input value reads 7.
5. Add a second Curves adjustment layer.
6. Click the curve to add a point to it, then move the point until the Input value reads 188 and the Output value reads 196.

   You can enter the Input and Output data manually, but it's better to drag the point to experiment and see different changes to the image.
7. Click to add a point near the bottom of the curve, then move it until the Input value reads 87 and the Output value reads 73.

   An S-curve always results in an increase in contrast.
8. Save your work, then close **Curves Skills Grayscale**.

Remove a color cast with curves

1. Open PS 10-15.psd, then save it as **Curves Skills Color Cast**.
2. Add a Curves adjustment.
3. Drag the white triangle left until the Input value reads 214.
4. Drag the black triangle right until the Input value reads 23.
5. Add a second Curves adjustment.
6. Click to add a point to the curve, then move it until the Input value reads 160 and the Output value reads 178.
7. Click to add a point near the bottom of the curve, then move it until the Input value reads 62 and the Output value reads 60.
8. Open the Info panel, then verify that the first readout is set to RGB.
9. Sample the petals of the flower.

   The petals are white—or should be white. Therefore, the RGB values should be relatively equal and high on the grayscale range. Wherever you sample the petals, you will find that the blue value is higher than the others, indicating a color cast.
10. Add a new Curves adjustment.
11. On the Properties panel, click the RGB list arrow, then click Blue to see the blue curve.
12. Add a point to the curve, then move it until the Input value reads 128 and the Output value reads 112.
13. Sample the petals of the flower.

    The RGB values are now relatively even; the blue color cast has been removed.
14. Save your work, then close Curves Skills Color Cast.

Use a channel as a mask

1. Open PS 10-16.psd, then save it as **Masking Hair**.
2. Open the Channels panel.
3. Click through each of the three channels, looking for the one that has the most contrast in the hair.

   The Red channel has the most range of tone in the hair.
4. Duplicate the Red channel, then name it **Mask for Hair**.
5. Target and show the Mask for Hair channel.
6. Enter [command] [I] (Mac) or [Ctrl] [I] (Win) to invert the channel.
7. Click Image on the menu bar, point to Adjustments, then click Levels.
8. Drag the black triangle to the right until the text box reads 69, then click OK.
9. Paint black to cover the white areas of the channel that are not hair.

   Your channel should resemble Figure 32.
10. Select all, copy, then click the RGB channel on the Channels panel.

Figure 32 Blacking out areas not to be affected

11. On the Layers panel, add a new Curves adjustment. Press and hold [option] (Mac) or [Alt] (Win), then click the layer mask on the Curves adjustment layer to see it.

12. Select all.

13. Click Edit on the menu bar, point to Paste Special, then click Paste Into.

    The Masking Hair artwork is pasted into the mask. It was necessary to first select all to get the Paste Into command.

14. Deselect, then click the Curves layer thumbnail to view the image.

15. On the Properties panel, drag the white triangle left until the Input value reads 165, then drag the black triangle right until the Input value reads 11.

16. Add two more points to the curve, then position them so your curve resembles Figure 33.

    The contrast is increased dramatically—but through the mask, so it's a subtle change. The increase in contrast has caused the hair to be more saturated

and it looks red. You can choose to not keep this shift to red.

17. Change the blending mode on the Curves layer to Luminosity.

    With the Luminosity blending mode, the adjustment affects only the Brightness values of the pixels below it; the color and saturation components do not get the same "bump."

18. Compare your result to Figure 34, save your work, then close Masking Hair.

Figure 33 Increasing contrast

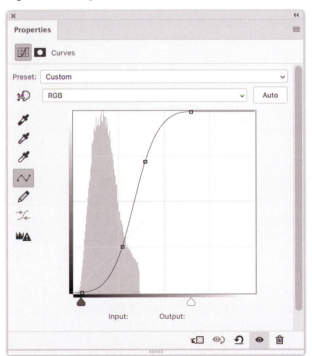

Figure 34 Effective and subtle adjustment to the hair

Jacob Lund/Shutterstock.com

Use the Clone Stamp tool

1. Open PS 10-17.psd, then save it as **Cloning Clouds**. The challenge will be to clone out the four birds using just the Clone Stamp tool and not any of the content-aware utilities. Content-aware utilities are relatively new to Photoshop, and for many years, designers had to tackle tough cloning challenges armed with just the Clone Stamp tool and strategic thinking. Cloning the birds out of this image will teach you the power of using the Clone Stamp tool with different opacity settings.

2. Click the Clone Stamp tool, verify that its Opacity is set to 100% and that the Aligned check box is checked.

3. Making multiple samples and multiple clones, remove each of the four birds from the scene.
Don't try to remove each bird with one move. Instead, create a patchwork of four or five clones to remove each bird. Don't try to make your work "perfect." The goal at this stage is just to remove the birds.

4. Set the Opacity of the Clone Stamp tool to 40%.

5. Sampling carefully, "build up" new clouds with multiple clones to cover the areas where you removed the birds.
Consider what you've learned about shadow-to-highlight tonal range. You can create new clouds that have a range from shadow to bright highlight.

6. Compare your result to Figure 35.
Figure 35 was created with only the Clone Stamp tool. Working with indefinite, nonspecific objects like clouds, smoke, or water gives you freedom to recreate the image using the Clone Stamp tool.

7. Save your work, then close Cloning Clouds.

Figure 35   New clouds created to clone out the birds

Explore content-aware features

1. Open PS 10-18.psd, then save it as **Content-Aware Skills**.
2. Click Image on the menu bar, then click Canvas Size.
3. Change the Width value to 9, then click OK.
4. Target the Desert layer.
5. Click Edit on the menu bar, then click Content-Aware Scale.
6. Press and hold [option] (Mac) or [Alt] (Win), then drag the middle-right handle of the bounding box to the right edge of the canvas.
7. Execute the scale.

   The content-aware scale expanded the scene without stretching the car or the sign. However, the bottom third of the signpost was distorted and needs to be fixed.

8. Click the Rectangular Marquee tool, then drag a box around the problem pixels at the bottom of the signpost. Include approximately ¼" of sand on each side of the post in your selection.
9. Click Edit on the menu bar, then click Fill.
10. Set the Contents to Content-Aware, verify that Color Adaptation is checked, then click OK.

    Because the signpost is so narrow, the content-aware fill might make the signpost disappear and replace it with sand. This may or may not happen in your image, depending on many factors, including how you made your selection. If the signpost is adversely affected by the content-aware fill, proceed to Step 11. If not, skip to Step 12.

11. Create a new layer, then use the Clone Stamp tool very precisely to clone the signpost down to the bottom of the canvas.

    In a real-world exercise, you would more likely just select the post with the Rectangular Marquee tool, then copy and paste what you needed to extend the signpost. For this exercise, however, use this as an opportunity to test your skills for working precisely with the Clone Stamp tool.

    TIP Press [caps lock] on your keypad to change the Clone Stamp tool cursor to a precision cursor in the shape of a plus sign. That allows you to better know exactly where you are sampling and cloning.

12. Compare your results to Figure 36.
13. Save your work, then close Content-Aware Skills.

Figure 36 Image scaled with a content-aware scale

(continued)

Retouch an image with the Healing Brush tools

1. Open PS 10-19.psd, then save it as **Healing Skills**.
2. Duplicate the Background layer, then name it **Spot Healing Brush**.
3. Click the Spot Healing Brush tool, set the Size to 40, then set the Hardness to 60%.
4. On the Properties panel, verify that the Sample All Layers option is checked.
5. Click and drag the Spot Healing Brush tool over all the blemishes one at a time on the forehead, nose, and eyelids.
   The Spot Healing Brush tool will do a good job at making the blemishes disappear, but the overall result will be blotchy and uneven in terms of the skin tone.
6. Create a new layer, then name it **Healing Brush**.
7. Verify that Sample All Layers is activated on the Options panel.
8. Working methodically from one side of the canvas to the other, use the Healing Brush tool to even out the flesh tones so the whole forehead is more consistent in color, as shown in Figure 37.
9. Save your work, then close Healing Skills.

Figure 37 Blemishes removed with the Spot Healing Brush tool; consistent skin tone created with the Healing Brush tool

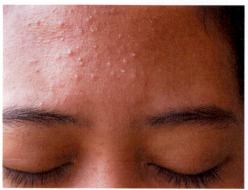

Duanjan J/Shutterstock.com

PROJECT BUILDER 1

1. Open PS 10-20.psd, then save it as **Red Boy**.
2. Assess the image.

   This is an image of a little boy who is blushing, maybe because he's embarrassed. It's cute, but the cheeks and especially the ears are too red.
3. Create a Hue/Saturation adjustment layer.
4. Set the blending mode to Overlay so the red cheeks, ears, and chin get darker and redder.
5. Duplicate the Green channel, then name it **Hot Spots**.
6. Invert the channel.
7. Click Image on the menu bar, point to Adjustments, then click Levels.

8. Drag the black triangle right to 53, then drag the white triangle left to 185.
9. Use the Brush tool to blacken out the areas that you don't want to be affected.

   Use Figure 38 as a guide.
10. Click the RGB layer thumbnail, then delete the Hue/Saturation adjustment layer.
11. Press and hold [command] (Mac) or [Ctrl] (Win), then click the thumbnail on the Hot Spots channel to load it as a selection.
12. Click Select on the menu bar, point to Modify then apply a 4-pixel feather.
13. Hide the selection.
14. Create a new Hue/Saturation adjustment layer.

   Because a selection was active, the selection is not the layer mask on the Hue/Saturation adjustment layer.
15. On the Properties panel, click the Master list arrow, then choose Reds.

   In this step, we are going to target the red hues specifically.
16. Drag the Hue slider to +10.
17. Click the same menu, then choose Master.
18. Drag the Hue slider to +2.
19. Click the Brush tool, set the Opacity to 20%, then paint white in the mask to increase the adjustment in areas you see fit.

   Your results should resemble Figure 39.
20. Save your work, then close Red Boy.

Figure 38 Blacking out areas not to be affected

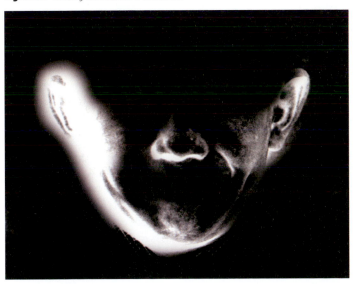

Figure 39 Comparing the reduced red areas

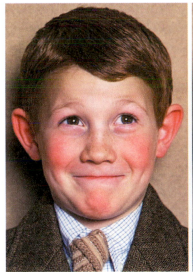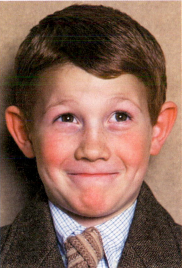

Barbara Maurer/Getty Images

This project is designed to give you more experience adjusting with Curves adjustment layers. Creating the best contrast possible with curves is something you'll need to do often, and the only true way to get good at it is to practice on lots of images and develop an eye for tonal range, both in black and white and in color images.

For this project, you've been given seven images in black and white and the same images in color. These are the same images you worked with in Chapter 5 when you learned levels.

All these images require adjustments for contrast. You may use multiple Curves adjustments when necessary, and definitely feel free to use layer masks to brush in adjustments to specific areas. Don't use any other adjustments, such as Hue/Saturation or Color Balance.

Work on the black and white images first. When you move to the color images, don't go back and check the adjustments you made on the black and white versions. Instead, remember what you learned on the black and white versions to inform you how to approach the color versions.

The goal for both the black and white and color images is to produce the best contrast and tonal range while maintaining reality and leaving no evidence of your involvement in modifying the images.

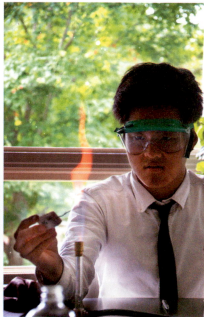

Figure 40 Color adjusted with curves

1. Open the folder named Project Builder Images, then open the folder named Grayscale.
2. Open all seven images.
3. Working methodically, use the skills you learned in Lesson 1 of this chapter to use Curves adjustments to improve the contrast in each image.

TIP You might want to page through Lesson 1 again for a refresher if you have difficulty or if you get stuck.

4. When you are done with each image, save a separate PSD (.psd) file for each.

5. Close each of the black and white images before moving on to the color images.
6. Open the seven color images in the Color Images folder.
7. Using what you learned when improving the black and white versions, adjust the color images for better contrast and, as a result, better color.
8. Save a separate PSD (.psd) file for each. Figure 40 shows one adjusted color image. Refer to the solution files for this project as examples of how these images can be adjusted.

NATIONAL GEOGRAPHIC STORYTELLERS | PRASENJEET YADAV

Prasenjeet Yadav wanted to explain science stories to non-scientists in an engaging and accessible way. At the time, no one was talking about science communication in India. But he was certain he could use photography to summarize scientific research visually.

Prasenjeet's first opportunity came when a friend invited him to create a photo study for a scientific paper. The research focused on the impact of wind farms on the wildlife of the Chalkewadi Plateau, where half of the area has windmills and half does not. Researchers found the density of fan-throated lizards was higher in the areas with windmills because the spinning blades kept away raptors that preyed on the lizards. Higher densities meant the lizards' home ranges were smaller, which resulted in fewer foraging opportunities, increased competition, and more fighting between the lizards. As a result, the lizards had higher cortisol levels due to stress.

To tell this story, Prasenjeet wanted to show a lizard juxtaposed with the windmills. He set up his camera and waited for the right shot. While not part of his original concept, the photo captures the lizard's unique courting behavior, with the male displaying his bright blue throat sack. In addition to being visually striking, the image alludes to one important finding of the study: stress can make a lizard's throat color less brilliant, which in turn affects its reproductive success.

This project proved that Prasenjeet could contribute to the larger academic community, not by engaging in scientific research, but by telling science stories. He learned that with a solid story and confidence in himself and his abilities, he could succeed in bringing these stories to a larger audience.

PROJECT DESCRIPTION

In this project, you will analyze and respond to Prasenjeet's image. You'll have the opportunity to investigate the different elements of the image and interpret the story for yourself. After looking at the photo closely, you will write a brief analysis consisting of your observations, your interpretation of the story, any questions you may have, and the messages you take away.

QUESTIONS TO CONSIDER

What stands out to you?

What is the focus of the image?

How do the foreground and background work together?

What is this image communicating about science?

Prasenjeet Yadav, Fan-throated lizard with windmills in the background, Chalkewadi Plateau, Western Ghats, India

GETTING STARTED

Reread what Prasenjeet learned about fan-throated lizards, their behavior, and the environment in which they live. Also consider the Chalkewadi Plateau and the role windmills play there. Having a better understanding of the subject and elements in the image will help you identify patterns and draw more accurate conclusions.

Think about the idea of cause and effect when analyzing this image. How does that relate to what is happening on the Chalkewadi Plateau? How does Prasenjeet convey these ideas in his photograph?

Mark specific parts of the image you want to focus on. This will help guide your analysis. Choose two to three elements you think play a key role in communicating an important science idea to include in your analysis.

Ps CHAPTER **11**

DESIGN WITH
MULTIPLE IMAGES

1. Create a Concept for a Poster
2. Position Images for a Background Setting
3. Integrate Multiple Images into a Single Background Image
4. Position Foreground Images
5. Integrate Foreground Images
6. Finish Artwork

Adobe Certified Professional in Visual Design Using Photoshop CC Framework

3. Organizing Documents

This objective covers document structure such as layers and managing document structure for efficient workflows.

3.1 Use the Layers panel to manage visual content.

  B Manage and organize layers in a complex project.

  C Recognize the different types of layers in the Layers panel.

CREATE A CONCEPT FOR A POSTER

▶ What You'll Do

In this lesson, you'll explore a scenario and background facts about a movie as part of brainstorming for a movie poster.

Creating a Poster

Fasten your seatbelts; you're in for a great ride. Throughout the six lessons in this chapter, you're going to build a movie poster—step by step, from scratch. This will be a real-world project, even though it's not a real-world movie. The poster size is that of a real mechanical. The images are all high-resolution stock images. The layout, the blending modes, and the methods used to build the artwork are all those you'd see if you were watching a real-world poster designer create this poster. This chapter won't ask you to make any design choices yourself. Instead, you will be instructed how to size images, where to position them, and which blending modes to choose. It's an invitation to you to follow along and get an inside view of the

choices and strategies a designer would rely on to build a complex image with multiple images.

Researching and Sketching a Concept for a Poster

Imagine you are an art director working for an agency that designs and produces first-run movie posters. You've just been brought in on a new project: *The King's Wager*. You will start at the sketch stage and work all the way to the end. This is what the client has told you about the movie:

- It's an American-produced film, but it was shot in England.
- It stars two respected actors playing a queen and a king.

- A popular American actress has the leading role.
- The actor is British, well-respected for both his stage and film work.
- The plot is as follows: The king has been away at battle for months. Believing that her jealous king is far away and may never come back, the queen falls in love with another man—a knight. Unknown to her, the king has actually returned and is masquerading as a servant in the castle.
  The queen's handmaiden alerts the queen to the king's ruse. To hide her admirer, she has him jailed as a thief who has invaded the castle. A battle of wills develops between the royals. Trying to test her, the king sentences the man to death, believing the queen will have no choice but to confess. To his surprise, the defiant queen accepts his gambit. Vowing vengeance, the "thief" is suited in armor and executed. After his death, stories begin circulating that a mysterious knight has been seen in the dark of night. The royals dismiss this as mere hysteria—until the queen's handmaiden is found dead.
- The marketing team has positioned this film in two important ways—first, as a historical thriller, with lots of action, suspense, and realistic sword battles between mounted knights and kings. However, it's also positioned as a costume drama and romance between beautiful people. The client's marketing team wants your agency to design a poster expressing both of these concepts.

After reading this background information, you would be provided with unit photography from the production. **Unit photography** is a collection of images taken on location by a professional photographer hired by the production company. Unit photography almost always includes images of the lead characters, photographed in costume in front of a solid backdrop in a photo studio. In fact, most movie posters you see use photos from these studio photo shoots far more often than they use the photography from the working set. That photography often comprises the background imagery for the posters.

At this point, you would look at as many images of other knight-related posters and campaigns as you could. Yes, professional designers get ideas from other designers' work all the time; it's not cheating.

Sketching ideas with pencil and paper is a key part of coming up with a concept for a poster. In our digital world, many designers want to skip this step and go directly into Photoshop; however, it's not a good idea to skip the sketch stage. With a pencil and paper, you have no limitations. Your mind is free to imagine what the poster could be. Whether or not you can draw doesn't matter; it's your mind that's doing the work—visualizing color, layout, and tone.

Figures 1, 2, 3, and 4 are examples you might draw for the poster. Based on the marketing strategy, you might determine that you want the following six elements in the poster: the queen, the king, the knight, a sword, a castle, and, of course, the title. The king and queen are the "star sell"—the famous actors that everybody likes and wants to pay money to see. The king is the title character, but the queen, as you've been informed, is the lead.

A knight in armor is so visually interesting, it's a good idea to use that image to define the mysterious, menacing quality the synopsis of the movie calls for. Working in concert with the beautiful queen and the rugged king, the three together generate the romantic aspect you've been asked to convey: a dangerous story of forbidden love and revenge.

Figure 1 Sketch for black knight element

Figure 2 Knight and castle sketch

Figure 3 King and queen sketch

Figure 4 Knight with sword sketch

POSITION IMAGES FOR A BACKGROUND SETTING

What You'll Do

In this lesson, you'll copy, paste, and position images for the background setting of the poster.

Loading Selections from Layered Artwork

When working with multiple images, it's most often the case that those images will be masked. Either they will be masked in your working file or they will have been masked in their own original file and brought into your working file as silhouettes without a mask.

When you have either masked or silhouetted artwork without a mask, you can always access a selection for them. To load a mask as a selection, press and hold [command] (Mac) or [Ctrl] (Win), then click the layer mask thumbnail on the Layers panel. A selection marquee will appear representing the entire layer mask as a selection.

To load a selection of silhouetted artwork that doesn't have a layer mask, press and hold [command] (Mac) or [Ctrl] (Win), then click the layer's artwork thumbnail on the Layers panel. The silhouetted artwork will be loaded as a selection.

Understanding X and Y Coordinates

Imagine that you had a 10 × 10 image at 100 pixels per inch. The total number of pixels would be 1 million (1000 × 1000 = 1,000,000). Photoshop has a number for every one of those 1 million pixels.

All pixels in a digital image are in a grid. Photoshop defines the top-left corner of the image as the point of origin for the grid. The location of all pixels is identified by their distance from the point of origin, expressed in terms of an X coordinate and a Y coordinate. The **X coordinate** indicates how far from the left edge the pixel is located. The **Y coordinate** identifies how far down from the top edge it's located. Therefore, a pixel with an X and Y coordinate of 10/10 will be 10 pixels in from the left edge and 10 pixels down from the top edge. The X and Y coordinate of the top-left corner of the image, or the point of origin, is 0/0.

Using X and Y coordinates, Photoshop can identify the location of any image or element on the page. Whenever you enter [command] [T] or [Ctrl] [T], a bounding box appears around the artwork. That bounding box has nine handles: eight around the perimeter and the center point. Those nine locations are represented on the Options panel by the **Reference point location icon** and the individual X and Y coordinates of a selected point.

Figure 5 shows the bounding box surrounding the word PARTY from a poster. Note the eight handles on the perimeter and the center point of the bounding box. The Options panel in the figure shows the X and Y coordinates of the center point of the bounding box. The center point is 864 pixels from the left edge of the image and 1,409 pixels from the top edge. The X and Y coordinates identify the location of the center point because the center point is chosen on the Reference point location icon to the immediate left of the X text box. If you want to know the X and Y coordinates of any of the other locations on the bounding box, simply click the corresponding location on the Reference point location icon.

You might be asking why X and Y coordinates are important or how they are used. One example would be for aligning artwork on the page. If you have three squares, and all

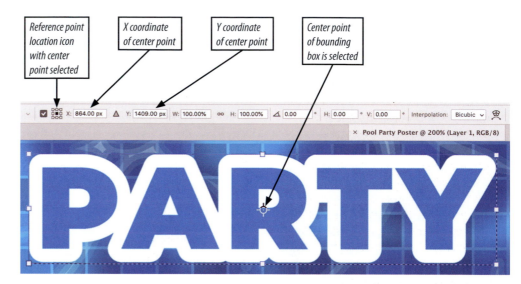

Figure 5 Transform bounding box and corresponding X and Y coordinates on the Options panel

three have the same Y coordinate for their top-left point, you know the top edges of all three are the same distance from the top of the image.

Another time X and Y coordinates come into play is when the need arises to align copies of artwork. In many circumstances, designers create preliminary designs using a half-size document size and low-resolution artwork. If that preliminary design is chosen to "go to finish"—to be produced—the document is resized to the actual size at high resolution,

and all the low-resolution images need to be replaced with high-resolution copies. X and Y coordinates make it easy to replace the low-resolution artwork with high-resolution artwork. Simply note the X and Y coordinates of the low-resolution artwork in position in the document, delete the low-resolution artwork, paste the high-resolution artwork, then enter the same X and Y coordinates (and scale percentage) on the Options panel. The high-resolution artwork will be in the same exact location as the low-resolution artwork once was.

Position images

1. Open PS 11-1.psd, then save it as **The King's Wager**.

   The file is built at 6.75" × 10". That makes it one-quarter the size of a standard movie poster, which is 27" × 40". If you were to build the file at actual size and resolution, the memory required would rapidly become too large to work with. Therefore, during the design process, designers work at one-quarter the size and just 150 ppi for the resolution. If the designer were to "go to finish"—meaning the client wants to produce the image as a poster—the low-resolution file would be rebuilt from scratch to size and at 300 ppi.

2. Invert the **canvas** to start with a black Background layer.

3. Click **View** on the menu bar, then click **Fit on Screen**.

4. Open Stars.psd, select all, copy, then close the file.

5. Paste the selection into The King's Wager file, then name the new layer **Stars**.

6. Open Billing.psd, select all, copy, then close the file.

7. Paste the selection into The King's Wager file, then name the new layer **Billing**.

   In the final version of this poster, you would recreate this layer as an editable live type layer, usually in Adobe Illustrator. This file is one you'll use just for positioning the type.

8. On the Layers panel, change the **blending mode** for the **Billing layer** to **Screen**.

   The Screen blending mode makes black pixels completely transparent.

9. Save your work, then continue to the next set of steps.

You pasted the Stars and Billing artwork into the poster. You set the blending mode on the Billing layer to Screen to make the black background transparent.

Position an image precisely

1. Open Big Knight.psd, show and target only the **Silo layer**, select all, copy, then close the file.

2. In The King's Wager file, target the **Stars layer**, paste the selection, then name the new layer **Big Knight**.

3. Hide the **Billing layer**.

4. Press **[command] [T] (Mac)** or **[Ctrl] [T] (Win)** to scale the image.

   Once you press [command] [T] (Mac) or [Ctrl] [T] (Win), the Options panel displays the physical attributes of the image within the bounding box, including its X and Y locations and its horizontal and vertical scale percentages. The X and Y locations indicate how many pixels a handle on the bounding box is from the left edge (X) and from the top edge (Y).

5. Verify that the **center point** is selected in the Reference point location icon on the Options panel.

   The X and Y coordinates now indicate the location of the center point of the bounding box.

6. Moving left to right, type **556** in the **X text box**, press **[tab]**, type **515** in the Y text box, press **[tab]**, type **80** in the W text box, press **[tab]**, type **80** in the H text box, then press **[tab]**.

   TIP To move through the Options panel in the reverse order, press [shift] [tab].

7. Click the **Move tool** , click **Apply** to execute the transformation, then compare your screen to Figure 6.

   The Big Knight image was scaled 80%; the location of its center point is 556 pixels from the left edge of the canvas and 515 pixels from the top.

8. Add a **Hue/Saturation adjustment layer**, clip it into the **Big Knight layer**, then drag the **Saturation slider** to **–50**.

Continued on next page

Figure 6 Positioning the big knight

9. Target the **Big Knight layer**, then set the **blending mode** to **Hard Light**.

Because the Hard Light blending mode makes the knight artwork transparent, the stars are visible through the knight and must be masked.

10. Add a **layer mask** to the **Stars layer**.

11. Press and hold **[command] (Mac)** or **[Ctrl] (Win)**, then click the **thumbnail** on the **Big Knight layer** to load it as a selection.

12. Click the **Rectangular Marquee tool** ⬚, press and hold **[shift]**, then add the **bottom of the canvas** to the selection.

13. Verify that the **layer mask** on the **Stars layer** is targeted, then fill the selection with **black**.

The stars are masked where they overlap the knight and at the bottom of the canvas.

14. Set the **blending mode** on the **Big Knight layer** to **Normal**, add a **layer mask**, then mask out everything except the head so your artwork resembles Figure 7.

15. Set the **blending mode** on the **Big Knight layer** back to **Hard Light**, then set the **Opacity** to **80%**.

16. Save your work, then continue to the next set of steps.

You used the X and Y text boxes on the Options panel along with the W and H text boxes to position the Big Knight artwork precisely. You used a selection of the Big Knight to mask the stars, then you used a layer mask on the Big Knight layer to mask out all but the Big Knight's head.

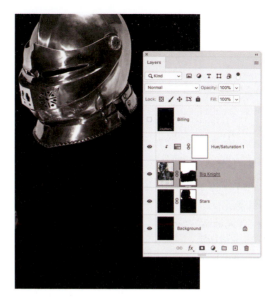

Figure 7 Masking the big knight

Position three background images

1. Open Castle.psd.

This is a stunningly beautiful image. Finding a reason to use an image this magnificent as part of your artwork is always a good idea. The photographer's great work only makes your poster look better.

2. Target the **Silo layer**, select all, copy, then close the file.

3. In The King's Wager file target the **Hue/Saturation adjustment layer** above the **Big Knight layer**, paste the selection, then name the new layer **Castle**.

4. Press **[command] [T] (Mac)** or **[Ctrl] [T] (Win)** to scale the image.

5. Type **692** in the **X text box**, press **[tab]**, type **1283** in the **Y text box**, press **[tab]**, type **63** in the **W text box**, press **[tab]**, type **63** in the **H text box**, then press **[tab]**.

6. Click the **Move tool** ✛ to execute the transformation, then click **Apply**.

Note the depth this image brings to the poster. We are seeing the castle from a distance, looking at it over a body of water. That water becomes the foreground for the poster, and the castle is moved deep *into* the poster.

7. Target the **Hue/Saturation adjustment layer** above the **Big Knight layer**.

8. Open Moon.psd, target the **Silo layer**, select all, copy, then close the file.

9. Paste the selection into The King's Wager file, then name the new layer **Moon**.

10. Press **[command] [T] (Mac)** or **[Ctrl] [T] (Win)** to scale the image.

11. Type **881** in the **X text box**, press **[tab]**, type **843** in the **Y text box**, press **[tab]**, type **52** in the **W text box**, press **[tab]**, type **52** in the **H text box**, press **[tab]**, then execute the transformation.

   Photo choice is so important. This is not a typical image of the moon; in fact, it looks more like some distant, unknown planet. The choice of this image gives the poster an otherworldly feel, adding an unsettling strangeness to the scene and keeping the setting from looking too much like romance novel artwork.

12. Open Small Knight.psd, target the **Silo layer**, select all, then copy.

13. In The King's Wager file, verify that the **Moon layer** is targeted, paste the selection, then name the new layer **Small Knight**.

14. Press **[command] [T] (Mac)** or **[Ctrl] [T] (Win)** to scale the image.

15. Type **946** in the **X text box**, press **[tab]**, type **738** in the **Y text box**, press **[tab]**, type **40** in the **W text box**, press **[tab]**, type **40** in the **H text box**, then press **[tab]**.

16. Execute the transformation.

17. Show the **Billing layer**, then compare your screen to Figure 8.

18. Hide the **Billing layer**.

19. Save your work, then continue to the next set of steps.

You pasted the castle, moon, and small knight artwork, scaled them, and positioned them precisely using X and Y coordinates on the Options panel.

Figure 8 Positioning the castle, moon, and small knight

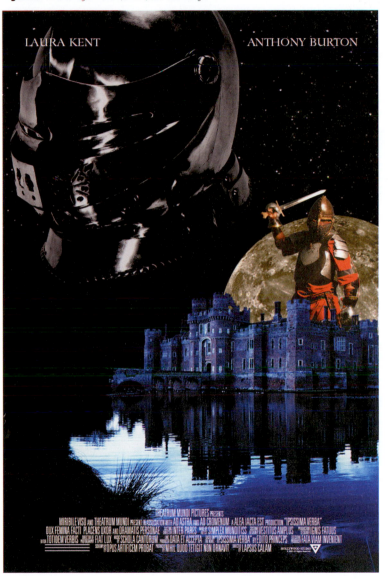

INTEGRATE MULTIPLE IMAGES INTO A SINGLE BACKGROUND IMAGE

▶ *What You'll Do*

In this lesson, you'll learn techniques for integrating multiple images into a background scene for the poster.

Understanding the Difference Between a First-Read and a Second-Read Element

Whenever you're designing with multiple images, it's important to identify which elements are most important. When creating a poster, like you are in this chapter, designers use the terms "first-read" and "second-read" to identify the hierarchy of elements.

First-read elements are those that you want the viewer to note immediately upon looking at the poster. In almost every case, these would include the title, important dates, and the most important images, such as the lead actors.

Second-read elements are, in many ways, more intriguing, because they are designed to hide in plain sight. Figure 9 shows a poster for a pool party. The image is an underwater image. Note the shimmery reflections of the water throughout. In fact, it's not only underwater; it's underwater in a swimming pool. Note the different blue-colored tiles across the entire background. These are all second-read elements. You might or might not note them on your first look at the poster, but your brain will

immediately relegate them as second priority and move instead to the bright white letters of the title treatment.

Figure 9 Identifying second-read elements in a poster

Ask yourself: where are those shimmery water reflections coming from? They're coming from the bright white flare in the top-left corner. Even though it's bright white and the light source for the whole poster, it's a second-read element. You might note it, but you can't help relegate it as less important than the first-read elements of the poster.

Another second-read element, and an interesting one, is the hat hanging on the letter P. It's cute, it's fun, and it's colorful. You see it, but you know immediately that it's not what the poster is about.

In the movie poster you will create in this lesson, the background images will provide atmosphere and tell part of the story of the movie. In this design, though, the background will be second-read much like the swimming pool tiles in the pool party poster. For the movie poster, you will mute the colors of the background elements, force a consistent color upon all of them, and darken everything to create a single background image that will sit quietly behind the first-read elements and not demand immediate attention.

Use adjustment layers to integrate artwork

1. Target the **Castle layer**.

   Note that the highlights on the small knight and the moon are much brighter than they are on the castle. If the viewer is to believe they all exist in the same world, then the light on them must be consistent. A Levels adjustment will help to brighten the highlights on the castle and put the castle into the same world as the small knight and the moon.

2. Add a **Levels adjustment layer**, clip it into the **Castle layer**, drag the **white triangle** left to **239**, then drag the **middle gray triangle** left to **1.24**.

3. Add a **Hue/Saturation adjustment layer** above the Levels adjustment layer, but do not clip it.

4. Drag the **Saturation slider** to **−64**.

This simple move does so much to integrate the artwork. Desaturated, the images all share a common look. Also, the setting is more realistic. With the desaturation, it is reasonable to believe that both the castle and the knight are illuminated by the moon. The next step is to make all the elements share a consistent color.

5. Click the **Create new fill or adjustment layer button** ⬤ on the Layers panel, then click **Solid Color**.

   The Color Picker opens.

6. Type **84/110/179** in the **R**, **G**, and **B text boxes**, respectively, then click **OK**.

7. Set the **blending mode** to **Color**, then set the **Opacity** to **50%**.

   With all elements sharing a consistent color tone, they are even further integrated into one world. The desaturation and the dark blue overall push the imagery back from the viewer, making it more of a background image.

Continued on next page

8. Show the **Billing layer**, then compare your canvas to Figure 10.

   Look at how successfully the disparate images have been integrated into one background using just three adjustments. They all exist in the same world, a blue twilight world lit up by the moon. The whole background is set back. Nothing is too bright, no one element really stands out from the others, and nothing calls attention to itself. Once the bright, colorful, and large foreground objects are placed in front, this background will become a second-read element.

9. Group **all the layers *except* the Billing and Background layers** into a group layer named **Background Setting**.

   TIP Select all the layers, then click the Create a new group button 🗀 on the Layers panel.

10. Hide the **Billing layer**, save your work, then continue to the next set of steps.

You used Levels and Hue/Saturation adjustment layers along with a Solid Color layer to integrate the background in terms of highlights, contrast, saturation, and color.

Figure 10 The integrated background

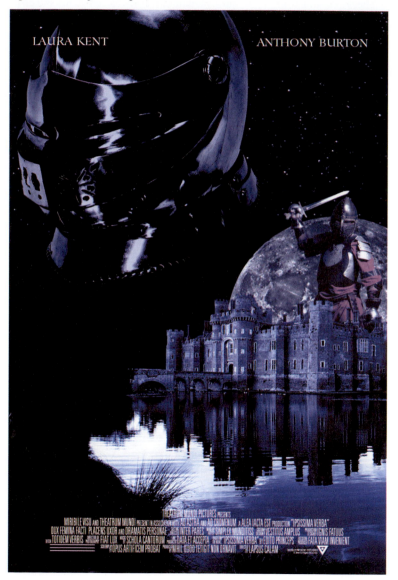

POSITION FOREGROUND IMAGES

Identifying and Creating First-Read Design Elements

Transitioning from background to foreground is always an interesting step when building a composite image. In many ways, it's like shifting gears. When working on the background, the focus of your work often involves pushing things back, making them less distinct, blurring the line between one image and another, muting colors, and so on.

The opposite is usually true when working with the foreground. Foreground elements are first-read elements. They are the first thing you want the viewer to see, even at a glance while just walking past.

Display text is always a first-read element of any design. Display text is qualified as text designed to dominate a layout, like the headline across the top of a newspaper, the masthead of a magazine, or the title treatment of a movie poster. When our brains see large type, we cannot help but read it and interpret the message being sent; it's involuntary.

Along text and size, brightness is a tool to identify a first-read element. Our eye naturally goes to bright elements in a layout; they convey the subconscious signal, "look at me first." Location, too, conveys hierarchy. The Western world reads left to right, so leftmost text in a layout takes on the higher profile, or "top billing." Similarly, we identify what is above

something else as being more important. Central locations in a layout also convey dominance.

Figure 11 shows the same pool party poster you viewed in the previous lesson. The headline POOL PARTY is the most dominant first-read element. It's not only text conveying a message; it is bright white and centered on the poster. Note that the flare is just as white and just as bright, but because it's been relegated to the upper-left corner, it can't compete for attention with the headline.

Figure 11 Identifying first-read elements in a poster

The same thing is happening with the logo at the top. Even though it is white and above the title, its smaller size and, in this case, lack of colors make it far less interesting.

After the headline, the date is likely the second of the first-read elements to catch the eye. The letters are white, and the fact that they are laid out as a wave immediately draws attention. Note too that the designer placed a darker blue field behind the date. This increased contrast draws the viewer's attention. Notice that the headline has a similar darker blue field behind it, in the form of a drop shadow, adding to the pull of the headline.

Compare the date to the logo at the top, which has no darker blue area behind it, and you can see that the date visually draws in the viewer so much more. Note too that the bright white letters of the date make it more dominant than the lime green letters below it, even though those lime green letters are also prominent and important.

All these subtle, not so subtle, conscious, and subconscious considerations go into the positioning, coloring, sizing, and lighting of elements in a layout. Speaking of subconscious, during this whole discussion, did you even once make a conscious note of those multicolored tiles scattered across the background?

Position the sword

1. Open Sword.psd., target the **Silo layer**, select all, copy, then close the file.

2. In The King's Wager file target the **Background Setting group layer**, paste, then name the new layer **Sword**.

3. Click **Edit** on the menu bar, point to **Transform**, then click **Rotate 180°**.

4. Press **[command] [T] (Mac)** or **[Ctrl] [T] (Win)** to scale the image.

5. Type **506** in the **X text box**, press **[tab]**, type **833** in the **Y text box**, press **[tab]**, type **69** in the **W text box**, press **[tab]**, type **69** in the **H text box**, press **[tab]**, then execute the transformation.

   Your canvas should resemble Figure 12.

6. Click **Layer** on the menu bar, point to **Layer Style**, click **Bevel & Emboss**.

7. Set the **Style** to **Inner Bevel**, then set the **Technique** to **Smooth**.

8. Set the **Depth** to **750%**, set the **Size** to **8 px**.

9. Set the **Opacity** of the **Highlight Mode** and **Shadow Mode** to **90%**.

10. Click the **Gloss Contour list arrow**, click the eighth contour named **Ring**, click the **Anti-aliased check box**, then click **OK**.

11. Add a **Levels adjustment layer**, clip it into the **Sword layer**, drag the **upper-white triangle** left to **235**, then drag the **upper-black triangle** right to **18**.

12. Create a **new group layer** for the **Sword** and its **adjustment layer**, then name the new group **Sword Group**.

Figure 12 Positioning the sword

Note that with the addition of the sword, the background has become the background, and the sword is instantly the "first-read" element of the poster because it's centrally located and it's the brightest object.

13. Save your work, then continue to the next set of steps.

You pasted, scaled, and positioned the sword artwork. You applied a Bevel & Emboss layer style with a Gloss Contour to add dimension and shine to the sword, then you used a Levels adjustment to brighten and add contrast.

Position the king

1. Open King.psd, target the **Silo layer**, select all, copy, then close the file.

2. In The King's Wager file target the **Background Setting group layer**, paste, then name the new layer **King**.

3. Click **Edit** on the menu bar, point to **Transform**, then click **Flip Horizontal**.

4. Press **[command] [T] (Mac)** or **[Ctrl] [T] (Win)** to scale the image.

5. Type **426** in the **X text box**, press **[tab]**, type **977** in the **Y text box**, press **[tab]**, then execute the transformation.

6. Add a **layer mask**, click the **Rectangular Marquee tool**, select the **entire right half of the canvas**, including the right half of the sword.

7. Fill the mask with **black** so that no part of the king image appears to the right of the sword, then deselect.

   Your canvas should resemble Figure 13.

8. Click the **Brush tool**, set the **Size** to **200 px** with **0% Hardness**.

9. On the left side of the sword, mask out the **king's hand**, the **gold handle**, and the **white cloth areas** of the king's costume.

10. Moving upward slowly and making small moves, mask the **king's black costume** so it merges with the shadows that surround the blue water, as shown in Figure 14.

    This is a great example of something called good luck. The king's black costume merges perfectly with the shadow that the castle casts on the water. It's as though the king and the water are one, like the king is emerging from the water. You really can't tell where the king ends and the shadows on the water begin. It's just good luck; you can't plan for these situations, but keep your eye out for them when they present themselves.

11. Save your work, then continue to the next set of steps.

You pasted, scaled, and positioned the king artwork and then masked it to integrate with the foreground scene of the castle artwork.

Figure 13 Masking the king on the right side of the sword

Figure 14 Masking the king to merge with the shadows

Position the queen

1. Open Queen.psd.

   The image of the queen will be a merge of two different images. In this case, you can imagine that the lead actress for the film was never photographed in a studio, so you are left with no choice but to merge an image of the actress's face with that of a stand-in posed in the queen's costume.

2. Starting with the Background layer, turn on each layer one by one to see how the merge was accomplished. You may hide and show the mask on the Damsel Copy layer to see the role it plays.

3. Show and target the **Silo layer**, select all, copy, then close the file without saving changes.

4. In The King's Wager file target the **King layer**, paste, then name the new layer **Queen**.

5. Press **[command] [T] (Mac)** or **[Ctrl] [T] (Win)** to transform the artwork.

6. Type **634** in the **X text box**, press **[tab]**, type **815** in the **Y text box**, press **[tab]**, type **93** in the **W text box**, type **93** in the **H text box**, then execute the transformation.

7. Add a layer mask, click the **Rectangular Marquee tool** [icon], select the **entire left half of the canvas**, including the left half of the sword.

8. Fill the **mask** with **black** so no part of the queen image appears to the left of the sword, then deselect.

9. Click the **Brush tool** [icon], set the **Size** to **25 px** and the **Hardness** to **0%**, then mask the **queen's dress** so your artwork resembles Figure 15.

You must work with what you've got, so the best move with the queen is to use the blue scarf for the edge of the mask. Perhaps it will be a good idea to fade it, but that's not a decision for now.

10. Save your work, then continue to the next set of steps.

You pasted, scaled, positioned, and masked the queen artwork.

Figure 15 Masking the queen

Figure 16 Positioning the title treatment

Position the title treatment

1. In The King's Wager document, verify that the **Queen layer** is targeted.

2. Open Title Treatment.psd. in a floating window beside or above The King's Wager document.

3. Drag the **Title group layer** into The King's Wager document.

   The Title group layer will be positioned in the Layers panel above the Queen layer.

4. Close Title Treatment.psd without saving changes.

5. In The King's Wager file, show the **Billing layer**.

6. Expand the **Title group layer** so you can see the three text layers (The, King's, and Wager).

7. Using Figure 16 as a guide, add **The King's Wager title** to the poster.

   You will need to move the Wager text to the right of the sword.

8. Save your work, then continue to the next set of steps.

You dragged the title artwork into the poster file and positioned it.

INTEGRATE FOREGROUND IMAGES

Investigating the Overlay/Desaturate Effect

Think of the thousands upon thousands of designers using Photoshop to make commercial art that is viewed by mass audiences. It only makes sense that designers will use Photoshop in similar ways to achieve specific looks, feels, or tones. One technique that has emerged and lasted for a long time is the Overlay/Desaturate effect.

The Overlay/Desaturate effect is achieved by applying a Hue/Saturation adjustment layer to artwork. The Hue/Saturation adjustment layer is used with the Overlay blending mode to create a substantial increase of contrast and vividness of color, then the Saturation slider is set to zero. The result is not a black and white image. Instead, it's a high-contrast image with darker, more muted colors. It's a gritty, "blown out" look that works really well for darker themes, such as crime, science fiction, horror, and war. In fact, entire films have been produced with this technique. Figure 17 shows the technique applied to an image.

In the movie poster you're working on, the background has been desaturated. The foreground elements of the king and queen are currently in full color, which puts them in an entirely different world from the background. They need to be desaturated, but you don't want a black and white king and queen as the first-read elements for your poster. Instead, you will use the Overlay/Desaturate technique.

Figure 17 The Overlay/Desaturate technique applied to a stock image

Yuri2010/Shutterstock.com

Use layer styles to integrate foreground artwork

1. Assess the image at this stage of design.

   It's an interesting poster with a "cool" factor. One success is the big knight in the background. Even though it's the largest element of the poster, it's very much a second-read element. It hides in plain sight. But once you notice it, it's a looming presence that menaces the scene. The small knight coming out of the shadows with his sword flashing in the moonlight contributes to that eerie feeling. And the castle image with its water foreground communicates the location perfectly.

   The next steps are to identify things to be fixed and improved:

   - The queen is crowding the small knight, so the small knight needs to move.
   - The sword and the title treatment can and must be integrated.
   - The sword is too flat against the king and the queen; there needs to be more dimension and depth.

2. Expand the **Background Setting group layer**, target the **Small Knight layer** and the **Castle layer**, click the **Move tool** 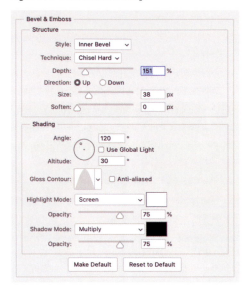, press and hold **[shift]**, then press the **right arrow key** on your keypad **four times**.

   The artwork is moved 40 pixels to the right, creating a comfortable space between the queen and the small knight.

3. Expand the **Title group layer**, target the **Wager layer**, then add a **Bevel & Emboss layer style**.

4. Enter the settings shown in Figure 18, then click **OK**.

5. Press and hold **[option] (Mac)** or **[Alt] (Win)**, then drag the 𝑓𝑥 **icon** from the **Wager layer** to the other two text layers.

   The Bevel & Emboss layer style is copied to the other text layers. The title treatment and the sword are now united; they are parts of a whole, even though they are technically two different elements. This move was a big step toward the goal of foreground consistency. Another big plus is that the shine on the metal of the small knight and the big knight in the background is the same shine that's on the sword and the type in the foreground.

Figure 18 Bevel & Emboss settings

6. Expand the **Sword Group layer**, then double-click the **Bevel & Emboss effect** to open the Layer Style dialog box.

7. In the **Styles list** on the left, click **Outer Glow**.

8. Click the **Set color of glow button** to open the Color Picker, then type **28/32/83** in the **R**, **G**, and **B text boxes**, then close the Color Picker dialog box.

   This is a subtle move. Since the background shadows are dark blue, it's a good idea to set the glow on the sword to a dark blue as well, rather than black.

9. Change the **blending mode** to **Multiply**.

10. Change the **Spread value** to **8**, change the **Size value** to **24**, then click **OK**.

    The glow creates the effect that the sword is casting a shadow on the king and queen, thereby creating the effect that the sword is in front of them by some distance, not on the same plane as they are.

11. Press and hold **[option] (Mac)** or **[Alt] (Win)**, then drag the **Outer Glow layer style** from the **Sword layer** to all **three type layers**.

    You cannot drag the *fx.* icon, because that would copy *both* the Bevel & Emboss layer style and the Outer Glow layer style to the type layers.

You didn't want to replace the Bevel & Emboss layer on the type layers, so you dragged only the Outer Glow style. Note how much the glow improves the relationship between the word Wager and the castle behind it. The dark glow behind Wager makes it much more distinct from the castle.

12. Compare your results to Figure 19, then save your work.

You added a Bevel & Emboss layer style to one part of the title then copied it to the other. You then added a dark blue outer glow to the sword to add a sense of distance between it and the king and queen behind it.

Figure 19   The sword and the type beveled and embossed and with an outer glow

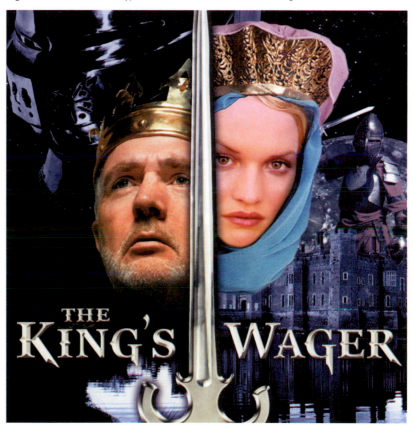

Use adjustment layers and blending modes to integrate foreground artwork

1. Assess the king and the queen as foreground elements.

   It works well that the king is looking up and only the queen is making direct eye contact with the viewer because she's the star of the poster. However, the king and queen photos are very different from each other. Even though he is a great character for the poster, and she looks terrific, his face is shadowy with lots of contrast, but her face has no shadows and is a little too red overall. Had they been photographed with the same lighting conditions in the same studio, they would be much more consistent. In addition to removing red from her, the two of them need to be desaturated to be more consistent with each other and with the background artwork.

2. Target the **Queen layer**, add a **Color Balance adjustment layer**, then clip it.

3. Click the **Tone list arrow**, click **Highlights**, then drag the **top slider** to **−10**.

4. Click the **Tone list arrow**, click **Midtones**, then drag the **top slider** to **−10**.

5. Click the **Tone list arrow**, click **Shadow**, then drag the **top slider** to **−10**.

6. Select the **King** and the **Queen** and the **Color Balance layers,** then create a **new group layer** named **Royals**.

7. Expand **Royals group layer**, target the **Color Balance adjustment layer**, then add a new **Hue/Saturation adjustment layer**.

8. Change the **blending mode** to **Overlay**.

9. Drag the **Saturation slider** to **−90**, then drag the **Lightness slider** to **8**.

10. Clip the **Hue/Saturation adjustment** into the **Color Balance adjustment layer**.

    The Hue Saturation adjustment affects only the queen.

11. Duplicate the **Hue/Saturation adjustment layer**, drag the **duplicate layer** down so that it's directly above the **King layer**, then clip it into the **King layer**.

12. Compare your artwork to Figure 20.

    The king and queen are desaturated, but not without color. Now that they share the same effect, they more believably inhabit the same space, even though his image has so much more contrast than hers. The desaturated effect is a giant step toward making them visually part of the same world as the background.

13. Save your work, then continue to the next set of steps.

You used a Color Balance adjustment layer to remove red from the queen's face. You then added a Hue/Saturation adjustment layer with an Overlay blending mode and desaturated the artwork to add a high-contrast, gritty look and better integrate the king and queen visually.

Figure 20  The king and queen overlayed and desaturated

FINISH ARTWORK

"Finishing" Artwork

If you're told to "finish artwork," it may sound like you're being told, "Get it done." In the design world, the word "finish" is used the way a carpenter would "finish" a table: he would apply "finish" as the last stage of his work to give the table a glossy sheen. Similarly, finishing artwork is the final design stage of a project.

The finish stage begins when all the elements are in place. Everything is sized in a way that works. Color correction has been done so that every element has good contrast and consistent contrast and color with all the other elements. Type components are also in place. You can think of the start of the finish stage as the poster being 85% or 90% done. All that's missing is the magic.

At the finish stage, the artwork starts talking to you. When you look at all the elements together, they begin telling the story of the poster, and included in that story is what's working and what needs a tweak. One element might convey that it's being squeezed in its space and needs to be scaled down slightly. Another might communicate that it's too bright and calling too much attention to itself. It's a fascinating, magical feeling when this relationship with your own artwork comes to life in this manner, and as a designer, you should consciously stop and tell yourself to let the artwork tell you which steps are next.

The finish stage has some ever-present components to it, like adding noise, which is the last step in almost every project that calls for some amount of a grainy texture. The following are some other common elements that show up at the finishing stage:

- **Flares**—If a project calls for a flare or similar dramatic lighting, a flare goes far in integrating the concept into one image. The flare becomes the light source for the entire canvas. Since all elements are affected by that light source, that conveys the sense that they're all in the same universe.
- **Shadows**—Shadows bring reality to layered artwork. If something is supposed to be in front of something else, then that something must cast a shadow onto that something else. Shadows create depth and prevent layered artwork from all appearing flat and on one plane. Also, when strategically used, shadows create bridges between elements, especially the foreground and background elements. In Chapter 8, you created a cast shadow between a waitress in the foreground and a wall of type behind her. The shadow brought the reality to the concept by building a bridge between the waitress in the foreground and the type on the wall in the background. Your brain was forced to accept as real the idea that if she was casting a shadow on the wall, she and the wall must inhabit the same space.

- **Smoke**—As long as there's been photography and moving images, smoke has been used to add atmosphere and mystery. In a multiple-image layout, smoke can be used to integrate all the images: as with shadows, if they all are in the same smoke, they must exist in the same world. Smoke is also useful for filling in empty areas or "holes" that might occur when you don't want to cram the layout with all kinds of different objects. Not every project calls for smoke, to be sure, but when it's possible, use smoke to create atmosphere.
- **Reflections**—You explored the power of using reflections in Chapter 6 when you reflected the zombie in the Hancock Tower. If one thing is reflecting something else, then those two things must exist in the same world.
- **Physical interactions**—If one element physically interacts with the position of another, logic tells the viewer that those two things exist together. You saw this with the Komodo attack artwork, also in Chapter 6. Paste the Komodo dragon behind the house, and it's just a Komodo dragon pasted behind a house in Photoshop. Curl the tail around and smash it through two windows, and suddenly you've got a story being told.

These are all ideas that might be inserted into the finishing process or enhanced at that stage. Other, perhaps less dramatic, techniques are also employed. The finishing stage is when all color and contrast considerations—and color effects, like hue/saturation adjustments—are finalized.

In many ways, finishing is everything, and everything leads up to finishing. It is the point at which you must distill your work into one cohesive piece of art in which all components are fully integrated and working together. Finishing is when the end product comes together as one piece of artwork. You might be surprised to learn that all high-end advertising agencies and art houses employ people whose job title is "finisher." These are highly skilled and highly paid artists and illustrators. Their job is to take a designer's low-resolution concept and finish every detail to perfection.

Use transparency to integrate foreground and background elements

1. Assess the foreground elements and their relationship with the background of the poster.

   Essentially, there is no relationship. The king and queen are simply in front of the background. The king is integrated with the background, but the queen is a floating head. One way to solve this is to fade her scarf into the background.

2. Add a **layer mask** to the **Royals group layer**.

3. Click the **Brush tool** , set its **Size** to **150 px** and its **Hardness** to **0%**.

4. Set the **Opacity** of the brush to **40%**; then, working from the outside, mask the **lower-right** and **bottom** of the **scarf** to resemble Figure 21.

   Along with addressing the problem that the queen was a floating head, fading her scarf creates a subtle transition between the queen and the background. It's a small first step.

Figure 21 Fading the queen's scarf

TIP Note that the Queen layer already has a complex layer mask. Masking the scarf on the group layer is a strategic move: with this method, the mask of the scarf is separate from the other masking done to the queen. Should we later want to edit it, having a separate mask for it would make that possible.

5. Save your work, then continue to the next set of steps.

You used a layer mask to fade the queen's scarf into the background scene.

Use a Lens Flare to integrate background and foreground elements

1. Hide the **Billing** and **Title layers**.

2. Collapse the **Sword Group layer**, target the **Sword Group layer**, then create a **new layer**.

   TIP Group layers must be collapsed so new layers can be made above them. Otherwise, the new layer will appear inside the group.

3. Name the new layer **Lens Flare**, then fill it with **black**.

4. Click **Filter** on the menu bar, point to **Render**, then click **Lens Flare**.

5. Click **105mm Prime** for the **Lens type**, set the **Brightness** to **105%**, then click **OK**.

   Note that the filter creates more than the single bright flare. There are other, smaller flares on the diagonal. These will need to be masked after the layer is screened.

6. Add a **Hue/Saturation adjustment layer**, then clip it into the **Lens Flare layer**.

7. Click the **Colorize check box**, drag the **Hue slider** to **219**, then drag the **Saturation slider** to **30**.

8. Change the **blending mode** on the **Lens Flare layer** to **Screen**.

9. Click the **Move tool**, then position the **flare** to the spot where the **highlight** on the **queen's crown** meets the **sword**, as shown in Figure 22.

   This is a case of the artwork telling the designer what to do. By sheer luck, the highlight on the queen's crown intersects with the sword,

making a perfect spot for *both* to reflect a hot white light. The flare unifies the sword with the queen's crown.

The flare plays a major role in integrating the poster. The flare creates a new light source. That light source is blue, just like the world of the background exists in a blue light. Psychologically, the viewer can't help but perceive that this light is shining on everything in the poster and casting a blue light; thus, all the elements are affected by the same light source.

10. Note the small flare to the lower right of the queen's eye, circled in the figure.

11. Add a **layer mask** to the **Lens Flare layer**, then use a soft brush to mask out the small flare.

12. Show the **Title** and the **Billing layers**, save your work, then continue to the next set of steps.

You added a lens flare, positioned it over the sword, then colorized it with a Hue/Saturation adjustment layer. You then masked out a secondary flare over the queen.

Figure 22 Positioning the flare

Use smoke to integrate background and foreground elements

1. Open Smoke.psd.

   Smoke.psd is a photograph taken of smoke against a black background. The smoke was illuminated by a strobe light to be captured in the camera.

2. Select all, copy, then close Smoke.psd.

3. Collapse and target the **Title group layer**, paste, then name the new layer **Smoke**.

4. Press **[command] [T] (Mac)** or **[Ctrl] [T] (Win)**.

5. Type **600** in the **X text box**, press **[tab]**, type **752** in the **Y text box**, press **[tab]**, type **53** in the **W text box**, press **[tab]**, type **53** in the **H text box**, then press **[tab]**.

6. Click the **Move tool** ✛ , then click **Apply**.

7. On the Layers panel, drag the **Smoke layer** below the **blue Color Fill layer** in the **Background Setting group**.

8. Change the **blending mode** to **Screen**, then set the **Opacity** to **60%**.

   The smoke fills many of the empty areas of the background. With the addition of the smoke, it has become more difficult to identify the moon artwork for what it is. It looks more like a random pattern than a moon, and it's also creating two distracting diagonal highlights in the queen's scarf where it fades.

9. Hide the **Moon layer**.

   This is another moment of the artwork speaking and an example of how the designer must remain open to change and not become "married" to any one component of the work. The moon had become visual clutter. It wasn't recognizable as a moon and appeared instead as some indistinguishable pattern behind the small knight. Without the moon, the small knight now emerges from smoke and darkness and is much more effective—and creepy. Even though it's a loss of a background element that has been part of the concept from the very beginning, removing the moon improves the poster as a whole.

10. Duplicate the **blue Color Fill layer** in the **Background Settings group**, drag it above the **Hue/Saturation adjustment** that is clipped into the **King layer**, clip it, then set its **Opacity** to **20%**.

11. Duplicate the **blue Color Fill layer** again, drag it above the **Hue/Saturation adjustment** that is clipped into the **Queen layer**, clip it, then set its **Opacity** to **15%**.

12. Expand the **Sword group**, duplicate the **blue Color Fill layer** again, drag it above the **Levels adjustment layer** above the **Sword layer**, then clip it into the Levels adjustment layer.

13. Set the **Opacity** on the **Color Fill layer** to **30%**.

14. Duplicate the **blue Color Fill layer** three more times, clip one into each of the title words (The, King's, and Wager), then set the **Opacity** on each to **50%**.

    Duplicating and clipping the blue Color Fill are the kind of last-minute moves that happen at the end of a project. It feels like it has been obvious the whole time, but it didn't become apparent until the end, when the whole poster was put together. Adding a slight blue tint to the king, the queen, the sword, and the type fully integrates all foreground elements into the overall blue color theme of the poster. This turns out to be perhaps the most crucial move in terms of integrating the poster, especially the king and queen. It would be unthinkable to undo it.

15. Create a **new layer** at the top of the Layers panel, then name it **Noise 16**.

16. Fill the layer with **50% Gray**, click **Filter** on the menu bar, click **Add Noise**.

17. Drag the **Amount** to 16, then set the layer's **blending mode** to **Overlay**.

18. Zoom in on the image and note how the consistent noise pattern across the whole of the poster does so much to integrate all the elements. A noise value of 16 is relatively high, but this artwork and the theme of the movie itself work well with this gritty noise effect.

19. Drag the **Noise 16 layer** below the **Billing layer**, then compare your result to Figure 23.

20. Save your work, then close The King's Wager.

You added an image of smoke to integrate the artwork, which resulted in the decision to remove the moon from the poster. You duplicated the blue color fill several times to colorize individual components with a customized blue hue. As a final move, you added noise to create a consistent texture across the whole of the artwork.

Getty images: Queen: Willie Maldonado; King & Big Knight: Erik Von Weber; Small Knight: Chip Simons; Castle: Pete Turner. Jupiter images: Moon: StockTrek; Stars: Paul Beard. Sword & smoke: Chris Botello

Figure 23 The finished poster

PROJECT BUILDER 1

This project builder is a background exercise that was used to create the image of the queen for The King's Wager poster. The project imagined a situation in which the actress playing the queen was not photographed in costume. As a work-around, a photo of the actress's face was "swapped" with the face of a different woman photographed in costume. This actually happens all the time with campaigns involving celebrities. Situations arise in which the famous person's face—or their entire head—must be merged with some other person's body.

This project offers the opportunity to do a complex head swap that demands subtle masking around the actress's hair and a careful paint job to produce a shadow that camouflages problems with the merge.

1. Open PS 11-2.psd, then save it as **Damsel Actress Merge**.
2. Add a layer mask to the Damsel layer.
3. Select the Brush tool, set the Size to 10 px, set the Hardness to 50%, set the Mode to Normal, and set the Opacity to 100%.
4. Mask the damsel's face as shown in Figure 24. Mask all the way up to the blue head scarf. Don't leave any shadow.

Figure 24 Masking out the damsel's face

5. Show the Actress layer, then drag it below the Damsel layer.
6. Scale the actress artwork 78%, rotate it −2°, then position it as shown in Figure 25.
7. Target the layer mask on the Damsel layer, then set the Brush tool Hardness to 0%.
8. Mask the Damsel to show the actress's blond hair, as shown in Figure 26.

9. Target the Actress layer, add a new layer above it, then name the new layer **Shadow Paint**.
The actress's face is inside the blue kerchief. The kerchief would cast a shadow on her face, so we need to add a shadow to reflect that. A shadow will also help to camouflage the compositing we have done so far. The Brush tool will be used to paint the shadow.

10. Paint a soft-edged black shadow on the right side of her face, like the one shown in Figure 27.
11. Fill the Background layer with white.
12. Mask the Actress layer so only the face shows.
13. Save your work, then close Damsel Actress Merge.

Figure 25 Positioning the scaled and rotated actress artwork

Figure 26 Masking in the actress's hair

Figure 27 Painting the shadow

If you were a designer at an agency and you were brought in to design ideas for *The King's Wager* poster, you would be expected to produce more than just one design, or one "look." You'd be working with a team, probably four or five other designers. All of you would be given the same unit photography and title treatment. From there, the team would be expected to produce 20 to 25 looks. That means you'd be expected to produce four or five.

This project asks you to imagine a different "color story" as an alternative look for the original *The King's Wager* poster design.

1. Open PS 11-3.psd, then save it as **The King's Wager alternate.**
2. In the Background Settings group layer, double-click the blue layer thumbnail on the Color Fill 1 layer to open the Color Picker dialog box.
3. Set the RGB values to 102/14/29, click OK, then increase the Opacity to 100%.
4. Drag the Color Fill 1 layer below the Hue/Saturation adjustment layer.
5. Change the blue Color Fill layers on the King layer and the Queen layer to the same red color.
6. Delete the blue Color Fill layers on the Sword and the three Title layers.
7. Target the Queen layer, then add a Hue/Saturation adjustment layer.

8. Drag the Hue slider to −165, then drag the Saturation slider to −43.
9. Add a layer mask, then paint in the adjustment so it affects only the queen's blue scarf and changes it to gold.
10. Scroll to the Lens Flare layer, double-click the Hue/Saturation adjustment layer, then drag the Hue slider to 51.
11. Duplicate the Hue/Saturation adjustment layer, drag it down so it's above the Smoke layer, then clip it into the Smoke layer.
12. Target the red Color Fill layer that's below the Smoke layer, then drag it down so it's immediately above the Castle layer.
    The red Color Fill layer will clip into the Castle layer.
13. Target the Small Knight layer, add a Hue/Saturation adjustment layer, then drag the Saturation slider to −46.
14. Compare your results to Figure 28.
    This alternate design works quite well. The red background signals danger, and the red water in the foreground is ominous. The bright gold color is effective for the smoke and even more so for the flare, and the gold and blood red complement each other. Comparing the two looks, the original is more sophisticated and finished, largely because the blue hue integrates everything so well. The red and gold alternate does not achieve the same degree of completeness, but it's a legitimate alternative to the original design.
15. Save your work, then close The King's Wager alternate.

Figure 28   An alternate "second look" for the poster

DESIGN PROJECT

This design project is your chance to design your own poster from scratch. Using the same supplied images—the king, the queen, the big knight, the small knight, the sword, the castle, the moon, and the stars—you will build your own version of the poster using your imagination. Feel free to use, or not use, any images you like. For example, you might want to remove the king entirely and make the poster feature only the queen. You may also add new photos to the mix, perhaps a knight on horseback or a fortune teller or a leviathan. You may also change the title and design your own title treatment.

1. Open 11-4.psd, then save it as **King's Wager Original Design.**
2. Access any of the images that were provided in this chapter.
3. Sketch ideas for a new, original poster.
4. Access any other images from other sources you might want to use.
5. Consider whether you want to stay with the same title or craft a new one.
   Build your own poster with the techniques and considerations you learned in this chapter.

WORK WITH
SHAPES, PATHS, AND VECTOR MASKS

1. Work with Shapes
2. Import Shapes from Adobe Illustrator
3. Work with Paths
4. Draw a Path Around an Image
5. Create Vector Masks

Adobe Certified Professional in Visual Design Using Photoshop CC Framework

1. Working in the Design Industry

This objective covers critical concepts related to working with colleagues and clients as well as crucial legal, technical, and design-related knowledge.

1.4 Demonstrate knowledge of key terminology related to digital images.

  A Demonstrate knowledge of digital image terminology.

2. Project Setup and Interface

This objective covers the interface setup and program settings that assist in an efficient and effective workflow, as well as knowledge about ingesting digital assets for a project.

2.4 Import assets into a project.

  B Place assets in a Photoshop document.

4. Creating and Modifying Visual Elements

This objective covers core tools and functionality of the application, as well as tools that affect the visual appearance of document elements.

4.1 Use core tools and features to create visual elements.

  B Create and edit vector images.

WORK WITH SHAPES

What You'll Do

In this lesson, you'll create and format a basic vector shape.

Understanding Bitmap vs. Vector Graphics

Images you work with in Photoshop are all bitmap graphics. **Bitmap graphics** are digital images made from different colored tiny pixels to reproduce a photographic image with the illusion of continuous tone from shadows to highlights.

Vector graphics are shapes created by your computer using straight and curved lines. The interiors of those shapes can be filled with color; their perimeters can take on a stroke of color. Vector graphics are often used in publishing and graphic design as simple geometric shapes—such as circles, ovals, and rectangles—but vector graphics can also be highly complex and accomplished artistic illustrations.

Figure 1 shows an illustration containing a variety of vector graphics. The bottom image shows the lines and curves that were drawn to create the illustration. The background is a simple rectangle with a red fill color. The bull, on the other hand, is a more complex shape filled with black. Curved lines create the type and the white object in the lower-left corner.

Figure 1 Illustration composed entirely of vector graphics

Zolotinka/Shutterstock.com

The entire illustration is created with shapes and fills. There are no pixels in the artwork; therefore, the artwork is resolution independent. **Resolution independent** is a term given to graphics that are not made up of pixels. All vector graphics are resolution independent. This means that a vector graphic can be reproduced at high quality at any size. For example, the file for this illustration could be printed at the same high quality on a postcard or on a 48-foot billboard.

Creating Vector Graphics in Photoshop

Although the bulk of the work people do in Photoshop is image editing and, therefore, pixel-based, when you're creating a layout in Photoshop, it often calls for vector graphics. For example, you might design a poster and want to have a star shape for a headline, a row of circles that contain photos, or a rectangle of color at the bottom as a background for text information.

When your work calls for a shape, Photoshop offers six vector-based tools: the Rectangle, Ellipse, Triangle, Polygon, Line, and Custom Shape tools. The Polygon tool is a many-shapes-in-one tool; you can use it to make pentagons, hexagons, octagons, and so on.

When you choose one of these tools, click the Tool mode menu on the Options panel, then choose Shape. You can apply a fill or a stroke color on the Options panel, where you can also set the stroke weight and stroke type, such as a dotted line. Shapes can be

reshaped by dragging the handles on the shape's default bounding box. Shapes can also be transformed like any other Photoshop graphic using the Transform commands on the Edit menu.

Shapes in Photoshop are created on their own layer on the Layers panel. The shape's layer functions like other layers in Photoshop: you can change the opacity, add a layer style, and use the shape as a clipping mask.

Editing and Combining Shapes

When you create a shape, Photoshop regards it as a "live" shape, meaning that you can edit the shape and perform other operations on it. The Properties panel, shown in Figure 2, displays all the information about the shape. Because the shape is "live," you can edit the shape on the Properties panel by inputting specific properties such as height, width, fill color, and stroke color. All your changes update immediately to the targeted shape.

Figure 2 The Properties panel showing information for a shape

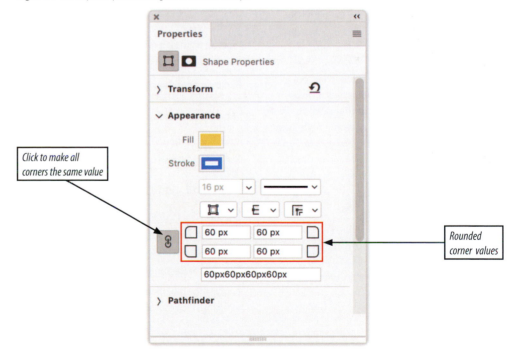

Another "live" feature of shapes is the ability to change angled corners to rounded corners. When you create a shape with angled corners, a small button called a **corner widget** appears at the angle. You can click and drag the corner widget to convert the angled corner to a rounded corner. The Properties panel also allows you to format angled corners as rounded corners.

All shapes are created with anchor points and lines that connect those points. The **Direct Selection tool** allows you to click and drag any anchor point on a shape, thus creating a new shape. For example, you could drag one anchor point on a square and reshape it into a kite shape. This is a great method for creating unique shapes. However, in Photoshop, when you alter a shape by moving one of its anchor points with the Direct Selection tool, Photoshop no longer recognizes it as a "live" shape. You'll no longer be able to modify it using the Properties panel, and you'll no longer be able to combine it with other shapes or apply round corners. The shape will be recognized by Photoshop as a traditional path.

Selecting and Moving Shapes

Once you've made a shape, use the Path Selection tool to select and move it. You also use the Path Selection tool to modify the shape by dragging the handles on the shape's bounding box.

Combining Shapes

The Options panel contains five path operations that control how shapes can be combined including the following:

New Layer: No combining of shapes occurs. Every shape you create appears on its own new layer.

Combine Shapes: Every new shape you make combines with previous shapes you made, always resulting in one combination shape.

Subtract Front Shape: Any shape you make over an existing shape is subtracted or removed from the first shape as though it is a hole or a negative space.

Intersect Shape Areas: The resulting shape is the intersection of overlapping shapes.

Exclude Overlapping Shapes: The intersection of overlapping shapes creates a hole in those shapes.

Combining shapes creates the ability to make an infinite number of new shapes.

Create, fill, and stroke a basic shape

1. Open PS 12-1.psd, then save it as **Basic Shapes**.
2. Set the **foreground color** to **white**, then set the **background color** to **black**.
3. Click the **Rectangle tool** on the toolbar.
4. Click the **tool mode list arrow** on the Options panel, then click **Shape**, as shown in Figure 3.

5. Target the **Background layer**, then create a **rectangle** of any shape anywhere on the canvas.

   The rectangle is created on a new layer automatically named Rectangle 1 and is filled with the current foreground color.

Figure 3 Rectangle tool and tool mode menu set to Shape

Tool mode menu

6. Double-click the **Rectangle 1 layer thumbnail**.

The Color Picker opens. When the Color Picker is open, the cursor becomes the Eyedropper tool when you float it over the image.

TIP Double-click directly on the thumbnail image to open the Color Picker. Double-clicking the blank area opens the Layer Style dialog box.

7. Click the **image** in different places to sample different colors.

Every time you sample, the rectangle's fill updates to that color and the new color is updated in the Color Picker.

8. Sample a **yellow color** from the yellow spool of thread in the lower-left corner of the image, then click **OK** to close the Color Picker.

9. On the Options panel, click the **stroke box** to show the available color swatches, then click a **royal blue swatch**.

10. Type **16 px** in the **stroke width text box**.

Your rectangle's fill color and stroke should resemble Figure 4. Its size and position will differ from the figure.

TIP When you're working with shapes, the Properties panel shows various formatting options for the targeted shape layer. You can choose to format a shape on the Properties panel or on the Options panel, or you can modify the shape directly.

11. Save your work, then continue to the next set of steps.

You used the Rectangle tool to create a rectangle shape. You applied a fill and a stroke color to the object.

Figure 4 Adding a fill and stroke to a shape

Format a basic shape and align it to the canvas

1. Click and drag any of the **handles** on the rectangle to make it larger.

   The bounding box on the shape functions the same as the bounding box that appears when you transform a selection. You can drag individual handles to resize the shape. You can also rotate the shape by floating your mouse pointer just outside of the bounding box.

2. On the Properties panel, type **3.25** in the **W text box**, then type **1.75** in the **H text box**.

   TIP Be sure you are working with inches, not pixels. If you see px in the W and H text boxes on the Properties panel, right-click the text box, then choose Inches from the pop-up menu.

3. On the **Options panel**, click the **Path alignment button** 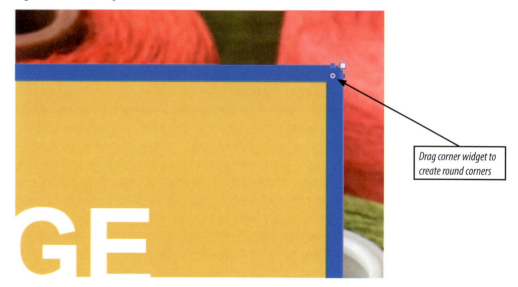.

   A panel opens with Align, Distribute, and Distribute Spacing options.

4. In the **bottom-right corner** of the panel, click the **Align To list arrow**, then click **Canvas**.

   When Canvas is chosen, selected shapes will be aligned in relation to the canvas (as opposed to aligning in relation to other objects).

5. On the panel, click the **Align horizontal centers button** ⊕.

   The rectangle moves left or right to align its center point to the horizontal center of the canvas.

6. Click the **Align vertical centers button** ⊩.

   The rectangle moves up or down to align its center point to the vertical center of the canvas. By clicking both buttons, the rectangle is now centered horizontally and vertically on the canvas.

7. Save your work, then continue to the next set of steps.

You specified an exact width and height for the rectangle, then you aligned the center of the rectangle with the center of the canvas.

Apply round corners to a shape

1. Note the **corner widget** on the rectangle's bounding box, which is identified in Figure 5.

2. Click and drag the **corner widget** toward the **center of the rectangle**, then release the mouse pointer.

   Dragging the corner widget toward the center creates round corners on the rectangle. The radius values of each of the round corners are noted on the Properties panel.

3. On the Properties panel, set the **corner radius** for all four corners to **60 px**.

Figure 5 The corner widget

Drag corner widget to create round corners

4. Click the **link icon**  on the Properties panel to deactivate it.

When the link is deactivated, each corner radius can be modified independently of the others.

5. Set the **top-left corner** to **0 px**, then set the **bottom-right corner** to **0 px**.

Your rectangle should resemble Figure 6.

6. Save your work, then continue to the next set of steps.

You dragged the corner widget on the rectangle to apply round corners to all four corners. You then used the Properties panel to apply a specific corner radius value to the rounded corners and then removed two of them.

Create a line as a shape

1. Click the **Move tool** , then target the layer named **GEORGE**.

2. Press and hold **[shift]**, then press the **up arrow** on your keypad two times.

3. Click the **Line tool** on the toolbar.

TIP The Line tool is hidden behind the current shape tool on the toolbar.

4. On the Options panel, set the **Fill color** to **white**, then set the **Stroke color** to **None** .

5. Click and drag a **horizontal line** of any length under **GEORGE**.

TIP Press and hold [shift] while dragging to create a straight line.

6. On the Options panel, type **440** in the **W text box**, then type **8** in the **H text box.**

When working with line shapes, the H text box determines the thickness of the line.

7. Click the **Path Selection tool** , then position the **line** as shown in Figure 7.

8. Save your work, then continue to the next set of steps.

You used the Line tool to create a line.

Figure 6 Removing the rounded corner from two corners

Figure 7 Positioning a line

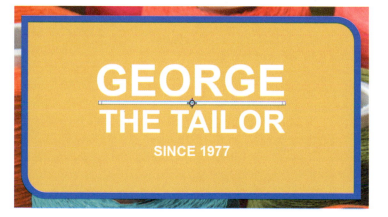

Apply layer styles and opacity to a shape

1. Double-click a **blank area on the Rectangle 1 layer** to open the Layer Styles dialog box.

2. Click the words **Drop Shadow** on the left-side column.

3. Enter the settings shown in Figure 8, then click **OK**.

4. On the Layers panel, reduce the **Opacity** of the Rectangle 1 layer to **75%**.

   The reduction of opacity affects the fill and stroke and the drop shadow. However, a nontransparent stroke would look better. This can be accomplished by creating a second rectangle.

5. Target the **Rectangle 1 layer**, then enter **[command] [J] (Mac)** or **[Ctrl] [J] (Win)** to duplicate it.

6. Rename the new layer **Stroke Only**, then set its **Opacity** to **100%**.

   The Stroke Only layer has the same Drop Shadow layer style, which is not needed.

7. Drag the fx on the **Stroke Only layer** to the **Delete layer button** 🗑 on the Layers panel to delete the layer style.

Figure 8 Drop Shadow layer style settings

8. On the Options panel, set the **Fill color** to **None** 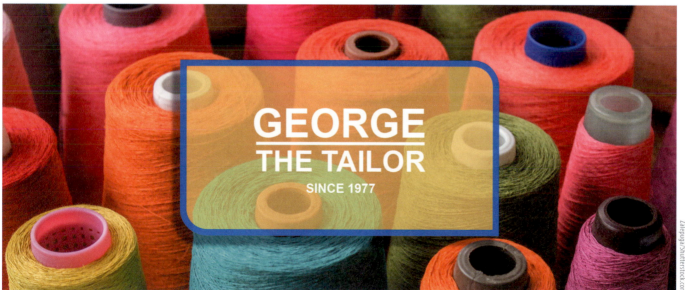.

   Your canvas should resemble Figure 9.

AUTHOR'S NOTE This result illustrates the benefits of working with shapes. First, it wouldn't be possible to create the two rounded corners with any of the selection tools, so this artwork is possible only with shapes. In addition to that, the shape is 100% editable. It can be easily resized, and the fill and stroke colors can be modified independently.

9. Save your work, then close Basic Shapes.

You applied the Drop Shadow layer style to the rectangle. When you reduced the opacity on the rectangle, you noted that it also reduced the opacity of the blue stroke, which was not the desired effect. You then duplicated the rectangle, set the Fill color to None, then set the Opacity to 100% to restore the blue stroke.

Combine shapes

1. Open PS 12-2.psd, then save it as **Combine and Reshape**.

2. Click the **Polygon tool** on the toolbar, then click the **canvas**.

   The Create Polygon dialog box opens.

3. Enter **500 px** for the **Width** and the **Height**, enter **5** for the **Number of Sides**, enter **100%** for the **Star Ratio**, then click **OK**.

   A pentagon shape is created on the canvas.

4. Click the **Path Selection tool** on the toolbar, then position the **pentagon** at the **center of the canvas**.

   The best way to move a shape is with the Path Selection tool. If you use the Move tool, the Options panel no longer shows info for the targeted shape.

5. Set the **Fill color** for the pentagon shape to **black**, then set the **Stroke color** to **None**.

6. Click the **Polygon tool**, then click the **canvas** again.

7. Change the **Width** and **Height** to **300**, then click **OK**.

Continued on next page

Figure 9 Transparent artwork with a drop shadow

GEORGE
THE TAILOR
SINCE 1977

Zalepugin/Shutterstock.com

8. Change the **fill color** of the **second pentagon** to **red**, then use the **Path Selection tool** ▶. to center the **red pentagon** over the black pentagon.

9. Target both **shape layers** on the Layers panel.

10. Click **Layer** on the menu bar, point to **Combine Shapes**, then click **Subtract Front Shape**.

    As shown in Figure 10, the front pentagon creates a hole in the black pentagon. The two layers on the Layers panel have become one layer, but the two shapes are not united as one. Both pentagons can be selected and modified independently.

Figure 10 Combining shapes to create a hole in one

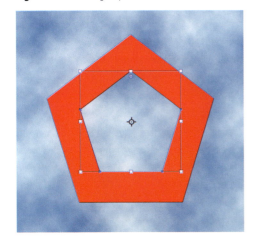

11. Click the **Path Selection tool** ▶. on the sky background to deselect the combined shape.

12. Click the **inside of the small pentagon**.

    Even though you are creating what is a negative space, the small pentagon is selected.

13. Click and drag the **corner widget** on the **small pentagon** to create round corners.

    Round corners are applied only to the small pentagon.

14. Save your work, then continue to the next set of steps.

You created two pentagons and used the smaller one to create a hole in the larger one. Noting that the two were still selectable independent of one another, you applied round corners to the smaller pentagon.

Reshape shapes with the Direct Selection tool

1. Click the **Path Selection tool** ▶. on the **sky background** to deselect.

2. Click the **Direct Selection tool** ▷., then click any **side edge of the red pentagon**.

    When you click the edge of a shape with the Direct Selection tool, the anchor points all turn white, indicating that each is selectable independent of the others.

TIP The Direct Selection tool ▷. is under the Path Selection tool ▶. on the toolbar.

3. Using the **Direct Selection tool** ▷., drag the **top anchor point** straight up.

    When you click and drag the first point, a warning dialog box appears that reads, "This operation will turn a live shape into a regular path. Continue?"

4. Click **Yes**.

5. Reshape the object as shown in Figure 11.

6. Save your work, then close Combine and Reshape.

You created a pentagon with the Polygon tool then used the Direct Selection tool to reshape it into an original shape.

Figure 11 Reshaped shape

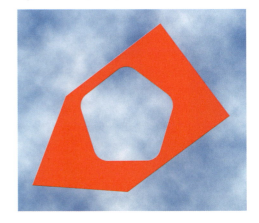

IMPORT SHAPES FROM ADOBE ILLUSTRATOR

▶ *What You'll Do*

In this lesson, you'll use a shape from Adobe Illustrator as part of a clipped and complex, three-dimensional effect.

SUNDAY 3PM · NBS

Importing Shapes from Adobe Illustrator

Shapes are a genuinely robust feature in Adobe Photoshop, offering you many practical options for creating basic and complex shapes for your layouts without having to leave Photoshop. That said, Adobe Illustrator is Adobe's preeminent drawing program, and some designers prefer to create their shapes in Illustrator and bring them into Photoshop. This is often the case for two reasons: either the designer is just more comfortable working in Illustrator, or the vector graphic is too complex to be created in Photoshop and requires Illustrator's greater sophistication and capabilities.

When you paste a shape from Illustrator into Photoshop, the Paste dialog box appears, asking how you want to paste the vector graphic as a Smart Object, Pixels, a Path, or a Shape Layer. Choosing Shape Layer pastes the object as a vector graphic, editable with the Path Selection and Direct Selection tools. Note, however, that a Shape Layer pasted from Illustrator is

not a "live" shape in Photoshop. It is simply a traditional shape made up of anchor points and lines connecting them.

EMBEDDING AND LINKING IMAGES

In addition to pasting images into Photoshop, you can also place them using the File menu. The two options for placing images from other programs are embedding and linking. When you embed an image in Photoshop using the Place Embedded command, the image becomes part of the Photoshop document and is no longer related to the original source file. If you link an image using the Place Linked command, the image is still linked to the original source file. If the source file is edited, the linked image will be updated with the new appearance. For example, if you place an image of a red apple from Adobe Illustrator into Photoshop using Place Linked and then update the color of the apple to green in Adobe Illustrator, the red apple will now appear green in the Photoshop document.

Paste an Adobe Illustrator object as a shape layer in Photoshop

1. Open PS 12-3.ai in Adobe Illustrator.

   This is an Adobe Illustrator file.

2. Click the **Selection tool** , then click the **star-shaped object** to select it.

3. Click **Edit** on the menu bar, then click **Copy**.

4. Return to Photoshop, open PS 12-4.psd, then save it as **Football Star**.

5. Set the **foreground color** to **red**, then target the **Star Template layer**.

6. Click **Edit** on the menu bar, then click **Paste**.

   The Paste dialog box opens, offering four options.

7. Click **Shape Layer**, then click **OK**.

   The star shape is pasted onto a new layer automatically named Shape 1.

8. Align the shape exactly with the star template.

9. Delete the **Star Template layer**.

10. Save your work, then continue to the next set of steps.

You pasted a shape from Adobe Illustrator into Photoshop as a shape layer.

Use a shape as a clipping mask

1. Show the **Fade Dark layer**, then set its blending mode to **Multiply**.

   The gradient darkens the background image.

2. Drag the **Shape 1 layer** below the **Lights layer** on the Layers panel.

3. Show the **Lights layer**, then clip it into the **Shape 1 layer**.

4. Show the **Player layer**, then clip it into the **Lights layer**.

5. Show the **Blue Tint layer**.

   Your canvas should resemble Figure 12.

Figure 12 Two images clipped into the star

6. Target the **Player layer**, then enter **[command] [J] (Mac)** or **[Ctrl] [J] (Win)** to duplicate it.

The Player copy layer is automatically unclipped.

7. Drag the **layer mask** on the Player copy layer to the **Delete layer icon** 🗑 on the Layers panel.

A dialog box appears asking if you want to apply the layer mask before deleting.

8. Click **Apply**.

9. Click **Layer** on the menu bar, point to **Layer Mask**, then click **Reveal All**.

10. Mask the **Player copy layer** so it appears he's leaping out of the star shape, as shown in Figure 13.

11. Show the **Type layer** at the top of the Layers panel.

12. Double-click a **blank area** on the **Shape 1 layer** to open the Layer Styles dialog box.

13. Click **Bevel & Emboss**.

14. Enter the settings shown in Figure 14, then click **Outer Glow** on the left column.

Continued on next page

Figure 13 Masking the player so it appears he's leaping out of the star

Adam Vilimek/Shutterstock.com; OSTILL is Franck Camhi/Shutterstock.com

Figure 14 Settings for Bevel & Emboss

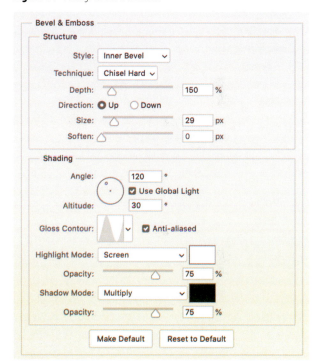

15. Enter the settings shown in Figure 15, then click **OK**.

The effect of the football player bursting through the star is cool, but the star itself is too uniform in shape and looks like exactly what it is: a standard shape from Illustrator. You will reshape it to make it unique. Also, note the point of the star peeking out from behind the player's arm. It is showing just enough to be distracting. It needs to be either showing fully or hiding completely, not "in between."

16. Target the **Shape 1 layer**, then click the **Direct Selection tool** .

17. Select the **anchor points** on each point of the star to make some points longer and some shorter.

Figure 16 shows one version of the modified star and the final artwork.

18. Save your work, then close Football Star.

You clipped images into a shape layer and applied a Bevel & Emboss and an Outer Glow layer style to the shape. You used strategic masking to create the effect of a football player bursting through the shape.

Figure 15 Settings for Outer Glow

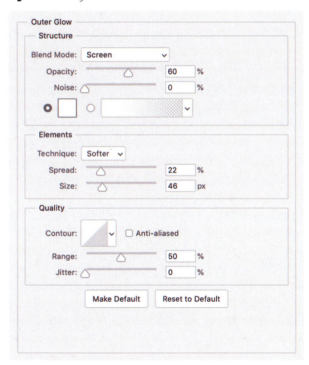

Figure 16 Reshaping the star

WORK WITH PATHS

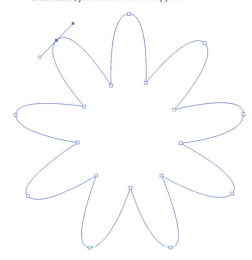

Working with Paths

Long before there were shapes and live shapes, there were paths. In fact, paths and the Paths panel go all the way back to the very first version of Photoshop.

A **path** is a simple vector object drawn with anchor points and lines that connect them. Those lines can be straight lines or curved lines. The object itself can be a traditional square or rectangle or circle, or it can be entirely unique.

When working with paths and shapes, inevitable questions arise as to what the difference between them is and why they both exist. It's important to clarify this, and the only way to do so is to briefly examine the history of Photoshop.

As stated, paths were a feature in Photoshop since the first version. For many iterations of the software, the only way to draw a path was with the Pen tool. You can use the Pen tool to draw straight lines or curved lines, making it possible to produce pretty much any shape you can think of. Then again, using the Pen tool to draw a perfect circle or a perfect square or a perfect isosceles triangle is about as difficult as trying to draw them with a pencil: it can be done, but it sure isn't easy.

At some point in Photoshop's more-than-three-decade history, designers started to express the

need to create quick circles, squares, triangles, and so on, and that's when the drawing tools like the Rectangle, Ellipse, and Triangle tools were added to the Photoshop toolbar. Note, however, that these tools can create *both* shapes and paths, depending on the tool mode you choose on the Options panel. If you choose Shape and draw an ellipse with the Ellipse tool, you create a new shape and a new layer on the Layers panel. If you choose Path, you do not create a new layer, but you do create a Work Path listed on the Paths panel.

All paths are only listed on the Paths panel. Paths are never placed on layers on the Layers panel. When you use one of the shape tools or the Pen tool to create a path, you must save the Work Path as a named path on the Paths panel.

This leads to another critical question: Why make a path? For most of your designs, you will likely rely on shapes more than you will rely on paths because you'll most often want basic circles, squares, and rectangles, which you can make quickly as shapes.

You will find yourself creating paths when you use the Pen tool to draw unique and original shapes. You can apply a fill or a stroke to a path. Paths offer one powerful option that shapes don't: you can stroke a path with the Brush tool using its current Size, Color, and Hardness settings. This can create many options for strokes and soft glows.

Draw a shape with corner points with the Pen tool

1. Open PS 12-5.psd, then save it as **Creating Paths**.

2. Click the **Pen tool** ∅, then, on the Options panel, verify that the **tool mode menu** is set to **Path**.

   The Pen tool can be used to create a shape, but in this case, we are using it to create a path.

3. On the Options panel, click the **Path operations menu** (next to Shape), then choose **Exclude Overlapping Shapes** ⬚.

4. Click the **top-center point on the star** to add an anchor point.

5. Moving clockwise, click **every point on the star** to trace it, then click the **first point** again to close the path.

   As you click, anchor points are added, and a path connects the points. When you return to the first point, a circle appears beside the Pen tool, indicating that clicking the first point will close the path.

6. Delete the **Star Template layer** from the Layers panel.

   The path continues to show.

7. Show the **Paths panel**.

   The path you created is listed as Work Path. A work path is an unsaved path.

8. Click the **Paths panel menu button** ≡, then click **Save Path**.

   The Save Path dialog box opens.

9. Rename Path 1 as **Star Corner Points**, then click **OK**.

   The Star Corner Points path is saved on the Paths panel.

10. Save your work, then continue to the next set of steps.

You used the Pen tool to trace a star on a layer. You noted that the path was listed on the Paths panel named Work Path. You saved the Work Path with a new name.

Convert corner points to smooth points on a path

1. On the Paths panel, verify that the **Star Corner Points path** is targeted, click the **Paths panel menu button** ≡, click **Duplicate Path**, name the new path **Star Smooth Points**, then click **OK**.

2. Verify that the **Star Smooth Points path** is targeted on the Paths panel.

3. Click the **Convert Point tool** ⌐ on the toolbar.

TIP The Convert Point tool ⌐ is located behind the Pen tool ∅.

4. If the anchor points are *not* showing on the path, the Convert Point tool will appear as an arrow; click the path with the arrow to make the anchor points appear.

5. Position the **Convert Point tool** ⌐ over the **top-center anchor point** of the star.

6. Click and drag **to the right** to convert the anchor point to a smooth point and create a curve on the path, as shown in Figure 17.

   The path continues through the point in a smooth arc, thus the name "smooth point." Smooth points have directional handles that define the arc of the curve.

Figure 17 Converting a corner point to a smooth point

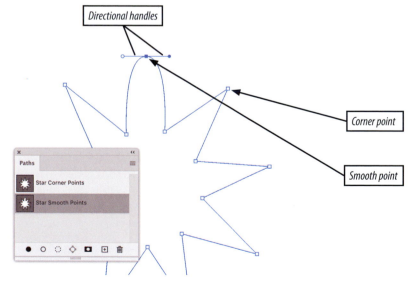

7. Working clockwise, convert all the points of the star to smooth points so that your canvas resembles Figure 18.

Every change you make to the path is updated to the path preview on the Paths panel.

8. Save your work, then continue to the next set of steps.

You used the Convert Point tool to convert corner points on the star to smooth points. You noted that directional handles associated with the smooth point determined the roundness and arc of the curve through the smooth point.

Create negative space in a path

1. Verify that the **Star Smooth Points path** is targeted on the Paths panel.

2. Click the **Ellipse tool** on the toolbar.

3. On the Options panel, click the **tool mode list arrow**, then choose **Path**.

You are using the Ellipse tool to create a path, not a shape.

4. On the Options panel, click the **Path operations button**, then verify that **Exclude Overlapping Shapes** is selected.

5. Verify that the **Star Smooth Points path** is targeted on the Paths panel and visible on the canvas.

6. Position the **Ellipse tool crosshair pointer** at the **center** of the path.

7. Using Figure 19 as a guide, press and hold **[option] (Mac)** or **[Alt] (Win)**, start dragging,

then press **[shift]** before you release the mouse pointer to create a perfect circle.

The circle is a negative space, or a "hole," at the center of the path. Note that the Star Smooth Points path has updated to show the negative space at the center.

8. On the Paths panel, click the **empty space** below the two listed paths so that no path is targeted.

When no path is targeted, no path is visible. Only the white canvas shows.

9. Save your work, then continue to the next set of steps.

You used the Ellipse tool as a path to create a hole in the larger outer path.

Figure 18 Nine points converted to smooth points

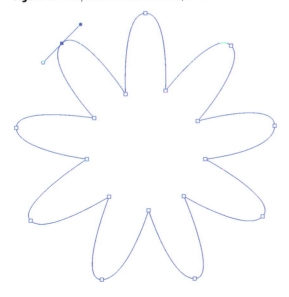

Figure 19 The circle is a negative space at the center of the path

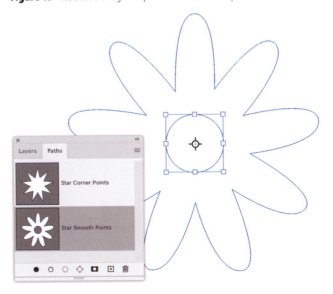

Fill and stroke a path

1. On the Layers panel, create a new layer, then name it **Flower**.

2. Target the **Star Smooth Points path** on the Paths panel.

3. Choose a **bright green color** as the **foreground color**.

4. On the Paths panel, click the **Fill path with foreground color button** ⬤.

   As shown in Figure 20, the path appears to fill with the green foreground color; however, it's important to realize that the path itself is not filled. Instead, the

Figure 20 Filling a path

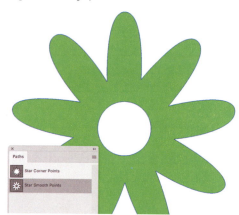

pixels on the Flower layer that is targeted are filled in the shape of the path with the foreground color.

5. Click the **Brush tool** 🖌 on the toolbar, set the **Opacity** to **100%**, set the **Size** to **15 px**, then set the **Hardness** to **100%**.

6. Choose a **bright orange color** as the **foreground color**.

7. Click the **Paths panel menu button** ☰, then click **Stroke Path**.

   The Stroke Path dialog box appears.

8. Click the **Tool list arrow**, click **Brush**, then click **OK**.

   An orange stroke is applied to the Flower layer. The stroke is applied with the foreground color and the Opacity, Hardness, and Size settings currently set for the Brush tool.

9. Save your work, then continue to the next set of steps.

You applied a fill and a stroke to the path, noting that the fill and stroke affect the pixels on the targeted layer, not the path itself.

Convert smooth points to corner points with the Convert Point tool

1. Hide the **Flower layer**.

2. Click the **Direct Selection tool** �, then click the **path** so that the anchor points become visible.

3. Click the **Convert Point tool** ⬐, then click the **top-center anchor point**.

   The smooth point is converted to a corner point.

4. Press and hold **[command] (Mac)** or **[Ctrl] (Win)**.

   Pressing [command] (Mac) or [Ctrl] (Win) changes the Convert Point tool ⬐ to the Direct Selection tool ▸.

5. Click the **Direct Selection tool** ▸, on the **next point to the right**.

   As shown in Figure 21, both directional handles appear because the point is a smooth point.

Figure 21 Directional handles on a smooth point

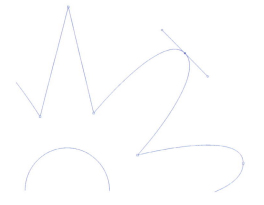

6. Use the **Convert Point tool** to drag the **right handle** to the location shown in Figure 22.

When you use the Convert Point tool to drag a directional handle, the smooth point is converted to a corner point. Using this technique, you can create any shape imaginable and redirect a path in any direction.

TIP Click the top of the directional handle to drag it.

7. Using the same method, reshape the current path into the path shown in Figure 23.

8. Save your work, then close Creating Paths.

You clicked the Convert Point tool on a smooth point, which converts the smooth point to a corner point. You then accessed the Direct Selection tool and clicked a smooth point to show its directional handles. You then dragged one of the handles with the Convert Point tool, which converted the point to a corner point and allowed you to reshape the path to your liking. Lastly, you repeated these techniques on the remaining anchor points.

Figure 22 Dragging the directional handle with the Convert Point tool

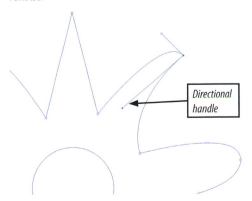

Directional handle

Convert a selection to a path

1. Open PS 12-6.psd, then save it as **Clay Jug**.

2. Click the **Magic Wand tool** on the toolbar, set the **Tolerance** to **16**, then verify that Anti-alias is checked and that the Contiguous option is not checked.

3. Click the **white background**.

4. Click **Select** on the menu bar, then click **Inverse**.

5. Click the **Paths panel menu button**, then click **Make Work Path**.

The Make Work Path dialog box opens, asking the Tolerance setting you want for the path. The Tolerance setting specifies how many pixels are used to determine the flatness of the curved path.

6. Accept the default **2.0 pixels**, then click **OK**.

As shown in Figure 24, a path is created from the selection. Note that an interior path is drawn

Figure 23 Redrawing the path with all corner points

inside the outer path to define the negative space inside the handle. The path is identified as a Work Path on the Paths panel, so it needs to be saved.

7. Double-click the **Work Path** on the Paths panel to open the Save Path dialog box.

8. Accept the default name, then click **OK**.

9. Save your work, then close Clay Jug.

You used the Magic Wand tool to make a selection. Then you converted the selection to a path using the Make Work Path command on the Paths panel.

Figure 24 Creating a path from a selection

Serg64/Shutterstock.com

DRAW A PATH AROUND AN IMAGE

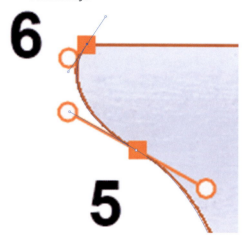

Isolating an Image with a Path

Figure 25 shows an image of a wooden chair that was photographed in a restaurant setting. If you wanted to paste a copy of just the chair into another image, like that of of the beach scene in the figure, you'd first have to remove the restaurant background and capture the chair on its own. All kinds of Photoshop lingo exists to describe this operation. You could say that you needed to "silhouette" the chair or "isolate" it. Or you could say you needed to "drop out" or "mask out" the restaurant background. Some people say they "cut a mask," while others say they "painted a mask."

Whatever phraseology you become comfortable with, dropping out a background to isolate an image is one of the fundamental challenges in Photoshop and one that every user must master. For most jobs, you will use a layer mask and the Brush tool to "paint out" a background, but the chair is an example of the type of image that is difficult to mask with the Brush tool. The long, curved sides leave very little room for error in consistency and smoothness of brush strokes you might paint, and because the isolated chair must be symmetrical, that creates another level of challenge.

The image of the chair was masked with the Pen tool. The elegant, curving arcs generated by the Pen tool can be easily aligned precisely to the edges of the chair. Once a path is drawn,

it can be converted to a selection, allowing you to copy the artwork to its own layer or into a different image.

Figure 25 Images with hard edges and long curves are good candidates to be masked with the Pen tool

Iakov Filimonov/Shutterstock.com

Generally speaking, hard-edged objects with long, curving arcs are better masked with paths than with the Brush tool.

Drawing a Path with Smooth Points and Corner Points

When you draw a path or trace an image with the Pen tool, you create anchor points and paths that connect the anchor points. The Pen tool creates two types of anchor points: smooth points and corner points.

Smooth points continue the existing path in a predictable direction. In Figure 26, the anchor points on the outside of the handle, circled in green, are all smooth points that trace the arc of the handle. When you draw a smooth point, you click and drag to reveal directional handles for the anchor point. You can drag the directional handles to adjust how the path aligns to the image you are tracing. By default, directional handles on a smooth point are paired: if you move one, the other moves in the opposite direction. This allows the path to continue "smoothly" through the anchor point.

Inevitably, when tracing an image, the path will need to change directions abruptly. In Figure 26, the red circles indicate areas where the path changes direction. The anchor points at those locations are corner points. When you use corner points to change the direction of a path, you use the Convert Point tool to "break" the directional handles to point in two different directions. You can see in the red circles that the directional handles for those anchor points are doing just that.

Figure 26 Smooth points and corner points

Sergf64/Shutterstock.com

Exporting an Image with a Clipping Path

Paths play an important role in exporting images as isolated objects. Using the image of the chair as a reference, once you draw and save the path, you can save the file with the saved path defined as a clipping path. A clipping path provides mathematical data that is saved with the file and defines the boundaries of the image for use in other software programs. In simpler terms, if you placed the image of the chair in a layout program like Adobe InDesign, only the chair would appear. Better still, InDesign can use the information from the saved clipping path to wrap text around the chair. Whenever you see images in magazines or on websites that show text aligning to the edge of an isolated image, that effect is created by saving a clipping path with the image.

Drawing a Path Around an Image with Negative Spaces

Figure 27 shows a path tracing the image of a pitcher with a handle. Note that it takes two paths to trace the pitcher: one path goes around the perimeter of the pitcher, and another traces the inside of the handle. The pitcher is an object with a negative space—the negative space being the space inside the handle. Similarly, if you were tracing an image of a donut, the hole in the donut would be the negative space you'd need to trace.

Figure 27 One image traced with two paths

Serg64/Shutterstock.com

When you draw a path around an object with negative spaces, you need to choose Exclude Overlapping Shapes from the Path operations menu once you select the Pen tool, as shown in Figure 28.

Isolate an image with a path

1. Open PS 12-7.psd, then save it as **Path for Urn**.

   The goals of this exercise are to use the Pen tool to create a path around the urn and to export the path as a clipping path for a text wrap in InDesign. When saving an image with a clipping path for use in Adobe InDesign or Illustrator, always save the file as a Photoshop (.psd) file.

2. Show the **Template layer**.

   The Template layer is a screenshot of a path that was drawn around the urn. You will follow this template to develop your skills for placing

anchor points strategically and dragging directional handles.

3. Show the **Hue/Saturation adjustment layer**.

   Because the Pen tool draws blue paths by default, it would be difficult for you to trace blue on blue. The Hue/Saturation adjustment makes the paths orange, which will be visually easier for you to work with.

4. Click the **Pen tool** .

5. Click **point 1** on the path.

6. In one move, click **point 2**, then drag directional handles that align with the orange directional handles on the template.

   As you drag the directional handles, you will be able to align the path between points 1 and 2 along the edge of the urn.

7. Using the same method, work your way through to point 5, adding points and dragging handles according to the template.

Figure 28 Choose Exclude Overlapping Shapes to create negative space on a path

8. When you get to **point 6**, use Figure 29 as a guide.

   The edge of the urn makes an abrupt change in direction at point 6. To align the path between points 5 and 6, you can't drag the handle at point 6 in the direction of point 7. Instead, you will need to drag the handle toward 1 o'clock, as shown in the figure.

9. Press and hold **[option] (Mac)** or **[Alt] (Win)**, then position the **Pen tool** over the **right-most directional handle**.

   The Pen tool changes to the Convert Point tool when positioned over the directional handle. You will use the Convert Point tool to redirect the path at point 6 to go toward point 7.

10. Using Figure 30 as a guide, use the **Convert Point tool** to drag the **handle** from 1 o'clock to 3 o'clock.

    "Breaking" the handles with the Convert Point tool converts point 6 from a smooth point to a corner point.

11. Press and hold **[shift]**, then click **point 7**.

    Pressing and holding [shift] connects the two points with a horizontal line.

12. Work your way to **point 11**.

13. When you get to **point 12**, just click a point.

    Sometimes you get lucky and don't need to drag out handles; the path just aligns with a click.

14. Click **point 1**.

    Points 12 and 1 connect with a straight line.

15. Click the **Add Anchor Point tool**, then position it over the **path** between points 12 and 1.

16. Click to add an **anchor point**.

By default, the new point is a smooth point; it has directional handles.

17. Click the **Direct Selection tool**, then drag the **new point** down to the anchor point at the bottom of the urn.

18. Hide the **Template layer**.

    Your canvas should resemble Figure 31.

19. Double-click the **Work Path** on the Paths panel to open the Save Path dialog box, then click **OK**.

    The Work Path is saved as Path 1.

20. Save your work, then continue to the next set of steps.

Following a template, you practiced skills for positioning anchor points and drawing a path to trace an image. You used the Convert Point tool to redirect the path at point 6, and you used the Add Anchor Point tool to add a point, which you used to reposition the path.

Figure 29 Drawing point 6

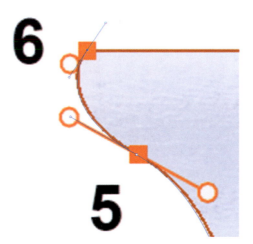

Figure 30 Redirecting the directional handle

Figure 31 Viewing the completed path

Make a selection from a path

1. Verify that the **Background layer** is targeted.
2. Click the **Paths panel menu button** 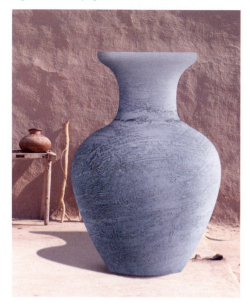, then click **Make Selection**.
3. Enter **0** in the **Feather Radius text box**, verify that **Anti-alias** is checked, then click **OK**.

   The selection is loaded from the path.
4. Click the **Create new fill or adjustment layer button** on the Layers panel, then click **Hue/Saturation**.

   A Hue/Saturation adjustment layer is created automatically with a mask representing the selection.
5. Drag the **Hue slider** all the way left to **−180**, then drag the **Saturation slider** to **−57**.

   Your artwork should resemble Figure 32.
6. Save your work, then continue to the next set of steps.

You used the Make Selection command on the Paths panel menu to convert a path to a selection. You used that selection as a mask for a Hue/Saturation adjustment to change the color of the selected object.

Figure 32 Modifying the hue and saturation

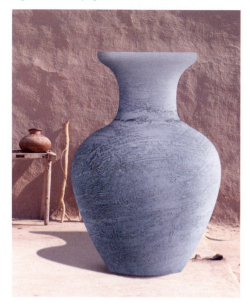

Save a file with a clipping path for a text wrap in InDesign

1. Click the **Paths panel menu button** , then click **Clipping Path**.
2. In the Clipping Path dialog box, verify that **Path 1** is chosen on the Path menu, type **3** in the **Flatness text box**, then click **OK**.
3. Save your work, then close the file.
4. Open PS 12-8.indd in Adobe InDesign, then save it as **Runaround the Urn**.
5. Click the **picture box** at the center of the page to select it.
6. Click **File** on the menu bar, then click **Place**.
7. Navigate to the **Path for Urn file**, then click **Open**.

   The image appears in the picture box.
8. Click **Object** on the menu bar, point to **Fitting**, then click **Fit Content Proportionally**.
9. Click **Window** on the menu bar, then click **Text Wrap**.

10. Enter the settings shown in Figure 33.

Note that the Contour Options setting is Photoshop Path and Path 1 is selected. InDesign is using the clipping path from the Photoshop file as the shape for the InDesign text to wrap to.

11. Click the **View menu**, point to **Screen Mode**, then click **Presentation**.

Your page should resemble Figure 34.

12. Press the **[esc] key**, save your work, then close Path for Urn.

You saved a file with a clipping path. You then placed the image in an InDesign layout, noting that only the part of the image that was inside the clipping path is visible in InDesign. You used the information from the clipping path to wrap text in InDesign around the shape of the placed image.

Figure 33 *Settings for the text wrap*

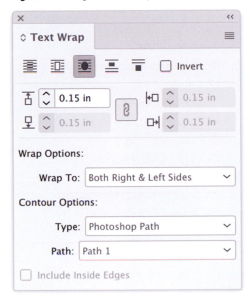

Figure 34 InDesign uses clipping path information for the text wrap

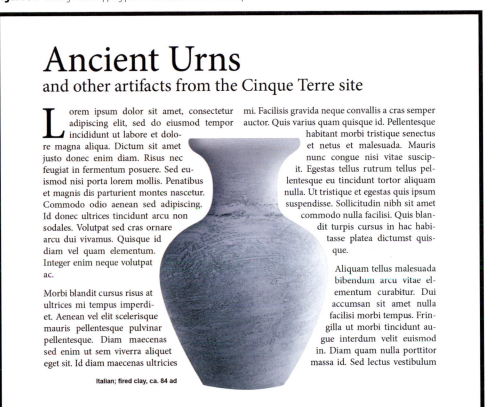

CREATE VECTOR MASKS

What You'll Do

In this lesson, you'll use paths as vector masks.

Working with Vector Masks

Shapes and paths can be used as masks on the Layers panel to isolate artwork. **Vector masks** are similar to layer masks, with a couple of exceptions. Vector masks are created with vector-based objects, not by painting pixels. Because the objects in a vector mask are objects drawn with anchor points and lines, the mask can be altered at any time by altering the vector graphic.

Figure 35 shows the chair isolated by a vector mask and positioned in a beach scene. The Pen tool was used to trace the edges of the chair, and the resulting path is being used as a vector mask to isolate the artwork. The vector mask on the Layers panel shows white to indicate what shows on the layer and gray to indicate what is hidden.

Figure 35 The chair isolated by a vector mask, listed on the Layers panel

Use a path to make a vector mask

1. Open PS 12-9.psd, then save it as **Kitchen Scene**.

2. Open PS 12-10.psd, then save it as **Vector Mask for Urn**.

   The goal of this exercise is to move only the urn from the desert scene into the kitchen scene using a vector mask to isolate the urn.

   TIP This set of steps will work best if these are the only two files open in Photoshop.

3. In the **Vector Mask for Urn file**, verify that **Path 1** is targeted on the Paths panel.

4. Target the **Urn layer**, click **Layer** on the menu bar, point to **Vector Mask**, then click **Current Path**.

   As shown in Figure 36, the path is used in a vector mask to make everything outside of the path not visible. The vector mask thumbnail on the Layers panel uses white to indicate what is visible and gray to indicate what is masked.

5. Click **Window** on the menu bar, point to **Arrange**, then click **Tile All Vertically**.

   Continued on next page

Figure 36 Vector mask on the Layers panel and the isolated image

6. Drag the **Urn layer** into the **Kitchen Scene file**, then position the **urn** where you think it looks best.

   As shown in Figure 37, the vector mask remains with the layer and continues to mask the desert background. The vector mask allows the urn to be believably part of this setting, with the exception that the urn has no shadows. You can use this as an opportunity to practice painting contact and cast shadows.

   TIP Drag the Urn layer from the empty gray area on the layer.

7. Add a **layer** below the Urn layer then, using the shadow information from the kitchen scene photo, paint in shadows for the vase.

8. Save your work, then close Kitchen Scene.

   You used a saved path to make a vector mask for the artwork it traced. You then dragged the layer with the vector mask to another image file, noting that the vector mask traveled with the layer.

Figure 37 Isolated image with vector mask

Sentelia/Shutterstock.com

Use a basic shape to make a vector mask

1. Open PS 12-11.psd, then save it as **Basic Vector Mask**.

2. Target the **Portrait layer**.

3. Click **Layer** on the menu bar, point to **Vector Mask**, then click **Reveal All**.

4. Click the **Ellipse tool** , then, on the Options panel, set the **tool mode menu** to **Path**.

5. Click and drag to create a **circle** of any size on the canvas.

   The circle is created as a vector mask.

6. Click the **Direct Selection tool**, click outside the circle to deselect, then select the **edge of the circle**.

7. Drag the **handles** on the circle to create an oval for the portrait.

8. Add an **Inner Shadow layer style** to the **Portrait layer**.

   Your artwork should resemble Figure 38.

9. Save your work, then close Basic Vector Mask.

You used the Ellipse tool to create an oval vector mask for an image, then you applied an Inner Shadow layer style to the artwork with the vector mask, noting that the layer style corresponded to the shape of the vector mask.

Figure 38 Finished portrait made with vector mask

Morguefile

Create and combine shapes

1. Open PS 12-12.psd, then save it as **Shapes Skills**.
2. Click the Eyedropper tool on the word Enter to sample the lime green color, then save that green as a new color swatch on the Swatches panel.
3. Click the Eyedropper tool, then sample a pink color from the hummingbird.

4. Target the Background layer, click the Rectangle tool, then draw a rectangle behind the word Enter.
5. Name the new layer **Enter Button**.
6. On the Options panel, add a 4 px stroke with the same green color as the word Enter.
7. On the Properties panel, set all four corners to 12 px round corners.
8. Target the Background layer.

9. On the Options panel, click the Path operations button, then click Combine Shapes.
10. Click the Rectangle tool, then draw three green rectangles that resemble those shown in Figure 39. Because Combine Shapes was selected, all three rectangles are combined on one layer.
11. Click and drag the corner widget on the third rectangle until it looks like the oval shown in Figure 40.

Figure 39 Drawing three rectangles to be combined

Figure 40 Using round corners to create the center oval

12. Set the Fill color to None, then set the Stroke color to the lime green color.

Your canvas should resemble Figure 41.

13. Save your work.

Import shapes from Adobe Illustrator

1. Open PS 12-13.ai, select the blue shape, copy it, then close the file.

2. In the Shapes Skills file, target the All Type group layer, then click Paste.

3. In the Paste dialog box, click Shape Layer, then click OK.

4. Scale the shape 40%, then position it as shown in Figure 42.

5. Name the new layer **Water Flower**.

6. Open PS 12-14.psd, select all, copy, then close the file.

7. In the Shapes Skills file, target the Water Flower layer, then paste the artwork.

8. Name the new layer **Shimmer**, then clip it into the Water Flower layer.

9. Clip the Hummingbird layer into the Shimmer layer.

10. Target the Hummingbird layer, press and hold [command] [J] (Mac) or [Ctrl] [J] (Win) to duplicate the layer.

The duplicated Hummingbird layer is not clipped.

11. Mask the bottom of the bird so it is clipped by the flower shape and the bird appears to be flying out of the water.

Your canvas should resemble Figure 43, shown on the following page.

12. Save your work, then close Shape Skills.

Figure 41 Line artwork created by combining three shapes

Figure 42 Positioning the shape from Illustrator

Chelsea Sampson/Shutterstock.com

Figure 43 The final graphic

Draw a path around an image

1. Open PS 12-15.psd, then save it as **Path Skills**.
2. Click the Pen tool, then zoom in on point 1 at the bottom of the path.
3. Click the point and draw a handle in the direction of point 2.
   All of the points on the pylon are smooth points except points 5 and 13, which are corner points. Click and drag directional handles for all points except 5 and 13.
4. When you complete the path, save the Work Path as **Path 1**.
5. Delete the Template layer, then save the file.
6. Click the Path panel menu button, then click Make Selection.
7. Enter **0** in the Feather Radius text box, verify that Anti-aliased is checked, then click OK.
8. Add a new Hue/Saturation adjustment layer.
   The selection automatically generates a layer mask for the adjustment.
9. Drag the Hue slider to −33.
   Your image should resemble Figure 44.
10. Save your work, then close Path Skills.

Figure 44 Adjusting the hue on the artwork

Morguefile

Create a vector mask and save a file with a clipping path

1. Open PS 12-16.psd, then save it as **Clipping Path Skills**.

   When saving an image with a clipping path for use in Adobe InDesign or Illustrator, always save the file as a Photoshop (.psd) file.

2. Target Path 1 on the Paths panel.

3. Click Layer on the menu bar, point to Vector Mask, then click Current Path.

A vector mask is added to the layer.

4. Target the Background layer.

5. On the Paths panel, verify that Path 1 is targeted.

6. Click the Paths panel menu button, then click Clipping Path.

7. Type **3** in the Flatness text box, then click OK.

8. Save your work, then close Clipping Path Skills.

9. Open PS 12-17.indd, then save it as **Runaround the Sign**.

10. Click the picture box at the center of the page to select it.

11. Click File on the menu bar, then click Place.

12. Navigate to the Clipping Path Skills file, then click Open.

    The image appears in the picture box.

13. Click Object on the menu bar, point to Fitting, then click Fit Content Proportionally.

14. Click Window on the menu bar, then click Text Wrap.

15. Enter the settings shown in Figure 45.

16. Click the View menu, point to Screen Mode, then click Presentation.

    Your page should resemble Figure 46.

17. Press the [esc] key, save your work, then close the file.

Figure 45 Settings for the text wrap

Figure 46 InDesign uses clipping path information for the text wrap

This exercise provides you five images to trace with the Pen tool. Moving from left to right, each gets more challenging. The first is the urn you worked with in the chapter, so this is a chance to trace it a second time, this time without the numbered template. Four of the images have handles and negative spaces, so you will need to remember to set the Pen tool to exclude negative spaces. This exercise should take at least an hour (if not two) for you to complete. Put the time needed into cutting paths for these images. Doing so will help you hone these important and powerful skills.

1. Open PS 12-18.psd, then save it as **Five Paths**.
2. Click the Pen tool.
3. Click the Path Operations button on the Options panel, then click Exclude Overlapping Shapes. Because four of the five images have handles and therefore negative spaces, you need this setting to be active throughout your work.
4. Zoom in and make a path that traces the first image.
5. On the Paths panel, save the Work Path as **Path 1**.

6. Before starting the second path, click below Path 1 on the Paths panel to deselect it.
   If Path 1 were to remain targeted, the second path you draw would be added to Path 1. With Path 1 not targeted, Photoshop creates a new Work Path for the new path you draw.
7. Draw a path around the second image.

8. Draw a path around the inside of the handle.
9. On the Paths panel, save the Work Path as **Path 2**.
10. Using the same method, create and save **Paths 3**, **4**, and **5** for the remaining objects.
    When you are finished, your Paths panel should resemble Figure 47.
11. Save your work, then close Five Paths.

Figure 47 Five paths on the Paths panel

This project builder follows up on the previous set of steps. You will save one of the paths you drew as a clipping path, but in InDesign, you'll have to confront an issue involving negative space in a clipping path. This makes for a good lesson on the differences between how you might need a version of a clipping path to function differently in InDesign than it does in Photoshop.

1. Open PS 12-19.psd, then save it as **Clipping Path Test**.

   If you completed Project Builder 1, you may use your own completed file for this exercise instead of this data file. If you do, you'll see the runaround in InDesign around your own path that you created yourself.

2. Click the Paths panel menu button, then click Clipping Path.

3. Choose Path 4 as the clipping path, set the Flatness to 3, then click OK.

4. Save the file, then close it.

5. Open PS 12-17.indd, then save it as **Runaround the Pitcher**.

6. Click the picture box at the center of the page to select it.

7. Click File on the menu bar, then click Place.

8. Navigate to the Clipping Path Test file, then click Open. The image appears in the picture box.

9. Click Object on the menu bar, point to Fitting, then click Fit Content Proportionally.

10. On the Text Wrap panel, enter the settings shown in Figure 48.

As you can see in the figure, there's a problem. Text is appearing inside the handle of the pitcher because InDesign identifies it as available space outside the clipping path, no different than the space that surrounds the perimeter of the pitcher. You'll need to make a change on the Text Wrap panel.

11. In the Wrap Options section, click the Wrap To list arrow, then click Largest Area.

    InDesign changes to wrap the text only around the largest of the two paths, and the text no longer runs through the negative space inside the handle.

12. Save your work, then close Clipping Path Test.

Figure 48 Text appears inside the handle where it is not wanted

This chapter presented you with so many options and techniques for working with shapes, paths, and vector masks. In this project, you will consider all that you've learned and apply it to re-creating your own layout using the images and ideas from this chapter. You can make your own version of the football player exploding from a shape or a new business identity for the image of the spools of thread. Create a new splash page based on the line art layout with the hummingbird or ovals with shadows clipped into a vector mask like the vintage portrait. Feel free to use any images from this or previous chapters. The goal of the project is that you incorporate shapes or paths or vector masks (or all three) to make a new layout that is visually interesting and complex.

Figure 49 Projects to be rethought and recreated

CREATING COMPOSITIONS TO TELL A STORY

Jen Guyton and Piotr Naskrecki, Watering hole, Gorongosa National Park, Mozambique

Scott Randall / National
Geographic Image Collection

Jen Guyton always knew she wanted to travel to Africa. Her mother loved Africa, and Jen heard a lot about it as she was growing up. Jen went to Africa for the first time in 2008 to study abroad in Tanzania. In 2011, after a research internship in South Africa, Jen visited a friend in Mozambique and learned about Gorongosa.

THE GORONGOSA RESTORATION PROJECT

Gorongosa National Park was badly damaged by Mozambique's long civil war. From 1977 to 1992, ninety percent of the large animals in the park were wiped out, and most of the predator species completely disappeared. Even though some trees were cut down, the habitat was largely undisturbed. In other words, its foundation was still there. After the war ended, the park was protected and given a chance to recover. In 2009, philanthropist and entrepreneur Greg Carr set up the Gorongosa Restoration Project to support this effort.

Jen felt incredibly inspired by the opportunity to rebuild an ecosystem from the ground up. She became a PhD student of Gorongosa scientific advisor Dr. Rob Pringle in order to become involved with the project. She lived in Gorongosa for five years as a graduate student and for an additional year as a *National Geographic* Fulbright Storyteller Fellow, participating in and documenting the project's work.

BIODIVERSITY IN GORONGOSA

Jen has always had an interest in photography. She especially likes the ability of still images to communicate a lot of information in an instant. To tell the story of biodiversity returning to the park, Jen chose an image composite technique. She felt that with intentional use and clear labeling, a composite photo could tell the story better than a time-lapse video.

For the location, Jen selected the last watering hole in the riverbed at the end of the dry season. She wanted to show how many animals visited it during a specific period of time and how they used this scarce resource. To create the image, Jen set up a camera trap to take a photo every five seconds for twelve hours. With no human presence, the camera captured thousands of images of more than 20 species of animals and birds exhibiting natural behavior.

It took patience and three months of persistence to find exactly the right conditions, with consistent light throughout the day and a representative sample of animals. Jen selected and compiled about 35 images from a single 12-hour period for the composition. For scientific accuracy, she did not move the position of any animal. She did not show any individual animal more than once. And she included at least one individual of every species that visited that day. The resulting image tells the story of Gorongosa's rich diversity of species, how the species interact, and the importance of this scarce water resource to them all.

CHANGING HEARTS AND MINDS

An image has the power to change hearts and minds, and pictures spread via the Internet and social media can bring a story to a worldwide audience. The popularity and awareness of Gorongosa has risen dramatically in the past 10 years for just these reasons. Storytelling and media play a huge role in this, Jen says, both internationally to raise awareness and funds for conservation, and on the local level to encourage people living near the park to care about and protect it.

JEN'S POINTS OF INTEREST

1. There is a lot of repetition of species in the composition, for example, the antelopes. The recurrence of the animals and their positions communicate a lot about their behavior in that specific environment.

2. The lighting and shadowing on the trees differ, which indicates that the activity is taking place over a period of time.

3. The still image captures a multitude of animals and displays them throughout the frame. Jen chose to include the baboons that are sitting up front in the right hand corner in order to make the viewer feel immersed in the scene.

PROJECT DESCRIPTION

In this project, you will analyze and respond to Jen's image. You'll have the opportunity to investigate the different elements of the image and interpret the story for yourself. Look at the photo closely. Take note of anything that catches your attention. You'll be writing a brief analysis, consisting of your observations, your interpretation of the story, any questions that come to mind, and the messages you take away. If you can, talk to your classmates and discuss your ideas. Decide which elements of the photo are impactful to you, and write a brief analysis of your findings.

QUESTIONS TO CONSIDER

What is the story?

What stands out to you?

What would you change? Why?

What questions do you have?

What caught your attention first?

Is there anything that seems confusing?

Do you like the image?

USE SOME OF THESE VOCABULARY WORDS

Asymmetrical: Parts that don't correspond to one another in shape, size, or arrangement; lacking symmetry.

Symmetrical: Made up of identical parts facing each other or around an axis.

Pattern: Repeated elements.

Repetition: Using a single element multiple times in a design.

Alignment: Being in correct or appropriate positions.

Variety: Purposeful absence of uniformity to create visual interest.

Harmony: Using similar elements in a scene.

GETTING STARTED

Start with the big picture, then work through the details. Glance over the whole image, taking in the overall feel and tone. Write down what you think the overarching theme and story might be. Then start to pick apart the details. Consider what elements make up the composition and how they interact with the space and each other.

Notice the biodiversity. There are various animals and environmental elements that make up this composition. Take note of the ones that stand out to you and the ones you have questions about.

This composition has a multitude of elements to analyze and take in. Identify different focal points to help break apart and absorb the story. For example, focus on the animals in the water first, and write down the messages you glean from that area.

SKILLS YOU'LL PRACTICE

Critical thinking

Giving feedback

Design analysis

Writing

Using design vocabulary

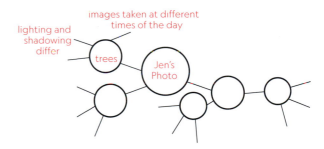

One way to organize your thoughts is with a graphic organizer. Here's an example of how you might use an idea web to capture your thoughts about the photo.

PROJECT DESCRIPTION

In this project, you will explore how to visually restore and tell the story of a damaged or changed location, environment, or ecosystem.

You will be creating a pair of still images using a collage technique that depicts an environment, what lives and frequents that particular place, why they do so, and how the environment has changed. One of your compositions should represent your chosen location from 10 to 50 years ago, while the other composition will represent your chosen location at present.

The goal of this project is to show the vast amount of life that exists in an individual location and how change occurs over time.

SKILLS TO EXPLORE

- Work with the layers panel
- Flatten and merge layers
- Create and move selections
- Explore content aware tool
- Cut and paste elements
- Use magic wand selection
- Work with channels panel
- Apply layer styles

FILES YOU'LL USE

- Ps_u3_reef.JPEG
- Ps_u3_nationalpark.JPEG
- Ps_u3_pollution.JPEG
- Ps_u3_city.JPEG

You will use Photoshop for this project to create an image that is inspired by Jen's photo composite work.

SKILLS CHALLENGE
EASY CUT AND PASTE OF A SELECTION FROM ONE IMAGE TO ANOTHER

Step 1: Use a selection tool to select the object you want to cut. You can use any of the lasso tools, the magic wand tool, or quick selection tools.

Step 2: Once you have selected the area you want to cut (you should see "marching ants" around the area), select Cut from the Edit menu.

Step 3: Open the composition you would like to paste the cut selection into and then select Paste from the Edit menu.

FOLLOW JEN'S EXAMPLE

1. Ask questions – a lot of questions. Sometimes the best way to find answers is by focusing on a few details, asking questions about them, then exploring them until they lead you to more information.

2. Find connections. When you feel like you've answered a question, don't move on. Use it as a launching pad to ask another question and find the connections and patterns between multiple variables.

GETTING STARTED

1. Using what is available to you, find out what your chosen location looked like many years ago. Compare that to an image or description of the location now. Look at the images side by side and mark them up. Compare and contrast the various elements that are present and/or absent in the images.

2. Map out your layout and establish your grid. You will likely be working with a vast amount of elements for your collaged still image, so planning a layout or grid will help you keep everything balanced and in harmony.

Inspired by an image of a reef, the student sketched points of interest to help bring focus to the vast topic.

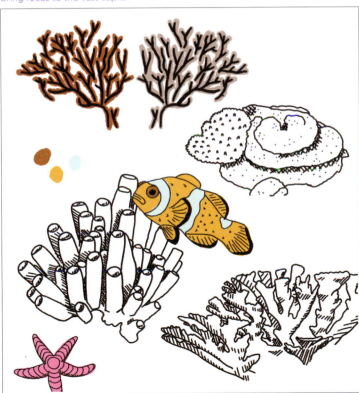

3. Exhaust your list of possible images. Create a folder on your local desktop or online drive. Search for images and articles about your location, and save any imagery, colors, patterns, text, and other resources you feel communicate the story to that folder. Don't worry about organization. Once you think you have enough to work with, go through all of your saved files and decide which ones you'll use as inspiration for your work.

After deciding to focus on reefs, the student brainstormed a possible grid and explored symmetry and color as ways to communicate change over time.

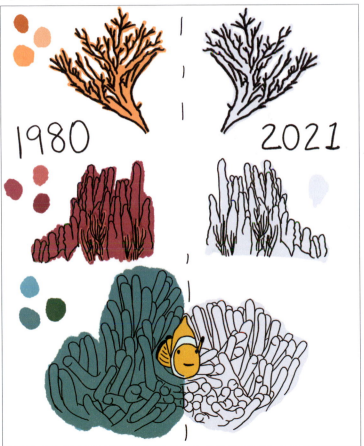

PROJECT DESCRIPTION

In this project, you will continue your exploration of visual restoration by telling a story of a location within your own community. This could be your classroom, the gym, your home, etc.

You will be creating a single still image using a collage technique that focuses on the life and activity of a familiar place. You will need to communicate information about the people, the objects and elements present in that particular location, and, most importantly, what role this place plays in your community.

The goal of this project is to create a composition that will teach viewers about a specific location and give them a better understanding of the biodiversity, importance, and activity of that location.

SKILLS TO EXPLORE

- Adjust layer opacity and fill opacity
- Create and manipulate masks
- Use level adjustments
- Apply autocorrection methods
- Explore hue and saturation
- Explore tools to repair and reconstruct images
- Create custom layer styles
- Use guides and grids

THINK LIKE JEN

1. Be patient and persistent. Communicating a complex story in a single still image is no easy task. Allow yourself time to test out ideas and get feedback.

2. Adjust your strategy. While doing your research and gathering information, you might discover something that you didn't know, or might uncover a pattern you didn't intentionally seek out. That's great! Run with it. Not all interesting stories are planned. Be flexible and adjust your original idea if needed.

SKILLS CHALLENGE
REPAIR AN AREA USING SAMPLED PIXELS

Step 1: Select the patch tool.

Step 2: Drag in the image to select the area you want to repair, then select Source in the options bar.

Step 3: Adjust the selection by holding down shift and dragging in the image to add to the existing selection.

Step 4: To extract the texture, select Transparent and adjust the Diffusion slider. Use a lower value for images with grain or a higher value for smooth images.

Step 5: Select your source image in the options bar, drag the selection border to the area from which you want to sample. When you release the mouse button, the originally selected area is patched with the sampled pixels.

GETTING STARTED

1. Brainstorm and create an exhaustive list of local places you might be interested in. Then cut that list in half so it only includes the places more familiar to you. This will help you narrow in on your topic and conduct efficient research.

2. This project is a great opportunity to try field research. Take a walk around your community, and note some places that might be of interest to you. Observe each location and keep a record of some of the activity going on. These initial observations might spark an interesting story.

3. When working on a story that involves various people and activities, it is crucial to gain different perspectives. Collaborate with classmates, teachers, and other people in your community to ensure an accurate picture.

To gain a unique perspective, the student walked around the park sketching different elements of the environment.

The student created a list of familiar places, then sketched possible scenes after deciding to focus on the park.

Robbie Shone, First water inlet, entrance passages of Veryovkina, the deepest cave in the world

© Robbie Shone

CHAPTER **13**

WORK WITH
SMART OBJECTS, ARTBOARDS, LIBRARIES, PATTERNS, AND WEB GRAPHICS

1. Export Layers from Illustrator to Photoshop
2. Work with Smart Objects
3. Work with Artboards and Libraries
4. Design Patterns
5. Prepare an Image for the Web

Adobe Certified Professional in Visual Design Using Photoshop CC Framework

2. Project Setup and Interface
This objective covers the interface setup and program settings that assist in an efficient and effective workflow, as well as knowledge about ingesting digital assets for a project.

2.4 Import assets into a project.
> **B** Place assets in a Photoshop document.

3. Organizing Documents
This objective covers document structure such as layers and managing document structure for efficient workflows.

3.1 Use layers to manage design elements.
> **C** Recognize the different types of layers in the Layers panel.

4. Creating and Modifying Visual Elements
This objective covers core tools and functionality of the application, as well as tools that affect the visual appearance of document elements.

4.1 Use core tools and features to create visual elements.
> **B** Create and edit vector images.

4.3 Make, manage, and manipulate selections.
> **A** Make selections using a variety of tools.

4.6 Modify the appearance of design elements by using filters and styles.
> **A** Use filters to modify images destructively or nondestructively.

EXPORT LAYERS FROM ILLUSTRATOR TO PHOTOSHOP

Exporting Layers from Illustrator

Adobe has done a lot to empower Photoshop's abilities for creating vector graphics. The shape tools are smart and versatile, and they provide you with enough options to get most of your vector work done without needing to leave Photoshop.

That said, Adobe Illustrator remains Adobe's powerhouse vector graphics software package, and there are so many things you can do in Illustrator that you can't do anywhere else, including in Photoshop.

When you make the commitment to learn Illustrator, your options in Photoshop multiply exponentially. In Chapter 9, you used Offset Path artwork from Illustrator to create the Jazz 2096 artwork in Photoshop. The Offset Path command exists only in Illustrator, and a complex piece of typographic art like the Jazz 2096 illustration can be created only with Illustrator being involved.

Like Photoshop, Illustrator has a Layers panel to organize and manage complex artwork on individual layers. Illustrator also offers the ability to export layers to Photoshop. The Export As command allows you to save Illustrator artwork as a Photoshop file in the PSD file format. As part of that export, you can choose to convert layers from the Illustrator file to layers in the exported Photoshop file. To export as layers, the Illustrator document color mode must be RGB.

Export layered artwork from Adobe Illustrator

1. Open PS 13-1.ai in Adobe Illustrator, then open the Layers panel.

   The artwork is composed of six layers.

2. Click **File** on the menu bar, then point to **Document Color Mode**.

3. Notice that **RGB** has been chosen as the color mode for this file, then release the mouse pointer.

   To export as layers, the Illustrator document color mode must be RGB.

4. Click **File** on the menu bar, point to **Export**, then click **Export As**.

   The Export dialog box opens. This is where you choose a file format, name your file, and choose where to store it.

5. Choose a destination folder for the file, click the **Format menu list arrow**, click **Photoshop (.PSD)**, then click **Export**.

   The Photoshop Export Options dialog box opens. Notice the Write Layers option button. This must be selected to export Illustrator layers as Photoshop layers.

6. Enter the settings shown in Figure 1, then click **OK**.

   The file named PS 13-1.psd is saved in your destination folder.

7. Navigate to the destination file, then open PS 13-1.psd in Photoshop.

   As shown in Figure 2, the file opens in Photoshop with all the layers from Illustrator.

8. Close PS 13-1.psd.

You used the Export As command in Adobe Illustrator to export layered Illustrator artwork as a layered RGB Photoshop document.

Figure 1 The Photoshop Export Options dialog box with the Write Layers option selected

Figure 2 Layered artwork from Illustrator layered in Photoshop

WORK WITH SMART OBJECTS

▶ **What You'll Do**

In this lesson, you'll use smart objects to explore various methods for editing nondestructively.

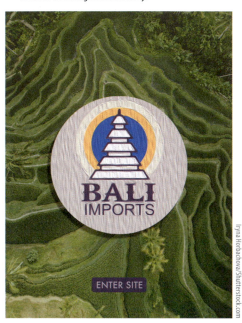

Iryna Horbachova/Shutterstock.com

Understanding Smart Objects and Nondestructive Editing

Nondestructive editing entails the work you do to a Photoshop file that is not permanent. The edits you made can be removed, and all images in the file can be restored to their original appearance.

Adjustment layers are a fundamental example of nondestructive editing. Rather than applying a Hue/Saturation or a Levels adjustment directly to an image, you use adjustment layers because they can be hidden or shown, and they can be deleted. Using adjustment layers, the image itself is never directly altered. The adjustment layers only change its appearance. If you hide or remove the adjustment layers, you'll see the original image again.

Converting an image to a smart object is another way to apply nondestructive operations to an image. **Smart objects** are layers that contain image data from raster or vector images, such as Photoshop or Illustrator files. Smart objects preserve an image's source content with all its original characteristics, enabling you to perform nondestructive editing to the layer.

For example, let's say you have artwork composed of 10 image layers and three adjustment layers. When you convert all those layers to a smart object, they become a single layer. You can do all kinds of operations to the smart object layer, including transformations, applying filters, distortions, and so on. What's important to understand is that none of the operations done to a smart object are destructive or necessarily permanent. The smart object is like a pointer to the original artwork, which remains unaltered. You can double-click the smart object, which will open the original layered artwork in a separate window. Any changes you make and save to the original artwork will be updated to the smart object. Smart objects give you the option to get back to where you started.

Pasting a Smart Object from Illustrator

Imagine your company's logo has been designed in Adobe Illustrator, and you have used that logo in hundreds of Photoshop files showcasing your company's products. Your company is going through a rebranding process, and you need to replace the old logo in all those Photoshop files with your new, rebranded logo. If you've used that logo in those Photoshop files, the changes will be fast and easy. If not, you will have a lot of work ahead of you.

When you paste an Illustrator file in Photoshop, you can paste it as a smart object. Once you do, you can scale it, distort it, apply adjustments to it, apply filters to it—you can pretty much do to it all that Photoshop has to offer. However, because it is a smart object, the original Illustrator vector artwork remains both untouched and accessible. Simply double-click the smart object on the Layers panel, and the original vector artwork opens in a separate file. Make any changes you like—for example, your company's rebranded identity. Then save the changes, and the artwork will be updated in the Photoshop file. The smartest way to use Illustrator artwork in a Photoshop file is to place it as a smart object, because no matter what you do to it, you can always rely on having access to the original artwork.

Scaling in Photoshop with Smart Objects

When working with digital images, it is important to remember that scaling changes the quality of the image. When the size of an image is reduced, pixels are discarded to achieve the reduction. Therefore, the image is rendered with fewer pixels than it was prior to the reduction.

Enlarging an image forces Photoshop to create new pixels to achieve the enlargement. Photoshop uses the existing pixel data to create the new pixels by a process known as **interpolation**. Thus, the enlarged image is composed of pixels that were not originally captured in the camera when the image was captured. The result is a lowering of the image's quality. Images with interpolated data will be blurred and will lack sharpness and fine detail.

Converting an image to a smart object makes it possible to scale an image with no loss in quality. Let's say you have an image in a layered file, and you reduce the image by 50%. If the image has been converted to a smart object, no data is lost with the reduction. The image appears to be half size, but no pixels are discarded to achieve the reduction. Therefore, the image can be enlarged to any size up to 100% with no loss of data or quality.

Enlarging an image beyond 100% of its original size requires interpolation, regardless of whether or not it has been converted to a smart object. However, with a smart object, if you restore the enlarged image back to 100%, it will be unchanged from its original status. In other words, it will be like reverting the image to what it was before any scaling was applied. Therefore, when working with layered artwork, it's always a good idea to convert every component image of the file to a smart object.

Merging Layers in Photoshop into Smart Objects

As you have seen throughout this book, complex Photoshop projects can result in files with dozens and even hundreds of layers. Often, all those layers can become cumbersome to manage.

You can convert layered artwork into a single smart object on one layer without losing access to the layers. This enables you to work with the single smart object layer with ease. You can transform it, apply adjustments and filters, and generally work with it like any other image in Photoshop. However, as a smart object, the single layer can be opened in a separate file with all the component layers accessible to be edited. After saving your work, all changes to the layers will be updated to the single smart object layer.

Paste Illustrator artwork as a smart object

1. Open PS 13-2.ai in Illustrator, select all, then copy.

2. Open PS 13.3.psd in Photoshop, then save it as **Illustrator Smart Object**.

3. Click **Edit** on the menu bar, then click **Paste**.

   The Paste dialog box opens.

4. Click **Smart Object**, then click **OK**.

   The artwork is pasted inside a bounding box.

5. Press **[return] (Mac)** or **[Enter] (Win)** to convert the pasted artwork to a smart object.

   The artwork is pasted as a smart object and named Vector Smart Object on the Layers panel. The smart object icon appears in the lower-right corner of the layer's thumbnail.

6. Press [**command**] **[T] (Mac)** or **[Ctrl] [T] (Win)**, scale the artwork **43%** on the Options panel, then press **[return] (Mac)** or **[Enter] (Win)**.

7. Name the new layer **BALI IMPORTS LOGO**.

8. Use any settings you wish to add a drop shadow layer style to the artwork.

   The pasted artwork functions like any other Photoshop element. You can apply layer styles, transformations, filters, and so on.

9. Click **Filter** on the menu bar, point to **Stylize**, then click **Oil Paint**.

10. Enter the settings shown in Figure 3, then click **OK**.

    Because the layer is already a smart object, the Oil Paint filter is applied as a smart filter—complete with a layer mask, should you need it.

11. Double-click the **thumbnail** on the **BALI IMPORTS LOGO layer**.

A new window opens in Adobe Illustrator. By default, the new window is named Vector Smart Object.ai. The artwork in the window is the original vector graphic. The smart object in Photoshop is based on this vector artwork, so any changes you make here will update the artwork in Photoshop.

Figure 3 Settings for the Oil Paint filter

12. Click the **Selection tool** ▶ on the toolbar, then click to select the **smaller of the two orange circles** on the artwork.

13. Click a **royal blue swatch** on the Swatches panel to give the selected object a blue fill.

14. Close the file and save changes when you are prompted to do so.

15. Return to Photoshop.

    As shown in Figure 4, the artwork in Photoshop is automatically updated with the new blue fill. The drop shadow layer style and the Oil Paint filter remain in place.

16. Save your work, then close Illustrator Smart Object.

You pasted artwork from Illustrator in Photoshop as a smart object. You applied a drop shadow layer style and a filter to the artwork, noting that the filter was automatically applied as a smart filter. You then double-clicked the artwork, which opened the original vector artwork in Illustrator. You made a color change, saved the file, and then returned to Photoshop to view the updated change.

Figure 4 Changes to the smart object are automatically updated

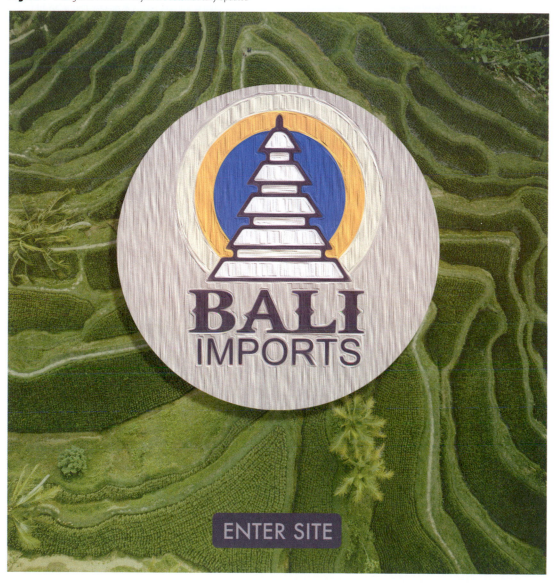

Scaling artwork as a smart object

1. Open PS 13-4.psd, then save it as **Scaling Smart Objects**.

   This artwork was created from scratch in Photoshop at this size. It has never been resized.

2. Target the **Left layer**, then enter **[command] [T] (Mac)** or **[Ctrl] [T] (Win)** to show the transform bounding box.

3. On the Options panel, verify that the **Maintain aspect ratio button**  is pressed, type **10** in the **W** and **H** text boxes, then press **[return] (Mac)** or **[Enter] (Win)**.

   The artwork is scaled to 10% of its original size; 90% of the original pixel data has been discarded.

4. Using the same steps, scale the artwork **1000%** to return it to its original size.

   As shown in Figure 5, the quality of the artwork is so degraded that it is unusable. The interpolation required to scale the image 1000% has resulted in an image that is 90% interpolated data.

5. Target the **Right layer**, click the **Layers panel menu button** ☰, then click **Convert to Smart Object**.

   The smart object icon appears at the lower-right corner of the layer's thumbnail.

6. Scale the **Right artwork 10%**.

7. Enter **[command] [T] (Mac)** or **[Ctrl] [T] (Win)** to show the transform bounding box.

8. On the Options panel, type **100** in the **W** and **H text boxes**.

   When scaling smart objects, the percentage you enter always relates back to its original size. Therefore, to scale this smart object back to its original size, you are returning it to 100% as opposed to scaling it 1000% as you did the non-smart object.

9. Press **[return] (Mac)** or **[Enter] (Win)**.

   The scaled artwork is in no way degraded and appears as it did in Figure 5. Pixel data is not interpolated when scaling smart objects, as long as the scale percentage is 100% or lower. When you scaled the smart object to 10%, only its physical size changed; no data was discarded. Therefore, when you returned it to 100%, there was no change.

10. Save your work, then close Scaling Smart Objects.

You scaled the first piece of artwork to 10%, then scaled it back to its original size, noting that the quality of the image degraded substantially. You converted the second piece of artwork to a smart object then applied the same two scales. The scaling had no negative impact on the artwork because pixel data is not interpolated when smart objects are scaled less than 100% of their original size.

Figure 5 Severe degradation of the image after scaling

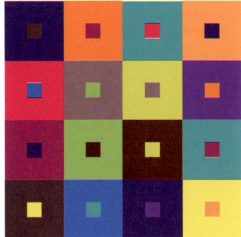

Merging layered artwork into a smart object

1. Open King's Wager.psd.

   This is the finished file from Chapter 11, complete with all the layers used to render the final image.

2. Open PS 13-5.psd, then save it as **iPad**.

   The challenge of this exercise is to place the poster artwork into the iPad to show a potential client how the artwork would appear in a real-world setting.

   TIP For this exercise, it's best if these are the only two files you have open in Photoshop.

3. Return to King's Wager.psd.

4. Target **all** the **layers** on the Layer's panel, click the **Layers panel menu button** ☰, then click **Convert to Smart Object**.

   All the layers are merged into a single smart object layer named Billing. Working with just one layer will be dramatically easier and more straightforward than working with the dozens of layers in the original document.

5. Rename the layer **Poster Smart Object**.

6. Click **Window** on the menu bar, point to **Arrange**, then click **2-up Vertical**.

   The two windows are positioned side by side.

7. Drag and drop the **Poster Smart Object layer** from the Layers panel in the King's Wager file into the iPad file.

   To move a smart object layer from one file to another, it must be dragged and dropped between the files. If you try to copy and paste it, the smart object would be pasted as traditional pixels, not a smart object.

8. Close the King's Wager file without saving changes.

9. In the iPad file, show the **Green Screen layer**, then clip the **Poster Smart Object layer** into the **Green Screen layer**.

10. Rotate the artwork **14.5%** (clockwise), then scale it **46%**.

11. Execute the transformation.

Your transformation should resemble Figure 6. Note that the type elements at the top and the bottom of the artwork are uncomfortably close to the edge of the iPad, and the artwork would look better for this presentation without them.

Continued on next page

Figure 6 Positioning the smart object inside the iPad artwork

xMarshall/Shutterstock.com

12. Double-click the **thumbnail** on the **Poster Smart Object layer**.

    A new window named Billing.psb opens, showing the poster as layered artwork.

13. Delete the **Billing layer**.

14. Target the **Noise layer**, click the **Create new fill or adjustment layer button**  on the Layers panel, then click **Hue/Saturation**.

    A Hue/Saturation layer is added.

15. On the Properties panel, drag the **Saturation slider** to **+20**.

16. Close the Billing.psb file, then save changes when prompted.

    As shown in Figure 7, the artwork in the iPad file is updated with the changes. The type at the top and bottom are gone, and the image is more saturated, as you would expect from a screen display.

17. Save your work, then close iPad.psd.

Your challenge was to paste a complex, multilayered document into another image. Rather than working with all those layers, you merged the entire document into one smart object. You dragged the smart object into the destination file, rotated it, and scaled it. Because it's a smart object, you were able to open it as a layered file, remove a layer, and add an adjustment layer.

Figure 7 Changes to the smart object automatically updated

WORK WITH ARTBOARDS AND LIBRARIES

What You'll Do

In this lesson, you'll use artboards to create canvases of different sizes in one document and use libraries to transfer and update artwork on the artboards.

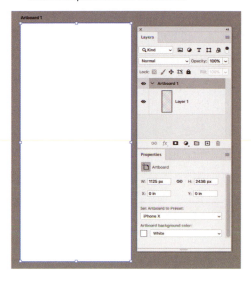

Understanding Artboards

Photoshop projects come in all shapes and sizes, and it's exactly for that reason—shapes and sizes—that artboards become so valuable. **Artboards** are multiple design layouts within one document. Some people refer to them as clipped containers, and others like to think of them as a type of layer group. Both descriptions are accurate. You can also think of artboards as multiple canvases with different dimensions all in one document window. Imagine you are designing 12 pages for a website. The pages are all unique, but they share the same elements, such as buttons, logos, and background images. You will have to copy and paste many of these shared elements from page to page and be sure to keep a consistent look and feel between pages.

Imagine trying to work on this project using 12 different Photoshop documents. You'd need to keep all 12 documents open simultaneously, and you'd be constantly clicking between them, having to remember which one you're in. With 12 individual documents open, there's no order of documents, so if you wanted to see the 12 pages as they progress through the site, you'd need to click through each file using only the filename to know you're doing so in the right order.

Working with artboards solves these and other challenges when working on multiple files at once. Artboards allow you to create multiple canvases at multiple sizes in one document. You can position the canvases in any orientation you like, for example, you might organize them sequentially from left to right. When you need to, you can drag and drop artwork from one artboard to another.

Figure 8 shows a layout of four artboards for four different devices: an Android 8 phone, a Microsoft Surface computer, a 38 mm Apple watch, and a 13" MacBook Pro. Photoshop offers dozens of preset templates for devices such as these, so generating artboards for them is quick and easy.

Note that all four artboards are in one document, and all are listed separately on the Layers panel. When you want to work on any given artboard, simply target the artboard layer on the Layers panel. Artboards are like group layers and contain all the artwork for that artboard.

Creating Artboards

When you create a new document, the New Document dialog box offers six categories of projects from which you can choose: Photo, Print, Art & Illustration, Web, Mobile, and Film & Video. Artboards are available for all six categories; however, when you choose Web or Mobile, the Artboards check box is automatically checked. This is because these two categories typically require multiple pages and sizes.

Figure 8 Four artboards in one document

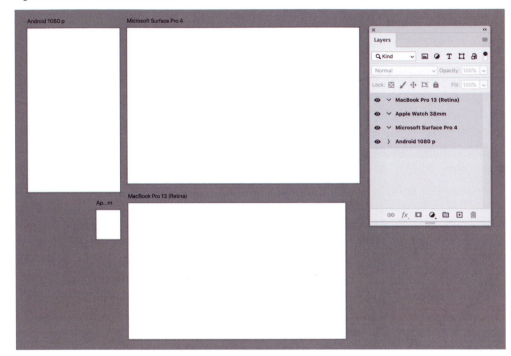

Figure 9 shows the New Document dialog box with the Mobile category selected and three mobile artboard templates below. On the right side are size specifications for the targeted template, the iPhone 8/7/6 Plus.

Once you create a document with an artboard, you have many options for creating additional artboards. One way is to click New on the Layer menu, then click Artboard. The New Artboard dialog box opens, shown in Figure 10, with a menu of all the preset templates for you to choose from.

Another way is to use the Artboard tool. The Artboard tool is positioned with the Move tool on the toolbar. You can create a custom-sized artboard simply by dragging the Artboard tool. When you do, the Options panel will list the same preset templates for you to choose from if you want to convert your custom artboard to a standard preset. You can move artboards around the document window using the Move tool.

Working with Libraries

The Libraries panel is one of the most powerful features in Adobe Creative Cloud. **Libraries** are created and kept in the Libraries panel. They allow you to store artwork you use often—such as a logo, a title treatment, or a repeating image—and make it available to be used in other documents. For example,

Figure 9 New Document dialog box with the Mobile category selected and available templates

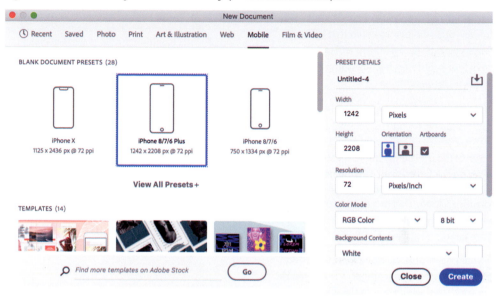

Figure 10 New Artboard dialog box

rather than everyone at the one company having to download the same logo file, it can be put into a library, where it will be available to everyone who has access to that library. Since you can share a library with anyone you choose, libraries become a great way for distributing documents.

You can add all kinds of artwork to a library, including images, type, adjustment layers, fill layers, patterns, shapes, and vector illustrations from Adobe Illustrator. Artwork placed in libraries is automatically converted to smart objects and stored in your account on Adobe Creative Cloud. This means the artwork is saved independently from any file you might have open.

You have two options when using artwork from a library in a document. If you drag the artwork from the library to the document, a link between the artwork in the document and the smart object in the library is established, which means if you alter the smart object in the library—change its colors, for example—the changes you make will be updated to all instances of that artwork in any open document. Linked artwork in closed documents will not be automatically updated. Instead, when you open those documents, you will be alerted that the library artwork has been modified and offered the option to update it.

You can also use artwork from a library *without* linking it. If you press and hold [option] (Mac) or [Alt] (Win) when dragging

artwork from a library into a document, no link will be created.

The option to link artwork from various documents to a library item is what makes libraries so powerful, especially for large-scale and multipage projects. Let's say you have been hired to design a website for a client, and you are working with a document that has 25 artboards, all of which have the client's logo. Should the client ask you to make changes to that logo and it is a library item, you could simply change the logo in the library, and it would change instantly on all 25 artboards. What a powerful solution!

Create artboards

1. In Photoshop, verify that no documents are open, click **File** on the menu bar, then click **New**.

2. At the top of the New Document dialog box, click **Mobile**.

   Preset sizes for various mobile devices are listed.

3. Click the **iPhone X preset**.

   As shown in Figure 11, the Width, Height, and Resolution text boxes on the right-hand side are for an iPhone X screen, and the Color Mode is RGB Color, which is standard for any on-screen presentation.

Figure 11 iPhone X artboard preset in the New Document dialog box

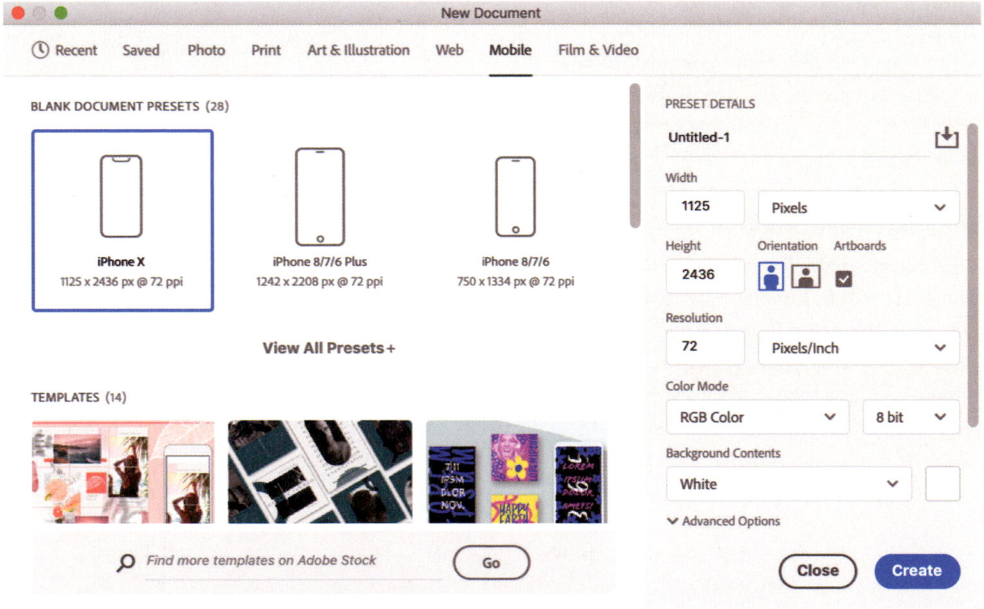

4. Click **Create**.

As shown in Figure 12, the new artboard, named Artboard 1, appears in the document window. The Artboard 1 layer appears on the Layers panel and includes one empty layer, named Layer 1. The Properties panel lists the preset size as iPhone X along with the preset pixel dimensions for width and height.

5. Rename the **Artboard 1 layer** on the Layers panel to **iPhone X**.

The name of the artboard is updated.

6. Click the **Artboard tool** ⬚, which is located behind the **Move tool** ✛ on the toolbar.

When an artboard is targeted on the Layers panel, clicking the Artboard tool causes plus signs to appear on four sides of the targeted artboard.

7. Click the **plus sign** to the right of the iPhone X artboard.

A duplicate artboard named Artboard 1 appears.

8. On the Properties panel, click the **Set Artboard to Preset list arrow**, then click **iPad Pro 12.9 in**.

9. On the Layers panel, change the name to **iPad Pro**.

Note that the new artboard was created without a layer. Only the artboard created with the New Document dialog box has a default layer.

10. Verify that the **Artboard tool** ⬚ is selected on the toolbar.

11. Click the **plus sign** ⊕ to the right of the iPad Pro artboard.

12. On the Options panel, click the **Size list arrow**, then click **Apple Watch 42mm**.

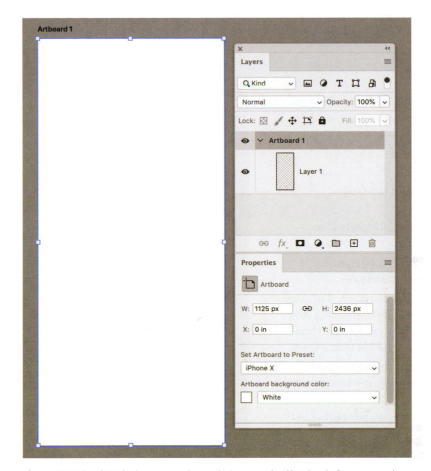

Figure 12 Artboard 1 in the document window, on the Layers panel and listed on the Properties panel

The new artboard changes to the size of a 42 mm Apple watch face.

13. Change the name of the artboard to **Apple Watch**.

14. Save the file as **Apple Layouts.psd**, and keep it open for the next set of steps.

You created three different artboards in one document. You used the Properties panel to set one to a preset for an iPad, and you used the Options panel to set the other to a preset for an Apple Watch. You noted that when you create new artboards, they are not created with layers.

Use libraries to store and transfer artwork

1. Open PS 13-6.psd, then save it as **Bali Imports Splash Screen**.

2. Target the **BALI IMPORTS LOGO layer**, click the **Layers panel menu button** ≡, then click **Convert to Smart Object**.

3. Click **Window** on the menu bar, then click **Libraries**.

4. On the **Libraries panel**, click **Create new library**.

5. Name the new library **Bali Imports**, then click **Create**.

6. Drag the **BALI IMPORTS LOGO layer** from the Layers panel into the Libraries panel.

   A thumbnail appears on the Libraries panel named BALI IMPORTS LOGO. On the Layers panel, a cloud icon appears on the layer, indicating it has been copied to your account on Adobe Creative Cloud.

7. Target the **Gradient layer**, click the **Layers panel menu button** ≡, then click **Convert to Smart Object**.

8. Drag the **Gradient logo** into the Libraries panel.

9. Click **File** on the menu bar, click **Save**, then close **Bali Imports Splash Screen**.

   The Libraries panel remains open.

10. In the Apple Layouts file, target the **iPhone X artboard** on the Layers panel.

11. Drag the **gradient artwork** from the Libraries panel onto the **iPhone X artboard**.

    The gradient artwork appears in a bounding box at the width of the iPhone X artboard.

12. Stretch the artwork so it covers the entire length of the iPhone X artboard, then press **[return] (Mac)** or **[Enter] (Win)** to execute the transformation.

Your canvas should resemble Figure 13. Note that on the Layers panel, the Gradient layer on the iPhone X artboard has a cloud icon on its thumbnail.

Figure 13 Gradient artwork on the iPhone X artboard

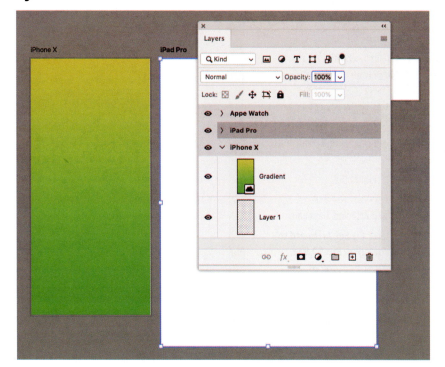

13. Target the **Apple Watch artboard** on the Layers panel, then drag the **gradient artwork** from the Libraries panel onto the **Apple Watch artboard**.

The gradient is added as a new layer on the Apple Watch artboard and has a cloud icon on its thumbnail.

14. Press and hold **[option] (Mac)** or **[Alt] (Win)**, then drag the **gradient artwork** from the Libraries panel onto the **iPad Pro artboard**, then use the **Move tool** 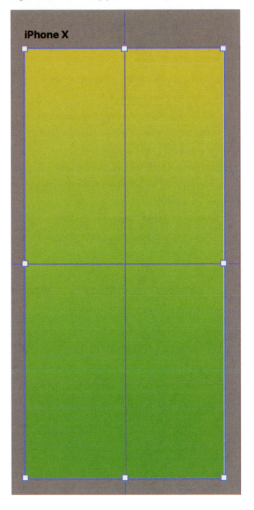 to position it so it fills the artboard.

Because you pressed and held [option] (Mac) or [Alt] (Win) when dragging the gradient artwork from the library, it is not linked to the Creative Cloud library. Note that there is no cloud icon on the Layers panel for the Gradient layer on the iPad artboard.

15. Save your work, then continue to the next set of steps.

You dragged the gradient artwork from the Libraries panel onto the iPhone and Apple Watch artboards—which, by default, creates a link to the Creative Cloud library. Then by holding [option] (Mac) or [Alt] (Win) as you dragged the gradient artwork onto the iPad layout, you did not create a link to the Creative Cloud library.

Create guides for artboards

1. Click **View** on the menu bar, point to **Show**, then verify that **Guides** is checked.

2. Verify that rulers are also showing.

TIP If you do not see rulers, click View on the menu bar, then click Rulers.

3. Target the **iPhone X artboard**.

When an artboard is targeted, a bounding box appears, making it easy to align guides to the vertical and horizontal centers of the artboard.

4. Drag a **vertically centered guide** and a **horizontally centered guide**, as shown in Figure 14.

The guides affect only the targeted artboard.

5. Repeat Step 4 to add guides to the iPad artboard.

Continued on next page

Figure 14 Intersecting guides on the targeted artboard

6. Target the **Apple Watch artboard**, click **View** on the menu bar, then click **Fit Artboard on Screen**.

   Only the Apple Watch artboard is in view.

7. Add **two centered guides** to the **Apple Watch artboard**.

   It is easier to add guides to the Apple Watch artboard at full screen size.

8. Click **View** on the menu bar, then click **Fit on Screen** to return to viewing all three artboards in the document window.

9. Drag the **BALI IMPORTS LOGO** from the Bali Imports library to the **center of each artboard**, scaling them as necessary.

   Your canvas should resemble Figure 15.

10. Save your work, then continue to the next set of steps.

You used the bounding boxes on each targeted artboard to position guides to identify the center of each artboard. You then dragged the logo artwork onto each artboard.

Figure 15 Logo artwork on all artboards

Modify library artwork

1. On the Libraries panel, double-click the **Gradient thumbnail**.

   As shown in Figure 16, the Libraries panel changes to show a thumbnail of the artwork and other information.

2. Click the **Open source document** icon ✎ at the top of the panel, then click **Edit**.

   The gradient artwork opens in a new window named Gradient.psb.

3. Click **Image** on the menu bar, point to **Adjustments**, then click **Invert**.

4. Close the Gradient.psb file, then click **Save** when you are prompted.

   As shown in Figure 17, the gradient artwork on the iPhone X and Apple Watch artboards is updated with the change. The gradient on the iPad artboard is not updated because it was not linked to the library when it was added to that artboard.

   Continued on next page

Figure 16 Gradient artwork on the Libraries panel

Figure 17 Gradient artwork updated on two artboards

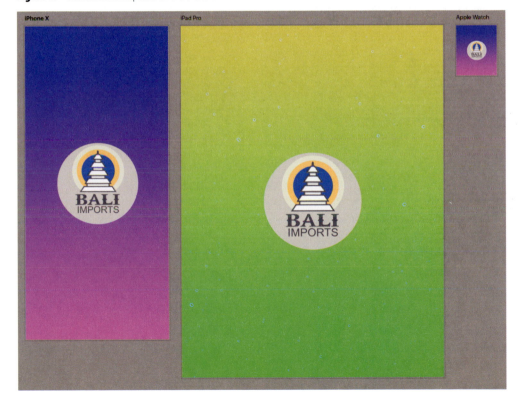

5. Save your work, then continue to the next set of steps.

You modified the gradient artwork on the Libraries panel and noted that the change was automatically updated on the iPhone X and Apple Watch artboards but not updated on the iPad artboard because it was not linked.

Export artboards as individual files

1. Click **File** on the menu bar, point to **Export**, then click **Artboards to Files**.

2. Click the **Browse button**, navigate to where you save your solution files, then click **Open**.

3. Enter the settings shown in Figure 18, then click **Run**.

As shown in Figure 19, an individual PSD file is created for each artboard.

4. Save the Apple Layouts file, then close it.

You exported the artboards as individual PSD files using the Artboards to Files export option.

Figure 18 Settings to export artboards

Figure 19 Individual PSD files created for each artboard

DESIGN PATTERNS

▶ What You'll Do

In this lesson, you'll design artwork for a tile to be used in a Pattern fill layer.

Designing Patterns

Patterns are smart, easy, fun, effective, and somewhat addictive. The best way to understand how patterns work in Photoshop is to think of a tiled floor. If each individual tile has a pattern and you use multiple tiles to cover the floor, the pattern on each tile is repeated across the entire floor.

Designing a pattern in Photoshop is remarkably similar. You aren't required to use a square document as your "tile document," but it's a good idea to do so, especially while you're learning about patterns. When you're satisfied with the artwork, click the Create new pattern button on the Patterns panel, and a new pattern swatch is added to the panel. You can name the swatch as you choose.

Patterns are applied in the same way as fill layers. In any open document, click the Create new fill or adjustment layer button on the Layers panel, then click Pattern. A pattern fill layer will be added, and the pattern will repeat as many times as necessary to fill the layout. Double-click the pattern fill layer to open the Pattern Fill dialog box, shown in Figure 20. Here you can scale and rotate the pattern, which can have a dramatic effect.

Figure 20 Pattern Fill dialog box

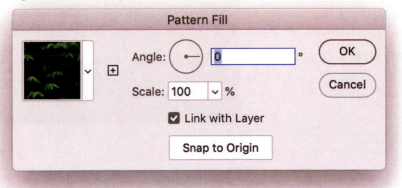

Many people tend to think of patterns as repeating shapes, like polka dots or hound's tooth. Shapes are great for patterns, but you can also use repeating imagery to make effective patterns. Figure 21 shows a leaf pattern that is currently available as a default choice in Photoshop Creative Cloud. The pattern design is so seamless, it's really difficult to tell that it's actually the same image repeated multiple times.

Design two polka dot patterns

1. Open PS 13-7.psd, then save it as **Polka Dot Pattern**.

   The canvas is 4" × 4". A circle is centered on the canvas.

2. Click **Window** on the menu bar, then click **Patterns**.

3. Click the **Create new pattern button**  on the Patterns panel.

   The Pattern Name dialog box opens.

4. Name the new pattern **One Dot**, then click **OK**.

   When you create a new pattern, the current visual status of the canvas is saved as a pattern.

5. Open PS 13-8, then save it as **Pattern File**.

Figure 21 Leaf pattern based on an image

6. Click the **Create new fill or adjustment layer button** on the Layers panel, then click **Pattern**.

   The Pattern Fill dialog box opens, and the canvas is filled with the current pattern chosen in the dialog box.

7. Click the **Pattern Picker list arrow**, then click the **One Dot pattern**.

8. Drag the **Scale slider** to **5%**, then compare your screen to Figure 22.

The pattern uses the original artwork like a tile that repeats in all directions. In this case, the tile is the white square with the blue dot in the center.

9. Click **OK**.

10. Click **View** on the menu bar, point to **Show**, then click **Smart Guides**.

11. Return to the **Polka Dot Pattern** file, then duplicate the **Ellipse 1 layer**.

12. Enter **[command] [T] (Mac)** or **[Ctrl] [T] (Win)** to show the bounding box.

    You are using the transform bounding box for its point of origin icon, which by default is at the exact center of the circle.

13. Click the **Move tool** 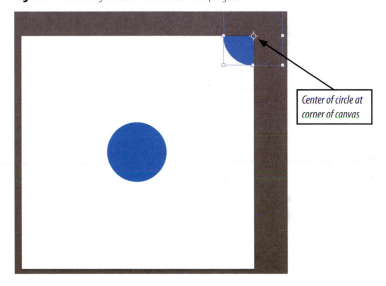 on the toolbar, then move the **circle** so the point of origin icon is exactly at the top-right corner of the canvas, as shown in Figure 23.

Continued on next page

Figure 22 Polka dot pattern scaled to 5%

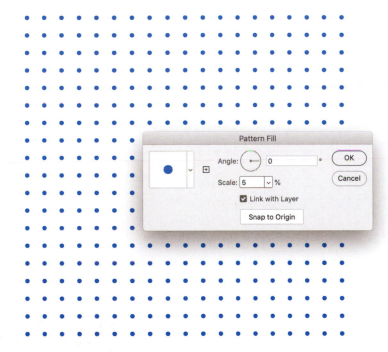

Figure 23 Positioning the center of the dot at the top-right corner

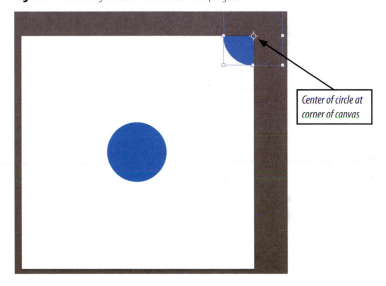

Center of circle at corner of canvas

TIP Horizontal and vertical pink smart guides will appear on the top and right edges of the canvas when the point of origin icon is exactly on the corner.

14. Repeat Steps 12 and 13 three times so a circle is in all four corners, as shown in Figure 24.

   Take a good look at the canvas as a tile for the pattern and imagine what will happen when the pattern repeats above, below, and to the left and right.

15. Click the **Create new pattern button** ⊞ on the Patterns panel, name the new pattern **Five Dots**, then click **OK**.

16. Switch to the Pattern File document.

17. Click the **Create new fill or adjustment layer button** ◑ on the Layers panel, then click **Pattern**.

18. Click the **Pattern Picker list arrow**, then click the **Five Dots pattern**.

19. Drag the **Scale** to **5%**, then compare your screen to Figure 25.

20. Click **OK**, then hide and show the **Pattern Fill 2 layer** to see the difference between the two patterns.

21. Save your work.

22. Keep the Pattern File document open, but close the Polka Dot Pattern file.

You designed two different tiles for two different polka dot patterns. First you made a simple pattern from a single dot at the center of the tile. You then created a more complex tile in which the dots extended the tile at each of the four corners. The result was a more complex and visually pleasing pattern.

Figure 24 A five-dot tile for a polka dot pattern

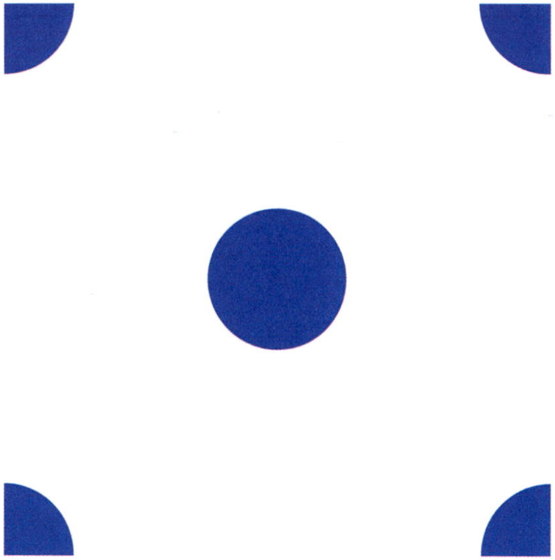

Figure 25 A complex polka dot pattern scaled to 5%

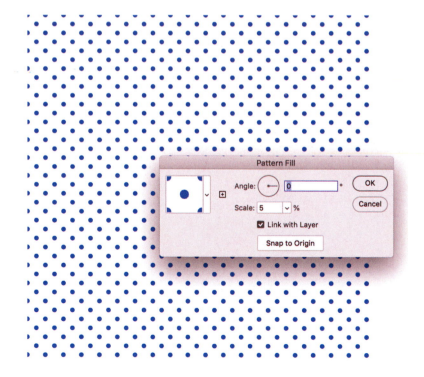

Design a pattern with images

1. Open PS 13-9.psd, then save it as **Flower Pattern**.

2. Target the **Daisy layer**, then enter **[command] [T] (Mac)** or **[Ctrl] [T] (Win)** to show the bounding box.

3. Move the **flower** so the point of origin icon is exactly at the top-right corner of the canvas.

4. Repeat Step 3 three times so a duplicate flower is at all four corners, as shown in Figure 26.

5. Click the **Create new pattern button** on the Patterns panel, name the new pattern **Hummingbird**, then click **OK**.

6. Switch to the Pattern File document.

7. Click the **Create new fill or adjustment layer button** on the Layers panel, then click **Pattern**.

8. Click the **Pattern Picker list arrow**, then click the **Hummingbird pattern**.

9. Drag the **Scale** to **24%**, set the **Angle** to **32°**, then click **OK**.

   Your canvas should resemble Figure 27.

10. Save your work, then close all open files.

You positioned the center of the flower artwork at all four corners of the tile. As a pattern, the four corners combine and repeat in a way that reconstructs the flower.

Figure 26 The flower positioned in all four corners

Chelsea Sampson/Shutterstock.com

Figure 27 The pattern scaled and rotated

Barbol/Shutterstock.com

PREPARE AN IMAGE FOR THE WEB

In this lesson, you'll use various operations to prepare an image to be used on the Web.

Specifying Resolution for Web Graphics

72 pixels per inch (ppi) is the target resolution for any image that is to be used on a screen. Therefore, for any website or slide show or even a television program, graphics you create should be at 72 ppi.

When creating web graphics from scratch in Photoshop, all you need to do is build them from the start at 72 ppi. On the other hand, if you receive a high-resolution image that needs to be resampled to 72 ppi, it's a good idea to create the web graphic as a copy and preserve the high-resolution image. **Resampling** is a term that applies any time you change the total number of pixels that make up an image. Pixels are resampled from the original resolution to the new resolution to reconstruct the image at a new size.

Specifying Web-Safe Colors

With 256 red, 256 green, and 256 blue shades available per pixel, Photoshop is theoretically able to create more than 16.5 million colors for you to choose from. However, not all those colors can be reproduced at high quality on every computer monitor or screen.

In 1996, a web-safe palette of 216 colors was created to address consistency and quality in reproducing colors on computer screens. At that time, most computer screens were 8 bit, meaning each monitor pixel could reproduce 2^8 colors, or 256 colors. Problems—specifically dithering—occurred when these screens tried to display large areas of color outside of that 256-color range.

Dithering is an on-screen form of pixelization in which individual areas of pixels become visible and create a distracting pattern. But a designer choosing from within the web-safe palette of 216 colors could be confident that no dithering would occur.

Flash forward to today's high-resolution and higher-bit-depth screens, and these problems have been greatly reduced. However, the Color Picker in Photoshop still offers a web-safe option. In Figure 28, note the Only Web Colors option and the reduced range of colors available on the Color Picker. If you choose the Only Web Colors option, the Color Picker offers only the 216 web-safe palette from which to choose colors.

Should you use the Only Web Colors option and limit your color choices? The question is, why not? If it's not critical that the purple color you are choosing has to be a specific purple, then why not use a purple from the web-safe palette? On the other hand, if the color you are choosing is critical—for example, a color strongly associated with a brand's identity—choose the color you need, then do some research online after the fact to see how it displays on different screens.

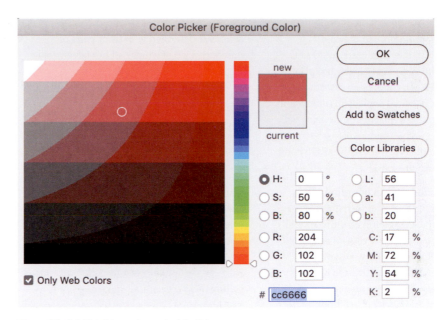

Figure 28 Only Web Colors option on the Color Picker

Choosing a Color Profile for Web Graphics

Remember this about the Internet and computers and digital image editing: they all existed before the consumer came along. The Internet was constructed in the 1970s, two decades before John Q Citizen began browsing. Computers existed before Steve Jobs and Steve Wozniak founded Apple in a garage, and yes, digital image editing existed before Adobe and Photoshop.

This is important to keep in mind because things we think of as "standard" in consumer-based computing aren't so standard if you look at the entire history. Take Adobe RGB, for example. When Adobe Systems built Photoshop, they programmed the color model Adobe RGB in which users could save Photoshop's color files. That's great, but prior to Adobe, the sRGB color model was standard for all screens, everywhere. People who understand this in depth (and with lots of enthusiasm) will tell you that you will get better color on screen for your web graphics if you use the sRGB color model instead of Adobe RGB.

sRGB is not a color model Photoshop offers, but you can specify that your web graphic use sRGB in the Export As dialog box. But should you? The best answer is to try it and see. If color is critical to your project, as it often is, and you're willing to put in the time necessary to pursue the best color you can get across different screens and devices, test it out. Export one version of your image with the Adobe RGB color model and another with sRGB. Put them side by side on different screens and decide which looks best.

Working with Hexadecimal Color

Like RGB, **hexadecimal** is a color model used to describe color mathematically. With RGB, color is described with three numbers, each of which can be one of 256 colors. Hexadecimal colors are described with three pairs of numbers, each of which can be sixteen colors.

ffffff is a hexadecimal value that describes the color white. For each of the six values, 16 characters are available: 0, 1, 2, 3, 4, 5, 6, 7, 8, 9, a, b, c, d, e, f. The first two characters (ff) represent the red component. Thus, the first two numbers offer 16 × 16 possibilities, for a total of 256. The same goes for the next pair and the next pair. Together, the three pairs offer 256 × 256 × 256 combinations, or 16.5 million colors. Interestingly, understanding the RGB color model helps you to understand the hexadecimal color model: each describes color with 256 shades; they just use different ways of getting there.

More comparisons will clarify this. Black in RGB is 0/0/0. Black in hexadecimal is 000000. RGB red = 255/0/0. Hex red = ff0000. RGB cyan = 0/255/255. Hex cyan = 00ffff. RGB gray = 128/128/128. Hex gray = 808080.

Hexadecimal color is another example of a technology that existed before the consumer came along. Long before there was Apple, Google, and Adobe RGB, computer programmers were specifying on-screen color in hexadecimal. Photoshop's Color Picker offers you the option to specify color in hexadecimal because professionals who code color for websites use hexadecimal to specify those colors. This has resulted in a big misconception: some Photoshop users assume that if they specify color in Photoshop in hexadecimal it is automatically a web-safe color. That is incorrect. Like RGB, hexadecimal color can produce more than 16.5 million colors. It's just another way of describing colors. If you want to limit the hexadecimal color model to only web-safe colors, you must click the Web Only Colors check box in the Color Picker.

Understanding Metadata

Metadata is a set of basic information about a file, such as who created it, the resolution, color space, copyright, and any keywords applied to it. Most digital cameras attach some information to an image file, such as the time the picture was taken, its height, width, and file format. Metadata is useful when you are working with hundreds of files and need a way of organizing them. Metadata is entered in the File Info dialog box and can be exported with your Photoshop file.

Resample an image for use on the Web

1. Open PS 13-10.psd, then save it as **Web Splash Screen**.

   Imagine that this is a graphic created by a designer in Photoshop at no specific size that you need to use as a splash screen for the client's website.

2. Click **File** on the menu bar, click **New**, then at the top of the New Document dialog box, click **Web**.

   The Web section of the New Document dialog box offers a useful list of size presets for various web documents. For this project you will size the Web Splash Screen document to Web Large, which is 1920 × 1080 pixels at 72 ppi.

3. Click the **Close button**.

4. Click **Image** on the menu bar, click **Image Size**, uncheck the **Resample** option, change the resolution to **72**, then click **OK**.

   By leaving the Resample option unchecked, the image was not resampled or interpolated with the change. You simply changed the resolution from 300 to 72 ppi, thus redistributing the pixels, not resampling them.

5. Open the **Image Size dialog box** again, check the **Resample** option, then change the measurement on the Width and Height text boxes to Pixels.

6. Type **1920** in the **Width text box**, then press **[tab]**.

   At 1920 pixels wide, the height is 1066 pixels deep, just slightly shorter than the 1080 needed.

7. Type **1080** in the **Height text box**, then press **[tab]**.

   At 1080 pixels in height, the width is 1945, which is 25 pixels more than the 1920 needed.

8. Click **OK**.

9. Click **Image** on the menu bar, click **Canvas Size**, enter the information shown in Figure 29, then click **OK**.

The image is now at the targeted size and resolution: 1920 × 1080 pixels at 72 ppi.

10. Save your work.

You resampled a high-resolution file to a specific resolution and pixel dimension. Once you achieved the desired number of pixels for the height, you cropped the image to achieve the desired number of pixels for the width.

Figure 29 Canvas Size dialog box

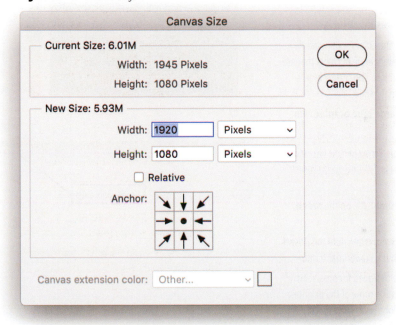

Specify the Only Web Colors option

1. Click the **Eyedropper tool** ✎. on the toolbar, then click the **large blue graphic** to sample its color.

   The client has informed you that this blue is their logo color. They've also told you that hexadecimal color 3366cc is the closest match for this blue for web graphics.

2. Click the **foreground color** on the toolbar to open the Color Picker.

3. Click the **Only Web Colors check box**.

   As shown in Figure 30, the Color Picker window displays a far more limited range of colors that are specified as web-safe colors. The closest blue is identified as hexadecimal 3366cc.

4. Click **OK**, then fill the **large blue graphic** with the new blue.

   TIP You'll need to preserve transparency on the layer to fill just the graphic so be sure to click the Lock transparent pixels icon on the Layers panel.

5. Click the **Eyedropper tool** ✎. on the **green stroke** to sample it.

6. Click the **foreground color**, then note the closest web-safe match, which is hexadecimal ccff66.

   Because web colors are designed for on-screen presentations, they include some of the brightest and most saturated colors, as is the case with this one, which is brighter than the original green.

Figure 30 Limited range of colors with the Only Web Colors option activated

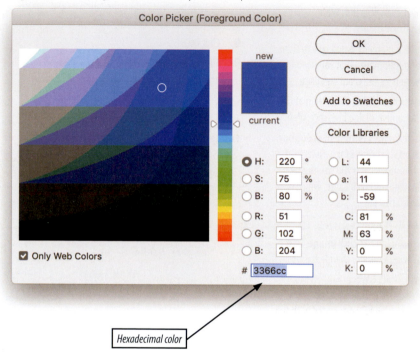

Hexadecimal color

7. Click **OK**, then fill the **green stroke** and the **ENTER TYPE layer** with the new color.

8. Using the same method, change the **pink button** to its web-safe match.

   Your canvas should resemble Figure 31.

9. Save your work, then continue to the next set of steps.

You used the Only Web Colors option to limit the Color Picker to only web-safe colors. You then replaced solid colors on the artwork with web-safe colors.

Export a Web graphic with metadata and the sRGB color profile

1. Click **File** on the menu bar, then click **File Info**.

   The File Info dialog box is where all data for the file is stored. The copyright info and the contact info in this dialog box can be exported with the file.

2. Close the File Info dialog box.

3. Click **File** on the menu bar, point to **Export**, then click **Export As**.

4. In the **File Settings section**, click the **Format list arrow**, then click **PNG**.

5. In the **Metadata section**, click the **Copyright and Contact Info option button**.

Figure 31 The artwork with only web-safe colors applied as solid fills

The copyright and contact info from the File Info dialog box will be exported as metadata with the file.

6. In the **Color Space section**, check and uncheck the **Convert to sRGB check box** to see the difference in color.

   The sRGB option offers far more vivid color in the image than does the default Adobe RGB color space.

7. Verify that the **Convert to sRGB check box** is checked, then click **Export**.

   The file is exported as Web Splash Screen.png.

8. Save your work, then close Web Splash Screen.psd.

You used the Export As dialog box to export an image as a PNG file with metadata using the sRGB color model.

This project builder will give you a review of working with a perspective warp, which you first explored in Chapter 8. In this project, you'll apply the warp to a smart object, which will allow you to work nondestructively. This is a great example of how the perspective warp allows you to use two images together that don't work until the perspective on one is altered.

1. Open **PS 13-11.psd**, then save it as **Smart Truck**.
2. Expand the Truck group, then hide and show each layer to see how the file has been built.
   The truck artwork was pasted into the file. Note that the Shadow layer is multiplied and set to 80% Opacity. The perspective of the truck is wrong for the road image. At this perspective, the truck would drive off the road.
3. Verify that all layers are showing.
4. Target the Truck group layer, click the Layers panel menu button, then click Convert to Smart Object.
   As a smart object, the shadow remains multiplied and transparent.
5. Scale the Truck smart object layer 86%, then click the Move tool to execute the transformation.
6. Click Edit on the menu bar, point to Transform, then click Flip Horizontal.
7. Center the truck left-to-right on the canvas.
8. Click Edit on the menu bar, then click Perspective Warp.
9. Draw a grid around the truck, as shown in Figure 32.

Figure 32 Drawing the grid around the truck

s_oleg/Shutterstock.com; Maciej Bledowski/Shutterstock.com

10. Click Warp on the Options panel.
11. Transform the grid as shown in Figure 33.
12. Press [return] (Mac) or [Enter] (Win) to execute the perspective warp.

    The one thing that needs to change is the passenger window on the truck. It shows the blue sky from the original image and needs to be masked so the desert landscape is visible.

AUTHOR'S NOTE When you apply a perspective warp to a smart object, it is applied as a smart filter. A smart filter is a way of applying a filter nondestructively. For example, on the Layers panel, the perspective warp can be hidden or shown. You will investigate smart filters further in Chapter 14.

13. Double-click the Truck smart object layer thumbnail.
    The layered artwork opens in a new window called Truck.psb.
14. Press and hold [command] (Mac) or [Ctrl] (Win), then click the thumbnail on the Paint layer.
    The artwork on the Paint layer is selected.
15. Hide the Paint layer.
16. Target the layer mask on the Truck layer, then fill the selection with black.
17. Save your work, then close the Truck.psb file.
    As shown in Figure 34, the change is updated in the Smart Truck file.
18. Save your work and keep the Smart Truck file open.

Figure 33 Warping the perspective of the truck

Figure 34 The smart object updated

Project Builder 2 is a review of exporting layered artwork between Illustrator and Photoshop, converting layered artwork into a smart object, using libraries to share artwork between files, and modifying and updating a smart object. It's a comprehensive overview of the techniques we covered in the chapter.

1. Open PS 13-12.ai in Adobe Illustrator, then show the Layers panel.
   The artwork is composed of three layers.
2. Click File on the menu bar, point to Export, then click Export As.
3. Type **Trucking Logo** as the filename in the Export dialog box.
4. Choose a destination folder for the file, click the Format menu list arrow, click Photoshop (.PSD), then click Export.
   The Photoshop Export Options dialog box opens.
5. Enter the settings shown in Figure 35, then click OK.
   A file named Trucking Logo.psd is saved.
6. Open Trucking Logo.psd.
   All elements from the Illustrator file are on three different group layers.
7. Target the X group layer, click the Layers panel menu button, then click Merge Group.
8. Using the same method, merge the other two group layers.
9. Apply a Bevel & Emboss layer style to each layer. Apply the styles to your liking. Figure 36 shows one example.

Figure 35 Settings for the export

Figure 36 Artwork with Bevel & Emboss layer styles

10. Create a new group layer for the three layers, then name the group **X Country Trucking**.
11. Click the Layers panel menu button, then click Convert to Smart Object.
    The folder and its contents are converted to a smart object.
12. Open the Libraries panel, then create a new library called **Truck Logo**.
13. Drag the X Country Trucking smart object into it.
14. Switch to the Smart Truck document, then drag the X Country Trucking smart object from the Libraries panel into the Smart Truck file.
15. Click Edit on the menu bar, point to Transform, then click Distort.
16. Distort the artwork to fit on the side of the truck, as shown in Figure 37.
17. On the Libraries panel, double-click the X Country Trucking thumbnail to show its information.
18. Click the Open source document icon ✐ above the image of the truck logo.
    The layered Photoshop file opens in a new window called X Country Trucking.psb.
19. Expand the X Country Trucking group layer, target the Truck layer, click the Lock transparent pixels icon on the Layers panel, then fill the Truck layer with black.
20. Save your work, then close the X Country Trucking.psb document.
    The change is updated in the Smart Truck document.
21. Save your work, then close Smart Truck.psd.

Figure 37 Distorting the logo onto the truck

PROJECT BUILDER 3

This project builder is an overview of pattern building. What makes this one different is that you'll incorporate a Bevel & Emboss layer style into the pattern.

1. Open PS 13-13.psd, then save it as **Layer Styles Pattern**.
2. Duplicate the Background layer, then name the new layer **B&E**.
3. Fill the new layer with 50% Gray.
4. Double-click a blank area on the layer to open the Layer Styles dialog box.
5. Add a Bevel & Emboss layer style with the settings shown in Figure 38.
   Your tile should resemble Figure 39.

Figure 38 Bevel & Emboss settings

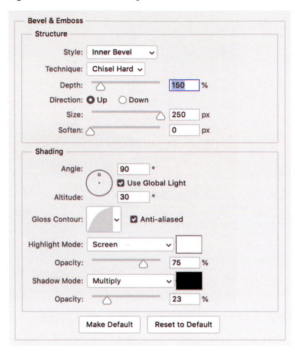

Figure 39 Bevel & Emboss tile

6. Click the Create new pattern button on the Patterns panel, name the new pattern **Bevel**, then click OK.
7. Save your work.
8. Open 13-14.psd, then save it as **Layer Styles Pattern Fill**.
9. Click the Create new fill or adjustment layer button on the Layers panel, then click Pattern.
10. Click the Pattern Picker list arrow, then click the Bevel pattern.
11. Drag the Scale to 25%, then click OK.
    Your canvas should resemble Figure 40.
12. Save your work, then close all open files.

Figure 40 The Bevel pattern scaled 25%

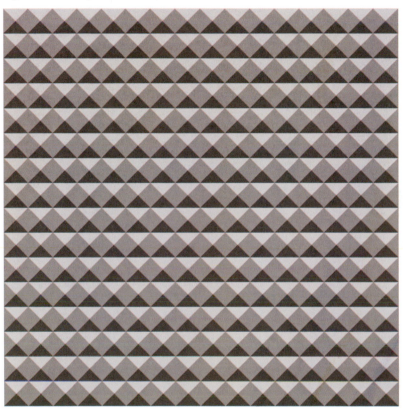

This design project offers you the chance to design a pattern of your own. You will be given some illustrations in Illustrator that you will use to build a tile for a pattern in Photoshop. This will be a complex and challenging project that will require you to manage scaling, positioning, and space

allocation along with the strategies of building a tile for a pattern.

1. Open PS 13-15.ai in Illustrator.
   This is an Adobe Illustrator file containing many illustrations.
2. Open PS 13-16.psd., then save it as **Floral Tile**.
3. Copy illustrations from the Illustrator file into the Photoshop file to create a pattern tile.

4. When you've designed the tile, create a new pattern in the Patterns panel.
5. Open PS 13-17.psd, then save it as **Floral Pattern**.
6. Add a Pattern fill layer, then scale it to your liking. Figure 41 shows one possible result, scaled at 110%.

Figure 41 One example of the Floral pattern

Ps CHAPTER **14**

CREATE COMPLEX SPECIAL EFFECTS

1. Create a Customized Solarize Effect
2. Create Mezzotint and Halftone Effects
3. Create Neon, Blur, and Lighting Effects
4. Create a High Dynamic Range (HDR) Composite
5. Create a Double-Exposure Effect

CERTIFIED PROFESSIONAL

Adobe Certified Professional in Visual Design Using Photoshop CC Framework

2. Project Setup and Interface

This objective covers the interface setup and program settings that assist in an efficient and effective workflow, as well as knowledge about ingesting digital assets for a project.

2.6 Work with brushes, styles, and patterns.

  A Open, browse, and search libraries of included brushes, styles and patterns.

  B Create, use, edit, and organize brushes, styles, and patterns.

3. Organizing Documents

This objective covers document structure such as layers and managing document structure for efficient workflows.

3.1 Use layers to manage design elements.

  C Recognize the different types of layers in the Layers panel.

3.3 Differentiate between and perform destructive or nondestructive editing to meet design requirements.

  A Nondestructive editing: Smart Objects, Smart Filters, and adjustment layers.

4. Creating and Modifying Visual Elements

This objective covers core tools and functionality of the application, as well as tools that affect the visual appearance of document elements.

4.3 Make, manage, and manipulate selections.

  A Make selections using a variety of tools.

CREATE A CUSTOMIZED SOLARIZE EFFECT

▶ What You'll Do

In this lesson, you'll use various curve adjustments to create customized solarize effects.

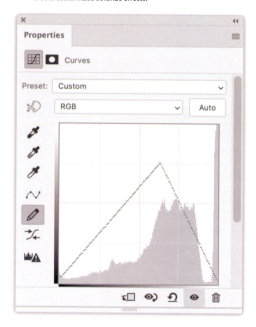

Creating Solarize Effects

Solarize is a filter that has been available since the first release of Photoshop; it mimics an effect in photography that's been around a lot longer: mixing a positive component of an image with a negative "x-ray" component.

It creates an interesting silver effect on black and white images. Figure 1 shows the image you will work on in color with the Solarize filter applied. Note the very alien, "sci-fi" effect it creates. The Solarize filter does not offer settings that you can adjust. It simply executes an algorithm, and you are left with the results.

Figure 1 The Solarize filter applied to a color image

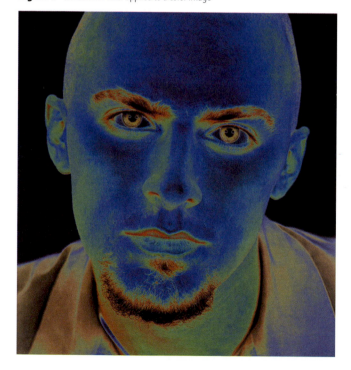

In terms of grayscale, the solarize effect is created by inverting only the top half of the grayscale range. Figure 2 shows a curve that completely inverts an image. The darkest pixels are white, at grayscale 255, and the lightest pixels are black, at 0. Figure 3 shows the same image with a solarize curve, which appears as an upside-down V. The bottom half of the grayscale is not inverted: from zero to 128, the image brightens. At the midpoint, however, the image inverts and gets darker. The top half of the grayscale goes from 129 to 0. This means that the top half of the image is inverted.

The solarize curve is created with the pencil tool in the Curves adjustment settings. You use this tool to draw straight lines in the Curves adjustment. Because the Solarize curve is an upside-down V, you can use the pencil tool to draw curves that are a different variation on that shape and, thus, different solarize effects.

Figure 2 Inverted curve inverts the whole image

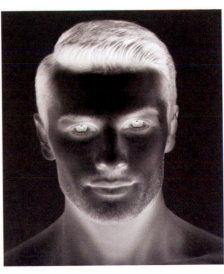

Figure 3 Solarize curve inverts only the top half of the image

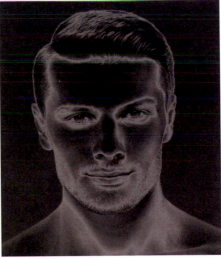

Solarize an image

1. Open PS 14-1.psd, then save it as **Solar Man**.

2. Target the **Solarize layer**.

3. Click **Filter** on the menu bar, point to **Stylize**, then click **Solarize**.

   With the Solarize filter, the light areas of the image—those in the top half of the grayscale range—are inverted, while the dark areas in the bottom half of the grayscale range are not affected. Note how the highlights in the image have become dark gray.

4. Hide the **Solarize layer**, then target the **Background layer**.

   You're going to use curves to create your own solarize effect on the image of the man on the Background layer.

5. Create a new **Curves adjustment layer**.

6. On the Properties panel, click the **pencil icon** ⟋, then click the **lower-left corner** of the grid.

   The pencil allows you to draw your own curve.

Figure 4 Drawing a solarize curve with the pencil tool

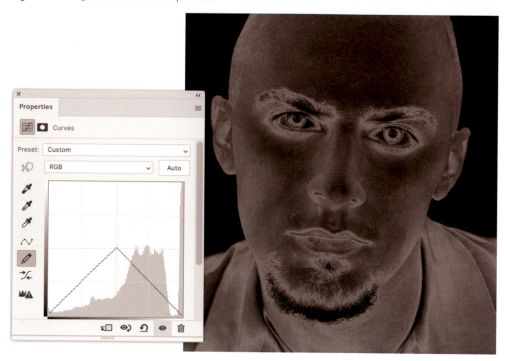

7. **[Shift]-click** the **center point** of the grid, then **[shift]-click** the **lower-right corner** of the grid so your curve resembles Figure 4.

   This curve is easy to read and understand. From 0–128, nothing has changed. From 129 to 255, everything has been inverted—the curve moves downward instead of upward, meaning the pixels move back toward black rather than toward white. Note the corresponding effect on the image. This inverted-V curve is essentially the same algorithm the Solarize filter uses, creating a very similar effect.

8. On the Properties panel, click the **lower-left corner**, then **[shift]-click** to redraw the curve so it resembles Figure 5.

   The shadow half of the curve is shortened, and the dark areas of the image are therefore darkened. It's an interesting move, but with a solarize effect, the goal is usually to create a "silver" person or image, which involves brightening, not darkening the image.

9. Using the same method, redraw the curve so it resembles Figure 6.

   This move is more in the right direction to achieve the silver effect and has a more interesting effect on the image than the standard Solarize filter did. Note how the cheeks, eyes, and eyebrows are starting to take on a distinct glow.

Figure 5   Darkening the solarize effect

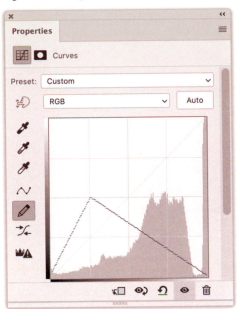

Figure 6   Brightening the solarize effect

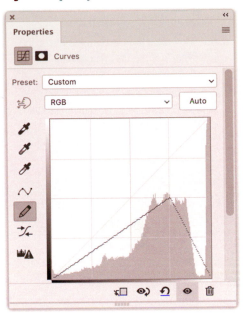

10. Redraw the curve to match Figure 7.

11. Add a new **Hue/Saturation adjustment layer** above the Curves adjustment layer.

12. On the **Properties panel**, click **Colorize**, set the **Hue** to **50**, set the **Saturation** to **75**, then compare your results to Figure 8.

    The yellow hue really works with the solarize effect. From this point, you could modify the curve again to adjust the solarize effect, or you could apply blending modes to the Hue/Saturation adjustment for alternate looks.

13. Save your work, then close Solar Man.

You learned that a solarize effect is done with a curve that resembles an upside-down V. You then used the pencil tool on the Curves adjustment to draw different solarize effects, some darker and some brighter. You created a very bright solarize curve, which created a silvery effect on the artwork. You colorized the effect with a Hue/Saturation adjustment for more impact.

Figure 7 Choosing a very bright effect

Figure 8 One version of the solarize effect with a yellow hue

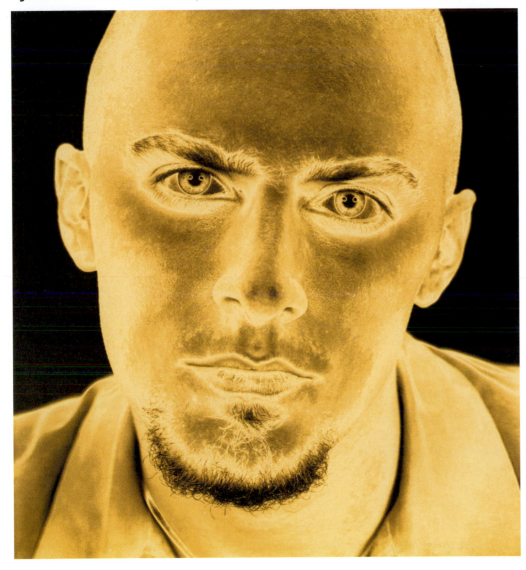

CREATE MEZZOTINT AND HALFTONE EFFECTS

Reproducing Images with Dots

Halftoning and **mezzotints** are long-established procedures in the world of printing and prepress. Of the two, you are certainly more familiar with halftoning from newspaper printing: a continuous-tone image is reproduced with dots of ink that are various sizes, and if you look closely enough, you can see the dots.

A **mezzotint** is a different screening technique you can use as an alternative to a conventional halftone. A mezzotint uses irregular shaped dots or lines to reproduce the image.

Reproducing images with dots of different sizes is a classic look that recalls comic books and old offset printing techniques. In today's digital world, the look has a certain retro charm to it, so incorporating halftone and mezzotint effects into your skills set can offer you some valuable options. Photoshop's Overlay and Soft Light blending modes have made it much quicker and easier to apply these filters in a way that *integrates* the effect with the original base image to create entirely new looks.

Create a Mezzotint effect

1. Open PS 14-2.psd, then save it as **Mezzotint**.
2. Duplicate the **Background layer**, then name the new layer **Mezzotint**.

3. Click **Filter** on the menu bar, point to **Pixelate**, then click **Mezzotint**.
4. In the **Mezzotint dialog box**, click the **Type list arrow** to see the different options available.

   As shown in Figure 9, the Mezzotint filter offers 10 different looks in three categories: dots, lines, and strokes. Be sure to experiment with each.
5. Click **Fine Dots**, then click **OK**.

Figure 9 Options for the Mezzotint filter

6. Zoom in on the effect so that you can see the pixels.

The effect produced by the Mezzotint filter renders the image with only black or white pixels. Though this file is in Grayscale mode—256 shades of gray available per pixel—there are no gray pixels that make up the filtered image. While it's visually interesting, it's not a look you would likely use on its own.

7. Set the **blending mode** to **Overlay**.

Overlayed over the original image, the Mezzotint effect produces a grainy, high-contrast image with bright whites, dark blacks, and very few midtones.

8. Change the **blending mode** to **Soft Light**, then compare your result to Figure 10.

Blending the Mezzotint effect over the original image with the Soft Light mode produces an elegant and charming grainy high-contrast image with bright whites and dark blacks. It would make for an excellent alternative to a simple grayscale image for the right project.

9. Save your work, then close Mezzotint.

You applied the Mezzotint filter to the image using the Fine Dots option. You then used the Overlay and Soft Light blending modes to produce practical alternatives to a traditional grayscale image.

Create a halftone effect

1. Open PS 14-3.psd, then save it as **Halftone**.

2. Duplicate the **Background layer**, then name the new layer **Halftone**.

3. Click **Filter** on the menu bar, point to **Pixelate**, then click **Color Halftone**.

4. Type **4** in the Max. Radius text box, click **OK**, then compare your result to Figure 11.

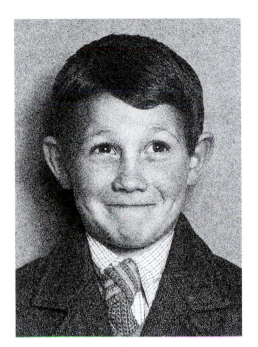

Figure 10 Mezzotint filter in Soft Light mode

5. Convert the file to **RGB Color mode**, then click **Don't Flatten** in the dialog box that follows.

TIP When working through the steps in this chapter, always click Don't Flatten when prompted.

6. Zoom in on the image so you can see the pixels.

Unlike the Mezzotint filter, the Color Halftone filter uses some gray pixels as part of the effect.

7. Click the **Magic Wand tool** , type **8** in the Tolerance text box, then verify that the **Anti-alias** and **Contiguous check boxes** are not checked.

8. Click a **white pixel**.

All of the white pixels in the image are selected.

Figure 11 Color Halftone filter

9. Click **Select** on the menu bar, then click **Inverse**.

All of the nonwhite pixels that make up the filtered image are selected.

10. Zoom out so you are viewing the image at 100%.

11. Copy the **selected pixels**, paste a new layer, then name the new layer **Halftone Transparent**.

With this step, you have isolated the filtered image on a transparent layer—the pixels that were originally white are now transparent.

12. Delete the **Halftone layer**.

Continued on next page

13. Open the file named **BRY Gradient**, select all, copy, then close the file.

14. In the Halftone document, target the **Halftone Transparent layer**, paste the **BRY Gradient**, then clip it into the **Halftone Transparent layer**.

15. Change the blending mode on the **Halftone Transparent layer** to **Overlay**.

16. Compare your result to Figure 12.

17. Zoom in to see the effect up close, as shown in Figure 13.

AUTHOR'S NOTE This is a really charming effect, and it's also unique. The gradient is visible only in the filtered artwork, and that makes this a unique variation, which is always a good thing. As a designer, you're always looking to find your own unique methods for producing new looks.

18. Save your work, then close Halftone.

You applied the Color Halftone filter to an image, then you copied all the nonwhite pixels onto a layer. Thus, parts of the layer were transparent. You then clipped a gradient into the halftone effect, then overlayed the dots to integrate the dots and the gradient into the main image.

Figure 12 Blue, red, and yellow gradient clipped into halftone effect

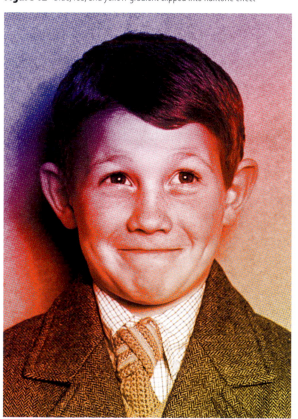

Figure 13 Blue, red, and yellow gradient is visible only in the filtered artwork

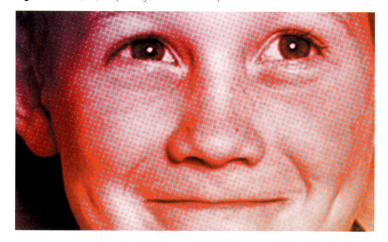

CREATE NEON, BLUR, AND LIGHTING EFFECTS

▶ *What You'll Do*

In this lesson, you'll create type that appears to be made of neon, you'll "paint light" to enhance an image, and you'll apply a motion blur as a smart filter to create a sense of movement.

Creating Neon Effects

Neon effects make for stunning special effects, and they're practical because they work so well with type. Neon is effective and it's classic: it can be used as a title treatment for many different types of projects.

Many books and manuals supply tips and tricks for creating simple neon effects—and that's the problem. They stop at the simple, which usually involves using basic Inner Glow or Outer Glow layer styles. These make for a serviceable neon effect, but they can be a bit "canned" and simple.

Working with paths is a great choice for designing neon effects, because you can use the Stroke Path command and apply a color stroke to a path using any of the paint tools on the toolbar. The ability to stroke a path with the Brush tool at different sizes and opacities creates many options for producing a more complex neon effect.

"Painting Light" in Overlay Blending Mode

You are already familiar with the Overlay blending mode from applying Noise and High Pass sharpening layers. In Overlay mode, gray pixels become invisible and have no effect on any underlying image. But that's only one component of the blending mode and not nearly all it has to offer. Things get interesting when you overlay black, white, and color.

Overlay is a transparent blending mode. All pixels on the layer with the Overlay blending mode will be transparent. An overlayed pixel either brightens or darkens the pixels beneath it. The degree to which it brightens or darkens is based on its grayscale value. Pixels above 128 brighten the underlying image, while pixels below 128 darken it. The further you go from the middle range, the more intense the brightening or darkening. Thus, white pixels with a grayscale value of 255 will brighten an image the most when overlayed, while black pixels at 0 will darken an image the most.

Figure 14 illustrates this concept. On the left is the original image. On the right, the image has been overlayed with black on the left and white on the right. The black and white pixels are transparent, and they darken and brighten the image to a great degree.

In addition to using just color fills, you can paint in Overlay mode. Create a new layer, set its blending mode to Overlay, then any painting you do, in any color, will brighten or darken the underlying image. You can think of this as "painting with light." It offers a powerful effect for selectively highlighting and shadowing specific areas of an image.

Using a Motion Blur to Create Movement

Think of an illustration of a colorful race car speeding past you. The artist conveys movement by creating trails of color to indicate how fast the car is going. The Motion Blur filter works to achieve the same effect. It scales or "stretches" an image in a direction and at a distance that you input. The image is blurred and stretched, mimicking the classic illustration of a speeding object.

Rather than apply the Motion Blur filter directly to an image, it's better to apply it to a copy of the image and then use blending modes and layer masks to specify how the effect interacts with the image.

Using Smart Filters

Adobe's commitment to nondestructive editing is evident in its Smart Filter feature. Instead of applying a filter directly to artwork, you can first specify the artwork as a smart object. With any smart object, the edits you make change the appearance of the artwork, but the original artwork remains unaltered.

The Convert for Smart Filters command on the Filter menu converts artwork to a smart object. When you apply the filter, it is applied as an item on the Layers panel that can be shown or hidden. The smart filter also produces a layer mask that you can use to selectively hide or show the filter. Figure 15 shows a Gaussian Blur smart filter on the Layers panel.

Figure 14 Overlaying black and white on an image

Figure 15 Gaussian Blur smart filter on the Layers panel

Copy and paste a path from Illustrator to Photoshop

1. Open the file named Squash Vegas.ai in Adobe Illustrator.

   This is an Illustrator file with type converted to outlines. When type is converted to outlines in Illustrator, the type forms are converted to paths. We are using paths from Illustrator for this exercise to give you experience with pasting Illustrator artwork as paths and not shapes in Photoshop.

2. Select all, copy, then close the file.

3. Open PS 14-4.psd, then save it as **Neon Type**.

4. Target the **Squash Court layer**, then paste.

   The Paste dialog box opens.

5. Click **Path**, then click **OK**.

   When you paste a path from Illustrator as a path in Photoshop, it is pasted as a vector mask on the targeted layer, whether you intend to use it that way or not. Because the vector mask now exists, it is also listed on the Paths panel, where it can be saved as a path.

6. On the Paths panel, double-click **Squash Court Vector Mask** to open the Save Path dialog box, then rename it as **Path 1**.

   A new path appears on the panel. Because the path is now saved on the Paths panel, you can delete the Squash Court Vector Mask, which was never needed. It was only a means to the end of saving the path.

7. On the Layers panel, delete the **vector mask** from the Squash Court layer.

TIP You can also delete the vector mask from the Paths panel.

8. Click **View** on the menu bar, point to **Show**, then click **Guides**.

TIP You can also press and hold [command] (Mac) or [Ctrl] (Win), then press the semicolon key (;) to show guides.

9. Click the **Path Selection tool** , float it over any **anchor point on the Squash Vegas path**, press and hold **[shift]**, then drag it straight up so it is positioned between the two guides.

TIP Use Figure 16 as a guide. If Path 1 becomes deselected on the Paths panel, select it, and then use the Path Selection tool and [shift] to reselect all the letters in Squash Vegas. Be sure you are *not* using the Move tool.

10. Hide the guides, save your work, then continue to the next set of steps.

You pasted a path from Illustrator as a path in Photoshop. You noted that it was pasted as a vector mask on the targeted layer. You saved the vector mask as a new path, then repositioned it. You then deleted the vector mask because it was no longer needed.

Figure 16 Positioning the path

Create a neon effect with paths

1. Verify that the **Squash Court layer** is targeted, then create a new layer named **60**.

2. Set the **foreground color** to **RGB 255/0/255**.

3. Click the **Brush tool** , set the **Size** to **60 px**, **Hardness** to **0%**, and **Opacity** to **100%**.

4. Click the **Paths panel menu button** , click **Stroke Path**, verify that **Brush** is listed in the Stroke Path dialog box, then click **OK**.

   As shown in Figure 17, the path is stroked with the foreground color using the Brush tool at the current Size, Hardness, and Opacity settings.

5. Set the **Opacity** on the **60 layer** to **60%**.

6. Create a new layer named **25**, set the **Size** on the **Brush tool** to **25**, then click the **Stroke Path button** on the Paths panel.

7. Set the **Opacity** on the **25 layer** to **50%**.

8. Create a new layer named **15**, set the **Size** on the **Brush tool** to **15**, then click the **Stroke Path button** on the Paths panel.

9. Keep the **Opacity** on the **15 layer** at **100%**.

10. Set the **foreground color** to **white**.

11. Create a new layer named **8**, set the **Size** on the **Brush tool** to **8**, then click the **Stroke Path button** on the Paths panel.

12. Set the **Opacity** on the **8 layer** to **80%**.

13. On the **Paths panel**, click the **white space below Path 1** to deselect it.

14. Target all **four neon layers**, click the **Create a new group button** on the Layers panel, then name the group **Neon**.

15. Show the **Player layer**, then compare your artwork to Figure 18.

16. Save your work, then continue to the next set of steps.

You stroked the path with the Brush tool at different sizes and different opacities to create a bright neon "tube" encompassed by a neon glow.

Use lighting techniques to illuminate an image

1. Assess the lighting in the squash court scene and on the athlete.

   While the room has interesting shadows, it's lit with a plain white light from overhead. There are no highlights on the skin of the woman playing. With the vibrant neon type now put in place, the entire scene must now "live in the same world" as the neon type.

2. Target the **Player layer**, click the **Create new fill or adjustment layer button** on the Layers panel, then click **Hue/Saturation**.

3. Clip the **Hue/Saturation adjustment** into the **Player layer**, then set the **blending mode** to **Overlay**.

Figure 17 Applying a stroke to the path with the Brush tool

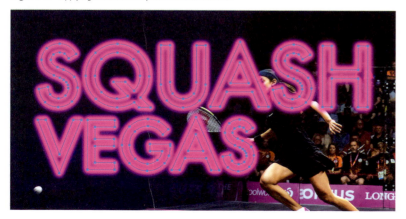

Figure 18 Neon effect created with four stroked paths

4. On the Properties panel, click **Colorize**, then set the **Hue** to **314**, the **Saturation** to **39** and the **Lightness** to **+31**.

   The Overlay blending mode adds contrast and makes the player more vivid. Note the highlights that now appear on her arms and legs. Colorizing her with a pink hue puts her into the world of the neon type, as though the pink neon light is now reflecting off her skin.

5. Target the **Squash Court layer**, create a new **Hue/Saturation adjustment layer**, then set its blending mode to **Hard Light**.

   The Hard Light blending mode increases the contrast dramatically. This is fitting for the image. The neon lights would create a high-contrast setting.

6. Create another **Hue/Saturation adjustment layer**.

7. On the Properties panel, click **Colorize**, set the **Hue** to **287**, then set the **Saturation** to **25**.

   The setting now takes on a purple hue, which would be expected from the bright purple neon lights.

8. Show and target the **Flare layer**, set the **blending mode** to **Screen**, then drag it above the two Hue/Saturation adjustment layers so that it's directly below the Neon group layer.

9. Create a new **Hue/Saturation adjustment layer**, then clip it into the **Flare layer**.

10. On the Properties panel, click **Colorize**, set the **Hue** to **244**, then set the **Saturation** to **25**.

11. Target the **Flare layer** and **its clipped adjustment layer**, press and hold **[option] (Mac)** or **[Alt] (Win)**, then drag the **two layers** to the **top of the Layers panel** so that they are above the Player layer and its adjustment layer.

12. Add a **layer mask** to the **Flare copy layer**, then fill the mask with **black**.

13. Using a large, soft brush, paint in the flare so it appears in front of the woman, as shown in Figure 19.

   AUTHOR'S NOTE Making the flare appear in front of the woman puts the woman *within* the light. The flare's source is behind her, but it shines through her bent arm and wraps in front of her. The flare also adds a sense of movement to the image, like the flash of a camera. It adds an aura to the woman; it makes her appear to be a sports star, and it adds glamour to the whole scene.

14. Save your work, then continue to the next set of steps.

You used Hue/Saturation adjustments to colorize and apply the Overlay and Hard Light blending modes to the squash court background and the player. You colorized a lens flare layer behind the player, then used a copy of it to paint light in front of the player.

Figure 19 Using a copy to brush the flare in front of the woman

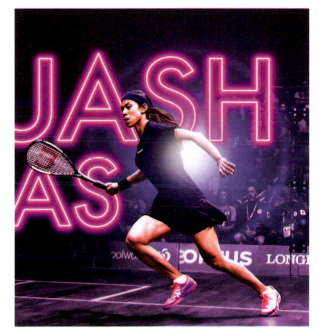
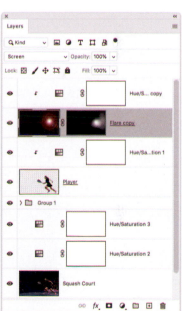

"Paint light" with the Overlay blending mode

1. Click the **Brush tool** , on the toolbar, set the **Size** to **50**, then verify that the **Opacity** is set to **100%**.

2. Target the **Hue/Saturation layer** that is above and clipped into the **Player layer**.

3. Click the **Create a new layer button** ⊞ on the Layers panel, then clip it into the **Hue/Saturation adjustment layer**.

4. Name the new layer **Overlay Paint**, then set the blending mode to **Overlay**.

5. Set the **foreground color** to **RGB 255/0/255**.

6. Using Figure 20 as a guide, paint "pink light" on the following areas of the Player layer: the forehead, hair, back of the neck, ear, shoulder, all the highlights on the clothes, the forearm holding the racquet, and the back of the sneakers.

7. Set the **foreground color** to **white**.

8. Still using Figure 20 as a guide, paint "white light" highlights on the **woman's cheekbones and legs**.

9. Save your work, then continue to the next set of steps.

You created a layer, clipped it into the Hue/Saturation adjustment layer, then set its blending mode to Overlay. You then painted pink and white "light" onto the player.

Figure 20 Overlaying pink paint to create highlights on the Player artwork

Create a Gaussian Blur using smart filters

1. Expand the **Neon group layer**, target the **60 layer**, click **Filter** on the menu bar, click **Convert for Smart Filters**, then click **OK** in the dialog box that appears.

   The dialog box informs you that the layer will be converted to a smart object.

2. Click **Filter** on the menu bar, point to **Blur**, then click **Gaussian Blur**.

3. Enter **20** in the **Radius text box**, then click **OK**.

   As shown in Figure 21, a Gaussian Blur Smart Filter is placed below the 60 layer, and a layer mask appears under the original thumbnail on the layer.

4. Click the **Eye button** 👁 next to the Gaussian Blur Smart Filter to hide it, and then click it again to show the filter.

Figure 21 Gaussian Blur smart filter on the Layers panel

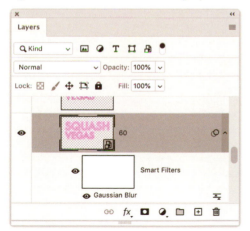

5. Double-click **Gaussian Blur**.

   The Gaussian Blur dialog box opens. Smart filters are editable and removable.

6. Type **24** in the Radius text box, then click **OK**.

7. Save your work, then continue to the next set of steps.

You converted a layer to a smart object to apply a Gaussian Blur filter nondestructively. You applied the filter, noting that a layer mask was provided and the filter effect could be turned on and off and edited.

Create a motion blur using smart filters

1. Hide the **Flare copy layer**.

2. Assess the appearance of the Player artwork.

   The Player artwork is comprised of the original silhouetted layer along with the Hue/Saturation adjustment layer and the Overlay Paint layer in Overlay blending mode. To create a motion blur for the Player artwork only, we need the artwork on a single layer. This can be done with the Copy Merged command.

3. Press and hold **[command] (Mac)** or **[Ctrl] (Win)**, then click the **thumbnail icon** on the **Player layer**.

   The artwork on the Player layer is selected.

4. Click **Edit** on the menu bar, then click **Copy Merged**.

5. Target the **Overlay Paint layer**, then paste.

   A copy of the Player artwork is pasted on a new layer named Layer 1. The artwork is pasted with the Hue/Saturation adjustment and the Overlay

Paint layer effects. Your Layers panel should resemble Figure 22.

6. Name the new layer **Player Merged**.

7. Click **Filter** on the menu bar, then click **Convert for Smart Filters**.

8. Click **Filter** on the menu bar, point to **Blur**, then click **Motion Blur**.

9. Set the **Angle** to **10**, set the **Distance** to **80**, then click **OK**.

Continued on next page

Figure 22 Layer 1 is the Copy Merged layer

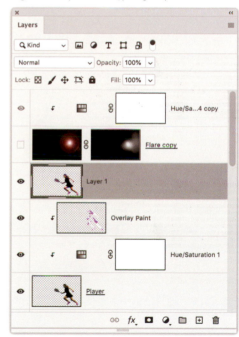

10. Change the **blending mode** on the **Player Merged layer** to **Lighten**.

    With the Lighten blending mode, the only pixels that remain visible are those with a Brightness value higher than the pixel beneath it. Therefore, only the brightest pixels of the motion blur artwork remain visible. The effect looks good, but the blur is not flattering to the woman's face, so you will use the layer mask to remove the blur from that area.

11. Target the **Motion Blur Smart Filters layer mask**, then use the **Brush tool** to paint **black** on the **front of the woman's face** (not her ear or side of her face) to remove the motion blur from that area.

    The effect works really well for the artwork. It's visible but also subtle. The only area that is lacking the motion blur effect is the racquet, where the effect is not easily seen. You will use a duplicate layer to strengthen the effect in just that area.

12. Target the **Player Merged layer**, press and hold **[command] [J] (Mac)** or **[Ctrl] [J] (Win)**, to duplicate the layer.

13. Target the **Motion Blur Smart Filters layer mask** on the **Player Merged copy layer**, then fill it with **black**.

14. Paint **white** in the layer mask to show the motion blur just in the racquet area.

    Your Layers panel should resemble Figure 23.

Figure 23 Layers panel with two Motion Blur smart filter layers

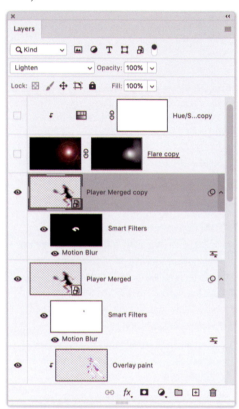

15. Show the **Flare copy layer**.

    This is exactly the type of artwork that calls for a noise layer to unify all the effects that have been applied.

16. Target the **topmost layer** in the Layers panel, click the **Create a new layer button** on the Layers panel, name it **Noise 10**, then fill it with **50% Gray**.

17. Click **Filter** on the menu bar, then click **Convert for Smart Filters**.

18. Click **Filter** on the menu bar, point to **Noise**, then click **Add Noise**.

19. Type **10** in the **Amount text box**, click the **Monochromatic check box**, then click **OK**.

20. Change the **blending mode** for the **Noise 10 layer** to **Overlay**.

    Your final artwork should resemble Figure 24.

21. Save your work, then close Neon Type.

AUTHOR'S NOTE For the fun of it, press and hold [option] (Mac) or [Alt] (Win), then click the Eye icon repeatedly on the Squash Court layer to see a before and after of the original artwork and how much can be done to enhance a simple image with lighting effects. From a simple image, you've created a photo illustration that could be used on a billboard or marquee to promote an event.

The goal was to create a motion blur of the player. The challenge was that the player artwork was being affected by an adjustment layer and a paint layer, so you used the Copy Merged command to create one merged layer. You applied the Motion Blur as a smart filter, then set its blending mode to Lighten. You then duplicated the Motion Blur and used a layer mask to show it only over the racquet. Lastly, you added a noise layer to integrate the artwork with one consistent texture.

Figure 24 The final artwork

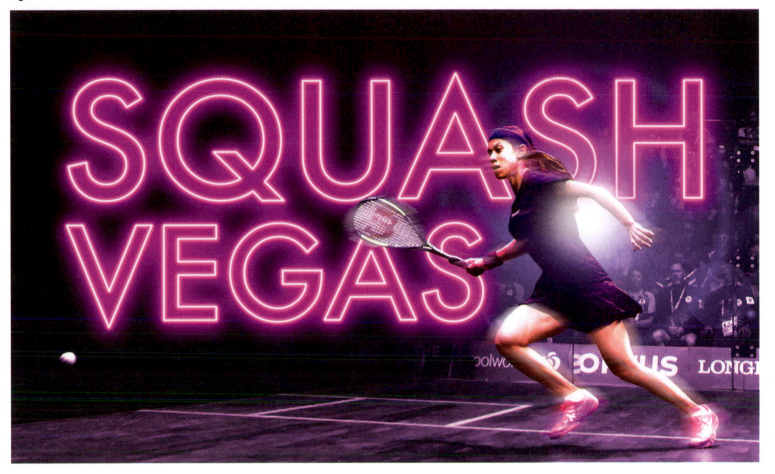

CREATE A HIGH DYNAMIC RANGE (HDR) COMPOSITE

In this lesson, you will use the Merge to HDR Pro utility to create an HDR composite.

Understanding High Dynamic Range Merged Photography

High Dynamic Range merged photography (HDR) is a great option for creating dramatic, highly detailed images and special effects. The basic concept of HDR is that you create one composite image from many source files—usually a minimum of three.

Here's how it works. You photograph the same image three times—once at normal exposure, once underexposed, and once overexposed. Each image has captured different ranges of detail from your subject. The underexposed image has captured subtle highlights, but no shadow detail. The overexposed image captures all the shadow detail, but with blown-out highlights. And the normal exposure captures the midrange.

In Photoshop, import those three source files into the Merge to HDR Pro utility. Automatically, it will create a composite image of the three, merging the tonal ranges from each to produce a composite image with a greater range of detail throughout the image than your camera could ever capture in a single shot.

The Merge to HDR Pro utility is a photographer's dream, but if you use Photoshop more as a graphic design package, the Merge to HDR Pro utility is very useful for you both as a powerful special effects generator and as a color manipulation device, working hand in hand with curves and levels.

Analyze source files for an HDR merge

1. Open PS 14-5.psd, which is shown in Figure 25.

2. Zoom in on the **top-left image**.

   This image is the most underexposed and, therefore, the darkest. Only the lightest areas of the scene have been captured, and they've been captured with crisp, clean detail. Note the inside of the library. There's a full range of detail from shadow to highlight, and the detail is so crisp that you can see each individual book. Other very bright areas—the moon and the light beside the tree—have also been captured. Note that none of the highlights are glaring—none are blown out. Other areas of the image are so underexposed that they're black.

3. Zoom in on the **top-right image**.

   This image is also underexposed, but if you compare this image to the first, you can see clearly that the photographer has allowed in enough light that many more areas of the image are visible. You can see substantially more sky, and the entire tree in the foreground is visible. More detail of the building can be seen, the shrubs in the foreground and in front of the building are suddenly visible, and the white bell tower on the building's roof has emerged from the shadows. The library interior is overexposed, and many areas are blown out to white.

4. Zoom in on the **bottom image**.

   The bottom image is at the complete opposite extreme. It is very overexposed. You can see

this in the highlight areas. The interior of the library, the light behind the tree, and the sky around the moon are all blown out. On the other hand, all the detail hidden in shadows in the other two images is exposed in this image. The sky, the trees behind the building, the branches above the building, and all the foliage in the foreground are visible.

5. Look at the three images, and try to see how together they show a full range of detail in the shadows, in the middle range, and in the highlights.

6. Keep the PS 14-5.psd file open.

   You opened a file containing three images that will be used to create one merged image. You assessed each image for its overall quality including shadows, highlights, and details.

Figure 25 Three source files at different exposures

Use the Merge to HDR Pro utility

1. Click **File** on the menu bar, point to **Automate**, then click **Merge to HDR Pro**.

   The Merge to HDR Pro dialog box opens.

2. Click **Browse**.

3. Select the three files **Hayden Library 1**, **Hayden Library 2**, and **Hayden Library 3**, then click **Open (Mac)** or **OK (Win)**.

   Your Merge to HDR Pro dialog box should resemble Figure 26. Note that the Attempt to Automatically Align Source Images check box is checked. Remember that HDR images are composites of multiple images. If any subject in your image moved between shots, or if the photographer moved slightly, Photoshop would use built-in algorithms to attempt to automatically align the source images. See the sidebar titled *Shooting Source Files for HDR*.

4. Click **OK**.

   Photoshop immediately begins the process of creating the composite image. When the processing is finished, the image will appear in a large Merge to HDR Pro dialog box.

   TIP If you see a warning dialog box about using Camera Raw, click OK. Photoshop is suggesting that you create the HDR merge with Camera Raw files instead of Photoshop PSD files. See the sidebar titled *About HDR and Camera Raw*.

Figure 26 Three source files imported

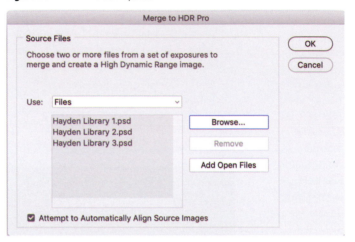

5. Compare the composite image in your Merge to HDR Pro dialog box to Figure 27.

The composite image shows a stunning range of detail throughout. It shows extraordinary detail in the sky, and you can even identify the color of the leaves in the trees *behind* the library. There's detail in the shrubbery and in the exterior of the building, and the highlight areas within the illuminated library interior and around the moon are not glaring or blown out. The detail throughout is so enhanced that the overall result is more a special effect than a representation of reality. Because everything is so very visible in the shadows, in the midrange, and in the highlights, the overall image seems to flatten out onto one plane. The result is pleasing—some would say beautiful—and somewhat surreal.

6. If the Mode is not already set to **16 Bit**, click the **Mode list arrow**, then choose **16 Bit**.

See the sidebar titled *About Bit Depth*.

7. Click **OK** to execute the HDR merge.

Photoshop processes the HDR merge and creates a new Photoshop file for the image.

8. Save the file as **Hayden Library HDR Merge**.

When you compare the composite image to the three source images, you can see that the composite image has utilized the best detail from the three source images.

9. Close PS 14-5.psd.

10. Close Hayden Library HDR Merge.

You used the Merge to HDR Pro utility on the Automate menu to merge three source files shot at different exposures into one high dynamic range image.

Figure 27 Composite HDR image

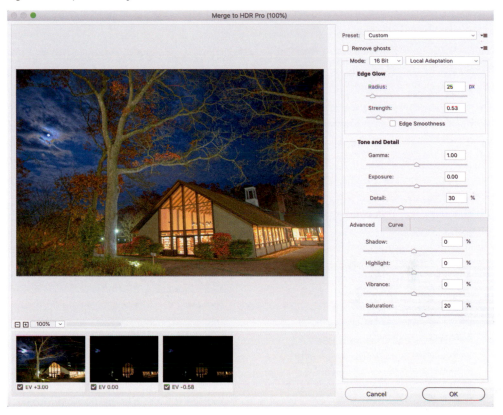

SHOOTING SOURCE FILES FOR HDR

When you're photographing images for source files for an HDR composite, you can use these guidelines.

- Use a tripod: The steadier your camera, the less variation you'll have among the source images.
- Don't vary the lighting between shots. Don't use a flash for one exposure but not another.
- To vary the exposure between source files, vary the shutter speed, not the aperture. Changing the aperture will change the depth of field between source files, which is a variation that you don't want to factor in.
- In terms of exposure differentiation, the exposure differences between source files should be two exposure values (EV) apart, roughly the equivalent of two f-stops.
- Take enough photos at enough exposures to capture the full range of detail in the shadows, midrange, and highlights. Generally speaking, you'll want to shoot a minimum of seven source files, even though you might not use them all in the final HDR merge.

ABOUT HDR AND CAMERA RAW

When downloading images from your digital camera, you can open the JPEG versions in Photoshop, or you can open the raw data files in Camera Raw. The raw data files give you access to the actual data captured when you snapped the photo, and the Camera Raw interface allows you to manipulate that data through a number of presets. When creating HDR files, you want to work with and retain as much of the original data as possible, so it's best that you use raw data files as your source files. Note, however, that you shouldn't make any adjustments to the source files in the Camera Raw interface because those settings are all automatically nullified as part of the Merge to HDR Pro process.

ABOUT BIT DEPTH

Bit depth is a term used to indicate the amount of computer memory allocated to each pixel in a Photoshop file. The bit depth for a given file is indicated and can be specified using the Mode command on the Image menu.

If an image is a 1-bit image, that would mean that only one byte of computer memory is allocated per pixel. Since a byte represents two things—on/off, black/white, positive/negative, etc.—a pixel in a 1-bit image could be either black or white. In a 2-bit image, pixels could be one of four colors: $2 \times 2 = 4$.

As you know, in a grayscale image, each pixel can be one of 256 colors, or shades of gray.

$2^8 = 256$. Thus, in a grayscale image, the bit depth is 8 bits. Each pixel is allocated 8 bits of computer memory, allowing it to be one of 256 colors.

An RGB image requires 8 bits per pixel per channel—that is, for one pixel, 8 bits in the red channel, 8 bits in the green channel, and 8 bits in the blue channel. Don't be confused and call that a 24-bit image. It's still an 8-bit image, 8 bits per pixel per channel. This is often noted as 8 bpc (bits per channel). Remember, the higher the bit depth per pixel, the greater the file size. That's why when you convert a grayscale image (one channel) to RGB mode (three channels), the file size triples.

By determining the number of different shades a pixel can be, bit depth determines the extent to which a range of detail can be captured in a digital file. When creating HDR composites, 8 bits per pixel per channel do not provide enough potential shades per pixel per channel to capture the broad tonal range accessed from the source files. To put it a different way, HDR composites contain a tonal range that far exceeds the range that an 8 bpc file can store.

Photoshop offers 16-bit and 32-bit options in the Mode menu. The Merge to HDR Pro dialog box allows you to work in 16-bit and 32-bit mode. You will find that 16-bit is broad enough to capture a satisfying tonal range in an HDR composite without creating an enormous file size. Nevertheless, only a 32–184 bpc file can store all the HDR image data.

CREATE A DOUBLE-EXPOSURE EFFECT

What You'll Do

In this lesson, you'll use two images and the Screen blending mode to mimic a classic double-exposure effect.

Eric Isselee/Shutterstock.com; kavram/Shutterstock.com

Understanding a Double-Exposure Effect

In traditional photography, a double-exposure effect is achieved when the photographer exposes the same frame of film to two different images. The two images are both burned into the film, merging the two images together in ways that can be beautiful, editorial, or informative.

In Photoshop, blending modes offer all kinds of opportunities for creating double-exposure effects. The Screen blending mode is particularly effective, because only the brighter pixels remain fully visible. Interacting with a darker image, the Screen blending mode often creates highly contrasting double-exposure effects.

Create a double-exposure effect

1. Open PS 14-6.psd, then save it as **Lion Double Exposure**.

2. Open PS 14-7.psd, select all, copy, then close the file.

3. In the **Lion Double Exposure file**, target the **Background layer**, then paste.

4. Name the new layer **Landscape**.

5. Verify that guides are showing.

   TIP Press and hold [command] (Mac) or [Ctrl] (Win) then press the [;] key to hide and show guides.

6. Scale the **Landscape layer** to **85%** and position it precisely inside the four guides.

7. Hide the guides.

8. Set the **blending mode** on the **Landscape layer** to **Screen**.

   Because anything screened with white becomes white, the landscape appears only inside the lion artwork.

9. Add a **layer mask** to the **Landscape layer**.

10. Using a big, soft-edged brush, mask out the landscape in the lion's face and other areas that you think it should be removed.

    Figure 28 shows one example, along with the layer mask that you can follow.

11. Show and target the **Gradient layer**, set its **Opacity** to **65%**, then set its **blending mode** to **Overlay**.

Your artwork should resemble Figure 29.

12. Save your work, then close Lion Double Exposure.

You screened a black and white image over a color image, creating a double-exposure effect. You masked the black and white image so it appeared in specific areas, then you applied a gradient with an Overlay blending mode to colorize the image.

Figure 28 Masking the Landscape artwork to integrate better with the lion

Figure 29 The final double-exposure effect

This project builder reviews and expands on the skills for creating a more complex Mezzotint effect than you would achieve just using the Mezzotint filter. You will experiment with seven different blending modes to explore the many color effects available to you with this technique.

1. Open PS 14-8.psd, then save it as **Color Mezzotint**.
2. Target the Silo Layer, then apply the Mezzotint filter with Fine Dots.
3. Zoom in on an area of the man's face so you can see white pixels easily.
4. Click the Magic Wand tool, set its Tolerance value to 4, verify that neither the Anti-alias nor the Contiguous check boxes are checked, then click a white area to select all the white pixels on the layer.

5. Click Select on the menu bar, then click Inverse.
6. Copy the selection, then paste.
7. Name the new layer **Black Pixels Only**, then zoom out to view the entire face.
8. Set the Silo layer's blending mode to Overlay.
9. Show the Gradient layer at the top of the Layers panel.
10. Clip the Gradient layer into the Black Pixels Only layer.
11. Target the Black Pixels Only layer.
12. Change the blending mode to Overlay.
13. Change the blending mode to Soft Light.
14. Change the blending mode to Hard Light.
15. Change the blending mode to Vivid Light.
16. Change the blending mode to Linear Light.
17. Change the blending mode to Pin Light.
18. Change the blending mode to Hard Mix, then compare your result to Figure 30.
19. Save your work, then close Color Mezzotint.

Figure 30 Mezzotint with the Hard Mix blending mode

PROJECT BUILDER 2

This project builder provides you with three additional professionally shot images to produce a stunning HDR merge. These provide you a good example should you choose to shoot your own images at different exposures for use in the Merge to HDR Pro utility.

1. Open PS 14-9.psd.
2. Assess the three images in terms of lighting, various exposures, and detail.
3. Click the File menu, point to Automate, then click Merge to HDR Pro.
4. Click Browse.
5. Navigate to the drive and folder where your data files are stored.
6. Select Pool 1.psd, Pool 2.psd, and Pool 3.psd, then click OK.
7. In the Merge to HDR Pro window, click OK. Photoshop begins the process of creating the composite image.
8. Click OK to execute the HDR merge.
9. Save the resulting file as **Pool HDR Merge**. Your result should resemble Figure 31.
10. Close the two open files.

Figure 31 HDR Merge of three images

Courtesy of Scott Barnhill

In Lesson 5, you screened a black and white image over the color image of the lion. In this lesson, you will screen a color image over a black and white image to create a double-exposure effect.

1. Open PS 14-10.psd, then save it as **Color Exposure**.
2. Open PS 14-11.psd, select all, copy, then close the file.
3. In the Color Exposure file, paste, then name the new layer **Forest**.
4. Screen the Forest layer.
5. Mask the Forest layer as you like.
   Figure 32 shows one example.
6. Add a Hue/Saturation adjustment layer above the Forest layer, then set its blending mode to Overlay.
7. Set the Saturation to +40, then set the Lightness to +9.
   Your artwork should resemble Figure 33.
8. Save your work, then close Color Exposure.

Figure 32 Masking the Forest layer

metamorworks/Shutterstock.com; Guenter Albers/Shutterstock.com

Figure 33 Final double-exposure effect

This design project offers you the chance to try your own hand at experimenting with different brush sizes and opacities to create your own neon effect.

1. Research neon images online to get a more complete sense of the different things people do with neon.
2. Open PS 14-12.psd, then save it as **Neon Design**.
3. On the Paths panel, note the paths that have been supplied to you for letters and for a border.
4. Regard Figure 34 as one example of how these paths can be stroked to create a neon effect.
5. Using different brush sizes and opacities, create your own neon effect using colors that you like.

Figure 34 Neon sign

NATIONAL GEOGRAPHIC STORYTELLERS

NADIA SHIRA COHEN

Nadia has always been fascinated by Japan. When she wanted to explore the issues of Japan's aging population and the resulting abandonment of many rural communities, she chose to focus on the town of Nagoro, an isolated mountain community on the island of Shikoku. Many families in the area have moved away and the few people who still live there are from an older generation.

To make the situation more visible, local artist Tsukimi Ayano creates life-size dolls and positions them all around town, engaging in life's activities. She puts a lot of care into how the dolls look, how they are placed, and how they interact with each other to show the roles of individuals in daily life and how they are no longer present in the town. People come from all over to see the dolls and learn about their stories.

In this image, the pair of dolls represents an old couple. From the road, Nadia only saw the dolls. When she moved around to find a good angle for the photo, she saw the vehicle as well. Nadia believes that the vehicle covered in vines juxtaposed with the dolls works perfectly as a symbol for the problems of aging and depopulation in Japan. It tells the story through a different lens.

PROJECT DESCRIPTION

In this project, you will explore the symbolic theme of aging and change over time. You will need to reflect on what you think it means to age and change, and the role that plays in your life and the life of the people in your community.

Collect various visuals, such as personal photos, media photos, pieces of writing, art, etc., and create an abstract still image of someone or something as it relates to age and change over time. The goal of this project is for you to creatively montage imagery in the form of an abstract still image to effectively tell a story.

QUESTIONS TO CONSIDER

❙ What stands out to you?

❙ What questions would you ask?

❙ What do you think the story is?

GETTING STARTED

Think beyond the obvious. We all know that a big part of aging is when people and things physically get older. This project is an opportunity to think more deeply about that by examining themes like maturity, experience, lessons, or even cultural change within a community.

Nadia Shira Cohen, A House Fit for a Samurai, Buried vehicle and life-sized dolls, Nagoro, Shikoku, Japan

After you ponder the theme of aging and change over time, decide what idea and perspective you want to focus on and how you are going to tell a unique story about it. Find your subject; you may choose a friend, a meaningful object, or even yourself. Create a moodboard where you can lay out all of your images, text, and other important visuals. Having everything visible on a single board will help you establish a focus, tone, and overall feel to the story.

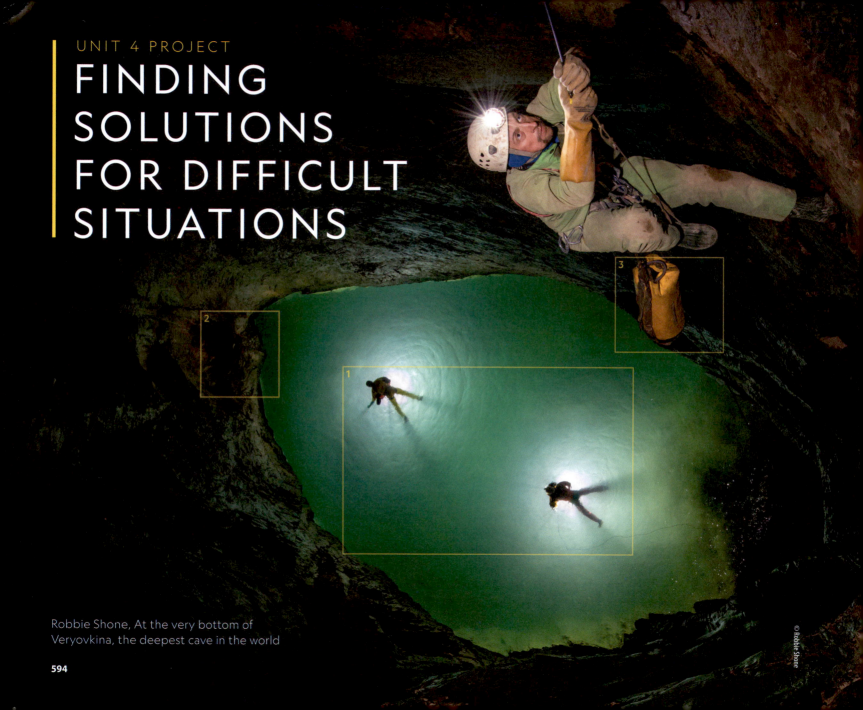

FINDING SOLUTIONS FOR DIFFICULT SITUATIONS

Robbie Shone, At the very bottom of Veryovkina, the deepest cave in the world

© Robbie Shone

© Robbie Shone

As one of the world's foremost cave photographers, Robbie Shone travels the globe to tell the story of Earth's remote and amazing places. As a student, Robbie practiced caving and learned the basics of cave photography in a tall vertical chamber called Titan in Peak Cavern, Derbyshire, England. Those skills became the foundation for his photographic process.

THE CHALLENGES OF CAVE PHOTOGRAPHY

It took Robbie three years to learn how to capture the image of Titan as he had envisioned it. Cave locations are often difficult to access while carrying the necessary photographic equipment. In many cases, the best vantage point for taking a photo is hanging from a rope while looking down into the void.

It is extremely complicated to take photos of immense, dark spaces. Because there is no light inside Titan—just a huge expanse of black space—Robbie needed to learn how light from flash bulbs and strobes works in caves and how to illuminate his photos in the most effective way. The long exposure time for the photos required a tripod to hold the camera steady. While hanging from a rope, Robbie bolted his tripod to the cave wall and pointed the camera straight down.

Robbie explored the composition and framing by drawing sketches of how he imagined the image would look and made technical drawings to plan the exposure. Most importantly, he learned to take advantage of unforeseen opportunities during a shoot.

THE DEEPEST CAVE IN THE WORLD

Between 2000 and 2019, a team led by Pavel Demidov* explored and mapped Veryovkina Cave in the Caucasus Mountains of Abkhazia, Georgia. In 2017, they descended to a depth of 7,257 feet (2,212 meters) below the surface, making Veryovkina the deepest known cave in the world.

In 2018, Pavel invited Robbie to join the expedition to visually document the deepest areas of the cave. It took the team four days to descend to the bottom. Once there, they spent two weeks underground. Then an unexpected storm above ground caused the cave to flood, forcing the team to climb for their lives to escape the rising water. They almost did not make it out.

TELLING THE STORY

To take this photo, Robbie used the same techniques he learned in Titan. Many of Robbie's photos do not have an end point, which allows the viewer to wonder what lies beyond. In this image, as Pavel climbs upward, the viewer sees the green lake at the bottom of the cave very clearly. Two swimmers with flash bulbs light up the water and the surrounding cave walls. Pavel is illuminated by his head lamp and from the side by a strobe, but the cave walls around him are in shadow. So while Pavel is in the foreground, the focal point of the image is the end point, the pool of water.

Yet even at the bottom of the deepest cave in the world, Robbie says, an explorer would see this as a challenge and a starting point for the next expedition: to find what lies below the surface of the lake. This is not the end of the cave—there is more to explore beneath the water.

*In August 2020, Pavel Demidov lost his life in a caving accident in the Caucasus Mountains, not far from Veryovkina Cave.

ROBBIE'S POINTS OF INTEREST

1. A unique aspect about photographing caves is that you rarely ever see an end point.

2. Despite various lights being held and mounted, the left side of the cave wall is still very dark, which shows the unique behavior of light in a cave environment and helps focus the viewer's attention.

3. Notice the texture of the cave walls. The appearance of the limestone shows just how rough a cave can be.

PROJECT DESCRIPTION

In this project, you will analyze and respond to Robbie's image. You'll have the opportunity to investigate the different elements of the image and interpret the story for yourself. Look at the photo closely. Take note of anything that catches your attention. You'll be writing a brief analysis consisting of your observations, your interpretation of the story, any questions that come to mind, and the messages you take away. If you can, talk to your classmates and discuss your ideas. Decide which elements of the photo are impactful to you, and write a brief analysis of your findings.

QUESTIONS TO CONSIDER

What is the story?

What stands out to you?

What would you change? Why?

What questions do you have?

What caught your attention first?

Is there anything that seems confusing?

Do you like the image?

USE SOME OF THESE VOCABULARY WORDS

Perspective: Representation of objects in a space.

Depth: The distance an object appears to be from the surface of something.

Scale: Refers to the physical size of an object; how big or small an element is in relation to another.

Tone: Relative lightness or darkness of a color.

Unity: The elements and principles of a piece working together.

Proximity: How closely elements are arranged.

Proportion: Size of an object as it relates to another object.

GETTING STARTED

Examine the perspective. Think about where Robbie would have had to be in order to get this angle, and what challenges he might have faced getting this shot.

Think about scale. Caves can be a bit deceiving because of the way light behaves inside of them. This shaft might not look that deep, but when you look at the man in the foreground in comparison to the divers in the water, the scale difference communicates that the hole goes down a lot deeper than it appears.

When it comes to understanding stories about difficult places, especially a cave, it is important to think about what you can't see as well. How much farther up does it go? How deep is the water? Was the water always there? How many lights are needed to light this space? All of these factors communicate the difficulty and intricacy of this challenging place.

SKILLS YOU'LL PRACTICE

Critical thinking   Using design vocabulary

Giving feedback   Writing

Design analysis   Using design vocabulary

Writing

One way to organize your thoughts is with a graphic organizer. Here's an example of how you might use an idea web to capture your thoughts about the photo.

PROJECT DESCRIPTION

In this project, you will be exploring unique perspectives and difficult places.

Using at least one of the images provided, create a series of three compositions that explore angles and perspectives. Think about scale and depth, and how they can influence the tone and feel of the piece. Consider how positions and perspectives emphasize different parts of your composition, and how that will affect the viewers' feeling about the image.

The goal of this project is to blend various visual elements such as distance, depth, angles, perspectives, etc., to create an interesting image that tells a compelling story about a place. This project is a good opportunity to experiment with unconventional angles and positions, and to explore the effects those techniques have on your composition.

SKILLS TO EXPLORE

- Duplicate an effect with saved curves
- Edit using Smart Objects
- Adjust layer opacity and fill opacity
- Create custom layer styles
- Move selected pixels
- Examine selection edges
- Explore vector selection tools
- Edit using Smart filters

FILES YOU'LL USE

- Ps_u4_cavelight.JPEG
- Ps_u4_city.JPEG
- Ps_u4_tree.JPEG
- Ps_u4_waterfall.JPEG
- Ps_u4_canyon.JPEG

You will use Photoshop for this project to create an image that is inspired by Robbie's photographic work.

SKILLS CHALLENGE
RECOVERING SHADOWS AND HIGHLIGHTS

Step 1: Right click on your layer, and click Convert to Smart Object.

Step 2: Go to Image in the Menu bar, point to Adjustments, then click Shadows/Highlights.

Step 3: A dialog box will pop up with two categories: Shadows and Highlights. Click on the Show More Options box in the bottom-left corner of the dialog box.

Step 4: Adjust the levels until you reach your desired shadowing and highlighting.

> **TIP:** Check the Preview button on the right side of the dialog box so you can see the adjustments as you are making them.

FOLLOW ROBBIE'S EXAMPLE

1. Familiarize yourself with the environment. Once you have a location in mind, take time to learn about it. Find out what it looks like from different views and angles.

2. Plan your image. Think about what you want to capture, how you want to capture it, and how these different elements will work together to tell the story of that specific place. Then, grab a pen and paper and map out your idea.

3. Embrace trial and error. Capturing stories of difficult places is not an easy task. Rise to the challenge and try something new. Experiment with new techniques and concepts.

GETTING STARTED

1. Find some inspiration. It can be hard to explore new ideas and concepts, especially when you are still getting used to what you just learned. Help yourself break out of your comfort zone by exploring more expressive and abstract visuals that might spark some ideas.

2. Write down ideas you think might work. It may be difficult to come up with the perfect concept off the top of your head. Write down some ideas and brainstorm before committing to a location. If it helps, discuss your ideas with a classmate or teacher.

Robbie created a rough sketch of the inside of a cave to map out essential factors such as where people might be placed and where lights might be mounted.

3. Avoid perfectionism. It's not uncommon for creatives to want their work to be absolutely perfect. In this project, perfection is not the goal, or even an objective. Let yourself pursue your concept relentlessly and try to tell the story of your chosen environment using whatever visuals necessary, no matter how abstract they might seem. This is a great opportunity to take some creative risks.

Robbie made a full sketch of what he wanted his image of the Titan Roof Dome to capture. Note the emphasis on depth and perspective.

PROJECT DESCRIPTION

In this project, you will continue to explore unique perspectives and difficult places, but you will focus your exploration on light and how it behaves.

In certain places, light doesn't always behave as one would expect. Using the series of compositions from your Design Project, you are going to work with and render light to enhance, adjust, or even change the tone of the story. You will be experimenting with adding, subtracting, adjusting, and filtering light as your main storytelling technique.

The goal of this project is to refine your ability to tell stories by blending various visual elements and experimenting with abstract techniques as a solution to working in challenging places.

SKILLS TO EXPLORE

- Explore hue and saturation
- Work with blending modes and filters
- Employ curves adjustments
- Make a default layer style
- Experiment with CMYK vs RGB vs Grayscale
- Use filters to modify images

THINK LIKE ROBBIE

1. Build off of what you know works. You don't always need to go back to the drawing board. If you find a technique that works for you, use it and apply it to other images and ideas.

2. Make observations about how certain techniques work. When using difficult and unconventional techniques, you can't always make accurate predictions. Take note of what works and what doesn't.

3. Reference other work. Return to other pieces you've done that you thought went well. Consider how you told a story in previous projects. How can you apply those same techniques and infuse meaning into this story?

SKILLS CHALLENGE
CREATE A GLOW EFFECT

Step 1: Make a copy of your background layer to work on.

Step 2: Use any selection tool (any of the lasso tools, the magic wand tool, or quick selection tools). Select the area you want to add a glow effect to and use the Refine Edge tool to make sure your selection is clean.

Step 3: Go to Filter in the Menu bar, point to Blur, then select Gaussian Blur. A dialog box will pop up. Use the Radius bar to adjust the amount of blur to be applied. The higher the value, the heavier the blur.

Step 4: Change the Blend Mode to Soft Light in the layers panel.

Step 5: For a stronger effect, change the blend mode to Overlay instead of Soft Light, then drop the opacity down.

GETTING STARTED

As you have done in previous projects, use your work from the Design Project as a starting point. Adding, subtracting, and adjusting design elements, in this case, light, can change the tone of a story completely. It can even change the perspective and focus. If you find yourself stuck on how to get started with this project, we recommend focusing on how you can work with light given the tools you have access to. Experiment with light using your tools on a blank artboard or a sample photograph. This will allow you to explore light in a creative way before applying it to your composition and story.

1. Get experimental. This is a great opportunity to try things you might not have been taught. Experiment with non-traditional ways of composing images.

Robbie made a technical drawing of a location inside Titan Cave, where he mapped out and marked important variables such as distance, format, tools, and important measurements.

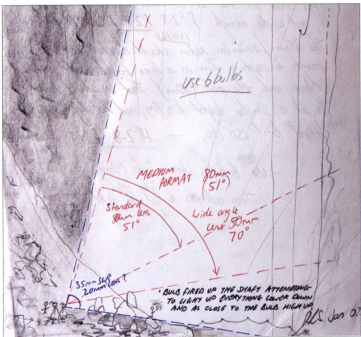

2. Work with your hands before jumping on the computer. It is often easier for your imagination to run freely when you are working with your hands and without limits. Sketch, paint, piece together, or try other crafty methods to develop an idea.

3. Think abstractly and don't judge your ideas. When we need to tell the story of a place where visibility is limited, creativity is a must. Think about what you can do in terms of angle, scale, light, texture, etc., to get your story across. Explore your tools and design concepts and how they can work together.

Robbie made a full sketch of what he wanted his image of a particular spot inside Titan Cave to capture. Note the focal point and how it interacts with the space.

GLOSSARY

A

Algorithm An ordered set of instructions to process data in a certain way.

Aliased edge A hard edge.

Alpha channel A grayscale image that Photoshop creates and uses to render the selection.

Anti-aliased edge A crisp but smooth edge.

Artboards Multiple design layouts within one document.

B

Base color The color of the pixel on the lower layer when a blending mode is applied.

Base layer The layer functioning as the clipping mask.

Bit depth Indicates the amount of computer memory allocated to each pixel in an image.

Bitmap graphics Digital images made from different colored pixels to reproduce a photographic image with the illusion of continuous tone from shadows to highlights.

Black point The very darkest pixel in an image.

Blend color The color on the layer in which the blending mode is applied. The blend color is above the base layer.

Blending modes Mathematical algorithms that define how pixels affect pixels on layers beneath them.

Bounding box A rectangle that surrounds an image and contains eight handles to click and drag in order to change the dimensions of the artwork.

Brightness A pixel's grayscale value. The higher the number, the brighter the pixel (the closer it is to white).

C

Camera Raw image A digital image that has not been compressed or otherwise processed.

Camera resolution The number of pixels per inch a camera can access to recreate an image.

Clipping Using artwork on one layer to mask the artwork on a layer (or multiple layers) above it.

Color model A mathematical model that describes how colors can be represented as numbers, usually as a way for computers to process color.

Color stops The colors that make up a gradient.

Composite image An image that brings together many different images to create one new image.

Contrast The relationship between shadows and highlights of an image.

D

Digital image A picture in electronic form.

Dithering An on-screen form of pixelization in which individual areas of pixels become visible and create a distracting pattern.

E

Edge The outline of a selection. The area of an image where highly contrasting pixels meet.

F

Feathered edge A blended edge.

Flipping Creating a mirror image of artwork by turning it horizontally or vertically.

G

Gradient A blend of two or more colors.

Grayscale image A single-color image, normally referred to as black and white.

H

Hexadecimal A color model used to describe color mathematically.

Highlights The lightest areas of an image represented by pixels in the top third of the grayscale range.

Hue The name of a color.

I

Image resolution The number of pixels per inch in an image file.

Image size The dimensions of a Photoshop file.

K

Kerning Increasing or decreasing the space between two letters.

M

Metadata A set of basic information about a file, such as who created it, the resolution, color space, copyright, and any keywords applied to it.

Mezzotint An alternative screening technique to a conventional halftone using irregular shaped dots or lines to reproduce an image.

Midtones Sections of an image represented by pixels in the middle of the grayscale range.

N

Noise Tiny, random, pixel-sized squares of color or gray applied to artwork to create texture over an image.

O

Opacity Determines the percentage of transparency. The lower the opacity, the more transparent it is.

P

Path A simple vector object drawn with anchor points and lines that connect them.

Pixels The smallest component that makes up a digital image.

Point of origin The point from which a transformation occurs.

R

Rasterize To convert type or vector artwork to pixels.

Radius A value that determines how many pixels to change on each side of an edge.

Resampling Occurs when the total number of pixels that make up an image is changed.

Resolution The number of pixels per square inch in a digital image.

Resolution independent Graphics, such as vector graphics, that are not made up of pixels.

Result color The color produced by blending the base and blend colors.

Rotating Moving an object clockwise or counterclockwise around a center point.

S

Sampling Taking information from a pixel or accessing its color.

Saturation The intensity of the hue. At 0% saturation, there is no color; full intensity or vibrance is at 100%.

Shadows The darkest areas of an image represented by pixels in the bottom third of the grayscale range.

Smart objects Layers that contain image data from raster or vector images, such as Photoshop or Illustrator files.

Snapshot A record of the project as it is at a given moment.

Stroke A basic artistic element that places an outline on an object.

T

Tracking Increasing or reducing the space between letters of a word.

Transform Change the shape, size, perspective, or rotation of an object or image.

U

Unit photography A collection of images taken on location by a professional photographer hired by a production company.

V

Vector graphics Shapes created from paths using straight and curved lines.

Vignette A visual effect in which the edge of an image, usually an oval, gradually fades away.

W

White point The very lightest pixel in an image.

X

X coordinate A location on the canvas that represents the horizontal distance from the point of origin (the top-left corner of the canvas).

Y

Y coordinate A location on the canvas that represents the vertical distance from the point of origin (the top-left corner of the canvas).

INDEX